070.9
D46w

126289

DATE DUE			

Windows on the World

Windows on the World

The Information Process In a Changing Society 1900–1920

Robert W. Desmond

University of Iowa Press Iowa City

University of Iowa Press, Iowa City 52242
© 1980 by The University of Iowa. All rights reserved
Printed in the United States of America

Library of Congress Cataloging in Publication Data

Desmond, Robert William, 1900-
  Windows on the world.

  Continues the author's The information process.
  Bibliography: p.
  Includes index.
  1. Journalism—History—20th century. 2. News
agencies—History—20th century. 3. European War,
1914-1918—Journalists. I. Title.
PN4815.D4   070'.9   80-19397
ISBN 0-87745-104-4

To Richard, Christopher, and Carolyn

Contents

Foreword

The importance of current information, promptly available to all persons, can hardly be exaggerated as being basic to a proper functioning of the social order. With it goes recorded information representing the history and wisdom of centuries.

Current information is the key to knowledge. Knowledge is the key to understanding. Understanding is the key to a civilized way of life for mankind.

With that as a thesis, this writer ventured to examine man's effort to understand his environment, beginning in the earliest of times, and recounted in *The Information Process: World News Reporting to the Twentieth Century*, published by the University of Iowa Press in 1978. This volume, a sequel, carries the story forward.

Eternally curious, adaptable and innovative, our forebears learned to cope with the world they knew. They obtained information as best they could and used it as seemed appropriate. It was no coincidence, however, that the pace of mankind's advance attained an unprecedented rate after the printing press appeared in fifteenth-century Europe. So at last it became possible to make facts and ideas known to many at small cost and to preserve knowledge for all time. With this, the face of the earth and the relationships between people have changed more in the five centuries since the Renaissance than in the fifty centuries preceding.

By 1900 a high level of literacy, culture, technology, and education existed over much of the globe. A society existed in which there was a need for current information. It was provided by a press organization that had evolved with growing effectiveness since about 1800, and especially since 1850, utilizing the wonders men of science had produced in means of communication and transportation by which most of the world and its peoples had been brought into close association.

The story of mankind's search for information never will end. As it proceeded prior to 1900, so it has proceeded since, within the context of events. That is the subject of the pages following. It proved possible to present the unfolding story of *The Information Process* extending over many centuries, to about 1900, in the single volume mentioned. The related events and changes in the world of the present century, now approaching its end, have been so complex, however, as to defy any such condensation. Each approximate period of about twenty years seems to form an entity of its own. Carrying the story forward, and seeking some proper logic of events and of time, the appropriate period to be viewed therefore seems to be from 1900 to about 1920, and a bit beyond.

That period began in a spirit of general public optimism, in a decade of constructive growth. The second decade, however, from 1910, brought a dismaying reversal, with a turn to military conflict, including the Great War of 1914–18 and the Russian Revolution. The Peace Conference following, in Paris, established a guarded hope for a better world to begin in the 1920s, shaped by peoples supposedly made wiser by the hardships so recently endured.

As in the preceding volume, *The Information Process*, the objective in this sequel, *Windows on the World*, is to bring together the diverse elements figuring in the reporting of public affairs internationally, of history-in-the-making from 1900 to 1920, and with a look at some elements following. The broad purpose, also, is to clarify the process of that reporting and to underline its significance as relating to the comprehension of events and situations as they affected the life of the times and, inevitably, of generations to come.

I wish to express personal thanks to several persons who have assisted in this study, having read the pages in manuscript and having made valuable comments and suggestions. These are Dr. Raymond B. Nixon, professor emeritus in Journalism and international communication, University of Minnesota, Minneapolis; Dr. Leslie G. Moeller, professor, School of Journalism, University of Iowa, Iowa City; Dr. John C. Merrill, formerly of the School of Journalism, University of Missouri, Columbia, but now at the Louisiana State University; Professor James W. Carey, School of Journalism, and Professor Lawrence E. Gelfand, Department of History, both of the University of Iowa. I also wish to express gratitude to my wife, Emily V. Desmond, for her support and assistance in this undertaking.

Robert W. Desmond
LaJolla, California

PART I
A New Century

_____

Public Information in a Changing World   1

New Year's Day of 1900 was a date to stir the minds and emotions of a generation.

Some accepted the day as marking the dawn of the twentieth century. Others argued that a new century could only begin with the figure "1," as in 1901. Logical as that was, the appearance of 1900 on the calendar had a magic of its own. It seemed to close the door on a familiar yesterday, with tomorrow yet a stranger. It was a time to look back, generally with a sense of gratification for net advances in the human condition, but also to look ahead with wonder, and usually with hope for even better things to come.

The world of 1900 was vastly different from what it had been in 1800. The earth's population had almost doubled, from an estimated 919 million to more than 1.5 billion persons. The manner of life had improved for most. Exploration, science, and technology had extended mankind's knowledge and mastery of his environment. A spirit of freedom had grown, public education and literacy were on the rise, standards of nutrition, sanitation and health were advanced, and religious tolerance was accepted. The power of steam and electricity had been harnessed to light cities and to perform many tasks. Industry and commerce had brought a degree of prosperity beyond anything previously known.

One of the most significant developments of the century just past was the vigorous growth of the newspaper and magazine press in many countries, and potentially in all. The application of the new technology to printing, communication, and transportation, as well as to industry, had changed the face of the globe. It opened new vistas in the realm of ideas and life styles. The boundaries of trade were extended. An earlier isolation of peoples in some areas was ended; places once remote were brought into the mainstream of affairs, regionalism and provincialism yielded to a new unity.

The newspaper press, news agencies included, growing in enterprise, prosperity and effectiveness, had brought most of the world into focus by 1900. Beyond 1900, the press organization was to proceed, with professional dedication, to open the windows ever wider, enabling almost all persons in settled areas to view the march of events and—assuming that they paid attention—to understand their meaning.

The information process was advanced with special vigor in the 1920s and 1930s. Magazines supplemented newspapers in reporting upon current affairs. There was a greatly extended use of photography, and of motion pictures and recordings, in acquainting the public with persons, places, and events. Especially important was the appearance of voice radio as a medium capturing interest and creating an unprecedented public awareness among the peoples of many lands of issues and events at home and abroad.

Events of the day, along with underlying and continuing circumstances and situations, form the subjects reported upon by the media of information. They are "covered" by representatives of those media. How effectively they are covered depends upon the number and competence of the representatives, their access to sources and opportunities to observe events as they occur, their actual freedom to report what they learn, and the manner in which their reports are presented by the media.

The first decade of the new century (1900–10) was relatively tranquil, in contrast to some previous periods and others to come. It was the last period in the experience of persons still surviving that could be called simple in the life style it permitted. There were, inevitably, incidents of disaster, both of nature and man-made. There were economic and social problems and times of crisis. There were wars, but of such scope and location as to affect only a limited number of persons. By and large, it was a decade during which a general belief prevailed that the world was growing better, and would continue to do so. The peoples of many nations were enjoying personal benefits and material comforts, with new conveniences and amenities, and had expectation of more to come.

The second decade (1910–20) was quite different, bringing a shocking mockery of those earlier expectations, and opening an era of crisis that has since occupied virtually all peoples of the earth. The crisis began with limited but ominous rumblings, followed by military confrontations in the Mediterranean and Balkan areas, and in Mexico. Then, quite suddenly, all of Europe exploded into a war in 1914, which was to continue for four years, and to involve much of the world. Unlike any within the memory of more than a few who had known the Franco-Prussian War of 1870–71, it was fought largely in settled and populous areas of Europe. Its casualties, destruction, and costs still overshadow today's world. Further, and coincidentally, the decade brought a revolution in Russia. The absolutism of czarist rule was well ended, but it was replaced by an equally absolute authoritarian communism with declared aspirations to shape the world in its own image.

The third decade (1920–30) began with a return of cautious hope, a determination that there must be no more war in the world, a confidence on the part of many that a proper application of reason and goodwill could solve existing economic problems, settle differences peaceably, and bring a better life to all peoples.

The press had gained a greater maturity and capability during the war years. By 1920 it was more widely prepared to provide a service of information contributing to the creation of a world climate in which all persons, given an improved understanding, might dwell happily, free of fear of further war. A League of Nations organization, created in 1920, was viewed as custodian of these bright hopes.

There were reasons for hope. Difficulties, including military conflicts surviving beyond the war and related thereto, were finding solutions. The League was, indeed, helpful in several instances. The shackles of old empires had largely been removed. Tensions remained in some areas, but the world was generally at peace. There were economic problems in some countries, but some others, including the United States, entered upon a prosperous new era. Japan's industry and trade were flourishing. The British Empire had become a Commonwealth of Nations. A World Court was prepared to deal with international problems. A crisis period in Germany itself seemed to have passed, with its economy recovering. International conferences had met and others were in prospect, looking toward a reduction in armaments. China, long loosely organized and a victim of exploitation, by 1928 seemed on the brink of a firm nationhood. The Union of South Africa was well established, and both Egypt and Turkey were on a new course. Prospects also seemed promising in the Philippines, Mexico, and much of Latin America.

Throughout that decade of the twenties and beyond, the media, where free of official restraint or censorship, were never more effective in opening the "windows on the world" so that the public might be informed and guided toward that general understanding supporting solutions of remaining problems. Radio, motion pictures, and advances in photography and magazine journalism combined to sharpen the acquaintance of all peoples with the world about them.

Unfortunately, there also were negative aspects. The war had left a heritage of hatred, suspicion and fear. The terms of the peace treaties were unrealistic in some respects, and especially in the cash reparation demands placed upon Germany. Modifications in 1924 and 1929 were helpful, but came too late. Economic problems stemming from the war defied solutions in some countries. Elements of nationalism were not suppressed, and led to political actions conflicting with the broader hopes for international amity. Combined with elements of intolerance, aspirations to individual power and political adventurism, those hopes were further undone. Even though a strong trend toward freedom and democracy had existed in 1920, it was countered by an aggressive communism in Soviet Russia and elsewhere, by a new fascism in Italy, and by comparable manifestations of authoritarianism emerging in Spain, Brazil, and later in Japan and Germany.

These influences and others, taken together, brought a whittling away of the first fine hopes of the decade. What proved a deceptive prosperity in the United States ended dramatically in a New York stock market crash in October 1929. The dominoes soon began to fall throughout the world, with a consequent decline in trade and a collapse of financial structures. The decade following thus became disastrous economically, politically, and socially.

The first breach of the peace came in 1931 and, in retrospect, marked the beginning of a second world war which continued until 1945. By 1939 the League of Nations came to an effective end. Those elements of actual warfare from 1931 form parts of the story of World War II and are not described in these pages. Mention must be made of some, but emphasis here relating to the 1930s will bear rather upon the information process itself as it carried over from the 1920s, and to the media and the personnel on the news fronts of the world in the years between the wars.

In those countries where authoritarianism dominated, beginning with the Soviet Union from 1918, and proceeding to Italy, Spain, Germany, Japan and others, the media of information were the first victims. This was significant. They reported only what they were permitted to report, and the peoples of their countries were ill-served. This left the media of the free countries to report what they could, increasingly obstructed in their efforts by closed sources elsewhere, by censorships, and by propaganda campaigns. Even with such handicaps, they presented reasonably effective accounts.

The successes of media contributions to public information through the years from 1900 to 1940 outnumbered the failures. Events themselves were such, however, as to deprive the media and the people of the world of that ultimate success: a permanent peace and well-being. The manner in which events conspired to bring that negative result, and the manner in which they were covered and portrayed by the media forms the subject matter of this account.

The Flow of News:
Decade One (1900–10) 2

The flow of news never ceases, since it is a reflection of human activity and concerns. Neither can news be confined within sure boundaries of time or place, in point of origins or effects. Thus in 1900 certain earlier and on-going events or news topics overlapped the January date, or were to have a bearing upon later events and later times.

For example, the Sino-Japanese War of 1894–95 and the Spanish-American War of 1898 were two events whose results were actively felt until beyond 1905; while the South African or Boer War which began in 1899 continued until 1902.

The results of the Spanish-American War quite suddenly gave the United States recognition as a world power. Even as that war was in progress, the Hawaiian Islands, by request of its people, became a U.S. Territory in 1898. The war itself gave the United States a position in Cuba until 1902 and somewhat beyond, in the Philippine Islands under force of arms until 1903 and then under a civil administration, and also in Puerto Rico, Guam, Midway, and Wake Islands. The Western Samoan Islands further became a U.S. Territory in 1899 by treaty with Great Britain and Germany. The Panama Canal Zone was added in 1904 by treaty with the Republic of Panama.

These circumstances resulted in a movement of U.S. newspaper correspondents to those areas of the world. They resulted in greater coverage of Washington as an administrative center by representatives of the national press, and also brought more foreign correspondents to the United States, particularly for the British press.

The Sino-Japanese War left a residual dislike in China for foreigners. With the private sanction of the Chinese Dowager Empress, Tzu Hsi, an extremist element was left free in 1899 to seek to drive foreigners out of the capital and out of the country. Bearing the name of I Ho Ch'uan, literally translated to mean Fists of Righteous Harmony, the group became known more simply, in international usage, as the Boxers, and its actions as the Boxer Rebellion or uprising. The league used riot, terror, and arms against foreign diplomatic personnel in Peking, foreign businessmen and missionary groups wherever located, and against Chinese who had become Christians. The disorders were not ended until 1901.

The Sino-Japanese War peace treaty in 1895 had given Japan as victor rights in Korea and Manchuria, extending to Port Arthur, Dairen, and other points on the Liaotung Peninsula within China. These rights were challenged in 1903 by czarist Russia in particular, and by Germany and France. Russia moved to establish a position of its own in Manchuria and Korea. When negotiations failed to bring a settlement Japan broke diplomatic relations with Russia on February 6, 1904, and directed a naval attack on units of the Russian fleet, then at Port Arthur, on February 8. The resulting Russo-Japanese War continued until May 1905, with military action in Manchuria and naval action in the adjacent waters. Japan was victorious, and the war ended in a peace treaty signed at Portsmouth, New Hampshire, in September 1905.

As with the victory of the United States in the Spanish-American War, Japan's victory in 1905 gained that country recognition also as a world power. Japan thus established a position in Manchuria and Korea, and in Formosa as well; it began a vigorous development in domestic industry and trade, looking to China especially as a great potential market for its products.

China's defeat in the Sino-Japanese War, its partial occupation by foreign troops in 1900–01, to bring an end to the Boxer Rebellion, the loss of Formosa and of control over parts of Manchuria and the Liaotung Peninsula, all moved Dr. Sun Yat-sen in Canton to initiate efforts to replace the ancient Chinese Empire with a new government under a republic. This change was to occur in 1911–12.

Russia's defeat of 1905 in the war with Japan contributed to stresses already existing in that country, and became a factor in ending the czarist government in 1917 through revolution, bringing into being a new Communist regime and a Soviet Union.

The Sino-Japanese War, the Boxer Rebellion, and the Russo-Japanese War together all gave such importance to China and Japan that the world press began a far more active coverage of events in those countries.

In another part of the globe, the South African War, already in progress in 1900, was a contest between Great Britain, along with forces from Australia and Canada, and the descendents of Dutch settlers for control of much of the southern part of the African continent. It was a contest triggered largely by the discovery in 1886 of rich deposits of gold in the Rand District of the Boer South African Republic, or the Transvaal. Victory in the war gave Great Britain control of the Transvaal and the adjacent Boer Orange Free State, which were added to the Cape Colony, yielded by the Boers in the 1830s, and to Natal, and Rhodesia, farther north. Most of this territory became the Union of South Africa in 1910, under the British flag, with the former Boer element sharing fully in the government. At the same time, the British position in Africa, along with Belgium, Portugal, France, and Spain, had brought Germany into colonial development on that continent in the 1880s. This was to become a matter of special concern, not unrelated to the crisis that escalated into World War I.

The Spanish-American War, which had begun in April 1898, ended with the signature of the Treaty of Paris in December of that same year. U.S. forces might have been withdrawn then from Cuba and the Philippines. They were, in fact, withdrawn from Cuba in 1902, after a period during which an independent republican government was formed. An unanticipated military involvement arose in the Philippines, however, with guerrilla warfare continuing until late 1903, followed by a generation of civil government administered by the United States.

As in Cuba, an independence movement had been active in the Philippines before the Spanish-American War began. Emilio Aguinaldo, leading the native insurrectionists, and his followers had assisted the forces of the United States from the time of the Battle of Manila Bay on May 1, 1898. With the end of the war in December, Aguinaldo became concerned lest the result be merely an exchange of Spanish control for a new control by the United States. He and his insurrectionist group therefore proclaimed on January 10, 1899, that the fight for independence would continue. Aguinaldo himself was captured in March 1901, but guerrilla action continued for more than two years beyond that time. Meanwhile, a civil government had been set up in 1902, with William Howard Taft as the first governor dispatched from Washington and serving until 1904.

The war itself had brought representatives of the U.S. press to the Philippines, establishing a basis for permanent coverage of the islands from Manila. Correspondents present, some having arrived in 1898 and some remaining after 1903, included John P. Dunning, David Morris, Robert M. Collins, and Harold Martin, all of the Associated Press;

Edward L. Keen, of the Scripps-McRae Press Association; Oscar King Davis of the *New York Sun* and its related Laffan News bureau; John Foster Bass and James Creelman for the *New York Journal;* George Bronson Rae and Frederick Palmer for the *New York World;* Stephen Bonsal, William Dinwiddie, and Francis D. Millet, an artist, all for the *New York Herald;* John T. McCutcheon for the *Chicago Record;* Richard Henry Little for the *Chicago Tribune;* and Martin Egan for the *San Francisco Chronicle.*[1]

Even as guerrilla warfare proceeded in the Philippines and also in South Africa, the Boxer uprising in China required coverage. Many foreigners were injured and some were killed, including the German envoy to China, Baron Klemens von Ketteler, and thousands of Chinese Christians were murdered. Order was restored only after 18,000 U.S., British, Japanese, French, Russian, and German military forces arrived in China and fanned out from the port of Taku to Tientsin, Peking, and other points. Peking was entered on August 14, 1900. Boxer elements were dispersed there and elsewhere, but not until September 1901 were the relief forces to leave the country, and it was 1902 before the Dowager Empress returned to the capital.

In the period from 1899 until the international military expedition arrived in June 1900 and reached Peking in August, the burden of news coverage rested chiefly upon Dr. George Ernest Morrison, representing the *Times* of London in Peking since 1895; and on Dr. Robert Coltman, a recent appointee there as a stringer or part-time correspondent for the *Chicago Record.* Both produced eye-witness reports of the Boxer attacks on legations and other actions there. Morrison was wounded.

To accompany the international expedition, several correspondents went from the Philippines to China, among them Morris and Collins for the Associated Press, and Egan, who also switched to the AP; Bonsal for the *New York Herald*; Davis for the *New York Sun* and the Laffan News bureau; and Palmer for the *New York World,* who also wrote for *Collier's Weekly.* Another early on the scene was Willmott Harsant Lewis, a young man of Welsh origin, who had recently become editor of the *North China Daily News* of Shanghai, but who also wrote for the *New York Herald.*

Others to arrive in China, some accompanying troops, were Charles E. Kloeber, manager of the Associated Press bureau in Washington,

---

1   For a detailed account of the Spanish-American War, its preliminaries and aftermath, including reference to the Philippines, see Robert W. Desmond, *The Information Process* (Iowa City: University of Iowa Press, 1978), pp. 386–401, and bibliographical references.

Thomas F. Millard for the *New York Herald,* Robert D. Paine for the *Philadelphia Press,* and Joseph Medill Patterson, son of R. W. Patterson publisher of the *Chicago Tribune,* who represented that paper during a summer interval from his studies at Yale.

For the British press, George Lynch of the London *Daily Chronicle* joined troops on the march to Peking. Dr. Emile Joseph Dillon, in St. Petersburg for the London *Daily Telegraph,* accompanied Russian troops moved by way of the Trans-Siberian Railway, then in its third year of operation. He remained with them on the advance to Peking. Gaston Chadourne of the French Agence Havas traveled with units of France's army on a long voyage from Marseilles to Taku and went on with them to Peking. Pierre Loti (Louis Marie Julien Viaud), known as a novelist, also was with French troops and writing for *Figaro* of Paris. Luigi Barzini of *Il Corriere della Séra,* Milan, who had reported the Sino-Japanese War, returned to prepare substantial reports on an expedition that was difficult and dangerous for all correspondents.[2]

The South African War, then in progress, had begun in October 1899 when the two Boer republics joined to battle the British of the Cape Colony and Natal. The Boers had early successes and put three cities of the Cape Colony under siege—Mafeking, Kimberley, and Ladysmith. Given time for British military forces to arrive from England, the situation was reversed, with the besieged cities all relieved by May 1900. The Boer capitals of Bloemfontein in the Orange Free State, Pretoria in the Transvaal, and Johannesburg as well were taken by the British between March and June. From that time, the Boers were able to conduct no more than a guerrilla campaign. That continued for two years, with peace only restored by treaty on May 31, 1902.

The war was reported by a large group of correspondents for the British press, five for the press of the United States, three for Australian dailies, and one for a Paris publication. A few British correspondents were present from the outset, others arrived early enough for some to be immobilized for as long as four months in the besieged cities. In the course of the war, thirteen were killed or died, thirty-seven were wounded, and several were captured by the Boers.

The British Reuter news agency and the *Times* of London were most actively represented, with correspondents including Henry M. Collins, William Hay Mackay, Roderick Jones, H. A. Gwynn, and Colonel

---

2 Desmond, *The Information Process,* pp. 415–17.

Robert Baden-Powell for the agency, and Leopold C. M. S. Amery, Lionel James, and Angus Hamilton for the paper.

Other correspondents included Winston Churchill and Edward Frederick Knight for the London *Morning Post;* Bennet Burleigh, Ellis Ashmead-Bartlett, and Percy Bullen for the *Daily Telegraph;* George Warrington Steevens, Charles E. Hands, and Edgar Wallace for the *Daily Mail;* John B. Atkins for the *Manchester Guardian;* Frederic Villiers for the London *Daily News* and *Graphic;* Melton Prior for the *Illustrated London News;* and Henry W. Nevinson for the *Daily Chronicle.* Correspondents for the U.S. press were John T. McCutcheon for the *Chicago Record,* who was previously in the Philippines, Richard Harding Davis for the *New York Herald,* Julian Ralph for the *New York Journal,* and George Denny and Richard Smith for the Associated Press.[3]

Among the correspondents so far mentioned, many had earlier experience on the news fronts of the world and others would serve into and beyond the fourth decade of the century. Winston Churchill had written from Cuba in 1895, and later from India and the Sudan. He gained special notice for his part in the coverage of the South African War, which led to his election to Parliament at the age of twenty-six and his subsequent career in public affairs. Special distinction also was to attach to the later careers of Frederick Palmer, Willmott Harsant Lewis, Joseph Medill Patterson, and Roderick Jones.

In the chronology of events, apart from those just noted as bracketing the year 1900, there were broad changes in progress significant of things to come, and of things that would be much in the news.

On January 2, 1900, for example, there appeared on Fifth Avenue in New York an "autostage," a motor-driven vehicle offering public transportation to as many as twelve persons. Even then, the internal combustion engine was a topic in the news. About a hundred motorized taxis were on the New York streets, as they also were to be seen in London, Paris, and Berlin. The R. E. Olds Company began producing "horseless carriages" in Detroit in 1900. There already were perhaps 4,000 throughout the United States, and others in Europe. They had been appearing since 1875 in Austria, Germany, France, and England. The names of Gottlieb Daimler, Karl Benz, René Panhard, and Sir Henry Royce were becoming familiar to newspaper readers, as the

---

3   Desmond, *The Information Process,* pp. 402–15.

names of Olds, Charles E. Duryea, and Henry Ford also soon were to become known.

There had been "road races" by motor cars between Paris and Rouen and Bordeaux as early as 1894 and 1895. A Grand Prix of 1903, for a Paris to Madrid race set a pace for others to follow. In the United States, the first organized race was on Long Island in April 1900. The first Vanderbilt Cup race was run in 1904, and the first Indianapolis Speedway race took place in 1911. The *New York Times* and *Le Matin* of Paris collaborated in 1908 to finance an automobile touring venture.

The Ford Motor Company, organized at Detroit in 1903, put its Model T on the market in 1908 and led both in the production and sale of cars in 1909. Ford was to introduce assembly line production in 1913, and in 1914 to raise the basic factory wage rate from $2.40 for a nine-hour day to $5 for an eight-hour day. It was the beginning of a second industrial revolution, and a social revolution was to follow in all countries after 1914. By then millions of motor vehicles were in use throughout the world. Highways were being constructed, time and distance were shrinking, motorists were encouraged to explore their areas and more remote regions. Advertising for motorcars and accessories was growing in volume, and service facilities were being made available. Steel production, rubber, the refining of gasoline and a variety of other industries were advanced as the motor age began and a new way of life introduced.

These early evidences of the motor age were matched also by the first signs of an air age. In September 1900 Orville and Wilbur Wright of Dayton, Ohio, tested a glider on the sands near the coastal town of Kitty Hawk, North Carolina.[4] Three years later, with a motor added, Orville Wright made the first successful test flight, again at Kitty Hawk. On the following day, December 18, 1903, the morning *Virginian-Pilot* of Norfolk, Virginia, reported the flight in major page-one space, with a photograph. Another two years passed and in 1905 Orville Wright flew for thirty-eight minutes over a twenty-four-mile circuit. A flight in France in 1906 by Alberto Santos-Dumont of Brazil, already known for balloon and dirigible developments, aroused special interest in Europe. When Wilbur Wright demonstrated a further improved "flying machine" in France and Italy in 1908 the world was at last prepared to accept the reality of flight by something other than a balloon, and the air

---

4 In England in 1900, H. G. Wells had written that "probably before 1950 a successful areoplane will have soared and come home safe and sound."

age may be said to have begun in earnest. From that time, daredevil pilots took their planes aloft at public fairs, and the press gave consistent attention to each new development.

James Gordon Bennett, Jr., publisher of the *New York Herald,* and an enthusiastic sailor and yachtsman since his youth, had established trophies for yacht racing. He did the same for automobile race winners and for notable flights. In London, Sir Alfred Harmsworth (later Lord Northcliffe) and his *Daily Mail* also offered trophies. Louis Blériot, a French aviator, thus was awarded a £1,000 prize when he flew a monoplane across the English Channel from Calais to Dover in 1909, so ending forever England's insular position.

Bennett and Harmsworth were not alone. The *Daily Telegraph* of London, the *New York Times,* and the *Chicago Record-Herald* joined in 1910 to sponsor an effort by William Wellman, a U.S. balloonist, to fly the North Atlantic, from west to east, in a dirigible. The effort failed, but Wellman kept in communication with the *New York Times* by wireless until shortly before he was forced down off the North Carolina coast.

The *New York World,* also in 1910, bestowed a prize of $10,000 upon Glenn H. Curtiss for the first continuous flight from Albany to New York, a distance of 137 miles, flown in 152 minutes. The first airplane takeoff from the deck of a U.S. warship occurred in November of that year, and thousands of persons also watched the first aviation meet in the United States at Los Angeles, with fliers from several countries setting new records. The first U.S. transcontinental flight was completed in 1911, although with many intermediate landings. By 1914 aviation was accepted as an important new means of transport. Both planes and dirigibles were put to serious tests and grim use during the next four years of war.

Still another evidence of things to come was the existence by 1900 in Paris, London, New York, and some other large cities of stores converted to display "moving pictures." In the United States they were sometimes referred to as "nickelodeons" because a nickel, five cents, was the price of admission for the brief showing.

The moving picture had been made possible, as distinct from some earlier versions, by the production in 1884 of a suitable rolled film by George Eastman of Rochester, New York, then manufacturing dry plates for photographic use. Thomas A. Edison, perpetually innovative and working in his New Jersey laboratory, devised a suitable camera, termed a Kinetoscope, using the rolled film to capture the movement of persons, animals, or objects. An apparatus to project the films in enlarged size on a white surface or screen was devised not only by Edison, but by Thomas Arnat of Washington, and another by Louis Lumiere of Paris. Novelty films were being shown from 1894.

The camera also was used to film events in Europe and elsewhere. Motion pictures were made in 1897 of President William McKinley's first inaugural in Washington. A motion picture photographer, J. C. Hemment, was in Cuba in 1898 during the Spanish-American War as a member of the *New York Journal* group of correspondents dispatched by its publisher, William Randolph Hearst.

In 1900 at least two newsworthy events in the United States were recorded in motion pictures: a fire in a Standard Oil Company refinery at Bayonne, New Jersey, and views of Galveston, Texas, virtually destroyed by a hurricane and tidal wave in September, with an estimated loss of 4,000 lives.

In Paris in 1909, Charles Pathé, a French pioneer in motion picture photography, introduced the "newsreel" *(acualités)* as a new medium in the information spectrum, producing films of current news events. He established branch offices in London and New York to arrange for making the films, dispatching them, and distributing them for weekly showings. In the United States, a comparable Hearst-Selig newsreel was produced in Chicago, beginning in 1914, and sponsored by William Randolph Hearst. It included views of World War I events as they occurred.

The year 1903 brought the production of the first film to tell a story, "The Great Train Robbery." Independent entrepreneurs soon were producing a variety of short films presenting simple stories or comic antics. Exchanges to handle their distribution for public showings were organized in the United States in 1904, and later in other countries. David Wark Griffith, an actor who had played in films made at the Edison studio in New Jersey, began to write and produce his own films in 1908. He originated many of the processes to be adopted generally by film-makers. In 1914 he produced one of the first multi-reel pictures, "The Birth of a Nation," telling a full and significant story of the American Civil War. It was presented in regular theaters, with an orchestral accompaniment, and attracted large audiences. This and other Griffith films following were greatly to advance the technical and substantive quality of the motion picture, with the public response soon justifying the construction of special cinema theaters in countries throughout the world.

Edison, having devised a means to light homes and cities by electricity, and having contributed to the effectiveness of the telegraph, cable, and telephone, and later to wireless communication as well as motion picture photography, also had devised and patented in 1877 a "phonograph or speaking machine," and later added a machine for office use permitting the dictation of speech. By 1905 both of the latter were reasonably effective.

The popularity of the phonograph (or gramaphone) grew from that time for home and school use, and a recording industry developed on a world scale. The voices of public figures were captured, and the greatest of musical artists and orchestras made recordings. Popular songs, novelty records, and dance tunes were made available. By 1910, from the music of the minstrel shows and the night clubs of New Orleans and elsewhere, there also came, in record form, the syncopated rhythms referred to as "ragtime," the "blues," and "jazz." In both classical and popular forms, recordings had an important world-wide cultural impact.

Edison's office "dictaphone" also became the key to the making of wire and tape recordings. Both were adapted, among other uses, to improved press and commercial communication practices.

Coincidental as it may have been, the fact that the Olympic Games took place in Paris in 1900 seems, in retrospect, to have sparked a new and enthusiatic world-wide public interest in sports, both in the participatory and spectator sense. The Olympic Games had been held in Greece at four-year intervals from 776 B.C. until A.D. 394. They did not occur again until 1896, when a new Olympiad took place in Athens, and received a certain amount of press attention. Meeting in Paris in 1900, however, the games received more attention, and still more in the traditional four-year intervals following to the present time, except as interrupted by two world wars.

After 1900, a general interest in track and field sports showed a steady growth and was fully reported in the press. Horse racing, boxing, wrestling, yacht racing, and rowing, all established sports, also gained increasing public attention. The "royal and ancient" game of golf had gained such popularity that international participation in cup competition began after 1900. Tennis, devised and patented in England in 1874, likewise had gained international acceptance, with the Davis Cup established as a trophy in 1900. Basketball, also an invented game, beginning in 1891, gained world acceptance after 1900.

Rugby football and soccer football became of such wide interest as to bring the formation in Paris in 1904 of an International Football Federation, with an annual Gold Cup competition since 1930. Inter-collegiate football, differing from England's rugby variety, became so popular in the United States that the first of many regional and inter-sectional championship games was played at the Rosebowl in Pasadena, California, in 1902. Professional teams were to come later. Baseball, perhaps dating from 1839 in the United States, became known as "the great American sport," played both by amateurs and professionals, with professional teams meeting in the first "World Series" in 1903. The game subsequently became literally a world sport, popular in Japan, Mexico, Cuba, and elsewhere. Lacrosse, derived from an Indian game, is said to be the oldest organized sport in North America, spreading from Canada to become international. Cricket, beginning in eighteenth-century England, became popular throughout much of the British Empire.

Angling and skeet-shooting, handball and swimming, bowling and ice skating, fencing and rowing, golf and tennis, skiing and cycling, and marathon running all tended to be participant sports or recreations. Yet some of those also have become spectator sports. Six-day bicycle races were introduced about 1900. The Tour de France began as an annual bicycle circuit in that country in 1903, with notable press attention, and comparable races followed elsewhere in Europe, in South America, and the United States.[5]

Handball became a spectator sport in a related version called jai alai. Rowing produced crew-races in England, the United States and elsewhere. Ice skating produced both races and exhibitions of skill, as well as ice hockey. Golf and tennis grew to become spectator sports, with international competitions, as did skiing and water sports. Sailing led to yacht races. Horse races, long popular, were matched by surrey races, automobile, motorcycle, and dog races, and aviation meets. Bowling and polo matches drew spectators. Bull fights may have grown up more as spectacles than as sport, but boxing matches were no less so, with million-dollar gates beginning in the 1920s.

Soccer and football matches, baseball and basketball, track and field events also were among sports gaining audiences. Great stadiums and arenas had been constructed long before the fourth decade to accommodate the sports followers.

Most of this growth in sports occurred largely because of public

---

5   Important in the development of the bicycle was the so-called "celeripede," produced in Paris in 1816 by Joseph Nicéphore Niepce, even then also engaged in research that was to produce the first successful photographic process a few years later. See Desmond, *The Information Process,* pp. 213–15. Orville and Wilbur Wright, sponsors of aviation, conducted a bicycle repair shop in Dayton, Ohio, as they worked on the problems of flight about 1900.

interest aroused by attention given the subject by the press and other media. Sports writers and columnists became major figures in the newspaper and periodical world. Special papers and magazines appeared, and even special news agencies to meet the public interest in sports. Coverage of sports events became virtually compulsory, ever broader in scope. Indeed, the media became captives of their own creation.

Much of the coverage was and is local, but sports events became of interest nationally and internationally. This produced special attention by news representatives from many countries at the Olympic Games through the first four decades of the century,[6] but on other occasions as well.

Sports were not alone in receiving greater press attention in the 1900–40 period. Music and the dance are, of course, deeply rooted in human experience, as are art, drama, literature, and science. With some exceptions and qualifications, however, it may be said that only since about 1900 has the press been sufficiently advanced to give such subjects consistent or substantial attention.

An urbanization of society permitted a growing patronage for theatrical and musical performances, exhibitions, and related forms of public entertainment, including sports. The performers themselves, such as writers, artists, and some scientists, gained fame and a following— notably personalities of the motion picture screen and in sports. In this, those figures of government and politics, finance and trade, formerly greatly prominent in the news, were joined by many others.

The first years of the century were notable also for a growing industrialization in Germany, Japan, and the United States, and to a lesser degree in France, Italy, Holland, Sweden, and Switzerland. This was accompanied by a development of shipping, in both passenger and cargo transport, by several of those countries. Great Britain, formerly dominant in industry and shipping, thus was faced by new competition.

These years were notable for changes in living standards, generally for the better, as well as the changes in production and trade. The press contributed to the changes and advances not only by the reports published, but by an advertising content creating an awareness and a desire for new products and services. These particular influences will be examined later.

---

6 The Olympic Games took place in Paris (1900), St. Louis (1904), Athens (1906), London (1908), Stockholm (1912), Antwerp (1920), Paris (1924), Amsterdam (1928), Los Angeles (1932), and Berlin (1936).

It is impractical here to review the history of the first decades of the new century in detail. Certain of the events already have been mentioned, however, and reference to certain others is appropriate as having been among subjects receiving major press attention.

In the United States, one such subject was the 1900 presidential campaign and November election of William McKinley, Republican party candidate, to serve a second four-year term. Theodore Roosevelt, a dramatic figure of the Spanish-American War, and then in the midst of a term as governor of New York, was his somewhat reluctant vice-presidential running mate. In the light of the new position of the United States as a world power, the election received greater press attention abroad then had been usual in the past. The McKinley-Roosevelt inaugural ceremony occurred on March 4, 1901.

Italy's King Humbert, on the throne since 1878, was assassinated by an anarchist at Monza, near Milan, in July 1900. He was succeeded by his son, Victor Emmanuel III. January 1901 brought the death of Queen Victoria at eighty-one. Since 1837 she had been ruler of Great Britain and Ireland, Empress of India since 1877, and a widow since the death in 1861 of her consort, Prince Albert of Saxe-Coburg-Gotha. So ended the "Victorian period" for Great Britain and the empire. Her son, Albert Edward, already sixty, succeeded to the throne as Edward VII, with his queen, the former Princess Alexandra of Denmark. Australia gained status as a commonwealth within the empire in that same year.

In September 1901 President McKinley, attending a reception during a Pan-American Exposition at Buffalo, was shot by Leon Czolgosz, a professed anarchist, and died eight days later. Theodore Roosevelt succeeded to the presidency, an office he would occupy until 1909.

Among events receiving international attention in 1902 was the eruption of Mount Pelée in the French West Indies island of Martinique. Volcanic activity began April 25, serious eruptions occurred on May 2 and 3, and on May 8 a rain of volcanic fire fell upon the largest city, the port of St. Pierre. The city was destroyed, along with all ships in the harbor; much of the island was devastated, and an estimated 40,000 lives were lost.

Prompt coverage was provided by three correspondents. Louis Seibold of the *New York World* was in the West Indies on another mission, and was quick to reach Martinique. Hamilton Peltz of the *New York Herald* arrived as head of a relief expedition. George Kennan, former assistant manager of the Associated Press bureau in Washington, arrived as a writer for *Outlook* magazine.

A situation, rather than a single happening, arose late in 1902 over a failure by Venezuela to pay certain debts to Germany, Great Britain, and Italy. Those three countries established a naval blockade off the Venezuelan coast, bombarded Porto Cabello, sank or seized several Venezuelan ships, took control of the custom houses at Caracas and elsewhere, and threatened occupation of the country.

Reminiscent of an 1896 crisis over determination of the Venezuelan-British Guiana boundary, with a threat of war between Great Britain and the United States over interpretation of the Monroe Doctrine, the 1902 confrontation presented a comparable danger to the peace. As in 1896, however, the crisis was reported soberly by press correspondents in Washington and London. No occupation occurred, and a settlement was reached early in 1903.

A long strike in 1902 by coal miners in Pennsylvania, with incidents of violence, was reported by the press. It was the first of a sequence of events bearing upon labor and management relations that were to preoccupy both government and press in the United States for years to follow. Out of them came congressional and court actions and prosecutions under the Sherman Anti-Trust Act of 1890, reinforced by the Clayton Anti-Trust Act of 1914. Public awareness of the serious and complex issues was advanced through those years by writers in periodicals and newspapers. This was true also of some other administrative and social problems in the United States during the first decade.

An event of 1903 was the death of Pope Leo XIII in Vatican City and the election of Guiseppe Sarto as Pius X. In this, the Associated Press scored a special news triumph. Salvatore Cortesi, the agency's Rome correspondent, who had a close relationship with the Pope's physician, was informed regularly of his condition through eighteen days of illness and of his death within minutes. Using a code arranged in advance with Charles T. Thompson, AP bureau chief in Paris, and with the New York headquarters office, the news of the Pope's death was transmitted immediately for publication in the United States. Rome itself and all of Europe learned of it only as Reuter cabled the report back from New York.

The same year brought Alphonso XIII to the throne of Spain at the age of sixteen. He had been sovereign under the regency of his mother since his birth, six months after the death of his father, Alphonso XII, in 1885. A much-publicized visit to France by Britain's Edward VII in 1903 was regarded as an important move to repair a less-than-cordial relationship between the two countries. It resulted in an entente in 1904 that was to be highly significant ten years later as World War I began. A treaty between the United States and Colombia also was important. It provided for the establishment of a Panama Canal Zone, supported by a treaty later in the year with a new Panama republic. Both made possible the construction of the Panama Canal linking the Atlantic and Caribbean to the Pacific. It was formally opened to traffic in August 1914. The year 1903 closed with a fire in the Iroquois Theater in Chicago, with 602 persons killed, and a need was demonstrated for special safety regulations in theaters and other public places.

Two other disasters occurred in the United States the next year. A fire destroyed much of the Baltimore business district in February 1904, with $80 million in estimated property damage. In June, an excursion steamboat, the General Slocum, burned and sank at Hell Gate in the East River between Manhattan and Long Island, with more than 1,000 lives lost.

In St. Petersburg an attempt was made to assassinate Viatscheslaf Plehve, Russia's minister of the interior, and a second attempt in July 1904 was successful, when a member of the Socialist Revolutionary party tossed a bomb into his carriage. Even as this occurred, the Russo-Japanese War was in progress.

As previously noted, Russian actions had deprived Japan of benefits conceded by China following its defeat in the Sino-Japanese War of 1894–95, and the failure of negotiations in 1903 led Japan to direct a naval attack on Port Arthur on February 8, 1904.

The Russo-Japanese War following was reported by about 200 press representatives. This was somewhat less than half the number actively engaged during the Spanish-American War, but probably set a new record for expense in international coverage.[7]

Most of the correspondents were writing for the press of Great Britain, the United States, and Europe. They had to be transported half way around the world, maintained for months, and their communications costs ran high. It was the first war during which wireless was used to transmit reports, and the first occasion when cables provided trans-Pacific communication between Asia and North America, supplementing earlier lines to points in Europe. One estimate put the total expenditure at $10 million for about fifteen months of coverage, with three-quarters of that borne by the Anglo–U.S. press.

---

7   For details of Russo-Japanese War coverage see Desmond, *The Information Process,* pp. 417–428.

Japan, whose modern press development began in the 1870s, had received reports from one correspondent during its occupation of Formosa (Taiwan) in 1874, and from several in the Sino-Japanese War. Many more were in the field during the 1904–05 war, however, representing Tokyo and Osaka dailies *Nichi-Nichi, Asahi, Mainichi,* and *Jiji.* They were permitted to witness more action than other correspondents. Russia's press, by contrast, then strictly controlled, appears to have been represented in the field by only one correspondent, a navy officer, Captain Nicholas Klado, writing for *Novoe Vremya* of St. Petersburg.[8] China, with a great stake in the outcome of the war, had not yet developed a strong vernacular press, and only one newspaper, the *Shih Pao* (Eastern Times) of Shanghai, just established in 1904, appears to have had a representative in the field. English-language,and other foreign-language papers in China, had no direct representation during the war, depending for reports mainly upon Reuter.

Correspondents already in Japan and China when the war began played parts in its coverage. Among them were Martin Egan and Robert M. Collins in Tokyo for the Associated Press, and later in the field with the Japanese. Thomas F. Millard for the *New York Herald* and E. J. Harrison for the London *Daily Mail* also were in Tokyo. For the *Times,* Dr. Morrison continued to write from Peking, and David Fraser had become a *Times* correspondent in Shanghai.

As the war began, correspondents traveled by ship to Japan. Some, with the Russians, arrived in Manchuria by way of the Trans-Siberian Railway. Of the first group, at least a score were kept waiting in Tokyo for four months. Some then were permitted to move to Manchuria, where land action centered. The delay, restrictions, and censorship so frustrated and irritated some that they departed, and only a few witnessed any fighting.

The use of wireless to report the war was a concept supported jointly by the *Times* and the *New York Times,* which had been conducting experiments since 1901 in a wireless exchange of news across the North Atlantic. Late in 1903, with the war still no more than a possibility, but with Russo-Japanese negotiations stalemated, Lionel James, an

---

8   An unverified report exists of a correspondent named Kraievsky for the *Russkoye Slavo* of St. Petersburg, said to have been in Tokyo for two months under the name of "Colonel Palmer," posing as a British or U.S. correspondent. He is said to have interviewed Japanese leaders, visited troops and military installations, even to have taken photographs, and then returned to the United States to write. If true, he may have been an espionage agent.

experienced correspondent for the *Times,* arrived in New York with authorization to purchase equipment from the American Wireless Telegraph Company, formed in 1902 by Dr. Lee DeForest, one of several pioneers in the advancement of wireless telegraphy.

James had the equipment transported to San Francisco for shipment to Hong Kong. He sailed aboard the same vessel, along with technicians to operate the transmitter. In Hong Kong, he chartered a 1,200-ton steamer, the *Haimun,* had the equipment installed, and a receiving station was set up at Weiheiwei on the China coast.

War by then had been declared in February 1904, and from March until June, James sailed the Yellow Sea in the *Haimun,* prepared to report such naval action as might occur. He had arranged for a Japanese naval officer to join him to clarify points that might arise and to advise on the handling of dispatches, uncensored though they would be, to assure accuracy and avoid unnecessary offense. Operators on the ship and others at the shore station, supervised by Fraser of the *Times,* handled a fair number of reports for the exclusive use of the sponsoring newspapers.

Two reports were of special value. In April, the Russian flagship *Petropavlosk,* venturing out of Port Arthur despite a Japanese blockade, hit a mine and sank with Admiral Stepan Osipovich Makarov and 800 crewmen. Then, in May, Japanese forces landed at Dairen to begin a siege of Port Arthur that was to bring its surrender seven months later.

Protests were made about the *Haimun,* chiefly by correspondents bottled up in Tokyo and by their newspapers, complaining of favoritism. The Japanese government made no objection, however, until June. At that time, the Russian government also protested, and the *Haimun* was forced to suspend operations.

Three other news craft were put to sea, although without wireless equipment, to report naval action and to carry dispatches to the China coast for transmission. For the Associated Press, Paul Cowles bought and used the *Genbu Maru* in this fashion. For the *Daily Mail,* Ernest Brindle used the *Chefoo* for a brief period. For the *Chicago Daily News,* Stanley Washburn and John Foster Bass used the *Fawan* for four months, with special success in carrying Bass's eye-witness report of the surrender of Port Arthur on January 1, 1905.

Correspondents long in Tokyo, some ultimately permitted to move to Manchuria to report Japanese action there, included Melton Prior, artist-writer for the *Illustrated London News,* and a senior member of the press corps, with experience dating from 1873; Frederick Villiers, artist-writer for the London *Graphic,* and active since 1876; Bennet Burleigh of the *Daily Telegraph,* and Edward Frederick Knight of the *Morning Post,* both also experienced war correspondents. Knight was minus an arm lost in coverage of the South African War.

The Anglo-American group included other veterans of war reporting. Among them were Richard Harding Davis and James H. Hare, a photographer, both for *Collier's Weekly,* with Hare also representing the London *Sphere;* Frederick Palmer for *Collier's* and the *New York World;* Percival Phillips for the London *Daily Express;* Ellis Ashmead-Bartlett, Lewis Etzel, and Gerald Morgan, all for the *Daily Telegraph,* with Morgan also writing for the *New York Tribune.*

Others in Tokyo were Fred A. Mackenzie, Charles E. Hands, and Harrison, all for the *Daily Mail;* Maurice Baring for the *Morning Post,* and William Maxwell for the London *Standard.* Reports were prepared for the *New York Herald* by Millard, Stephen Bonsal, William Dinwiddie, and Willmott Harsant Lewis, and for the *New York Sun* and Laffan News Bureau by Oscar King Davis and John T. Swift. John T. McCutcheon, formerly of the *Chicago Record,* but since 1903 a political cartoonist for the *Chicago Tribune,* was present as an artist and writer for that paper. Alfred Curtis represented the *Chicago Daily News,* George Kennan wrote for *Outlook* magazine of New York, and Jack London, famed as a novelist, was on special assignment for the *New York Journal* and other Hearst newspapers.

Reuter had correspondents on both sides in the war. The same was true for the Associated Press. Egan and Collins were with the Japanese. Howard N. Thompson, proceeding with Russian forces from St. Petersburg, later was relieved in Manchuria by Henry J. Middleton of the Paris bureau. George Denny, Frederick McCormick, W. Richmond Smith, Christian Hagerty, and Nemirovich Denchenko all were AP correspondents with the Russians in Manchuria. Denchenko also produced a notable report from Port Arthur.

The press was further represented with the Russians by Francis McCullagh, moving from St. Petersburg for the *New York Herald* and the *Manchester Guardian,* and by Richard Henry Little, on temporary leave from the *Chicago Tribune* to report from Manchuria for the *Chicago Daily News.*

For the Agence Havas, Georges LaSalle was with the Russians. The French press also was represented in Manchuria and at the surrender of Port Arthur by Ludovic Naudeau of *Le Petit Parisien,* and by Raymond

Recouly of *Le Temps*. For *Il Corriere della Séra* of Milan, Luigi Barzini returned again to the Far East. He produced a notably perceptive report of the great Battle of Mukden during February–March 1905.

There were casualties among Japanese correspondents, who were given greater opportunity than others to move with troops. Lewis Etzel, an American writing for the *Daily Telegraph,* was killed during the bitter fighting in Manchuria. Middleton of the Associated Press died of illness at Liaoyang in June 1904. Little of the *Chicago Daily News* and McCullagh of the *New York Herald* and *Manchester Guardian* were captured by the Japanese and held for some weeks as prisoners of war.

The war came to a formal end in a treaty signed September 5, 1905, at Portsmouth, New Hampshire, pursuant to an invitation by President Roosevelt to meet there.

The conference, beginning in August, brought together, along with the negotiators, a group of correspondents prepared by experience to deal with matters of high politics and diplomacy, as distinct from the reporting of overt events of war. The occasion also brought into the world arena of journalism, for the first time, representatives of the Japanese and Russian press, writing specifically for *Asahi* and *Nichi Nichi* of Tokyo and the *Novoe Vremya* (New Times) of St. Petersburg.

The press group at Portsmouth included Howard N. Thompson, Associated Press correspondent at St. Petersburg, who had been in Manchuria briefly during the war; Dr. Emile Joseph Dillon, St. Petersburg correspondent for the London *Daily Telegraph;* Dr. George Ernest Morrison, Peking correspondent for the *Times;* Sir Donald Mackenzie Wallace, experienced as a correspondent and editorial executive for the *Times;* and George W. Smalley, Washington correspondent for the *Times,* and previously long in London for the *New York Tribune.* Also present were Melville E. Stone, general manager of the Associated Press, and Salvatore Cortesi, Rome correspondent for the agency. A considerable number of Washington correspondents were included in the gathering.[9]

Among happier news subjects of 1904 was the election in the United States of Theodore Roosevelt to a second term as president, a full term of his own; the founding of the Bethlehem Steel Corporation; and the opening of the New York subway system. There also was a settlement

---

9   Desmond, *The Information Process,* pp. 417–28.

of a long conflict of interests in Morocco between Spain and the Sultan of Morocco, and also between Spain and France. The treaty signed in October included related agreements giving Great Britain and Russia trade rights there, with an Anglo-Russian entente that was to have importance in 1914. Further, the treaty promised an end to a century-old problem with brigands, the so-called Barbary pirates operating out of Morocco, Algeria, and other African Mediterranean points to seize and hold ships and men for ransom.

Most of those pirate depredations had ended by 1900, and even the promise of 1904 was not wholly realized. Walter Burton Harris, correspondent for the *Times* in Morocco from 1887 until 1933 and based in Tangier had been captured and held shortly after 1900 by Shereff Ahmed ibn-Muhammed Raisuli, Berber leader of the Riff hills tribesmen, who held himself above and independent of the sultan.

In 1904, as negotiations were proceeding between the Sultan Abd-el Aziz and representatives of Spain and France, Raisuli captured an American citizen of Greek origin, Ion Perdicaris, and held him for ransom. The United States, which had landed Marines on the "shores of Tripoli" to restrain such practices in 1801–05, and again in 1815, was now once more involved. In Washington, Secretary of State John Hay made a sharp demand for "Perdicaris alive or Raisuli dead," a phrase suggested to him by Edwin Milton Hood, then chief of the Associated Press bureau in the capital. A U.S. naval squadron was dispatched, and Perdicaris was freed without ransom.

Such troubles still were not ended. In 1907 Raisuli captured Sir Henry McLean, a British subject serving as commander of the sultan's bodyguard. The British government paid more than £17,000 (about $100,000) for his release. Raisuli later was forced to refund most of that payment. He lived until 1925, presenting Riff tribal threats to Spanish control in Morocco at that period, and once more a subject of active press coverage.

Germany, having gained territorial positions in eastern and western Africa since 1884, also manifested an interest in Morocco in 1904. It raised questions about the treaty and trade rights gained there by Spain, France, Great Britain, and Russia. Kaiser Wilhelm had alarmed Great Britain in January 1896 by an expression of sympathy with the Boers in South Africa. Germany also was competing with Great Britain in trade, maritime commerce, and naval ship construction. Its interest in Morocco added further tension to the equation.

In 1905 the kaiser himself sailed into the port of Tangier in his yacht and formally expressed the hope that all of Morocco might remain under the sovereign authority of the sultan. In this, the kaiser did not realize his hope, and a new German demand was made that led to an international conference in 1906 at the Spanish port of Algeciras, adjacent to Gibraltar. Germany and Austria were represented, along with Spain, France, Great Britain, other European powers, and the United States. Germany sought to block a reform program for Morocco, as prepared by France, objecting that it would make Morocco virtually a French protectorate. In this effort, Germany failed again.

A considerable group of correspondents covered the Algeciras conference. Harris of the *Times,* also an adviser to the British delegation, drew upon his long experience in Morocco. Sir Donald Mackenzie Wallace, another long with the *Times,* but sometimes representing the British Crown on foreign missions, was present. Others included Ellis Ashmead-Bartlett of the *Daily Telegraph;* Granville Fortescue, a retired U.S. Army officer representing the London *Standard;* and Charles T. Thompson, Associated Press bureau chief in Paris.[10]

The French and Spanish positions in Morocco were virtually unchanged by the Algeciras meeting. French and British fears of German intentions persisted, however. One alarm was touched off by a revolt of Moorish tribesmen in Morocco in 1907 and the situation escalated, with French *gendarmarie* taking control in many areas, and with the sultan's brother, Mulai Hafid, leading a revolt in 1908 that made Abd-el Aziz a refugee, with Hafid replacing him at Fez, the capital of the French section. Another crisis arose in September 1908 when six deserters from the French Foreign Legion took refuge in the German consulate at Casablanca, but who were arrested by a French patrol as they were about to board a ship bound for Germany. Referred to The Hague Court, this resulted in a Franco-German agreement in 1909 giving Germany economic opportunities in Morocco, even though France held political control.

A more serious alarm was raised in 1911 when French forces in Fez acted to put down anti-foreign disturbances. Germany contended this action had the effect of abrogating the Algeciras agreement. It also led Germany to send the gunboat *Panther* into the port of Agadir in the French zone on July 1, ostensibly to protect Germans there. Since no protection was required, the action was viewed as a veiled threat that Germany was prepared to establish a position of its own in Morocco. It

---

10   Not to be confused with Howard N. Thompson, formerly of the AP bureau in St. Petersburg.

led to an agreement in November by which Germany received full control in a part of the French Congo in return for such claims as it might have advanced in Morocco.

These events, echoing in all the capitals of Europe, and receiving careful press attention, contributed to the deterioration of relations between Germany, on the one hand, and France, Great Britain, and Russia on the other. Two interviews granted by the kaiser in 1908, and one in particular, contributed further to that deterioration.

Anglo-German differences were causing great unrest in London and elsewhere by 1908. With an asserted desire to compose those differences, Kaiser Wilhelm agreed to an interview in September with an English friend, Colonel Edward Stuart-Wortley. A diplomat, rather than a journalist, Stuart-Wortley was assisted in writing the account of the interview by E. Harold Spender, then Berlin correspondent for the London *Daily News*. The kaiser, shown the text, approved it with only minor changes. It also was examined by the German Foreign Ministry, with little further change and no objection.

When the interview was published in the *Daily Telegraph* of October 28, however, it aroused anger and disquiet not only in Great Britain, but in France, Russia, Japan, and in Germany itself. One of the dubious statements by the kaiser was that most of the German people wanted war with Great Britain, and that he alone stood between them as England's friend. It was not the only tactless remark the kaiser made in those years, but it became an element in the situation that was to result in World War I in 1914.

What might have been even more explosive, had it ever been published, was the substance of a two-hour interview granted by the kaiser about a month after his meeting with Stuart-Wortley. On that occasion, William Bayard Hale of the *New York Times* met with the German emperor aboard his yacht, off the coast of Norway.

Hale, then thirty-nine and a former Episcopal clergyman, had turned to journalism in 1900, had been managing editor of the *Philadelphia Public Ledger* from 1903–07, and in 1908 had been appointed as Paris correspondent for the *New York Times*. One of his first acts was to go to Germany, where the newspaper was as yet unrepresented, to write a series of articles. He was given the opportunity to meet with the kaiser.

Without any prompting, the emperor talked of many things. He spoke harshly of Great Britain and British leaders, of Japan, and of the Roman Catholic Church. He said he expected Germany to go to war, sooner or later, with Great Britain, and made other statements so extreme that

Hale felt it would be unwise to publish the interview. He consulted with the United States ambassador in Berlin, with German Foreign Ministry officials, and he made his doubts known to the editorial executives of the *New York Times*. They in turn discussed the matter with President Roosevelt. All agreed that the interview should not be published.

Hale prepared a greatly modified version of the interview, however, as an article for the conservative *Century Magazine,* a New York monthly. By that time, the Stuart-Wortley interview had appeared in the *Daily Telegraph*. The German Foreign Ministry, learning of the prospective *Century* article, urgently requested that it not be published. Although the magazine even then was in production, the presses were stopped, the article withdrawn and a piece of fiction substituted. The concern in Berlin was still such that a German cruiser was sent on a special voyage to New York. There, by agreement, it took aboard those first copies of the magazine containing Hale's article, along with the plates from which the printing had been done, and all were thrown overboard in mid-Atlantic as the ship returned to Germany.[11]

News coverage in Russia had improved somewhat between 1900 and 1905 in terms of access to information and its international distribution, but a setback came in 1905 following Russia's defeat in the war with Japan.

The war had brought a growing discontent among Russian business and professional men and, even more, among workers and peasants, whose conditions of life were extremely difficult. On Sunday, January 22, 1905, with the war going very badly for Russia, a procession of workers and members of their families marched to the great square in front of the Winter Palace in St. Petersburg to make a peaceful petition to Czar Nicholas II for reforms to ease their problems. They were blocked by guards, however, and fired upon, with 1,500 killed or wounded. This "Bloody Sunday" event became symbolic of ending hope for an orderly transition in Russia from autocratic rule to a liberal society comparable to that in Western Europe.

In July of 1904 a bomb had killed Plehve, the minister of the interior. In February 1905 a bomb also killed the Grand Duke Sergius in the area of the Kremlin itself. In May the war with Japan was lost. The czar

---

11   Not until 1934, twenty-six years later, did Hale's son, William Harlan Hale, also a writer, tell the story of the interview and the subsequent action in two articles in the *Atlantic Monthly*. Not until 1939 did the *New York Times* itself present some parts of Hale's original text of the interview.

promised to convene a national assembly or Duma, supposedly to permit the people at last to participate in their own governance. But in August a new law provided only for a consultative body, with all essential powers still to be held by the czar and the Imperial Council. The results of the Portsmouth Peace Conference in September were not reassuring. Unrest throughout much of the country led to a general strike in October, and an insurrection by workers in Moscow in December.

The czar in an October manifesto had reassured the people that the proposed assembly would be granted real legislative power and, on that basis, order was restored in the country by early 1906. Members of the Duma were elected, and the parliamentary body assembled in St. Petersburg in May. Its prospective effectiveness was compromised even before it met, however, by the promulgation of laws under which the czar remained all-powerful, and the Duma was dissolved in July, with nothing accomplished. Other meetings took place in 1907 and later, but without benefit to the people.

These events in Russia between 1905 and 1907 were poorly reported within the country. Because of limited educational opportunities, except for the privileged few, illiteracy was widespread. It was the largest country in the world, occupying nearly one-seventh of the land area of the globe. Its first census, taken in 1897, gave it an estimated population of nearly 130 million, representing many races and creeds, and a variety of languages and dialects. But the country had no more than 800 newspapers of which only about fifty were dailies, and about a dozen of those were in St. Petersburg. They were small and all were under a censorship occasionally relaxed. Since the controls precluded excellence, no paper was outstanding and they reached a limited readership.

The best known of the existing dailies were the *Novoe Vremya* (New Times) and *Ryech* (Speech), both of St. Petersburg, privately published, but carefully supportive of government policies, and the *Moskovski Vedomosti* (Moscow Gazette), an official government organ. They made little effort to provide direct coverage of news, depending chiefly upon official government releases for domestic reports, with world reports received through the Wolff news agency of Germany or rewritten with great caution from foreign newspapers and publications.

In 1894 the Rossiyskoye Telegraphnoye Agenstvo (RTA or Rosta) (the Russian Telegraph Agency) had been formed in St. Petersburg. A news agency holding semi-official status, it was a subsidiary of the Wolff agency, with its service going to Russian newspapers. Count Serge Julievich Witte, Russia's minister of finance, in 1902, believed that Wolff was withholding from its service certain economic and financial reports that he regarded as important. By his action, another agency was formed in that year. Known as the Torgova-Telegraphnoye Agenstvo (TTA or KTA) (Commercial Telegraph Agency), it also received the Wolff world report, but combined with it material provided through the Ministry of Finance.

Two years later, in 1904, the Rosta and TTA agencies were merged by official edict, and designated the Sankt-Petersburgskoye Telegraphnoye Agenstvo (Viestnik or Westnik) (St. Petersburg Telegraph Agency). It continued to receive the Wolff report, and in 1909 became an acknowledged official agency, jointly directed by the Council of Ministers, with special representation for the Ministries of Finance, Interior, and Foreign Affairs. It was subject to restrictions affecting news presentation throughout the country.

Liberal and even revolutionary papers were attempted in Russia, but invariably were suppressed, although some were circulated underground. Other such papers were published abroad by refugees and sometimes smuggled into Russia. As a result, in 1900 *Iskra* (Spark) was established in Geneva, and produced later in Nuremberg and in London. A Socialist paper, it was edited until 1903 by Vladimir Ilyich Ulyanov, later to become known as Nicolai Lenin. In 1903, the Russian Socialists split, with one group, the Bolsheviks, in the majority, taking an extreme revolutionary position, as contrasted to the Mensheviks, a more moderate minority.

In 1905 a paper supporting the Bolshevik position was attempted in Russia, sponsored by Lenin from his emigré base in Zurich, Switzerland. It was edited by Josef Vissarionovich Dzhugashvili, then twenty-six, who became known in 1913 as Josef Stalin. Titled the *Novaya Zhizn* (New Life), it was permitted to appear openly in the climate existing in Russia in 1905, but was soon forced underground. In 1910 it was replaced by *Zvezda* (Star) in St. Petersburg, with Stalin still as its editor, but in 1912 its name was changed again to *Pravda* (Truth). *Pravda* sometimes appeared openly, but was often suppressed and operated underground. It became the chief organ of the Bolsheviks, the Communist party, and the new Soviet government at Moscow in 1918.[12]

For the rest of the world, events in Russia in the first decade of the century were reported chiefly by correspondents in St. Petersburg.

---

12 During the 1905–09 period 400 Russian journalists were reported jailed; from 1906–13, fines totalling $280,000 were assessed against papers. See L. M. Salmon, *The Newspaper and Authority* (New York, 1922), pp. 105–06, 266–67.

George Dobson was dean of the corps there in 1905. He had replaced Donald Mackenzie Wallace for the *Times* in 1878, but wrote primarily for the *Daily Mail* after 1897 and until 1913. Dr. Dillon, representing the *Daily Telegraph* since 1886, remained until 1914.

Dudley Disraeli Braham, who had replaced Dobson for the *Times* in 1897, was expelled in 1903, charged with "hostility" to the government and "the invention of false news." His actual offense was to report a pogrom at Kichinev in Bessarabia, with frightful atrocities, property damage, and many Jews killed or wounded. The *Times* objected to Braham's expulsion as unjustified, and waited for three years before naming Robert Wilton as a successor. It did so then only after receiving assurances that the charges against Braham had been withdrawn, and that Wilton would be well received. Actually, Wilton had been reporting earlier for the *Glasgow Herald* and unofficially for the *Times* since Braham's departure. He continued to represent the *Times* until 1917.

The *Times* also sought news of Russia through other sources. Harold Williams, a staff member who was to become foreign editor in 1919, was assigned to cultivate the Russian emigré groups in Germany, France, and Switzerland. Information also was obtained through Theodor Herzl, Paris correspondent for the Vienna *Neue Freie Presse* and a leading Zionist, with personal sources in Russia. Further reports were received from a Mr. McKenna, writing in code from St. Petersburg and Riga under the pseudonym of "Justyn Paul."

Howard N. Thompson, the first Associated Press correspondent in St. Petersburg, appointed in 1904, remained only through 1905. He was absent even during that period, first on a brief assignment in Manchuria during the Russo-Japanese War, and again to report the Portsmouth Peace Conference in 1905. During those intervals he was replaced by John Callan O'Laughlin, formerly of the *New York Herald,* who came from the AP bureau in London, and by Dutch-born, U.S. educated Hendrik Willem Van Loon. Van Loon had moved quickly, following graduation from Cornell University, through the AP bureau in Washington, and then to Warsaw and St. Petersburg. O'Laughlin succeeded Thompson in St. Petersburg in 1905, followed by Seymour Beach Conger, moving from the London bureau early in 1906 and remaining in St. Petersburg until 1911. He was followed then by Roger Lewis.

John Foster Bass, who had reported the first part of the Philippines campaign for the *New York Journal,* moved to St. Petersburg in 1901 as correspondent for the *Chicago Daily News.* He went to the Far East to report the Russo-Japanese War for that paper, but then returned to

St. Petersburg, where he remained until 1915. Stanley Washburn, with Bass for the *Daily News* during the war, went to Constantinople in 1905. There he chartered a dispatch boat and visited the Black Sea ports of Odessa and Batum in the south of Russia, ostensibly to deliver dispatches to U.S. and British consular officials, but also to gather news in that part of the czarist realm. This he transmitted from neutral ports in Rumania and Turkey for use by the Chicago paper and the *Times* in London.

Other correspondents in St. Petersburg during these years included Guy Beringer for Reuter; M. Giaccone for the Agence Havas; Francis McCullagh representing both the *Manchester Guardian* and the *New York Herald* before and during war coverage in the Far East and in Russia until after the revolution; Henry W. Nevinson for the London *Daily Chronicle* and *Harper's Weekly* of New York; and Charles E. Hands for the *Daily Mail*. William T. Stead, editor and publisher of the London *Pall Mall Gazette* and the monthly *Review of Reviews*, was present briefly.

Wallace of the *Times*, who had been that paper's first resident correspondent in St. Petersburg from 1877–78, returned in 1906 as a special emissary of King Edward VII, representing the crown in official negotiations that included direct relations with the czar. His special position gave him access also to sources within the growing political left in the country. Through seven months in the capital he acted as a correspondent for the *Times*, although unofficially. When he returned to London, he did so with a belief that a revolution would occur in Russia. Living until 1919, he saw his prediction come true.

Apart from these continuing situations revolving around Morocco, Germany, and Russia, the chronology of events receiving wide attention following the end of the Russo-Japanese War in 1905 included a demand at that time by residents of the Island of Crete for union with Greece. This had had its roots in an insurrection against Turkish rule in 1896–97. Despite objections by European powers to the desired union, it was proclaimed by the Cretans in 1908, and became official in 1913.

The year 1906 brought news of the destruction of much of San Francisco by earthquake and fire on April 18–19, with 500 persons dead or missing, 500,000 made homeless, and an estimated $350 million in property damage. The newspaper offices of the city were wrecked and communications interrupted, but eye-witness coverage was provided. German-born Karl H. Von Wiegand, then manager of the western division of the Associated Press in San Francisco, was one who produced reports. Jack London, living in Oakland, across San Francisco Bay, wrote a report for *Collier's Weekly*. Will Irwin, formerly of the *San Francisco Chronicle*, but then a member of the *New York Sun* staff, used early and fragmentary reports as the basis for a nostalgic piece in the *Sun* headlined "The City That Was." It survives as a kind of newspaper classic.[13]

June of 1906 brought a dissolution of a union existing since 1814 between Sweden and Norway. Prince Charles of Denmark assumed the Norwegian throne as Haakon VII. The new nation had a parliamentary government, woman's suffrage, and its capital in Christiania (renamed Oslo in 1925). In Sweden at the same time, Oscar II abdicated, and his son succeeded as Gustavus V.

A variety of reports on the odd and sometimes illegal activities of titled and privileged personalities in the world, and of financial and social leaders, received attention on both sides of the Atlantic, especially in the popular press. Illustrative was the occurrence in late June 1906 when Harry K. Thaw, a wealthy New York playboy, shot and killed Stanford White, a prominent and respected architect. The action occurred in the presence of scores of persons in the roof garden restaurant of Madison Square Garden, then at 23rd Street and Broadway. Thaw asserted that White had seduced his wife, Evelyn Nesbit Thaw, a former showgirl. The case, in and out of the courts for several years, received persistent press attention.

In March 1907 in the United States a financial panic began which cast a long shadow. It brought action leading in 1913 to the passage by Congress of the Federal Reserve Act, and ratification of the sixteenth amendment to the Constitution providing for a federal income tax.

The Boy Scout movement, to become worldwide, began in England in 1907, sponsored by Lord Baden-Powell, who had played a role as a correspondent for the *Daily Mail* during the South African War. The Girl Scout movement followed. A vigorous campaign for the right of women to vote, long debated in England, began to assume militant form at this time, increasing through the years until approved in an election of December 1918.

New Zealand attained dominion status within the British Empire in September 1907. A Second Hague Peace Conference met from June to

---

13 Men and women engaged in news work in San Francisco at the time made it traditional to gather annually on the anniversary of the event to reminisce. Although their numbers naturally have declined, the ceremony continues.

October of the year, carrying forward the efforts of the first conference in 1899, and a Central American Peace Conference met in Washington in November. In December 1907, most of the ships of the United States Navy, painted to form a "Great White Fleet," departed on a world cruise, both as a good will mission and as a show of force.

Two natural disasters received press coverage in 1908. An earthquake in Jamaica was reported by Percival Phillips of the London *Daily Express,* who had just arrived there for a conference of cotton planters. The second was a quake and tidal wave that decimated Calabria in the south of Italy, with an estimated 85,000 deaths and as many more casualties in the area of Messina, Sicily. Joseph Pierce of the Associated Press was killed in covering the event.

Austria's assumption of sovereignty in the same year over Bosnia and Herzegovina, former Turkish provinces in the Balkans, was significant in providing the tinder for World War I. Also significant was the assassination in Lisbon, early in the year, of King Carlos I and the crown prince. Succeeding to the throne was the king's younger son, who became Manoel II. In 1910, however, an insurrection forced him to flee to England, and a Portuguese Republic was then proclaimed.

In sports, the Olympic Games took place in England in 1908. Jack Johnson, a Negro, became heavyweight boxing champion of the world. A presidential campaign in the United States brought the election in November of William Howard Taft, the Republican party candidate. Taft had been secretary of war in the Roosevelt cabinet and was favored by Roosevelt as his successor. He was inaugurated in March 1909. A month later, Roosevelt left the United States on a year's scientific expedition to Africa, sponsored by the Smithsonian Institution. He was accompanied, among others, by John Callan O'Laughlin, AP correspondent in St. Petersburg in 1905, but then in Washington for the *Chicago Tribune,* and serving as assistant secretary of state during the last two months of the Roosevelt administration.

An early event of the 1909 was the deposition in Turkey of the Sultan Abd ul-Hamid, succeeded by his brother, Mohammed V. A major topic of the news was the final attainment of the North Pole after the failure of more than 500 previous expeditions. Commander Robert E. Peary of the United States Navy, in his own sixth attempt since 1886, became the first man to reach the Pole. This he did on April 6, 1909, along with five members of his party.

Peary had received financial support on earlier ventures from James Gordon Bennett of the *New York Herald.* Such support was not forthcoming, however, when he was preparing his new expedition in

1908. But he did receive $4,000 from the *New York Times,* with the understanding that the paper would have exclusive rights to his own story of the attempt, successful or not.

Having reached the Pole, five months were required for Peary and his party to reach Indian Harbor, Labrador, on the return journey, and further time to proceed to Newfoundland and Nova Scotia. The first report of his success was cabled from Indian Harbor on September 7, 1909, and immediately made known to the world. Walter Scott Meriwether of the *New York Times* staff wrote the first reports for that paper and then set out for Nova Scotia to meet Peary for follow-up stories, and to handle the preparation and transmission of the explorer's own account. This was published in the *New York Times* in three installments on September 9, 10, and 11, and also made available by syndication to other newspapers in the United States and abroad.

The Associated Press also sent four staff members to Nova Scotia to interview Peary and others in his party. These four were W. C. Jeffards, J. W. Regan, John Quinpool, and W. G. Foster.

The North Pole story was complicated, however, by the fact that just a week before Peary reached Indian Harbor, another experienced Polar explorer had arrived in the Shetland Islands with a claim to having reached the North Pole on April 21, 1908, almost a year before the date Peary presently was to report. This was Dr. Frederick A. Cook, originally of Brooklyn, whose message was transmitted from the Shetlands to Brussels.

Cook, a surgeon, had been attached to two of the earlier Peary expeditions in 1891 and 1902, and also to a Belgian Antarctic expedition in 1897–98. He had led other expeditions and, in undertaking a new North Pole attempt in 1907, had received $25,000 from Bennett and the *Herald.* Returning from the Arctic, Cook reached Copenhagen on September 4, three days before Peary reached Indian Harbor. He was received with great acclaim, and hailed as the first man to reach the Pole. His story was published in the *New York Herald* and other newspapers.

With the Peary claim coming in the next few days, the world was puzzled as to which to accept. Just as reporters hastened to Nova Scotia to interview Peary, so they sought out Cook in Copenhagen. One who did so was Philip Gibbs, an experienced newsman, of the London *Morning Chronicle.* He conceived some doubts about Cook's claim of having reached the Pole, made further investigations which supported his doubts, and wrote detailed reports of his findings. Cook held to his claims, was received enthusiastically in New York on September 21, and had the full support of the *New York Herald.*

By December, however, it had become officially accepted that Cook had not reached the North Pole, but that Peary had done so. The University of Copenhagen, which had conferred an honorary degree upon Cook in September, cancelled that action. He was expelled from the Arctic Club and from the Explorers Club of New York, of which he had been president. Even the *New York Herald* was forced to concede that he had failed.[14]

Efforts had proceeded since 1840 also to explore the Antarctic regions. Ernest Henry Shackleton, a British explorer, conducted an expedition to the southern polar area during 1907–09, and returned to New Zealand in the summer of 1909, several months before the Peary-Cook claims were heard. He had not attained the South Pole, but he did bring important new knowledge of the Antarctic. An account of his expedition was transmitted in the longest cable dispatch yet moved between New Zealand and London, occupying four and one-half columns in the *Daily Mail*.

Shackleton's experience, combined with Peary's success, provided an incentive for Roald Amundsen, Norwegian Arctic explorer, to turn to the Antarctic. He had been there with Cook on the Belgian expedition of 1897–99. In 1910–11, however, he led his own party, and on December 14, 1911, became the first man to reach the South Pole, with four companions. Naturally, the exploit received great press attention, with the London *Daily Chronicle* carrying an exclusive personal account.

Captain Robert Falcon Scott, a British explorer, reached the Pole about a month later, on January 18, 1912, also with four companions. B. J. Hodson, of the London Central News agency, anticipating Scott's return, went to New Zealand to obtain a full account. Tragically, however, the Scott party encountered difficulties on the return journey; all perished in March, with their remains only found the following November.

On another level of news concern, the British government in 1909 was confronted with unusual budgetary costs for naval construction to keep pace with German building, and also for social reforms. A proposal for greatly increased taxes on persons of means became a controversial issue leading to a general election in January 1910 and another in December. The Liberal party, controlling the government since 1905, lost seats in

---

14   Cook disappeared for a time, but later wrote and lectured on the Arctic. He also spent more than six years in prison for violation of the postal laws in an oil promotion scheme. He died in 1940, outliving Peary by twenty years.

Parliament, but still retained a majority. Serious economic problems remained, however. One result was a series of strikes in 1911–12 among rail and transport workers and coal miners. This was further complicated by a growing demand for Home Rule in Ireland, and somewhat comparable demands in Wales.

The year 1910 also brought the death of King Edward VII in May.[15] Former U.S. President Roosevelt, who had made an almost triumphal tour of Europe following his return from Africa in February, represented the United States at the king's funeral ceremonies in London. George V succeeded to the throne. His queen was Mary, daughter of the Duke and Duchess of Teck.

In the same month in 1910, Halley's comet, passing the sun on May 18, was one of the first science stories to receive wide public attention both before and after the event. Some persons were prepared to believe that the earth, passing through the tail of the comet, might come to an end.

It was a year during which the Carnegie Endowment for International Peace was established, with a fund of $10 million from Andrew Carnegie, successful in the manufacture of steel through the introduction of the Bessemer process in the United States. It was not his first benefaction, and it was followed in 1911 by the establishment of the Carnegie Foundation, endowed with $135 million, for the "advancement and diffusion of knowledge and understanding." This foundation was surpassed financially in 1913 in the establishment by John D. Rockefeller, Sr., Standard Oil Company director, of a Rockefeller Foundation. It was intended to operate beneficially on an international basis, beginning with an endowment of almost $242 million.

The Nobel Prizes, awarded in Sweden since 1901 for accomplishments in science and literature and for contributions to peace, had been established under the will of Alfred Bernhard Nobel, inventor and manufacturer of high explosives from 1867 until his death in 1896. The Nobel awards began to receive particular attention throughout the

---

15   The United Press Associations (UP), formed as a second news agency in the United States in 1907, had established a few resident correspondents in Europe in 1909. One of the London representatives was Fred L. Boalt, former editor of the *Portland News* in Oregon. Boalt had gone to Buckingham Palace to make a routine inquiry about the king's condition, since it was known he was ill. Identifying himself, he said "I am the UP man." Unfamiliar with the new agency, those he spoke to apparently assumed him to be a medical specialist or technician, as with an "X-ray man." On this assumption, presumably, he was passed along until he met the king's physician, who told him "the King is dying." Thus the United Press gained advance knowledge and was able to provide an early report.

world after 1910. Indeed, Guglielmo Marconi had received the prize in physics in 1909 for his invention of wireless telegraphy.

The first decade also closed on three other cheerful and constructive events. The Union of South Africa was formed in 1910 and became a dominion, healing the scars left by the South African War of 1899–1902, with Louis Botha, Boer commander at the close of that war, as the first premier. A fourth Pan-American Conference met in Buenos Aires, and the Cunard liner *Mauretania* (31,937 tons) set a new transatlantic speed record that stood for twenty-two years, crossing from Queenstown to New York in 4 days, 10 hours, 41 minutes.

Such events and circumstances as noted above, possessed of sufficient importance or general interest as to warrant public attention in many parts of the globe, may be referred to for that reason as "world news," as distinct from those reports of more limited local or regional interest. It is the variety that forms the basis for the examination of press and media procedures in the pages following. The media of information were to make it their business, increasingly, to report such newsworthy events and situations, and to do so as accurately, promptly, and effectively as possible.

Changing Perspectives in the Press 3

A new adjacency of peoples and nations in the first years of the twentieth century was very real. It was built upon the creation since about 1850 of a network of communications, rail and steamship lines, an organized postal exchange, and the beginning of an extended highway system to accommodate a growing motor traffic.

The needs of an unfolding industrial and commercial complex, especially in Europe and the United States, but in Japan and some other areas as well, contributed to these advances. Wider educational facilities were required to support the evolving economic, political, and technical structure of society. No less important was the provision to the public of a reliable service of current information by a press organization already well developed.

Thousands of newspapers and periodicals were appearing throughout the world by the first decade of the century. They were made to meet every sort of public need and interest. A newspaper, by definition, is a paper of news; that is the reason for its existence, whatever else may appear in its columns. A magazine, or periodical, might be concerned with any subject. Published weekly, monthly or otherwise, it could hardly report the news in the manner of a daily newspaper. Some magazines published news-related, topical articles, however, and a few were concerned with current affairs. Great changes would come later, but in 1900 those magazines not made to serve special interests or particular groups tended to be literary or critical in content.

Most newspapers were published weekly and were small in size and circulation. They usually served small communities and retained some characteristics of the printer-owned papers of the early nineteenth century. There were, however, hundreds of daily papers appearing in many countries during the 1900–10 period. It is accepted that to be classified as a daily a newspaper must be published at least five days a week; most appear six days and many seven days. By 1900–10, a considerable number were large in circulation, with a few approaching or exceeding a million a day. Even for such leaders, however, a twelve-page paper was fairly standard, except on special occasions, or in Sunday editions, when they might be produced in two sections or more.

It is elementary to note that some dailies are published for morning distribution, others for distribution in the afternoon. Traditionally, the morning newspaper has been the more important and the more prestigious. Taking advantage of the longer interval for preparation and distribution provided by the hours of the night, the morning paper was able to present more news, including a reasonably full account of the previous day's events. It could add editorials (or "leaders," in the British usage) relating to those latest events, and it could be made available to subscribers or newsstand buyers over a wide radius by the breakfast hour. In these circumstances, morning papers usually have been circulation leaders.

The afternoon newspaper, by contrast, normally would produce its main edition, among several, at about 4 P.M., or earlier. This was before the conclusion of the day's activities, locally, but necessarily so to permit delivery of the paper to the homes of subscribers before the dinner hour, and for sale to home-bound workers. Time still did not permit delivery over so wide a radius as the morning paper, thus reducing its circulation potential. The growth of urban communities, however, and the use of motor vehicles for distribution made substantial circulations possible, and even leadership for some. Considering time zone differences, it was even possible for many afternoon papers to present a full budget of the day's news originating in most of the world. Many smaller cities had only an afternoon paper. The larger the city, the greater the possibility that it would have two or more dailies.

Advertising and Press Distribution

The effectiveness of the afternoon paper in terms of reader service, and as an advertising medium, was demonstrated by Edward W. Scripps, world pioneer in the development of group newspaper publication. Beginning in Cleveland in 1878, he controlled more than twenty dailies in the United States at the time of his death in 1926, all of them afternoon papers. In those years, he saw the population of the country double. The number of morning papers rose from 438 to 504, circulating 15 million copies a day, but afternoon papers increased from 533 to 1,612, circulating 25 million copies.

Scripps recognized that many persons had more time to read a newspaper in the evening than in the morning. Men usually left home early each day to go to their work. Women remained at home, for the most part. An afternoon paper, purchased by the man on his way home, or home-delivered, usually not later than 5 P.M., provided later news and was available for all members of the family to read in the evening. Scripps made it a point to publish material in his papers that would be of interest to women as well as to men, and perhaps even to younger members of the family. This was not always so in the morning papers. He also was aware that women usually were the purchasing agents for their families in matters of food, clothing, and furnishings. The woman, with an opportunity to read the newspaper in the evening, could discover what was being advertised in the shops for the following day, could discuss with her husband possible purchases, and could plan her time for the next day to take advantage of special sales. This she might not be able to do on the basis of an advertisement seen in the morning paper and calling for prompt action. It made the afternoon paper a particularly effective retail advertising medium. Retailers themselves were induced to give thought to the use of advertising in the press, whether morning or afternoon.

Retail advertising was a well-established feature in newspapers of the United States and Great Britain in the 1900–10 period, although less so in the press of most other countries. The volume of advertising, retail and otherwise, had grown in ratio to the growth of cities and changes in the economy. As business and industry learned to use advertising effectively to advance the volume of trade and services, assisted by a growth of advertising agencies, more pages were required to accommodate the advertising messages in the individual newspaper. The papers grew larger in number of pages, and a proportion of that added space went to the publication of more news and editorial matter. The division of space by about 1910 was approximately 40 percent advertising and 60 percent news-editorial. It was a ratio, incidentally, to be more than reversed in later decades.

The progressive growth in advertising proceeding in the first decade was not only a spur to retailing and business in general, but a service to the public, providing useful information about goods and services. Equally important, it brought revenue to the newspaper through the sale of advertising space far exceeding the revenue from subscriptions and the sale of the papers themselves. This enabled the newspaper to engage more staff members to gather, write, and edit the news, to prepare substantial editorial articles, to afford news agency and syndicate services, and thus to improve the general service to readers.

At the same time, the newspaper organization changed. It had long ceased to be an enterprise dominated by a printer-owner, as in the eighteenth century and before, and had become the expression of an editor-owner's personality and interests. The late nineteenth and early twentieth century brought it into a third phase, however, with a concern for production costs, advertising revenue, circulation promotion, and delivery. Management problems called for the attention of a business-wise publisher-owner. With the enterprise growing in size, he became an administrator assisted by an editor and managing editor, specifically concerned with news and editorial content, managers in charge of advertising and circulation, others in charge of mechanical production, an accounting staff, and a general housekeeping staff. Each of these functions had its own special and subordinate divisions.

As the newspaper grew in size to accommodate the greater volume of advertising, it became essential that that volume be maintained or increased to support the technical and mechanical investment and staff organization. The circulation also had to be maintained or improved if the newspaper's finances were to be kept in balance.

Newspapers were being published competitively in many cities during the 1900–10 period. Other things being equal, the paper with the largest circulation would be the favored advertising medium, might set the highest advertising rate because it reached more potential customers, and might therefore expect to enjoy the greatest prosperity. But only one paper could be the leader in circulation and naturally wished to maintain that position. Other papers sought to maintain positions strong enough to attract and hold a volume of advertising to assure survival at the very least. This competition gave great importance to reader-appeal as the key to building and retaining a level of circulation, lacking which a newspaper would tend to lose favor as an advertising medium, and could be forced out of business.

Enterprising editors and writers through the years had found new subjects and better or more appealing ways of treating old subjects to win readers. Per-copy prices and subscription prices had been cut to the lowest possible figure, and copies of papers were made easy to obtain through street sales and home delivery. The drama of events and the manner of their reporting had established before 1900 a public habit of reading newspapers. An element of sensationalism added to news reporting from about that period in a number of countries made for some very large circulations, if not always for the most admirable kind of journalism. Such so-called popular newspapers at one extreme were matched by so-called quality papers at the other.

As the term suggests, the quality paper is serious, effective, and responsible in its performance. It gives major emphasis to "hard news," meaning that which is most significant—news of substance. It presents well-informed and non-partisan interpretation and guidance through special articles and editorials reflecting a concern for public understanding and welfare. It maintains high standards as to the advertising accepted for publication. Its typographical dress is conservative and tasteful. Usually, it is a morning paper.

The quality paper, quite properly, is highly respected, viewed as the best paper where it exists. There are few of them, actually, because relatively few readers are prepared to appreciate so exclusive an emphasis upon serious and sometimes complex subjects, with no concessions to entertainment. Few will take the time to read such a newspaper as it deserves to be read. For that reason, the quality paper rarely leads in circulation. In its ultimate expression, it cannot even exist except in a very large city, possessing enough readers to support it and, even then, usually also because it is received by others living outside the city of publication. The quality paper has one special advantage. Because it is known to be faithfully read by persons of intellect and talent, and often of power, position, and wealth, its advertising rate is high in proportion to its circulation.

The popular paper, by contrast, shapes its content and typographical display to capture the attention and interest of that far larger segment of the population unprepared to give close attention to serious subjects, and which is seeking entertainment beyond substance, or at least along with substance.

It must be said, however, that a popular paper is not necessarily to be faulted because it does not meet the standards of the ultimate quality paper. There is nothing wrong with a newspaper being interesting or providing entertaining material, so long as it maintains a reasonable balance. Since there are so few true quality papers, every other paper, almost by default, is forced into some lesser category, yet many are excellent and responsible in undertaking to inform their readers. Better that a person read a responsibly made popular paper than no newspaper at all. Many persons who might appreciate a quality newspaper do not live in an area where it is available. Others may prefer a brighter newspaper. Some read both. The reader of a popular newspaper, gaining new maturity in the course of experience, may discover at some point that the quality newspaper no longer seems dull.

Where the popular newspaper becomes objectionable is when it resorts deliberately to sensationalism in the selection of material for publication, to forms of display and headline use carrying a distortion of emphasis, to writing involving an invasion of personal privacy, to bad taste, or to substituting trivia to the exclusion of substance. A paper sacrifices respect when it so panders to a segment within the readership as to stress the more regrettable manifestations of human behavior. It may even lose the right to be called a newspaper if it elects to win readers by overburdening its pages with entertainment features, forcing out informative matter. Falsification and partisanship would be the ultimate sins.

As a proper distinction may be made between a popular paper that is objectionably sensational or trivial and one that is acceptably interesting and responsible, so a distinction may be made between the more serious papers. A serious paper is not necessarily a quality paper. It may also exist as the voice of a government or group. It may or may not be admirable, but it could be significant, exercising an influence in shaping opinion within a community, a nation, or the world. Such papers existed earlier, and they were usefully classified in 1968 by Dr. John C. Merrill, professor of journalism at the University of Missouri. He introduced the term "élite press" to include forty newspapers at that time, including the few unquestioned quality papers along with others significant within twenty-five countries.[1]

Differentiations had to be made also in the 1900–10 period, and still must be made, between the information paper and the political paper, and between local, regional, and national newspapers.

The information paper, the most representative, stresses the news, whether in quality or popular style. The political paper, while also presenting news, is identified with some political party, splinter group, or political figure, and usually is so partisan in character as to outweigh its informational value. Most political papers have been small in size and circulation, and read mainly by the party faithful. Such papers have been most numerous in European capitals, with Paris a prime example.

As a special-interest publication, the political newspaper is not alone.

---

1   John C. Merrill, *The Elite Press: Great Newspapers of the World* (New York, 1968).

There also are religious papers, financial papers, sports papers, theatrical and literary papers, and papers presenting society news and gossip. Some of the latter are weekly rather than daily publications. There also are information papers owned in whole or in part or controlled by governments or by industrial or corporate groups. Such control may or may not be known to the public. The contributions to knowledge by all such special-interest papers may only be·judged on their merits.

Those papers classified as local, regional, and national are so designated simply by way of describing their areas of distribution and readership. Most newspapers always have been local, being distributed primarily in and near the place of publication. The regional paper, obviously, is distributed over a wider radius. A national newspaper is distributed pretty much throughout a particular country, and on the date of publication. To make this possible, the size of the country, the available means of transportation, and the time available for distribution become the controlling factors. The area within which it is distributed naturally bears upon its potential influence, its total circulation, and its prosperity.

In Great Britain by 1900, it was already possible to distribute London morning and Sunday newspapers by rail to reach most parts of the United Kingdom by breakfast time or mid-morning, except for northern Scotland and Ireland. The morning *Manchester Guardian* was similarly distributed. The national newspaper made its first appearance in this fashion in Great Britain. It gave very large circulations to the *Daily Mail* and some other popular daily and Sunday papers, and it added appreciably to the readership of such quality papers as the *Times,* the *Guardian,* the *Sunday Times,* and the Sunday *Observer.*

The system was extended to France. With Paris at the hub of a national rail network, morning papers of the capital could be delivered to most parts of the country for morning readership, and gave some such papers very large circulations. The system also was adopted in Japan, with newspapers of Tokyo and Osaka receiving national distribution. Morning dailies of Tokyo, Paris, and London now long have had circulations far exceeding others in the world by reason of such distribution, further advanced by the establishment of branch publishing plants and communications technology.

In even smaller countries, it was easier to distribute newspapers nationally. Thus, in Holland papers of Amsterdam, Rotterdam, and The Hague were read throughout the country; in Denmark, papers of Copenhagen; in Belgium, those of Brussels and Antwerp; and in Switzerland, those of various cities were interchanged.

Within larger countries, it was not possible in 1900, or for long after, to distribute a newspaper nationally on the date of publication. Regional distribution was the best that could be attained. This is not to say, of course, that some newspapers did not circulate widely or even nationally, but with delays.[2]

Magazines

Periodicals in great variety were appearing in many countries by 1900. Some gave attention to current subjects and were making increased use of photographs. Writers included experienced newspaper reporters and correspondents; some served as editors. Given time and space to deal with subjects at length, and with a magazine having a longer life in a home than a daily newspaper, some articles had great impact, inducing political, economic, and administrative action, and shaping social behavior.

Magazines gained special importance in the United States at this period. The country at last had been settled, from coast to coast, with rail service connecting virtually all cities and towns. It was thus possible to distribute weekly and monthly magazines nationally, to reach newsstands and subscribers on or before the cover date, and to reach a literate and prosperous audience.

The appeal of certain magazines, available at low cost, won impressive circulations, attracting a substantial volume of advertising, and making the magazines themselves highly profitable. This in turn enabled them to engage the best qualified editors and writers, and the finest artists and photographers. With the publications thus made increasingly satisfying, circulation and advertising grew further.

The national distribution of such magazines had a social importance. They created a public awareness and interest in matters of significance. Their wide readership helped build a national unity, modified what otherwise would almost certainly have been a devisive regionalism in so large a country, and reduced what would have been a marked parochialism.

---

2 Only since about 1950, through air delivery and the use of electronic means of facsimile transmission of pages for reproduction at branch plants, has remote same-day distribution or publication of newspapers become possible in the United States, the Soviet Union, or other large countries.

The effectiveness of the advertising messages reaching a national audience was enormously important, economically and socially. A national market was created for consumer goods and services, with products made available to a buying public through local retail outlets and department stores, and also through mail-order firms, which grew large at this time. As with the magazines themselves, the products advertised were distributed nationally by rail and through the postal service. This contributed to the industrial growth of the nation, and also educated the people in a way of life more attractive, more satisfying, and more constructive.

What happened, as a result of magazine growth in the period just before and after the turn of the century, is well described by Theodore H. White in a novel.[3] Reference is made to a fictitious printer-publisher-editor entering the magazine business in New York. One of White's characters describes what followed in the next half century:

> ... They'd just finished building the railways across this country. ... Now any factory anywhere can ship its goods from coast to coast for the first time. The whole country is one market, ... but only if you can find a way of talking to the whole country at once. They need a big horn ... that will reach everybody.
>
> ... Not only that. Everything was beginning to fit together then. They were developing high-speed rotary presses that could throw off a couple of million copies of a magazine in a few days ... someone develops half-tone photo-engraving so magazines can use pictures, cheap. ... All of it ... coming together, with industry screaming for a way to sell pianos, baby carriages, kerosene lamps, stoves from coast to coast. They want a horn to talk to the market.
>
> ... Do you know what happened when national magazines started to develop? ... They had to invent a new kind of person to run them! It was the first time anybody except the President of the United States had to sit in an office and think about this whole damned country all at once. Some editor had to think not just what the local people in Chicago, or New York, or Charleston, or San Francisco wanted to read, but what would hold an audience together across the whole land. ... The first time somebody sat in this kind of office in New York and started to play with the mind of the country, things started to happen. ... For the past fifty years anything this country has done, the magazines kicked them into doing—the magazines closed up the trusts, cleaned up the cities, put through food-and-drug acts, amended the Constitution, closed off immigration. ...

---

3 Theodore H. White, *The View from the Fortieth Floor* (New York, 1960), pp. 106–07.

Allowing for a certain hyperbole, the "big horns" did appear, with the results mentioned. The fictitious publisher or editor could have been any one of a number: Samuel S. McClure, Frank A. Munsey, Cyrus H. K. Curtis, Edward W. Bok, George Horace Lorimer, Joseph Palmer Knapp, and several others.

Among the first magazines to attain national distribution were *Collier's Weekly* of New York, and the *Ladies' Home Journal* and the *Saturday Evening Post* of Philadelphia.

Collier's, originally called *Once-a-Week,* dated from 1888, established by Irish-born Peter Fenelon Collier. Robert J. Collier, son of the founder, edited *Collier's* from 1896–1902. He was followed by Norman Hapgood to 1912, by Collier again until 1914, by Mark Sullivan to 1917, and by Finley Peter Dunne until 1919. At that time, Joseph Palmer Knapp, a successful printer and publisher of other magazines, took control as publisher.

Collier's was perhaps the first magazine in the United States to venture directly into the coverage of news, as it did at the time of the Spanish-American War and the Russo-Japanese War, with photographers in the field, and with both Frederick Palmer and Richard Harding Davis reporting the latter war. Mark Sullivan, already an experienced investigative reporter at thirty-two, joined the staff in 1906, and contributed important articles in the years before becoming the magazine's editor from 1914–17.

Cyrus H. K. Curtis, formerly in the advertising business, established the *Ladies' Home Journal* in 1883 as a magazine for women. Successfully edited by Mrs. Curtis until 1889, it was directed from that time until his retirement in 1919 by Edward W. Bok. Coming to the United States from his native Holland as a small boy, Bok had previously edited the *Brooklyn Magazine* and conducted a syndicate in New York for three years. As editor of the monthly *Ladies' Home Journal,* he made it far more than a magazine for women. It was extremely influential in advancing the role of women in public affairs, and contributed to the constitutional change by which they gained the right to vote.

In addition, however, Bok helped through the magazine to raise the standards of taste in dress, home architecture, and furnishing. He acquainted readers with the best in literature. As early as 1892, he began a campaign against patent medicines, nostrums of no intrinsic value, and went on to help raise the standards of public health. He explored matters of nutrition and examined the improper labeling and advertising both of pharmaceutical and food products, of packaging and adulteration, and of other matters involving public safety and welfare.[4] In this effort, Bok was supported by Mark Sullivan and Samuel Hopkins Adams writing in *Collier's* in 1905–06, and by Upton Sinclair acting independently to describe unsanitary conditions in Chicago meat-packing houses in his book, *The Jungle* (1906). The result of these exposés was the passage by Congress of the Pure Food and Drug Act in 1906. Under Bok's direction, the *Ladies' Home Journal* became one of the first national magazines to gain a million in circulation, and it was highly profitable as an advertising medium, drawing a great response from its readers.

Curtis also bought the *Saturday Evening Post,* a languishing Philadelphia weekly, in 1897. Founded in 1821, it never had any connection with Benjamin Franklin, as implied in its years under Curtis. George Horace Lorimer, with brief experience as a reporter in Boston, was employed in 1898 when he was thirty-two and made editor of the *Post* in 1899. Until 1936 he continued as editor-in-chief and made the magazine one of the most successful and prosperous. By 1912 it had nearly two million circulation and more than seven million dollars in advertising revenue and grew beyond that. The popularity of the magazine was advanced by readable short stories and serial fiction, combined with articles of substance on public affairs. It was attractively printed, with inviting covers by Norman Rockwell and other talented artists. It sold at only five cents a copy. The *Post* paid its writers well and had its choice of the best. Staff writers included Samuel G. Blythe, former *New York World* bureau chief in Washington, and Isaac F. Marcosson, formerly of the magazine, *World's Work.*

Other weeklies giving attention to public affairs and subjects in the news included *Leslie's Weekly* and *Harper's Weekly.* The first, known as *Frank Leslie's Illustrated Newspaper* for many years after its establishment in 1855, continued until 1922. *Harper's Weekly,* appearing from 1857 until 1916, was edited by Richard Harding Davis from 1890–94. During that time, following association with the *New York Evening Sun,* Davis also traveled widely as a writer for the magazine, producing articles on newsworthy subjects in the United States, Latin America, and Europe. He stressed personalities and colorful aspects of the places visited.

The *Nation,* established in 1865 by Edwin Lawrence Godkin, was a weekly of opinion which continued under his direction until 1899 and

---

4 Bok tells his own story of those years in an autobiography, *The Americanization of Edward Bok* (New York, 1920), which won a Pulitzer Prize in 1921.

then by Oswald Garrison Villard until 1934. It was substantial and important, but not in the popular category. It was matched after 1914 by the *New Republic,* edited by Herbert Croly and financed by Dorothy Payne Straight and Willard D. Straight. He was a former U.S. diplomatic representative in China, Korea, and Japan, acting chief of the Division of Far Eastern Affairs in the Department of State, and later a representative in China for an American banking group. In 1904–05 Straight had represented both Reuter and the Associated Press as a stringer in Tokyo, Seoul, and Manchuria. The Straights also financed *Asia* magazine. Croly, former editor of the *Architectural Record,* was editor of the *New Republic* until his death in 1930. In the first years he had Walter Lippmann as associate editor, and Charles Merz, formerly of *Harper's Weekly,* became Washington correspondent in 1916 and associate editor in 1919.

The *Outlook,* established as a religious weekly in 1867, was transformed in 1893 under Lyman Abbott to become a magazine of public affairs. It received articles from various capitals and centers of news activity, and also used articles by leading personalities, including Theodore Roosevelt, a contributing editor after leaving the presidency. George Kennan, formerly of the AP, and builder of a portion of what became the Great Northern telegraph line across Siberia, already has been mentioned as a contributor.

Another weekly, the *Pathfinder,* begun in Washington in 1894, was unusual in that its main concern was with the news, which it rewrote from newspapers, adding entertaining miscellany. Folksy in style, it was directed to readers in small towns and rural areas. Printed on newsprint and offered by subscription at a dollar a year, its circulation was substantial, as was its advertising content which ran heavily to mail order offerings and patent medicines. In a sense the first news weekly, it survived into the 1950s, with latter-day bureaus in New York, Chicago, and some foreign cities.

Made to appeal to a more sophisticated audience but also placing stress upon matters in the news, the *Literary Digest* was established in 1890 by Dr. Isaac K. Funk and Adam W. Wagnalls, both former clergymen and book publishers. It gained importance after 1905 under the editorship of William Woods Seaver. Each week it summarized the news and newspaper editorial comment on the news, adding photos and a selection of political cartoons and some material reprinted from publications of various countries. By 1910 it was solidly successful both in circulation and advertising volume.

A number of other magazines established in the nineteenth century gave at least some attention to public affairs and carried over into the new century. Among them was the *National Geographic Magazine* originating in 1888. It took a new direction in 1905, stressing photographs, and began a long advance in circulation and advertising continuing to the present time. Others were the *Atlantic, Harper's, Century, North American Review, Scribner's, Cosmopolitan,* the *Forum, McClure's, McCall's, Munsey's, Pearson's, Everybody's,* and the *Review of Reviews.* Most were published in New York City.

The *Review of Reviews,* established in 1891, was edited by Dr. Albert Shaw, a former editorial writer for the *Minneapolis Tribune.* He believed the public needed help in sorting out the complexities of world affairs, and the magazine was made to summarize and condense the news and to present interpretations in accompanying editorials.

Another monthly, *World's Work,* was established in New York in 1900 by Doubleday, Page and Company, book publishers. It was edited by Walter Hines Page until 1913, when he was appointed United States ambassador to Great Britain. The magazine was concerned with the "activities of the newly organized world, its problems and even its romances." Isaac F. Marcosson was a staff member, assigned to Washington before he moved to the *Saturday Evening Post.* The magazine was absorbed by the *Review of Reviews* in 1932, then edited by Frank H. Simonds, and the *Review of Reviews* was absorbed by the *Literary Digest* in 1937.

A group of magazines, both old and new, including some mentioned, attained importance and performed usefully in the early years of the century providing manifestations of investigative reporting. They were circulated nationally, enjoying the advantage of low postal rates set for all publications in 1879 by congressional action, and inexpensive and widely read. Two had been established in 1893, *Munsey's* and *McClure's,* both monthlies. Frank A. Munsey was primarily interested in profits, which he later also realized from newspapers and from a first chain of (Mohawk) grocery stores. Samuel Sidney McClure, already directing one of the early syndicates, sought writers qualified to produce articles of depth and substance on subjects of importance and in the public interest.

The emphasis in *McClure's* magazine, beginning in 1902, was on aspects of the growing industrial and corporate structure in the United States and on the conduct of government at all levels. Writers included Ida M. Tarbell, Lincoln Steffens, and Ray Stannard Baker. Miss

Tarbell, already known for carefully researched biographies, produced a series on the history and business operations of the Standard Oil Company and on John D. Rockefeller, its founder and director. Steffens, formerly of the *New York Evening Post* and the *New York Commercial Advertiser,* wrote a series titled "The Shame of the Cities," detailing corruption and misgovernment in several. He followed with a series on state governments. This also was carried forward by George Kibbe Turner, formerly of the *Springfield Republican* of Massachusetts. Baker, formerly of the *Chicago Record,* examined labor problems, with attention to wages and hours, safety, the employment of women and children, unionism, and the position of Negroes in the changing economy.

McClure's also published articles by Burton J. Hendrick on abuses in the direction of life insurance companies, contributing to a major inquiry in 1905 resulting in new laws and bringing Charles Evans Hughes into public life through his action as counsel for the committee of investigation. He became governor of New York in 1906 (defeating William Randolph Hearst), Supreme Court justice from 1910–16, Republican candidate for the presidency, secretary of state from 1921–25, and chief justice of the Supreme Court from 1930–41. William Allen White, editor and publisher of the *Emporia Gazette* in Kansas, and known for his political writing, became a contributor. Samuel Hopkins Adams and Will Irwin, both formerly of the *New York Sun,* served on the staff, although both also wrote later for *Collier's.*

In 1906 Baker, Steffens, Tarbell, and John S. Phillips, all identified with *McClure's,* joined to buy control of the *American Magazine,* with a heritage going back to 1870. For the next several years, with Phillips as editor, they made it a vehicle for further articles of inquiry. Control of the magazine went in 1911, however, to Joseph Palmer Knapp, head of what had become known as the Crowell Publishing Company of Springfield, Ohio, to which *Collier's* was added in 1919. Both publications changed direction but proceeded successfully along with the *Woman's Home Companion,* a Crowell monthly publication since 1897, and chief competitor of the *Ladies' Home Journal.*

In the years of the first decade, David Graham Phillips, formerly of the *New York World,* wrote a series of articles for *Cosmopolitan,* then recently purchased by Hearst, which were critical of practices in the United States Senate. Charles Edward Russell, formerly of the *Minneapolis Journal,* followed up on the articles by Steffens and Turner in *McClure's* by writing further in *Cosmopolitan* of flaws in state governments. Alfred Henry Lewis, formerly Washington correspondent for the *Chicago Times* and the *New York Journal*, wrote of the so-called "beef trust" and of Wall Street practices in *Everybody's*, then one of the largest magazines in circulation. He later examined the International Harvester Company for *Cosmopolitan*.

The generally critical tone of so many of the articles published in these magazines led President Roosevelt to refer to them as "muckraking"—the term deriving from *Pilgrim's Progress*. It was not to suggest that the articles were inaccurate, improperly sensationalized, or undeserving of serious public attention. Some of them, indeed, gave support to the president's own "trust-busting" program. The impact of the articles was powerful and brought benefits to the nation and respect to the writers.

Newspapers and some magazines had published articles and editorials previously that were informative and strong, and they continued to do so. An example was the exposure and breakup of the corrupt Tweed ring in New York in the 1870s by the *New York Times* and *Harper's Weekly*, including the appearance in the latter publication of powerful cartoons by Thomas Nast. But the appearance of articles in magazines circulating nationally and continuing month after month had impressive results. They brought passage by Congress of the first Pure Food and Drug Act, tighter controls and higher standards in the insurance business, broke up trade combinations, forced improvements in factory operations and working conditions, with new measures of safety and sanitation, hastened the right accorded to women to join in the democratic process by casting their votes, and contributed generally to the public welfare by improving the administration of government.

The period of muckraking did not continue in its original form beyond 1910. From that time, however, there always were periodicals of general circulation in the United States presenting fully topical material, sometimes scarcely distinguishable from what might conceivably have appeared in a newspaper. What the magazines had accomplished through their advertising pages in stimulating the distribution and sale of products nationally was fully supported by the daily newspapers in their own communities by publishing the advertising messages of the local distributors of those products, as well as by their own quota of national advertising for the products and services. Newspapers and magazines alike continued to turn attention to faults in the general society, and to contribute thereby to their recognition and correction.

As magazines were entering upon a new role in their contributions to public information in the United States during the first decade of the century, they were doing the same in some other countries, notably

France, Italy, Great Britain, and Germany. Periodical publications had begun to appear in those countries in the seventeenth century. By 1900 magazines existed in most major countries. None matched certain of those in the United States during that decade or later in the circulations attained. It would be several decades before any approached U.S. publications in advertising volume, or influence upon the markets for goods or services.

Many of the magazines in other countries were literary and critical in their content; a number placed emphasis upon illustrations, although accompanied by text; some were primarily for entertainment. There were, however, a number concerned with public affairs, political and economic.

Among the more important publications in the various categories appearing in the first decade in Great Britain were the *Edinburgh Review* (1802), the *Quarterly Review* (1809), *Blackwood's Magazine* (1817), the *Fortnightly Review* (1865), and the *Cornhill* (1860), the first to use serial fiction. Among many others were a London *Review of Reviews* established in 1890 by W. T. Stead, the *Strand Magazine* (1891), more popular, with fiction, articles, and illustrations, the *Sphere* (1900), the *Tatler* (1901), *Punch* (1841), and three weeklies, the *New Statesman,* the *Spectator,* and the *Economist.* The *Illustrated London News* (1842) long had been a major weekly presenting reports and sketches from the "news fronts." The *Graphic* (1869) and the *Sketch* (1892) were comparable but less important.

In France, the magazines at the time included *l'Illustration,* the *Revue des Deux Mondes,* the *Mercure de France,* the *Revue de Paris,* and a new (1909) revue, *NRF.* Germany had, among others, the *Illustrirte Zeitung,* one of the early illustrated periodicals. Italy had *La Critica,* a new (1903) bimonthly established by Benedetto Croce.

Syndicates

Apart from news agency services which were well established by 1900, commercial syndicates existed to provide newspapers with a variety of materials to supplement the news. Such syndication began in England and the United States, possibly as early as 1820, certainly by the 1840s, but increasingly after about 1865.

By some interpretations, Samuel Topliff, conducting the Merchants' Reading Room, a Boston coffee house, in the 1820s, may have pioneered in syndication when he distributed reports personally written from

Europe for use in Boston newspapers. Charles A. Dana, then a *New York Tribune* staff member, may have been another such pioneer when he arranged to have copies of letters written from Europe in 1848 distributed for use by several newspapers in the United States. The sharing of news reports coming from India at considerable cost for use by London morning dailies in the 1840s also may have amounted to syndication.

In a more precise sense, however, the first real syndicate is rather commonly accepted as having been formed in Chicago in 1865 by Ansel N. Kellogg, then former publisher of the weekly *Baraboo Republic* in Wisconsin. There and elsewhere in the United States during the Civil War period from 1861 to 1865 weekly and small daily papers sometimes were short of writers and printers and lacked for news and other material to fill their columns. They established a system for the exchange of material with papers in other towns, and sometimes even of material already standing in type.

This experience induced Kellogg to establish the A. N. Kellogg Newspaper Company in 1865. From Chicago, the company provided newspapers with ready-printed sheets to form pages two and three of a four-page weekly, such as then were common in small towns. Referred to as "patent insides," and delivered in the desired number of copies, the printer-publisher then could prepare and produce the other side of the sheets to form pages one and four with local news and advertising. The Chicago company filled the inside pages with general news and feature material rewritten from Chicago, New York, and Washington papers, and added some advertising for its own profit. As the company proceeded, it added electrotype plates with text that could be laid in the form ready for printing on the flatbed press, half-tone cuts for photos or cartoons, special articles for use when required, and every other sort of aid for a busy publisher.

In 1906 the Kellogg company was purchased by the Western Newspaper Union (WNU), a comparable enterprise established in 1872 in Des Moines, Iowa, which had prospered and was to absorb still other companies in the printing field. Moving its headquarters and production to Chicago, a more conveniently located center, as Kellogg had found, the WNU went forward to provide small newspapers with every requirement. It even entered into advertising representation, soliciting paid advertising for national products and services for the use and added profit of newspapers and handled on a commission basis. Changing technology in the newspaper business eventually brought the WNU to an end in 1952, but certain of its advertising services survived even then.

The use of short stories and serial fiction was regarded by many newspapers in the 1870s and as late as the 1920s as helpful in building and holding circulation. This was an early practice among dailies in Paris, with major novels by such writers as Emile Zola and Jules Verne given first publication in that fashion. There the daily installment or *feuilleton* would appear in the same position each day, occupying perhaps half of an inside page. In France they were not syndicated. In the United States, however, Irving Bacheller, briefly a reporter in New York, began in 1883 to distribute fiction and then other material to newspapers. This he continued to do with great success until 1896, and also became a novelist himself. He joined the staff of the *New York World* during the 1898–1900 period, but after that he turned entirely to the writing of fiction. He lived until 1950.

Edward Bok, prior to becoming editor of the *Ladies' Home Journal* in 1889, had conducted his own Bok Syndicate Press for three years in New York. He began in 1886 by distributing weekly letters written by the Reverend Henry Ward Beecher, for many years pastor of the Plymouth Congregational Church of Brooklyn. He added other articles on theological subjects, letters on literary topics, and particularly a full page of material designed to be of special interest to women. It was this that brought him to Curtis's attention.

The first syndicate to represent both permanence and variety was established in New York in 1884. This was the S. S. McClure Newspaper Features, beginning with a distribution of short stories and serial fiction, as Bacheller then was doing. McClure supplemented this by an Associated Library Press in 1892, and the selection of material then became considerable. He directed the syndicate until about 1914, meanwhile also establishing and conducting *McClure's* magazine from 1893 until about 1910.[5]

From 1895 William Randolph Hearst began to syndicate material originated by and for the *New York Journal,* which he had purchased that year, and by his *San Francisco Examiner.* This included articles, special columns, cartoons, and comics. The Hearst Syndicate became the King Feature Syndicate (KFS) in 1914 and continues as one of the largest.

The *New York World* and the *New York Herald* both entered syndication in 1895, distributing their own features and special news reports. Other newspapers also entered into a similar distribution of

---

5 McClure lived to be ninety-two, his death occurring in 1949. He wrote an autobiography in 1914 and, although he owned *McClure's* magazine again briefly in 1924, the last decades of his life were devoted largely to personal writing projects.

their own news reports, and sometimes also cartoons and photographs. This was so with the *Sun* papers of New York, and with the Laffan News Bureau, a creation of the publisher, William M. Laffan. It operated from 1897 until 1916. The *Chicago Record* service, begun in 1899, was transferred to the *Chicago Daily News* in 1901, and also was available through syndication.

In 1902, Edward W. Scripps converted an earlier and limited service into the Newspaper Enterprise Association (NEA). It was based in Cleveland, originally to serve the Scripps newspapers, but was made available commercially in 1909 and later became NEA-Acme, providing a great variety of material, including photographs.

Curtis Brown, former editor of the *New York Press,* organized a Curtis Brown Syndicate in 1900, with offices in New York and London, to distribute articles and fiction. Louis H. Moore, a staff member of the old United Press news agency (1882–97), was the syndicate's representative in London from 1900–07. He was succeeded by John S. Steele. The New York based syndicate was reorganized in 1914, becoming the Edward Marshall Feature Syndicate.

World War I brought new activity to syndicates, and their numbers and offerings multiplied after the war. The services of individual newspapers, some of which had been made available to other newspapers before the war, were made increasingly available through syndication in the later years. This applied chiefly, however, to the services of newspapers in the United States, where distances made it possible for many newspapers to use the same service without their circulations overlapping.

News Agencies

From 1900, it was the information newspapers, both quality and popular, along with the news agencies, that performed the important service of gathering and publishing current reports, and they did so with ever-growing speed and effectiveness.

The well-made information paper covered the news of its own community, with its reporters observing events and exploring news sources in the city of publication, the area surrounding, and sometimes farther afield. The news of the nation and of the world reached that paper through one or more news agencies, possibly augmented by other services or syndicates, and in some instances by a paper's own stringer or staff correspondents. Thus, the news of the world is that which transpires in any one community raised to some power approaching infinity.

Beginning about 1800 a few newspapers in London ventured to send staff writers to France, Germany, and Spain. So began an effort to bring some orderly reporting to the affairs of the world. Wars interfered with such enterprise, however, until after 1840. By that time two or three New York dailies also were showing comparable initiative.

Until about 1850, nevertheless, most newspapers depended for news from beyond their own communities largely upon the receipt of other newspapers, whose contents they then rewrote or reprinted so far as they wished. Delivery of such newspapers delayed by days, weeks and months because of distances meant that nearly all news was late when published. There was little recourse for newspapers until telegraph and cable lines permitted prompt reports and, for most, until news agencies were formed to provide such reports with the transmission costs so prorated as to make them affordable. While telegraph services began to become available in the 1840s, and cable service from the 1850s, it was not until after 1870 that a world service of news began to flow.

A newspaper sufficiently prosperous, and willing to send its own reporters into the field to report events of war and peace, or to take up residence in other cities and capitals, as some did in the 1840s and 1850s, referred to them as "special" correspondents, "staff" correspondents, or as "our own" correspondents. News agencies were to do the same after about 1860. Correspondents sometimes were shared by two or more non-competitive newspapers or news agencies. Or a staff member of a local newspaper in a city or capital might provide reports to others. Such non-staff reporters were referred to as "stringers" or "stringer correspondents."

These practices, terms and differentiations still apply with reference to reporters for newspapers and news agencies. So far as readers were concerned, such correspondents remained anonymous figures virtually until the period of World War I. Exceptions were rare. A major change began at that time, however, with an identity given to many through the attachment of their names or "bylines" to their reports, or sometimes pseudonyms or initials, usually above but sometimes concluding the dispatches.

London dailies, following their pioneering efforts to produce original reports from beyond the boundaries of the country, were represented abroad by a considerable number of correspondents after 1870. Certain New York newspapers by then were somewhat active in the same manner. No individual newspaper in any country, however, was as yet able to afford the provision of original coverage on a world scale. This was where news agencies were able to serve effectively, using staff and stringer correspondents. Even they were able to do so only by arranging after 1870 for an exchange of news between three of the first agencies. These three, Reuter (Great Britain), the Agence Havas (France), and the Wolff Büro (Germany), became known as world agencies, and as the big three. They not only exchanged news among themselves, but they obtained news through a group of associated national agencies, one of which was the New York Associated Press. All formed an Alliance of News Agencies, commonly referred to as the "Ring Combination," its members bound by contracts or "treaties," renewable at periodic intervals. In 1900 that alliance included twenty-eight news agencies in as many countries.

The news agencies began as private commercial ventures, with Havas as the first in 1835. The Wolff agency, beginning in 1849, and the Reuter agency in 1851, both offered business and financial reports and only entered general news distribution in 1855 and 1858, respectively. In later years, the Havas and Wolff agencies obtained financial support from their governments, French and Prussian (the Imperial German government after 1870), and to this extent became at least semi-official agencies, even though not necessarily admitting to that status.

The New York Associated Press, having had its beginning in 1848, went through two reorganizations prior to 1900, first in combination with the Western Associated Press (1867–93), and then as the Associated Press of Illinois (API) (1893–1900), when it became known more simply as the Associated Press, a cooperative, nonprofit agency owned by its member newspapers.

As the Ring Combination news agencies existed in 1900, they were either (1) privately owned commercial enterprises, with Reuter as the largest of these; or (2) cooperative, with the Associated Press then virtually alone in that category; or (3) semi-official, as with Havas and Wolff; or (4) fully official, as with some existing in countries where the national press was not large enough or prosperous enough to provide full support. There government support was required if an agency was to exist at all. Such an agency had to be regarded as official, and at least potentially subject to governmental direction in the handling of news subjects touching upon high policy or some controversial matters.

There were other agencies unrelated to the Ring Combination. They were small, usually operating exclusively within their own countries, or even within cities. Some dealt with general news on a limited scale, but many were concerned with specialized reporting of financial, political, sports, or religious news. This only began to change in 1907, and further in 1909, when the United Press Associations and International News Service were formed in the United States.

The technology of newspaper production was, of course, a matter of continuing concern. The first decade of the new century carried forward the advances of the past, with improved press facilities to help keep pace with rising circulations and broader distribution. The quality of printing and of photoengraving advanced. There were to be changes in the manner of news writing and presentation during the first four decades, and the technology of communication was to be greatly advanced.

Communications and the Electronic Age

As the twentieth century began, the countries and continents of the world were linked by a network of electrical communications created approximately within the previous fifty years. Each advance in communication, as in transportation, reduced dependence upon the horse and the sailing vessel. Each advance had been reported by the press, used by the press, and sometimes assisted by the press.

Telegraph, cable, and telephone lines were widely extended by 1900, and wireless was the newest wonder. Even as the world was on the verge of a motor age, an air age, and no less a new industrial age, it also was on the verge of an electronic age. All that had gone before, great as it was, was merely prologue.

One of the first advances of the decade was the completion of an electronic bridge across the Pacific. Two bridges, to be precise. A major gap in the world's cable network in 1900 was the absence of any direct line between North America and points in the Far East. This was corrected with cables placed in service in 1902 and 1903.

The first of these, jointly sponsored and owned by the governments of the United Kingdom, Canada, Australia, and New Zealand, ran from the Canadian port of Vancouver to Sydney and Brisbane, Australia, by way of Fanning Island, Suva, and Norfolk Island, with a spur from there to Auckland, New Zealand. From New Zealand and Australia, a connection through the existing British-owned Eastern Extension, Australasia and China Telegraph Company lines provided for communication with most places in Asia and Europe. Another Canadian-based cable was laid later.

The second Pacific cable was completed in 1903 by the Postal Telegraph-Commercial Cables Company. The Postal Telegraph Company, formed in 1881 and based in New York, was supplemented in 1884 by the Commercial Cable Company, providing service across the North Atlantic. Both companies at that time came under the direction and control of John W. Mackay (who had made a fortune in silver in Nevada's Comstock Lode) in association with James Gordon Bennett, Jr., publisher of the *New York Herald.* A separate Pacific Cable Company was formed to extend a Pacific cable. Mackay died in 1902 as arrangements were proceeding, and the companies then came under the direction of his son, Clarence H. Mackay.

The new Pacific cable, placed in service the following year, ran from San Francisco to Manila by way of Honolulu, Midway Island, and Guam. From Manila, a link was available to Shanghai and other Asian points, including Tokyo, by way of the existing British Eastern Extension Company cable.

As part of the Pacific Cable Company service, a spur line was completed in 1904–05 between Guam and Yokohama by way of the Bonin Islands. Construction of this line went forward in great secrecy, for the Russo-Japanese War was in progress, and by special wish of the Japanese government, to assure uninterrupted communication with the rest of the world if the Russian navy should manage to cut the cables then existing between Japan and the China coast. This did not happen and the spur cable was operating in 1905.

Wireless
Communication
Established　　At this same period, experiments were proceeding in the use of wireless, stemming from earlier work by Michael Faraday in England, Heinrich Hertz in Germany, and Guglielmo Marconi's successful operation in Italy. Messages in code had been moving over short distances since 1898, with the press of Ireland, England, and the United States giving active support to Marconi. Working with him in his British Marconi Wireless Telegraph Company, formed in 1900 in a reorganization of his first companies of 1897, were James A. Fleming and C. S. Franklin. Their problem was to extend the range and clarity of the wireless signals.

In the United States, experiments also were being made. Prominent among those at work were Reginald Aubrey Fessenden, Canadian-born engineer with the Westinghouse Electric and Manufacturing Company of Pittsburgh; Thomas A. Edison at his New Jersey laboratory; Dr. Lee DeForest, who had completed undergraduate and graduate study in 1899 at the Yale Sheffield Scientific School; Irving Langmuir, with the

General Electric Company research laboratory at Schenectady, New York; and Swedish-born Ernst F. W. Alexanderson, also with the General Electric Company, whose alternator improved international wireless communication.

Fessenden had made important early contributions adding to the power of wireless signals by inventions in 1901 and 1906, at a time when he was general manager of the National Electric Signal Company in Massachusetts. His equipment was used in 1901 for news transmission by the Publishers' Press Association, a New York based regional news agency established in 1898. Fleming and Franklin in England, and Edison, working with German-born Emile Berliner, added vital elements. DeForest also devised improvements on existing equipment and in 1902 set up his own organization, the American Wireless Telegraph Company, to manufacture transmitters and receivers.

Under contracts with the U.S. government in 1903, DeForest built wireless stations for use at the U.S. Naval Observatory at Arlington, Virginia, at Pensacola and Key West, Florida, at Guantanamo Bay, Cuba, and in Puerto Rico and the Panama Canal Zone. His equipment was used by Lionel James, London *Times* correspondent, aboard the steamer *Haimun,* to report events during the early months of the Russo-Japanese War. In 1906 DeForest devised the audion tube, which became the basis for advances in every area of communications and for modern electronics in its broadest application.

Meanwhile, since 1901 the *Times* and the *New York Times* had been conducting experiments in wireless transmission across the North Atlantic. The first news message had been moved successfully on December 26, 1902—a twenty-five word dispatch to the *Times* from George E. Parkins (later Sir George Parkins), stringer correspondent for the paper in Toronto. The two papers joined in financing and sharing James's wireless dispatches during the Russo-Japanese War.

It was possible, from the outset, to transmit messages over short distances, as from ship-to-shore or between ships at sea. Recognizing the potential value of such use as contributing to safety at sea, Marconi had worked with Lloyd's of London, specialists in marine insurance, almost from the time of his arrival in England from his native Italy in 1896. In 1900 a Marconi International Marine Communications Company was formed, shore stations established, and wireless equipment put aboard some ships.

From about 1903, it was possible for messages to be relayed across the Atlantic from ship to ship. This method was used in 1905 to carry to London for the *Daily Telegraph* a shipboard interview conducted by its correspondent, Dr. Emile Joseph Dillon, with Russia's foreign minister, Count Sergei Yulievich Witte, when both were en route to the Portsmouth Peace Conference following the Russo-Japanese War.

It was 1907 before wireless became sufficiently reliable to permit a fairly regular exchange of news messages between the *New York Times* and the *Times* of London. This was done, however, with Glace Bay, Newfoundland, and Clifden, Ireland, as the points of transmission and reception for the North Atlantic traffic. Existing cable and telegraphic connections completed the circuits between London and New York and Toronto. On October 17 of that year, a commercial service began, utilizing Marconi stations. A press rate of five cents a word was set, in contrast to the ten-cent cable rate then in effect. Uncertainties and delays still persisted, however, and restricted general use of wireless for news exchange, particularly where urgency was a factor. The *New York Times* nevertheless received quite regularly some less urgent matter, intended for use in its Sunday editions.

By 1912 the technical difficulties at last were sufficiently solved to permit the New York paper to receive all of its dispatches from London by wireless, including some relayed from points on the European continent and beyond. The *Times* also received all of its dispatches from the United States and Canada in the same fashion. Other newspapers and news agencies made some use of the facilities. The *New York Herald* in that year also established a transmitter in New York to broadcast news bulletins to ships at sea, with some reports posted or printed for the information of passengers.

In August 1912 the White Star liner *Titanic* sank in mid-Atlantic after striking an iceberg. More than half its passengers and crew members were lost. Had it not been for wireless communication between the *Titanic* and the Cunard liner *Carpathia*, the loss of lives might have included all aboard the *Titanic*. Even so, there had been faulty and interrupted wireless signals. Marconi himself, in New York when the *Carpathia* arrived, went aboard to learn what he could about those failures.

An International Radiotelegraph Union (IRU) had been formed at a Berlin conference in 1906. A second conference met in London late in 1912 while the *Titanic* disaster was still fresh in the minds of all persons. One of its main objectives, accordingly, was to establish a firmer allocation of frequencies for coastal and ship wireless transmitters, with strict regulations to prevent users straying from their assigned wavelengths, and to prevent unlicensed transmitters or careless operators from causing interference and confusion on the air. A supplementary International Conference on Safety at Sea met in London in 1914 to give further point to these measures, but it was interrupted by the outbreak of World War I.

Governments were actively interested in wireless communication, not only for use by ships at sea but for diplomatic and military use. Just as the United States Navy contracted with DeForest in 1903 to construct wireless stations, so the British General Post Office (GPO), administering all communications in the United Kingdom, had a wireless station constructed near Rugby. The British Admiralty had its own station for naval communication. The French government established a powerful station on the Eiffel Tower; the German government erected a station at Nauen, a few miles west of Berlin; and the Dutch government built a transmitter, the most powerful at the time, to permit communication with its possessions in the East and West Indies.

Wartime military considerations brought suspension in 1914 of nongovernmental wireless transmission across the North Atlantic through British and French stations. The exchange of press messages over that routing therefore ceased and was not resumed until after the Armistice in 1918. The German transmitter at Nauen remained in use, however. It moved press messages between Germany and the United States until 1917. The Dutch transmitter also was put to some use by the press.

Beginning of Radio Broadcasts

A significant advance in communication began during the early years of the century, with pioneering experiments in the transmission by wireless of voice and sound.

Fessenden appears to have been the first to produce what became known as "broadcasts." In 1906, while with the National Electric Signal Company in Massachusetts and continuing his experimentation, a program of music went out on Christmas Eve from his laboratory at Brant Rock. Wireless operators aboard some ships within several hundred miles of the coast were astonished to hear voices, singing, and the sound of a violin coming from their headsets.

Two years later, DeForest broadcast in Paris an experimental program of voice and music from the Eiffel Tower. It was heard more than 500 miles away. In January 1910 he also broadcast a program from the stage of the Metropolitan Opera House in New York, with Enrico

Caruso, famed operatic tenor, among those heard within a limited radius by the few then possessing the necessary equipment.

The first radio broadcasts to be heard regularly in the United States, and possibly in the world, began in 1909, arranged by Charles David Herrold in San Jose, California, where he conducted the Herrold College of Engineering and Radio to instruct telegraph and wireless operators. In experiments of his own, he was able to place a transmitter and aerial atop the Garden City Bank building in San Jose. He and Mrs. Herrold broadcast music from phonograph records, with a microphone placed before the machine. The audience at that time was limited to amateur or ham operators in the central California area, and to wireless operators on ships off the Pacific coast.

As Herrold proceeded, the San Jose station was designated as FNFN, and bore other experimental designations until 1921. In 1912 he added a transmitter at the Fairmont Hotel in San Francisco. In 1913, collaborating with the Navy Department, he erected a transmitter at Mare Island, near Vallejo, and another at Point Arguello, in the south, near Lompoc.

At the time of the Panama Pacific Exposition in San Francisco in 1915, DeForest gave demonstrations there of wireless and radio technical developments. Herrold and his San Jose and San Francisco stations played a part in these demonstrations. By 1921 when radio was gaining public interest, the San Jose station was licensed under the call letters of KQW, with broadcasts originating both in San Jose and San Francisco. It became an affiliate in the Columbia Broadcasting System network in 1928, and was redesignated as KCBS in 1948.[1]

Although radio broadcasting, like wireless itself, was ruled out for civilian use in the allied countries during the war years of 1914–18, including the Herrold station, at least one other experimental broadcast was produced domestically by DeForest when the United States was still neutral. In this, he may also have become the first radio news broadcaster. From a transmitter at Highbridge, New York, in November 1916 DeForest used news bulletins provided through the *New York American* to report election returns when President Woodrow Wilson was elected to a second term in the White House.

Despite Fessenden's priority in 1906, DeForest's three broadcasts in 1908, 1910, and 1916, his invention of the vitally important audion

---

1   Long unrecognized in the history of radio development, Herrold's part in its evolution was revealed by Gordon B. Greb, a member of the San Jose State University faculty. See Gordon B. Greb. "The Golden Age of Broadcasting." *Journal of Broadcasting* (Winter 1958–59), 3–13; also Terrence O'Flaherty, *San Francisco Chronicle,* April 3, 1959.

amplifier tube, and numerous other contributions to electronics gained him informal designation as the "father of radio."

Radio developments put to practical tests during the war were given wide application almost immediately after the return of peace. In 1919 Dr. Frank Conrad became one of the first to operate an experimental radio transmitter. From his home garage in Pittsburgh, Pennsylvania, he broadcast phonograph records, as Herrold had done ten years before on the West Coast. As assistant chief engineer of the Westinghouse Electric and Manufacturing Company, Conrad also held some 200 patents in electronics. He moved his transmitter to better quarters in 1920, then licensed as KDKA, Pittsburgh, a Westinghouse station.

In November of that year, KDKA broadcast returns in the presidential election during which Senator Warren G. Harding, the Republican candidate and editor and publisher of the *Marion Star* of Marion, Ohio, won election over James M. Cox, the Democratic candidate and publisher of the *Dayton Daily News*.[2] Their vice-presidential running mates, both later to serve in the presidency, were Calvin Coolidge, former governor of Massachusetts, and Franklin Delano Roosevelt, assistant secretary of the navy in the Wilson administration.

At times referred to as the first radio station and as the first to broadcast news, KDKA actually was neither. The Herrold station in San Jose certainly had preceded it, and possibly what became WHA in Madison, Wisconsin, broadcasting from the University of Wisconsin campus. Not only had DeForest broadcast news of the presidential election in 1916, but the *Detroit News,* with an experimental station, 8MK, later to become WWJ, had been broadcasting news since August 20, 1920. Station KDKA, nevertheless, was undeniably a pioneer in broadcasting and may have been the first to do so on a regular schedule. These developments, bringing an important new dimension to the information process, will be examined later in greater detail.

---

2   Horace Greeley, editor and publisher of the *New York Tribune* and candidate of a splinter Liberal Republican party and of the Democratic party for the presidency in 1872, is the only other journalist ever to have run for that office. He was defeated by Ulysses S. Grant, Republican party candidate, running for a second term. Greeley died on November 29, 1872, less than a month after the election.

The devices produced by Fessenden, DeForest, and others to improve wireless transmission were applicable to telegraphic, cable, and telephonic communication, adding speed and clarity. The rights to the DeForest audion tube were sold in 1912 to the American Telephone & Telegraph Company. With applications conceived by John J. McCarty, AT&T engineer, it produced improvements in long-distance telephone use and experimental demonstrations in wireless telephony in 1915. Alexander Graham Bell, the inventor of the telephone, then sixty-eight, and his coworker in Boston of 1876, Thomas A. Watson, then sixty-one, again conversed, but over a distance of 3,000 miles, rather than between adjacent rooms, as they had first done. Bell was in New York and Watson in San Francisco. The U.S. Navy station at Arlington, Virginia, also spoke by telephone that year to the Eiffel Tower in Paris, and with navy installations in San Diego and Honolulu.

The telephone and the typewriter had become important adjuncts in the gathering, preparation, and transmission of news. Indeed, the typewriter, introduced in 1873, was triply important. Its principles were adapted to the operation of Ottmar Mergenthaler's Linotype in the 1890s to set type by machine. The typewriter was used not only by newsmen to write their accounts more rapidly and legibly, but by telegraphers to transcribe code messages directly into typewritten form, with carbon sheets added to produce duplicates; and it was adapted to teleprinter machines after about 1912, providing for the automatic delivery by telegraph of typewritten news reports between news agency and newspaper offices.

Agency reports and other messages reaching newspaper offices long had been delivered over a network of leased wires. This required the presence in each office of telegraphers to read the incoming Morse code and transcribe the messages. There was a variation of this method in New York, where copies of news agency dispatches were distributed to newspapers by pneumatic tube. In London and Paris, such reports were distributed by messengers either in the form of "flimsies," thin sheets produced in multiple written copies by the use of a stylus, or as printed sheets to be scissored apart at the receiving end, with separate stories selected, prepared for use and sent to the printer.

A second variation involved the use of the telephone. Some newspapers in small cities could not afford to receive their news reports by telegraph. From London, as early as the 1880s, the Reuter agency had served some such papers in the surrounding area by telephoning brief items for their use. In the United States, Kent Cooper, bureau manager in Indianapolis in the 1890s for the Scripps-McRae Press Association, also had devised a plan for telephoning the news to small newspapers. Later, with the Associated Press in New York in 1910, Cooper as traffic manager introduced the same system on a larger scale.

The telephone service by then was more widely extended and improved. It was possible to set up a link between an Associated Press bureau in a major city and small newspaper offices within a radius of one hundred miles or more. With the circuit established at a scheduled time, and the costs pro rated, an editor in the AP bureau would read a prepared report of news at dictation speed, the items following without pause. In each of the newspaper offices, a listener would copy the items, possibly in the form of notes or shorthand, or directly on a typewriter. They then would be rewritten. This so-called "pony service" was being used throughout the United States within a few months of its introduction by the Associated Press, and was adopted by the United Press as well.

The ultimate solution for prompt and accurate news distribution, however, awaited the appearance after about 1912 of the automatic printer or teleprinter, activated by telegraph over a leased wire network, but without the need to employ telegraphers to transcribe the reports. It was thus affordable even by smaller newspapers.

Experiments had been conducted since the introduction of telegraphy on systems to convert the code signals into written or printed form. In the United States, in the first years of the telegraph, short and long pencil marks were made separately but automatically on a running tape, coincidental with the code transmission, to be read as the dots and dashes of the code. The system was promptly abandoned, however, when it became clear that the operators could read the sounds themselves with greater speed.

In England, as early as 1838, Sir Charles Wheatstone patented a so-called Dial printer, or chronometric telegraph, activated by telegraphic impulse and producing printed letters on tape. It was slow, however, and therefore went unused. Improved devices were introduced later by Lord Kelvin (formerly Sir William Thompson) and by Alexander Bain. Other systems were produced in France by Louis François Clément Breguet and Jean Marie Emile Baudot, and in Germany by Johann Georg Halske. Royal E. House, an American, made his entry in 1846, patenting a device both in the United States and Europe. David Edward Hughes improved upon it in 1855, while Edison, Frank L. Pope, and Elisha Gray also made their contributions.

Stock market and commodity market reports began to be distributed to New York bankers, brokers, and others, in visual form on tape in 1866. In that year, Dr. S. S. Laws, a former Presbyterian minister who had become vice-president of the Gold Exchange in New York patented a device operated by telegraph to report the price of gold in a service reaching subscribers in their offices. A year later, Edward A. Calahan improved upon the system, delivering quotations in printed form on a running paper tape. A Gold and Stock Telegraph Company, formed in 1868, took over the Laws device and improved upon it, utilizing inventions by Edison, Pope, and Calahan. It was referred to as a "ticker tape" because of the sound made in the recording process. The company became a subsidiary of the Western Union Telegraph Company in 1870 and expanded considerably.

The system also was extended to Great Britain in 1869, and became the basis for the formation in 1872 of the Exchange Telegraph Company (Extel) of London, but with a minority ownership held in New York. It distributed reports of the London Stock Exchange on tape, and in 1884 added a limited news report. Reuter made arrangements with Extel to use the instrument itself to deliver news to London newspapers, although the rate of transmission still was hardly more than ten words a minute.

Transmission of telegraph messages became mechanized in those years. As a telegrapher sent a message, the electrical impulses not only activated a sounder-key matching the dot-dash signals, but also caused a paper tape to be punched. Each letter, numeral, or symbol was represented by individual patterns of small holes, originally three in number, but later five. That tape punched at the point of message origination, perhaps at a relay point and at the receiving end, could be fed into a transmitter to send, resend, or relay the signals automatically and at greater speed than by direct manual transmission because they moved without pause. Electrical contacts made through the holes in the tape caused the appropriate signals to move over the circuit. This system continues to be used, with numerous refinements and adaptations—one of the first was its application to the operation of the automatic teleprinter.

Essential to that device was an adaptation of the typewriter. The first effective typewriter was produced in 1867 by Christopher Latham Sholes, editor of the *Milwaukee Sentinel* during 1861–63, along with two associates, Carlos Glidden and Samuel W. Soulé. After further experimentation and improvement, the machine was placed in production in 1873 by E. Remington & Sons of Ilion, New York, manufacturers of rifles. Under the Remington name, it was progressively improved. Other machines also appeared. From about 1880, telegraphers used the machine to transcribe code messages directly into readable typescript.

The typewriter became an element in experimentation looking toward an automatic teleprinter that would reproduce news reports and other messages, not only on running tape but in typewritten form on a full-width sheet. Such experimentation had been conducted during the nineteenth century in Germany by Halski, Carl Friedrich Gauss, Wilhelm E. Weber, Johann Philipp Reis, and Ernst Werner von Siemens; in England by Sir William Fothergill Cooke, Frederick George Creed, and Donald Murray; in the United States by Edison, Pope and Gray, and by Amos E. Dolbear, George W. Phelps, German-born Edward E. Kleinschmidt, and Charles L. and Howard Krum.

The first machines to perform effectively were activated by prepunched tape transmitting telegraphic code signals and producing typewritten matter on paper eight inches wide, moving automatically from a continuous roll. The machines were introduced between 1900 and 1906 by Murray in England; by von Siemens in Germany; and by Kleinschmidt and Krum in the United States.

In the earliest practicable machines, the transmission was all in capital letters, but the use of caps and lower case soon became possible. The use of tape permitted a steady transmission, with messages moving at an original rate averaging forty words a minute, later increased to sixty, or 3,600 words an hour, the effective maximum for many years, compared to an average of about thirty-five words moved in manual transmission and transcription by telegraphers.[3]

A news agency delivering a service to a newspaper for teleprinter reception could send story after story, line after line, single-spaced, double-spaced, or triple-spaced, punctuated and paragraphed. The rolls of paper, interleaved with carbon sheets, permitted delivery of two or three copies for use or record. Service messages to editors could be included, beginning a day or night transmission with a schedule of major stories to come, so far as available or predictable, notifying them of a time for release of a public address or document transmitted in advance, making corrections and inserts, adding new lead paragraphs for later editions or where an event took a new turn and required updating, and indicating other changes or cautions. The incoming matter was to be torn from the roll at intervals, ready for selection, editing, headlining

---

3   By 1978 the rate of teleprinter transmission was 1,200 words a minute.

and dispatch to the composing room to be set in type and placed in the page form, ready for publication.[4]

In one transmission over a leased wire network by 1912 to 1915, a report could be delivered in any number of newspaper offices at the same time. If one teleprinter was not enough to receive the full service required by a newspaper, or if two or more news agency services or special reports were received regularly, the number of printer machines in an office could be increased accordingly. It became usual for a daily newspaper, and news agencies as well, to have a battery of such machines in use.

Teleprinters, sufficiently perfected about 1912 to assure reliable service, were used not only by news agencies and newspapers, but by telegraph companies to move all commercial messages. As a generic name, the teleprinter sometimes was referred to also as a teletypewriter or a newsprinter. The term "Teletype" also came into use, but this was a trademarked name. They also were referred to by the names of their manufacturers.

The Murray machine, manufactured by Creed & Co. of London, was put to use in England in 1912, and commonly referred to as a "Creed." The U.S. rights were sold to the Western Union Telegraph Company. Western Union also used the Kleinschmidt Telegraph Typewriter, produced in the United States by Kleinschmidt, Inc. Improvements were made with a Murray Multiplex in 1923, adding speed, capacity, and reliability. It was a product of the Creed company, of Western Union, and of the Western Electric Company of Chicago, a subsidiary of AT&T. The Creed also was used in France and other parts of western Europe. In Germany, a Siemans-Halske machine was put to use soon after 1912 and was used in Austria and other parts of central and northern Europe.

Quite independently in these years, Charles L. Krum, a Chicago engineer, and his son Howard, had developed a teleprinter machine in 1906. With financial support from Mr. Joy Morton, director of the Morton Salt Company of Chicago, a machine combining their names was on the market in 1914. Called the Morkrum Telegraph Printer, but commonly referred to as the "Morkrum," it was adopted for use by the Postal Telegraph Company, competing with Western Union. European rights were purchased by Donald Murray, and it was put to use on that side of the Atlantic. The Associated Press adopted the Morkrum

---

4 Again, as a matter of record, the newspaper production process has been revolutionized since about 1960.

machine to distribute news reports in the New York City area, replacing the pneumatic tube. Both the Associated Press and the United Press put it into use nationally in 1915.

By the end of World War I, teleprinter machines were in general use in most countries for the distribution of news reports. In the United States, the Kleinschmidt and Morkrum machines were about equally accepted, but neither company was prospering. The two were merged in 1924 as the Morkrum-Kleinschmidt Company, and then reorganized as the Teletype Company, with "Teletype" registered as the name of the machine. In 1930 that company was taken over by the American Telephone and Telegraph Company, but operated separately as the Teletype Corporation, with Kleinschmidt, Inc., as a manufacturing subsidiary.[5]

The AT&T set up special switchboards to handle teleprinter circuits throughout the United States, with ties to Canada and Mexico, but connected by telephone wires rather than telegraph wires. Over these circuits moved virtually all teleprinter service for the press, and then later for radio and television networks as they were established and extended, along with a vastly expanded Teletype service for business and government. A comparable concentration occurred in Great Britain and other countries of the world, but with the teleprinter networks controlled by governments through their postal and telegraph departments or ministries, rather than by private enterprise.

Cable and wireless reports were integrated into the teleprinter transmissions. Until the 1930s, longline cable transmission and wireless or radiotelegraphic transmission, as "wireless" became more commonly known, required the use of a Wheatstone sender linked to a siphon recorder or undulator at the receiving end. Under that system, rather than a dot-dash code sounding in signal form, or a tape being punched, a stylus traced hill-and-dale, square-cornered undulations on tape in the receiver. That tape moved before an operator, who "read" the undulations, short and broad, decipherable as dots and dashes of code, and from that he transcribed the message in typewritten form.

This changed by the mid-1930s, however. The placement of amplifiers at intervals throughout the length of new cables, along with the introduction of a feed-back system through a regenerator devised in 1921 by Edwin H. Armstrong of Columbia University, gave greater strength to cable and radiotelegraphic transmission. It opened the way

---

5 Edward E. Kleinschmidt lived to be 101 years old. He died August 9, 1977, at his Illinois home.

for direct teleprinter reception and automatic relay of such messages moving over the greatest distances.

Further, a high-speed, automatic printer developed by William G. H. Finch of the Hearst organization, along with A. M. Stevens and William A. Bruno, was placed in operation in 1930. It used a radiotelegraphic signal rather than a wire-borne signal to activate the teleprinters linked in the circuit. A message written on an electrically integrated typewriter, at whatever speed the operator could attain, was transmitted directly by wireless and reproduced at the same rate written. The system was known in the United States and Canada as the "TWX" and in Great Britain as the "telex." A tape also could be punched and when fed into the transmitter permitted reception at the increased rate of eighty words a minute.

A comparable machine was devised in Germany in 1930 by Dr. Rudolph Hell and known as the "Hellschreiber." The great difference was that in its reception the message was reproduced on a tape and by a facsimile process, rather than in typewritten form on a full-width sheet. Both machines were adaptable for use, however, in the wide transmission by radiotelegraphy of messages in a multiple address system to be described later.

Manual telegraphic transmission and transcription by Morse operators did not end as teleprinters came into general use after 1915. There was a long period when both means of transmission and communication continued. From about 1930, however, mechanization and the use of punched tapes inevitably made the Morse operator a victim of the new technology. A coaxial cable also technically advanced was introduced in 1935 and, with progressive improvements, carried many messages simultaneously in both directions, including voice, sound, and pictures, as well as text, and with freedom from any sort of external interference.

Rates and Regulations

Telegraph, cable, and telephone services were as well advanced in most major countries of the world in the 1900–14 period as the technology of the time permitted. For underdeveloped and peripheral areas much remained to be done.

More than half of the world's cable mileage was British-controlled. The United States stood second in that respect, and its position had been strengthened by the addition of the Pacific cables in 1903 and 1905. In 1910, further, the Western Union Telegraph Company, in cable communication in the Key West–Caribbean area since 1873, negotiated a one hundred-year lease for the use of the five North Atlantic cables then operated by the pioneer Anglo-American Company, and of joint U.S.–British ownership. Western Union absorbed that company. Even though in North Atlantic competition with the U.S.-owned Commercial Cable Company and with German, French, and Italian lines, it felt secure enough to raise certain rates.

German interests by 1910 controlled five North Atlantic cables, plus six short lines between German and British shores, and one South Atlantic cable, with spurs from the Azores to New York in one direction and to Liberia and other west African points in the other. Shorter cables linked German possessions in Asia and the Pacific, with lines centering on the German-held island of Yap, in the Pelew Islands group.

Two French cables had spanned the South Atlantic since 1874 and 1879, the second with landings in the West Indies. An Italian cable was in operation from the Italian shore to New York, and another across the South Atlantic to Buenos Aires and intermediate points.

The regulation of international communications had been necessary since telegraph messages began to cross national frontiers in the 1840s. Bilateral treaties had become regional and then international. Since 1865, regulation centered in a permanent bureau of the International Telegraphic Union (ITU), with headquarters in Berne, Switzerland. It was recognized by all governments, as was the International Postal Union, also established at Berne in 1875 for the administration of that form of communication. As cable and telephone services were added, they came within the authority of the ITU bureau by agreement, as wireless and radio later also were to be included.

The International Telegraphic Union organization met in conferences approximately every five years, reviewed the regulations previously established to assure orderly transmission and payments for service, and made such modifications as seemed desirable. Certain principles were maintained governing rates to be charged for various classifications of service.

In the United States and, originally, in some other countries, the communications facilities were owned and operated by private companies, but government ownership was far more common and became almost universal. In that circumstance, the ITU ruled that full voting membership in the organization was open only to countries in which the communications facilities in fact were owned and/or controlled by the government. This did not preclude the attendance of representatives of other countries or even of private companies at the ITU conferences, or prevent them from speaking, but they had no votes. In practice, this created no serious problem for a country such as the United States, which was generally able to abide by the ITU regulations. But there could be no guarantee that problems might not arise.

The rates for transmission of messages by telegraph and cable were established originally on a per-word basis, whether by government or private company, and bore a relation to the distance over which the message was to be transmitted. A "word" was interpreted to mean ten letters. There was a basic standard or "regular" rate. More immediate handling, or priority in handling, could be assured by payment of a higher "urgent" rate, and even a "double urgent" rate. This sometimes was important for press use if news developments warranted, or when factors of time and deadlines existed, or competition recommended its use.

Private telegraph companies in the United States, beginning in the 1840s, set their rates quite arbitrarily. They not only tended to be high, such as fifty cents a word between Boston and New York, but also inconsistent, with one company charging much more (or less) than another for messages moving over approximately the same distance. It was common to set ten words as the minimum message length or charge. Competition between companies provided the greatest assurance of a reasonable rate, but competition did not always exist, and companies also might agree to maintain a high rate. The original cable rates also were high on almost any long line, with nearly ten dollars a word set for the first effective North Atlantic cable in 1866, and with a minimum charge assessed for ten words. Such rates soon were reduced progressively through negotiation if not competition, but still remained high in many instances.

Once the telegraph and cable lines existed, with a few of the more prosperous newspapers using them even to a limited extent, all other newspapers were virtually forced to do the same if they were to provide an equivalent service to readers and survive in competition with the few. The rates set by government-owned lines in Europe usually were far lower than those charged by private companies in the United States, but they added up in either case, if any volume of news was transmitted. This provided the incentive for the establishment of news agencies. A news agency could pay one original transmission fee for a report, with the total cost divided among the newspapers sharing that dispatch at a rate to each that most could afford. Prosperous and enterprising newspapers, such as the *Times* of London and the *New York Herald,* nevertheless continued to set a pace for others by publishing exclusive reports received by telegraph and cable from their own correspondents.

A fourth meeting of the International Telegraphic Union, and one of its most important, took place at St. Petersburg in 1875. A recognition existed of the important role of the press in the provision of public information, and also of the financial burden placed upon the press to meet telegraphic and cable costs. The ITU meeting therefore approved a special "press" rate, recommended to be half the "regular" rate, which was generally accepted in all countries. At such a rate, however, the lowest priority applied; press messages filed at that rate would be moved only after all regular-rate messages had been moved.

The press nevertheless received some concessions beyond the ITU provision, in part because of the growing volume of dispatches. In the United States, a few companies set even lower press rates for news reports transmitted during the night, interpreted to mean from 6 P.M. to 6 A.M., when general traffic was light. This was helpful to morning newspapers, whether individually or as served by a news agency. Uniformity in telegraph rates in terms of distance did not arise in the United States, however, until regulatory action was taken after 1887 by the newly formed Interstate Commerce Commission.

It had long since become possible by that time, as a measure of economy, for the New York Associated Press in association with regional news agencies to lease telegraph lines for the transmission and exchange of news, paying for the time those lines were in use rather than for the number of words moved. This permitted a considerable economy.

In cable transmission, a per-word charge continued, but the rates were reduced progressively in every classification, including "press." For example, by 1884 the original ten dollar word rate on the North Atlantic cable had been adjusted to provide a press rate of seventy-five cents per word. Competition provided by the new Commercial Cable Company line in that year brought the press rate down to twenty-five cents, and briefly to twelve cents, before it was stabilized at forty cents. This rate did not continue for long. Pursuant to agreement at an ITU conference in Berlin in 1885, a new North Atlantic cable press rate of ten cents became effective in 1886, and continued into World War I. When a wireless service became available over the same London–New York or Toronto routing in 1908, it provided a five-cent rate.

Costs on some other long lines were higher. The Berlin–New York press rate was fourteen cents. The press rate from Shanghai or Peking to London over the Great Northern Company telegraph line across Siberia was $1.62 a word, with an additional ten cents to New York. The "urgent" rate from Hong Kong to New York by that routing or by cable was $6.37 a word; from Manila to New York it was $2.37 a word, but the press rate was eighty-five cents. When the new cable of 1903 went into operation across the Pacific it provided for a one dollar press rate between China or Japan and San Francisco, plus ten cents to New York, and another ten cents to London. The regular rate across the South Atlantic was $8 a word at the outset in 1874. It was still $3.40 in 1882, but half that at the press rate. The rates between North America and South America remained high.

An ITU conference in London in 1903 approved a press rate, day as well as night, at half the regular rate within the European area. This was extended to apply to world transmissions by action of a Lisbon conference of the ITU in 1908. That conference further ruled that "urgent" messages for press use could be sent at the "regular" rate, but retaining the higher priority for handling.

Special favorable rates were made available on British-owned cables for the exchange of news within the empire. Thus, for example, the Australia-London press rate, which had been the equivalent of $2.59 a word, with a minimum of ten words, when that cable connection was two years old in 1875, was down to fifteen cents under rates made effective for the empire press in 1913. At the same time, the India-London press rate was eight cents, South Africa–London seven and one half cents; and the Canada-London rate continued at ten cents.

Through most of the years since about 1870 the volume of news transmitted by cable had become substantial. Newspapers and news agencies had exercised their own economies by moving their basic dispatches between correspondents and bureaus and headquarters in the briefest possible form. This meant the omission of full names and titles of persons regularly in the news, of non-essential articles, prepositions, and conjunctions. It meant a telescoping of two or more words into a single word. Referred to as "cablese," and likely to be incomprehensible to a layman who might see it, this permitted a message to be conveyed at a substantial saving in the number of words actually transmitted. Considering the total volume of copy moved, these usages resulted in a major financial saving of charges based on word count. An editor at the receiving end restored the omitted words and reconverted the cablese into a full-length account, making it ready for use by the newspaper or for transmission by the news agency to its member papers.

The telephone, although used increasingly for news purposes, did not share in the advantage of press rates. Time, rather than words, was the basis on which charges were made for the use of that instrument. When telephone lines were only beginning to cross frontiers, an ITU conference at Berlin in 1885 agreed upon a five-minute time unit as a basis for charges, and a call was to be limited to ten minutes if there were other demands for use of that wire. By 1896, when the next ITU conference met at Budapest, the demand for telephone time commonly exceeded the facilities then available, and a three-minute time unit was set, with a six-minute maximum if other demands existed. By 1903, with the ITU conference in London, telephone lines were far more extensive, but the three-minute time unit was retained, and has continued to apply on long-distance connections. With the increased facilities available, it was possible, however, for the ITU to eliminate the ruling establishing a maximum time for the use of wire.

The technical difficulties of conducting properly audible conversations over long distances restricted the growth and use of telephone service. Cities within the United States had been linked early in the century, but in nothing even approaching a national network. In Europe, connections were established between Berlin and Amsterdam in 1903, Rome and Paris in 1906, and Paris and London in 1910, with a telephone cable beneath the English Channel. Advances came more rapidly after 1910. All European capitals were in communication by 1915, and a 3,000-mile New York–San Francisco circuit was opened, using a system of wireless telephony. Long-distance lines were operating by then in all parts of the United States and Canada, in parts of South America, Africa, Australia, and New Zealand, and in some areas in Asia, where Japan was the most progressive in its service.

The fact that telephones were installed and lines extended did not in itself mean that the quality of the service was perfected. There remained great frustrations in the use of the instrument in some cities and countries of the world. Not until the late 1920s and early 1930s was service between capitals in Europe sufficiently advanced to provide prompt connections and clarity of tone. Although the telephone had been used extensively for news purposes in many cities for at least a decade before that period, it was used increasingly from about 1930 for press communication between the countries in Europe and on other long-distance circuits.

The American Telephone and Telegraph Company, in some financial difficulties just prior to 1907, had revived quickly after that time under the direction of Theodore N. Vail. In 1909 the AT&T bought a controlling interest in the Western Union Telegraph Company, which had had some lean years. The two companies kept their separate identities, but Vail held the presidency of both until 1913. Then threatened with a U.S. government anti-trust suit, the AT&T divested itself of the Western Union, but the two companies nevertheless were to work in collaboration to extend and improve communications. Newcomb Carlton, an experienced telephone executive, replaced Vail in the presidency of Western Union. Both companies were very much aware of the advances in wireless technology and the impact it might have upon telephony, telegraphy, and cable communications, and they were to play their own roles in the unfolding electronic revolution.

The appearance of wireless as a new communications method had led the German government to sponsor a Preliminary Radiotelegraphic Conference in Berlin as early as August 1903, with nine countries represented. The announced purpose was to chart preliminary studies of means to regulate wireless communication at a time when it already was apparent that uncontrolled transmission of signals would mean such chaos on the air that message reception would become impossible. An underlying element at the conference was a sharp conflict affecting British and German wireless activities, with a need to find a solution.

Technical improvements in transmission, as devised soon after that conference by Fessenden, DeForest, and others, pointed toward possible solutions to the problems discussed at Berlin. The conference there had included a proposal by the German government that a second meeting should be held. Accordingly, a full-dress Berlin Radio Conference met in October 1906, with delegates present from twenty-nine nations. Because wireless, unlike the telegraph, cable, and telephone, used the airwaves rather than wires, with the obvious need to maintain order on the air, the United States government regarded the medium as properly subject to its regulation nationally. Whereas U.S. representatives had attended ITU conferences merely as unofficial observers, official representatives went to Berlin as active participants.

The result of the 1906 Berlin conference was the formation of an International Radiotelegraph Union (IRU), with a radiotelegraph convention drafted and made effective July 1, 1908, for a period of time then undefined. The Berne bureau of the International Telegraphic Union was designated to act also for the IRU. The United States Senate did not ratify the IRU convention until 1912, but the United States government, like others, accepted the regulations from the outset as they bore upon wavelength frequency allocations, transmitter station licenses, and other matters intended to contribute to orderly and effective wireless transmission.

A conference of the IRU met in Lisbon in 1908 along with the ITU, and the IRU met in London in 1912 in its own first full conference.[6] As noted earlier, the *Titanic* disaster led to the establishment in 1912 of a firmer allocation of frequencies for coastal and ship wireless transmitters and measures to assure that wavelengths would be maintained to prevent unlicensed transmitters from causing signal interference and confusion on the air over land or sea.

As communication circuits spun an ever-tighter web around the world between 1900 and 1915, and continued through the war years, great advances also were made in photography and motion pictures, in photoengraving, in the phonographic recording of voice and music, and in the technology of printing, with ever-faster rotary presses producing newspapers and magazines, some replete with color. The net result was an unprecedented service of information available after the war to the peoples of most nations.

---

6   The IRU and ITU agreed upon a merger at a joint meeting in Madrid in 1932, effective in 1934. The International Telegraphic Union thereupon became the International Telecommunications Union, still the "ITU," and with the ITU bureau continuing in Berne. To deal with matters of wireless, radio, radiotelegraphy, and later with television, separate sessions, within the ITU, met as required, and regional conferences also were held. After World War II the ITU was transferred to Geneva.

Washington Becomes a Major News Center

5

Washington gained importance as a world capital and news center after 1900, almost exactly a century after the government of the new nation had moved to the District of Columbia, following its temporary interval in New York City in 1789–90 and in Philadelphia until 1800. George Washington, whose name the new city on the Potomac bore, had served his two terms as the first president of the United States in 1789–97, when John Adams succeeded him to become the first president to reside in the new specially created capital. Washington had died at nearby Mount Vernon in 1799 at sixty-seven. Two years later in 1801 Thomas Jefferson became the third president and the first to be inaugurated in the permanent capital.

There were only twenty-four daily newspapers in the United States in 1801, and the nation itself remained concentrated along the Atlantic seaboard, with a population of 5,308,483. By 1901, however, the population was more than 105 million, the nation was settled from coast to coast, and daily newspapers numbered 2,331.

In the years between 1789 and the 1840s, the basic news reports on government activities were derived belatedly from the columns of newspapers published in New York, Philadelphia, and then Washington. Indeed, the modern period in Washington news coverage may be said to have begun only in the administration of President William McKinley, inaugurated in 1897. It was a period dominated by news of the Spanish-American War, its preliminaries and aftermath. It was the period that brought the sudden new recognition to the nation as a "world power." This had a double result in that foreign press representation was increased in the United States, while the press of the United States also increased its own coverage both of Washington and of the world.

The contrast between the reporting from Washington as a young capital in 1800 and that beginning in the period after 1900 is illustrative of the great social and technical advances of the time, and of the changes in the information process.

Press coverage of Washington began in simple fashion with the establishment there in October 1800 of a tri-weekly paper, the *National Intelligencer,* published by Samuel Harrison Smith, formerly of Philadelphia. In that city, he had purchased the *Independent Gazetteer* from Joseph Gales, Sr., changing its name to the *Universal Gazette.* He became a friend of Jefferson, who was secretary of state and vice president in the Washington and Adams administrations, and supported him for the presidency in 1800. With the prospective move of the government to the new village of Washington, Jefferson persuaded Smith to move his newspaper there. Retitled the *National Intelligencer,* it had some of the qualities of an official journal during Jefferson's presidency (1801–09), reporting the news of the executive branch of the government and providing the only reports of debates in Congress.

In 1810 Smith retired, and the *National Intelligencer* was purchased by Joseph Gales, Jr., son of the former publisher of the Philadelphia *Independent Gazetteer.* In 1812 he was joined by his brother-in-law, William W. Seaton. In 1813 the two made the *National Intelligencer* a daily newspaper, and conducted it for nearly fifty years. Both men were shorthand reporters, occupied desks in the House and Senate chambers, and held the exclusive right for some years to produce records of the proceedings, either personally or through their employees. Until 1835 almost all reports of congressional or government affairs, as published in newspapers of the United States and other countries, were derived from the columns of the *National Intelligencer.*

Other newspapers appeared in Washington, however, including the *United States Telegraph* in 1826,[1] the *Washington Globe* in 1830, and the *Madisonian* in 1837. The first two were established to advance the political fortunes of Andrew Jackson, and the other one to support James Madison. They also reported the news of Congress and its proceedings, and became added sources of information for newspapers in other places.

There was at the time no official record of congressional debates. From 1824 to 1837 the *National Intelligencer* republished its daily

---

1   Although the electric telegraph did not appear in any form prior to 1837, and is commonly dated from 1844, newspapers bearing the name "Telegraph" were established in Buenos Aires, Boston, and Washington in the years between 1801 and 1826. It derived from the semaphore telegraph, devised in France in the late eighteenth century by the Abbé Claude Chappé, and used widely in Europe between 1794 and more than sixth years thereafter to transmit messages, including news reports.

accounts in a separate *Register of Debates in Congress.* The *Washington Globe* did the same in a *Congressional Globe* from 1834 to 1873. Only then was the official *Congressional Record* at last started, published by the Government Printing Office. In the earlier years, it was sufficiently in the interest of the government, however, to have the reports published by the newspapers to justify the allotment of Treasury funds to compensate them for the preparation of the debates and of some other official papers. Those funds varied between $90,000 and $330,000 a year.

The *Baltimore American,* established in 1799 in that city so near to Washington, was the first outside the capital to undertake direct coverage of Congress, as it did from 1801. Facilities for press representation in the small House and Senate chambers of that time were virtually nonexistent. Except for the *National Intelligencer,* other reporters were only reluctantly permitted to make notes while seated in the area assigned to visitors, and were denied even that right in the Senate chamber until 1802.

There were reporters in Washington from the beginning, and editors and writers visited there. They were permitted to go where they wished, and to develop news sources where they could. In so small a capital, it was possible for them to approach members of Congress and of the cabinet, and to know them and other officials personally. The president and the White House, however, received little direct attention.

This is not to say that the presidents and public officials failed to recognize the importance of the press in its news and editorial treatment of their activities and as an influence in the process of government. One of the great concerns of writers, however, was with the "game" of politics, sometimes complicated by partisanship and an insufficient recognition of public responsibility. An adversary relationship between press and government, between journalists and officials, soon made itself felt. The Federalist administration of John Adams struck back by passing the repressive Alien and Sedition Acts in 1789. Ten or fifteen convictions resulted, of which eight brought fines and imprisonment to printers and writers. The laws may have been unconstitutional, but lapsed in 1801 before receiving a court test. Jefferson, upon becoming president and representing what then was a Democratic-Republican party, pardoned all those convicted under what he called an "unauthorized act of Congress," and the fines were restored with interest.

The first amendment to the Constitution became effective in 1791, providing that Congress should make no law "abridging the freedom of speech, or of the press." This did not assure that the press would use its freedom with full responsibility. Neither did excesses of partisanship end. Problems of access to information in Washington were rare, however, and a growing maturity on the part of the press was accompanied by a more substantive reporting of government affairs.

In his scholarly study of *The Presidents and the Press* (1947), James E. Pollard examines the relationship between the presidents and representatives of the domestic press. He makes it clear that until the administration of Theodore Roosevelt (1901–09) the relationship lacked form and usually rested upon personal associations between a president and individual editors or newsmen, often antedating his election and inauguration.

Examples of these relationships included President Washington's friendship and correspondence with Matthew Carey, publisher of the *American Museum,* a Philadelphia magazine, and of the *Pennsylvania Evening Herald.* He also felt a sufficient confidence in David C. Claypool, editor of the Philadelphia *Pennsylvania Packet and Daily Advertiser,* to hand him personally for publication an advance copy of his "Farewell Address" of September 1796.

John Adams, as a young man, had written for the *Boston Gazette,* and he wrote for other papers at various periods throughout most of his life, including the *Mercure de France* of Paris in 1780 and other European papers. As president, however, his relations with the press were unpleasant, since he was the victim of some of the worst partisan journalism in the history of the country. This accounted in part for the passage of the Alien and Sedition Acts at that time.

Jefferson, on the other hand, although also badly treated by some newspapers, in the later period of his administration, was a strong advocate of press freedom. He had a personal relationship with several editors, including Thomas Ritchie of the *Richmond Enquirer* in his native Virginia; James Cheetham of the *American Citizen* in New York; William Duane of the *Aurora* in Philadelphia, who also had published a paper in Calcutta, India; and, of course, Samuel Harrison Smith of the *Universal Register* in Philadelphia and the *National Intelligencer* in Washington.

Both Gales and Seaton, succeeding Smith in the conduct of the *National Intelligencer* after 1810 paid periodic visits upon President Madison and his secretary of state, John Quincy Adams, to gather news and also to give news. J. Q. Adams himself, as sixth president, met with Peter Force of the *National Journal* of Washington, and had good relations with the *Intelligencer.* Adams is popularly supposed, although erroneously, to have been forced to grant an interview to Anne C. Royall, publisher of a Washington weekly, *Paul Pry,* when she found him swimming in the buff in the Potomac River and sat on his clothing until he consented to answer her questions.

A close relationship existed between Andrew Jackson and Francis P. Blair, a Kentucky banker and plantation owner, who established the *Washington Globe* in 1830 to support Jackson. Associated with him were John C. Rives and Amos Kendall, later of the *New Orleans Picayune.* Duff Green, a St. Louis lawyer and journalist, had established the *United States Telegraph* to support Jackson in 1826. He turned against him, however, and Blair took up Jackson's cause in the *Globe.* James K. Polk, president from 1845–49, also was on good terms with Blair.

By the period of the 1820s, during the Monroe administration, there were perhaps a dozen reporters writing regularly from Washington for papers in parts of the United States, still a country of less than ten million, within twenty-four states, all east of the Mississippi River, except for Louisiana and Missouri. One Washington reporter, Elias Kingman, wrote for several of the papers from 1822 to about 1860, conducting what Frank Luther Mott, press historian, surmises to have been "probably the first Washington news bureau." Others included Robert Walsh for the *National Gazette* of Philadelphia, Nathaniel E. Carter for the New York *Statesman,* and both Matthew L. Davis and James Gordon Bennett for the *New York Courier and Enquirer,* one of the leading newspapers of the time. Davis also wrote as a stringer for the London *Times.* Appointed in 1820, he appears to have been the first foreign press representative in the United States.

Bennett played an important role in advancing the quality of Washington correspondence. For the *Courier and Enquirer* in the late 1820s, he produced some of the more readable capital reports up to that time, pioneering new territory in the treatment of economics as well as politics. He helped break down some of the barriers to news, and gained experience which he turned to account after he established the *New York Herald* in 1835.

For the *Herald,* Bennett in about 1840 introduced what may have been the first office or "bureau" in the capital for any one newspaper published in another city. Robert Sutton, who was in charge, also may have become the first correspondent to have had special entrée to the White House, although not necessarily to the president. Bennett had had a formal visit with President Van Buren at the White House in January

1839 and published in the *Herald* on January 12 what was purported to be the first interview with a president in office. Pollard describes it as little more than a report of a visit, but some direct quotes were used. It was the *Herald,* nevertheless, that became the first non-Washington paper to gain the right to give direct coverage to congressional debates. This it did in 1841 during the Tyler administration, and so opened the way for other newspapers to do the same, with facilities made available in larger House and Senate chambers.

Presidents Fillmore and Pierce, in the years between 1850 and 1857, appear to have had few direct associations with the press, although the *National Intelligencer* once again assumed a semi-official position with reference to Fillmore. Pierce and Buchanan had a comparable relationship with the *Union,* as the *Madisonian* was retitled. Buchanan was on good terms with John W. Forney, publisher of the *Philadelphia Press* and later of the *Washington Chronicle,* and he also corresponded with Gerard Hallock, publisher of the *New York Journal of Commerce.*

By the late 1850s, the White House was at last receiving some coverage, with presidential press secretaries as sources of information. Correspondents also were admitted to await reports after meetings of the cabinet.

Abraham Lincoln, before his election to the presidency in 1860, had been on friendly terms with Joseph Medill, editor of the *Chicago Tribune,* and with Henry Villard, a fellow resident of Springfield, Illinois, and a stringer for the *Tribune* and also for the *Cincinnati Commercial.* In the White House, Lincoln was in regular contact with Noah Brooks, whom he also knew in Springfield, and who was virtually a member of the family, but serving, too, as Washington correspondent for the *Sacramento Union* in California. Mrs. Lincoln gave her confidence to Chevalier Henry Wickoff of the *New York Herald,* and was sometimes indiscreet in discussing official matters with him.

The New York Associated Press, still relatively young as a telegraphic news agency, had established a Washington bureau headed by Lawrence A. Gobright. He was on good terms with the president. It was through his action that the world first learned of Lincoln's assassination in 1865. J. M. Winchell of the *New York Times* had at least two interviews with Lincoln. Horace Greeley, editor of the *New York Tribune,* fancied himself as an unofficial adviser to the president, and he did indeed receive special information for "use and guidance" in a generally cordial relationship. Lincoln also had correspondence with such editors as Henry J. Raymond of the *New York Times* and William Cullen Bryant of the *New York Evening Post.*

Resident correspondents in the capital, and visiting newsmen, had more meetings with Lincoln than with any preceding president, but his remarks were casual and friendly, rather than newsworthy in themselves. He received and talked with William Howard Russell, then widely known as a correspondent for the London *Times,* when he arrived in Washington in March 1861 prior to a tour of the southern states in the month before the Civil War began. Henry E. Wing, a youthful correspondent for the *New York Tribune,* and a witness of the Wilderness Battle, carried the first news of that Union victory to an anxious Washington, and was hurried to the White House to give the details to Lincoln personally.

President Andrew Johnson, succeeding Lincoln, gave the first real White House interview, as Pollard recounts. In an exclusive meeting, he talked for more than an hour with Alexander K. McClure, editor of the *Franklin Repository* of Franklin, Pennsylvania, and later founder of the *Philadelphia Times.* The interview was republished in the *National Intelligencer.* Simon P. Hanscom, editor of the *Washington Republican,* was one of several newsmen who saw Johnson regularly. Before leaving office in 1869, he gave other interviews to correspondents for the *New York Herald,* the *World* and *Citizen,* the *Boston Post,* the *Cincinnati Commercial,* and others.

President Grant had reasonably good relations with correspondents during his period of command in the Civil War. Sylvanus Cadwallader, of the *Chicago Times,* one of those correspondents, continued to see him at the White House. DeBenneville Randolph Keim, of the *New York Herald,* was another former war correspondent who had his confidence, and even went on special missions for the president to far parts of the world. Charles Nordhoff, also of the *New York Herald,* saw him frequently. William J. Murtagh, editor of the Washington *Republican* had good relations with members of the administration. When Grant toured the world in 1877, following his presidential years, he was accompanied by John Russell Young, then with the *New York Herald.*

President Hayes, formerly of Cincinnati and former governor of Ohio, maintained a close personal friendship with William Henry Smith, founder of the *Cincinnati Evening Chronicle* in 1867. He was general agent of the Western Associated Press during the Hayes administration and later. Hayes also corresponded with Whitelaw Reid, publisher of the *New York Tribune,* another former Cincinnati friend, and with Murat Halstead of the *Cincinnati Gazette,* W. D. Bickham of the *Dayton Journal,* J. M. Comly of the Columbus *Ohio State Journal,* and others.

Hayes was under fire, however, from the *New York Sun,* which called him "the fraudulent president" because of the electoral college vote that gave him his election over Samuel J. Tilden in 1876. He was the victim of a hoax in 1878 when the *Philadelphia Times* published what was presented as an interview with the president by George Alfred Townsend, which was based upon nothing more than a conversation overheard at a reception.

President Garfield, like Hayes, had cordial relations with Whitelaw Reid, but he was assassinated four months after entering office. Chester Alan Arthur, succeeding to the presidency, had Charles R. Miller, editor of the *New York Times,* as a close friend and companion.

President Cleveland, serving two terms, separated by four years during which Benjamin Harrison was in the White House, suffered at the hands of the press. He set a precedent, nonetheless, before his first election by submitting to daily questioning by reporters. Later, he also permitted correspondents to prepare written questions to which he would respond through his secretarial staff, answering some and ignoring others.

Cleveland talked freely at times with Francis E. Leupp of the *New York Evening Post,* Francis A. Richardson of the *Baltimore Sun,* and L. Clarke Davis, editor of the *Philadelphia Inquirer* and later of the *Philadelphia Public Ledger.*[2] Another newsman in Cleveland's confidence was George F. Parker, managing editor of the *New York Press.* As his second term began in 1893, Cleveland invited Parker to take charge of press relations at the White House. In doing so, Parker became the first presidential assistant specifically concerned with such matters. He conferred with the president six days a week and made news available to the press.[3]

Like some other presidents, Cleveland resented press interest in his private affairs, including reports before his first election that he had sired an illegitimate son, and persistent attention to his marriage in the White House in 1886 and to the honeymoon. Despite unhappy relations with the press, Cleveland gave interviews to writers for the *Baltimore Sun* and the *Philadelphia North American,* and to Robert Lincoln O'Brien of the *Boston Transcript,* Ballard Smith and Manton Marble of

2 Davis's son, Richard Harding Davis, was even then beginning his own career in journalism in Philadelphia.

3 From 1895 to 1905 Parker wrote for the London *Times* and for magazines during a period when he also was serving in England as U.S. consul in Birmingham and commissioner for the Louisiana Purchase Exposition of 1901–04.

the *New York World,* Harold Frederic, then editor of the *Albany Evening Journal,* E. Prentiss Bailey, editor of the *Utica Observer,* and others. He also appointed Daniel Manning, editor of the *Albany Argus,* as his secretary of the treasury in 1885, and Hoke Smith, publisher of the *Atlanta Journal,* as his secretary of the interior in 1893.

Harrison, president from 1889–93, between Cleveland's two terms, was equally disturbed by press attention to his private life, as Chester A. Arthur had been also, despite generally good relations with newsmen. Harrison's son was the publisher of the *Montana Daily Journal* of Helena. He selected several journalists for diplomatic assignments, one of whom was Whitelaw Reid of the *New York Tribune.* Described as "cold and aloof," the only person present to say a farewell to Harrison on the morning he left the White House in 1893 was the Washington correspondent for a group of newspapers in Indiana, his home state. Julian Ralph of the *New York Sun,* who had tried to interview him the day before, was sharply rebuffed.

McKinley, in the White House from 1897 until his assassination in 1901, had been a member of Congress from Ohio from 1876–91, and then governor of the state. He had acquaintances among editors and publishers and among Washington correspondents, by whom he was well liked, and he reciprocated that sentiment. He named John Hay, formerly of the *New York Tribune,* as his secretary of state, and Charles Emory Smith, editor of the *Philadelphia Press,* as postmaster general. Smith in turn named many editors to postmasterships.

Press relations at the White House proceeded in a somewhat haphazard fashion under McKinley. Even with the Spanish-American War in progress, it was not regarded as a source of news warranting special coverage. Newsmen would go there when special announcements were anticipated, or would put questions to members of the secretarial staff. They rarely saw the president and then did not approach him unless invited to do so. Occasionally, he gave items of news to groups of correspondents or even summoned a number of them to make a formal statement. These were not news conferences, however. He never was questioned at any length, much less interviewed, although he complained that some papers had published purported interviews.

Certain advances in press relations, nevertheless, were made during the McKinley period. A corner of the outer reception room in the executive wing of the White House was equipped with a large table and a number of chairs for the use of reporters. There they gathered on days when a cabinet meeting was scheduled. There some observed the visitors admitted to see the president and might question them before or after the visits. There they also received reports and talked with members of the secretarial staff.

This arrangement was further improved by John Addison Porter, secretary to the president. Former editor and proprietor of the *Hartford Post* of Connecticut, he introduced the practice of meeting with reporters at 10 P.M. to discuss events of the day. George B. Cortelyou, who succeeded Porter in April 1900, continued the practice. Informal as they were, and at a somewhat awkward time, these meetings have been characterized by Pollard as "the germ of regular White House news conferences." For the first time also copies of public addresses to be made by the president were available to the press in advance to permit their publication both promptly and accurately.

In the same period, John Hay at the State Department introduced the practice of receiving four or five selected correspondents and speaking with them informally and in confidence so that they might write more knowledgeably of foreign affairs.[4] These evidences of trust between officials and correspondents, and a recognition of the importance of the press in its provision of public information, were greatly significant.

Hearst's *New York Journal* since 1896 had never ceased to attack McKinley. This took a strange turn in 1901. On February 3, 1900, William Goebel, recently elected Governor of Kentucky, died of gunshot wounds received as he was approaching the state capital in Lexington. On February 4, 1901, the anniversary of his death, Ambrose Bierce, then writing a weekly column for the Hearst papers in New York and San Francisco, produced a quatrain published in the *Journal:*

> The bullet that pierced Goebel's breast
> Can not be found in all the West;
> Good reason, it is speeding here
> To stretch McKinley on his bier.

In April, also, the *Journal,* in an editorial directed against McKinley, said: "If bad institutions and bad men can be got rid of only by killing, then killing must be done."

When McKinley was shot in September at Buffalo, a copy of the *Journal* containing another attack on the president was reported to have

---

4 Hay, whose uncle Milton Hay had been Abraham Lincoln's law partner in Springfield, became one of Lincoln's private secretaries at the White House in 1861 when he was twenty-three. Later he was a biographer of Lincoln. Subsequently, he served in diplomatic assignments in Paris, Madrid, and Vienna, and was U.S. ambassador to Great Britain in 1897–98. From about 1870 to 1875 he was a staff member of the *New York Tribune*. This experience gave him a special understanding in his relationship with newsmen and enabled him to be particularly helpful to them.

been in the pocket of Czolgosz, his assassin. These circumstances brought public condemnation of Hearst and his newspapers. He had responded by changing the name of the morning *Journal* to the *New York American* soon after the Bierce verse appeared, and made the *Journal* an afternoon paper. The total affair nevertheless turned many papers away from imitation of the more sensational practices of the Hearst papers, successful as they had been in winning readers.

With McKinley's death on September 14, 1901, eight days after the shooting, Vice-President Theodore Roosevelt succeeded to the presidency.

Roosevelt, more than any of his predecessors, had a sense of public relations and of the potential value of the press in the advancement of public understanding of government. He also was aware that the United States had entered a new era. One of his first acts as president was to summon to his office the heads of the three U.S. news bureaus in Washington. At that time, these were Charles L. Boynton, Associated Press, Edward L. Keen, Scripps-McRae Press Association, and David Barry, Laffan News Bureau. He explained that he would be available to them and would keep them informed, but also that he would depend upon them to show discretion in what they wrote. He only asked that his family be granted privacy.

Even though space had been made available earlier for correspondents in the executive wing of the White House, Roosevelt is credited with having made it possible for them to have actual working quarters there. The story is that, on a cold and rainy day, the president happened to observe William W. Price, then a member of the AP staff, standing outside in the bad weather to speak to visitors entering or leaving. With an addition about to be made to the executive wing, Roosevelt directed that it should include a room adjacent to the entrance foyer for the use of reporters regularly assigned to covering the White House. This was done, and a working press room resulted, equipped with desks and telephones, typewriters and reference books.

Roosevelt demonstrated an understanding of the press and a personal grasp of news values. His relations with correspondents were informal but useful. He did not limit his contacts to the three news agency representatives, but saw others individually and in groups. There were no regular meetings or news conferences, but he would invite correspondents to his office when he had something he wished to communicate to the press and the people. As many as fifty might respond; more commonly, he saw no more than a half dozen at a time. When he was being shaved in the morning, he sometimes saw one or two and talked with them frankly.

If he wanted full public attention to a subject, he was known to release the relevant information on a Sunday, aware that it would be likely to receive more prominent display in the Monday morning papers, when competition for space usually was reduced because of the weekend suspension of normal business and government activities.

Roosevelt sometimes suggested news subjects himself, and even indicated what he regarded as suitable phraseology. Correspondents learned that he could not be trapped into making indiscreet remarks or persuaded to grant an interview unless it suited him to do so. If he did not want to answer a question, he might explain frankly, but in confidence, his reason for refusing, and he expected his confidence to be respected. Despite his request that his family be granted privacy, his four sons made news, and the marriage of his daughter, Alice, to Nicholas Longworth, a member of Congress from Ohio, in a White House ceremony in 1906 received full attention.

The president in his relations with the press insisted that, unless he gave specific permission, he was not to be quoted directly. To break that rule meant that a correspondent would be barred from other meetings. When statements were attributed indirectly to the president, if inaccurate or proved merely to be inexpedient, the writer ran the risk of being denounced as having been untruthful. During his administration enough correspondents were so branded as to form what they themselves called the "Ananias Club."

Among correspondents regularly at the White House in this period, Oscar King Davis of the *New York Times* saw the president two or three times a week and talked with him on every sort of subject. John Callan O'Laughlin of the *Chicago Tribune* received an appointment as assistant secretary of state during the last two months of Roosevelt's administration, and accompanied him to Africa after he left the presidency.

Others at the White House, regularly or frequently, included Price of the Associated Press; Leupp of the *New York Evening Post;* George Hill, *New York Tribune;* Sumner Curtis, *Chicago Record-Herald;* Gus J. Karger, *Cincinnati Times-Star;* Judson C. Welliver, *Des Moines Leader;* and Sam Blythe, *New York World,* and later of the *Saturday Evening Post.* Other magazine writers included Henry Beech Needham, formerly of the *New York Evening Post,* but then writing for *McClure's* and *World's Work;* Isaac F. Marcosson, then also of *World's Work;* Lincoln Steffens of *McClure's;* and Mark Sullivan of *Collier's.*

Correspondents in Washington for the domestic press had become numerous by this time. It had long been a practice for such reporters to conduct their news-gathering task throughout all branches of government. As the White House became a greater source, however, so did some other departments of the executive branch. Reference has been made to the practice introduced at the Department of State by John Hay of receiving correspondents. When Elihu Root followed Hay in that office in 1905–09, he continued to meet with newsmen almost daily. William Howard Taft, secretary of war from 1905–09, met regularly in his office with those few correspondents covering that department, and was helpful to them.

As president from 1909–13, Taft was less accessible to correspondents, and less helpful. For a time after entering the White House, he conducted weekly conferences in the cabinet room. The meetings were arranged by Major Archie Butt, who had been an aide to Roosevelt and continued under Taft. Correspondents attended by invitation. The rules were much as they had been at the meetings with Roosevelt, including a ban on direct quotation without permission. Moderately helpful so long as they continued, the meetings became infrequent and then ceased.

Taft discovered that he preferred to meet with newsmen individually, and this became the practice. Special favor went to Karger of the *Cincinnati Times-Star,* a newspaper owned by the Taft family. Others included Price, formerly of the AP but then of the *Washington Star* and a personal friend of Taft's, and Oscar King Davis, of the *New York Times,* who had been a Roosevelt favorite.

New members of this special group were Richard V. Oulahan of the *New York Sun,* Robert T. Small of the Associated Press, J. Frederick Essary of the *Baltimore Sun,* and Louis Seibold of the *New York World.* Seibold was granted an exclusive interview with Taft in 1912, during the presidential campaign of that year. It was not a real interview because Taft simply dictated answers to questions Seibold had prepared, or to such of them as he chose to answer. In the end, Taft withheld his approval of the effort and nothing ever appeared in print.

At the Department of State under Taft, Philander C. Knox, succeeding Hay and Root, held no conferences with correspondents. He did talk with some individually, but usually at his home in the evening.

News reporting at the executive level thus lost some of the gains made during the Roosevelt administration. It proceeded with considerable vigor in other areas of the governmental structure, however, and was to gain further during the presidency of Woodrow Wilson, beginning in 1913.

By 1870 there were enough news writers in Washington to make it difficult to determine who among the group were in fact to be regarded as *bona fide* representatives of the press. Where London, Paris, and some other capitals were great cities, as important for commerce, industry, banking, and cultural activities as they were as seats of government, the main concern in Washington was then, as it is now, the business of government itself, with its related political concerns. It became important to know which information services and which correspondents were properly eligible for admission to report the debates in Congress and deserving of the time and attention of government officials and staff members.

To meet this need there was established, by agreement of press and government, a self-regulating United States Congressional Press Gallery, which took form in 1871. Having been judged eligible by a committee of his peers, a reporter or correspondent was granted membership in the Press Gallery, and so was accredited to report debates in Congress from assigned space in the House or Senate chamber or, as for most members in actual practice, to report other activities of government in any of its branches. It was determined at the time that 143 reporters writing for newspapers in sixty cities of the United States, including Washington itself, and for news agencies, were entitled to such accreditation.

The number accredited rose slightly from year to year until after 1914. The Press Gallery membership in 1899, the Spanish-American War period, was only 156. This became 213 in 1909. The number rose sharply after 1914, during World War I and the postwar years, but surged forward after 1933, and the total membership now stands in the thousands.

Members of the Press Gallery prior to 1914 included writers for news agencies and for newspapers, some of the latter representing two or more papers. Aside from reporters for Washington dailies, they were expected to be writing for telegraphic transmission. This excluded stringers writing by mail, writers for magazines, most writers for syndicates, and photographers. Not until after 1935 were the regulations modified to give recognition to such journalists, or to radio news reporters or broadcasters and, later, to television news personnel. This was accomplished by establishing separate galleries for several categories, but the effect was nevertheless to provide recognition or accreditation to more writers for more media, and for photographers.

From 1911 correspondents in the United States for foreign newspapers and news agencies were made eligible for membership. They were few in number at that time and most of them were based in New York, visiting Washington only occasionally. Although their numbers now are far greater, most of them still make New York their center.

The total membership in the press galleries became a section appearing in the *Congressional Directory,* a reference source for any who might need to verify the *bona fide* of a reporter or correspondent in the capital, or reach such a person by mail or telephone.

The growth in coverage of news in the United States by the foreign press paralleled, on a more modest scale, the extension of such coverage by the press and other media of the United States itself.

The first effort by any foreign newspaper to arrange for original investigation and reporting of events in the United States seems to have come in 1820 when the London *Times* engaged Matthew L. Davis, a reporter in Washington for the *New York Courier and Enquirer,* to act for it as a stringer there. Years passed, and the *Times* appointed J. C. Bancroft Davis as a stringer in New York from 1854 to 1861, and C. Edwards Lester also in the mid-1850s.

A very marginal type of reporting developed in 1842 when Charles Dickens, already known as a novelist and to become briefly the first editor of the London *Daily News* in 1845, arrived in Boston in one of the early steamships. For several months he traveled in New England, the Middle Atlantic states, the South, and parts of the north central states. He lectured along the way, was enthusiastically received, and met with President Tyler at the White House. The journey involved hardships, his impressions were not all favorable, and his later accounts presented in *American Notes,* published in London, were not appreciated by readers in the United States. His novel, *Martin Chuzzlewit* (1843), based on his experiences did no more to endear him to American readers.

Dickens was to dare a return to the United States in 1867–68, more famous than ever for his novels, from which he gave readings in many cities, earning nearly $100,000. He also met with President Andrew Johnson. A new volume of impressions, *Letters and Times,* was more favorably received in the United States than were the fruits of his first visit.

In point of chronology, another British visitor to the United States, possibly in 1851, was Henry Labouchere. Then recently graduated from Cambridge, he came as an adventurer and traveled for two years with a circus, followed by further wanderings in Europe before he returned permanently to England. There he became part owner of the London *Daily News,* which he represented in besieged Paris during the

Franco-Prussian War of 1870–71, and later was publisher of a lively British periodical, *Truth.* Labouchere wrote nothing specific, however, based on his observations in the United States.

Five members of the *Times* staff visited the United States in 1856, one of whom was John Delane, editor of the paper. The others were Robert Lowe, Lawrence Oliphant, L. Filmore, and Thomas Gladstone. Gladstone went as far west as Kansas Territory to write of the conflict there between free-soil and pro-slavery advocates over whether slavery should be permitted in the new territory.

J. C. Bancroft Davis was succeeded briefly as New York stringer for the *Times* in 1861 by Charles Tuckerman. He was replaced by Charles Mackay, a British citizen who had visited the United States in 1857, and wrote for the paper from New York as a resident correspondent through the Civil War period to 1865. He wrote in a spirit more friendly to the South than to the North.

William Howard Russell, famed as a correspondent for the *Times* during the Crimean War in 1854–55, and on important assignments elsewhere, arrived in New York in March 1861. Received by Lincoln in Washington and then making a tour of the southern states, he was back in the capital when the Civil War began, and in the field during the Battle of Bull Run on July 21. His account of that Union defeat, published in the *Times* of August 6, upon reaching New York and Washington made Russell *persona non grata* in the North. He spent the winter in Canada and returned to London in April 1862.

Apart from Mackay, the *Times* also was represented in the United States during the war years by Antonio Gallenga, who had reported for the paper in his native Italy and elsewhere since 1859, and by Francis (Frank) Lawley, briefly in Richmond in 1863. He was followed by a Mr. Alexander, possibly P. W. Alexander, formerly of the *Savannah Republican.* Their reports from the Confederate capital reached London through the French consulate in Richmond and by way of Paris.

Other British newspapers were represented in the United States for the first time during the war. Edwin L. Godkin, British-born but a resident of the United States since 1856, reported for the *Daily News,* as he also had done during the Crimean War. The *Daily Telegraph* received reports from George Augustus Sala and from Edward James Stephens Dicey, who also wrote for two London magazines, *Macmillan's* and the *Spectator.* The *Morning Herald* was served by Samuel P. Day, with the Confederates. Frank Vizetelly, artist-correspondent for the *Daily News,* also was in the South. George Alfred Lawrence, intending to write from there for the *Morning Post,* was arrested as he sought to cross into Confederate territory and returned home.

When the war began in April 1861, Reuter sent James McLean to New York as its first agent in the United States. He arranged to receive information through the New York Associated Press, with which Reuter had formed its news exchange arrangement in 1856, and also from other sources, even in the South. He depended heavily upon reports from Washington by Lawrence Augustus Gobright, NYAP representative.

McLean prepared summaries of the news, and operated on a schedule whereby those dispatches, along with clippings and copies of newspapers were placed aboard every mail ship outbound from New York for England, with the fastest crossings of the Atlantic then requiring eleven days. The most consistent reporting of the war for the British press was provided through Reuter in this fashion, and also for the European press through the Reuter association with the Havas and Wolff agencies, and their associations, in turn, with other national agencies.

Reuter scored a particular news triumph just after the war's end in 1865, through the efforts of Gobright and McLean, in providing British and European newspapers with a report of President Lincoln's assassination. Hiring a tug to pursue an outbound mail ship and toss a canister aboard containing the Gobright-McLean report, Reuter was able to disseminate the news a full week before any other account reached the other side of the Atlantic.

The Paris press also received its first original reports from the United States during the war years. They were prepared by Frederick Gaillardet, editor of the New York French-language *Courier des Etats-Unis,* acting as a stringer for *La Presse* and *Le Constitutionelle.* Other reports were provided by Michel Chevalier, an economist, writing for *Le Journal des Débats,* also of Paris.

In the years following the war, Mackay was succeeded in New York for the *Times* during 1865–67 by Louis John Jennings, formerly in India for the paper. He was to become editor of the *New York Times* from 1867–76, after which he returned to his native England, where he was to write and become a Member of Parliament. Joel Cook, an American, and former Civil War correspondent for the *Philadelphia Public Ledger,* succeeded Jennings as a stringer for the *Times,* serving from 1867 until 1907. He usually wrote two letters a week, with Philadelphia as his base through most of those forty years.

McLean remained in New York for Reuter until 1893, another long period of service of more than thirty years. He then was replaced by S. Levy Lawson, who retained that post until World War I. The Reuter news exchange with the NYAP continued through the changes wherein the NYAP-WAP combination developed in 1867, to become the API in 1893 and the AP in 1900. The original dependence upon Gobright in Washington became a dependence after 1877 upon other staff members and, after 1900, notably upon Edwin Milton Hood, which continued until his retirement in 1920. Not only did Hood become chief correspondent for the AP in Washington, and dean of the press corps, but he was a confidant and adviser of presidents and others. Franklin Delano Roosevelt, assistant secretary of the navy in President Wilson's cabinet in 1920, when Hood retired, referred to him as "one of the grandest men who ever lived."

George Augustus Sala, in the United States as a representative of the *Daily Telegraph* during the Civil War, returned in 1888 and journeyed across the country. He was not the first foreign newsman to do so. William Simpson, an artist-correspondent for the *Illustrated London News,* on a world journey, reported aspects of the Modoc Indian War in California and Oregon in 1873. The last Indian War, in South Dakota in 1890–91, received attention from John Merry LeSage of the *Daily Telegraph,* and A. K. Zilliacus, writing for a European paper.

C. F. Moberly Bell became manager of the *Times* in 1890. Reviewing the paper's coverage of much of the world through its "own correspondent" system, he felt the time had come to appoint a resident staff correspondent in the United States. On the recommendation of James Bryce (later Viscount Bryce), British historian, author, and diplomat, whose book, *The American Commonwealth* (1888) was already a classic, and who was soon (1907–13) to serve as ambassador to the United States, Bell gave thought to offering the post to Theodore Roosevelt, at that time a member of the U.S. Civil Service Commission in Washington. Instead, however, he persuaded George W. Smalley to take the position.

A native of Massachusetts, and a Civil War correspondent for the *New York Tribune,* Smalley had been that paper's correspondent in London since 1866. He was widely known there and highly respected. In 1895, by then sixty-two years old, he accepted Bell's offer to join the staff of the *Times* as correspondent in New York, even as Cook continued as a stringer in Philadelphia. One of his first acts was to go to Washington to meet with Richard Olney, then secretary of state, to discuss the critical Anglo-American confrontation of the time over determination of the British Guiana–Venezuelan boundary and its relation to the Monroe Doctrine.

The United States was still in a sharp economic recession following a panic of 1893, caused in part by the failure of the Baring Bros. banking house of London, with British investors selling American securities and so causing a serious drain on U.S. gold reserves.

A strong demand by some in the United States for a compensatory renewal of the free and unlimited coinage of silver, which had been halted in 1891, became a lively issue in the contest for the presidency in 1896. William Jennings Bryan, Democratic party candidate, spoke eloquently for a free silver plan. William McKinley, the Republican party candidate, supported a continued adherance to the gold standard, and he was elected in November, to assume office in March 1897.

British and European investors and traders took an unprecedented interest in the issue at stake in the campaign, in the New York stock market behavior, in shipping, in railroad development, in some agricultural enterprises, and in economic matters in general. Smalley and Cook both provided reports for the *Times*. In addition, the London *Daily Mail,* newly established by Alfred Harmsworth, sent a young correspondent, George Warrington Steevens, to give special coverage to the 1896 campaign.

So far as most foreign newspaper readers were concerned, interest in news from the United States prior to 1896, except for the years of the Civil War, related primarily to the more superficial, fantastic, and violent aspects of life. Newspapers and magazines of other countries commonly had portrayed the United States as a place of Indians and cowboys, of oddities and natural wonders in a far land, of bandits, and of eccentrics using sudden wealth in strange ways.

In fairness, it must be said that the press of the United States favored equally trivial and distorted stories from Europe, Latin America, Africa, and Asia. The entire international exchange of information suffered in this fashion prior to World War I. Not all publications were guilty, but the fault was notable in the popular press, for which it was criticized with little result. Such stories provided entertaining reading, attracted readers, and it was difficult to argue with success.

In the United States, New York long had been the chief news center. As the largest city, the major port, the financial base, the place of publication for the most enterprising newspapers and leading magazines, and the hub of communications and transportation, it was the logical place for foreign reporters to work. Even as late as 1914 it was said, not without a certain justification, that "there was nothing known in Washington that was not known in New York the day before." News flowed there, not only from Washington, but from all parts of the country and from abroad.

In 1900 there is reason to believe that stringers were writing from Washington for five British newspapers, but for very few other foreign media. Correspondents in New York sometimes visited Washington, just as Smalley did. The Reuter bureau in New York depended on the Associated Press for its reports from there. The French Agence Havas had recently established its own agent and bureau in New York, and so had the Wolff bureau of Germany, but that was chiefly to be close to the AP headquarters, as a convenience in the selection and exchange of news.

One of the British stringers recently arrived in Washington was A. Maurice Low (later Sir Maurice Low), who wrote for the *Morning Post* of London. Very soon he was named a regular staff correspondent for the paper, the first resident foreign staff correspondent in Washington. There he continued until his retirement shortly after 1930.

Late in 1901, C. F. Moberly Bell, manager of the *Times,* visited the United States. In Washington he talked with President Roosevelt, only recently in office following McKinley's assassination. Smalley was in New York then and went to Washington when it seemed desirable. By 1904, however, Bell had become persuaded that Washington was one of the most important capitals of the world and deserved permanent staff representation. Valentine Chirol, director of the *Times* foreign department, and a visitor to the United States in 1903 and again in 1904, shared that view. He proposed that Smalley be transferred to Washington; Bell agreed, and the move was made.

Both executives of the *Times* hoped that, based in Washington, Smalley might give greater attention than in New York to political and administrative matters bearing upon international affairs. Smalley by then was well acquainted with Roosevelt and Hay, but still he seemed unable to produce reports reflecting the kind of insight into diplomatic policy that Bell and Chirol wanted for the paper. He helped cover the Portsmouth Peace Conference in 1905, following the Russo-Japanese War, working in company with Sir Donald Mackenzie Wallace, a *Times* veteran eight years younger than Smalley, and with Dr. George Ernest Morrison, the paper's Peking correspondent, nearly thirty years younger. Again, Smalley's contributions did not measure up to what his very demanding London editors wanted, and they began to consider replacing him in Washington.

They thought of Morrison, for one, but of other *Times* correspondents: Henry Wickham Steed in Vienna; George Saunders in Berlin; and William Lavino in Paris. The man finally named was Robert Percival Porter of the paper's London staff. Smalley left the *Times* in

1906, aged seventy-three, after ten years with that paper, added to more than thirty years with the *New York Tribune.* He did not retire happily, however, but returned to London to pass the last years of his life. He died there in 1916.

Porter was English-born, but had lived in the United States through his boyhood and until he was fifty-two. He began his newspaper career on the *Chicago Inter-Ocean,* with later experience on the *New York Tribune,* and he was co-founder of the *New York Press* in 1887. An economist and specialist on monetary matters, taxation, and transportation, he also had been a U.S. tariff commissioner and director of the census, all prior to returning to England in 1904. There he joined the *Times* staff as editor of a special engineering supplement.

Back in Washington as resident correspondent for the *Times* from 1906 to 1910, Porter gave special attention to economic subjects and to politics and diplomacy, as the paper wished him to do. In 1910, however, he returned to London as director of supplements for the *Times,* each one virtually a book on its special subject and usually republished as such. In that assignment, Porter traveled over much of the world and wrote extensively until his death in 1917.

Control of the *Times* passed in 1908 to Lord Northcliffe, as Harmsworth had become in 1905. He was already publisher of the popular *Daily Mail* and other newspapers and periodicals. Walter Fred Bullock had opened a *Daily Mail* bureau in New York in 1906. From 1908 he also represented the *Times* there, continuing for both papers until 1923, the year following Northcliffe's death.

Meanwhile in Washington, Porter was succeeded briefly in 1910 by Charles R. Hargroves and then by Arthur Willert (later Sir Arthur Willert). With the *Times* since 1906, and recently down from Oxford, Willert had been in the Paris and Berlin bureaus until 1908, and then in the London office acting also as a stringer for the *New York Evening Post.*

Willert was the *Times* resident staff correspondent in Washington from 1910 until 1921. He exemplified the type of man the paper valued as its representative in a foreign capital—highly informed, urbane, and almost as much a working diplomat as a working journalist. It was a combination of talents possessed by such other staff members as Wallace, Chirol, Steed, and Harris.

Foreign correspondents who visited the United States or remained in the early years of the century included Gaston Chadourne of the Agence Havas. He had gone from his post in Rome to report the Boxer relief expedition in China in 1900, but returned to Europe in 1901 by way of

Canada and the United States. The Agence Havas in 1900 named an American, Henry Sweinhart, as special representative in Washington. Dr. George Barthelme became a stringer in Washington at this approximate period for the Cologne *Gazette* and other European papers. Otto von Gottberg represented the *Berliner Lokal-Anzeiger,* although he was in New York nearly as much as in the capital.

One correspondent who remained long in the United States was Percy S. Bullen, of the London *Daily Telegraph.* A representative of that paper during the South African War, and later in Paris, Rome, and Berlin, he started for Japan early in 1904 to report the situation that erupted almost immediately as the Russo-Japanese War. In traveling by way of the United States, the tension in the Far East had eased temporarily between the time he left London and his arrival in New York. His paper cabled him to wait there for further instructions, and soon he was asked to remain as correspondent in New York, rather than proceed to the Far East.

The *Daily Telegraph* established what became a permanent bureau in New York, and Bullen served as correspondent until his retirement in 1934. When he began in 1904, however, it was not yet certain that his base necessarily would be in New York, and he made a journey to Washington within a few weeks. There he paid a formal call at the White House, attired in striped trousers, a morning coat, and top hat, and was admitted to see President Roosevelt. The President greeted him cordially and remarked that "It's high time you fellows began to discover America." McLean and Lawson of Reuter, Smalley of the *Times,* and Low of the *Morning Post* already had "discovered" it as resident staff correspondents. Bullen became the fourth. H. T. Cozens-Hardy, representing the London *Morning Leader,* became a fifth. Formerly in Paris for that paper, he established a bureau in New York in 1905 and remained until 1914, going occasionally to Washington, as Bullen was to do. Bullock of the *Daily Mail* arrived in 1906, when Porter succeeded Smalley for the *Times* in Washington.

Foreign correspondents in Washington, whether staff or stringer or visitors from New York bureaus, were as free as representatives of the domestic press to seek out news sources wherever they might be found. They were not eligible to sit in the congressional press galleries, but they could hear debates from the visitors' galleries. They did not have direct access to the president, except in such formal meetings as Bullen had with Roosevelt, but they could query his secretaries. They might be able to see the secretary of state or other top officials by appointment, and Hay and Root, at least, received them on occasion, along with domestic press representatives, to respond to questions.

There were so few foreign correspondents in Washington prior to 1910, even as visitors, that they were not considered for membership in the congressional Press Gallery by way of giving them full accreditation. That changed in 1911, when membership was opened to them in the Press Gallery organization.

As with domestic correspondents reporting public affairs, the number of foreign correspondents increased after 1914. Most of them still chose to make New York their operating base. After about 1930 some, responding to a world interest in motion pictures, established themselves in Hollywood, usually as stringers, and in sufficient numbers to warrant the formation of a special association of correspondents in Los Angeles.

The United States
Discovers the World

6

The press organization of the United States gained in vigor and prosperity after 1900. The events of the Spanish-American War period brought both an added world attention to the United States and a greater attention by its press to the rest of the world. A growing industrialization and activity in world trade required that the people look beyond the frontiers.

Among daily newspapers, many were providing strong local and national coverage of the news, and some in New York and Chicago had undertaken independent foreign reporting on a limited scale. Where a number of London dailies had demonstrated enterprise in that respect increasingly from 1800 the *New York Herald* had led among U.S. dailies almost from the time of its establishment in 1835. The *New York Tribune* had been notably effective in the early 1870s. The *New York Sun,* the *New York World,* and since 1895 the *New York Journal* had made their contributions.

In the new situation following the Spanish-American War, the *Chicago Record* led the way in original coverage beyond the frontier. Significant efforts were made during the first decade also by the Associated Press and by several other dailies, notably the *New York Times,* the *Christian Science Monitor,* established in Boston in 1908, the *Chicago Tribune,* and, in a small way, by the *New York Evening Post.* Further, two news agencies had their beginnings. The United Press Associations (UP) was formed in 1907, and the International News Service (INS) in 1909, both with headquarters in New York, both competitive with the Associated Press, and both soon entering into independent world news reporting.

The *Chicago Record* was a morning paper, paired with the afternoon *Chicago Daily News*. Both were published by Victor F. Lawson. The *Daily News* had been first in the field, established in 1876 by Melville E. Stone, then twenty-eight, but already experienced in journalism in Chicago and Washington. It was the first penny paper in Chicago. Short of operating capital in its first year, it was saved when Stone persuaded Lawson to join in the venture. Although only twenty-three, Lawson already had made a fortune in Chicago real estate. Well educated at Phillips Academy and Andover, and with a good sense of business he turned the *Daily News* into a profitable enterprise, with Stone as editor. In 1881 they established the *Chicago Morning News,* but promptly changed its name to the *Chicago Record.* In 1888, Stone dissociated himself from the newspapers to enter the banking business, and Lawson became owner and publisher of both.

With an interest in the larger world, one of Lawson's first acts as an independent publisher was to send William E. Curtis, formerly of the *Chicago Inter-Ocean* staff, as a roving correspondent in Central and South America. Curtis wrote a series of substantial articles for the *Record* on political, economic, and social matters in a part of the world rarely mentioned in the press of the United States or Europe. They were influential in bringing about the establishment in 1890 of an International Union of American Republics, with a permanent Bureau of American Republics in Washington. From this was to come a series of Pan-American Conferences, the formation in 1901 of a Pan-American Union in Washington, and the Organization of American States in 1948.

Curtis himself became director of the Bureau of American Republics in 1890–93, and went to Spain and Italy on special missions. He wrote several volumes on Latin American subjects. In 1897, he also wrote from Europe for the *Record,* along with William Sumner Harwell, including reports from Sweden, another area previously neglected in the world press.

Meanwhile, the *Record* sent Omar Maris to Alaska in 1896 to report on the resources of that territory, and he was in Canada in 1897 to report on gold discoveries just made in the Klondike. Trumbull White, formerly with the *Chicago Times,* was sent to Australia and New Zealand for the *Record* in that same year on an assignment similar to that of Curtis in Latin America nine years before. Curtis, White, and three others, Crittenden Marriott, Charles M. Faye, and Charles E. Crosby, made a serious study of Cuban affairs in 1897. Crosby was killed by Spanish fire while with the insurrectionists seeking independence for the islanders. Other correspondents went on brief journeys for the *Record* to London, Paris, Peking, and Tokyo.

During the Spanish American War, the *Record* was one of the most active newspapers in coverage, with about twenty correspondents directed from Key West by Trumbull White. His wife, Katherine Short, also provided reports while serving as a nurse aboard a Red Cross steamer plying between Key West and Cuba. The *Record* received reports on the Battle of Manila Bay as observed by John T. McCutcheon, political cartoonist for the paper, who happened to be on a journey aboard a U.S. revenue cutter when the war began, with the ship diverted to Hong Kong and then to Manila with Admiral Dewey's fleet. McCutcheon remained in the Philippines until 1899, with a side journey to Asia, and later was to report aspects of the South African War for the paper.

Melville E. Stone had returned to the news field in 1893 as general manager of the Associated Press of Illinois (API), formed in that year in a merger of the New York Associated Press with the Western Associated Press based in Chicago, and taking over the NYAP news exchange arrangement with the Reuter agency.

Stone and Lawson were impressed in 1898 by the situation they recognized as confronting the United States after the Spanish-American War because of the new territorial interests gained by the nation in the West Indies and in the Pacific.

In a letter to Charles H. Dennis, then editor of the *Record,* Lawson wrote:

> . . . the nation henceforth must shoulder the responsibilities and discharge the duties of a world power. As a protection against errors by our government and against aggression upon our rights and privileges by other governments, we as a people must keep abreast of events in foreign countries. We cannot afford longer to ignore what other nations think of us and of one another. We Americans must know the world better than we ever have known it in the past.
>
> That being the situation, the *Record* is confronted with a duty and an opportunity. The American people require, and we are entitled to have a world-wide news service conducted for their enlightenment and in the American spirit. The *Record* will establish such a service. It is no longer desirable, or even safe, for public opinion in this country to rely, as it now does, almost exclusively upon foreign agencies, most of them subsidized by foreign governments, for their own news of other countries.[1]

---

1   Charles H. Dennis, *Victor Lawson, His Time and His Work* (Chicago, 1935), p. 264.

This latter reference bore upon the exchange arrangement with the British Reuter agency taken over by the Associated Press of Illinois and providing virtually the only source of world news for the press of the United States, including the *Chicago Record* itself. Reuter depended in turn upon its exchange with the Havas and Wolff agencies of France and Germany and other national agencies of Europe forming the Ring Combination, many of which were indeed official or semi-official agencies of their governments.

Lawson had been intimately involved in the formation of the Associated Press of Illinois in 1893, and was its president, as Stone was its general manager. But Lawson wished to supplement its service with reports for his own newspaper and prepared, as he put it, "in the American spirit," somewhat as Reuter, several years before had "anglicized" its service.

Lawson and Dennis proceeded to organize such a supplementary service for the *Record*. Curtis, who had been Washington correspondent for the paper in 1897–98, returned to South America, where he had been ten years before, "to arrange for a complete representation at the leading cities and points of news interest." In Manila McCutcheon arranged for two stringers there, and traveled to Hong Kong, Peking, Saigon, Bangkok, Rangoon, Colombo, Calcutta, and back to Manila by way of Korea and Japan to arrange representation. Dr. Robert Coltman, appointed in Peking, reported the Boxer Rebellion in 1899–1900. George Ade, of the paper's Chicago staff, was sent to Europe and the Balkans to arrange coverage.

By July 1899 Lawson was able to say that the *Record* had "between 85 and 90 correspondents in Europe and the Orient," plus men at "two or three points in South America." Most of them were stringers, but by the end of that year the service was winning such a reputation that William C. Reick, then managing editor of the *New York Herald,* acting on instructions from Bennett, the publisher, invited Lawson to consider consolidating the *Record* service with that of the *Herald,* long regarded as the best in the United States. Lawson went to Paris, where Bennett had his home, to discuss the matter, and for a time the two papers made their reports mutually available. Lawson ended the trial, however, when he became convinced that the *Record* was gaining little of value.

Early in 1900, Lawson reiterated his belief in the need for a special foreign service to supplement that received through the API. His philosophy was outlined somewhat more fully in Dennis's book:

> Heretofore the few American newspapers that have undertaken to gather an individual service of foreign news have depended chiefly upon placing a man in London and having him clip from the London morning papers the most desirable news and cable it to New York. This is the simplest and most economical plan of getting foreign news, but like some other things that are cheapest, it is not the best plan.
>
> There are two objections to it. First, the news printed in London papers is naturally only that news as is wanted by English newspaper readers. American interests, as they may be involved in foreign happenings, are only incidentally and partially reported in such a service, when they are reported at all. Second, English interests not infrequently give color and general character to the news itself.
>
> In continental countries, particularly in Germany and France, the criticism is made that the news of all Europe, as printed in the American press, is in too large a measure drawn from London, and is therefore naturally presented in an undue degree from the English point of view. London is the greatest news center in the world, and yet that fact seems only to emphasize the wisdom of supplementing and correcting London news by the news and views of the rest of the world.
>
> It is worth remembering also that, leaving out of account the interests of American newspaper readers in general, a large proportion of our citizenship is composed of natives of the continental countries of Europe, and they are therefore particularly interested in an accurate, if not sympathetic, presentation of news from "the fatherland."[2]

Acting on these views, Lawson and the *Record* in 1900 sent a permanent correspondent to London, the paper's first resident staff representative. He was Edward Price Bell, an able member of the Chicago staff, who remained in London until 1923 directing the European service. In those years, Bell won such respect that he was referred to by Lord Northcliffe, most successful British publisher of the period, as "the best American newspaperman London ever had." J. L. Garvin, respected editor of the *Observer,* the London Sunday quality paper, called him "the best unofficial ambassador the American people ever sent to our people." In this, he received praise comparable to that bestowed in his time upon George W. Smalley, *New York Tribune* correspondent in London from 1866 to 1895.

In 1901 the morning *Chicago Record* was sold by Lawson to Herman H. Kohlsaat, a Chicago businessman owning wholesale bakeries and

---

2 Dennis, *Victor Lawson,* pp. 267–68.

restaurants. He already owned the morning *Chicago Times-Herald* and merged the *Record* with that to make the *Chicago Record-Herald*.[3]

In selling the *Chicago Record,* Lawson retained its foreign service and made it a part of his afternoon paper, the *Chicago Daily News.* Although most newspaper foreign services have been associated with morning dailies, the *Daily News* service became an exception and soon among the most important and respected. It was made available also through syndication to other newspapers in noncompetitive circulation territories.

Frederic William Wile, a member of the Chicago staff of the *Record,* had followed Bell to London in 1900 as an assistant, but was reassigned to Berlin in 1901 and served there as *Daily News* correspondent until 1906. He then transferred to the service of the London *Daily Mail,* remaining in Berlin until 1914. Succeeding him for the *Daily News* in Berlin was Albert C. Wilkie, who earned high praise for his work. John Foster Bass, an experienced journalist most recently representing the *New York Journal,* was assigned to St. Petersburg for the *Daily News* in 1901 and remained until 1915, except for the period of the Russo-Japanese War, when he was in Manchuria and also aboard the paper's dispatch boat *Fawan* off Port Arthur. Stanley Washburn, son of former U.S. Senator William Drew Washburn of Minnesota, was with Bass at that time as a war correspondent, and after 1905 was in the south of Russia, where he also wrote for the London *Times.*

Lamar Middleton was assigned to Paris for the *Daily News* in 1901. Upon his death there in 1910, he was succeeded by Paul Scott Mowrer of the Chicago staff, then twenty-three and only two years out of the University of Michigan.

One reason certain newspapers were more popular than others was because they gave news attention to local events, to news of persons and places familiar to readers. They published reports from the national capital and from foreign places, along with editorials and serious articles, but it was recognized by editors that relatively few readers paid much attention to such matter, except in a quality paper.

The *Chicago Daily News* was made in a sufficiently popular pattern to attract a considerable readership. But it had some of the characteristics of a quality paper, notably in its foreign service. Even within the office, however, this was regarded as a whim of Lawson's,

---

3   Kohlsaat also owned the *Chicago Evening Post* from 1894–1901, had a partial interest in the morning *Chicago Inter-Ocean* in 1891–93, and again became its publisher from 1912–14, when he merged it with the *Record-Herald.*

with doubt as to how generally such reports actually were read. Indicative of an attitude then prevailing in the United States, Mowrer's colleagues on the *Daily News* staff attempted to dissuade him from accepting the Paris post when it was offered to him in 1910.

Glamor, adventure, and even fame might come to a war correspondent. For example, Richard Harding Davis had become a kind of idol for an upcoming generation of newsmen in the United States, in part because of the prominence he had attained in reporting wars since 1897. For Mowrer to go to Paris as a peacetime correspondent, concerned with subjects regarded as of no intrinsic interest to most readers, could mean he would be forgotten, some of his friends believed, and so sacrifice an otherwise promising career in journalism.

Mowrer chose to accept the Paris assignment, nevertheless, and remained there until 1935. Far from being forgotten, he gained a great reputation. He did cover wars in that time, but reputation came equally through his reporting of international political and economic subjects. Recognition of his work included a Pulitzer Prize in 1929. Reputation came to him and others because the world changed greatly after 1910, with foreign news ultimately to dominate page one in virtually all newspapers. Long before Mowrer returned to Chicago to become editor of the *Daily News* from 1935–45, some of his colleagues of 1910 and their juniors were eagerly seeking appointments as foreign correspondents.

Associated Press

Lawson was not alone in recognizing that the new position of the United States in the world after 1898 recommended special enterprise by the press organization in providing substantive reports on public affairs at home and abroad. Stone, his friend and associate, encouraged Lawson in developing the special service for the *Record* and *Daily News,* and also contemplated extending foreign coverage for the Associated Press of Illinois, under his direction since its formation in 1893.

The API already had some stringer correspondents of its own in Europe in 1899, and representatives in Havana and Manila since the Spanish-American War. It had a strong bureau in Washington, and its own representative working with Reuter in London. It provided coverage of the Boxer uprising in China in 1899–1901, followed by the placement of two correspondents in Tokyo.

Desirable as it seemed to Stone and others in the API at that time to build upon the agency's limited foreign representation, such action had to wait. The API had become involved in a legal contest in 1898 with the *Chicago Inter-Ocean* and its editor, George Wheeler Hinman, relating to the restrictions on membership in the agency and other bylaws. An adverse ruling by the Illinois State Supreme Court in February 1900 led to a decision by the API to end its existence as an Illinois corporation, and to reincorporate in New York state. This it did, renamed more simply as the Associated Press (AP), effective in September 1900, with its headquarters in New York City and with Stone continuing as general manager.[4]

As 1901 began, Stone at last was able to give purposeful thought to the subject that had interested him, as it had interested Lawson in 1898–99.

As Lawson in 1898 had discussed with Stone his interest in establishing a special service for the *Chicago Record,* Stone had asked Walter Neef, London representative of the API, to express his views on the contemplated *Record* service. Neef responded in January 1899:

> It must be acknowledged that the matter we [the API] receive through Reuters from Havas, Wolff and the other agencies is usually a colorless statement of fact, and American correspondents sending the same news from the various continental centers would treat the matter from a different point of view and include just the things that would interest our people. Thus if the *Record* has American correspondents all over, or intelligent people who are on the lookout for news that will especially interest America, they undoubtedly will get some items which we shall not.[5]

This reply, shown to Lawson at the time, encouraged him to proceed with his plan. But it also gave Stone and the directors of the API something to consider with reference to the agency service. It suggested that the API also might provide its own direct coverage of world news, tailored to inform the people of the United States more effectively. It

---

4 The long and complex story of this controversy and change was related to the formation and activity of the old United Press (1882–97). That agency had derived from the Hasson News Association of Philadelphia (1869–70), the American Press Association (APA) of New York (1870–77), and a National American Press Company operating the National Associated Press (NAP) of New York (1877–82), all headed by John Hasson. The old United Press emerged in 1882. Its story, along with the transformation of the New York Associated Press (NYAP) and the Western Associated Press (WAP) into the Associated Press of Illinois in 1893, and the conflict with Hinman and the *Inter-Ocean,* is told in Desmond, *The Information Process,* pp. 359–68.

5 Dennis, *Victor Lawson,* p. 266.

could supplement, or perhaps even replace the Reuter-Havas-Wolff and Ring Combination service.

Lawson by 1901 had made a good beginning in the formation of a special service for his *Chicago Record,* with the service transferred in that year to his afternoon *Chicago Daily News.*

The Associated Press had a full staff in New York, an effective coverage in Washington, and representatives in most major cities of the United States, some of them division points in the organization to route the news reports over the leased wire network. The agency also had at that time eighty-seven stringers in capitals and cities abroad, with actual staff representation in London, Havana, Manila, and Tokyo. Even so, the AP remained essentially a national agency, dependent upon Reuter for world reports.

Stone was not alone among directors of the AP in believing that resident staff correspondents should at least be assigned to some foreign posts beyond the four mentioned. Actually, Neef was alone in London, and his function was merely to select and process excerpts from the Reuter service. The other three occupied their posts chiefly as a result of the Spanish-American War and the Boxer incident in China, with no clear decision that those assignments would necessarily be permanent.

The great volume of foreign reports reaching the United States since colonial times had come from European capitals, and especially from or through London. With that in mind, Stone caused inquiries to be made about such access as correspondents for the AP might have to news sources in those capitals, if assigned there, about possible censorship, press rates and other costs, and about the quality of the communications facilities.

At length, in 1902, Stone was ready to go to Europe himself to explore the possibilities. His first stop was in London, where no great problem was anticipated and none encountered. A beginning of increased coverage was made there, with the transfer to London, to serve with Neef, of Elmer E. Roberts, veteran of the API Spanish-American War coverage and then correspondent in Havana.

From London, Stone went to Paris. In 1903 he returned to Europe to visit Rome, Berlin, and St. Petersburg. In his approach to government officials in each capital, seeking assurances of clear news channels, he had support from John Hay, then U.S. secretary of state. Hay was in sympathy with Stone's purpose and understood his needs. Stone also had the support of members of the U.S. diplomatic corps and of ambassadors in the United States from the countries visited.

The missions were precedent-making. It is unlikely that any spokesman for the press ever before had made representations to government officials and to monarchs advancing the *right* of the people to have information about public affairs.

In Paris in 1902, Stone put his case before Minister of Foreign Affairs Théophile Delcassé and other cabinet members. He said, in part:

> If The Associated Press is to gather the news of France at first hand then our correspondents must be absolutely free and there must be no attempt to influence them. I understand, of course, that in order to be useful the representative of The Associated Press accredited to any capital must be on friendly terms with the government at that capital, but under no condition will he be a servile agent of that government.
>
> The Associated Press will not surrender the right to a free and accurate statement of the news, and anything the association may do in the future must be done with the distinct understanding that the government of France will not attempt to influence the impartial character of the service.
>
> If the French government can see its way to expedite our dispatches on the state telegraph system, if it will throw open all departments of the government to us so we can obtain the facts, then I shall be glad to establish a full-sized bureau in Paris, and take all our French news from Paris direct.[6]

Despite these rather boldly stated demands, the French government agreed to abide by the terms Stone outlined. France's relations with Great Britain were not wholly amicable at the time. It welcomed an opportunity to be represented to the American public more directly, rather than through the interposition of the British Reuter agency. It was agreed that French officials would provide information directly to AP correspondents, even bypassing the Agence Havas, which had been the channel for Reuter. Stone was assured that officials would respond to questions on matters of particular interest to the people of the United States, and that the Ministry of Poste and Telégraphes would assist by preparing special telegraph and cable forms to identify AP dispatches as an aid to more rapid handling.

With these agreements, Stone made Charles T. Thompson head of a new bureau in Paris. Henry J. Middleton, formerly a stringer for the AP, remained a member of the bureau. Stringers in other cities of France, then and later, directed their reports to the Paris bureau.

The French government, in the months following, was pleased by what it regarded as an improved presentation of the news of France in

---

6   Oliver Gramling, *AP, The Story of News* (New York, 1940), pp. 165–66.

the United States. It volunteered its assistance in advancing similar arrangements for coverage by the Associated Press in Italy and Spain. The practical possibilities of such aid were enhanced by the considerable control then exercised by the French Agence Havas in the direction of the Agenzia Telegrafica Stefani of Italy and the Agence Espagñole et Internationale of Spain.

The Paris bureau was made a relay point for news from Italy and Spain, cabled from there direct to New York rather than by way of London as before. This reduced the time interval for transmission from several hours via London to about twenty-one minutes direct from Paris. It also saved added charges on the Paris–London leg.

Returning to Europe in 1903, and going first to Rome, Stone met with officials of the Italian Foreign Ministry, with King Victor Emmanuel, and with Pope Leo XIII, then in the last year of his life. He spoke very much as he had in Paris and with generally comparable results. The AP bureau established in Rome was placed under the direction of Salvatore Cortesi, a stringer there for the agency since 1895, and he was to head the bureau until his retirement in 1931. British-born William A. M. Goode, who had served as an API correspondent in Cuba during the Spanish-American War, was assigned to assist him as second man in the bureau. The early success of these two, along with Thompson in Paris, in producing the first knowledge the world received of the death of Pope Leo XIII on July 20, 1903, has been described. Cortesi had such good relations with the Italian government, the Vatican, and sources throughout Italy that the AP enjoyed a special advantage through the years.[7]

From Rome, Stone went to Berlin. Following previous procedure, he saw officials in the German Foreign Ministry and also met with Kaiser Wilhelm II. Again, arrangements followed for coverage by AP correspondents. A new Berlin bureau was placed in charge of Elmer E. Roberts, moved from the London bureau, and who remained as Berlin chief until 1911, assisted by Robert E. Berry, a Scotsman.

Late in 1903, Stone arrived in St. Petersburg. Czarist government restraints made it the most difficult of the major European capitals for news coverage. Correspondents for the foreign press were relatively few,

---

7 Cortesi's personal standing was demonstrated in 1913 at a time when all AP bureau heads were bonded as a technical requirement for handling funds. Two character references were needed and Cortesi cited "Guiseppe Sarto, Pope, Vatican Palace, Rome" (Pius X), and "Victor Emmanuel of Savoy, King, Quirinal Palace, Rome." Although listed in a spirit of fun, the references were legitimate, and both the pope and the king responded with friendly and favorable reports on Cortesi's responsibility.

handicapped by lack of ready access to information sources, a controlled and inferior local and national press, a heavy censorship on outgoing reports, high transmission rates and poor service, and by the possibility of expulsion from the country, without recourse, if a report displeased officials.

Stone was aware of the problems he was to meet in seeking admission for Associated Press correspondents on the terms he regarded as essential. He had gained some support from Count Arthur Cassini, Russia's ambassador in Washington. He hoped, also, that the position established for the AP in London, Paris, Rome, and Berlin might be further basis for acceptance of his proposals in St. Petersburg.

What he encountered was evasion and delay. Count Vladimir Lamsdorff, minister of foreign affairs, disclaimed responsibility in matters of censorship and communication. Viatscheslaf Plehve, minister of the interior and also head of the czar's secret police, told Stone outright that he was "not prepared to abolish the censorship," and that it would be imprudent to do so because there was great unrest in Russia. He referred to riots that had occurred, plots to overthrow the government, and cited a history of political assassination.

It was true that there was unrest. Also, Czar Peter III had been deposed and murdered in 1762, Czar Paul had been killed in 1801, Czar Alexander II had been assassinated in 1881, and Plehve's predecessor in the Ministry of the Interior had been assassinated the year before.[8] Plehve told Stone that he had no authority in the matter of communications and referred him to the minister of finance, then Count Serge Julievich Witte, who was hardly more helpful than either of the others. Stone also knew that William T. Stead, editor of the London *Review of Reviews* and formerly editor of the *Pall Mall Gazette,* had visited St. Petersburg earlier in 1903 to seek an end to the censorship. Despite a personal friendship with Plehve and an audience with Czar Nicholas, his effort had failed.

Even with so unpromising a beginning, Stone was persistent enough to win assurances from some ministries that they would deal helpfully with any AP correspondent assigned to St. Petersburg. He also was promised a satisfactory arrangement for handling and paying for the transmission of dispatches. He had about resigned himself to failure in obtaining any concession on censorship, however, and was in some doubt as to whether it would be useful to place a correspondent in the Russian

---

8 Plehve himself became a target of two attempts on his life in 1904, one a few weeks after his talk with Stone, and the second in April when a bomb killed him.

capital. In that mood, he was about to leave St. Petersburg early in January 1904, when suddenly he received notice that an earlier request for an interview with the czar had been granted.

Czar Nicholas, then thirty-five and nearly ten years on the throne, heard from Stone, who was twenty years older, his wish that the Associated Press might report the news of Russia through its own efforts, rather than continuing to receive such reports by indirection, with attendant risks of distortion. That news had been reaching the AP and the people of the United States through Reuter, which had a correspondent in St. Petersburg. The Agence Havas also had a representative there, and the Wolff agency had an exchange arrangement with the Russion Telegraph Agency, Rosta (Rossiyskoye Telegraphnoye Agenstvo), formed in 1894, and with the Commercial Telegraph Company, TTA (Torgova-Telegraphnoye Agenstvo), as formed in 1902 by action of the Ministry of Finance. Much of what the Wolff, Havas, and Reuter agencies reported, even through their correspondents, was based upon what was permitted to appear in the Russion press, representing a distortion at the source.

"We come as friends," Stone said to the czar, "and it is my desire that our representatives here shall treat Russia as a friend; but it is the very essence of the proposed plan that we be free to tell the truth. We cannot be the mouthpiece of Russia, we cannot plead her cause, except insofar as telling the truth will do so."

The czar appeared to accept this concept, and asked Stone to explain the arrangements he wanted to see made effective. Stone reiterated much that he had said in other capitals and reverted to the matter of censorship. He said:

> Censorship is not only valueless from your point of view, but works a positive harm. A wall has been built around the country, and the fact that no correspondent for a foreign paper can live and work here[9] has resulted in a traffic of false Russian news that is most hurtful.
>
> Today there are newspapermen in Vienna, Berlin and London who make a living by peddling out the news of Russia, and it is usually false. If we were free to tell the truth in Russia, as we are in other countries, no self-respecting newspaper in the world would print a dispatch from

---

9   This was not accurate. There had been foreign correspondents in St. Petersburg for more than 20 years and in 1903 there were correspondents there for Reuter, Havas, and Wolff, for the London *Daily Telegraph* and *Daily Mail,* for the *Manchester Guardian,* the *New York Herald* and the *Chicago Daily News.* The London *Times* correspondent had been expelled a few months before Stone arrived, but another representative was serving the paper unofficially.

Vienna respecting the internal affairs of Russia because the editor would know that, if the thing were true, it would come from Russia direct.

All you do now is to drive a correspondent to send his dispatches across the German border. I am free to write anything I choose in Russia, and send it by messenger to Wirballen, across the German border, and it will go from there without change. You are powerless to prevent my sending those dispatches, and all you do now is anger the correspondent and make him an enemy, and delay his dispatches, robbing the Russian telegraph lines of revenue they should receive. So it occurs to me that the censorship is inefficient, that it is a censorship which does not censor, but annoys.[10]

At the czar's request, Stone put his proposals in the form of a memorandum. He soon learned that Plehve, informed of this new statement, still opposed the proposals. But he also learned that the czar had approved them, and had specified that any Associated Press correspondent would be permitted to transmit reports without censorship.

Stone had left Russia by that time, but he sent word that the AP did not want any such favored treatment. He pointed out that if other correspondents were to remain subject to censorship this could be interpreted to mean that the AP had reached an agreement to report only that which had the approval of the government, thus defeating the value of the reports. Within forty-eight hours, probably to Stone's surprise but also to his gratification and that of others, censorship restrictions were declared rescinded for all accredited foreign correspondents in St. Petersburg.

The result was that a new Associated Press bureau was established in St. Petersburg early in 1904. It was headed by Howard N. Thompson,[11] still another of the former API Spanish-American War correspondents, and successor to Roberts in Havana. Thompson had not been long in St. Petersburg when the Russo-Japanese War began. He crossed Siberia on the Trans-Siberian Railway and was with Russian troops in Manchuria for a time. From St. Petersburg in 1905 he also accompanied the Russian delegation to the Portsmouth Peace Conference.

The Russian press itself remained under restraint, but correspondents in St. Petersburg for the foreign press were able to operate with unprecedented freedom during the 1904–05 period.

"We found ourselves able to present a daily picture of life in Russia that was most interesting and edifying," Stone wrote later. Even during the Russo-Japanese War, he said:

---

10   Gramling, *AP,* p. 172.

11   Not to be confused with Charles T. Thompson in Paris.

The Russian authorities gave the largest possible latitude to our correspondents. They turned over to us in St. Petersburg, daily, without mutilation, the official reports made to the Emperor and to the War Department, and the world was astonished at the frank character of the despatches coming from Russia.

Ninety per cent of the real news concerning the war came in bulletins first from St. Petersburg, and later in detail from the field, and there was no attempt on the part of the Government to influence the despatches, or even to minimize their disasters, when talking officially to our correspondents, who made daily visits to the War, Navy, Foreign and Interior offices, and were given the news with as much freedom as in Washington. Until Port Arthur was invested January 1, 1905, we found that we were able to receive despatches with extraordinary speed.[12]

During Thompson's first wartime absence from St. Petersburg he was replaced there temporarily by John Callan O'Laughlin from the AP London bureau. When he went to the Portsmouth Conference, Thompson was replaced by Hendrik Willem VanLoon, a young correspondent moving from London by way of Warsaw. Returning to St. Petersburg in September 1905, Thompson remained only a short time, succeeded again by O'Laughlin and by George Denny, who had reported the war.

With the problems that overtook Russia after its defeat, news coverage within the country became progressively more difficult, and most of the gains for correspondents were erased by 1906. The AP bureau remained in St. Petersburg, nevertheless. Even before the end of 1905, however, O'Laughlin and Denny moved to other assignments, and Seymour Beach Conger, transferring from London, assumed direction of coverage in Russia until 1911.[13]

Stone never visited the Far East, but he had authorized the establishment of an Associated Press bureau in Tokyo in 1901, even as he was investigating prospects for the European bureaus. Correspondents there were Robert M. Collins, an API correspondent in the Philippines in 1899, and Martin Egan, also present in the Philippines for the *San Francisco Chronicle*. Those two had joined in covering the

---

12 Melville E. Stone, *Fifty Years a Journalist* (New York, 1921), pp. 277–78.

13 O'Laughlin left the AP at this time to serve as Washington correspondent for the *Chicago Tribune* and then the *Chicago Herald* between 1905 and 1917, except for an interval in 1909–10. In those years he served, first, as an assistant secretary of state during the last weeks of the Roosevelt administration and then accompanied the former president on his expedition to Africa and returned with him by way of Europe. Leaving the *Chicago Herald* in 1917 for military service in World War I, O'Laughlin subsequently bought the *Army and Navy Journal,* a publication he conducted in Washington until his death in 1949.

Boxer Rebellion in China for the API in 1899–1900, and in 1901 they established the bureau in Tokyo, with Egan as chief. Together they covered the Russo-Japanese War from Tokyo and in the field, and were joined in Tokyo by George Denny.

In 1905, following the war, Denny joined O'Laughlin in St. Petersburg but they were replaced by Conger. O'Laughlin left the agency service, but Denny returned to Tokyo to replace Collins, who was appointed at that time to succeed Walter Neef, retiring as bureau chief in London. There Collins remained until 1920. Egan left Tokyo and AP service in 1907 to become editor of the *Manila Times*. He continued in that position until 1914, when he moved to New York as public relations adviser to J. P. Morgan & Co., in banking and investments, until his death in 1938.

With Egan's departure from Tokyo, he was replaced for the AP by J. Russell Kennedy. Irish-born but U.S. naturalized, Kennedy had been with the *Toronto Mail* and the *Washington Post*. For fifteen years before going to Tokyo, however, he had been a personal assistant to Stone both in the API and the AP. From 1907 to 1913 he was bureau chief in Tokyo. He then became managing director of a newly formed Japanese news agency, Kokusai Tsushin-sha (International News Agency), which received the Reuter news service for distribution in Japan, and he himself also became chief correspondent for Reuter. He was replaced in Tokyo for the AP by Joseph E. Sharkey, a member of the Paris bureau since 1907.

The establishment of bureaus in Tokyo, Paris, Rome, Berlin, and St. Petersburg, with the far older but growing bureau in London, plus representation in Havana and Manila, and stringers elsewhere abroad, had placed the Associated Press on the road to becoming a world news agency by 1905. It then was providing the press and people of the United States with a great volume of information, supplementing that provided by Reuter, to meet some of the specifications envisaged by Stone and Lawson alike as they began to make their plans in 1898. A strong Washington bureau, with Edwin M. Hood as chief, added substance to the agency's daily report.

---

*Scripps
Forms
the UP
1907*

Recognition of the new concern in the United States with the larger world after 1898 was not reflected solely in the extended activities of Lawson's *Chicago Record* and *Chicago Daily News* and the Associated

Press. There was a growing effort by other dailies to provide supplementary reports of their own from abroad, plus that development in the field of magazines and syndicates described, and a more active coverage of Washington. But a new era also was manifest in the formation of agencies to vie with the Associated Press.

The new Associated Press of New York, like the former API, was a cooperative news agency providing service to member papers only. This meant that nonmember papers had to look elsewhere for a general news service. With the old United Press suspended in 1897 that particular alternative source was gone, and AP service or membership was not to be had merely by application.

William M. Laffan, business manager of the *New York Sun,* had formed a Sun News Service to provide news and feature stories written by reporters and staff and stringer correspondents for the morning and afternoon *New York Sun* papers. Under the editorial direction of Charles A. Dana, until his death in 1897, the morning *Sun,* in particular, had gained repute for its writers and writing. The afternoon *Sun* also had an able staff, including Henry R. Chamberlain in London, who was greatly respected and provided a good foreign report drawn from London and European papers. With a five-hour time difference between London and New York, his dispatches arrived for use in the morning *Sun* and for distribution by the Sun News Service to subscribing papers. Laffan added to the foreign staff, and also sent writers on special missions at home and abroad.

Following Dana's death and the suspension of the old United Press, both occurring in 1897, Laffan became publisher of the *Sun* papers. The Sun News Bureau was retitled the Laffan News Bureau. With a creditable output, it was active until 1916, seven years after Laffan's death. The *Sun* papers then were purchased by Frank A. Munsey. The morning *Sun* was suspended, along with the Laffan bureau.

Meanwhile, a better news service and a permanent one, available to any newspaper on a commercial basis, was brought into being in 1907 by Edward W. Scripps. Called the United Press Associations because it was a merger of three regional agencies, it was known more simply as the United Press or UP.

Scripps, with sound experience gained on the *Detroit News,* established and directed by his half-brother, James E. Scripps, had undertaken to develop papers of his own after 1878, beginning with the *Cleveland Press* and the *Cincinnati Post.* He added others to form the first group of papers in the world. In 1902 he also formed the Newspaper Enterprise Association (NEA) of Cleveland, one of the early syndicates.

From 1890, Scripps chose to make his home in California, permitting his associate, Milton A. McRae, to exercise general direction of the Scripps-McRae Newspapers from Cincinnati. Although living in semi-retirement, Scripps remained active and added a number of separately and personally owned papers on the Pacific coast. In that period he could have had membership for some of his papers, at least, in the Western Associated Press, which became the API, or in the Old United Press. He declined because those services were designed primarily for morning papers, while all of his were published in the afternoon, and also because he objected to some of the bylaws of the WAP–API. He showed favor to the old United Press, however, and some material intended for publication in his papers was moved by special arrangement over the United Press leased wires. After formation of the Laffan News Bureau, he arranged to use its service.

Prior to 1895, the Scripps papers were without service from any agency, concentrating rather on local news in their areas, supplemented by an exchange of materials originating within the group, obtained from stringers in Washington and elsewhere. With the notable exception of articles written from Europe, North Africa, Mexico, and Cuba at various times between 1881 and 1889 by Scripps's half-sister, Ellen Browning Scripps, very few original foreign reports appeared in the newspapers prior to the Spanish-American War period.

With the end of the old United Press obviously approaching late in 1896, a Scripps-McRae Press Association (SMPA) was formed in Cincinnati in January 1897. It provided telegraphic news reports to seventeen Scripps-McRae afternoon papers in the Midwest. Although operating domestically for the most part, Edward L. Keen became a wartime representative in the Philippines in 1898.

To serve his Pacific Coast newspapers, conducted independently of those in the Midwest, Scripps also formed a Scripps-Blades Service, incorporating the name of Paul H. Blades of the *Los Angeles Record,* one of his papers established in 1895. With the departure of Blades, the service became known as the Scripps Western Report, and then the Scripps News Association (SNA), based in San Diego.

As Scripps had acted when the old United Press was nearing its end, so the suspension of that agency in April 1897 led J. B. Shales, a New York publisher, to bring together in New York City the directors of a group of afternoon papers in the state to form a Publishers' Press Association (PPA). Incorporated in March 1898 and based in New York, it arranged to receive a limited foreign report from London, presumably from the Exchange Telegraph (Extel) agency. It also included a report from Washington, reports from stringers in the eastern states, and formed an exchange arrangement between member papers.

Through Scripps's initiative, an exchange of news began after 1898 between his own two services in the Midwest and West and the Publishers' Press Association in the East to produce a national telegraphic service available to any newspaper wishing to subscribe. The Laffan News Bureau service obtained at $250 a week was added.

In 1906, Scripps bought control of the Publishers' Press Association for $150,000, possibly to forestall its purchase by William Randolph Hearst, then expanding his holdings. By that time, Scripps was publishing twenty-six afternoon papers, seventeen in the Midwest Scripps-McRae League, and the others on the Pacific Coast. He merged the three regional agencies in 1907 to form the United Press Associations, but operating as the United Press or UP. Even though this revived the name of the older, discredited United Press of 1882–97, it was Scripps's decision, and there was no relationship.

The new United Press, operative in June 1907, had its headquarters in the offices of the former Publishers' Press Association in New York. It was directed by John A. Vandercook, former editor of Scripps's *Cincinnati Post*. Vandercook died in 1908, and Hamilton B. Clark, former manager of the Scripps News Association on the West Coast became president of the UP. He was soon followed by Clayton D. Lee, former treasurer of the PPA, who served until 1913, and was succeeded by Roy Wilson Howard.

Roy Howard had started his news career in 1902 as a reporter for the *Indianapolis News,* but he soon returned to his native state of Ohio to join Scripps's *Cincinnati Post*. In 1906, at twenty-three, he was appointed manager in New York for the Scripps-McRae Press Association, but moved almost immediately into the same position with the PPA. With the formation of the UP in 1907 he became general manager of the headquarters office in New York. In 1908, he was made general manager of the UP itself, and in 1913 followed Lee both as president and general manager of the agency. He held this position until 1920, at which time he became a partner with Robert Paine Scripps, son of Edward W. Scripps, in what also became the Scripps-Howard Newspapers in a reorganization of the former Scripps-McRae League of newspapers.

The United Press service was intended at the outset primarily for the Scripps-owned afternoon newspapers. It soon was made available, however, on a commercial basis to other afternoon newspapers noncompetitive with the Scripps papers, and without any such membership restrictions as were set by the Associated Press. There was a demand by morning papers also for the UP service, either because they were denied AP service or wanted a supplementary service. A morning service was introduced therefore by the UP by the end of its first year, and its reports were going to 247 dailies in the United States, both morning and afternoon. The number doubled within the next few years and continued to rise.

The United Press placed emphasis on human interest material and introduced a lighter and more lively style in the news, by contrast to the sober treatment demanded by Stone in the AP service. It recruited reporters and stringers who were young, eager, and aggressive and so provided sharp competition for the older agency in the pursuit of news and its earliest possible delivery. It was a service welcomed by many newspapers, AP members papers among them.

The vigor and success of the new United Press was such that S. Levy Lawson, manager in New York for the Reuter agency, proposed to his London office as early as 1909 that, when the time came to renew its contract in 1913 with the Associated Press, an alliance with the United Press be considered instead. In 1912 Lawson and Roy Howard went together to London to meet with Herbert de Reuter to discuss such a possible alliance.

Whatever the view of the Reuter directors may have been, the United Press management decided against seeking an alliance. It would have meant payment of a large differential for the Reuter world service at a time when the UP was still only beginning to establish itself. That cost also would have required the agency to curtail plans for a foreign service of its own. Further, Howard had surveyed the operations of the Ring Combination and concluded that for the UP to enter an alliance with agencies, many in an official or semi-official relationship with the governments of their countries, would compromise the quality of the world news report to be distributed. For these reasons, the United Press chose to proceed independently.

While working to develop a domestic service, Howard had been giving attention since 1909 to the development of a foreign report as well. The Laffan News Bureau service was dropped, but the UP arranged to receive reports from the Louis Hirsch Telegraphisches Büro of Berlin, the Exchange Telegraph Company (Extel) of London, and the Fournier agency of Paris, the latter providing a specialized business and financial report.

A London bureau was established by the United Press in 1910. Edward Leggett Keen, who had been in the Philippines in 1898–1900, first for the Scripps-McRae Press Association and then for the Publishers' Press Association, and who had been manager of the UP bureau in Washington since 1907, was assigned to London as the agency's European manager. He continued there and later in Paris until 1925. He also became a vice-president of the UP in charge of foreign coverage from 1919 until his retirement in 1940.

Fred L. Boalt, former editor of the *Portland News* in Oregon, was a UP correspondent in London in 1910 and for some years after. William Philip Simms arrived in Paris in the same period, the first UP representative there. He remained throughout World War I and continued a lifetime career in foreign reporting for the UP, and for the Scripps-Howard Newspaper Alliance, formed in Washington in 1920 as a supplementary service of the Scripps-Howard Newspapers. Simms's first assistant in Paris was André Glarner, a native of France, who had been in the United States for several years, but soon became Paris correspondent for the British Exchange Telegraph Company, a post he occupied until his retirement in 1952.

Hearst Forms the INS 1909

A second new agency formed was the International News Service (INS), which appeared in 1909 as an adjunct to the growing publishing empire of William Randolph Hearst.

Starting with the *San Francisco Examiner* in 1887 and the *New York Journal,* purchased in 1895, Hearst in 1909 controlled seven morning and afternoon papers in Chicago, Los Angeles, Boston, San Francisco, and New York. The *San Francisco Examiner* held membership in the API and then in the AP.

The *Journal,* established in 1882, never had been admitted to any of the agencies. Hearst, in acquiring the paper in 1895, arranged for his own leased wire to facilitate the exchange of news and features between San Francisco and New York. Having the means to do so, he also sent reporters, correspondents, and special writers on assignments at home and abroad, usually for the *Journal*. The exclusive reports were sold to other papers in noncompetitive areas, and a news exchange arrangement was made with some of those papers. Lawson's *Chicago Record* was among them until Hearst established his own afternoon *American* in Chicago in 1900, with a morning *Examiner* added in 1902. The *New York Journal* was changed from morning publication to afternoon in 1901, with a morning *American* established in that city. A morning *Los Angeles Examiner* was added to the Hearst group in 1903, and an afternoon *Boston American* in 1904.

The original special wire became known in 1904 as the Hearst News Service, providing material to the four morning newspapers and to other non-Hearst papers. A Publisher's Press was announced to serve the three Hearst afternoon papers and others. This latter was unrelated to the Publishers' Press Association, dating from 1898, which Scripps purchased. Conceivably, Hearst might have subscribed to that service or even bought it, but did neither.

What Hearst did do in May 1909 was to form a new American News Service (ANS), supplanting both the Hearst News Service and the Publisher's Press. He also established a separate Hearst Syndicate to handle the sale and distribution of special features originated or controlled by his papers, including Sunday "comics." In August 1909 the ANS was split, the name itself was dropped, and a National News Association (NNA) was formed to serve the afternoon papers; an International News Service (INS) provided news reports to the morning papers. This was the beginning of the Hearst-owned International News Service. In January 1910 the NNA and the INS were combined to form a single agency, the International News Service, Inc., serving both morning and afternoon papers.

With its headquarters in New York, the INS was directed at the outset by C. J. Mar, who had headed the ANS. He was succeeded within a few months by Richard A. Farrelly, who was manager until 1916, at which time Barry Faris became editor-in-chief.

Meanwhile, the Hearst Syndicate became the King Features Syndicate (KFS) in 1914, directed by Moses Koenigsberg. In 1918 he assumed the joint direction of KFS and of the INS, but Faris continued as editor of the agency, by then serving 400 newspapers.

As the UP and INS entered the field, with their services available to any newspaper, the limitation on membership maintained by the AP ceased to be the problem it had been to non-member papers in earlier times. Both of the new agencies extended their coverage year by year and added foreign reports. Many of the AP member papers also subscribed to one or the other, and some to both. The events of World War I brought great advances in coverage by all three of the U.S. news agencies. By the 1920s they were world agencies providing reports at least equal to those of the original big three, Reuter, Havas, and Wolff.

However perceptive other U.S. newspapers publishers may have been in 1898–1900, none matched Lawson in a purposeful extension of foreign coverage until 1908 and later. A number had a token representation in London or Paris, and coverage in Washington had been strongly developed by a considerable group.

The *New York Times,* a respected morning daily from its establishment in 1851, was also influential and profitable until the early 1890s. A period of drift in its direction set in after the death in 1891 of George Jones, the only survivor among the three founders of the paper forty years before, and its business director through most of those years. The panic of 1893 had an adverse effect. Vigorous new competition in the New York morning newspaper field, marked by the sensationalism of the *New York Journal,* then purchased by Hearst, and by the *New York World,* the circulation leader, suddenly placed the *Times* on the verge of bankruptcy and suspension.

The paper was saved when it was purchased in 1896 by Adolph S. Ochs, then thirty-eight and successful publisher of the *Chattanooga Times* in Tennessee. He also was founder of the regional Southern Associated Press and its president until its merger in 1893 with the Associated Press of Illinois. In addition he was founder and president of a business periodical, *The Tradesman,* circulating in the southern states.

Ochs proceeded to work what has been described as a miracle in reviving the *New York Times.* Holding to the paper's conservative traditions, making few immediate changes in personnel, but stressing substantial news reporting, he accepted a slogan already adopted, "All the News That's Fit to Print," and tried to make it so.

Coverage in New York and Washington was strengthened. The *New York Times* never had undertaken any consistent or extensive coverage abroad, but Harold Frederic, former editor of the *Albany Evening Journal,* had been a resident correspondent in London since 1884, and continued there until his death in 1898. By an existing arrangement, he processed the service of the London *Times* for use in New York, wrote a weekly cable letter, and wrote occasionally from the continent. Another cable letter came from a stringer in Paris.

The paper was not sufficiently recovered financially in 1898 to match most other New York dailies in sending its own correspondents to report the Spanish-American War. As a member of the API, however, it made good use of the wartime reports provided in what Stone, as its general manager, called that agency's "first notable achievement." It also received the Reuter world report through the API.

Ochs did make two gestures toward foreign coverage in 1897. In the summer, at a cost of $5,000, he purchased fifty photographs of Queen Victoria's Diamond Jubilee celebration. These were presented in a special sixteen-page supplement printed on high quality paper to assure satisfactory reproduction at a time when that was not possible on relatively coarse newsprint passing through high-speed rotary presses. The *New York Journal* had sent Mark Twain and Richard Harding Davis to London to provide reports of the Jubilee, and the *World* and *Herald* also had special coverage. But the *New York Times* venture gained favorable notice. Of less general interest, but deemed of importance to some influential readers, the full text of a commercial treaty between the United States and Spain was cabled in that same year from Madrid for publication in the *Times* at a cost of $8,000.

By 1901, under the direction of Ochs and with the talents of Louis Wiley, brought from the *New York Sun* as business manager, the *New York Times* was again on solid financial ground. So much so that Ochs was able in that year to buy the *Philadelphia Times,* dating from 1875, and place it under the management of his younger brother, George Washington Ochs (his name legally changed in 1917 to George Washington Ochs-Oakes). In 1902, he also bought the *Philadelphia Public Ledger,* established in 1836 and long the city's most successful daily, published by George W. Childs and Anthony J. Drexel. With it he merged the *Philadelphia Times,* and his brother continued as editor of the resulting morning *Ledger* until that paper was sold in 1913 to Cyrus H. K. Curtis, publisher of the *Ladies' Home Journal* and *Saturday Evening Post*—two of the most successful national magazines. Construction also began about 1903 on a new twenty-story building for the *New York Times* on a triangular site where Broadway crosses Seventh Avenue just above West Forty-second Street. The building was occupied in 1905, with the wide area to the north designated as Times Square. Within ten years, it became necessary to add an annex nearby in West Forty-third Street as the main building, which was constantly enlarged in the years following to become the paper's headquarters.

Late in 1901 the *New York Times* formalized an agreement for the exchange of news with the London *Times*. The two papers became associated at the same time in experiments in the transmission of news by wireless across the North Atlantic.

These same early years brought to the editorial staff of the *New York Times* a number of men who figured prominently in the development of news reporting at home and abroad. Frederick T. Birchall, a native of Lancashire, England, became night city editor. Carr V. Van Anda, a man of rare talents, was brought from the *New York Sun* in 1904, and was managing editor until 1925, when he was succeeded by Birchall. Charles M. Lincoln and William C. Reick were brought in 1907 from the *New York Herald*. Reick long had served that paper, and was once editor of its Paris edition. He also was president of the New York Herald Company from 1903–07. As an aide to Ochs, he played a particular role in moving the *Times* into a direct coverage of foreign news. He also held part ownership until he became owner of the *New York Sun* from 1911–16. Lincoln, also thoroughly experienced, was later to become foreign editor.

Reick went to Europe in 1908 to engage correspondents for the *New York Times*. British-born Ernest Marshall was named to head the London bureau, which was to be the administrative center for the paper's coverage of Europe for the next decade. W. Orton Tewson, also British but with experience in New York, was made assistant to Marshall.

William Bayard Hale was appointed to establish a Paris bureau. A former clergyman, with a pastorate at Middleboro, Massachusetts, an earlier reference has been made to Hale's visit to Germany and his interview with Kaiser Wilhelm. Hale remained in Paris only a year, was with *World's Work* magazine in New York from 1909–13, went to Mexico as a special representative for President Wilson in 1913–14, and then to Berlin for the International News Service. The *New York Times,* following Hale's visit to Germany, engaged Frederic William Wile as its correspondent in Berlin. Assigned there originally by the *Chicago Daily News* in 1901, he had switched in 1906 to the London *Daily Mail,* and represented both that paper and the *New York Times* in Berlin from 1908 to 1914.

In New York, Russian-born Herman Bernstein was added to the *Times* staff in 1908 and made several journeys to Europe between then and 1912, with St. Petersburg among the capitals visited as a basis for special reports of ongoing situations in the news.

The *New York Times* had been represented in Washington virtually since its establishment. Charles Willis Thompson was correspondent there during the first years of the new century, and Oscar King Davis was assigned there in 1907. Formerly writing for the *New York Sun* and the Laffan News Bureau in the Philippines and China in 1899–1900, and for the *New York Herald* during the Russo-Japanese War, Davis was in Washington until 1912 for the *New York Times* and for the Ochs-owned *Philadelphia Public Ledger.*

Christian
Science
Monitor

The *Christian Science Monitor,* established in Boston in 1908, set some standards later adopted by other newspapers, and contributed notably to public understanding.

This was a period when a trend toward an extreme form of popular journalism, sometimes described as "yellow" journalism or "sensationalism," was winning readers in cities of the United States, including Boston. It followed upon excesses introduced by the *New York Journal* and the *New York World* in the period prior to and during the Spanish-American War. Its effectiveness in gaining circulations of up to a million a day for the first time, with advertising patronage following, brought such profits as to invite imitation, especially in larger cities with competitive newspaper situations.

What this meant was a kind of contrived ferment in print bearing upon the more bizarre, violent, and gaudy aspects of human behavior, including crime and moral lapses of individuals, particularly of those possessing some degree of fame, wealth, and social or political prominence. It was an emphasis accentuated by glaring typographical display, colored inks, a selection of photos, posed or otherwise, imaginative art work, and an overblown prose style. The effect was to put values out of balance and to distort essential truth. Apart from the questionable taste involved and a cynical pandering to the crowd, this suggested a new application of Gresham's law, with the "bad" newspapers threatening to drive the "good" out of business, to the total disadvantage of the public welfare.

The trend disturbed many persons in and out of journalism. Among them was Mary Baker Eddy, founder in 1879 of the First Church of Christ, Scientist, in Boston. Mrs. Eddy directed that the church should sponsor the publication of a daily newspaper for general circulation and readership, countering the trend toward sensationalism, that would be properly informative, constructive in purpose, made "to injure no man, but to bless all mankind." She directed that it be called the "Christian Science Monitor."

Some with whom she consulted recommended that the words "Christian Science" be omitted from the title. They believed it was bound to suggest a "religious" publication, a "church" paper, rather than a newspaper in the full sense as intended, and so would defeat its purpose by failing to reach a general audience on its own merits. They argued that the name would frighten off readers not of the faith, and even invite a prejudice or intolerance depriving it of broad acceptance. Mrs. Eddy was insistent, however, and the full name was retained. What resulted was a newspaper that might properly be called unique.

The first issue of the *Christian Science Monitor,* an afternoon paper, appeared November 25, 1908, with Archibald McLellan as editor and Alexander Dodds as managing editor. McLellan was one of five directors of the Mother Church, a lawyer by profession, previously associated for almost twenty years in Chicago with a financial agency that became Dun and Bradstreet, Inc. He had been in Boston since 1902 as editor of weekly and monthly Christian Science publications before becoming a director of the church. Dodds had been in journalism in Pittsburgh since his youth, becoming managing editor of the *Pittsburgh Post* and *Pittsburgh Sun.* Also a member of the church, he was invited to take full charge of organizing the new paper in Boston.

Others on the news staff in the first years included John J. Flinn, for many years with the *Chicago Inter-Ocean.* He was an early adviser in planning the *Monitor,* and the first director of its editorial page. Frederick Dixon of London, long a writer there for *Macmillan's Magazine,* became associate editor of the *Monitor* for several months, director of its editorial office in London from 1909 to 1914, and then returned to Boston as editor of the paper, succeeding McLellan, and served until 1922.

Original or early staff members also included Oscar L. Stevens, formerly of the *Boston Transcript;* John Phillips, the *Chicago Examiner;* John L. Wright, the *Boston Globe;* Forrest Price, the *Pittsburgh Chronicle-Telegraph;* Amos Weston, the *Boston Herald;* and Paul S. Deland and Ernest C. Sherburne, both with Boston newspaper experience. Among these, Price, Weston, Deland, and Sherburne remained with the *Monitor,* with increasingly responsible assignments for more than thirty years prior to retirement.

From the outset, the *Monitor* received service from the equally new United Press, of which Dodds became a vice-president from 1909–12, and from the Associated Press from 1909. It received a special service through the London bureau organized by Dixon in 1909. There eight or ten persons produced original material and gleaned information from the British and European press to form a world report. Such material in those first years was forwarded to Boston by ship mail, rolled in a fashion which the London bureau called the "Boston sausage."

In Washington, W. W. Germane acted as a stringer from 1909 to 1915. Arrangements were made for weekly articles received by mail from Edward C. Butler in Mexico, William D. McCracken in Switzerland, and Charles H. Gibbs and Albert Cope Stone in Australia. This was, of course, only a beginning. From the time of World War I the *Monitor* developed its own service of staff and stringer correspondents in Washington and other parts of the United States and abroad. Whatever appeared, whether news, editorials, or special articles, was exclusive to the paper, aside from news agency reports and some photographs, and this gave it a character of its own.

The emphasis was on substantive news and solid information. It was a quality newspaper, and could not expect to build a large circulation. This was recognized and accepted. Published in Boston six days a week, and only incidentally a local newspaper, it was intended for distribution throughout the United States, Canada, Great Britain, and other English-speaking countries, but with copies going to almost every other country as well. It depended upon subscriptions, rather than direct sales. Beyond Boston, delivery was by mail. This meant that an edition of any given date would not reach more than a few readers until a day to a month or more later.

News is a perishable commodity, and the late delivery meant that the *Monitor* would be a second paper to most readers. It meant that staff members had to plan the content and find a way of treating news and current affairs in such a manner that the paper would still be worth reading, however late it might be in arriving. It took some time to solve this problem, and was done by putting stress on the "why" and "how" of events, their "meaning" and "significance," with the addition of background and supplementary information to provide a frame of reference within which readers could gain a real understanding of events and acquaint themselves with individuals figuring in them. Maps, charts, diagrams, and photos were added. More than that, the *Monitor* found subjects and areas of information not treated in other newspapers, examined situations that had not yet erupted into the kind of happenings that made news for the average newspaper or news agency.

Writers for the paper were dedicated to factual, accurate, and objective reporting. But they demonstrated what many others then believed impossible: a fusion of objectivity and background material to provide an interpretation of events that was wholly factual, without overstepping the boundary of subjective, editorial treatment.

Most dailies were made on the assumption that unless reports arrived by telegraph and cable they were not news. The *Monitor* demonstrated that much useful information might arrive by mail, presented with full detail that would have been impermissible, for reasons of cost, if transmitted by wire. The time soon came when readers with special interests in Asia, South America, Africa, the Pacific, and even parts of Europe and the United States, discovered that the *Monitor* was providing them with information not available from any other source.

This pioneering made late delivery irrelevant to those readers who appreciated a quality newspaper. Accordingly, the *Monitor* not only was read, but it had a long period of secondary value, with copies passed along to others, with stories and articles saved, clipped, posted, and quoted. It was a new concept of journalism, giving readers a far greater understanding of the world.

The *Monitor* readership was always selective because of its late delivery and consequent status as a second paper for most, and the name unquestionably was a restrictive influence, as some had seen from the start. As a quality paper, it lacked elements of entertainment demanded by some readers. Even so, its circulation in April 1909, five months after the paper began, was 43,000, then approximately equal to the London *Times,* commonly regarded as the best newspaper in the world.

The *Monitor* circulation grew several-fold in later years. Always small in contrast to the popular papers, it maintained a reasonable equality with other quality papers of the world. It was read with attention and respect by persons whose education, taste, and professional or occupational talents and responsibilities made them leaders in their communities. Public officials were among them, and editors of other newspapers, who often quoted the *Monitor,* reprinted material, and adopted some of its practices. It went to libraries, universities, and diplomatic posts throughout the world. With such readership, it attained influence and prestige far beyond what its circulation figures might suggest, and its staff representatives were well received wherever they went.

The national and world distribution of the *Monitor* required the publication of several daily editions to serve readers in various geographical areas. Augmenting the basic news and editorial pages and departments, each edition included matter of regional interest, and also provided opportunity for regional advertising or for advertising messages directed to such regions, with rates commensurate with the circulation of the edition. This was something offered by no other publication, and the international edition in particular held special interest for the variety of its advertising. These editions produced in Boston ultimately became five each day, beginning with a Pacific edition, then the Central edition, the Atlantic edition, the New England edition, and the International edition, for delivery in Great Britain, Europe, and elsewhere in the world.

Because of the time required for mail delivery throughout the United States, the *Monitor* did not meet the specifications of a truly national newspaper. Except for that technicality, however, it was such a paper. Its broad concern with international affairs, and its actual international distribution, was to result in the addition in 1917 of the subordinate line under its page-one title describing it appropriately as "An International Daily Newspaper." It was the only newspaper that could make such a claim, and the line became even more fully justified in the years following as the *Monitor* also developed one of the more extensive services of staff and stringer correspondents attached to any newspaper.

Chicago
Tribune

The new concern in the United States after 1900 with national and international affairs, while reflected most notably in the developments so far described, was manifested in other ways and by other newspapers.

In the Midwest, the *Chicago Tribune* long had occupied a strong position in the morning newspaper field. It was actively represented in the coverage of the Civil War and the Spanish-American War. Staff writers had ventured afield on other occasions, one being Henry Norman in the Hawaiian Islands in 1898, but then soon sent to London as the paper's first resident correspondent abroad. In the first decade of the new century, he was followed there by Arthur L. Clarke.

Beginning in that first decade, the *Tribune* arranged for a considerable coverage in Washington and abroad, although much was done by stringers. Its own activity was stimulated by the enterprise of the *Chicago Record* and *Chicago Daily News,* and by the entrance of Hearst into the Chicago newspaper field with his afternoon *American* in 1900 and morning *Examiner* in 1902. This marked the beginning of a keen war for circulation.

Joseph Medill, long active as editor and publisher of the *Tribune,* died in 1899. His son-in-law, Robert W. Patterson, managing editor since 1874 but already directing the paper, became its publisher, sharing the ownership with Medill's grandson, Medill McCormick. James Keeley, English-born, had succeeded Patterson as managing editor, and became copublisher with Patterson in 1903. Under their vigorous direction, the paper gained effectiveness in news reporting and editorial leadership. Although a popular paper, it also had substance and proceeded with great strength even after Patterson's death in 1910. In 1911 it chose to call itself "The World's Greatest Newspaper," and added that line beneath the page-one title.

In that first decade, it received reports not only from the London bureau, but from D. B. McGowan in Berlin, Grace Corneau in Paris, Oscar Durante in Rome, W. L. Hubbard in Vienna, David Macbeth in St. Petersburg, James R. Jackson in Bucharest, F. W. Anderson in Constantinople, Richard Lachman in Frankfurt, Charles J. Bart in Leipzig, and R. W. Emerson in Tangier.

John T. McCutcheon, artist-writer for the *Chicago Record* during the Spanish-American War in the Philippines and later in South Africa, became the *Tribune's* political cartoonist in 1903. He also went abroad for the paper as a writer-artist during the Russo-Japanese War, and was in Africa in 1909–10, part of the time with former President Roosevelt on his hunting expedition there. Professor Frederick Starr of the University of Chicago wrote a series of articles from the Congo, illustrated with photographs. Reports also were received from Mexico and a number of capitals in South America.

From Washington, the *Tribune* had received reports since 1894 from Raymond A. Patterson, son of the paper's publisher, who had joined the staff following his graduation from Yale in 1878. He remained in Washington until his death in 1909. Richard Weightman wrote editorial page articles from the capital. John Callan O'Laughlin, who had been in Washington for the *New York Herald* from 1893–1903, and with the Associated Press in London and St. Petersburg from 1903–05, then returned to Washington for the *Chicago Tribune* until 1909. He was succeeded by Arthur Sears Henning, who had been an assistant in the bureau. From about 1914 its own foreign service developed.

Several newspapers already known for special coverage in Washington and overseas continued or extended those efforts.

The *New York Herald,* a leader in news enterprise, remained among the most active in that respect under the direction since 1866 of publisher James Gordon Bennett, Jr. He had made his home in Paris in 1877, with the Paris edition of the *Herald* published there since 1887. Bennett also had established the *New York Evening Telegram* in 1867.

The *Herald* traditionally had maintained an effective coverage in Washington. The Paris bureau, by reason of Bennett's residence there, was especially important. Correspondents in Paris during the first years of the century included Charles Inman Barnard, Albert Stevens Crockett, and George Dickin. Milton V. Dryden was in London, and others writing from there included Crockett, Ralph D. Blumenfeld, Julius Chambers, and British-born George Allison. Sidney Whitman was in Berlin. Richard Harding Davis wrote for the paper during the Spanish-American and the South African wars, and Joseph L. Stickney, naval affairs editor, also wrote during the first of those wars, and during the Russo-Japanese War. Francis McCullagh was in St. Petersburg before and after the Russo-Japanese War, and in Manchuria during the war. He also wrote for the *Manchester Guardian* through the same period. Thomas F. Millard wrote from China in 1900, and E. J. Harrison from Tokyo from 1909–13. He also represented the London *Daily Mail* and edited the *Japan Advertiser.* Very active for the paper through all of those years were Stephen Bonsal and Aubrey Stanhope, a British citizen; both had roving commissions that took them about much of the world for the coverage of major stories.

The *New York Sun* had its own representation in Washington and some original coverage abroad even before 1900. Joseph Pulitzer, yet to establish the *St. Louis Post-Dispatch,* wrote for the morning *Sun* from Europe in 1878. Arthur Brisbane, later long-identified with the Hearst newspapers, became London correspondent for the *Sun* in 1884, at the age of twenty, for four years. Richard Harding Davis, after brief experience in Philadelphia, became a reporter for the *Evening Sun* and laid the foundation for his later successes. Henry R. Chamberlain became London correspondent in 1892, and Julian Ralph, one of the morning *Sun*'s ablest reporters, covered the Sino-Japanese War in 1894–95.

William M. Laffan, business manager of the paper and sponsor of the *New York Evening Sun*'s establishment in 1887, became the owner and publisher of both *Sun* papers in 1897. He had established the Sun News Service in 1893 to syndicate material produced by reporters and correspondents for the papers, and retitled it in 1897 as the Laffan News Bureau.

Under Laffan's direction until his death in 1909, the *Sun* increased its news representation. William C. Reick, formerly of the *New York Herald,* and more recently with the *New York Times* from 1907–12, with a share in its ownership, became owner of the *Sun* from December 1911 until 1916, and then president of the *New York Journal of Commerce.* Purchased by Frank A. Munsey in 1916, the morning *Sun* was merged with the *New York Press,* which he had purchased in 1912. The *Evening Sun* was continued, but the Laffan News Bureau was suspended.

In those years Richard V. Oulahan was the *Sun's* Washington correspondent from 1897 until 1911, with David Barry also in the bureau. The paper had reported the Spanish-American War with Oscar King Davis in the Philippines and later in China to report the Boxer uprising before he joined the *New York Herald* and later the *New York Times.* Chamberlain retired as London correspondent in 1905. He was succeeded by British-born Frank B. Grundy, with Ambrose Lambert as an assistant. Grundy moved to Paris for the paper in 1911, with Oulahan moving from Washington to take the London post in 1911–12.

The *New York Tribune* had occupied a position of leadership in foreign reporting in 1870–71, with notable coverage of the Franco-Prussian War directed by George W. Smalley, London correspondent from 1866 to 1895. The *Tribune* had been owned since 1873 by Whitelaw Reid, former Civil War correspondent and associate editor during the years just prior to the death in November 1872 of Horace Greeley, its founder. From 1897 until his own death in 1912, Reid was greatly engaged in diplomacy and out of the country. The paper, then operated under a so-called "regency," lost much of its earlier vigor, although it was still respected.

Waiting in the wings were others who would restore the *Tribune's* position. One was Reid's son, Ogden, who was educated at Bonn and Yale, and was a member of the New York bar. He had been a member of the paper's staff since 1908 and became managing editor in 1912. Another was Arthur Draper, who had joined the paper in 1905, just out of college, and who became city editor in 1912.

With Smalley's departure from London in 1895 to become correspondent in New York and later in Washington for the London *Times,* Isaac N. Ford, long a member of the *Tribune* staff went to the

London bureau. There he remained until 1900, followed by Frank Marshall White until 1914. Gerald Morgan, who reported the Russo-Japanese War, writing also for the London *Daily Telegraph,* was one of a very few other overseas correspondents for the *Tribune* during the first decade of the century, and he was chiefly in Europe. Frederick Moore was in Paris, but went to China for the AP by 1914. In Washington at various periods were William McPherson, Frank L. Simonds, and George Hill.

The *New York World,* dating from 1860, had been purchased in 1883 by Joseph Pulitzer, by then also publishing the *St. Louis Post-Dispatch.* A Sunday edition was added in 1884, and an *Evening World* in 1887. The morning *World* became an entertaining and popular newspaper, but was also enterprising and responsible in its news and editorial content. By 1895 it had gained circulation leadership in New York and in the nation. In that same year, William Randolph Hearst purchased the morning *New York Journal.* With great financial resources, he challenged the *World* for circulation leadership and both papers entered a period of sensationalism centering in considerable part upon the plight of Cuban insurrectionists and the Spanish-American War. By 1900, however, Pulitzer had steered the *World* back to its earlier relative sobriety, with substance and value in its news and editorial content.

The World had maintained a careful Washington coverage before the war, and supported some limited reporting from Europe. It had taken a constructive part in bringing a peaceful solution of the British Guiana–Venezuelan boundary dispute of 1895 that threatened a British–U.S. confrontation over interpretation of the Monroe Doctrine. The *World* was actively represented in coverage of the Spanish-American War, with a staff directed by Henry C. Cary and correspondents including Percival Phillips, Louis Seibold, George Bronson Rae, and Sylvester Scovel in the Cuban area, and Edward W. Harden in the Philippines, where he was joined later by Rae and by Frederick Palmer.

Pulitzer was a perceptive man and after the war, possibly with the same motivation as that of Lawson in Chicago, he approved the establishment of a *World* bureau in London in 1899. British-born James M. Tuohy was its director until 1922, the same length of time as Edward Price Bell represented Lawson's *Chicago Daily News* in the British capital. Wythe Williams joined the bureau in 1910, and Harrison Sprague Reeves became Paris correspondent at the same time.

Frederick Palmer had reported the Yukon gold rush for the *World* in 1897, and then the Spanish-American War aftermath in the Philippines.

He reported the Boxer rebellion in China in 1900 and also covered the Russo-Japanese War. On those assignments, he wrote for *Collier's Weekly* as well as for the *World*. Louis Seibold was on roving assignments for the paper, but wrote chiefly from Washington, producing substantial reports on matters of politics and government. Samuel G. Blythe also wrote from Washington, while David Graham Phillips and Irvin S. Cobb were among others on the New York staff to gain distinction as reporters. The paper maintained a news-exchange relationship with the *Chicago Tribune*.

William H. Merrill, formerly of the *Boston Herald,* had been appointed as editor of the *World* editorial page in 1888. In prospect of his retirement in 1904, Pulitzer had Samuel M. Williams, a member of the staff, tour the country to find a man both to succeed Merrill and to take some of the burden off Pulitzer's shoulders. Williams recommended Frank I. Cobb, then thirty-four and an editorial writer for the *Detroit Free Press*. Cobb served with distinction from that time until his death in 1923. He kept the *World* on the course charted by Pulitzer both before and after the publisher's death in 1911. The direction of the New York papers then passed to his sons, Ralph and Herbert Pulitzer, for Joseph Pulitzer, Jr., gave his attention to the St. Louis paper, originally under the tutelage of Oscar K. Bovard, managing editor and editor until 1938.

The *New York Journal,* dating from 1832, became a new entry in competition among the city's dailies in foreign reporting following its purchase by Hearst in 1895. A Sunday and an evening edition were added to compete with the *World* in those fields. The policies and content of the *Journal* in particular brought the term "yellow journalism" into the lexicon, reflecting a stress on news of crime, general sensationalism, typographical extremes, entertainment features, and practices deplored by many, but successful in winning readers.

Hearst lured writers and editors of demonstrated talent away from other newspapers by offering high salaries, and engaged big-name writers for special assignments. Sam S. Chamberlain was brought to New York from the *San Francisco Examiner* as managing editor. Arthur Brisbane and Morrill Goddard were brought from the *New York World* as editor and Sunday editor, and Richard F. Outcault as a cartoonist. James Creelman was lured from the *New York Herald* and Julian Ralph from the *New York Sun.*

Richard Harding Davis, known for his work on the *Sun,* but also for his fiction and subsequent writing for *Harper's Weekly,* of which he also was editor, was sent to Moscow in 1896 to provide special reports on the coronation of Czar Nicholas II, and then to Budapest to report that city's millenial celebration. Both Davis and Stephen Crane, author of *The Red Badge of Courage,* went to Greece in 1897 to report the Greco-Turkish War. Later in the same year, Davis and Mark Twain went to London to report the Diamond Jubilee of Queen Victoria.

The *Journal* led in coverage of the Spanish-American War, with James Creelman and many others in Cuba, and John Foster Bass later in the Philippines. Julian Ralph, its London correspondent, also reported aspects of the South African War, and Jack London, famed as a novelist, provided special reports on the Russo-Japanese War.

Matter published in the *Journal* in 1901 was regarded by some as having influenced Leon Czolgosz to assassinate President McKinley. The resulting public outrage induced Hearst to rename the paper the *New York American,* although he continued the *Evening Journal.* Both papers had obtained their basic national and world reports from the Associated Press. After 1901, they depended almost entirely upon the AP for such reports, except during the Russo-Japanese War, and until Hearst established his own International News Service in 1909. Its reports then were added to those of the AP, and took precedence in all of the Hearst newspapers whenever a choice existed.

The *New York Evening Post,* established in 1801, and the oldest existing daily in the city, had many of the characteristics of a quality paper, based on good local reporting, Washington coverage, a sober editorial page, and notable attention to the arts. Allied with it was a weekly magazine of opinion, the *Nation,* established in 1865 by British-born Edwin Lawrence Godkin, who had reported both the Crimean War of 1854–56 and the American Civil War for the London *Daily News,* but who had made his home in the United States from about 1860.

Financial control of the *Evening Post* had been gained in 1881 by Henry Villard. Born Heinrich Hilgard, he had changed his name upon coming to the United States in 1853 and settling in Springfield, Illinois. There he wrote for German-language papers, but also for the *Chicago Tribune,* the *Cincinnati Commercial,* and other newspapers. He reported upon the Colorado gold rush in 1858–59, covered the Lincoln-Douglas debates of 1858, became well acquainted with Lincoln, reported the Republican party convention of 1860 and the campaign and election of that year, and followed Lincoln to Washington. There he remained to report the Civil War for the *New York Herald* and then for the *New York Tribune.* Immediately after the war he went to Europe for the *Tribune* in 1866 to cover the Austro-Prussian War. That was soon over, but he remained in Europe for a time, engaged in personal studies, and then returned to New York to become involved in railroad and electrical developments. In 1881 he was president of the Northern Pacific Railroad Company, remaining as a director after 1889, and then organized the General Electric Company, an Edison enterprise, of which he also was president.

Villard's purchase of the *New York Evening Post* and of the *Nation* was almost incidental to his other activities in 1881, and the editorship of both publications was undertaken by Godkin from 1882 until his retirement in 1899. Following Villard's death in 1900, his son, Oswald Garrison Villard, became editor of the *Evening Post* until 1918 and of the *Nation* until 1934. He also wrote, during those years, from Washington and Europe.

The *Evening Post* received reports from Paris at various times during a period of about sixty years from the 1870s to the 1930s from Stoddard Dewey, a stringer serving a number of papers. Francis E. Leupp was Washington correspondent from 1889 until 1904, when he became commissioner of Indian Affairs. The paper had four correspondents reporting the Spanish-American War. In general, however, it depended upon the AP for most of its reports until after World War I, when it sponsored a foreign service of its own.

One other New York daily, the *New-Yorker Staats-Zeitung,* among the leading German-language newspapers of the country, developed a limited service. Published by Herman Ridder, a banker but also a member of the Associated Press board of directors, it had Gunther Thomas in London as one of its representatives. Ridder also supported the development and use of the Intertype, which was introduced in 1913, and was competitive with the Linotype as a machine for the composition of type. From the parent paper in New York, Ridder's three sons, after his death in 1915, extended their activity by purchasing the *New York Journal of Commerce* in 1926 and proceeded in the development of a coast-to-coast group of newspapers and radio-TV stations.

The British and Empire Press

7

The United Kingdom and the British Empire were at the height of their power and prestige in 1900. London was the financial and commercial center of the world, the communications center, and the greatest news center. The British press, long the most enterprising and effective in the pursuit of news and in the editorial treatment of public affairs, led in the reporting of international events.

The Reuter news agency, one of the first in existence, was based in London. It had formed and continued to occupy a major position in a League of Allied Agencies or Ring Combination in gathering, exchanging, and distributing world news through an association of agencies in many countries.[1]

As the century began, several British newspapers were commonly regarded as the best in the world. They were served by their own correspondents in other lands. A variety of services and periodicals contributed further to the volume and quality of information made available to the British public and, indirectly, to the peoples of the world. Any news agency or newspaper of another country seriously concerned with global affairs looked to London. There Fleet Street, focal point of the publishing district, was lined with offices representing the press of many nations. Their very presence made London an even greater pool of information.

Reuter's Telegram Company

Reuter's Telegram Company, Ltd., the fourth news agency to be established in the world, had its origin in London in 1851. Then known

---

1 The origination and organization of the Ring Combination, dating from 1870, is described in Desmond, *The Information Process*, pp. 158–68.

merely as "Mr. Reuter's Office," it was reorganized in 1865 as the Reuter's Telegram Company, Ltd. Formed by German-born Paul Julius Reuter, it began as a service of financial and commercial information, but entered the general news field in 1858.

An informal exchange of reports existed virtually from the outset between the Reuter office and the Agence Havas of Paris, the first news agency, and the Wolff'sche Telegraphen Büro in Berlin, the third agency, which had its beginning in 1849. From 1856, Reuter also exchanged news with what then was known as the New York Associated Press, which began in 1848 as the second agency. These relationships became increasingly formalized after 1859 and led to the establishment in 1870 through Mr. Reuter's effort of the Ring Combination, bringing into the news exchange relationship several national agencies formed during the 1860s and later.

The exchange between the member agencies within the Ring Combination was governed by contractual arrangements. The Reuter, Havas, and Wolff agencies, early and successful in the business, and long referred to as the "big three," were free to gather news wherever they wished. But they divided the world among themselves, in effect, for the redistribution of that news and the news they exchanged. Each had areas in which it held the exclusive right to provide a total world report to individual newspapers published there or, more commonly, to national agencies in an exchange for the news contributed by those agencies from their more limited areas. The exchange also involved payment of a cash differential to the "big three" agency in recognition of the fact that a comprehensive world report was being received in exchange for a limited local or national report.

The Reuter agency became highly successful. Reuter himself retired at sixty-two from its active direction in 1878, but he lived until 1899 and continued in an advisory role to that time. He was long known as Baron de Reuter, a title conferred upon him in 1871 by the German Duke of Saxe-Coburg-Gotha and given formal recognition by the British Crown in 1891. Herbert Reuter, his only son, succeeded his father in the direction of the agency in 1878. He also succeeded to the title upon his father's death but never used it, and was always known more simply as Herbert de Reuter.

The agency obtained news from beyond British shores through stringers and correspondents appointed more and more widely as the years passed, and through its exchange arrangements with Havas, Wolff, and the Ring Combination agencies. It reported the news of London through its own office there. No facilities existed, however, for coverage of British news outside London other than to rewrite matter published in the provincial newspapers, those appearing in other cities of the British Isles. Most of those papers received Reuter's world service, but until 1868 they themselves had no telegraphic reports of news of the British Isles, except as briefly attempted by two private telegraph companies with uneven results.

The British provincial press had grown in numbers of daily newspapers since 1855, when restrictive government taxes on publications and advertising were greatly reduced. Editors of some of the papers began a telegraphic exchange of news among themselves in 1865. In 1868 a cooperative, non-profit service was organized to formalize and extend that exchange. Known as the Press Association, Ltd. (PA), it was largely the creation of John Edward Taylor, publisher of the morning *Manchester Guardian,* along with John Lovell, who managed the service until 1880 when he became editor of the *Liverpool Mercury.* Sir Edmund Robbins, then manager, was succeeded in 1914 by his son, H. C. Robbins.

In addition to providing a properly organized report on events throughout the British Isles, the Press Association added a special London report. Its service was welcomed by daily papers throughout the country. The private services previously conducted by telegraph companies ceased. An arrangement also was made for the distribution of the Reuter service to the provincial press through the new agency. By 1900 the Press Association was strongly entrenched, and its relationship with Reuters had become close. It also formed a working relationship with the Exchange Telegraph Company (Extel) formed in London in 1872 as a financial service, later adding some national and foreign reports. Extel itself was directed by Sir William Creyke King for many years prior to his death in 1943.

Following its entrance into the general news field in 1858, the Reuter coverage increased in Europe and beyond. Sigismund Engländer was its agent in Europe from the outset, with James McLean in New York from 1861, M. J. M. Bellasyse in South Africa from 1861, Henry M. Collins in India and Australasia from 1865, W. F. Bradshaw in South America in 1871, and a Mr. Virnand in Egypt by 1873.

With interests gained in national news agencies in Denmark, Holland, Belgium, and Spain from 1865–75, Reuter established a world-wide position for the coverage, gathering, and distribution of general news. It never ceased to maintain a strong service of financial and commercial information, the basis of its formation, and it operated a private commercial telegraph service between London and Berlin from 1866 until 1870.

Despite its growth and general success, Reuter also had its share of problems.[2] Among these in the 1890s and early 1900s, it was under some stress arising, in part, from unusually high communications costs for reports from the Far East, and for coverage of military campaigns in the Sudan and South Africa. It therefore sought other sources of income. An advertising subsidiary was established in London in 1891 and another in Sydney in 1893. The London branch was suspended in 1894. More important, a Telegraph Remittance service was established in 1891 to handle the transfer of money between London, India, and Australia. Through use of a code system, the rates were lower than those set by established banks, and the service prospered so that in 1910 a Banking Department was added to aid in the transfer of funds and in the conduct of commercial business. This department, located in London, became known in 1912 as the Reuters Bank and in 1914 it became the British Commercial Bank, with shares offered to the public.

The Reuter staff itself went through changes just before and after the turn of the century. George Douglas Williams, chief editor since 1880, retired in 1902. He was succeeded by Frederick W. Dickinson, a staff member since 1874. S. Levy Lawson succeeded McLean as manager of the New York bureau from 1892 until after World War I. E. A. Brayley Hodgetts, who had established the agency's first bureau in Berlin in 1891, was replaced there in 1900 by Austin Harrison. In 1904 he was succeeded in turn by Valentine Williams, elder son of the former chief editor, who remained until 1910, when he joined the *Daily Mail* staff. Andrew Pooley, replacing him, was transferred to Tokyo in 1911, with Lester Lawrence then taking the Berlin post.

Edward Buck went to Calcutta in 1897 to direct coverage in India, following Henry M. Collins's move to Australia. Remaining until his retirement in 1933, Buck attained great stature, personally and professionally, and was knighted. Henry Satoh, made the first permanent agent in Tokyo in 1907, was succeeded in 1911 by Pooley, transferred from Berlin.

Coverage of the South African War in 1899–1902 had many Reuter representatives active, with two killed. H. A. Gwynne, who directed the agency staff, was named director of the London-based Reuter Foreign Service in 1904, but left almost immediately to become editor of the London morning *Standard* and later of the *Morning Post* from 1911 until the paper was merged with the *Daily Telegraph* in 1937. Roderick

---

2 See Graham Storey, *Reuters: The Story of a Century of News-Gathering* (New York, 1951). See also Desmond, *The Information Process.*

Jones, also a member of the war staff, was in the London office in 1902–05, returning then to direct the South African service until 1915. At that time, he became managing director of the agency in London.

W. H. G. Werndel and Fergus Ferguson, already veterans, continued in the Balkans and Middle East after 1900. William J. Moloney, who was to have a long career in the service, was then also in the Middle East. Joseph Watson and George Jeffreys Adams were in Paris, but Adams switched to the Paris bureau of the *Times* in 1913. Guy Beringer was in St. Petersburg.

Reuter Subsidiaries: India

Three agencies—in India, South Africa, and Japan—all of which became subsidiaries of Reuter for various periods of time, had their beginnings after 1900.

In India, Reuter had provided reports to newspapers since 1860, and had bureaus, stringers, and staff correspondents there. Asia was its exclusive territory under the Ring Combination contracts, except for Indo-China, which became Havas territory in 1890, in exchange for Egypt, which became Reuter territory.

Edward Buck, in Calcutta for Reuter and also writing for the *Englishman,* a Calcutta paper dating from 1821, formed an Indian News Agency (INA) soon after 1900. It undertook to gather and distribute news on the subcontinent. Associated with him in the effort was Everard Cotes of the *Statesman,* founded in Calcutta in 1875 and later to absorb the *Englishman.* The two worked closely with Lord Curzon, then Viceroy of India, who had himself written from China and the Middle East for the *Times* ten years earlier as George Nathaniel Curzon. The INA service to the Anglo-Indian press had something of a semi-official character. Reuter provided some financial support, held a share in the ownership, and the Reuter world report was distributed as part of the service.

In 1905 K. C. Roy, a Bengali Brahmin associated with the *Indian Daily Mail* of Calcutta and other newspapers, established a second service. This was called the Associated Press of India (API), with headquarters in Calcutta and offices in Bombay and Madras. It offered reports to the vernacular press of India, but to English-language papers as well.

These two agencies were in some competition until 1910. In that year the API absorbed the INA. Because Reuter had had a financial interest in the INA, it retained an interest in the API. Buck withdrew, but Cotes remained with the API and produced a special service for officials in India.

Differences soon arose between Cotes and Roy, and Roy withdrew from the API. He established another agency, the Indian News Bureau (INB), to provide a service exclusively to vernacular papers.[3] After a short period, however, the two men resolved their differences, Roy returned to the API and suspended his INB.

From that time, the API proceeded with considerable success. Aided by an amendment to the Indian Telegraph Act, press messages were moved at reduced rates, and the agency found new clients. Newspapers that had made it a practice when news developments warranted to send their own reporters to Calcutta and then to Delhi—New Delhi when that city became the capital of India in 1912—or to other places, generally abandoned that procedure and depended upon the API for news of India. Reuter retained its interest and continued to provide world news reports for API distribution.

In 1915, with World War I in progress, Cotes returned to England. Reuter purchased his interest in the API. Added to its own interest, carried over from the original INA, this give Reuter full control of the API, which became an affiliate and subsidiary. The API continued to operate under its own name, however, and Roy remained as manager and chief editor until his death in 1931. He was succeeded by Sir Usha Nath Sen. The API continued to function as a Reuter subsidiary until 1949.

Reuter Subsidiaries: South Africa

A second Reuter subsidiary was in South Africa. Reuter had been the only news agency ever to operate in that part of the world, its coverage beginning in 1861 at Durban, in 1876 at Capetown, and in 1884 at Pretoria, the capital of the Transvaal. In 1910 the Union of South Africa

---

3 The vernacular press, as it developed, included newspapers in Bengali, Hindi, Urdu, Gujarathi, Tamil, Marathi, Telagu, Sinhalese, and other languages, of which fourteen were recognized as "official" by the government of India after 1948.

was formed as a political entity, with Dominion status in the British Empire.

Certain of the South African newspapers, particularly those published in the Afrikaans language, deriving from the Dutch, had sought to contest the Reuter domination in 1908 by establishing a new agency, the South African Amalgamated Press, with an independent cable report from London. It proved too costly to continue beyond 1909, but a compromise arrangement was reached with Reuter, which joined with both English and Afrikaans newspapers in a partnership to form the Reuter South African Press Association (RSAPA) in 1910. Whereas Reuter had maintained its chief bureau at Capetown since 1876, the RSAPA headquarters was at Johannesburg. Reuter held a sixty percent interest in what was, in effect, a subsidiary directed until 1915 by Roderick Jones, previously director for Reuter in Capetown. With Jones in London after 1915, the RSAPA was directed by James Dunn, also previously in Capetown since 1902.

The strength of the press in South Africa had become such by 1938 that a reorganization of the RSAPA was in order. The partnership was converted into a cooperative, non-profit arrangement comparable to the Press Association, Ltd., of Great Britain, or the Associated Press in the United States, with membership control vested in dailies in the Union of South Africa and in Southern Rhodesia, notably the Argus South African Newspapers group headed by John Martin. The name "Reuter" was eliminated from the title, and it operated independently as the South African Press Association (SAPA), but with Dunn continuing as general manager and also as chief representative for Reuter. The Reuter world service continued to be distributed through SAPA.

Reuter Subsidiaries: Japan

The third agency to become a Reuter subsidiary was in Japan, outside the British Empire. There the Kokusai Tsushin-sha (International News Agency), formed early in 1914, was a Reuter affiliate until 1923, then independent until 1926 but still distributing the Reuter world service.

Even though the Kokusai agency existed under that name for no more than twelve years, from 1914 to 1926, the circumstances of its origin, operation, and disappearance, though complex, are significant. They relate to other aspects of Japanese press development and to the general flow of news internationally. The Reuter position in the story was vital, but the Associated Press also played a part.

The Japanese daily newspaper press had its beginning in 1872. By 1914 it was very considerably advanced, with major papers in Tokyo, Osaka, and Yokohama. The first cable had reached the shores of the island empire in 1873, and Reuter offices were established at Yokohama, then at Nagasaki and Tokyo. Under the Ring Combination contracts, Asia—Japan included—was an area exclusive to Reuter for distribution of a world news service.

For some years the Reuter service as provided by cable was too costly for the young press of Japan to afford, but an alternate mail service was provided, even though the news was inevitably less recent when published. Later an omnibus service was provided by cable at an intermediate cost, presenting a series of brief items subject to expansion.

By 1907, however, Japan's position in the world had greatly changed. Industry and trade had grown, and victory in the Russo-Japanese War had given the country status as a great power. General literacy had increased and a number of dailies were sufficiently prosperous to afford the Reuter cable service. Henry Satoh was appointed in that year as the agency's first permanent agent in Japan, based in Tokyo. In 1911 he was replaced by Andrew Pooley, formerly in the Berlin bureau. Pooley remained until 1914, serving both as administrator of the service and as chief correspondent for Reuter.

Reuter had removed Satoh from his position as agent because he also was writing as a stringer for the Associated Press. Pooley's reports, however, were offensive to Japanese officials and to members of the business community. A direct censorship was not acceptable at the time, but outgoing dispatches found objectionable by the Japanese were so garbled in transmission, by design, as to be useless. Then, on January 30, 1914, Pooley was arrested and charged with blackmail in connection with his reporting of a bribery case relating to certain Japanese naval officers and an armament firm. The matter was raised in the British House of Commons and figured in a diplomatic exchange. Pooley was released from prison on March 23, presently left Japan, and apparently left the Reuter service. He was replaced as Tokyo correspondent for the agency by J. Russell Kennedy.

Kennedy, although Irish-born, was a U.S. naturalized citizen. He had worked for the *Toronto Mail* and the *Washington Post* and then, for fifteen years, had been in Chicago and New York as an assistant to

Melville E. Stone, managing director first of the Associated Press of Illinois and then of the Associated Press. In 1907 he had been assigned to Tokyo to succeed Martin Egan, AP correspondent there since 1901, and served until 1913.[4]

Writing from Tokyo between 1907 and 1913, Kennedy's reports were judged by AP editors in the New York headquarters to have become over-sympathetic to Japanese policies, both political and economic. A decision was reached in New York to transfer him to St. Petersburg, although he never did go, and Joseph E. Sharkey arrived in Tokyo to replace him as correspondent and remained until 1921. The reports that Kennedy had been sending to New York for the AP, so different from what Pooley had been writing for Reuter, were viewed favorably in Tokyo, even if not by the AP management in New York.

Japan's new position in the world was of concern to officials and business leaders of that nation. It disturbed them that the news of the world reaching the Japanese press and people was coming almost exclusively through the British Reuter agency, and that the news of Japan in turn was reaching the rest of the world through that same channel. They were not satisfied, on either score, and the reports by Pooley had been a particularly sore point.

These leaders did not wish to end the Reuter service, but they did believe that a Japanese national news agency should be formed to handle the internal distribution of that service as in other countries, with some selection and editing possible, rather than to have it go directly to the newspapers. They also would welcome news from sources other than Reuter. Further, they believed that a Japanese agency might send its own correspondents to cover some national and world news at the source. But they particularly wanted to see a national agency provide news written to portray Japan in a more satisfactory way, with that news made available to Reuter in an exchange whereby it might receive world distribution.

There were news agencies in Japan, but none was doing what the officials and business leaders envisioned, and none had any relation to

---

4 In 1909 Kennedy became owner-of-record of the *Japan Advertiser,* an English-language paper then published in Yokohama. As such, he was acting as an agent for Benjamin W. Fleisher, a former Philadelphia businessman, who also had arrived in Japan in 1907. Fleisher, in buying control of the *Advertiser* in 1908, also acquired an interest in the *China Press* of Shanghai, for which he acted as business manager until 1913. Disposing of his interest in that paper, he moved to Japan and moved the *Japan Advertiser* to Tokyo, where it was an important and prosperous daily until Fleisher was forced by the Japanese government to sell it in 1940 at a fraction of its value.

Reuter. The first agency in Japan had been the Shimbun Totasu Kaisha (Newspaper Service Company), formed in 1886. It was merged in 1888 with another, Jiji (Current News), then only just established, to form the Teikoku Tsushin-sha (Empire News Agency), with official status, which continued until 1927.

The Nippon Dempo Tsushin-sha (Dentsu) (Japanese Telegraph Agency) began in 1901 and continued until 1936. In 1906 it annexed an advertising agency, the Kokoku Kabushiki Kaisa (Japan Advertising Company, Ltd.), thus becoming both a news agency and an advertising agency, comparable in that respect to the Agence Havas in France.

A small agency, Toho Tsushin-sha (East Service), was organized late in 1914, with a subsidy from the Japanese government. It actually was based in Peking and its purpose was to provide a news service to papers in China, at little or no cost, in order to shape the views of readers there in a fashion suiting Japan's policies and interests during World War I. It continued after the war with the same propaganda purpose, but its headquarters was moved to Tokyo in 1923.

Kokusai Tsushin-sha, also organized in 1914, became the most important of the national agencies. Viscount Eiichi Shibusawa of the Japanese National Bank was especially influential in its formation. It was intended to accomplish those purposes mentioned as being of concern to government officials, industrialists, and other business leaders, and it had their financial backing.

Planning the agency in 1913, its sponsors consulted with J. Russell Kennedy, then in his sixth year as Tokyo correspondent for the Associated Press. It was not only that they were pleased with his reports of Japanese affairs as transmitted to the AP, but they were aware both of his Irish birth and of his long personal association with Stone, general manager of the AP. They requested that he go as an emissary for Kokusai to London and to New York to seek rights for the proposed agency to distribute in Japan the service of Reuter and the growing service of the Associated Press as well, and to propose an exchange involving an incorporation in those services for world distribution of reports on Japanese affairs to be provided by Kokusai. If granted, this would modify the concern of the founding group about the British flavor of the world report reaching the Japanese press and people through the Reuter service alone. It would give Kokusai opportunity to determine what was to be distributed in Japan, and it would permit the addition of a Japanese flavor to outgoing reports.

Kennedy, aware that Sharkey had been sent to Tokyo to replace him as a correspondent for the AP, had personal reasons for yielding to the persuasions of the Japanese group. He did go to London and New York on the mission set for him. Because Japan was within the exclusive territory to be served by Reuter, and because the Associated Press as an agency within the Ring Combination was obliged to observe that limitation, Kennedy was unable to obtain for Kokusai the right to receive the AP service. This could hardly have surprised him. He did, however, gain the right for Kokusai to handle distribution of the Reuter service in Japan, as national agencies did in other countries, with the desired opportunity to control what actually went to the newspapers. It had the effect of making Kokusai a member of the Ring Combination.

In London, further, Kennedy won appointment as chief correspondent for Reuter in Japan, succeeding Pooley, and also ending his relationship with the AP. More than that, on his return he was appointed managing director of Kokusai, thus wearing two hats, so to speak. It meant that his own reports, written for Reuter rather than for the AP, were incorporated in the total world report, thus meeting another desire of the Japanese sponsors of the new national agency.

Under these circumstances, the Kokusai agency began operations early in 1914. Between that time and 1923, under Kennedy's direction, it distributed the Reuter service and it developed a strong original coverage of news within Japan, which became a part of the Ring Combination exchange, supplemented by Kennedy's own reports. The agency's sponsors thus had reason to be pleased with the results. Reuter also had reason to be pleased. If not technically a subsidiary, Kokusai was at least an affiliate under the direction of the Reuter correspondent and tied to the Reuter service.

Soon after World War I, however, Kokusai encountered financial difficulties. It also was guilty of some inaccuracies that brought protests. The business group in control was led to consider whether it might be desirable for Japan to have a news agency wholly its own, independent of Reuters and the Ring Combination, and with its own correspondents abroad. Such an agency, it was believed, might be able to distribute its own service in China and elsewhere outside Japan. Precedents for such independent action by then existed in the two U.S. agencies, the United Press and the International News Service.

A new member of the Tokyo business community, with certain professional qualifications in the news field, became an informal consultant at this juncture on the direction Kokusai might take. He was Yukichi Iwanaga, who had established the Y. Iwanaga Information

Bureau in Tokyo in 1920, a syndicate distributing a selection of articles obtained from a New York syndicate and provided in translation to subscribing newspapers in Japan.

Iwanaga, then thirty-eight, was the fourth son of Dr. Sensai Nagoya, head of the Health Department in the Ministry of Foreign Affairs and founder of the Medical School at the University of Tokyo. Iwanaga had been adopted at the age of eight by an uncle, Shoichi Iwanaga, whose name he took, and who was one of the chief industrialists of the Meiji era and managing director of the Nihon Yusen Kaisha (NYK) steamship line.

Educated in the law, Yukichi Iwanaga, was further advised and sponsored by Count Shinpei Goto, a friend of his father's and president of the South Manchurian Railway. Iwanaga entered the employ of that railroad in 1909 at Changchun, Manchuria. In 1917 he returned to Tokyo as private secretary to Count Goto, by then minister of the National Railroad Department in the government. When Goto left that post in 1918, he and Iwanaga traveled together in postwar Europe and the United States until 1920. Meanwhile, Shoichi Iwanaga had died in 1913. From this uncle and father-by-adoption Yukichi Iwanaga had inherited the equivalent of about one million dollars. Returning from the United States in 1920, he opened his Tokyo Information Bureau, or syndicate.

Perhaps upon Iwanaga's recommendation, and certainly with his approval, Aisuke Kabayama, president of the Kokusai agency, and Viscount Shibusawa, still representing the business group concerned, proposed to the other members that Kokusai undertake distribution of its service in China and Korea. Kennedy, as managing director, reminded them that Kokusai, as a member of the Ring Combination, could not distribute news in any other Asian areas, all of which fell within Reuter's exclusive territory.

The directors of Kokusai, balancing this obstacle against the possibility of a greater financial return and a possible national advantage if its service were extended, decided upon a reorganization that would free the agency from Ring Combination ties. Discussion of ways and means began in 1921. Iwanaga was brought in as a member of the Kokusai board of directors. Later in the year he went to the United States to report the Washington Naval Conference for the agency in its first overseas representation. There he became acquainted with Frank B. Noyes, publisher of the *Washington Star* and president of the Associated Press. He also visited the offices of the AP in New York. In 1922 Noyes was in Tokyo, and from him Iwanaga learned more about the cooperative, nonprofit system under which the AP operated. The concept of such an organization for Kokusai was explored. The management of Reuters was brought into the discussion by correspondence.

On September 1, 1923, Japan was rocked by a great earthquake, with fires adding to the death and destruction in Tokyo and other cities. One result was the suspension of Iwanaga's Information Bureau. Despite the disaster, the earlier discussions with Reuters brought Sir Roderick Jones, its managing director, to Tokyo several weeks after that occurrence. Negotiations began, the result of which was that Kokusai paid 200,000 yen (about £20,000, or almost $100,000) to acquire what were referred to as the "franchise rights" of Reuters in Japan, effective in November 1923. This meant that Kokusai became an independent agency, no longer even technically a subsidiary of Reuters, as it had been, in effect, since its formation in 1914, and no longer a member of the Ring Combination.

Kennedy retired as managing director of Kokusai, and was replaced in that position by Iwanaga. Kennedy nevertheless continued as chief correspondent in Japan for Reuters until February 1925. At that time he was succeeded by Malcolm Duncan Kennedy, unrelated despite the name. J. Russell Kennedy remained in Japan, where he served in 1927–28 as correspondent for the *Chicago Daily News*. He died in Tokyo in 1928, aged sixty-eight, honored by the government and the Emperor of Japan.

Kokusai, continuing independently from 1923 to 1926, still received the Reuters world service and distributed it nationally. Although then free to sell its own service outside Japan, without reference to any Ring Combination contracts, it never actually did so. In 1924 Iwanaga made another journey to the United States, visited the Associated Press headquarters again and sought a greater understanding of that agency's form of organization and operation. Dedicated to an improvement of press standards in Japan, he believed the AP system could be applied with advantage to Kokusai. He spent much of his personal fortune in that effort, but not under the Kokusai name, as it happened.

In 1925, following a recommendation by the Ministry of Foreign Affairs, Kokusai absorbed the small agency, Toho Tsushin-sha, government-supported since its formation in 1914. More important, Kokusai itself was substantially reorganized in 1926, taking the new name of Nippon Shimbun Rengo-sha (Rengo) (Associated Press of Japan), with Iwanaga continuing as director and the entire Kokusai staff taken over. By Iwanaga's planning, it was patterned after the Associated

Press of the United States as a cooperative and nonprofit agency, with eight Tokyo and Osaka dailies forming the core of the membership. The service, still including the Reuters world report, was distributed to twenty-six papers. In 1927 Rengo absorbed the Teikoku Tsushin-sha agency, dating from 1888. This left only one other independent agency in the country, Nippon Dempo Tsushin-sha (Dentsu), founded in 1901, with its advertising subsidiary, Kokoku Kabushiki Kaisa.

Even though patterned after the Associated Press, Rengo differed from the AP, and Reuters as well, in three important respects. First, it received government support, as Kokusai also had, through the Ministry of Foreign Affairs. The contributions varied, but examples included a payment of $180,000 in 1929 and $225,000 in 1930. Second, it added an advertising subsidiary comparable to that maintained by Dentsu, and by the Agence Havas in France. Third, it did not undertake any foreign coverage through correspondents of its own, whether staff or stringer.

This latter Rengo might conceivably have done eventually, but another reorganization interfered. The world economic crisis that began in 1930 caused problems in Japan, as it did in other countries. By 1931 a belief arose within the government that its position might be improved and budgetary costs eased if there was one national agency rather than two, with that one agency strong enough to be represented abroad as well as serving the established national radio stations. This concept suggested a merger of Rengo and Dentsu. The Ministry of Foreign Affairs was partial to Rengo. The national military establishment, gaining strength, had a preference for Dentsu. Neither Iwanaga, architect and managing director of Rengo, nor Hoshiro Mitsunaga, founder and director of Dentsu, favored a merger, nor did the Japanese newspapers, generally. The issue therefore went unresolved until 1936 when the two were nevertheless merged to form the Domei Tsushin-sha (Domei) (Allied News Agency), with Iwanaga as its director.

The Reuter agency itself, becoming identified with Kokusai early in 1914, and already conducting the API in India and the RSAPA in South Africa, was at a high point in its effectiveness and prosperity. Contributing to its financial well-being was its subsidiary British Commercial Bank.

The beginning of World War I in the summer of 1914, followed by the death in 1915 of Herbert de Reuter, director of the agency, brought problems and a reorganization of the enterprise. These circumstances will be examined later, in the chronology of events.

The Times

Among newspapers of the world, the London *Times* stood highest in prestige in 1900, as it had for a half century before. As a quality newspaper, however, it was by no means a leader in circulation. Inexpensive, popular papers, making great advances in the early years of the first decade, left it far behind in that respect. Resultant losses in advertising volume created a serious financial problem.

For those persons of London and the United Kingdom who needed and appreciated the best-informed news and editorial treatment of the most important topics, with a full view of domestic and world news developments, the *Times* was essential reading. Its readers, if not the most numerous, were among the best educated, formally or otherwise, and included those in responsible government posts, executives in commerce and industry, and educators and leaders in every professional field. They were thinkers and doers, creators and directors in the social community, members largely of the more prosperous segment of society, of the upper classes and, in sum, of what later came to be known as "The Establishment."

These readers were notably responsive to what they read in the *Times*, giving it their trust and loyalty. They tended to be faithful readers, and so were among the best informed. One of the distinctive features of the paper was its publication of letters from occupants of the highest positions in British affairs, and sometimes in the affairs of other countries: letters on every sort of subject, sometimes greatly informative, occasionally amusing, but all indicating the importance their writers attached to the *Times* as a medium of information and guidance, almost as a national institution.

The *Times* had become a reluctant subscriber to the Reuter news service in 1858. Its great pride and strength even then was in its reporting of the news by the paper's "own" correspondents, and the Reuter reports were used only secondarily or in special circumstances. The news staff by 1900 had so grown in size, professionalism, specialization, and in general quality that a *Times* representative was likely to be received with special confidence wherever he sought information, and sometimes was consulted, cajoled, flattered, and even feared because of his own character, as well as because of the status of the newspaper.

Nowhere was this more an element in the paper's prestige than in its reporting from abroad. The *Times* foreign service was the largest identified with any one newspaper. Its writers, resident in foreign capitals, sometimes operated on a level scarcely distinguishable from that of British diplomatic representatives. Even though writing anonymously, they were known and respected in the capitals where they lived and worked.

No less qualified were *Times* writers in London itself. Those covering the courts usually were themselves legally trained. Others covering the ministries and agencies of government, the affairs of business, industry, finance, politics, science, education, sports, literature, the arts, or whatever other subject, had background and experience enabling them to conduct their inquiries and write with solid authority. The same was true for leader writers and those contributing to special supplements.

Other London and British newspapers were not lacking in staff members as highly qualified, but they were fewer in number. The standards of personnel and performance set by the *Times* were important in raising press standards generally, and not in Great Britain alone.

The *Times* in 1900 was under the chief proprietorship of Arthur Fraser Walter, great-grandson of John Walter, the founder of the paper in 1785. Charles Frederick Moberly Bell, a former correspondent in Egypt, had been managing director since 1890, and George Earl Buckle had been editor and editorial (leader) page director since 1884. Valentine Chirol in 1899 had just replaced Sir Donald Mackenzie Wallace as head of the foreign department, with Wallace turning to the editorship of the tenth edition of the *Encyclopaedia Britannica,* then a *Times* enterprise. Flora Louisa Shaw, formerly of the *Pall Mall Gazette,* had headed the colonial department since 1890.

With Chirol on a journey to the Far East in 1900–01, L. S. Amery substituted as foreign editor. Formerly in the paper's Berlin bureau, and then directing the *Times* staff in South Africa during the Boer War, Amery had returned to London in September 1900, with that war still in progress. In 1902 he became colonial editor when Miss Shaw, then fifty-one, left the paper to marry Sir Frederick J. D. Lugard (later Lord Lugard), noted as a British colonial administrator and later Governor of Hong Kong, Governor-General of Nigeria, and a Privy councilor. In 1910 Amery moved from the colonial department to substitute again for Chirol, then away for reasons of health. He might have become foreign editor permanently, since Chirol was to leave the paper in 1912,[5] but Amery himself had left in 1911 to serve as a Member of Parliament, proceeding in a political career that included service as secretary of state for the dominions and colonies.

---

5 Chirol was knighted in 1912, and held government appointments through World War I. He retired in 1918 and wrote several books before his death in 1929 at seventy-seven.

Among the *Times* correspondents as the century began was Henri de Blowitz in Paris, as he had been since 1871. He was long known for his reports not only on French affairs but on political developments throughout Europe. In 1902 Blowitz retired at seventy-seven and died in 1903, resulting in several personnel shifts. William Lavino, who had been in Vienna for the paper since 1892, replaced Blowitz in Paris, where he remained until his death in 1908. Henry Wickham Steed, in Rome since 1897, replaced Lavino in Vienna, where he remained until 1913. William Francis Hubbard, in Madrid since 1899, followed Steed in Rome, where he gained the assistance of William K. McClure, who succeeded him in 1915.

Lavino's death in Paris in 1908 triggered a second series of staff changes. George Saunders, in Berlin since 1897, moved to Paris, and remained until his retirement in 1914. He was succeeded by George Jeffreys Adams, formerly in Paris for Reuter. F. E. O'Neill, who had been Lavino's assistant both in Vienna and Paris, had replaced Saunders in Berlin in 1897. Within a year, however, he was replaced in turn by Hubert Walter, whose uncle, Arthur Fraser Walter, became proprietor of the paper. Hubert Walter had been with the paper since 1894 in Spain, Portugal, and France. His term in Berlin was brief and the post was assumed within a year by Frederick A. Mackenzie, formerly of the *Daily Mail*. He remained until the outbreak of war in 1914.

Meanwhile, Dudley Disraeli Braham, with Saunders in Berlin, moved to St. Petersburg in 1897, as Saunders moved to Paris. Braham was expelled in 1903, and it was 1906 before the *Times* replaced him officially with Robert Wilton, who remained in Russia until 1917. George W. Smalley, correspondent in New York and Washington since 1895, retired in 1906. He was succeeded in Washington by Robert Percival Porter until 1910, and then by Arthur Willert.

Other *Times* correspondents in 1900 included Walter Burton Harris in Morocco for the paper since 1887, where he remained until his death in 1933; James David Bourchier in the Balkans since 1892 and based in Sofia until 1915; Dr. George Ernest Morrison in China since 1896 and based in Peking until 1912; Captain Frank Brinkley, a stringer in Tokyo from 1892 to 1912, followed by Charles R. Hargroves until 1914; Percy F. Martin, formerly in India, but in Mexico City from 1900 to 1915; and Dr. George E. Parkins (later Sir George Parkins), a stringer in Toronto from 1900 to 1910, followed by John Stephen Willison (later Sir John Willison), editor of the *Toronto Evening Star*.

Correspondents appointed in those first years of the century also included David Fraser at Shanghai, who was to succeed Morrison in

1912; Philip F. Graves, who went to Egypt in 1907, and later to Constantinople to cover the Near East and Middle East; and Gordon Browne, also in Constantinople in 1909–10. In 1904 A. W. Jones, recently down from Oxford, was named correspondent in Australia.

The *Times* received reports during the South African War of 1899–1902 not only from Amery, but from Angus Hamilton and Lionel James. James also served the paper during the Russo-Japanese War of 1904–05, and is notable for his use of wireless to provide coverage. Wallace, Morrison, and Smalley reported the Portsmouth Peace Conference following that war. Stanley Washburn, an American serving the *Chicago Daily News* during the war, wrote both for that paper and for the *Times* from the south of Russia in 1905.

Military correspondents, as distinct from war correspondents, had written as specialists for the *Times* since the mid-nineteenth century. Among them at the turn of the century were Sir George Clarke (later Lord Sydenham) and until 1903 Colonel Lonsdale Augustus Hale, R. E. (later Sir Lonsdale Hale). On January 1, 1905, Colonel Charles à Court Repington became the paper's military correspondent. He had been writing on such subjects since 1884, but mostly for the *Army Review*, of which he was editor. He wrote for the *Times* through World War I. In the same period, the *Times* had James Richard Thursfield (later Sir James Thursfield) as a naval correspondent.

The Times Goes to Northcliffe

As a business enterprise, the *Times* had been in difficulties since 1889. At that time it lost a libel action brought against the paper by Charles S. Parnell, Irish political leader and head of the National Land League of Ireland, which was seeking land reform there, including the breakup of great estates. The *Times* had accused Parnell, editorially, of having had a part in crimes committed in that cause. Loss of the case cost the paper more than £200,000 (nearly $1,000,000) in damages and expenses.

Under this serious financial burden, the *Times* sought various means to bolster its income as a measure of survival. Its sponsorship of the *Encyclopaedia Britannica* was one such effort. It also made its respected foreign service available through syndication for use by newspapers outside the United Kingdom, including the *New York Times,* the *Chicago Tribune,* and *Le Matin* of Paris. The monetary return was limited, however, and none of the financial efforts was notably successful. The *Times* refused, even so, to compromise on the quality of its service to the public, making no concessions to popularity, but actually strengthened its costly foreign service. It also conducted experiments in wireless news exchange with the *New York Times* across the Atlantic and in the Russo-Japanese War zone.

In the first years of the century, further, the *Times* as a quality paper was feeling the impact on its own fortunes caused by the growth and public favor won by the *Daily Mail* and other inexpensive popular dailies competitive in the morning field for readership and advertising patronage. It had become evident by 1906 that some drastic action was required if the paper was to survive at all. This conclusion was inescapable by 1908, when the circulation of the *Times* was down to a mere 38,000 a day, with advertising volume and revenues proportionately reduced.

Various plans were considered, and several offers were received for the purchase of the *Times,* but were dismissed because of fear that those making the offers would be unable or unwilling to maintain the quality and character of the paper. This the directors could not bear to contemplate.

One of those interested in gaining control of the *Times* was Lord Northcliffe (as Sir Alfred Harmsworth had become in 1906). Highly successful in publishing since 1888, he had purchased the London *Evening News* in 1894, and established the *Daily Mail* as a morning paper in 1896. He had acquired the *Weekly Dispatch* in 1903 and converted it into the *Sunday Dispatch* as a weekend edition of the *Daily Mail* and similar in style. He had also established the *Daily Mirror* in 1903 as a morning illustrated tabloid, half the page size of the standard newspaper and the prototype of modern newspapers in that format. In addition he had established the *Continental Daily Mail* as an English-language morning daily in Paris in 1905, and in that same year had bought the *Observer,* a London Sunday newspaper of quality dating from 1791.

There was concern as to whether Northcliffe, identified almost entirely with popular journalism, could be expected to respect and maintain the sober traditions of the *Times* if he controlled it. Circumstances were sufficiently desperate, however, that Moberly Bell, manager of the *Times,* acting on his own initiative, ventured to open discussions with Northcliffe. These talks gave him reassurance that he communicated to others in the *Times* organization.

The result was that majority control of the *Times* passed to Northcliffe in 1908, with a payment of £320,000 (about $1,455,000). Arthur Fraser Walter retained some shares and remained as chairman of the Board of Directors. A new member of the board who gained a small interest was William Flavelle Monypenny. He was a former assistant to George Earle Buckle, the editor, and had been a correspondent for the paper during the first weeks of the South African War before entering military service himself. He was subsequently editor of the *Johannesburg Star* from 1902 to 1906.

The sale of controlling interest in the *Times* to Northcliffe assured its survival. The financial stress on the paper was ended, and its quality was improved. Northcliffe made no sweeping changes, preserved its traditions, and provided funds to strengthen its service. The 38,000 circulation of 1908 had surged upward by 1914 to 318,000, a large figure for a quality newspaper and for one selling at a higher price than any popular paper. It was a readership figure that again made the *Times* an attractive advertising medium, reaching an especially prosperous and influential audience, and the new advertising volume added substantially to revenue.

Only four changes in the internal staff organization of the paper occurred at any early period by reason of Northcliffe's control. First, Reginald Nicholson was brought from the *Daily Mirror* in 1909 to act as assistant manager under Moberly Bell. Second, some correspondents for the *Daily Mail* also became representatives for the *Times,* among them Walter Fred Bullock in New York, and George Dobson in St. Petersburg. Third, the foreign and colonial departments became a single imperial and foreign department, with two divisions. The foreign division, under Chirol, was concerned as before with the assignment and work of correspondents in foreign places. The imperial division was, in effect, what had been the colonial department, concerned with what remained of British colonial areas and with the dominions. Amery continued as director until he left the paper in 1911. He was succeeded by Edward William Macleay Grigg (later Lord Altrincham), who had been with the paper since 1903.

Other changes, of course, were inevitable. Arthur Fraser Walter died in 1910 and his shares and position as chairman of the board passed to his son, John Walter, V. Managing director Moberly Bell died at his desk in 1911. Nicholson, assistant since 1909, took over direction until 1915. The responsibilities then were divided between Howard Corbett as manager and William Lints Smith as associate manager. In 1920 Corbett was succeeded as managing director by Campbell Stuart (later Sir Campbell Stuart) in a curious arrangement by which he also was managing editor of the *Daily Mail,* with Smith exercising greater responsibility than before in the *Times* organization. This arrangement continued until 1924, when Stuart became a director of the paper, with

Smith as manager until his retirement in 1937, and with Christopher Shotter Kent as assistant manager.

Chirol retired as foreign editor in 1912. Henry Wickham Steed, correspondent in Vienna, was named to the post and also as director of the imperial and foreign department. However, his concern with events of the Balkan wars, then in progress, kept him in Vienna, Constantinople, and Paris, until late in 1913. Braham, who had worked in the foreign department or division since his expulsion from St. Petersburg in 1903, carried on the work as assistant foreign editor until Steed reached London. Braham then left the paper to go to Australia, although he later returned to London and the staff in 1929. Steed served as foreign editor and director of the division from 1913 until 1919. In that period, Charles R. Hargroves, who had been briefly in Washington, and then Hugh Byas, served as stringers in Tokyo.

George Earle Buckle retired in 1912, after twenty-eight years as editor of the *Times*. He was succeeded by Geoffrey Robinson (later Geoffrey Dawson), a member of the staff only since the previous year. Robinson had distinguished himself as a scholar at Oxford, had served in the Colonial Office, and had become private secretary to Lord Milner, High Commissioner and Governor of the Cape Colony from 1897 and High Commissioner for South Africa after the Boer War.

When William Flavelle Monypenny left the *Johannesburg Star* in 1906, Robinson succeeded him as editor and as correspondent there for the *Times* until 1910. In London for Christmas of that year, he was offered a post on trial in the office of the *Times*. He accepted and began work in February 1911. Within a year he was to win the warm approval of Buckle and Northcliffe for the quality of his work, and gained the personal friendship of John Walter, V. His appointment as editor, to succeed Buckle, followed.

In 1917, as a condition of his inheritance of an estate in Yorkshire, Geoffrey Robinson changed his name to Geoffrey Dawson. Differences with Northcliffe led to Dawson's resignation in 1919, at which time Steed became editor of the *Times*. Steed, in turn, resigned late in 1922, three months after the death of Northcliffe, and Dawson returned as editor of the paper until his retirement in 1941.

The Daily Mail

London had more enterprising and important newspapers during the early years of the century than any other city. While the *Times* was unique, the *Daily Mail* was a leader at that period and beyond. Its circulation alone made it important among dailies, although subject to criticism for some of the very things that made it a popular paper. Its enterprise in news-gathering at home and abroad and its editorial initiative gave it certain merit. It was, of course, the creation of Lord Northcliffe.

Born Alfred Charles William Harmsworth, near Dublin in 1865, he moved with his parents to London in 1867. In his youth, he contributed articles used in the *Morning Post* and in 1888, at twenty-three, he established a weekly paper, *Answers to Correspondents,* which was conducted and promoted with imagination and originality and soon became both popular and profitable. Other periodicals were added, with financial returns permitting him to purchase the London *Evening News* in 1894, and to establish the morning *Daily Mail* in 1896 as an inexpensive, innovative, and interesting addition to the London press. Much as Hearst's *New York Journal* was working a revolution in journalism in the United States at the same time, so the *Daily Mail* introduced the popular newspaper in the United Kingdom. It did for a new generation what the London *Morning Herald* had done by introducing human interest in the news some seventy years before. As then, the success of the effort invited imitation and adaptation locally and in other cities and countries.

In 1904, as a reflection of his success, Harmsworth was created a baronet. He was raised to the peerage in the king's honors list in 1905, styling himself Lord Northcliffe. In 1917, in recognition of his wartime activities, he became Viscount Northcliffe. Joined with him in his ventures from the early years was his brother, Harold Sidney Harmsworth, three years younger. He was knighted in 1910, became Lord Rothermere in 1914, and in 1918 Viscount Rothermere, following wartime service as minister of air.

From its inception, the *Daily Mail* had reported the news with vigor, including original coverage from abroad. With its low price, lively appearance, content, and national distribution, it was selling a million copies a day by 1910, the largest circulation consistently maintained for any daily newspaper in the world at that time, and it was influential as well as profitable.

Already a recognized success in 1900, although only four years old, the *Daily Mail* was well represented in the coverage of the South African War, then in progress. E. J. Pryor directed the service, with Charles E. Hands, Edgar Wallace, Frederick Slater Collett, and George Warrington Steevens in the field. Collett and Steevens lost their lives. It also received reports from two U.S. correspondents, Richard Harding Davis, who also wrote for the *New York Herald,* and Julian Ralph of the *New York Journal.*

From north China, Henry George W. Woodhead, editor of the *Peking and Tientsin Times* in Tientsin, was a stringer for the *Daily Mail* from 1902 to 1911. Ernest Brindle also wrote from China during the Russo-Japanese War, and E. J. Harrison was in Tokyo from 1897 until 1913. Tom Clarke, reporting from Hong Kong and Tokyo between 1909 and 1913, continued in a long career with the London paper.

Walter Fred Bullock, formerly in Berlin for the *Morning Post,* became chief correspondent for the *Daily Mail* in New York from 1906 until his retirement in 1922. He also represented the *Times* there after 1914. George Dobson, who had written from St. Petersburg for the *Times* between 1878 and 1897, represented the *Daily Mail* there from 1897 to 1913. Later he again wrote for the *Times*. Andrew M. Pooley had been in Berlin for the *Daily Mail* prior to 1906, when he joined the Reuter staff there. The *Daily Mail* then engaged American-born Frederic William Wile, in Berlin since 1901 for the *Chicago Daily News* and for the *New York Times* from 1908. He continued there until 1914, after which he served in the *Daily Mail* London office through the war years. George Ward Price, who joined the paper in 1908 after leaving Cambridge, was Wile's assistant in Berlin in 1909, but was transferred to Constantinople in 1910. He continued with the paper on foreign assignments until the 1950s. William McAlpine was in Paris in the early 1900s until 1910.

The *Continental Daily Mail,* established in Paris in 1905, became competitive with the *New York Herald* edition there. Its first editor was Norman Angell Lane, who had served the *Daily Mail* in Berlin and Paris. He was to become known for articles and books under the name of Norman Angell. Knighted in 1931, he was awarded the Nobel Peace Prize in 1933.

Northcliffe's successful *Evening News* was strictly local in its distribution. The *Daily Mirror,* established in 1903, made a slow start, but did well later in terms of circulation, although it was insubstantial in content. The *Sunday Dispatch* matched the style and success of the weekday *Daily Mail*. The Sunday *Observer,* 114 years old when acquired in 1905, was then extremely sober and financially weak. James L. Garvin, formerly of the *Daily Telegraph,* became its editor in 1908 and put it on the way to becoming an important and influential quality paper, but its real distinction came only after its sale by Northcliffe in 1911 to U.S.-born William Waldorf Astor (later Viscount Astor), and its inheritance in 1919 by his son, the second Viscount Astor, with Garvin continued as the paper's editor.

The Daily Telegraph

Most nearly approaching the *Times* in terms of quality among London daily newspapers after 1900 was the morning *Daily Telegraph,* established in 1855 and very soon passing to the ownership of Joseph Moses Levy. It was edited almost from the outset by his son Edward Levy, who also became proprietor and director of the paper upon his father's death in 1888. In 1875, by way of meeting a stipulation in the will of an uncle, Lionel Lawson, from whom he received an inheritance, he added his uncle's name to his own, becoming Edward Levy Lawson. In 1892 he was made a baronet, and in 1903 was raised to the peerage, becoming Lord Burnham. He retired from active direction of the paper at that time, with his son Harry Lawson then assuming all responsibilities. When his father died in 1916, he in turn became owner of the paper and also inherited the title.

The *Daily Telegraph* was the first penny paper in England. It also was more politically liberal than the *Times* or the *Morning Post* and was brighter in content but still informative. For these reasons, it took the lead in circulation among London dailies almost at once, dislodging the *Times* from a position held for about forty years. The *Daily Telegraph* kept the lead until it was dislodged after another forty years, in 1896, by the *Daily Mail,* selling at one-half penny. Like the *Times,* however, the *Daily Telegraph* maintained high standards in the reporting and editorial treatment of public affairs.

John Merry LeSage, later Sir John LeSage, an experienced correspondent of the first decade of the century became editor of the paper. Edwin Arnold, principal of Sanskrit College at Poona, India, after leaving Oxford, returned to England at twenty-nine to begin forty years of association with the *Daily Telegraph* in 1861. Also a poet and author, he was made a baronet in 1888, and spent some years in Japan, but his skill as an editor contributed greatly to the quality of the paper in the years prior to his death in 1904. James L. Garvin was another talented staff member from 1899 until 1908, when he became editor of the *Observer.*

The *Daily Telegraph* provided good domestic news coverage. For its world report it placed greater dependence upon Reuter than did the *Times,* but was second only to that paper in the development of its own service from abroad, particularly after about 1880.

Dr. Emile Joseph Dillon, in St. Petersburg from 1886 until the time of World War I, held a roving commission that took him to all parts of Europe and beyond. A notable linguist and investigator, he wrote of international affairs with some of the same special insight and knowledge characteristic of Blowitz for the *Times*. His inquiries took him to Crete, to China at the time of the Boxer uprising in 1900, and to the Portsmouth Peace Conference following the Russo-Japanese War. His effectiveness in Russia was somewhat reduced after the retirement in 1906 of his friend, Count Witte, long prominent in the czarist government. But his service to the paper continued until the Paris Peace Conference of 1919, following which he retired to live in Mexico and Spain until his death in 1933.

Correspondents for the paper during the South African War included Bennet Burleigh, Percy S. Bullen, and Ellis Ashmead-Bartlett, then beginning a long career. Burleigh and Ashmead-Bartlett also reported the Russo-Japanese War, as did Gerald Morgan, writing for the *New York Tribune* as well, and Lewis Etzel, an American, who was killed in Manchuria.

Bullen, following the South African War, served the *Daily Telegraph* in Paris, Berlin, and Rome, and then became the paper's first resident correspondent in the United States in 1904, based in New York, until his retirement there in 1934. Percival Landon, who had reported the South African war for the *Times,* joined the *Daily Telegraph* soon after and remained until his death in 1925. In those years he covered a journey of the Prince of Wales (later George V) to India in 1905, moved in the Middle East, Russia, Egypt, and the Sudan until 1911, and also returned to India for a three-year period of residency.

Edwin H. Wilcox was another correspondent long active with the paper. Assigned to St. Petersburg shortly after 1900 as an assistant to Dillon, he later was based in Berlin, returned to Russia at the time of World War I, and was in Paris from 1934 until his retirement in 1938. Campbell Clarke, Paris correspondent since the late 1870s, was knighted in 1897 and, as Sir Campbell Clarke, remained at the Paris post until his death in 1902. He was succeeded by James W. Ozanne. H. H. Bashford was in Berlin for the paper in the early years of the century, followed by Wilcox. Eustace B. F. Wareing served for more than forty years in various European capitals. Sir Archibald Hurd was named the paper's first military correspondent at the time of the Russo-Japanese War and continued through World War I. The paper also sent staff members on special assignments to various areas of the world and, without becoming resident correspondents, some nevertheless remained in certain capitals and countries for extended periods.

Other British Publications

Another London newspaper providing substantial reports from abroad, as well as domestic coverage, was the *Daily News*. Dating from

1846, it had gained special distinction for its accounts of the Franco-Prussian War, in an association with the *New York Tribune,* and during the Russo-Turkish War of 1877–78. It had maintained an active, if somewhat limited coverage since that time, particularly in Europe.

In 1902 the *Daily News* came into the effective control of the Cadbury family, manufacturers of cocoa and chocolate products. They also were Quakers. Reflecting the humanitarian, liberal, and pacifist inclinations of that group, the paper was directed until 1930 by George Cadbury, Henry Taylor Cadbury, and Edward Cadbury.

In 1912 the *Daily News* acquired two other London papers. One, the *Morning Leader,* dating from 1892 as London's first half-penny paper, was merged with the *Daily News.* The other was the *Star,* an afternoon paper started in 1888 by T. P. O'Connor, former Paris correspondent for the *Daily Telegraph* and a stringer there for the *New York Herald.* Acquired in 1908, the *Star* was continued.

The *Daily News* correspondents in these early years of the century included Mrs. Emily Crawford, one of the few women active in that capacity up to the time. Formerly writing from Paris for the *Weekly Dispatch,* she represented the *Daily News* there from 1897 to 1901 and her reports were regarded as among the best. Charles Tower and then Henry Woodd Nevinson were in Berlin for the paper between 1900 and 1914. H. T. Cozens-Hardy, in Paris for the *Morning Leader* in 1904 and then in New York for that paper during 1905–12, remained there for the *Daily News* when the *Leader* was purchased and merged with the *News.* In 1914 he went to France for the *News* as a war correspondent.

The *Daily Chronicle,* established in 1877, was at its best between 1904 and 1918, edited by Robert Donald (later Sir Robert Donald). It had Martin Donohoe in Paris in those years, sometimes relieved by Philip Gibbs (later Sir Philip Gibbs). It was Gibbs, moving to Copenhagen in 1909 to meet Dr. Frederick A. Cook upon his arrival from the Arctic with a claim to having reached the North Pole, who raised the first question as to the validity of that claim, later rejected in favor of Commander Robert E. Peary's coincidental claim. The *Daily Chronicle* was acquired in 1918 by a group including David Lloyd George, Liberal party leader and even then prime minister.

The *Morning Post,* established in 1772 and the oldest existing London daily of general circulation in 1900, was a conservative quality paper and had a small but active foreign service. Well represented in coverage of the South African War then in progress, its most publicized correspondent was Winston Churchill.

Edward Frederick Knight, an experienced correspondent, formerly with the *Times,* represented the *Morning Post* both in the South African and Russo-Japanese wars. He lost an arm as a result of a wound received in South Africa. Provost Battersby, a military writer on the London staff, replaced him there. George Alfred Ferrend, of the *Post* staff, was killed in that war, and John Stuart was among the correspondents caught in the siege of Ladysmith.

Maurice Baring, son of Lord Revelstoke, British financier and banker, was a *Post* correspondent along with Knight during the Russo-Japanese War. Formerly in the diplomatic service, although briefly, and later known as a novelist and poet, Baring also represented the paper in St. Petersburg during 1905–08 and in Constantinople in 1909. He later wrote for the *Times* in the Balkans in 1912.

William Miller represented the *Post* in Rome for many years and was an able correspondent. A. Maurice Low (later Sir Maurice Low), became the first permanent resident correspondent in Washington for any foreign newspaper, arriving there for the *Post* in 1900 and remaining until his retirement in 1930. Walter Fred Bullock was in Berlin for the paper prior to 1906, when he joined the *Daily Mail* as its New York correspondent. Henry George W. Woodhead was a stringer in Tientsin, also representing the *Daily Mail* and other services.

In 1911 the editorial direction of the *Morning Post* was assumed by H. A. (Howell Arthur) Gwynne, a former *Times* correspondent, briefly foreign director of Reuter in 1904, and editor of the morning *Standard* from 1904–11. Gwynne edited the *Morning Post* from 1911 until 1937, when it was merged with the *Daily Telegraph.*

The morning *Standard* began as an afternoon paper in 1827, but had changed to morning publication in 1857, although an *Evening Standard* was continued. The morning *Standard* attained some importance, providing original coverage throughout the South African and Russo-Japanese wars. For forty years, from 1867 to 1907, it was represented in Paris by T. Farman. John Black Atkins and Arden Hulme Beaman also provided Paris coverage between 1906 and 1914.

In 1904 ownership of the morning *Standard* and the *Evening Standard* passed to Cyril Arthur Pearson (later Sir Arthur Pearson), also a magazine publisher and founder of the London *Daily Express* in 1900 as a half-penny popular paper competitive with the *Daily Mail.* When he was forty-four, Pearson's eyesight began to fail; he later became blind and turned increasingly to efforts to assist others so afflicted until his death in 1921. In these circumstances, he sold the morning *Standard* in 1910 to Davison Dalziel (later Lord Dalziel), previously engaged in the direction of a news service in London, and competitive for a time with Reuter. Gwynne, editor of the *Standard* since 1904, went to that same position with the *Morning Post* in 1911. Pearson retained the *Evening Standard,* but with it he merged the afternoon *St. James's Gazette,* established in 1880, and under his ownership since 1903. In 1913, however, he sold the *Evening Standard* to Sir Edward Hulton, already possessing publications of his own. In that same year, Pearson also sold the *Daily Express* to Canadian-born William Maxwell Aitken.

In 1902, two years after its establishment, an American newsman was engaged as editor of the *Daily Express.* Ralph D. Blumenfeld, Wisconsin-born, began his professional career in Chicago. He was in London as a representative of the *New York Herald* in 1890–92 and returned in 1894. He was present in 1897 for the old United Press to report Queen Victoria's Diamond Jubilee celebration of that year. With the *Daily Mail* in 1900–02, he then joined the *Daily Express* and remained with that paper as an executive after Aitken took it over in 1913 and as a director until his retirement in 1933.

Another American joining the *Daily Express* staff in 1901 and remaining until 1922 was Percival Phillips. Entering journalism in Pittsburgh, he began a career as a foreign correspondent by covering the Greco-Turkish War of 1897 for the *Chicago Inter-Ocean* and the Spanish-American War for the *New York World.* For the *Daily Express,* Phillips covered the Russo-Japanese War, World War I, and many other foreign assignments. He had become a British citizen, and was knighted for his coverage of World War I. As Sir Percival Phillips, and transferring to the *Daily Telegraph* in 1922, he continued actively until his death in London in 1937.

The *Daily Express* had John Nathaniel Raphael in Paris in 1908, and staff or stringer coverage in other European capitals, but the development of the paper had been slow prior to its sale to Aitken in 1913. Born in Canada in 1879, Aitken had made a fortune shortly before 1910, when he was thirty-one. As a broker and member of the Montreal stock exchange, he had been asked by the Bank of Montreal to interest himself in the merger of three cement companies. His success in bringing about the amalgamation brought him under attack, but also made him wealthy. He retired from business, moved to England in 1910, and there also promptly won a seat in Parliament. He became private secretary to Bonar Law, likewise Canadian-born, and a strong figure in the Conservative party and its leader in the House of Commons in 1911, the year Aitken was knighted.

Between 1913 and 1917, Aitken turned his attention to the *Daily Express*. Lacking in journalistic experience, he nevertheless studied the business and soon put the paper on the way toward a success matching that of the *Daily Mail,* and ultimately passed it in circulation. His role, and that of his newspaper in World War I gained him title as Lord Beaverbrook in 1917. He had gone personally to the French front with Canadian troops to provide "eye-witness" reports for his newspaper, and became a special representative of the Canadian government. He also became minister of information in the British Cabinet in 1918. After the war he gave full attention to the *Daily Express,* added a *Sunday Express* in 1921, gained a position in the London afternoon newspaper field as well by purchase from Hulton of the *Evening Standard* in 1922, and later acquired the *Glasgow Evening Citizen.*

The London afternoon newspapers appearing in the 1900 period were reduced in number in the years following. The *St. James's Gazette* was merged with the *Evening Standard* in 1905, with the *Standard* continuing under Pearson to 1913, under Hulton to 1922, and then under Beaverbrook. The *Star* also survived after its sale to the *Daily News* in 1909. The *Westminster Gazette,* started in 1893 with John Alfred Spender as editor from 1896 to 1922, attained importance, but became a morning paper in 1922. It was sold in 1928 to the morning *Daily News* and merged with that paper. The *Pall Mall Gazette,* dating from 1865, had some remarkable staff members, including William T. Stead as editor from 1880 to 1890, when he founded his own monthly *Review of Reviews.* The *Pall Mall Gazette* had been sold to William Waldorf Astor (later Lord Astor) in 1892 and continued until 1925, when it was purchased by Beaverbook to be merged with the *Evening Standard.* From that time, the London afternoon newspaper field was occupied by the *Star,* the *Evening Standard,* and the *Evening News.* The latter was conducted by Lord Rothermere, brother of Lord Northcliffe, whose death occurred in 1922, and the paper was known more simply as the *News.*

Newspapers of the United Kingdom outside of London, forming the provincial press, were numerous by 1900, and some were excellent in content. The *Glasgow Herald* and more particularly the *Manchester Guardian,* both morning dailies, had undertaken some direct coverage abroad. The *Guardian* and two popular Sunday papers in Manchester, *People,* established in 1881, and the *Empire News,* founded in 1884, were circulated nationally along with the London morning and Sunday papers.

The British Sunday papers were well established in 1900 and became increasingly important in the decades following, representing a special form of journalism, usually popular in style and commonly exceeding daily newspapers in circulation. With the exception of the *Weekly Dispatch,* which became the *Sunday Dispatch,* in effect a weekend edition of the *Daily Mail,* and the *Sunday Express,* allied with the *Daily Express,* the others were independent weekly papers. Smaller in number of pages than most of the bulky Sunday editions of newspapers in the United States, they still tended to be larger and more costly than the weekday editions of British papers.

The *Observer* was one of the important quality London Sunday papers. The *Sunday Times,* dating from 1822 but unrelated to the *Times* of weekday publication, also was a quality paper. It attained special importance after 1915 under the direction of William and James Berry, whose role in British journalism was soon to match that of the Rothermere brothers, and who became Lord Camrose and Lord Kemsley, respectively, in the 1940s.

Another independent London Sunday paper was the *News of the World,* established in 1843. Edited from 1891 until his death in 1941 by Sir Emsley Carr, it was owned during those years by George Allardice Riddell, who became Lord Riddell in 1918. Stressing crime and sports and making a generally popular appeal, the paper passed the million mark in circulation soon after 1900 and attained the eight-million mark in the 1950s, the largest circulation to that time of any daily or weekly newspaper in the world.

Other London Sunday papers included *Reynolds News,* established in 1850 as a publication representing the cooperative movement in Great Britain, and the *Sunday Graphic* and the *Sunday Pictorial,* both started in 1915, the latter as a Sunday edition of the *Daily Mirror.* Like the *People* and the *Empire News* of Manchester, nearly all of the popular Sunday papers attained circulations in the millions.

The *Manchester Guardian* was the one provincial daily to attain a national circulation, although it was relatively moderate because of its high quality. In that respect, it was on a par with the *Times,* and preferred by some because of its more liberal political leaning. Started as a weekly in 1821, the *Guardian* became a morning daily in 1855. From 1871 to his death in 1905, the publisher and proprietor was John Edward Taylor, who also was the moving force in the establishment in 1868 of the Press Association, Ltd. The editor of the *Guardian* from 1872 until his retirement in 1929 was Charles Prestwich Scott, a cousin of Taylor's, and his successor in the proprietorship after 1905. The two made the *Guardian* one of the most highly respected newspapers in the world, and as carefully read as the *Times.*

Beginning shortly before 1900, the *Guardian* introduced a limited foreign coverage. John Black Atkins, formerly of the morning *Standard,* reported from Cuba during the Spanish-American War, and later helped report the South African War. Edward Daniel Scott, son of C. P. Scott, the editor, was killed there. Francis McCullagh, in St. Petersburg in 1904, and also writing for the *New York Herald,* went to report the Russo-Japanese War and was captured by the Japanese, but returned to St. Petersburg after his release. He remained until about 1919 and was jailed by the communists. John G. Hamilton also reported the Russo-Japanese War, and later served as correspondent in Paris for nearly ten years.

Charles Edward Montague, son-in-law of C. P. Scott, and with the paper from 1890 until his death in 1928, exercised an important influence as an editor and writer, while also winning acclaim as a novelist and essayist. Others contributing to the paper included Thomas Vaughan Nash in India in 1900, and G. Lowes Dickinson, writing from the Far East. Dickinson also was the author of scholarly books.

The *Manchester Evening News,* established in 1868, came under the *Guardian* ownership in 1924. Strictly local in circulation, it was a highly profitable paper and contributed revenue to the corporate structure that enabled the *Guardian* itself to extend its coverage.

Other British provincial dailies of substance included the *Leeds Mercury,* dating from 1717 and originally a weekly; the *Yorkshire Post* (1857) also of Leeds; the *Birmingham Post* (1857); the *Sheffield Telegraph* (1855); the *Western Morning News,* Plymouth, somewhat active in foreign reporting; the *Liverpool Daily Post* (1855), which absorbed the *Liverpool Mercury* in 1904; the *Scotsman* of Edinburgh, a daily since 1855; the *Glasgow Evening News;* the *Dublin Evening Mail;* and others. Although a few efforts were made by five or six provincial papers to provide some coverage of foreign events, the *Guardian* alone did so consistently or substantially. The Sunday papers also made some such efforts, but the *Observer* and the *Sunday Times,* chiefly through stringer correspondents, did so most effectively.

Apart from foreign reports provided by staff and stringer correspondents for the *Guardian* and the London morning and Sunday papers noted, the British provincial press until after 1930 was dependent for its world reports upon the Reuter service, and for coverage of the British Isles upon the Press Association, Ltd., plus Reuter reports from London;

upon the Exchange Telegraph Company, Ltd. (Extel) for some financial, domestic, and miscellaneous foreign reports; and upon Central News (CN) for some supplementary domestic and foreign reports.

The Central News, Ltd., had been established in London in 1863, as the Central Press of the United Kingdom. The title was changed in 1871, and it became a limited company in 1888. An advertising service was added at that time. In 1908 control of the CN passed to stockholders in the United States, with the Empire Trust Company of New York as the largest owner of shares. The second-largest shareholder was Melvin J. Woodworth, financial editor of the *Spur,* a smart-set magazine published in New York. He was also controlling owner of the New York News Bureau, which published Ticker Topics, Inc., a financial report, and was further identified with Doremus & Company, an advertising agency in the financial field. Not until 1937 did control of the Central News revert to British ownership. Although the service had been moderately active in foreign reporting between about 1890 and 1900, it contributed little in that respect after the turn of the century.

Among British periodicals, the weekly *Illustrated London News,* dating from 1842, had presented reports and sketches from its own artist-correspondents at home and abroad, particularly since the time of the Crimean War in 1853–55. For later times, Melton Prior, active in the field since 1873, reported both the South African and Russo-Japanese wars, with Lester Smith also present as an artist in South Africa. The *Graphic,* an illustrated weekly established in 1869, had been similarly active. Frederic Villiers, an artist-correspondent, began his association with that publication in 1876 and was regularly in the field as late as World War I. In 1926 these two publications, along with *Black and White,* established in London in 1891, and *Sketch,* started in 1892, which added photographs after 1900, were brought together in one organization, Illustrated Newspapers, Ltd., directed by William Harrison.

On a somewhat different level, but still directly concerned with public affairs, the *Review of Reviews* was a monthly established in 1890 by William T. Stead. It continued after his death in 1912, presenting substantial background on both foreign and domestic subjects. There were similar journals of opinion, although more political and partisan in approach.

In India, the first newspapers appeared in 1780. There were two, both in English and both appearing in Calcutta, the headquarters of the British East India Company. These were the *Bengal Gazette* and the *Indian Gazette*. The first lasted briefly, the second for more than fifty years. Others appeared in Bombay and Madras before 1800.

The East India Company's trading activities became the basis for the establishment of British control of the subcontinent. That control passed to the crown in 1858, with direct imperial administration made effective. Queen Victoria was proclaimed Empress of India in 1877. Calcutta remained the capital until 1912, when Delhi was selected as the site of a new capital, later designated as New Delhi by reason of construction and development of adjacent areas.

The progressive growth of British trade and commerce, military and administrative activities, missionary and educational developments, and the extension of transportation and communications, notably after about 1850, brought a great influx of British residents. A press development began even earlier, first in English, but with a vernacular press beginning in 1818. The percentage of literacy among the people of India was low, but the population was so large that the total number of those who were literate, even though divided among a variety of languages, warranted the publication of newspapers in those languages, and some in two languages. British publishers owned vernacular papers, as well as English-language papers, and Indian publishers owned English-language papers as well as vernacular papers. From about 1860, the British Reuter agency began to provide a world news report for newspapers of the country, with that service increasing as telegraph and cable communication was introduced.

Among papers important in the first decade of the century were the *Statesman* and the *Indian Daily Mail* in Calcutta; the *Times of India* in Bombay; the *Hindi* in Madras; and the *Tribune* in Ambala. There also were the *Civil and Military Gazette* of Lahore and the *Pioneer* of Allahabad, for both of which Rudyard Kipling, born in Bombay in 1865, wrote during his youth. The first of the vernacular papers was *Samachar Darpan* in Bengali, started in Calcutta in 1818 and made bilingual in 1829. The *Amrita Bazaar Patrika,* established as a Bengali-English daily in Calcutta in 1860, was published wholly in English after 1878. In that year, however, the *Ananda Bazaar Patrika* was founded in Calcutta as a Bengali daily and became highly successful.

In Colombo, capital of Ceylon (now Sri Lanka), which was important in commerce, shipping, and communication, the *Ceylon Observer* and the *Times of Ceylon,* among the early papers, attained standing. So did *Dinamina,* following its establishment in 1909 as a vernacular paper in Sinhalese.

With the activities of the East India Company and other British commercial interests extending eastward from India both before and after the cable completion in 1872–73, other English-language papers were established in larger places. Among those existing in 1900 were the *Straits Times* at Singapore, dating from 1845, and the *China Mail,* established in 1845 at Hong Kong, a Crown Colony since 1842. Beyond the empire itself, British traders and missionaries established publications in China and later in Japan.

The extension of the empire to Australia and New Zealand brought the establishment of dailies, including the *Sydney Morning Herald* in 1831 as the first; the *Sydney Evening Post* and the *Daily Telegraph,* in 1879; the *Argus* (1846), the *Age* (1854), and the *Herald* (1840), all of Melbourne; the *Advertiser* of Adelaide (1858); the *Telegraph* of Brisbane (1872); and the *West Australian* (1833) and the *Daily News* (1840), both of Perth. A weekly paper, *Truth,* started in Sydney in 1890, and nationally distributed, gained importance. Other daily and Sunday papers appeared throughout Australia, some before 1900, but many after that date.

In New Zealand the first daily was an afternoon paper, the *Taranaki Herald* of New Plymouth, established in 1852. The morning *Taranaki Daily News* appeared there in 1857. The *New Zealand Herald* of Auckland began in 1863, and the afternoon *Auckland Star* in 1870. In Wellington, the capital, the *Evening Post* began in 1865, and the *Dominion,* an important morning paper, in 1907. The *Christchurch Star* was established in 1868, the *Dunedin Star* in 1863, the *Otaga Daily Times,* also of Dunedin, in 1861, and dailies further appeared in a number of other places, including Ashburton, Blenheim, Gisbourne, Greymouth, Hamilton, and Hastings.

The cable reached Australia in 1873, was soon extended to New Zealand, and linked to telegraph lines already existing in both countries. World news service was provided by Reuter, which had maintained a Sydney bureau since 1861. It was directed for many years prior to 1899 by Henry M. Collins, through whose efforts the agency's service also had been extended to India and beyond from 1867. Representatives of the Australian and New Zealand newspapers took up residence in London in 1873 to process the Reuter service and supplement it.

A New Zealand Associated Press, Ltd., had been formed in 1878, with headquarters in Wellington, receiving a world service in an exchange with Reuter. In Australia, small services for regional or special news exchange were maintained by individual cooperating newspapers, with national services introduced after 1930.

The Australian press itself was directly represented on the world news fronts for the first time during British involvement in the Sudan in 1898 and in the South African War of 1899–1902. Correspondents for the Melbourne *Argus,* the Melbourne *Age,* and the Sydney *Evening Post,* on those occasions, included Donald McDonald, John Revelstoke Rathom, William John Lambie, and Horace H. Spooner. Lambie and Spooner were killed in South Africa, and Rathom went on to a long and active career in news work in the United States. From 1900 the number of Australian and New Zealand journalists active as correspondents on world fronts increased greatly.

The British presence in South Africa began in 1795, when a garrison was established to safeguard the sea route around the Cape of Good Hope to India; it was subsequently re-established in 1806 in the Cape Colony and extended to Natal on the east coast in 1824. The first news publication appeared at Capetown in 1800 in English, and in Afrikaans for Boer readers. Organized news coverage began in 1861 through a Reuter office at Durban, which became the first cable point in the south of Africa in 1879. Meanwhile, a main Reuter office had been established at Capetown in 1876. From 1884, coverage also was maintained by the agency at Pretoria, capital of the Boer South African Republic or the Transvaal, in nearby Johannesburg, a gold-mining center, after 1886, and in Bloemfontein, capital of the Boer Orange Free State.

The press was developed in South Africa after 1824. Newspapers of importance during the 1900–10 period included two in Capetown, the *Cape Argus,* dating from 1857, and the *Cape Times,* from 1876. There also were two Afrikaans dailies in Pretoria, *Zuid Afrikaan,* one of the earliest, having been established in 1830, and *De Volkstem,* in 1873. Others included the *East Province Herald* of Port Elizabeth, dating from 1845; *The Friend* (1850) of Bloemfontein, edited briefly during the South African War by Rudyard Kipling; the *Natal Mercury* (1852), and the *Natal Daily News* (1878), both of Durban; and the *Diamond Fields Advertiser* (1878) of Kimberley. The gold-mining activities in the Rand district of the Transvaal brought a number of papers into existence, among them the *Johannesburg Star* in 1887, an afternoon paper, and the morning *Rand Daily Mail,* established in 1902, with an associated *Sunday Times* in 1906. World news reports for the South African press were provided through the Reuter agency. Its position in the area has been described in earlier pages.

A British presence had been established at Alexandria, Egypt, in 1801–03, and was reinforced in 1807, when military forces were landed. A closer association followed the opening in 1869 of the Suez Canal, which provided a shorter sea route to India. Most of the shares in the canal came under British control in 1875. British-owned cables touching at Alexandria after 1872 added to Egypt's ties to London. From 1882 the administration of the country was in British hands. In a trade with the Agence Havas, Egypt after 1892 became a territory exclusive to Reuter for the distribution of world news. Egypt and the Sudan were greatly in the news because of military action during the 1890s. Although never strictly a part of the empire, Egypt was designated a British protectorate from 1914 to 1922.

Both Reuter and the *Times* had staff and stringer correspondents in Alexandria and Cairo from the 1870s or earlier. The first newspaper in Egypt had appeared at Cairo in 1798 during the French campaign there under Napoleon. Known as *Le Courrier de l'Egypte,* it did not survive but was the first of a number of French-language papers, some of which existed during the period of 1900 and later. They were produced by the Société Orientale de Publicité (SOP). Despite its name, the SOP was owned by a British resident of Cairo, Oswald Finney. It also published English-language papers, including the *Egyptian Gazette* (1880) of Alexandria, and the *Egyptian Mail,* published chiefly for British military forces in the country.

The *Egyptian Gazette* had been established by C. F. Moberly Bell, who was born in Egypt of British parents in 1847. He was correspondent in Alexandria for the *Times* from 1866 to 1873, and again from 1882 to 1890. While in private business during those intervening years, he established the *Gazette*. It also was a period when his brother, John Scott Bell, replaced him as correspondent for the *Times*. When Moberly Bell was summoned to London in 1890 to become manager of the *Times,* his Alexandria newspaper continued to appear, published by the SOP, and was regarded for a time as the official voice of the British government in Egypt.

Arabic dailies included *Al-Ahram* (The Pyramid), founded at Alexandria in 1875, and transferred to Cairo in 1899. Published in the first years of the century by Gabriel Takla Pasha, it introduced the most modern methods of production, arranged for special news reports from points in the Middle East and beyond, and attained great importance and a substantial circulation. Another Cairo morning paper of almost equal status was *Al-Misri* (The Egyptian), owned by Mahmoud Abdul Fath, and circulated throughout the Middle East. An afternoon paper,

Al-Balagh (Information) of Cairo, serious in character, was greatly respected.

Canada, largely explored, settled, and administered by France and the French in a long epoch from the sixteenth to the eighteenth centuries, although not without British participation, became a part of the British Empire in 1763 as a result of Anglo-French wars in Europe and North America. It gained dominion status in 1867. French ethnic influences, strong in the eastern part of the country, produced an active French-language press there.

The first newspaper established was the weekly *Halifax Gazette* (1751) in Nova Scotia, and the press developed steadily from that time. Among early newspapers still appearing in 1900 was the *Morning Chronicle* of Quebec, technically dating from 1847, but deriving from others originated as early as 1764. Another was the *Montreal Gazette,* tracing its origin from 1788 as the *Gazette Littéraire* published by Fleury Mesplet, a printer trained and backed financially by Benjamin Franklin, an absentee cofounder of the paper shortly before his death in 1790.

Other important dailies in the early years of the century, most still appearing, included the *Toronto Globe* (1844); the *Toronto Mail and Empire* (1872), a morning paper; the *Toronto Evening Telegram* (1876); and the afternoon *Toronto Daily Star* (1892). There were also the *Montreal Star* (1869), and the French-language *La Presse* (1884), also of Montreal. Both were afternoon papers. The city also had the Sunday *La Patrie (1878), with Le Devoir* established in 1910. Quebec had two afternoon French-language papers, *Le Soleil* (1896) and *l'Action-Quebec* (1907).

Ottawa, had the *Ottawa Citizen* and the *Ottawa Journal.* Also in Ontario, there were the *London Free Press, Hamilton Spectator, Brantford Expositor, Pembroke Observer, Chatham News,* and *Sarnia Observer,* all established between 1844 and 1885. In New Brunswick, there was the Fredericton *Gleaner* (1880); in Nova Scotia, the *Halifax Herald* (1872); and in Newfoundland, the St. John's *News* (1894).

Settlement of the western areas of Canada brought the establishment, among others, in British Columbia of the *Colonist* (1858) and the *Times* (1884) at Victoria, and the *Province* (1898) at Vancouver. There also were the Winnipeg *Free Press* (1874), and the *Tribune* (1890); the *Leader-Post* (1883), as it later became, at Regina; and the *Herald* (1883) at Calgary. The *Star-Phoenix* appeared in Saskatoon and the *Albertan* in Calgary in 1902, the *Journal* in Edmonton in 1903, the *Herald* in Lethbridge in 1907, and the *News* at Medicine Hat in 1910.

As the press gained strength, certain newspapers developed special services of their own. It has been noted earlier that many arranged to receive reports through the Western Associated Press of Chicago, with the Reuter world report channeled to some even earlier through the New York Associated Press and, after 1893, through the Associated Press of Illinois and then through the reorganized Associated Press after 1900.

In 1903, newspapers of Ottawa, Montreal, and Toronto formed a Canadian Associated Press (CAP), with cable service from London and a representative assigned there in a direct association with Reuter. The Canadian government provided a grant of $8,000 annually to assist in communications costs. At the same time, a regional association was formed, the Eastern Associated Press (EAP), to serve papers in the Maritime provinces—Nova Scotia, New Brunswick, and Prince Edward Island. In 1907 a second regional association was organized, with headquarters in Winnipeg. Known as the Western Associated Press (WAP), but unrelated to the earlier agency of that name in the United States, it was a cooperative serving newspapers in Manitoba and other western provinces.

In this same period, the Canadian Pacific Railway Telegraph Company was operating a commercial news service, and gained the right to distribute the Associated Press service of the United States in Canada. In 1910, however, Canada's Western Associated Press entered an appeal to the Dominion Railway Commission protesting the rates charged by the telegraph company. The result was that the company withdrew from the news field and released to the Canadian newspapers the right it had held to distribute the AP service.

To assure continuation of that service with the Reuter reports, newspapers joined to form a new agency in 1911, the Canadian Press, Ltd. The other associations, CAP, EAL and WAP, continued independently as regional services until 1917. In that year, a Dominion charter granted to the Canadian Press, Ltd., made it a national association with a government subsidy of $50,000 a year to help cover leased wire charges, and the regional associations were merged into the new agency.

A second reorganization came in 1923 when the Canadian Press, Ltd., grown stronger, became The Canadian Press (CP), a cooperative agency owned by member newspapers. With an effective exchange of domestic news among the papers, and the full AP-Reuter service available for distribution, the CP rejected the government subsidy after 1924. Its own full coverage of Canadian news was made available to the AP and to Reuter, and it became a part of the Ring Combination report. The CP also placed its representatives in London, New York, Washington, and elsewhere to provide not only for an exchange of news reports but for direct CP coverage.

By that period in the 1920s the *Montreal Gazette,* the *Toronto Star,* a Saturday *Toronto Star Weekly,* established in 1910, and one or two other papers were receiving reports also from their own correspondents, both staff and stringer, in Canada, the United States, Europe, and sometimes beyond. With the Canadian newspaper and periodical press entirely free of any government restrictions and with a fully literate readership, the people of Canada were as well served as any in the world.

The World Press 8

The press of the United States, Great Britain, and British Empire countries, provided turn-of-the-century readers with a good service of domestic and world information. The same was true for the press of some other countries, although with differences and variations. Shortcomings, where they existed, were chiefly attributable to government restrictions on freedom of expression and publication, to a low rate of literacy, to economic circumstances denying many persons the means to afford publications, and sometimes to the opportunity to obtain them.

While it is not practical to examine in detail the situations existing in every part of the world during the 1900–10 period, a proper balance in the examination of information services requires attention to some.

*France
and the
Paris Press*

On the European continent, where the general literacy level was high in many areas, Paris long had been a major center of journalistic activity, and second only to London as a world news center. Administrative base for a French colonial empire, the capital of a nation moving into industrial greatness, a cultural center, a crossroads in transportation and communication, and a place to which "everybody" came, it was a focal point of information.

So many writers for the world press had made Paris a center of coverage by 1879 that an Association Syndicale de la Presse Étrangère à Paris had been formed in that year to give its members official standing in their relationship to the government and other sources. It was one of the first correspondents' associations in any capital, and the first of several in Paris. A Syndicate de la Presse Étrangère à Paris, almost the same in title, was formed in 1883. A continental branch of the British Union of Journalists, based in London, was formed by British correspondents in Paris in 1896, with an original membership of forty-seven.

There were to be others, but one of the most important was formed in 1907 by Paris correspondents for eighteen newspapers and four news agencies of Great Britain, nine newspapers or services in the United States, and staff members of the two existing Paris English-language newspapers. In December of that year twenty-five members of that group met in the Paris offices shared by the London *Daily Chronicle* and the *Chicago Daily News* to form the Association de la Presse Anglo-Américaine de Paris, or the Anglo-American Press Association, with both versions of the name to be used. T. Farman, correspondent for the London morning *Standard* in Paris since 1867, and dean of the foreign press corps, declined the presidency because he was about to retire. That office went, instead, to James W. Ozanne of the *Daily Telegraph*. The second president, named in 1908, was Howard N. Thompson of the Associated Press, and the presidency has alternated annually since that time between British and U.S. news representatives.

Since 1631, when the *Gazette de France* appeared originally as a weekly in Paris and the first newspaper in the country, the press had been active. For most of its years, however, it had operated under government restrictions, with only brief periods of freedom until 1881. Then under the Third Republic, a new press law permitted almost complete liberty of expression. It was not surprising, therefore, that the number of daily and weekly newspapers and periodicals doubled by 1900. There were 240 papers in Paris alone, more than in any other city of the world, and many of them were dailies, with 2,160 in 540 other cities and towns of the country.

Some of the best newspapers appeared in provincial cities. But the Paris press received greater attention, in part because certain of the papers were more authoritative, enterprising, and controversial in editorial expression, but also because many received national distribution over a railroad network of which Paris was the hub. That distribution was handled through a single commercial organization, the Messageries Hachette. Those papers distributed nationally had the larger circulations and were the more profitable, as with London morning papers so distributed within the United Kingdom.

Paris journalism, unlike that in London, was greatly political. Many papers, daily or weekly, were identified with political parties or splinter groups. Publishers and editors often were involved in politics, or aspired to be, with their papers and their writing commonly reflecting a personal or partisan view. Most papers of this sort were small in size, circulation, and income. They were commonly printed commercially, rather than in their own shops, and were frequently short-lived.

Because of the great number of such partisan papers, rarely warranting classification as *news*-papers, a distinction was made in Paris between the "political" press and the "information" press, between "journals of opinion" and those "journals of information" which provided a reasonably substantial budget of news and had a broader readership. The volume of advertising in the political papers was almost nil. It was small even in the information papers, still numerous enough to discourage advertisers, and seldom larger than eight pages, although some exceeded that in later years. With such limited space, they could present only a fraction of the material to be found, for example, in a London or New York newspaper.

Although the newspapers were inexpensive, a Paris reader whose interests were broad, would be obliged to buy several to obtain the information he could find in a single paper in either of those other cities. For the equivalent, he would have to spend more to buy one or two information papers, at least one political paper, a financial paper, a sports paper, and others, perhaps including a daily or weekly offering theatrical, cultural, literary, and social news. Retail advertising and classified advertising (*petit annonces*) was in small volume, and such general advertising as he might see would more likely be in a magazine.

The Paris newspaper reader, further, might be unaware that some of the papers were receiving alternative financial support from political or industrial groups, or from individuals with personal interests finding reflections in what was published, or indeed omitted, thereby casting doubt on the validity of the service. Worse, some were "gutter sheets," given to blackmail of individuals, business firms, or even governments, or with their columns for sale to financial operators or others using the space for their own advantage.

Rarely was a Paris newspaper taken by subscription or received through direct delivery. Rather, it was purchased afresh each day at a street stand or kiosk. A device commonly used to win and hold readers under this arrangement was for a paper to publish a daily installment of a novel by a known and respected writer. This *feuilleton* appeared across the bottom half or third of an inside page.

Neither the Paris nor the French provincial press in the period of 1900 included a daily of quality, nor did it yet include popular papers in the

London or New York sense, although there was a tendency to borrow
some of those latter characteristics as a means to capture attention and
win readers. Some political writers known for their vigorous and
effective prose, polemical though it might be, and using their names or
pen names, provided an appeal that held readers both to political and
information papers.

Paris dailies of major importance in the first years of the century
included *Le Temps,* dating from 1861, and *Le Journal des Débats* from
1789. Both were morning papers, well-informed, with partisanship
muted, dull in appearance, but carefully read by an important group,
including government officials and news correspondents. They would
have been *élite* newspapers, in the sense later introduced by Dr.
Merrill.

Political papers of a more partisan variety included two established
and conducted by Georges Clemenceau: *l'Aurore,* begun in 1903, and
l'Homme Libre in 1913, four years before Clemenceau became wartime
premier of France. Jean Jaures, Socialist party leader, published *Le
Populaire* and *l'Humanité* as party organs while he served in the
Chamber of Deputies until assassinated in 1914, a few days before
World War I began. Other Paris political dailies of importance included
Le Figaro, established in 1854; *La Liberté* in 1864; *l'Oeuvre* in 1893;
and *l'Action Française,* a Royalist paper.

The leading information dailies of Paris, sometimes referred to as the
"big five," in part because of their circulation leadership, included *Le
Matin,* established in 1884 by Samuel S. Chamberlain, an American
and former editor of the Paris edition of the *New York Herald.* He
edited the paper for two years, selling it then to French owners, and
returned to the United States, soon to begin a long career with the
Hearst newspapers. Others were *Le Petit Parisien* and *Le Petit Journal,*
both established in 1876; *l'Echo de Paris* in 1884; and *Le Journal* in
1892.

Informative, but specialized, were such journals as *Excelsior,*
primarily a society paper; *La Journée Industrielle* and *l'Information,*
business papers; and *l'Auto,* a sports paper. Among foreign-language
papers, were the Paris edition of the *New York Herald,* dating from
1887; and the *Continental Daily Mail* from 1905.

In the French provinces, particular merit attached to such regional
information dailies as *Le Progres de Lyon, Le Petit Marseillais, Le Petit
Provencal,* also of Marseilles; *Le Petite Gironde* of Bordeaux; *l'Est
Républicaine* of Nancy; *Le Journal de Rouen; Le Petit Niçois* of Nice;
l'Echo du Nord of Lille; and *Le Petit Dauphinois* of Grenoble.

Among periodicals, *l'Illustration,* somewhat comparable to the *Illustrated London News,* entered news coverage outside of France during the period of the South African and Russo-Japanese wars, with Reginald Kann as its representative in the field on both occasions. Among other important periodicals giving attention to current topics were the *Revue des Deux Mondes,* dating from 1829, and *Le Mercure de France* from 1728.

Prominent among individuals associated with the Paris dailies was Adrien Hebrard, editor of *Le Temps* for forty-seven years from 1867 to 1914. André Tardieu also helped to make that paper important as a contributor and foreign editor prior to becoming minister of foreign affairs. Pierre Comert was its correspondent in Berlin, and succeeded Tardieu as foreign editor. Raymond Recouly reported the Russo-Japanese War for the paper. The *Journal des Débats* had Maurice Pernot in Rome and then in Vienna.

For *Le Matin,* Maurice Bunau-Varilla became chief proprietor after Chamberlain's departure, with Marcel Knecht and Stéphane Lauzanne both prominent in the organization. Lauzanne, a nephew or, by some accounts, the natural son of Henri de Blowitz, long-time Paris correspondent for the *Times,* was correspondent for the paper in London in 1898–01, editor-in-chief in 1901, and its political editor for nearly forty years thereafter. Married to Camille Gros of San Francisco, he was regarded as one of the great friends of the United States in France. A M. Caro was correspondent in Berlin for the paper. Jules Hedeman, a successor to Lauzanne in London, became foreign editor and developed the best foreign service available in any French paper prior to World War I, in a period when the circulation had reached a million a day.

The *Petit Parisien* attained the million mark by 1904, and half-again as much by the eve of the war. Having been established by Jean Dupuy in 1876, ownership remained in the family and passed to Charles Alexandre Dupuy, three times premier of France and made a senator-for-life in 1900. Ludovic Naudeau, long a correspondent in St. Petersburg, also reported the Russo-Japanese War for the paper, although later transferring to the staff of *Le Journal.*

The *Echo de Paris* had André Geraud as a correspondent in London from 1908 to 1914. Foreign editor of the paper from 1917 to 1938, he became widely known and influential as a writer on international affairs under the name of "Pertinax." The paper also had Condurier de Chassaigne in London, where he served as president of the Foreign Press Association shortly before the war.

Pierre Loti (Louis Marie Julien Viaud), to become known as a novelist, had written for *Le Figaro* from Indo-China in 1883, but also reported the Boxer Rebellion in China in 1900. The paper had a M. Bonnefon in Berlin.

Several Paris journals of information instituted the practice of assigning a staff correspondent, or perhaps two or more, to make an investigation, or *enquête,* of a subject at home or abroad under a system or procedure also referred to as *grand rapportage.* Rather than reporting findings day by day, time was allowed to gather all essential information, observe, interview, and conduct such research as might be required to gain a full understanding of a subject or situation. Only then would the writing begin, with a special series of articles resulting. Some such inquiries were so useful and substantial as to warrant republication in book form. It was a system to be adapted by newspapers of other countries, and one contributing usefully to public understanding.

Four or five Paris information papers became particularly active in this form of investigation, and Albert Londres, Henri Béraud, Georges Le Fèvre, and Louis Roubaud were among reporters who earned reputations for such writing during the first quarter of the century.

Even though some such highly competent correspondents represented certain of the Paris dailies, the French press as a whole was chiefly dependent for its national and international news reports upon the service of the Agence Havas, with its own correspondents and ties to the Ring Combination agencies.

Charles Lafitte was managing director of the Havas agency from 1897 until his death in 1924. He also exercised control on behalf of Havas over the Agenzia Telegrafica Stefani in Italy; the Agence Espagñol et Internationale, often referred to as Fabra, in Spain; and shared the Belgian news field with Reuter. Henri Houssaye was in general charge of the agency's news service in 1900, and moved about Europe. His nephew, Charles Houssaye, was in Buenos Aires from 1902 directing the service in South America, but moved to the directorate in Paris in 1915 when his uncle retired. Elié Mercadier, with the agency since 1870, exercised a major control over the foreign service from 1875 and continued to do so through World War I. Leon L. Pognon, in Bucharest from 1876, and wounded while reporting the Russo-Turkish War of 1877, was director-general in Paris prior to the World War.

Among Havas correspondents, Georges Vayssié, the first agency representative in Morocco in 1890 and based in Egypt after 1896, continued in service until 1919. Robert Raynaud, director of the newspaper *Dépêche* in Tangier, also became a Havas stringer there in

1881. Laurent Rabanit was a stringer in Algiers. His son, Henri Rabanit, was resident correspondent in Tangier in 1906, but was killed in 1909. George Fillion, in the agency service from 1889 until his death in 1912, reported from Indo-China, Vienna, the Balkans, Berlin, and Lisbon, and then was in Paris in charge of communications services.

Gaston Chadourne, who had reported the Greco-Turkish War of 1897 and then was in Athens and Rome, had gone from that post to report the Boxer Relief Expedition to Peking in 1900, returning to Europe by way of Canada and the United States. Georges de La Salle reported the Russo-Japanese War in 1904. A M. Giaccone, correspondent in St. Petersburg since 1887, died there in 1907. He was succeeded by Alexandre Gorline, followed in turn in 1913 by Horace Trouvé. A M. Guillerville, in Berlin from 1890, was reassigned to Rome in 1905, and replaced in Berlin by André Meynot, who was succeeded there in 1913 by Ludovic Péricard. A M. Cartier was in Vienna, Rome, and Stockholm in those early years of the century. Jean Maury was in Turkey and the Balkans in 1908–09. American-born Henry Sweinhart was a stringer in Washington in 1909. The first permanent Havas bureau in the United States was established in New York in 1913, headed by M. Collin-Delavaud, who was succeeded in 1914 by M. Delmas.

Germany and the Berlin Press

Germany as a united nation after 1871 became increasingly important as a European and world power, with an empire extending to parts of Africa and the Pacific. Its growth as an industrial nation, participation in world trade, shipping, and scientific advances, and its creation of a large naval and military establishment by the end of the first decade of the century all combined to make Berlin a news center of importance. From about 1890, in particular, the corps of foreign correspondents there grew steadily. They formed an organization in 1906, the Verein der Ausländischen Presse zu Berlin (Berlin Association of Foreign Correspondents).

News sources were reasonably open to correspondents by the twentieth century, and the press of the country was sufficiently informative to be helpful. By then more newspapers were appearing in Germany than in any other country, although most were small and some only represented title changes on various editions of the same newspaper circulating in adjacent communities. Most were information papers, some of quality, enterprise, and substantial readership. Some, however, were political papers. A press law of 1874 assured freedom, but government restraints nevertheless survived from earlier times. Some papers were controlled and even owned by the government, but informed persons recognized these relationships and the papers were read with that awareness.

Unlike the British and French press where the major dailies appeared in the capitals, the Germany press included important dailies in cities other than Berlin. Those most active in direct coverage in the early years of the century, with staff correspondents in other European capitals, although rarely elsewhere, included the *Berliner Tageblatt,* dating from the 1880s; the *Kölnische Zeitung* of Cologne, dating from 1804; and the *Frankfurter Zeitung* of Frankfurt-am-Main, a daily since 1856, but with a heritage stemming from 1615. It had had Theodor Curti as a correspondent in Paris as early as 1870. Dr. Harry Stuerman moved about Europe in the first decade of the new century. Paul Weitz was variously in The Hague, Constantinople, and London in the years between 1869 and 1920. Through a close friendship with Baron Alfred Hermann Marschall von Bieberstein, who held diplomatic appointments in those capitals, and whom he followed, Weitz produced many reports exclusive to his paper. These three papers were read carefully both for their news and editorial content.

Other dailies read with attention included three in Berlin, the *Lokal Anzeiger,* dating from 1883; the *Berliner Zeitung* from 1877; and the *Vossische Zeitung,* named after its founder, Christian Voss, in 1705. Among those published in other cities were the *Hamburger Nachrichten,* dating from 1792, and then active in some of the earliest European news-gathering enterprise; the *Allgemeine Zeitung,* established at Tübingen in 1798, but moved later to Munich, with Heinrich Heine, poet and essayist, as its representative in Paris in the 1830s; the *Münchner Neuste Nachrichten,* also of Munich and dating from the 1880s; and the *Augsburger Zeitung,* established in 1798.

Apart from special articles and editorial content, the German dailies depended primarily upon the Wolff agency for world news reports. As the third news agency in the world, established in Berlin in 1849 by Dr. Bernhard Wolff, formerly an assistant in the Havas agency in Paris, the German service had been known originally as the Berlin Telegraphische Anstalt. It distributed commercial information until 1855, when it also entered the general news field. The agency went through organizational and title changes until 1865, when it formed a combination with a national agency, the Continental Telegraphen Compagnie, gained Prussian government support and supplementary financing, and became at least a semi-official service. From that time it operated as the Wolff'sche Telegraphen Büro-Conti-Nachrichten Büro (WTB-CNB), but was commonly known internationally as the Wolff bureau.

The Wolff, Havas, and Reuter agencies exchanged news from 1859 and became associated after 1870 in the alliance of news agencies generally referred to as the "Ring Combination," with an exchange of world news. Within this association, Wolff had its exclusive territories for the distribution of its reports, including the German Empire, as it became after 1871, the dual empire of Austria-Hungary, and much of northern and southern Europe.

The strength of the Wolff agency was not equal to that of Reuter and Havas, largely for lack of its own correspondents in more than a few major capitals. It was bolstered, however, by its control of the Svenska Telegrambyrå of Sweden from its establishment in 1867; a similar control of the Norsk Telegrambyrå of Norway, from its formation in that same year, until 1879 when its ownership became totally Norwegian; a small interest in the Ritzaus bureau of Denmark; a close working arrangement with the official agencies in Austria and Hungary, the K. K. Telegraphen-Korrespondenz-Büro and its associated Ungarische Telegraphen-Büro; and also with two agencies in czarist Russia, the semi-official Rossiyskoye Telegraphnoye Agenstvo established in 1894, and the Torgova-Telegraphnoye Agenstvo established in 1902.

Dr. Wolff retired in 1871, with direction of the agency assumed by his associate, Richard Wentzel, who was succeeded in 1887 by Dr. Heinrich Mantler, as managing director through the period of World War I. Since the reorganization of 1865, the actual ownership of the Wolff-CNB agency had rested with the Bleichröder Bank of Berlin, headed in 1900 by Dr. Paul von Schwabach, personal banker to Kaiser Wilhelm II. The bank stood in a semi-official relationship to the government. This in itself gave a semi-official status to the agency as well, but also gave it special access to official news and favorable arrangements for the use of government-owned communications facilities.

The Wolff agency was represented by correspondents in London and Paris, but their function was chiefly to scan the Reuter and Havas reports to select items to be forwarded to Berlin. Beyond that dependence for added news matter was largely upon stringers and upon exchange arrangements with those national agencies within Wolff's own exclusive territories. This arrangement was criticized by the government as inadequate when the century began, resulting in some extension of direct coverage, but to no great effect.[1]

As tensions arose in Europe after 1910, the German government made the first modern moves toward the use of propaganda as a force or weapon in the conduct of international relations. In doing so, however, it was only following general practices introduced by the former Chancellor Otto von Bismarck. The Wolff agency became a pawn in the nation's designs. The government, along with a group of industrialists, also formed a wireless news service to be used in the same fashion. This Syndikat Deutscher Uberseedienst, formed in 1913 and renamed in 1915 as the Transozean Nachrichten, used the new wireless transmitter at Nauen, near Berlin, to send reports available for use without cost by any publication in any country, while serving the interests of Germany in the prewar and wartime period from 1913 to 1918.

Italy and Southern Europe

Italy, for centuries a center of civilization and culture, and an area of great interest to much of the rest of the world, had contributed to the growth of the press. "Gazette," one of the most widely used names for newspapers, derived from the *gazetta,* a sixteenth-century Venetian coin and the price of a newssheet. The establishment of Italy as a unified kingdom, with Rome as its capital from 1871, coincided with the beginning of a better organized coverage of news throughout the world and brought correspondents there in growing numbers. News interest had attached to the Vatican for many years, and that enclave of Rome also received greater attention.

The Agenzia Telegrafica Stefani, the fifth major news agency in the world, had been formed in 1853 by Guglielmo Stefani, with its headquarters in Turin until 1881, when it was moved to Rome. From that time until 1899 it was directed by Ettore Friedlander, and had a working association with the French Agence Havas from 1861 until 1917.

---

1   Four other small Berlin agencies had existed for many years, but provided no world reports to the German press. These were the Herold Depeschen Büro, formed in 1862, and three formed in 1868, the Bösmans Telegraphen Büro, Korrespondenz Hofmann, and the Telegraphisches Büro Louis Hirsch. The Hofmann bureau continued until 1917, the others until 1928.

The leading Italian daily in 1900 was *Il Corriere della Séra* of Milan. Established in 1876 as an afternoon paper, as the name suggests (The Courier of the Evening), it became a seven-day morning paper under the direction of the Crespi brothers, textile manufacturers, who acquired ownership in the early years of the paper's existence. Luigi Albertini, its editor from 1898 until 1925, who became a member of the Italian Senate, gave it great distinction. By 1900 its circulation was about 100,000, the largest in the country and doubly remarkable because it was a quality newspaper, serious and responsible, making no attempt to gain general popularity. It also was remarkable because although distributed throughout Italy, its publication in the north meant that, by reason of the conformation of the Italian peninsula, its delivery in the extreme south was delayed. Its quality further earned it readership in other parts of Europe, despite language differences.

In its first year of publication, the *Corriere della Séra* established a resident correspondent in Paris, always the most important foreign news center for the Italian press. It also developed an excellent national coverage, and by 1900 was represented in other European capitals. Guglielmo Emanuel was in London through about a decade prior to 1919. The paper also sent correspondents farther afield. Luigi Barzini, related to the Crespi family, provided distinguished correspondence from China during the Sino-Japanese War of 1894, the Boxer Rebellion in 1900, the Russo-Japanese War, and remained active for the paper through World War I.

A second newspaper of quality in Italy was *La Stampa* of Turin, established in 1868. It was edited in the first decade by Alfredo Frassati, and continued under his direction until 1926. *Il Messaggero* of Rome, established in 1878, was a third daily of high quality. Important also were *Il Mattino* of Naples, established in 1891; *Il Giornale d'Italia* of Rome in 1901; and others in Florence, Venice, Genoa, Bologna, and elsewhere.

The *Osservatore Romano* (The Roman Observer) was established in 1861 under private ownership at the suggestion of Pope Pius IX to combat anticlericalism and support the Roman Catholic Church. It was acquired by the Vatican in 1890. Pope Leo XIII at that period appointed Gianbattista Casoni, a Bologna lawyer, as editor. He made it a paper of special importance published to speak for Vatican City and the Vatican. Succeeding to the editorship in 1920 was Count Guiseppe Dalla Torre, who had published a Catholic paper in Padua, and who was to direct the Vatican paper for the next forty years.

Rome was a useful listening post on events in the Balkans, but Vienna was even better and an important cultural and educational center as well. Foreign correspondents had been in residence there since about 1850, and were more numerous in the period of 1900. From there they kept watch on and sometimes visited Budapest, capital of the Hungarian kingdom within the dual monarchy, Bosnia-Herzegovina, Serbia, Montenegro, Albania, Rumania, Bulgaria, Greece, and Turkey. There also were staff or stringer correspondents in Athens, Constantinople, Bucharest, and Sofia.

Some daily newspapers in this part of Europe were useful supplementary sources of information, with two or three in Vienna represented by their own correspondents in a few other capitals. Of these, the *Neue Freie Presse,* dating from 1864, was regarded as the best of the Austrian papers through 1914 and was the most successful. It was represented in Paris in some of those years by Dr. Theodor Herzl, later one of the founders of Zionism; and also by Dr. Paul Goldmann, who was in Berlin for a long period, as late as 1938, at which time he was dean of the foreign press corps there. The *Neues Wiener Tageblatt,* established in 1865, became the leader in circulation and advertising volume, and had Max Goldschieder in London among its correspondents. The *Arbeiter Zeitung,* a Socialist party paper established in 1889, had importance, as did *Die Reichspost,* started in 1893, a Christian Socialist party voice. The *Wiener Zeitung,* dating from 1780, even then a merger of two earlier papers, was recognized as a government organ.

The leading dailies in Budapest were *Pesti Hirlap,* dating from 1841, first edited by Lajos (Louis) Kossuth, widely known as a Liberal political spokesman, and *Pesti Naplo* (1850), another carefully read paper. In Prague, then also within the Austrian-Hungarian Empire, *Narodni Listý,* established in 1860, was a respected daily.

In Rumania, the leading paper was *Universul* of Bucharest, dating from 1882, and in Bulgaria, it was *Vecherna Poshta* of Sofia from 1900. In Greece, the *Akropolis* of Athens, a daily since 1884, and *Makedonia,* started in Salonika in 1908, were the most important in the first years of the century. One of several new national news agencies established in the years between 1900 and 1914 was the Agence d'Athènes (AA) formed in 1905, with headquarters in Athens. It became a member of the Ring Combination, and was provided with a world news service through Wolff. In Turkey no substantial press development occurred until after World War I.

Spain and Portugal had received considerable news attention from Napoleonic times, particularly through the French and British press. Most coverage was provided by stringers or visiting correspondents, rather than resident staff representatives. After 1870, the Iberian Peninsula was part of the Havas exclusive territory for world news distribution.

The first Spanish news agency was founded in 1865 by Nilo Maria Fabra y Deas and known from 1867 to 1870 as the Agencia Telegrafica Fabra, and then was operated until 1879 as a combined Havas-Reuter service. Under Havas control from 1879, it extended its service to Portugal, operated under other names until 1893, when it took a fourth name, the Agence Espagñol et Internationale, continuing as such until 1919, still Havas-controlled. Fabra retained an interest until his death in 1903.

Newspapers were neither free of government restraint nor highly developed in either country. The first authorized papers in Spain appeared in 1810. They tended to be political, however, and were subject to censorship. This meant that many were short-lived and rarely gained importance or attained prosperity. Those possessing a relative effectiveness in the early years of the century were the *Diario de Barcelona,* surviving from 1792, partly because it was published in Catalonia and escaped most of the censorship; the *A.B.C.,* a conservative, tabloid-format, illustrated paper established in Madrid in 1904, and perhaps the most prosperous; and the *Gaceta de Madrid,* a government paper started as a monthly in 1661, and only becoming a daily in 1890. In Portugal, two Lisbon dailies were most effective, the *Diario de Noticias,* established in 1864, and *O Seculo* founded in 1880.

Switzerland and Northern Europe

Switzerland, Luxembourg, Belgium, Holland, Denmark, Norway, Sweden, Poland, and Finland were countries seldom receiving direct coverage by foreign correspondents. Such coverage usually was provided for the world press through the Ring Combination news exchange or by stringers. Most of those countries possessed high standards of education and literacy, however, with the peoples served by some of the best daily and weekly newspapers in the world, certain of them nationally distributed and carefully read. The language barrier, however, placed

limitation upon the readership of most such newspapers beyond the
frontiers of their own countries.

English, French, German, Italian, and Spanish were widely read, if
not always spoken, throughout Europe and beyond. This circumstance
gave extra-national distribution to some papers of Switzerland, a
tri-lingual country using German, French, and Italian, and some of the
papers of Belgium published in French, but not those in Flemish. For
lack of general familiarity with the languages, newspapers published in
countries in the south using Magyar, Czech, Rumanian, Bulgarian,
Greek, and Portuguese, had limited extra-national readership. The same
was true for northern European newspapers, however well made,
appearing in Dutch, Danish, Norwegian, Swedish, and Finnish, not to
mention Polish and Russian.

For Switzerland, news was exchanged between the Agence Havas and
the Agence Télégraphique Suisse (ATS), formed in 1894, with its
headquarters in Berne, and operating also under German and Italian
versions of that title, the Schweizerische Depeschenagentur (SDA) and
Agenzia Telegrafica Svizzera (ATS), to serve newspapers in the
appropriate sections of the country.

Special merit attached to the *Neue Zürcher Zeitung* (NZZ) of
Zurich, dating from 1780, and gaining a considerable European
distribution; *Der Bund* (1850) of Berne, another respected paper; the
Tages-Anzeiger (1893) of Zurich; the *Gazette de Lausanne* (1798); the
Journal de Genève (1826); the *Tribune de Genève* (1879); the *National
Zeitung* (1842) of Basle; and possibly the two oldest existing Swiss
papers, both established in 1738, the *Feuille d'Avis de Neuchatel* and
the *Feuille d'Avis de Lausanne.*

In Belgium, the Havas and Reuter agencies shared in coverage and
distribution of news from 1870 until 1920, except for the 1914–18 war
interval when the country was under German military occupation.
Newspapers of importance included *Le Soir,* established in 1887, *La
Patriote* (1885), and *La Dernière Heure* (1906), all of Brussels and all
in French. Three papers in Flemish were the *Het Laaste Nieuws,*
established in Brussels in 1886, *De Gazet van Antwerpen* (1891), and
Volksgazet (1894), also of Antwerp. All had merit but were rarely seen
outside the country because of the language.

In Holland, Reuter had established an early position and maintained
it for the coverage and exchange of news. Foreign correspondents also
sometimes reported from Amsterdam and from The Hague—official
capital and the setting for two international peace conferences in 1899
and 1907. From that latter year, the Hague was the home of the Peace

Palace and the International Court of Justice and Permanent Court of Arbitration.

Important dailies included *Algemeen Handelsblad* of Amsterdam, dating from 1828; *De Telegraaf* (1893) of Amsterdam, but tracing its origin to 1619; *Het Vrije Volk* (1900), a Socialist daily of Amsterdam; the highly respected *Nieuw Rotterdamsche Courant* (1843) of Rotterdam, commonly referred to as the NRC; and two dailies published in The Hague, *Het Vaderland* (1868), and the *Haagsche Courant* (1883).

In Denmark, the Ritzau bureau dating from 1866 maintained a news exchange, first with Reuter and then with Wolff. Among leading newspapers one was the *Berlingske Tidende,* established in Copenhagen in 1749 and bearing the name of its founder, Ernst Heinrich Berling. It became a daily in 1841 and was a government paper for some time, until that relationship ended in 1901. The *Politiken,* also of Copenhagen, dated from 1884. Both were morning papers favorably regarded.

In Norway, the Norsk Telegrambyrå, established at Christiania (later Oslo) in 1867 by A. H. E. Fich, a Dane and former Ritzau associate, had Wolff support until 1879, and a news exchange continued beyond that time. Wolff had a similar relationship with Sweden's Svenska Telegrambyrå, also established in 1867.

Among more than 400 Norwegian newspapers in the period of 1900, leaders included the *Aftenposten* (1860), the *Morgenbladet* (1819), the country's first daily, and the *Dagbladet* (1868), all of Christiania, as well as dailies in Bergen, Stavanger, and elsewhere.

In Sweden, leading papers of the period in Stockholm included *Aftonbladet,* established in 1830, the *Dagligt Allehanda,* beginning as a weekly in 1766 but becoming the first daily in 1769, the *Dagens Nyheter* (1864), and the *Svenska Dagbladet* (1884). The *Handels och Sjöfarts Tidning,* established in Göteborg in 1832 as a commercial paper, became a respected general newspaper commonly referred to as the *Göteborg Tidning.* Important also was a Malmo daily started in 1872, the *Sydsvenska Dagbladet-Snällposten.*

Finland, using both the Finnish and Swedish languages, had established a bilingual news agency in 1887, the Suomen Tietotoimisto-Finska Notisbyran (STT-FNB). It exchanged news with the Swedish agency and also with Wolff. The country, in the period of 1900 was a grand duchy within the authority of Czarist Russia and the press had a difficult time. Virtually the only newspapers of importance had been established in Helsinki (Helsingfors, in the Swedish version), and included *Uusi Suomi,* dating from 1847, and the *Helsingin Sanomat,* established in 1889. They placed stress on news reports, rather than on editorial commentary or political subjects. Russia permitted a breath of freedom after 1905 and the press flourished, but renewed controls after 1908 reversed the trend. Not until after Finland declared its independence in 1917 and became a republic in 1919 did matters improve.

Poland, by reason of its historical divisions, had newspapers in German and Russian, as well as in Polish, but few were able to operate freely. The *Gazeta Warszawski,* dating from 1774, was among those of relative importance in the first years of the century, and the Wolff agency provided existing papers with a world news report.

Russia, overspreading a great area of Eastern Europe, nearly twice as great an area in Asia, and touching the Middle East on the south, was the largest country in the world in 1900 and still is, occupying nearly one-seventh of the landmass of the globe. Its first census in 1897 gave it an estimated population of nearly 130 million persons of many races and creeds, speaking a variety of languages and dialects but with limited literacy.

An epoch in the history of Russia began in the sixteenth century with Ivan IV, also known as Ivan the Terrible, the first to take title as czar (or tsar) of all the Russians, with Moscow as his capital. More than a century later, Peter I, or Peter the Great, founded a new capital in 1703 at St. Petersburg (Petrograd after 1914, and now Leningrad) on the Neva River and Gulf of Finland. Referred to as a "window on the west," it marked a beginning of close association with Western Europe. Western advisers were brought to Russia, intermarriages began between the royalty of Russia and Western European countries, and with others enjoying wealth and privilege. Many European Russians established educational, cultural, and personal ties to Western Europe, and made French a second language.

Telegraph and cable lines and railways, as they were extended in Europe, brought Russia into that network. A personal interest also was held by Czar Alexander II in the Danish-owned Great Northern Telegraph Company (Det Store Nordiske Telegraf-Selskab). Its line was completed across Siberia in 1868, linking Vladivostok to St. Petersburg, with an added link in 1871 to Shanghai and other cities in China. From St. Petersburg, the line ran to Copenhagen and so to all of Europe. A Trans-Siberian Railway, the longest in the world, began operating in 1897. Joining Moscow to Vladivostok, with access to the

Pacific, spurs were added later to Port Arthur and elsewhere in the East, as well as to St. Petersburg.

Czar Nicholas II, coming to the throne in 1894, inherited foreign debts, hunger, and unrest among the people, and faced a growing revolutionary sentiment. Russia's defeat in the Russo-Japanese War, along with the "Bloody Sunday" massacre of January 1905 outside the Winter Palace in St. Petersburg, added to public discontent and forced some concessions by the government.

Because of limited educational opportunities in Russia under the czars, illiteracy was widespread. Newspapers were few and small, and freedom of expression, oral or printed, had long been restricted. The first newspaper had appeared in 1703, the *Vedomosti* (Gazette) of Moscow, sponsored by Peter I. By 1910 there were more than 800 papers in the country, but only about fifty were dailies, with about a dozen in St. Petersburg itself. All had been under censorship from the outset. This was relaxed at times, but individual newspapers made little effort to produce original news coverage at home or abroad.

Some slight representation by the Russian press had existed during the Crimean War in 1853–56, during the Russo-Turkish War of 1877–78 when the telegraph system moved reports to Moscow and St. Petersburg, and during the Russo-Japanese War and the Portsmouth Peace Conference following. For the most part, however, the press of the country depended for domestic reports upon official government releases of information, and upon material rewritten from Russian and foreign newspapers. It also depended upon the world service provided by the Wolff agency directly to individual newspapers between about 1870 and 1894, and then by an exchange with the new Russian agencies, Rosta, TTA, or Westnik, established between 1894 and 1904.

None of the Russian papers was outstanding, since the government controls precluded excellence. Those most effective in the first years of the century, however, were *Novoe Vremya* and *Ryech*, both privately published in St. Petersburg and carefully supportive of government policies. *Moscovski Vedomosti* in Moscow was an official government organ. Liberal and even revolutionary papers were published both in Russia and abroad, but inevitably were suppressed in Russia itself, although some were distributed clandestinely.

Direct and increasingly active world press attention to Russia may be said to have started in 1856–57 when William Howard Russell of the London *Times,* fresh from his pioneering activities in coverage of the Crimean War, went to Moscow to report the coronation there of

Alexander II, and remained to write a series of articles about cities and the life of the country. From 1871 to 1873, and in 1877, Januarius Aloysius MacGahan was in Russia, first for the *New York Herald* and later for the London *Daily News.* Donald Mackenzie Wallace was appointed as resident correspondent in St. Petersburg for the *Times* in 1877, and Dr. Emile Joseph Dillon for the *Daily Telegraph* in 1886. From those years both staff and stringer correspondents wrote from Russia for the British, U.S., French, and German press. More numerous after about 1904, but never to approach the numbers in other major capitals, the correspondents worked under difficulties relating to access to sources and to censorship. Beginning with Wallace himself in 1878, several were expelled long before any such action was taken by any other government. They nevertheless helped to open Russia to the world through their coverage.

China and the Asian Press

China had devised the means and methods for printing from movable type, including proper paper and ink, four centuries before Johann Gutenberg introduced modern printing in Europe. China had its early publications and books, but they were intended exclusively for officials and scholars. While something akin to news was made available to that favored group from the first century A.D., the general public in China and Asia saw nothing comparable to a printed newspaper until the early nineteenth century. This was a reversal of the previous situation since by then the peoples of the western world had become familiar with printed newssheets and publications in various forms through two preceding centuries.

Illiteracy, vast distances, and official restrictions in China prevented the development of vernacular newspapers until late in the nineteenth century. The official *Tching-pao* (Capital Report) started as a handwritten monthly in about 756 A.D. Later block-printed, then a type-produced weekly in 1361, it became a daily in 1830 and continued until 1911, the end of the empire. Commonly referred to as the *Peking Gazette,* it thus appeared in one form or another for nearly 1,200 years, the publication of longest existence. But it was neither a newspaper in its content nor in general distribution.

The first real newspaper in China awaited the extension of the British East India Company trading enterprise, when the *Canton Register* was established in that port city in 1827 by James Matheson. By treaty with the Chinese imperial government, Great Britain in 1842 acquired the island of Hong Kong at the mouth of the Canton (Pearl) River and made it a Crown Colony in 1843. In that same year Matheson moved his Canton paper to the new location as the *Hong Kong Register,* and it continued until 1859.

The *China Mail,* also a weekly, was established at Hong Kong in 1845 by Andrew Shortrede. Made a daily in 1876, it sponsored in 1872 a vernacular edition, *Wah Tse Yah Pao,* sometimes Chinese-owned as it proceeded. The first daily in Hong Kong was the *Daily News,* beginning in 1853, with a vernacular edition, *Chung Ngoi San Pao,* added in 1858. Among papers appearing there in the first decade of the 20th century were the *Hong Kong Telegraph,* started in 1891, and the *South China Morning Post,* which gained special prestige after its establishment in 1903.

Meanwhile, Hong Kong became a great port city and trading center, augmented by rights acquired in 1860 on the Kowloon Peninsula standing opposite on the Chinese mainland, and the further leasing in 1898 of adjacent "New Territories." In other treaties with the Chinese government between 1842 and 1860, British citizens gained the right to reside and do business in five "treaty ports"—Canton, Shanghai, Amoy, Foochow, and Ningpo. Similar rights were extended later to Tientsin, Hankow, and Peking, the capital, along with the right to travel in China. Under these provisions, traders, missionaries, educators, and journalists were among those who became residents of China.

The treaties were extended to benefit peoples of other nations, including France, Germany, Japan, and the United States. The extraterritorial rights permitted foreigners to maintain their own courts in China to handle matters involving their own nationals and to supervise their own interests. They became the basis for the establishment of an International Settlement in Shanghai, including a "French Quarter," a French "Concession" in Tientsin, a comparable foreign enclave in Hankow, and a "Legation Quarter" in Peking. In such areas the entire administration was directed by foreigners; the Chinese government had no jurisdiction. These special rights, continued until World War II, gave status and protection to foreign persons living and working in the areas, and in China generally.

It was from 1842 that English-language newspapers began to appear, and then some in other languages. This soon brought the beginning of news reporting by foreign residents of events and situations in China for use by newspapers in England and other countries. Most such reporting was done by stringers, usually editors or staff members of the papers appearing in the Chinese cities. As in Hong Kong, some of those papers also added vernacular editions, published in Cantonese in the southern areas and in Mandarin in the north. The Chinese government placed restrictions on the publication of vernacular papers, but if such a paper was published in a treaty port or an international settlement, registered at a foreign consulate, with a foreigner named as managing director, it was free to appear, "flying the foreign flag," as the phrase went. Newspapers, however owned, if delivered through the Chinese postal system, could be blocked in distribution outside the settlements, but this circumstance did not arise for many years.

The London *Times,* in keeping with its early news enterprise, was the first foreign newspaper to send a resident staff correspondent to China. George Wingrove Cooke was there from 1857–60. He was followed by Thomas William Bowlby, who was captured and killed late in 1860 when covering the T'aiping Rebellion, in which Chinese contested the presence of British and French troops in Peking.

Even earlier reports from China had been provided by a visiting correspondent, Bayard Taylor, who was a staff writer for the *New York Tribune.* He also had been perhaps the first correspondent to visit Japan, having accompanied the United States Navy expedition in 1853 under Commodore Matthew Perry seeking to open trade negotiations there. He went on to China in 1854 and later to India and the Middle East and Africa in a pioneering journalistic venture for the press of the United States.

Telegraphic and cable communications between China and the western world were established between 1871 and 1873, first when a spur from the Danish Great Northern Telegraph company line across Siberia was extended southward to China, and second when the British cable from the English shore to India was extended to China and Japan. British telegraphic communication rights already had been obtained in China in 1870. The British Eastern Extension, Australasia and China Telegraph Company, Ltd., formed in 1896, further established cable ties between London and Hong Kong, Shanghai and Tokyo. That company also joined with the Danish Great Northern company in the same year in an agreement whereby they became joint partners in the China communications field, with the Chinese imperial government brought into the association in 1904. Agreements with U.S. interests and with a joint German-Dutch company gave all foreign companies privileges in China.

The existence of telegraphic and cable communications facilities from 1873 sped a news exchange within some parts of China, as well as Japan, and between those countries and the rest of the world. This ended the great delays previously attendant upon an exchange of information by ship. It also brought Reuter representatives to both countries, with the Reuter world report made available to existing newspapers able to afford the service.

Stringers, if not staff correspondents, provided more reports from China for the press of the western world as foreign activities increased. They were identified with the growing foreign-language press in China. In Shanghai's International Settlement, the *North China Herald* started as a weekly in 1850 added a supplement later, the *Daily Shipping and Commercial News*. This became so important that in 1864 the *Herald* and the supplement were combined to form a new paper, the *North China Daily News*.

The first important vernacular paper in China was established in the Shanghai International Settlement in 1872 by Frederic Major, a British tea merchant. Known as the *Shun Pao* (Shanghai Gazette), a weekly, it became a daily within three months and attained great success, in contrast to most vernacular papers which presented mostly trivia and gossip and published no more than a few hundred copies of any one edition. A second successful vernacular daily, *Sin Wan Pao* (News Gazette), flying the foreign flag, was established in the International Settlement in 1893 by a Chinese merchant. Both papers continued until 1937, each by then claiming 150,000 circulation, whereas the largest of the English-language papers distributed no more than 10,000 copies daily.

A growing interest in China by traders and missionaries of the United States was reflected in the publication of a *Shanghai News-Letter* from 1867–69 by two U.S. citizens, John Thorne, agent in China for Wells, Fargo and Company, and Howard Twombly, engaged in missionary work. In 1869 this became part of a British-owned *Shanghai Evening Courier,* itself later absorbed by the *Shanghai Mercury,* established in 1879, and which became the *Evening Post & Mercury* in a 1931 merger.

Thomas F. Millard, who had arrived in China in 1900 as a correspondent for the *New York Herald,* to report the Boxer Rebellion, remained in the Far East, engaged both in journalism and in business. In 1911 he entered into partnership with Dr. Wu Ting-fang, former Chinese envoy to the United States, to establish the *China Press* as a

Shanghai daily and the first U.S.-owned newspaper in China, apart from missionary publications. Financial support came also from Charles R. Crane, Chicago manufacturer, later to become U.S. minister to China in 1920–21, and from Benjamin W. Fleisher, formerly in business in Philadelphia and also owner since 1909 of the *Japan Advertiser,* then of Yokohama. Fleisher was business manager of the *China Press* until 1913, when he disposed of his interest and moved permanently to Japan. Millard served as editor of the paper until 1917. He then established a weekly periodical in Shanghai, *Millard's Review of the Far East,* again with financial aid from Crane. John B. Powell, recently graduated from the University of Missouri School of Journalism, arrived in Shanghai specifically to edit the magazine, which he purchased in 1919.

Most of the early English-language papers in China stressed matters of business and shipping, but some were political and others were produced by missionary groups. Most were short-lived; those surviving were concerned with general news. One that did so successfully was published in the French Concession in Tientsin, the *Peking & Tientsin Times,* started in 1894. Henry George W. Woodhead, who was editor from 1916–30, also served during those years as a stringer for Reuter and for individual newspapers in Great Britain and the United States.

A British-owned weekly in Tientsin, the *Eastern Times,* established in 1885, was edited until 1891 by Alexander Michie, also a stringer for the *Times.* Affiliated with it was a vernacular paper, established in 1886, the *Shih Pao* (Eastern Times), published by Gustav Detring, German commissioner of the Chinese Imperial Maritime Customs. Both papers were suspended in 1891, but another paper titled *Shih Pao* appeared in Shanghai in 1902.

The most successful vernacular paper in China was established in Tientsin in 1902 by Ying Lien-chih, a convert to Catholicism and a reformer who had left Peking because his activities offended the imperial government. Known as the *Ta Kung Pao* (Impartial Gazette), it had a long life, was widely distributed and carefully read, although it was of such quality that its circulation hardly exceeded 50,000, contrasted to *Shun Pao* and *Sin Wan Pao* of Shanghai claiming three times that figure.

The *Shih Pao* of Shanghai, established in 1902, was published by Ti Ch'h-ch'-ing, a scholar and a man of influence. His paper actually lasted only a few years, but it demonstrated greater news-gathering enterprise than any other in China, regardless of language, and it was the first vernacular paper to give its readers a broad view of the world. Its own correspondents covered the Russo-Japanese War, and it had stringer correspondents in important cities of China, and in London, New York, San Francisco, and other foreign cities. It received newspapers from Tokyo and elsewhere, from which it selected, translated, and published a variety of material. Some other vernacular papers did the same, but not with equal accuracy or selectivity. These high standards, unfortunately, were not maintained, and the *Shih Pao* did not outlast the decade.

In addition to *Millard's Review of the Far East,* a comparable periodical, but a monthly, had been appearing in Shanghai since 1912. Titled the *Far Eastern Review,* it had been established in Manila in 1904 by George Bronson Rae, a correspondent for the *New York Herald* in Cuba from 1895–97, and then a Spanish-American War correspondent there and in the Philippines for the *New York World.* Rae published his journal in Manila until 1912, when he moved to Shanghai. In both places, he also became associated in governmental and private business affairs in an advisory and public relations capacity. In later years, and particularly after 1931, Rae and the *Far Eastern Review* alike were viewed as speaking for the Japanese government, and Rae himself became a representative of that government in Washington, supporting its interests in Manchuria.

Growing British interests in China, supported by the improved communications facilities after 1873, revived the earlier concern of the *Times* for the provision of news coverage from that part of the world. Archibald Ross Colquhoun in 1883 became its first resident correspondent in Peking since Bowlby's death in 1860. He remained there for more than ten years, although also ranging over other parts of Asia. Thomas Cowen was a stringer in Tientsin in the 1890s, and T. H. Whitehead wrote from Hong Kong in the same period. George Nathaniel Curzon, later to become viceroy of India and British secretary of state for foreign affairs, wrote occasionally from China and the Middle East from 1892–94.

Dr. George Ernest Morrison, an Australian, and medically trained, had made an adventurous journey in China, had written of his experiences, and was engaged as correspondent there for the *Times* in 1896, succeeding Colquhoun in Peking. Serving with distinction, and becoming known as "China Morrison," he remained until 1912, at which time he was appointed adviser to the first president of the new Chinese Republic, Yuan Shih-k'ai, until the president's death in 1916. Meanwhile, David Fraser had become correspondent for the *Times* in

Shanghai in 1903, and Colin Malcolm MacDonald followed Morrison in Peking in 1912.

Few other newspapers, not even Reuter, were actively represented in China until the Sino-Japanese War of 1894–95. One exception was the London *Standard*, for which Valentine Chirol, then only twenty-three, was in the country in 1875. By 1894, Chirol was correspondent for the *Times* in Berlin, but he returned to China to report the war of 1894–95. Two *Times* stringers in Tokyo, Captain Frank Brinkley and Colonel Percy Palmer, provided war reports. Frederic Villiers, experienced correspondent for the London *Graphic,* also hastened to China. Three New York newspapers established their first representation in China, with James Creelman arriving for the *New York World,* Stephen Bonsal for the *New York Herald,* and Julian Ralph for the *New York Sun.* Luigi Barzini of the Milan *Corriere della Séra* also provided distinguished reports.

The war centered in Korea and southward to Port Arthur. Action continued for almost eight months on land and at sea. Chinese correspondents did not exist, and no correspondents of any nation were permitted to move with Chinese forces. Japanese correspondents were in the field for virtually the first time. Accompanying that country's forces, they provided most of the reports reaching the peoples of the world. Japan's military command kept foreign correspondents under restraint. They did see some action, however, with Canadian-born James Creelman producing notable reports of the capture of Port Arthur in November 1894. His *New York World* account of the massacre by Japanese troops of much of the civilian population shocked readers of all nations and reflected seriously upon Japan.

As victor in the war, Japan was awarded Formosa (Taiwan) and the adjacent Pesdacores Islands in a peace settlement in April 1895. The independence of Korea was recognized, but with rights granted there to Japan. Japan also gained control of southern Manchuria, including the South Manchurian Railroad, and other rights on the mainland of China.

Even as the Boxer Rebellion of 1899–1901 had stemmed from the Sino-Japanese War, later objection and conflict over the exercise by Japan of peace treaty rights, as raised particularly by Russia in 1903–04, became the issue contested in the Russo-Japanese War of 1904–05. Battle action then was at sea and in Manchuria and, again, at Port Arthur. Although these latter areas formed parts of China, there was no Chinese participation in that war, and the newly established *Shih*

Pao of Shanghai was the only Chinese publication making any effort to provide direct coverage.

There was strong world interest in China during the Sino-Japanese War and the Boxer Rebellion, with direct coverage by the press of several countries. Interest also centered greatly on action in Manchuria during the Russo-Japanese War. From 1905, however, with Japan's victory in the latter war, news emphasis tended to shift to Japan and did not return to China in any major degree until about 1925.

Japan and Press Growth

Japan was not in the mainstream of world affairs until after 1868. Trade relations between Europe and Asia had their effective beginning between 1489 and 1503, when Vasco de Gama established Portuguese trading posts in India, with others at Macao and Nagasaki. The British East India Company made its first approach to India in 1609, later acquired the port of Bombay, previously held by the Portuguese, and controlled all of India by the eighteenth century, with its base at Calcutta. Ferdinand Magellan, a Spanish navigator, discovered the Philippine Islands in 1521. Settlement was begun there in 1565, Manila established in 1572, and trade developed. The Dutch East India Company attained a position in India in that period, but more particularly at what became Batavia (now Djakarta) in Java, and the East Indies in 1603. In 1605 the Dutch were granted a license to trade in Japan. Meanwhile, the Portuguese had brought Jesuit missionaries to the country. Their activities and success in converting many Japanese to Catholicism resulted ultimately in the expulsion of all Portuguese from Japan in 1647. The Dutch remained, however, and continued in a trade relationship, although still limited to Nagasaki. Neither the British nor the Spanish succeeded to obtaining trading rights in the country.

These Pacific areas did not figure in the news for many years. The Dutch were sufficiently established in the East Indies by the eighteenth century, however, to sponsor small newspapers in Batavia, including the *Batavaise Nouvelles* in 1744, and the *Bataviasche Courant* in 1816, which became the *Javasche Courant* in 1828 and continued for more than a century. Spanish-sponsored Manila papers appeared after 1811, and British-sponsored newspapers began to appear in India. The first daily in Manila and the Philippines was *La Esperanza* in 1846, followed by the *Diario de Manila,* an official paper, in 1848, *El Comercio* in

1858, and a paper in Tagalog, the language of the islands, *Putnubay Nang Catolica* in 1890. Emilio Aguinaldo, leader of the native independence movement, established *La Independencia* in 1898, and the Spanish-American War of that year brought the first English-language daily, the *Manila Times,* under U.S. sponsorship.

In Japan, the Dutch trade relationship produced a request from the Japanese government late in the seventeenth century that the Dutch prepare an annual report on events in the rest of the world for the information of the emperor and officials. This continued for more than a century, and in 1861 the report became more elaborate and was made a printed monthly publication in 1862. It became known as the *Batavia Shimbun* (Batavia Newspaper) because the content was translated from the Batavia *Javasche Courant* and from other newspapers reaching Batavia and forwarded to Nagasaki, where the paper was prepared.

From 1862 to 1864 the *Batavia Shimbun* appeared each month, produced by Hikozo Hamada, sometimes credited with having introduced modern journalism to Japan. A sailor in his youth, he had been shipwrecked off the coast of Formosa in 1850, was picked out of the water by an American vessel bound from China to San Francisco, and had no choice but to make the voyage. Arriving in California, then only just admitted as the thirty-first state in the union and in the midst of the gold rush, Hamada found friends, learned English, received some education, acquired the name "Joseph Hikozo," or "Joseph Heco," and was naturalized as a citizen of the United States.

In 1853 Hamada returned to Japan with Commodore Perry's naval squadron, no doubt as an interpreter. Having observed the press in the United States and having become bilingual, he remained in Japan and was drawn into the preparation of the *Batavia Shimbun* in that 1862–64 period. In March 1864, with two friends, Ginko Kishida and Senzo Homma, he also established a paper intended for general distribution, the first of its sort in Japan. Known as the *Shimbunshi* (News), it consisted largely of material translated from foreign newspapers and publications. After the tenth issue, however, it was suppressed by the government. Hamada then soon returned to the United States, while Kishida went to China, both taking advantage of changes that permitted Japanese to travel abroad, and with all restrictions on such travel ending in 1868.

The visit of Commodore Perry to Japan in 1853, and his return in 1854 with a larger naval squadron, brought a beginning of reforms in Japan that advanced at a great pace after 1868. That was the first year of the Meiji era, the name signifying the year, meaning "Enlightened

Government," and selected to apply to the reign of a new emperor, Mutsuhito, who had succeeded to the throne in 1867. Then only fourteen years old, his reign continued for forty-five years, until 1912. The capital had been moved in 1603 from Kyoto to Yedo. In 1868, Yedo was renamed Tokyo (Eastern Capital).

From that time, Japan began to emerge from its isolation. Trade and diplomatic relations were opened with all nations. Japanese emissaries familiarized themselves with other countries, and foreigners were freely admitted to Japan. Domestic, industrial, and business enterprises were established and grew strong, supported by a system of education that brought a high level of literacy to the people within a generation. This opened the way for a growth of newspapers and other publications. An ordinance of June 1868 established laws to govern the press, with amendments added in 1873 and subsequent years. A telegraphic system was extended, and Japan was brought into communication with the rest of the world by cable in 1873, with a news exchange following.

The first modern style vernacular newspapers of general circulation appeared in Japan in 1872. There were three, all in Tokyo. The first was *Nissin Shinji-shi* (Japan-China News). It was established by F. da Rosa, possibly of Portuguese heritage, with John Reddie Black, an experienced British newsman, as editor. Stressing current news and well made, it might have continued successfully had not an 1874 amendment to the 1868 press law specified that foreigners could not conduct vernacular newspapers. Even though da Rosa had government support originally, he was obliged to suspend the paper.

The second paper was *Hochi Shimbun* (News), originally known as *Yubin Hochi* (Postal News). Using a relatively simple system of ideographs, it was designed for easy reading and became a popular newspaper, successful under changing ownerships.

The third paper became the most important. This was *Nichi-Nichi* (Today-Today, or Day to Day), started as a Tokyo daily in February 1872 by Genichiro Fukuchi, an educator. It was edited by Ginko Kishida, a former associate of Hamada, returned from China.

Like most successful Japanese newspapers to follow, *Nichi-Nichi* had support from at least one prominent public official using the paper to advance his own interests, and also from a major business group. It presented current news when that was still a novelty in Japan, and it also was the first to publish reports received by mail from its own representatives outside the country.

Prince Tomomi Iwakura went on a mission to the United States and Europe in 1871–73 with about fifty persons in his party "to study the institutions of civilized nations" and also to explain conditions in Japan with a view to the establishment of formal diplomatic relations with other countries. Whether from a correspondent or a stringer, at least one report was published in *Nichi-Nichi* describing the mission's presence in Salt Lake City. In 1874, when Japanese forces landed in Formosa following the murder there of a Japanese seaman whose vessel had been wrecked off the shore of the island, Kishida accompanied the expedition and wrote reports. The paper was represented in the field again during the Sino-Japanese War of 1894–95, one result of which was to be the formal ceding of Formosa to Japan by China; and it was represented again during the Russo-Japanese War and at the Portsmouth Peace Conference following.

A fourth Tokyo daily, the *Yomiuri* (The Call, or Town Crier) was established in 1874. It was written in simple style, comparable to the *Hochi Shimbun,* and also gained a popular following.

Osaka became the second city in Japan to be served by a newspaper. The *Osaka Nippo* (Osaka Daily Report) was established in 1876. It was purchased in 1888 by Hikoichi Motoyama, an industrial leader, and the name was changed to the *Mainichi Shimbun* (Every-day Newspaper, or Daily Newspaper). By 1892 it had staff correspondents in Europe and Australia, and its own direct Tokyo-Osaka leased wire by 1898. In 1910 the *Mainichi Shimbun* bought the Tokyo *Nichi-Nichi.* The papers continued separately, but with their operations integrated. Editions of the *Mainichi* were established also in Nagoya and at Moji, on the southern island of Kyushu.

Another daily to become equally important and successful was *Asahi* (Rising Sun), established at Osaka in January 1879 by Ryuhei Murayama, a journalist of great skill and professionalism. An edition was added in Tokyo in 1888, and others later at Nagoya and Kokura. The *Asahi* gained prompt reader-acceptance and showed high enterprise, with more correspondents in foreign capitals providing excellent reports than any other Japanese newspaper. It also arranged to use the reports of the London *Times.*

Two business dailies destined to become important were established in 1876 in Tokyo. One, the *Chugai Shogyo* (Journal of Commerce), was sponsored by the Mitsui industrial group. The other was the *Nippon Keizai Shimbun* (Japan Economic Newspaper).

Another paper of quality, the *Jiji Shimbun* (Current Affairs Newspaper) was established in Tokyo in 1882. It was the first to appear seven days a week, the first to use modern rotary presses, and the first to engage women as staff members. It published substantial articles on foreign affairs and was more balanced than most others in its news and references concerning the western nations of the world. Two papers founded soon after in Tokyo were the *Miyako Shimbun* (Capital Newspaper) in 1884 and the *Kokumin* (The Nation) in 1890.

All of these newspapers survived in the first decade of the twentieth century and beyond. Directed to what already had become the most literate public in Asia, to a public whose interest was spurred by events, including the wars of 1894–95 and 1904–05 in which Japan was involved, and distributed nationally, either directly or through regional editions, most of the papers gained substantial circulations. With the development of advertising nationally, they were commercial and financial successes enabling them to provide good news services, including the full Reuter world report.

A Reuter office had been established at Yokohama when the first cable reached Japan's shore in 1873, and branch offices soon existed in Nagasaki and Tokyo. The cost of the cable service was high for the newly established Tokyo newspapers at that time, but an alternative mail service was made available, and then an omnibus service offering an economy. The full cable service was reaching most of the dailies by 1900, however, and Reuter established Henry Satoh as its first permanent resident agent in Tokyo in 1907. He was followed by Andrew M. Pooley from 1911 to 1914, by J. Russell Kennedy until 1925, and then by Malcolm Duncan Kennedy. Some of the papers also developed their own foreign services.

The formation of domestic news agencies to serve the Japanese press, beginning in 1886, has been described, including those functioning after 1900, notably the Nippon Dempo Tsushin-sha (Dentsu) (Japanese Telegraph Agency) established in 1901, and Kokusai Tsushin-sha (International News Agency) established in 1914. The latter was reorganized in 1926 as Nippon Shimbun Rengo-sha (Rengo) (Associated Press of Japan), and again reorganized in 1936 as Domei Tsushin-sha (Domei) (Allied News Agency) in a merger with the Dentsu agency.

The rapid increase in foreign trade and general relationship with other countries of the world that began with the introduction of the Meiji era in 1868 brought many foreign residents to Japan. As it had in China, this resulted in the publication of foreign-language newspapers.

The first concentration of such residents was in Nagasaki, the port so long used by the Portuguese and Dutch and directly across the China Sea from Shanghai. There an English-language *Shipping News and Advertiser* established in 1861 was moved to the port of Yokohama, serving Tokyo, and was renamed the *Japan Herald*. Others appeared in

Osaka, Kobe, and Tokyo itself. Most were in English, but others were in Portuguese and German. Most were small and often short-lived, and importance and longevity came later. Again, as in China, the editors and staff members of these papers became stringer correspondents for newspapers in London and New York, and for news agencies.

The *Tokyo Times* was established in 1877 and edited for the next three years by Edward Howard House. A native of Boston and part-owner in 1854 of the *Boston Courier* (1824–60), House also worked for the *New York Tribune* and the *New York Times* before going to Japan in 1870. He also had collaborated with Dion Boucicault in play writing and production in New York. In his first years in Japan he taught English at the University of Tokyo. As editor of the *Tokyo Times* and later, he wrote as a stringer for the *New York Herald* and the *New York World*. Among his other talents, he was a musician, and in his later years prepared and conducted the first orchestral concerts heard in Japan and also directed the Imperial Court Orchestra. He received high recognition from the government prior to his death in 1901 at sixty-five.

The *Japan Mail* was established in Yokohama in 1881 by Captain Frank Brinkley. Irish-born, he had gone to Japan as an officer in a detachment of guards for the new British legation in Tokyo. He made himself an authority on Japan, married a Japanese woman in 1878, and became an adviser both to the Ministry of Foreign Affairs and to the Nippon Yusen Kaisha (NYK) steamship line. In establishing the *Japan Mail,* he received government financial aid, but insisted that his editorial independence was in no way compromised. His paper was regarded, nevertheless, as a consistent defender and advocate of all things and policies relating to Japan. While editing the paper, he also was a stringer for the London *Times* from 1892 until his death in 1912. Honored by the Japanese government, he ranked among the 300 "highest personages" in the country.

The *Japan Advertiser,* started by a U.S. citizen and printer as an advertising bulletin in Yokohama about 1890, was to become the most important foreign-language paper in the country. Some news was added to the bulletin in 1891 and it developed with a number of changes of ownership until 1907. In that year E. J. Harrison became its editor and publisher. In Japan since 1897, he had worked for the *Japan Herald,* the *Japan Chronicle,* and the *Japan Times,* three other English-language papers, the latter unrelated to the earlier *Tokyo Times.* He also had served as a correspondent for the London *Daily Mail* during the Russo-Japanese War.

In 1907 Benjamin W. Fleisher arrived in Japan and became familiar with the *Japan Advertiser*. In 1909 he bought the paper from Harrison, who nevertheless continued with it until 1913, while also acting as correspondent in Japan for the *Daily Mail* and for the *New York Herald*. Fleisher was interested in the press situation in Shanghai as well as in Japan, and he arranged for J. Russell Kennedy, Tokyo correspondent for the Associated Press since 1907, to act as the owner-of-record of the *Advertiser* from 1909 to 1913. In that interim, Fleisher gave some financial support to Thomas F. Millard and Dr. Wu Ting-fang in the establishment in Shanghai in 1911 of the *China Press*. He remained as business manager of that publication until 1913, then disposed of his interest and returned to Tokyo to take direct charge of the *Advertiser*. Kennedy, whose relation to the paper had been minimal, likewise ended his relationship with the Associated Press in 1914 to become director of the new Japanese Kokusai news agency and to assume responsibility at the same time as Reuter correspondent in Tokyo.

Fleisher moved the *Japan Advertiser* from Yokohama to Tokyo in 1913, where it continued under his direction as publisher until 1940. Editors of the paper in the first two years included Cecil Gray, formerly of the London *Standard,* who served briefly, and Charles R. Hargroves, formerly a correspondent in Washington for the *Times,* and who was a stringer for that paper in Tokyo. He was succeeded in 1914 by Hugh Byas, British-born and with London news experience. Except for an interval in 1917–18 and another in 1922–26, when he represented the *Advertiser* in London, Byas edited the paper until 1930, serving through most of the years also as correspondent in Tokyo for the *Times* and for the *New York Times*.

The *Advertiser* became a training ground for many who were to become correspondents in Japan and China. The *Advertiser* also was in competition with two other English-language papers mentioned. One was the *Japan Chronicle* of Kobe, edited by A. Morgan Young also serving as a stringer for the *Manchester Guardian,* the *Baltimore Sun,* and papers in Australia. The other was the *Japan Times* of Tokyo, established in 1897 as the third paper to bear that name. It was founded by Motosada Zumoto, who edited it in 1904 and again in 1911–14. The paper was in fact a government organ, and Zumoto was himself identified with the government.

Educated at Yale, Zumoto had been a press attaché in the Japanese Ministry of Foreign Affairs during the Russo-Japanese War. He then became private secretary to Prince Ito, resident-general in Korea, and there he established the *Seoul Daily Press* in 1906. Next, he founded an Oriental Information Bureau in New York, the announced purpose of which was to provide "intelligent information to the American people with regard to Far Eastern Affairs." In 1916 in Tokyo, he established the *Herald of Asia,* an English-language weekly, and he served as a member of the Diet, the Japanese parliamentary body.

Significant as relating to the work of foreign reporters in Japan, Zumoto formed an International Press Association in Tokyo in 1909. It had government support and correspondents were required to become members to gain recognition as properly accredited. Only then would a correspondent, whether staff or stringer, be received in government offices and, most important, be permitted to file reports for transmission at press rates and on a receiver-to-pay basis.

The announced purpose of the International Press Association was to protect the public "from unscrupulous newspapermen who misrepresent Japan" and "to improve the standards of correspondence from Japan to outside journals." Bearing no comparison to those *bona fide* correspondents' associations then existing in London, Paris, and Berlin, it was in fact a censorship and propaganda agency in keeping with some of Zumoto's other activities. Backed by the government, it was intended to shape and control reports written by western correspondents in Japan. Except for the accreditation provision and that relating to the filing of dispatches, there would have been no reason for any correspondent to become a member. As it was, they had no option. Zumoto himself retained the presidency of the association for several years and, as such, attended international conferences of journalists as its representative.

Until 1894 most news reaching the rest of the world from Japan had come through such stringers as House for the *New York Herald* and *New York World,* Brinkley for the *Times,* and the small Reuter offices existing since 1873. The Sino-Japanese War of 1894–95 brought increased coverage, and by 1898 there were enough stringers and staff representatives for the western press in Japan, chiefly in Tokyo, to warrant the establishment of an International Association of Journalists—not to be confused with Zumoto's International Press Association of 1909. The backbone of its membership came from the foreign-language newspapers.

More correspondents appeared after 1900, including some who had reported from the Philippines and from China during the Boxer Rebellion. Among them were Martin Egan, who became the first representative for the Associated Press in Japan, and Robert M. Collins, his assistant. Others were Millard for the *New York Herald,* who soon went to China, and John T. Swift for the *New York Sun* and Laffan News Bureau, who arrived in 1904.

Japan's participation in the Boxer relief expedition in 1900, along with the signature of an Anglo-Japanese Alliance of 1902, gave the country new prestige in the West, repairing the bad impression left by the Port Arthur massacre during the Sino-Japanese War. Its victory in the Russo-Japanese War did even more to advance direct news coverage by the world press. Some correspondents who had reported that war remained and others arrived, including Satoh for Reuter, J. Russell Kennedy for the AP, and Gray for the *Standard*.

At the same time, Japanese government officials and business and industrial leaders developed a concern for the nation's image throughout the world. Foreigners in Japan were placed under police surveillance, and not least foreign journalists. The formation in 1909 of Zumoto's International Press Association was evidence of the desire to control correspondents. The arrest of Andrew Pooley, Reuter correspondent, in January 1914 was additional evidence, and the formation of the Kokusai agency was a further result of the new spirit in the country.

The Japanese press itself was subjected to progressively more serious restraint. Under the press law of 1868 as amended, editors could be arrested, and the distribution and sale of any issue of a publication could be halted by any one of four ministries of the government. Any printed matter could be seized and destroyed. Supervision and authority over the press rested with the director of the Tokyo Metropolitan Police Board, operating within the authority of the Home Ministry, and with local police authorities throughout the country.

A revised Constitution of 1890 provided for a free press "within the limits of the law." Those limits were defined by imperial ordinances, and all freedom could be nullified, as it was during the Sino-Japanese War and the Russo-Japanese War. The government also began the practice of calling "voluntary" conferences of newspaper editors at the home, foreign, and war ministries and others to discuss what news should appear, and how it should be treated. Attending such conferences, editors sometimes gained their own first knowledge of certain matters when they were instructed not to mention them. Or they might be able to confirm what previously had been only a vague report or rumor, yet might then also be instructed to remain silent on the subject.

The Tokyo Metropolitan Police Board issued instructions to editors, also conveyed through police prefectures throughout the country. Any procurator of a district court might issue such instructions. A publication might be suspended for a specified period because a local police or judicial official judged something in its pages to be "prejudicial to the peace of society," to "public morality," or as "endangering foreign relations."

Generally speaking, a newspaper was not permitted to engage in editorial discussion of current political subjects unless it had posted a bond in advance to insure payment of any fine that might be assessed for offenses that remained open to subjective interpretation by police officials. A newspaper judged guilty might be suppressed, with printed issues confiscated; it might be suspended for a day or for weeks; it might be fined or its editor jailed. Suspensions and confiscation could be costly, both in lost revenue from circulation and advertising, and also in wasted newsprint, most of which had to be imported. In practice, however, an order for confiscation of an edition frequently came only after distribution had been completed. The letter of the law was satisfied by surrendering to the police a token bundle of papers, with an assurance that no more of that edition would be printed.

Faced with the prospect of a fine or jail sentence, Japanese editors chose to remain anonymous. From 1890, the editor-of-record for a Japanese newspaper was not necessarily or even probably the real editor. By convention and as an accepted practice, a paper had a "dummy editor" or so-called "jail editor" who would go to prison if the law required. Although a member of the newspaper organization, he had few if any real duties, and was paid very little. Also, if a paper was fined even a moderate amount, it might let the "jail editor" serve a sentence, rather than pay the fine, assuming a choice existed, and assuming the directors of the paper objected to paying the fine. Japanese publishers and editors understandably found these regulations and procedures onerous, and attempts were made periodically to have them modified, but without success.

It was in part to exercise further control over the manner in which foreign reports were presented to the readers of Japanese newspapers, and at the same time to control what the people of the world were to be told about Japan in their own newspapers, that action was taken to form the Kokusai Tsushin-sha news agency in 1914. The officials of government and leaders of industry sponsoring the agency were reasonably satisfied with the results, but a desire for an even more effective news exchange led to the 1926 reorganization by which Kokusai was transformed into the Nippon Shimbun Rengo-sha agency, and led to the merger of Rengo and Dentsu that resulted in the formation of Domei in 1936.

That portion of the Western Hemisphere below the thirtieth parallel north latitude, which was explored and settled primarily by Spain and Portugal during and after the sixteenth century, became known as Latin America because the Romance languages were used by the new masters of the vast area. France, Great Britain, the Netherlands, and Denmark gained some territorial positions, but the ties and traditions related almost exclusively to the two countries of the Iberian Peninsula. As in North America, immigration to the areas brought people from Italy, Germany, Africa, and even from Japan, and in smaller numbers from other countries.

Some of the same changes and sentiments arising in North America as the decades passed were felt in Latin America. The revolution by which the British colonies in North America gained independence in the late eighteenth century, with the French Revolution following, fed growing discontent with administrative policies imposed from Madrid and Lisbon. The involvement of Spain and Portugal in the Napoleonic campaigns in Europe, and the preoccupation of those countries with domestic problems brought further stirrings. There had been some sentiment for independence in parts of South America as early as 1721, insurrections also had occurred, but outright wars began in 1806. These efforts grew and by 1825 virtually all of Central and South America was free of Spanish domination, with new nations taking form. The last remnant of Portuguese control ended in Brazil in 1889, and the last of Spanish rule ended in Cuba and Puerto Rico in 1898.

As in the United States and Canada, the press in Latin America followed patterns chiefly borrowed from Europe—Madrid, Lisbon, Paris, and London. The first printing press had been set up in Mexico City early in 1535, more than a century before the first had appeared in Massachusetts Bay Colony in 1639. Another was set up at Lima, Peru, in 1584 or 1586, when that city was a center for Spain's colonial administration in the new world. Except for a single issue of a newssheet in Mexico City in 1541 and a single issue in Boston in 1690, however, no regular publication of news began in the Western Hemisphere until 1704 in Boston and 1722 in Mexico City.

Much as in North America, the important development of newspapers, including dailies, began in Latin America after 1800. Until independence was gained, and often later, the press there was subject to restraint and censorship. Among older newspapers surviving in 1910 few had appeared for more than fifty years. Older papers in Brazil included the *Diario de Pernambuco* of Recifé, which had been established in 1825. Three morning dailies in Rio de Janeiro, were the *Jornal do Comercio* (1827), the *Jornal do Brazil* (1891), the *Correio da Manhã* (1901), and an afternoon paper, *A Noticia* (1894). In São Paulo, there was the morning *O Estado de São Paulo,* which began in 1875, and two afternoon papers, the *Diario Popular* (1884), and *A Gazeta* (1906).

In Argentina, the important dailies were *La Prensa* (1869) and *La Nación* (1870), both appearing in the morning in Buenos Aires, and regarded as the leading newspapers of Latin America. An afternoon paper, *La Razón,* had been established there in 1905. There was a German-language *Deutsche La Plata Zeitung* (1868), and a British-directed English-language *Buenos Aires Herald* (1876). Substantial dailies also were published in other cities of the country, among them *La Capital* (1867) in Rosario, *Los Andes* (1882) in Mendoza, and *El Dia* (1884) in la Plata.

In Chile, there appeared *El Mercurio,* with editions at Valparaiso from 1827 and at Santiago from 1900, and the afternoon *Las Ultimas Noticias* at Santiago from 1902. Competing papers were *La Unión* of Valparaiso (1885), and *El Diario Ilustrado* of Santiago (1902). Colombia had *El Espectador,* established at Medellin in 1888 but later moved to Bogotá, and *El Tiempo,* founded there in 1911, which became an important daily. Peru had *El Comercio* (1839) at Lima, and *La Prensa* (1903). Uruguay had *La Tribuna* (1879) and *El Dia* (1886), both morning papers at Montevideo. Ecuador had *El Comercio* (1906) at Quito, and Venezuela had *El Universal* (1909) at Caracas. British Guiana had the *Evening Post & Sunday Argosy* (1880) and the *Chronicle* (1881), both at Georgetown. Cuba had the *Diario de la Marina* (1832) and *El Mundo* (1901), both of Havana.

Mexico remained under the dictatorial government of Porfirio Diaz from 1876 until 1911. Such publications as existed lacked freedom and substance. The best appeared in Mexico City and included *El Imparcial* (1896), a government-subsidized morning paper, and the afternoon *El Mundo* soon to follow, but soon retitled as *El Heraldo;* both were published by Rafael Reyes Spíndola. Another in the capital was *El Siglo II,* established in 1898 by Plutarco Elías Calles, who later became president of the country. Others were *El Pais* and *El Diario,* and the English-language *Mexican Herald.*

Except for Mexico, Cuba, and the West Indies, there were few direct relations for news purposes between Latin America and North America even as late as 1910. There was routine diplomatic association, limited commercial and financial relations, and contacts bearing upon the

Pan-American Union formed in 1901. Otherwise, matters of communication and transportation were conducted largely on a triangular course by way of Europe. This only began to change during World War I.

Such national, and even hemispheric information as the Latin American press could provide to its readers prior to 1860, and for some time later, was gathered in the local communities, and perhaps regionally, plus some received by telegraph or rewritten from other newspapers received belatedly by mail. The French Agence Havas had undertaken coverage of news in South America in 1860, originally from Rio de Janeiro, and also sought to provide world news reports to the press on that continent, using telegraph lines as they were extended. Although cable communication had been established across the North Atlantic in 1866, no cable was to cross the South Atlantic until 1874.

When the Havas agency joined with Reuter and Wolff in 1870 to begin an exchange of news through what became the Ring Combination, with the assignment of exclusive territories for the distribution of a world report, the Agence Havas was given exclusive rights in South America, where it already had established a position. As it happened, however, the Franco-Prussian War of 1870–71 obstructed the efforts of Havas to extend its service. Indeed, there was some possibility that the agency itself might collapse. In the circumstances, the Reuter agency came to its support, and the two worked in close collaboration in South America until 1876 and, in some respects, until 1890. In addition, Reuter joined Havas in the earlier relationship it had had with the Fabra agency in Spain, which was operated as Reuter-Havas from 1870 to 1879.

News exchange was advanced when the first South Atlantic cable was completed in 1874 by the British-owned Western Telegraph Company. The cable ran from British shores to Recifé, Brazil, by way of Portugal, the west African coast, Madeira, and the Cape Verde Islands. It was soon extended southward from Recifé to Rio de Janeiro and to São Paulo, Montevideo, and Buenos Aires. Other companies provided telegraphic service overland, across the Andes, between Buenos Aires and Santiago, thus including the west coast of South America. The cable later was extended northward from Recifé to the West Indies and ultimately to Halifax, Nova Scotia.

With the cable and the Andes telegraph lines forming a juncture in Buenos Aires, the main bureau in South America for the Havas-Reuter service was moved there from Rio de Janeiro about 1882, and Buenos Aires became a news communications center for all of South America, as Mexico City was to become such a center for Central America. A Havas agent represented both agencies in Buenos Aires and a Reuter agent, established at Valparaiso, Chile, represented both agencies on the west coast. They were occupied with gathering news of South America, and with the distribution there of a jointly-sponsored world service under the name Agencia Telegrafica Reuter-Havas. In 1876, after the Havas crisis was past, this became simply Agencia Havas.

When the cable began operation in 1874, the Havas agency established its first bureau in London. A Havas agent there prepared reports of British news derived from the full Reuter and Press Association services to be combined with Havas reports from its own general service. A Bureau Amsud (South American bureau) became a part of the London operation for the receipt and dispatch of news in the South American service. This designation was dropped in 1876, but the Havas London bureau continued, and so did the shared relationship of the two agencies in South America. In 1882 Havas and Reuter correspondents were added in Montevideo and other capitals, with the news service strengthened accordingly. This relationship continued until 1890, when new agreements left Havas in exclusive control of world news distribution in South America. It also was largely dominant in Central America, although Reuter continued to share that territory for distribution of its news and commercial services.

Cables from points in the United States reached Cuba, Puerto Rico, Jamaica, Trinidad, and Colombia in 1870, and others were to follow. A French cable across the North Atlantic in 1879 had spurs to the West Indies and Brazil. A German cable came later, running from Emden to Buenos Aires by way of the Azores, with spurs from those islands to New York and to Liberia on the African coast. An Italian cable to Buenos Aires came still later. A so-called "back-door cable" with telegraphic connections was extended between 1881 and 1891 to give the United States a communication link by way of Mexico and Central America to the west coast of South America and over the Andes to the east coast.

It was not until 1900 that the first independent news agency was established in South America. This was the Agencia Noticiosa Saporiti (ANS) at Buenos Aires. It was a family-owned commercial service intended for provincial papers in Argentina. Always with a very limited report, it still exists. No other agency of any scope was attempted in Latin America for many years. Some newspapers established their own coverage of the news, regionally, nationally, and even abroad. This was done most notably by *La Prensa* and *La Nación* of Buenos Aires, with reports made available to other newspapers in noncompetitive areas. Until about 1916, that was the nearest thing to any service supplementing the world report provided by the Havas agency.

Speaking generally, the newspapers of Latin America gave as much space or more to international news reports as to the news of events in their own countries. There were political papers, and papers which gave a certain partisan treatment to political matters. But the major emphasis was on news. There were not so many papers but some of them at least were effective advertising media and, for that reason, as large in number of pages as many dailies in the United States and Great Britain. The stress on international news, provided through Havas, had a certain safety factor because it did not bring a newspaper into controversy with the government of its country through publication of local news, possibly of a sensitive political nature. Further, it was justified because the domestic economy of almost any Latin American country was affected by events and conditions elsewhere in the world.

The literate public, a minority of the total population, was nevertheless greatly concentrated in the larger cities. Such readers were personally concerned, directly or indirectly, with matters that might affect the world markets for coffee, beef, sugar, nitrates, cotton, oil, copper, and other products whose export and current prices determined their own income and what they themselves might be able to import. Foreign capital investment also figured in the development of most countries, and continued to be important, relating to railroads, mines, plantations, orchards, packing, petroleum, communication, highway construction, building, retailing, and commercial enterprises. Historical and cultural ties with European countries, along with the presence of large first- and second-generation immigrant groups, assured a further continuing interest in world news.

Newspapers made to satisfy such interests tended to be serious, *la prensa seria,* as they were called, and perhaps dull by some standards, but they included an unusual number of high quality ones. Contrary to the situation in most other parts of the world, many of these quality papers were circulation leaders in their own countries.

No newspaper better exemplified this standard than *La Prensa* of Buenos Aires. Although following certain practices viewed by some as peculiar, and at times criticized as reflecting the special interests of families of wealth and privilege, estimated at about 2,000 in number and as "owning" Argentina, *La Prensa* nevertheless became a symbol of the best in journalism, a model for all serious papers in Latin America. It was accepted by those familiar with it as one of the great newspapers of the world, widely recognized for its merits. It also was one of the most successful as a business enterprise. From the time of its beginning in 1869, but particularly in the years from about 1900 to 1930, its story was one of great accomplishments.

Established as a morning paper by Dr. José Clemente Paz, *La Prensa* demonstrated enterprise from the outset. It spared no expense to get the news. It arranged for stringer correspondents in cities and towns throughout Argentina, eventually numbering about 2,000, with branch offices in the larger cities. It received the Havas world service. It did not at first develop an extensive foreign service of its own, but it did send staff members to other countries in South America and Europe, from time to time, to write special reports. It commissioned special articles by government leaders and by authorities in many fields of knowledge elsewhere in the world. From the time of World War I, it established resident correspondents in Paris and London, and arranged for stringers in such capitals as Rome, Berlin, Madrid, Rio de Janeiro, Montevideo, Santiago, and New York. They had instructions to "Argentinize" the news, that is, to write it to make clear its importance to readers in Argentina.

Even before the cable existed, *La Prensa* was the first paper in Latin America to obtain and publish a report of the critical Battle of Sedan in 1870 during the Franco-Prussian War. It had the first report published anywhere of the Portsmouth Peace Conference settlement in 1905 following the Russo-Japanese War, with the details obtained and cabled by Camillo Cianfarra, an Italian journalist representing the paper at the conference. Special efforts were exerted to obtain information, almost regardless of expense, even on subjects of minor importance, if likely to be of particular interest to some readers.

As the years passed, *La Prensa* became a paper of record and used the telegraph and cable extensively to obtain full texts of important speeches and documents. It prided itself upon its accuracy.[2] Its standards of news were such that, unlike papers in most countries, *La Prensa* published no reports of lawsuits involving any sort of personal accusations. It printed only court verdicts, without coverage of prior details, and then with emphasis on the juridical aspects of the cases. Its treatment of crime news was equally restrained. Divorce actions were ignored; suicides were

2   Perhaps apocryphal but illustrative is a story that on one occasion *La Prensa* did publish an erroneous report of the death of a Spanish baritone. Later, as the account goes, the singer appeared in a Buenos Aires concert, but *La Prensa* refused to acknowledge his presence, declining to publish an advertisement announcing his appearance and making no mention of the concert.

rarely reported, such reports being viewed as "prejudicial to society." If the person committing suicide were of such importance as to require some mention, death was reported as having come "in an unexpected manner." The private life of an individual, whatever his official position or social status, was not referred to because it would constitute an invasion of privacy, and "serve no useful purpose." There was no such thing as society news.

Apart from its large budget of general news, *La Prensa* presented an editorial page of high order. It held itself above political partisanship and, whatever position it took on controversial subjects, demonstrated fact and reason determined its policy. As a further aid to public understanding, it added a special midweek section and also a Sunday section presenting substantial articles by world authorities on current economic, social, and political subjects, and on science, art, literature, and history. For some time, *La Prensa* also sent a weekly eight-page feature supplement (El Suplemento Semanel) to 175 smaller newspapers in Argentina for inclusion with their own Sunday or weekend editions as a means of extending more widely the same variety of understanding. When rotogravure photo reproduction of a superior variety became technically possible about 1914, a "roto" section was added to the Sunday edition of *La Prensa*.

Standards governing the quality of advertising and the conditions for its acceptance were as strict as those relating to the paper's news and editorial content. No advertising solicitors were employed; all advertising was submitted voluntarily for insertion. Then every such advertisement was examined by a special control section . If the control section disapproved of a product, as it did of breakfast cereals and chewing gum, for example, advertising for that product was rejected. Claims or promises considered extreme would bring rejection, as would uses of type or illustration judged tasteless. Any person wishing to insert a classified advertisement was required to identify himself, as well as to meet certain standards. These precautions were taken to guard readers against being misled or defrauded.

Advertising from the Argentine government or from official agencies or institutions usually was rejected lest its publication seem to compromise the paper's independence or impartiality. It was accepted only when it was judged to contain information in the public interest. Even then it had to be paid for in cash, since no commercial credit was granted to the government or to public offices. No advertising was accepted from public officials or administrative offices if it contained elements of opinion, lest readers suppose that the paper necessarily agreed with those opinions. Advertising for political parties and candidates also was rejected on the ground that if the content of such advertising were of news-worthy importance it would be published as news, rather than as paid advertising, and also that acceptance of such advertising might seem to be favoring one party or candidate over another and so compromise the political impartiality of the paper.

La Prensa was particular about its circulation as well. The paper was readily available through street sales and in shops. Subscriptions were equally available, but only to individuals for home delivery. Bulk subscriptions from government departments or offices were not accepted lest they be interpreted as a form of government subsidy to the paper. Delivery of the paper to government officials had to be to their homes, rather than to their offices.

An absolute separation was maintained between the news-editorial function of *La Prensa* and its advertising, circulation, and business functions. Its standards of production and mechanical equipment were as high as for the other departments. The paper had its headquarters in a large and handsome building on the Avenida de Mayo, in the heart of Buenos Aires, and had two supplementary printing plants elsewhere in the city. It also had a branch in La Plata, capital of Buenos Aires province, as well as offices in other cities. Staff members enjoyed special amenities in the main building, including a restaurant, library, social room, and a billiard room. The building also included luxurious apartments placed at the disposal of distinguished visitors to the capital. Members of the organization were encouraged and helped to extend their acquaintance with the best practices in journalism, in all aspects, including opportunities for travel and observation throughout the world. In the interests of the paper's independence, however, they were not to become involved in political or controversial matters or with organizations so involved.

Utterly serious in its news and editorial content, and selective in its advertising, *La Prensa* made no concessions in the use of popular appeals that had gained large circulations for some newspapers. Even in appearance, it was as conservative as possible. Until after World War I, it was made up as was the London *Times,* with advertising occupying the first and last pages, and with the main news page and the editorial page facing each other on the two middle pages, but without any advertising; news and advertising content shared the other pages. Its headlines were small and tended to be little more than labels indicating the general subject matter. This style was only modified after the century was well advanced, when *La Prensa* was made more nearly to resemble the *New*

York Times, with news on page one, but still presented in a conservative manner.

The careful coverage of national and world news in *La Prensa,* its editorial fairness and constructive content, and the reliability of its advertising combined to attract a wide and loyal readership, despite its plain exterior. Reaching an urban population more literate than in other parts of the continent, but distributed throughout Argentina and beyond, and reaching the most prosperous and influential persons in Latin America, the paper led in its circulation of approximately 250,000 in 1930. Since long before that, however, it had been a favored advertising medium at rates more than commensurate with its circulation, with a heavy volume both of display and classified advertising making it a newspaper of substantial size.

The financial return from advertising, as well as sales and subscriptions, produced revenue that enabled *La Prensa* to serve its readers without consideration of costs. It was independent of private or official pressures. It also was able to offer public services unique among newspapers of the world. As publisher, Dr. Paz established a precedent whereby a generous proportion of the paper's profits was devoted to purposes which would advance the community and the nation and would assist individuals. This practice continued in the years following his death in 1912.[3]

To assure that *La Prensa* would continue on the course set by its founder, Dr. Paz prepared his son, Ezequiel Pedro Paz, to take over the direction of the paper. He began work in the newspaper office in 1893 when he was twenty-one, and took full charge in 1898, although his father remained available for consultation until his death fourteen years later. Don Ezequiel took the paper to new successes.

The people of Buenos Aires and of Argentina were favored by the existence of a second morning daily virtually equal to *La Prensa* in quality, and which followed many of the same practices. *La Nación* was established January 4, 1870, a few months after *La Prensa,* by Dr. Bartolomé Mitre. Born in Buenos Aires in 1821, he became involved in

---

3 These services, over and beyond *La Prensa's* performance as a medium of information, included (1) a free medical, surgical and dental clinic, (2) a free legal consultation service for persons of limited means, (3) a free employment service, (4) an agricultural consultation service, (5) a musical conservatory offering free training and public concerts, (6) a library of 90,000 volumes open to students and the public, (7) an Institute of Popular Lectures offering addresses by national and world authorities, (8) a postal service in Argentina for letters sent in care of the paper, (9) literary prizes, and (10) a special annual award of 1,000 pesos to any person able to prove he had taught the greatest number of illiterates to read.

journalism early in life and was editor in 1848–49 of *El Mercurio* at Valparaiso, Chile's main seaport. The paper was started there in 1827 by Pedro Felix Vicuna and Ignacio Silva, with the assistance of a United States citizen, Thomas G. Wells. Mitre, aside from his journalistic bent, had had military training. Returning to Argentina by 1852, he served as an officer in campaigns leading to the formation of the United Provinces preliminary to the establishment of a republic, of which he became the first president from 1862–68.

La Nación, founded two years after he left the presidency, gained immediate recognition under Mitre's direction. It proceeded on much the same lines as *La Prensa,* although on a scale slightly more modest. Both papers received the Havas service, both resembled the London *Times* in general appearance, and *La Nación* also developed a national coverage by stringers, although about half the number serving *La Prensa.* In later years it also added a superior Sunday editorial supplement and engaged stringers in Europe.

As conservative as *La Prensa* in its news treatment, *La Nación* also avoided references to the private lives of public figures, with the right of privacy guarded for all persons, especially women. This latter concern again meant that no such thing as society news appeared. Neither did "letters to the editor" in those or other Argentine newspapers. Such letters were discouraged. Nevertheless, any letter received, if from a person of importance or making a valid point, might be rewritten as a news story or used as a special article, but no letter ever appeared, as such.

The news itself was presented, as in *La Prensa,* without display or headlines intended to excite undue interest, or even help readers judge of a story's importance. Much of the news in *La Nación* was departmentalized, and a "Chamber of Deputies" line would be sufficient, for example, to head a report of almost any nature concerning legislative action. An equally wooden label-type head might top a story of an event of great importance. Such practices were in effect throughout most of Latin America until World War I. Upon the death of Dr. Mitre in 1906 at eighty-five, full direction of *La Nación* passed to his son, Jorge A. Mitre, already long active in the paper's management.

Importance was attached in Latin America to the major ABC Powers—Argentina, Brazil, and Chile. For Chile, the press had had its effective beginning in February 1812 with the appearance of *La Aurora de Chile* at the port of Valparaiso. Its printing press was the first in the country and had been brought from the United States the year before through the initiative of José Miguel Carrera, a leader in the independence movement, and with the assistance of Joel Poinsset, the U.S. consul in Valparaiso. Four printers also came from the United States to help set up the office.

The oldest newspaper surviving in Chile in 1910 was *El Mercurio* of Valparaiso, dating from 1827, and one with which Mitre had gained experience. Established originally by Pedro Felix Vicuna and Ignacio Silva, they also had assistance from a U.S. citizen, Thomas G. Wells.[4] A Santiago edition was established in 1900, the creation of Agustin Edwards (MacClure); who gained ownership of the paper at that time. Edwards added a third edition in 1906 at Antofogasta, a more northerly seaport. In 1902 he also had established *Las Ultimas Noticias* as a companion afternoon paper in Santiago. Proceeding from that period under the Edwards family direction, the *Mercurio* papers all were recognized as quality publications, and all succeeded, with the Santiago edition of the *Mercurio* leading in circulation among newspapers of Chile.

Aside from the ABC countries, press development in Latin America prior to World War I was most advanced in Uruguay, Colombia, and Peru. For some others, there remained handicaps based upon communications costs, a high incidence of illiteracy, inadequate revenues, transportation problems, and government curbs on freedom of access to information and freedom to publish.

Uruguay, the smallest of the South American republics, possessed one of the highest literacy rates, was socially progressive, and had a press operating under conditions of freedom, with *El Día* of Montevideo especially respected. In Colombia the constitution adopted in 1886 guaranteed freedom of press and assembly, and the press did operate freely, with *El Espectador* of Bogotá recognized as well made. In Peru *El Comercio* of Lima was regarded as one of the most important dailies of Latin America. Conducted by José Antonio Miró Quesada, and from 1905 to 1919 by his son, Dr. Antonio Miró Quesada, who was also a member of the Chamber of Deputies and Peru's minister to Belgium, it was a liberal and informative daily. Another Lima morning paper, *La Prensa,* was well conducted by Dr. Agusto Durand from the time of its establishment in 1903 until his death in 1923.

Prior to 1917, the press and peoples of Latin America continued to

4 See Ramon Cortez Ponce, "The Chilean Press: Past and Present," *Journalism Quarterly* (June 1946), 221–23.

depend primarily upon the Agence Havas for world reports, and most of what the rest of the world learned about Latin America was channeled in a reverse flow by way of Paris and London through Havas and the Ring Combination of news agencies.

Representatives of the world press rarely visited Latin America in those years. There were exceptions, however. Reports had been produced by correspondents in Mexico for the press of the United States during the 1846–48 war between the two countries. Attention went to the attempt by France to establish a position in Mexico between 1863 and 1867, with Austria's Archduke Maximilian a puppet emperor. The first telegraph line linking Mexico with the United States in 1851 and cable extensions between 1870 and 1891 encouraged a somewhat accelerated flow of news with reference to Mexican affairs and those of Cuba, Puerto Rico, the West Indies, and the west coast of South America.

Efforts by residents of Cuba and Puerto Rico to gain independence from Spain, beginning in 1868, were viewed with sympathy in the United States and received press attention. This included reports on the "Virginius affair" in 1873, when that American-registered filibustering vessel was captured by a Spanish gunboat while carrying supplies for the Cuban insurrectionists, with eight U.S. citizens among those later executed. It was a story that took at least three U.S. correspondents to Cuba—Januarius Aloysius MacGahan of the *New York Herald* and Julius Chambers and Ralph Keeler of the *New York Tribune*. Keeler vanished never to be heard of again.

Disorders in Peru in 1891, an element in a long series of boundary disputes with Chile, Brazil, and Ecuador, were reported by John P. Dunning of the Western Associated Press. An important breakthrough in advancing a direct flow of news between Latin America and the United States, as well as in general relations, had occurred in 1888 when William E. Curtis of the *Chicago Record* visited Central and South America and produced a series of probing accounts contributing to a greater awareness of common hemispheric interests.

Meanwhile, the insurrectionists in Cuba and Puerto Rico moved with renewed vigor in 1895. This situation was seized upon by the *New York Journal,* just purchased by William Randolph Hearst, as a subject of special attention. The *New York World* was drawn into the matter, which received increasing coverage, not only by the press of the United States but by some London newspapers. Emotions aroused by the situation and also by its treatment in the press led to the Spanish-American War of 1898. From that time, Havana remained a news center regularly covered by and for the press, as Manila also became a news center across the world in the Philippines.

In those years there had been episodes centering in Venezuela in 1895 and 1903 relating to interpretations of the Monroe Doctrine and holding a potential for conflict between the United States, on the one side, and Great Britain, Germany, and Italy on the other. The *New York World* played a constructive role in the settlement of the first dispute.

The interest of the United States in an interocean canal across Central America territory turned attention before 1900 to Nicaragua and then to the Isthmus of Panama, where a French canal-building effort begun in 1879 was abandoned in 1902. The United States acted in 1903 to conclude treaties and mark out a Panama Canal zone. Construction of the canal proceeded, with its opening in August 1914.

There were problems of concern to the United States in the Dominican Republic in 1905–07, incidents in Honduras and Nicaragua, and a growing unrest in Mexico under the Diaz dictatorship which ended in 1911. These matters all received press attention. Even earlier, there had been Latin-American conferences at intervals between 1826 and 1889, including one convened in 1828 by Simón Bolivar, already known as the "Liberator," who was paired with José de San Martin as authors of Latin American independence. An 1856 conference also met in Washington and received some attention from the U.S. press. This was exceptional, however. Not until after the formation of the International Union of American Republics in 1890 were the joint North American and Latin American sessions regularly reported by representatives of the press. After the first such gathering in Washington in 1889–90, Pan-American conferences occurred at Mexico City (1901–02), Rio de Janeiro (1906), Buenos Aires (1910), Santiago (1923), Havana (1928), Montevideo (1933), Lima (1938), and others later. They received increasing press attention.

From 1900 some U.S. newspaper and magazine representatives visited Mexico, Central America, and the West Indies. In addition to coverage in Havana, there were stringers in Mexico City and in the Panama Canal Zone from 1914. Mexico received more consistent attention after that same year. No such direct coverage was given consistently by the U.S. press to the countries of South America until about 1916–17, and only gained volume after about 1930. That came coincidentally with the development of radiotelegraphy, radiotelephony, and commercial airline service.

Part II
A World at War

The Flow of News:
Decade Two (1910–20)

The second decade of the century was one of war, revolution, and fundamental change. As the decade began the world scene was one of deceptive tranquillity. Pockets of unrest existed in an aggressive German policy holding a threat to Great Britain, in deep discontent within czarist Russia, and hardly less in Mexico, China, and the Balkans. The year 1910 brought the death of Britain's Edward VII and succession to the throne of his son George V, along with Queen Mary. It brought the formation of the Union of South Africa. One overt event in the United States arising from labor trouble affecting the press was a dynamite explosion in the *Los Angeles Times* building causing a fire, great damage, and twenty-one deaths.

The first military action of the decade came in Mexico. Since the overthrow and execution of the French-supported Emperor Maximilian in 1867, Mexico had made considerable progress as a republic, first under a government headed by Benito Juárez and then, after a disorderly interval from 1872–77, under Porfirio Diaz until 1880 and again from 1884 to 1911. Such advances as had taken place under the thirty-year Diaz regime had been accomplished within the context of a thinly-veiled dictatorship and at the expense of the agrarian and working classes. Resentment within these groups and among liberal-minded persons generally led at last to a revolution that unseated Diaz in 1911. Then eighty-five, he resigned and departed for Paris where he died in 1915.

Francisco Madero, leader of the revolution and educated at the University of California and in France, was a member of a wealthy family with estates and mining property in northern Mexico. He became head of the government in 1911, first as provisional president and then by election, with Pino Suárez as vice-president. The administration lost effectiveness, however, in part because of sectional revolutionary activity, with regional leaders, usually military men, contesting for power. This brought a new revolution in Mexico City itself in February 1913. General Victoriano Huerta, commander-in-chief of the army, turned against Madero and seized control. Madero and Suárez in being taken to prison on February 22 were killed by their guards, and were generally believed to have been assassinated on Huerta's order.

A presidential election in October 1913 confirmed Huerta in the presidency. The election was so obviously controlled, that the United States refused official diplomatic recognition of the Huerta government. Dissatisfaction with the election among the people of Mexico also resulted in localized revolts under other leaders. Among them were General Venustiano Carranza, heading a so-called Constitutionalist party, Francisco ("Pancho") Villa, who had been one of Carranza's officers and also had supported Madero, General Alvaro Obregón, and General Emiliano Zapata.

The U.S. had moved 20,000 troops to the Mexican border in March 1911 as the Madero revolt proceeded, but withdrew them in June after Diaz resigned. As the internal turmoil resumed in 1913–14, the U.S. became directly involved when a small party of marines went ashore at Tampico in April 1914 to purchase supplies and were arrested. This brought on a U.S.–Mexican confrontation we shall examine later.

Across the world in Africa, France gained a special position in Morocco in 1911. A crisis arose there in July when the German gunboat Panther put in at Agadir. This and Germany's effort to develop a Berlin-to-Baghdad railroad raised concern in Italy, as well as elsewhere. With its own ambitions to develop a colonial empire, Italy had failed in Ethiopia in 1896 and in China in 1898, and had been rebuffed by Turkey in efforts to obtain commercial concessions in parts of North Africa then still remaining within the Ottoman Empire. In a somewhat desperate move, Italy undertook a military campaign against Turkey in September 1911. This was to bring an involvement with Austria and other European powers, and to touch upon separate wars in the Balkans in 1912–13. As with the U.S.–Mexican relationship, these circumstances call for later consideration.

In the chronology of the times, attention turned to China in October 1911, with a revolutionary outbreak there that brought an end to the empire in February 1912. China was so vast a country, and so ill-served in matters of transportation and communications beyond the treaty ports and the capital, that it was not possible to report events occurring in remote areas. For example, floods along the Yangtze River in 1911 later were believed to have caused 100,000 deaths, yet went virtually unreported at the time. Even as late as December 1920, an earthquake in Kansu province, deep in the country, caused an estimated 180,000 deaths, but again was virtually unreported.[1]

The Manchu rulers of Imperial China had been losing power since about 1860, partly because foreign influences were growing in the country, and partly because regional warlords were gaining power in their own districts. China's defeat in the Sino-Japanese War of 1894–95 was a serious blow to the authority of the imperial government. The events of the Boxer Rebellion of 1899–1901 brought foreign troops into China and further weakened its prestige. The death of the Dowager Empress Tzu Hsi in 1908 brought succession to the throne of three-year-old Hsüan T'ung (Pu Yi), under the regency of his father, Prince Chun. This administration was as weak as that of the late dowager empress.

The concept of a republican form of government for China already had gained some advocacy, beginning certainly as early as 1895 in the wake of the Sino-Japanese War. Most active and influential, and later to become known as "the father of the republic," was Dr. Sun Yat-sen (Sun Wen), graduated in 1894 from medical school in Hong Kong and the first Chinese to enter modern medical practice. Born in 1867, son of a farmer living on the island of Macao, he had been raised as a Christian and received part of his education in Honolulu, where an elder brother lived.

Dismayed by the results of the Sino-Japanese War as they affected China, Sun Yat-sen was diverted almost immediately from medical practice to revolutionary activities looking toward the formation of a republic based on "nationalism, democracy and socialism" to replace the Manchu regime. In 1898 at Canton, he established the Kuomintang (National People's Party) to give support to the plan for the republic and recruited members. Between 1896 and 1911 he toured the world three times to collect funds and organize a Chinese Revolutionary League. The imperial government put a price on his head. He was kidnapped in London in 1896 and held at the Chinese Legation, but was released following British government representation.

In October 1911 the revolution began. In January 1912, with the approval of a Kuomintang national convention, Sun Yat-sen took the

---

1 By contrast, a fire in the Triangle Waist Company clothing factory in New York City in March 1911, with 145 fatalities, became an instant and major subject of news. It was even more promptly reported than usual because William G. Shepherd, formerly of the *St. Paul Daily News,* but an early member of the United Press staff in New York, happened to detect the fire personally. Like the Iroquois Theater fire in Chicago in 1903, it produced legislation to safeguard the public, with special regulations for factories.

oath as provisional president of a new republic. On February 12 the abdication of the boy-emperor was announced in Peking, with an edict also announcing a republican government to replace the monarchy. Dr. Sun soon resigned voluntarily as president, however, in favor of Yuan Shih-k'ai, the former viceroy under the monarchy. Dr. Sun regarded him as being in a better position to bring about unification within the country and to give strength to the republic. At this juncture, Dr. George Ernest ("China") Morrison, correspondent in Peking for the *Times* since 1895, was appointed as an adviser to the new president and served until Yuan's death in 1916.

The republic encountered difficulties from the outset. District warlords, guarding their own prerogatives, blocked unification. Dr. Sun also became persuaded that Yuan was not acting to build an effective republic, but was preparing to make himself a new emperor. Sun therefore sponsored a new revolution in 1913. This Yuan was able to halt, and Sun took refuge in Japan. He did not return to China until 1917, a year after Yuan's death. Meanwhile, the republic continued, but not very effectively.

The presidency of the republic was assumed in 1916 by Li Yüan-hung, a military man who had been vice-president. He was forced to resign a year later in favor of Fèng Kuo-chang, who had become the new vice-president. In 1918, Fèng yielded the presidency in turn to Tuan Ch'i-jui, who served until 1920, and was followed by Hsu Shih-ch'ang until 1922. Li Yüan-hung then was recalled as president. As Yuan had named Morrison as an adviser in 1912, so in 1922 Li named Thomas F. Millard, who was experienced as a correspondent for the *Chicago Tribune* and the *Manchester Guardian* and as editor of the *China Press* and *Millard's Review of the Far East*. When Li left the presidency again in 1923, he was succeeded by Ts'ao Kun until 1925. Millard continued as an adviser until that time, following which he became staff correspondent in Shanghai for the *New York Times,* a post he held until early 1941. With Ts'ao Kun's departure from the presidency, a three-man coalition conducted the affairs of the government. These were Fèng Kuo-chang and Tuan Ch'i-jui, both former presidents, and Marshal Chang Tso-lin, a Manchurian warlord and the actual power behind the government of the republic since 1921.

Dr. Sun Yat-sen on returning to China in 1917 was dissatisfied with the manner in which the republic was being conducted. He reactivated the Kuomintang and undertook to establish a separate, independent republic. This he declared to be the lawful government of China under his leadership. The effort was ineffective, however, for lack of cooperation by military leaders in Canton where he had again made his headquarters. By 1923, nevertheless, Dr. Sun's persuasions, combined with the dubious performance of the government in Peking, had gained for him the backing of workers and students in the south of China, and also had gained the backing of troops from the neighboring provinces of Kwangsi and Yunnan. This began a new chapter for the Kuomintang and for China and the republic. It became part of the story of the third decade of the century. Circumstances in China in 1912 under the new republic had been so uncertain that the United States sent troops to Tientsin to protect national interests and safeguard missionaries and other American citizens.

Italy's 1911 move against Turkey in a Tripolitan War continued into 1912. There followed what became known as the First Balkan War in October-December 1912, which resumed in February-May 1913, and the Second Balkan War in June-August 1913.

The growing Anglo-German tensions occasioned a visit to Berlin in 1912 by Lord Haldane, then a member of the Privy Council, in an unsuccessful British effort to persuade Germany to curb its naval construction and general military expansion. The failure added to alarm, not only in Great Britain, but also in France and Russia, as to Germany's intentions. Visitors to Berlin in 1912 and 1913 were returning with stories of arrogant public behavior by German officers, and their toasts to "Der Tag," which was taken to mean the day when Germany would "march." An aggressive attitude also had been demonstrated at least since 1908 by the government of neighboring Austria-Hungary, relating especially to the Balkan area.

Such portents of trouble brought a rush by nations in Asia, as well as in Europe, to enter into a series of treaties of "alliance" and "non-aggression," or to confirm existing treaties. It also brought military maneuvers, increased budgets for military construction, and a shifting of naval units, including a transfer of British ships of war from the Mediterranean to the North Sea, even as French vessels moved somewhat in reverse from the Atlantic to the Mediterranean, thus facing Germany in the first instance and Austria and Italy in the second.

Even as these events transpired, the Olympic Games took place in Stockholm in 1912. That year brought the death of Japan's Emperor Mutsuhito, who had ruled since 1868, and marked the end of the Meiji ("Enlightened Peace") era during which Japan had made great advances. He was succeeded by his son Yoshihito, whose reign was titled Teisho ("Great Righteousness") and continued until 1926.

A further important administrative change in 1912 was implicit in a presidential campaign in the United States. Woodrow Wilson, former president of Princeton University but then Governor of New Jersey, was nominated as the Democratic party candidate, and President Taft by the Republican party. Many Republicans, however, rallied to the support of former President Theodore Roosevelt, who had become disenchanted with Taft and therefore sought and gained nomination by a new Progressive or "Bull Moose" party. In the course of his campaign, while visiting Milwaukee in October, he was shot but only slightly wounded, and made a dramatic platform appearance only minutes after the incident. With the Republican vote split between Taft and Roosevelt in November, Wilson was elected and took office in March 1913.

The tragic death of Captain Robert F. Scott and four companions occurred on their return journey after reaching the South Pole in January 1912.

An even greater tragedy occurred on April 14–15, 1912, when the 46,000 ton White Star liner *Titanic,* then the largest and presumably the safest ship afloat, struck an iceberg late at night on her maiden voyage from Southampton to New York and sank within four hours. Of 2,224 passengers and crew, 1,513 were lost. There were no working reporters aboard the *Titanic,* but several identified with the press were among the victims of the disaster. They were William T. Stead, editor and publisher of the London *Review of Reviews* and former editor of the *Pall Mall Gazette;* John Jacob Astor, IV, whose cousin, William Waldorf Astor, had purchased control of Stead's *Pall Mall Gazette* in 1893 and in 1911 had bought the Sunday *Observer* from Lord Northcliffe; Francis D. Millet, a painter and formerly artist-correspondent for the *New York Herald, Harper's Weekly,* and the London *Times;* and Major Archibald Butt, recently a personal aide both to Presidents Roosevelt and Taft, but with experience as a Spanish-American War newspaper correspondent.[2]

The *Titanic* was within two days of arrival in New York when it struck the underwater extension of the iceberg at about 10:30 P.M. of Sunday, August 14. Equipped with wireless, the ship's CQD distress signal was heard at a Marconi station at Cape Race, Newfoundland, by operators at the Charleston Navy Yard station near Boston, by other land stations, and by ships at sea. An Associated Press bulletin from Cape Race reached New York and was relayed to London. By that hour, the London Monday morning papers had gone to press. In New York, most editors, believing the *Titanic* "unsinkable," used the bulletin in the

---

2   Millet and Butt were commemorated by a fountain erected in Washington in 1913.

Monday morning editions, but expected later reassuring reports to follow. None ever did.

At the *New York Times* office, managing editor Carr Van Anda was no less hopeful than others. Nevertheless, he put members of the staff to work immediately to prepare the most complete report possible on the basis of what little was known. With Frederick T. Birchall, then night city editor, helping to shape the account, a full story of the ship and the notable list of passengers was prepared, photos obtained, and phone calls made to useful sources in New York, Halifax, and Montreal. On Van Anda's judgment, the headline over a broad page-one display in the final edition of the Monday morning paper, coming off the presses at 3:30 A.M., dared to say that the *Titanic* was sinking. The *Times* outdid any other newspaper in the first reports.

The Tuesday morning paper naturally was far more complete. By then, there was confirmation that the ship had indeed gone down. News also was received by wireless, again through Cape Race, that the Cunard liner *Carpathia,* responding to the original CQD, had rescued survivors and was continuing on its way to New York. Other ships were known to be in the area of the sinking and still searching.

The *New York Herald* did almost equally well in reporting the event. James Gordon Bennett, its publisher, making his home in Paris, had intended to sail in the *Titanic,* but changed his plans and had arrived in New York a few days before the disaster. Always concerned with ships and the sea, he took personal charge of organizing the *Herald* coverage.

Learning of the *Carpathia*'s rescue of some passengers, Bennett obtained a list of those aboard that ship. He discovered that one was a young woman, May Birkhead, who had been in Paris shortly before he departed and had been the subject of an interview in the Paris edition of the *Herald.* He sent her a wireless message asking her to "Wireless all operator can take on *Titanic.*" She had no newspaper experience, but nevertheless was soon sending interviews with survivors, and also persuaded some to prepare sketches from memory of scenes aboard the sinking liner.

When the *Carpathia* arrived in New York on Thursday night, reporters for newspapers and news agencies swarmed aboard. The *Herald* arranged to have Miss Birkhead escorted promptly to the paper's office to tell her own story, deliver the drawings, more copy, and even some photographs. With this beginning, May Birkhead became a member of the *New York Herald* staff in its Paris edition until 1926.

The *Times* and the *Herald* led all other newspapers with their accounts of the *Titanic* sinking. Eye-witness accounts and photographs were obtained from many of the 711 survivors brought by the *Carpathia*. The equally active Associated Press included accounts by two who had jumped from the stern of the ship as it was near its final plunge. Guglielmo Marconi, in New York when the *Carpathia* arrived and with a special concern over the part of wireless in the event, went aboard with a *New York Times* reporter, James Speers—one of sixteen from that paper working on the story. Bennett's part in directing coverage, his last personal news work in New York and his last visit to the city, was directly responsible for filling several pages in the *Herald*.

The *Titanic* sinking, although especially dramatic, was not the only ship disaster in those years. The *Principe de Asturias,* a Spanish steamer, had been wrecked off the coast of that country a month before, with 500 drowned. A Japanese ship, the *Kichemaru,* sank off the coast of Japan in September 1912, with a loss of 1,000 lives. The *Calvados,* a British ship, went down in the Sea of Marmara near Turkey in March 1913, with 200 lost. The Canadian ship, *Empress of Ireland,* sank in the St. Lawrence River in May 1914 following a collision with a collier, with 1,024 fatalities. And 812 were lost when the excursion steamer *Eastland* overturned in the Chicago River on a Saturday in July 1915. This latter disaster occurred two months after the Cunard liner *Lusitania* (31,550 tons) was torpedoed off the Irish coast in May, one of the critical events of World War I, with 1,198 persons lost.

In 1912–13 the First and Second Balkan wars were fought and, ironically, the Palace of Peace was dedicated at The Hague. That year the new Wilson administration began in the United States. The early part of 1914 brought a meeting in Brussels of the International Socialist Bureau, with five men among those present destined to head the governments of their various countries in later years. These were Nicolai Lenin (Soviet Russia), Friedrich Ebert (German republic), Thorvald Stauning (Denmark), Karl Hjalmar Branting (Sweden), and J. Ramsay MacDonald (Great Britain). The Panama Canal was opened in August. President Wilson's wife, Ellen Louise Axson Wilson, died in that same month. He was remarried in December 1915 to Edith Bolling Galt of Washington, a widow.

In April 1914 the United States had become involved in the controversy with Mexico arising from the Tampico incident. On June 28 the heir to the Austrian throne was assassinated at Serajevo, and a month later World War I began. The United States was able to maintain a neutral position in the war until 1917. Meanwhile, however, the people and the government were under pressure both from the Allied and Central Powers, with propaganda programs more highly organized than ever before in the history of international relations. From the time of the sinking of the *Lusitania* in May 1915, in particular, there was concern in the United States over German submarine activity threatening U.S. ships and commerce, and with British naval searches of U.S. ships.

The war had other repercussions in the United States. These included in 1915 a bomb explosion in the Senate reception room in Washington, and the shooting and wounding of J. Pierpont Morgan, a New York banker representing British financial and contract negotiations in the United States; in July 1916 the sabotage of ammunition in huge explosions on the docks at Toms River island, near Jersey City, and in January 1917 damage to a munitions plant in New Jersey.

Unrest in the Caribbean and Central America led the United States to make Haiti a U.S. protectorate in 1915, and marines were landed in Santo Domingo in 1916. In an extension of the earlier Mexican confrontation, a concentration of troops on the Texas border in 1916–17 included a punitive expedition into Mexico itself. Denmark and the United States also signed a treaty in 1916 by which the United States acquired the Danish Virgin Islands in the West Indies for a payment of $25 million, effective in 1917. In that same year Puerto Rico became a U.S. Territory. Meanwhile, in 1916, U.S. Brigadier General John T. Thompson developed a new and lethal portable submachine gun (the "Tommy gun").

As World War I began in 1914, Japan immediately declared its solidarity with the Allied powers and proceeded without delay to seize German territories and enterprises in China and in the Pacific. It not only restrained the Chinese Republic from declaring also for the Allies, but demanded special rights in Manchuria and Shantung province and moved troops into both areas. When China protested, Japan in 1915 served the Republic with what became known as the "Twenty-one Demands," tantamount to an insistence upon full control in China. These were first made known to a world otherwise preoccupied by the war in Europe by Frederick Moore, formerly in the *New York Tribune* Paris bureau, but in 1915 an Associated Press correspondent in China. The demands seemed so outrageous when received in the New York AP headquarters offices that they were discredited, and Moore himself was dismissed.[3] Once the reality of the demands was confirmed, however, outcries of disapproval arose from so many sources that they were largely abandoned for the time by the Japanese government. British protests brought a withdrawal of Japanese military forces from Shantung. In 1917, China at last was able to align itself with the Allies and was later represented at the Paris Peace Conference. Even so, Japan gained rights at that conference, some at the expense of China, thus adding to the problems of that still-young republic.

In 1916 President Wilson was re-elected to a second term, defeating Charles Evans Hughes the Republican party candidate, and was inaugurated in March 1917.

Because of the involvement of the United States with Mexico in 1914 and again in 1916, and because of the pressures of World War I, it had seemed prudent for the country to build its military strength. "Preparedness" was the operative word, and a Preparedness Day Parade in San Francisco in July 1916 intended to advance public awareness of that need was interrupted by the throwing of a bomb in protest. Ten persons were killed and forty wounded.

In February 1917 it became known that the German ambassador in Mexico, acting officially in response to instructions from Berlin, had proposed a German alliance by which Mexico might be assisted in recovering much of the western territory of the United States ceded in the settlement following the U.S.–Mexican War of 1845–48. By then, the United States had severed diplomatic relations with Germany because of its submarine attacks against neutral shipping. In April 1917 the United States declared war on Germany, associating itself with the Allies.

Industrial production, much of it war-related, had been soaring in the United States since 1915. Motor cars, trucks, and airplanes were coming off the production lines, as well as munitions in great volume. Yet advances were made in such other areas as medical science, including vitamin research in a new departure in nutrition and public health. In a related concern for social order, twenty-four states by 1916 had prohibited liquor sales, and Congress passed the eighteenth amendment to the Constitution in 1917 to halt the manufacture and sale of all alcoholic beverages. The amendment was ratified by the necessary two-thirds of the states in January 1919, and became effective as law on

---

3   Ironically, Moore was taken into the employ of the Japanese government, whose interests he represented as a lobbyist and propagandist. See Randall Gould, *China in the Sun* (Garden City, N.Y., 1946).

June 30 of that year. As time was to demonstrate, this action held the potential for trouble, as did a charter granted by the state of Georgia in 1915 permitting a revival of the Ku Klux Klan, originally a creation of the Civil War period supporting violent action by hooded bands moved by intolerant beliefs.

The people of the United States and of other lands were increasingly occupied by the events of the European war and war-related matters. The scope of the war itself, including its financial aspects, was such that the future of all peoples and nations seemed to hinge upon its outcome, as indeed it did. This meant that the press concentrated its effort above all upon reporting the course of the war from 1914 through 1918, including the related revolution in Russia, and the peace-making through 1919 and into 1920.

Rehearsals for Armageddon 10

Political unrest had been bubbling throughout much of the world at the turn of the century. In the decades bracketing 1900 six wars had been fought. These were in the Sudan, Korea and China, Greece, Cuba and the Philippines, South Africa, and in Manchuria and the seas adjacent to Japan. More than that, there was the Boxer uprising in China, disorder in Russia, conflict in Turkey and the Balkans and in Africa and parts of South America, and revolution in Mexico. Yet two international peace conferences had met at The Hague, and a Peace Palace had been erected there.

Spain had lost the last of its great colonial empire in 1898, and Portugal had lost its position in Brazil. The ancient Chinese empire ended in 1912, the almost equally ancient Ottoman empire was a fraction of its former size, and the three-hundred-year-old czarist government of Russia was under pressure.

The British, French, Dutch, Belgian, Portuguese, Danish, and German colonial positions seemed secure. Great Britain and France felt threatened, nonetheless, by an aggressive Germany supported by the Austrian-Hungarian Empire as it built a military and naval establishment, contested for world trade and shipping leadership, and looked for more positions of strength in Africa, the Middle East, and the Pacific. This complex situation resulted in a network of new treaties and alliances among nations. Many were defensive in nature and to be invoked in the event of hostile action by another nation or a combination of nations.

The year 1908, in retrospect, was important in setting the stage for a violent decade to follow. In Turkey, a western-educated group referred to as the "Young Turks" seeking to make the country strong, more democratic, and an influence in international affairs, staged a revolution. This brought concessions from the Sultan Abd ul-Hamid II, who was nevertheless deposed in 1909 and replaced by his brother as Mohammed V.

In Austria, the government in October 1908 boldly proclaimed the annexation of Bosnia and Herzegovina, directly to the south, which were Balkan provinces long under Turkish rule. It used its power to induce Turkey, then in disarray, to accept the transfer of sovereignty in return for a payment in 1909 of the equivalent of $10.3 million. This annexation was much to the displeasure of adjoining Serbia, which had gained its independence of Turkey under the terms of the Treaty of Berlin in 1878 and objected to Austria's unilateral action affecting the two neighboring Slav states.

In 1908 also publication in the London *Daily Telegraph* of an interview with Germany's Kaiser Wilhelm II caused wide concern in other countries. His interview with William Bayard Hale of the *New York Times* soon after, even though withheld from publication, was known in substance to some government leaders and was equally disturbing. At the same time, Germany seemed to be flexing its muscles in Morocco and making overtures to Turkey in looking toward the construction of a Berlin-to-Baghdad railway.

Turkey retained its power in the Middle East in 1908, except for most of present-day Saudi Arabia and Iran, and in a part of Europe beyond the Bosphorus extending to Adrianople (Edirne) on the Bulgarian frontier. It also retained that portion of the North African coast including Tripolitania and Cyrenica, with Fezzan in the south, an area known in its entirety as Tripoli (now Libya); and in the Dodecanese Islands, including the large and historic island of Rhodes, just off the Turkish coast. It continued to contest with Greece for retention of its earlier control of the island of Crete.

The Ottoman empire, at its height in the sixteenth century, had then extended from the Caspian Sea in the east to include the African coast of the Mediterranean westward to the Atlantic. It then also extended deep into Europe, including the Balkan Peninsula westward to the Adriatic, and nearly all of what later became Hungary, Rumania, and much of southern Russia, almost surrounding the Black Sea, plus most of the islands in the eastern Mediterranean.

Conflict had attended the loosening of Turkish controls over much of this area, beginning in the seventeenth century, but it still continued in parts of the Balkans, as well as the Middle East. The very word "balkan" is Turkish for "mountains," and describes some sections of terrain. Where the Turks were forced out, the Hapsburgs of Austria commonly moved in from their base in Vienna, a center of the old Roman empire, except in Greece, which had regained its own independence in 1833 after some four centuries of Turkish control.

A conflict with Russia arose in 1850 over the protection of Christians in the Turkish-held Danubian principalities of Rumania, Bulgaria, Serbia, Montenegro, and Albania. In this, Turkey received the support of France, Great Britain, and Sardinia. Russia's refusal to accept Turkish control in certain of those areas, its bombardment on November 30, 1853, of the Turkish Black Sea port of Sinop, and destruction there of a Turkish squadron, led to the Crimean War (1853–56). In this, Russia was defeated by those other countries. For the time, it ceased to challenge Turkey on the position of Christians in the Danube area or in Turkey itself, and Turkey became more involved in European affairs.

In 1859, however, the Danubian principalities were encouraged by France and Russia to unite. Rumania took form in 1861, as the principalities of Wallachia and Moldavia joined, but still under Turkish control. Montenegro, Herzegovina, and Serbia, responding to an ethnic pan-Slav movement centering in Moscow, revolted in 1861–62 against Turkish control. This failed of its purpose, which was to gain independence, but in 1867 British and Dutch pressure induced Turkey at least to withdraw its military forces from Serbia.

The death of Sultan Abd ul-Mejid brought a change in Turkey in 1861. Abd ul-Aziz, the new ruler, was confronted with unrest not only in Serbia, but also in Crete, where a union with Greece was demanded. This was suppressed, but led to a diplomatic break with Greece, ended by a conference of ambassadors in Paris in 1869, where Crete also was granted autonomy under its own Christian governors. Egypt also maneuvered the sultan into approving a favorable change in the Egyptian succession, with the viceroy to bear title as the "khedive," or prince.

It became clear at this period, that the Turkish treasury was seriously depleted. This introduced a financial crisis that became worse in 1873, when a world economic depression so complicated matters that the European powers viewed Turkey as actually bankrupt. The sultan himself had become despotic in his conduct of government and the generally favorable position that Turkey had enjoyed internationally as the Crimean War ended in 1856 had become greatly eroded. France by then was weakened because of its defeat in the Franco-Prussian war of 1870–71. Germany and Russia were correspondingly stronger. Russia remained concerned about the position of Christians within the Turkish realm, and also was friendly to the Pan-Slav concept that had its appeal to Serbia and others in the south of Europe.

Russia had encouraged an insurrection in 1866 against Turkish control in Bulgaria. Later unrest there was put down harshly by the

Turks. Atrocities accompanying such action in May 1876, and verified in the summer, led Russia again to assume a position as defendant of civilization and Christianity and to declare war on Turkey in April 1877. The events in Bulgaria and the Russo-Turkish War of 1877–78, in which Turkey was defeated, had turned European opinion against that country. Internally, also, Abd ul-Aziz had been dethroned in May 1876, and committed suicide. His nephew Murad V succeeded him as ruler for only three months, and then was deposed as insane. His brother became Abd ul-Hamid II, and remained on the throne from 1876 until 1909.

The Russo-Turkish War ended with the signature of the Treaty of San Stefano in March 1878. This specified, among other things, an independent status for Serbia and Rumania. A separate Turkish agreement with Great Britain in June assigned the Mediterranean island of Cyprus to that country. A treaty signed at the Congress of Berlin in July 1878 put a capstone on the Russo-Turkish War settlement. It confirmed the independence of Serbia and Rumania, and Montenegro as well. Bessarabia and Dobrudja, adjacent to Rumania, were ceded to Russia, and reforms were promised in other areas.

The terms of the Berlin Treaty were not fully observed, however. Out of this, for example, a revolt occurred in 1890 on the island of Crete, still Turkish-controlled, but still favoring union with Greece. This led in due course to the Greco-Turkish War of 1897. The Greeks were defeated, but intervention by European powers, fearing a wider conflict, brought an end to the war. Greece paid a financial indemnity and Crete was put under international control, with Prince George of Greece as governor. It was, in fact, to become a part of Greece in 1913.

Despite the Berlin Treaty of 1878, Turkish administration continued in Macedonia, a loosely defined area of the Balkans overspreading portions of northern Greece and southern areas of Bulgaria and Serbia. Political partisans there resisted despotic Turkish rule, yet efforts by European powers to bring reform and order failed to move either party.

Serbia meanwhile found. that, although assured of independence in the 1878 Berlin Treaty, it had only exchanged Turkish domination for Austrian. Attempting to make its independence real, it took purposeful action after 1905 in an effort to unite all Slavic peoples of southern Europe. In this it had some encouragement from Russia, where the Slavic strain was important. The concept called for a union of Serbia, Montenegro, Bosnia, Herzegovina, the two Hungarian provinces of Croatia and Slavonia, and even parts of Austria. If actually brought together as a union, it would include about twenty-seven million persons, more than half the population of the Austrian-Hungarian empire.

The Hapsburg rulers of Austria, not unnaturally, looked with disfavor upon this Pan-Slav movement. As one important measure to obstruct the concept, and citing removal of surviving Turkish controls as the objective, Austria took police and military action in October 1908 to support its formal annexation of Bosnia and Herzegovina to the empire.

This exercise of power affronted Turkey and Serbia alike, but neither was in a position to resist or reverse the action. In itself a breach of the 1878 Berlin Treaty, the action also offended Russia, Great Britain, France, and Italy. Only Germany, equally opposed to the creation of a Pan-Slav state, stood with Austria. Italy, although alarmed by the concept, had ambitions of its own. It was more concerned lest Austrian influence block those ambitions than in contesting the Bosnia-Herzegovina seizure. No nation, in fact, was prepared to contest that seizure to the point of initiating military action. The annexation succeeded, but within it was that invitation to disaster which overtook the world in 1914.

Italy felt disadvantaged among the nations of Europe, lacking a colonial position. It had observed France's recent extension of power in Morocco, with nothing more serious than a gesture of German disapproval at the Algeciras Conference of 1906. It noted that even general disapproval had not reversed Austria's gain in the Balkans. Italy had failed to establish a position in Abyssinia in 1896. The Rome government considered that time was running out if it were to gain its own place in the larger world. It sought to take advantage of Turkey's current weakness and preoccupation with domestic affairs by seizing some of that country's remaining empire in North Africa, in the Mediterranean, and in Albania, just across the Adriatic.

Thus began the Italo-Turkish War, or Tripolitan War of 1911–12. It almost merged, in point of time, with the First Balkan War of 1912–13, and with the Second Balkan War following almost immediately in 1913.

Somewhat coincidentally, although out of a completely different set of circumstances, the revolution in Mexico in 1911 led to a military involvement there by the United States from 1914 to 1917 that was to overlap the larger war then already in progress in Europe, and which was an outgrowth of the Balkan territorial contest.

In the summer of 1911, the Rome government demanded that Turkey recognize Italian commercial rights in Triopli. A Turkish compromise proposal was rejected. On September 28, Italy demanded Turkish consent to its military occupation of Tripoli, with an ultimatum calling for a reply within twenty-four hours. Turkey did not respond and on September 29 Italy declared war.

An Italian naval squadron, already in position, bombarded the port of Tripoli. Italian forces landed on October 5 were reenforced and by the end of November the city of Tripoli was secured. A desert campaign proceeded slowly through the winter and much of 1912, with some sharp and bloody encounters. By late 1912, however, Italy had established its control in the area.

Meanwhile, Italian naval action had proceeded against Turkish ships and islands in the Mediterranean, with the Dodocanese Islands, Rhodes included, occupied in May 1912. The Dardanelles, the strait between the Aegean Sea and the Sea of Marmara, leading in turn to the Bosphorus, the city of Constantinople, and the Black Sea, already had been closed by action of Italian ships of war.

Turkey, beset by its domestic problems, was unable to halt the Italian aggression. The neutral powers of Europe, however, some with their own interests in the Mediterranean and Balkan areas, were alarmed lest the unilateral Italian action disturb the delicate balance in the Balkans and bring on a general war.

Russia objected to the closing of the Dardanelles, through which its own ships passed between the Black Sea and the Mediterranean, and the strait, closed in April, was reopened to traffic in May. Austria, by blocking Italian naval action in the Aegean and in the Adriatic, prevented any contemplated landing in Albania. Great Britain and France, disapproving Italian action, brought pressure to end it. The signature of the Treaty of Ouchy, relating to Tripoli, and the Treaty of Lausanne on October 18, 1912, ended the war. Italy, nevertheless, had established a position in Tripoli (Libya) and in the Dodocanese Islands and Rhodes that was to remain effective for more than thirty years.

The Italo-Turkish War was not well covered by the press, although its political aspects were reported by correspondents in Rome, Constantinople, and Vienna. Largely a naval operation, no correspondents were with the ships. Such land action as occurred, notably in and beyond Tripoli, was almost impossible to report directly. It appears that only three correspondents undertook such coverage. These were Bennet Burleigh and Ellis Ashmead-Bartlett, both of the London *Daily Telegraph,* and Percival Phillips of the *Daily Express*—all experienced in war reporting.

The group of "Young Turks" gaining power in that country in 1908 did so with the object of introducing reforms of a liberal nature. Differences arose, however, resulting not only in a change in the sultanate, but in a massacre of Armenian Christians at Adana, in south central Turkey in 1908. An attempt to extend Moslem influence throughout the country, still overspreading most of the Middle East, at the expense of Orthodox Christian elements, caused further bloodshed. Turkish forces also suppressed elements demanding greater autonomy in Albania.

These events, and general harsh and illiberal practices in areas under Turkish control, combined to alarm leaders in the Balkan countries. Bulgaria proclaimed its independence in 1908, but this brought incidents of violence. A desire for autonomy and independence in Macedonia, and for a clear definition of Macedonian territory, received support from Austria and Russia, and from Bulgaria as well. But this brought only greater Turkish repression.

The result was that several of the countries managed to subordinate their racial, religious, and political differences and join in a Balkan League in 1912, looking toward united and defensive action. The members included Greece and Bulgaria, which concluded a treaty of alliance, and Serbia and Montenegro. Austria proposed to the European powers that pressure be brought equally on the Balkan states and on Turkey for reforms in Macedonia as a means of keeping peace, and Austria and Russia were commissioned to act in accordance with this proposal. Before they could do so, however, Bulgaria acted separately.

Bulgaria in August 1912 demanded that Turkey grant autonomy to Macedonia. Receiving no satisfactory response, Bulgaria formed an agreement with Serbia a month later to join in a war on Turkey, which was itself even then involved in war with Italy. Several weeks passed with no supporting action, but a formal end to the Italo-Turkish War was nearing. Montenegro, the smallest country in the Balkans, and closely allied to Serbia, was actually the first to declare war on Turkey on October 8, 1912. Turkey, which already had announced military maneuvers near Adrianople, on its own frontier with Bulgaria, declared war on that country, but without reference to Montenegro. Greece and Serbia then declared war on Turkey. So began the First Balkan War on October 18, the same day the Italo-Turkish War ended with the signing of the Treaty of Lausanne.

Turkish forces attacked first in Bulgaria, westward from Adrianople (Edirne), but were defeated on October 22. Bulgarian forces then advanced toward Constantinople, gaining victories between October 28 and November 3, but were blocked in a drive toward the Turkish capital on November 18. Meanwhile, the Serbians gained victories in October and November, establishing control of northern Albania to the Adriatic coast and the port of Durazzo (Durrës), as the Montenegrins also advanced to the port of Scutari (Shkodra).

The Serb and Montenegrin positions on the Adriatic coast brought opposition and a threat of intervention from Austria, with Italian support, not unrelated to its own private interest in Albania. Germany and Great Britain supported Austria and Italy, but Russia, with French adherence, gave support to Serbia and Montenegro. In no case did this involve military support, but an international crisis was threatened, with Austria and Russia both beginning mobilization. Russia was unprepared for war, however, and modified its advocacy of the Serbian-Montenegrin cause.

An armistice in the Balkan confrontation was declared on December 3. It was observed by Turkey, Bulgaria, and Serbia, but not by Greece or Montenegro, whose forces continued to clash with Turkish troops in various areas. A peace conference opened in London on December 17, but broke down early in January because of Turkey's refusal to make certain concessions. The armistice ended, and the war resumed in February 1913.

The second phase of the war began with further victories for the Balkan allies. On March 18, at the recently captured Turkish port of Salonika, King George I of Greece was assassinated by a drunken man, himself a Greek. On March 26, Bulgaria established military control of Adrianople in Turkish territory, and a new armistice with Turkey was concluded on April 16. The peace conference, resuming in London in May, brought an end to the war. Under the terms of the treaty signed May 30, Turkey was to withdraw completely from the Balkans, from the island of Crete, and certain Aegean islands. The treaty specified that future control of those islands and of Albania was to be determined by the European powers. Austrian pressure already had resulted in a denial to Serbia and Montenegro of the gains they had made in Albania and the use of its ports of Durazzo and Scutari. The settlement thus left a residue of discontent in those countries, and in some others as well. The result was a Second Balkan War, which began just a month after the Treaty of London had ended the first.

By decision of the European powers, Crete was assigned to Greece, effective in December 1913, and also the port of Salonika and Macedonian areas adjacent. Earlier, almost immediately after the May treaty signature in London, the powers ruled that Albania, freed of Turkish control, should become a principality under the protection of those neutral powers, but actually under the tutelage of Austria. Montenegro stood between Albania on the south, and Austrian-held Bosnia and Herzegovina on the north. It was the only Balkan country other than Albania with a good Adriatic port, Scutari. This it made available for use by Serbia, otherwise a land-locked country. The neutral powers, however, also ruled that Scutari must be ceded to Albania, supporting the Austrian and Italian protest against any outlet to the Adriatic by any independent Balkan country. The Serbian-Montenegrin successes of 1912 were thus completely erased.

Further, Bulgaria, which had stood with Serbia in September 1912 to demand Turkish reforms in Macedonia, had concluded its own unilateral armistice with Turkey in April 1913. Since then, it had refused to satisfy Serbia's expectation under the 1912 agreement that it might annex a portion of Macedonia in the event of victory over Turkey, such as indeed had occurred.

Three times denied the fruits of victory, including access to the Adriatic ports of Durazzo and Scutari, as well as frustrated in its earlier desire to form a Pan-Slav Union, Serbia had hoped at least to establish a corridor by which it might have access to the sea through the Greek port of Salonika on the Aegean. Greece was willing to grant such use. The corridor would have to pass through Macedonian territory, however, and Bulgaria refused to grant any cession to make that possible, despite what Serbia believed to have been the understanding in 1912.

Serbia sought a review and revision of the treaty agreements to provide for such a corridor. It was supported in this by Greece in a treaty of alliance concluded June 1, 1913. Bulgaria proposed that the matter be referred for arbitration to Russia's Czar Nicholas II. Even as the issue was pending, the commander of Bulgaria's armed forces, instigated by Austria and Germany, but acting on his own initiative, directed a sudden and totally unexpected attack on Serbia and Greece, both Bulgaria's allies in the first war. So began the Second Balkan War on June 29, 1913.

Serbia and Greece rallied to meet the Bulgarian attack. The Bulgarian government denied having approved that attack, but could not, or did not turn back. Turkey also entered the war, this time allied with Serbia and Greece, its former foes, but again opposed to Bulgaria, to which it had lost Adrianople in the first war.

This second war, although short, was in three phases. The first phase was quickly over, with Bulgarian forces defeated on several fronts and checked by July 10, only twelve days after the first shots were fired. The second phase began at that time, with Rumania entering the war as a new member of the alliance against Bulgaria. Rumania had been angered by Bulgaria's refusal, after the first war, to make what it regarded as a proper frontier settlement. The European powers agreed. An ambassadorial conference at St. Petersburg had awarded the town of Silistria on the lower Danube to Rumania (a nonbelligerent in the first war) as compensation for gains made by victorious Bulgaria in the settlement.

By the end of July Rumanian forces, having taken advantage of Bulgaria's earlier defeats, were on the outskirts of Sofia, the capital. From the south, Turkey also took advantage of the situation to move back into Adrianople, a city of about 30,000 on the Turkish-Bulgarian frontier. On July 31 Bulgaria surrendered.

An interlude followed during which two peace treaties were signed. By the Treaty of Bucharest of August 10, Serbia and Greece were permitted to retain those parts of Macedonia they had occupied in the war. With Greek control reaffirmed in Salonika, as gained in the first war, the desired Serbian corridor to the Aegean also was made possible. Rumania, for its part, gained Dobrudjan territory, extending its Black Sea coast north of Bulgaria. A Treaty of Constantinople, on September 29, confirmed Turkey's position in Adrianople and set the Maritza River as the boundary between Turkey and Bulgaria.

The third phase of the war, beginning in September, despite the treaties, was equally brief. Rumania had withdrawn, but Albania entered as a sixth participant. Albania had been conducting raids into territory assigned to Serbia under the 1878 Treaty of Berlin. Serbia responded by invading Albania on September 23. Greek forces then also were in southern Albania. As in 1912, Austria again intervened with an ultimatum of October 18 demanding Serbia's evacuation of Albania. That evacuation was completed a week later. An Austro-Italian note of October 30 also demanded a Greek evacuation of southern Albania, to be completed by the end of the year. In this case, British intervention on behalf of Greece, relating to its position in the Aegean Islands, had the effect of delaying the Greek departure from Albania until the spring of 1914.

The war which had started June 29 ended, in effect, with Bulgaria's surrender on July 31, 1913, and with the treaties following. The third phase of September-October was of such a nature as to require no additional peace treaty. The expectation by Austria and Germany that their irregular support of Bulgaria's original attack in June would pay dividends had been dashed, however. Their concern lest a Pan-Slav state be established in the south of Europe, with Russian support, was in no way abated. Serbia remained irritated by Austria's domination of Balkan affairs, including its own exclusion from Adriatic ports and its forced retirement from Albania. Bulgaria and Rumania were at odds. Relations between Greece and Turkey were poor, despite their recent alliance against Bulgaria. Turkey had no reason to feel friendship toward Italy, which had deprived it of territory in the war of 1911–12. It all added up to a situation that was to explode in the summer of 1914.

*Press
Coverage of
the Balkan
Wars*

Archibald Forbes, who had won distinction as a correspondent for the London *Daily News* during the Franco-Prussian, Russo-Turkish, and other wars and expeditions, had opened many a conversation by predicting that "There'll be trouble in the Balkans in the spring." He knew that area from experience, and often enough there was trouble, whether in the spring, summer, or fall.

Trouble in the Balkans on all occasions had held the potential for becoming trouble throughout Europe, and the danger was never of more concern than it was during 1911–13. For that reason the great powers used their influence to confine the conflicts to the narrowest possible geographical area and to bring them to an end as rapidly as possible.

Some publishers and editors recognized that Balkan conflicts had significance warranting careful attention. Since unrest and military action had been common in the area, even as Forbes said, there were editors, particularly in far parts of the world, who did not understand the complex issues and dismissed events and even military action in the area as of minor importance, hardly worth any space. Most readers were equally disinclined to pay attention to what some regarded as episodes of comic opera in some vague Graustarkian area.

This attitude was not shared, however, by news correspondents in such capitals as Rome, Vienna, Sofia, Belgrade, Athens, and Constantinople. They understood the problems and so did some editors in Europe. The result was that, even though the Italo-Turkish War was scarcely reported from the field, the two Balkan wars following were covered by a considerable group of newsmen.

Among correspondents thoroughly familiar with the Balkans were W. H. G. Werndel and Fergus Ferguson, both of Reuter, who specialized on the area for more than thirty years. Dillon, St. Petersburg correspondent for the *Daily Telegraph* for twenty years, knew Crete and the Balkans intimately. James D. Bourchier of the *Times* had been in Vienna and Sofia for fifteen years. Steed, also of the *Times*, had been in Vienna since 1902 and in Rome before that. Appointed as foreign editor of the paper in 1912, he delayed his return to London for a year because he regarded the Balkan situation as so important that he wished to remain in Vienna.

Other correspondents well acquainted with the situation included Melton Prior, dean of the corps and artist-correspondent for the *Illustrated London News,* Bennet Burleigh and Ashmead-Bartlett of the *Daily Telegraph,* and Percival Phillips of the *Daily Express.* All three had reported in the field some parts of the Italo-Turkish War of 1911–12. Frederic Villiers, almost Prior's equal in field experience, represented the *Graphic.* Also richly experienced was Lionel James of the *Times.*

Younger newsmen reporting the wars included Valentine Williams in Vienna and G. Ward Price in Constantinople, both for the *Daily Mail;* Cyril Campbell in Belgrade, and Philip P. Graves and David Loch in the field, all three for the *Times;* Percival Gibbon of the *Graphic;* Alan Ostler of the *Daily Express;* Henry W. Nevinson and Martin Donohue of the *Daily Chronicle,* along with Philip Gibbs, on his first war assignment for that paper.

In Rome, an important listening post on the Balkans, there were such established resident correspondents as William Miller of the *Morning*

Post, William Francis Hubbard of the *Times,* and Salvatore Cortesi of the Associated Press.

All of these correspondents, except Cortesi, represented the British press. The press of the United States was served by Stephen Bonsal of the *New York Herald,* Frederick Palmer, writing for the *New York Times,* George Abel Schreiner of the Associated Press, and James H. (Jimmy) Hare, news photographer for *Collier's Weekly,* and representative for the London *Sphere.* All were familiar with the Balkans and had previous experience in war coverage. Other U.S. correspondents included Herbert Adams Gibbons of the *New York Herald,* and three representatives of the *Chicago Daily News:* Paul Scott Mowrer, its Paris correspondent, Lewis Edgar Browne, and Constantine Stephanove, Belgrade stringer. E. Alexander Powell represented the *New York World.*

More correspondents for the press of countries other than Great Britain and the United States were present for the coverage of the Balkan wars than for any other previous event. The Agence Havas was particularly represented by Jean Maury, Constantinople correspondent moving widely in the field, Horace Trouvé in Belgrade, Ludovic Péricard leaving his Berlin post to play a part, and by André Meynot. Bellanger moved to Athens from Tripoli, where he may have reported the Italo-Turkish War. Cartier was in Vienna; Vassenhove in Sofia.

Three German correspondents are known to have been in the field, including a Herr Goteborg of the Berlin *Lokal Anzeiger.* At least eight wrote for the Austrian press, five of them army officers. One was a Lieutenant Hermenegilde Wagner writing for the *Reichspost* of Vienna. Bourchier of the *Times,* unsuccessful in having any one of his own assistants in Sofia attached to the Bulgarian army, depended somewhat upon Wagner for information. Regrettably, Wagner was neither accurate nor impartial, yet he was quoted throughout Europe and Reuter carried his reports to the world.

Those correspondents undertaking to describe the action of the wars sought attachment either to the Turkish forces or to one of the other belligerent armies. Those with the Turks naturally made Constantinople their center. Most of the others, perhaps as many as one hundred in the course of the wars, gathered at Sofia, the Bulgarian capital. No more than half that number actually went into the field. Those who did, however, followed earlier precedents for war coverage and moved with considerable equipment, including horses, wagons, and servants to assist them. The correspondents with Turkish forces were fewer in number, but Turkey was inclined to be more helpful than the other governments.

For those in the field there was danger and hardship. They were under fire at times and faced the hazard of being mistaken for spies and mistreated or executed. Fortunately, nothing of that sort happened. But unless they had their own transportation, they were likely to be immobilized. Even if they did, the terrain was rough and unmarked for directions. Food was difficult to obtain, and usually costly. The weather was unpredictable, and shelter was not always available or adequate. Communications were uncertain and subject to interruption. Censorships were strict and often inconsistent. The correspondent needed to be in good physical condition, or retire from the field.

In the field or not, some of the correspondents reported both wars from beginning to end. Among them were James of the *Times,* Ashmead-Bartlett of the *Daily Telegraph,* Ostler of the *Daily Express,* and both Price and Williams of the *Daily Mail.* A considerable number of the correspondents became actively engaged once again in the Great War so soon to overwhelm all of Europe and the world itself.

U.S.–Mexican Expeditions, 1914–17

The revolution in Mexico that ended the long dictatorship of Porfirio Diaz in 1911 was followed by an internal contest for power. As 1914 began, Victoriano Huerta occupied the presidency of the republic, but had been denied diplomatic recognition by the government of the United States because the validity of his election to office was questioned.

The United States became directly involved in the continuing Mexican struggle wholly by chance when a small party of U.S. Marine officers and men went ashore at Tampico in April 1914 to purchase ship supplies. Normally, a routine procedure, they were arrested and held for an hour or two. Although released, with apologies, the commander of the U.S. naval squadron to which they were attached demanded a formal salute of the U.S. flag by Mexican troops. This was refused by President Huerta himself. Three days later, President Wilson ordered units of the U.S. fleet to Tampico Bay, with congressional approval of his request for authority to use the armed forces to obtain what was deemed proper "recognition of the rights and dignity of the United States."

U.S. naval forces soon went ashore also at Vera Cruz, 250 miles south of Tampico, and off the Bay of Campeche. Marines occupied the city, and the custom house was seized to prevent the landing of military supplies from Germany for the Huerta government. This action brought Mexican opposition and some exchange of fire, with casualties on both sides. Mexico severed diplomatic relations with the United States in a situation that might have led to war. Argentina, Brazil, and Chile, through their diplomatic representatives in Washington, offered to arbitrate the dispute. Settlement was reached in an ABC Conference from May to August at Niagara Falls, New York.

Meanwhile, U.S. forces remained in Vera Cruz. The Navy and Marines were relieved there by elements of the U.S. Army under Brigadier General Frederick Funston, who also acted as military governor until November when the forces were withdrawn.

In that period, Huerta had been formally elected to the Mexican presidency on July 5, 1914. A continued refusal of the United States to accord recognition to his government, however, made his position untenable, as he himself conceded, and he resigned on July 15 and left the country. He was arrested in New Mexico in 1915, charged with attempting to organize a new revolution in Mexico. He died at El Paso in January 1916.

With Huerta's departure from Mexico in July 1914, General Venustiano Carranza assumed the presidency on a provisional basis. He was promptly recognized by the United States, and later by Great Britain and seven Latin American states. His position was not secure, however. Francisco ("Pancho") Villa, formerly a military aide, had split with Carranza, declared opposition to his government, and established an effective control in the north of Mexico. Carranza had control in the south, including Mexico City, with General Alvaro Obregón as his new military commander, but with General Emiliano Zapata in opposition.

Civil strife continued in Mexico from 1914 to 1916. By that time the Carranza position was improved. Most of Villa's followers had left him and he had been declared an outlaw and a bandit. Seeking supplies and money to support his continuing campaign, nevertheless, he led a small force that stopped a train in January 1916 at Santa Isabel, a short distance south of the Texas border, and shot eighteen U.S. mining engineers who were aboard. On March 9, he led about 400 men in a raid across the border at Columbus, New Mexico, burning the town and killing eight U.S. soldiers and nine civilians.

Earlier fighting in the north had affected U.S. interests in Mexico itself and President Wilson had warned Carranza that unless order was maintained the United States might feel obliged to intervene. The

Tampico-Vera Cruz episode had ended in November 1914, but less than a week after the Villa raid of 1916, and this time with the consent of the Carranza government, a U.S. punitive expedition of 12,000 men crossed into Mexico with the object of capturing Villa. Funston, now a major-general based in El Paso, was in command at the border. Command of the troops was assigned to Brigadier General John J. Pershing, a career officer promoted to major-general while on the Mexican assignment during the months following.

Despite his original consent to the expedition, Carranza soon protested the presence of U.S. forces on Mexican soil. In April 1916, a clash occurred at Parral, about 450 miles south of El Paso, between Carranza forces and a U.S. contingent. To avoid more serious trouble, the U.S. forces retired north of the border. In May, however, Villa raided again, killing three more U.S. soldiers and two civilians. This led President Wilson to send more troops to the border and to order all National Guard troops mobilized, with some assigned to the Mexican front. A number of detachments again moved south in pursuit of Villa, and again met some armed opposition from Carranza forces.

This confused situation never was solved in any clear-cut fashion, militarily or politically. United States troops, growing to 150,000, remained at the border until February 1917. The raids did not cease. There were others in 1918 and 1919, and U.S. detachments made brief forays into Mexico. They were unsuccessful in capturing Villa even though he was operating near Juárez, just across the border from El Paso. Offenses against U.S. citizens continued sporadically until 1920.[1]

The situation on the Texas-Mexican border was quiet during the winter of 1916–17. Public attention in the United States was by then greatly directed to the war in Europe, and by late 1916 it was affecting the United States in ways that made the Mexican border problem seem almost irrelevant.

A German declaration of unrestricted submarine warfare to begin on February 1, 1917, along with serious U.S. shipping losses already

---

1   In 1920, Carranza's military commander and minister of war, General Obregón, turned against him, drove him from Mexico City, and he was assassinated in May. In June, Villa surrendered to Obregón and was permitted to retire to private life. Obregón was formally elected to the presidency in December 1920. About three years of relative order followed. In 1923, Villa participated in a new revolt, this time against Obregón, and was himself assassinated in July. Obregón continued in the presidency until 1924, and was succeeded by General Plutarco Elías Calles from 1924–28. Obregón was elected in 1928 to serve another term but was assassinated before taking office. Emilio Portes Gil, a lawyer, then was elected by the Mexican Congress as provisional president.

experienced, led the United States to break off diplomatic relations with Germany on February 3. Other U.S. ship sinkings followed in February and March. Earlier, the United States had uncovered efforts by Germany to sabotage industrial production and advance propaganda efforts. One result was a demand for the recall of two German military attachés in Washington, Captains Franz von Papen and Carl von Boy-ed. Later in February 1917, it became known that Germany was seeking to encourage Mexico to make war on the United States, and was prepared to assist. Mexico's reward would be to regain areas of Texas, New Mexico, and Arizona lost in the U.S.–Mexican War of 1845–48.

In light of the growing impact of the European war on the United States, Pershing had been recalled from the Mexican border late in January 1917 for assignment in Washington. Most of the troops were withdrawn in February, including National Guard units, to be regrouped and prepared to form part of an American Expeditionary Force (AEF) in France, if war were declared.[2]

In April 1917 the United States declared war on Germany and joined the Allies, designated in accordance with President Wilson's insistence as an "Associated" power. Pershing arrived at Liverpool in June and proceeded immediately to Paris. Assigned to command the AEF, he was made a full general in October. Meanwhile, the first members of the AEF arrived in France on June 26. Others followed, but it was about a year before any U.S. troops entered into active combat.

Coverage of the U.S.–Mexican Expeditions

The events that took U.S. military forces to Vera Cruz and to the Texas border in 1914–17 were tangential to the internal contest for control of the government in Mexico. This contest was reported before, during and after the period of U.S. involvement, by staff and stringer correspondents, chiefly in Mexico City, for the Agence Havas, Reuters, the Associated Press, the United Press and a number of U.S. newspapers. Others, of course, moved to report the military action in which the United States was involved.

2   In February, also, Major General Funston, who had been in command on the border, died in San Antonio. Known also for his service in the Philippines immediately after the Spanish-American War, he had captured Emilio Aguinaldo, leader there of the insurrectionist-guerrilla forces.

Among correspondents, Robert H. Murray had been in Mexico City for the *New York World* since 1910 and remained until 1919. Stephen Bonsal of the *New York Herald* had taken a sabbatical in 1911 to visit the West Indies and Latin American countries for the *New York Times*. He was in Mexico when Porfirio Diaz was forced out of the presidency that year and remained for a time. Other visiting journalists in Mexico shortly after the departure of Diaz included David Lawrence and Burge McFall, both of the AP; Hamilton Peltz, *New York Herald;* Earl Harding, *New York World;* Guy Core, *Omaha Bee;* and John Reed, *El Paso Herald,* acting also as a stringer for the UP. Others in Mexico City before 1914 included G. F. Weeks, who arrived in 1913 for the *New York Herald* and remained until 1920, and Paul Wootan, a stringer for the *New York Times* while serving on the staff of the English-language *Mexican Herald.* Norman Walker was present for the AP and Ralph Turner for the UP, until moved to France in 1918.

The incidents at Tampico and Vera Cruz in 1914 brought newsmen to Mexico in considerable numbers, including photographers and newsreel cameramen. Some had previous experience in reporting military action, but others represented a new generation of correspondents.

The group included William G. Shepherd of the United Press, who was first with reports of the U.S. Marine landing at Vera Cruz. George Abel Schreiner, who had been in Europe for the AP, also was at Vera Cruz, along with Walter C. Whiffen and Kirke Simpson of that agency. Novelist Jack London, with experience in reporting the Russo-Japanese War, was present for *Collier's Weekly.*

Three visiting writers were arrested while en route to Mexico City, although traveling under a "safe conduct" pass to interview President Huerta, but were released through the good offices of the British ambassador to Mexico. They were Richard Harding Davis, by then a seasoned war correspondent, representing the Wheeler Syndicate which was established in 1913 in New York by John Neville Wheeler, formerly of the *New York Herald* staff from 1908–12; Frederick Palmer, also an experienced war correspondent, then writing for *Everybody's Magazine;* and Medill McCormick of the *Chicago Tribune,* one of its stockholders and briefly the paper's publisher before 1910 but to become a congressman (1917–19) and a U.S. senator from 1919 until his death in 1925.

Other correspondents reporting some parts of the Vera Cruz occupation from April to November of 1914 included John T. McCutcheon, cartoonist-correspondent for the *Chicago Tribune,* and

Joseph Medill Patterson, also of the *Tribune,* who was a correspondent during the Boxer Rebellion in China in 1900. He was a cousin of Medill McCormick and very soon became copublisher of the *Tribune* along with Robert R. McCormick, also his cousin and younger brother of Medill McCormick. A third representative of the *Tribune* at Vera Cruz was Floyd Gibbons, a reporter on the paper's local staff since 1912.

McCutcheon had previous experience during the Spanish-American War and the South African War as a member of the *Chicago Record* staff, and in the coverage of the Russo-Japanese War for the *Tribune.* He interviewed Francisco Villa and made a sketch of him before he became an outlaw. Gibbons also became acquainted with Villa and covered some of his later activities in northern Mexico prior to 1916.

James H. (Jimmy) Hare, photographer for *Collier's Weekly,* experienced in the Spanish-American and Russo-Japanese Wars, photographed Mexican leaders, including Villa. Gregory Mason of *Outlook Magazine* covered the activities of Villa and Carranza alike. So also did John Reed, by then for the *New York Times.* Still other correspondents reporting this period of the U.S. controversy with Mexico were Vincent Starrett, *Chicago Daily News;* Thomas P. Costes, *New York American;* Robert (Steed) Dunn, also known as an explorer, *New York Evening Post;* and Caspar Whitney, *Harper's Weekly.* So far as is known, the only representative present in Vera Cruz for the press of any country other than the United states was Oliver Madox Hueffer of Central News, London.

With the war in Europe commencing about August 1, roughly three months before U.S. forces were withdrawn from Vera Cruz, some correspondents left Mexico to cross the Atlantic. Among those who did so were Richard Harding Davis, Shepherd, Palmer, McCutcheon, Schreiner, Whiffen, Joseph Medill Patterson, and Hare. They were followed soon after by Robert Dunn, John Reed, and Oliver Madox Hueffer.

The second period of U.S.–Mexican involvement began two years later, when General Pershing was in command of the U.S. punitive expedition moving south from the Texas border. With U.S. troops concentrated on that frontier in 1916–17, correspondents gathered in the El Paso area, the base of operations under General Funston.

George L. Seese of the Associated Press, who knew Mexico well and something of Pancho Villa's movements, was in Columbus, New Mexico, when the Villa raid of March 1916 occurred. The AP also was represented by Howard K. Blakeslee, later known as a science writer, and by Sumner N. Blossom, later editor of the *American Magazine.*

Edward T. Conkle, Chicago bureau chief for the United Press, was in charge of that agency's coverage. U.P. staff members included Hal O'Flaherty, who had been manager of the Milwaukee bureau, Webster (Webb) Miller, recently of the *Chicago American* staff, and Harold D. Jacobs, later to become UP cable editor in New York.

The Hearst newspapers, and through them the International News Service, received reports from Damon Runyon, Alfred Henry Lewis, and Wallace Smith.

Floyd Gibbons was present as a representative of the *Chicago Tribune* along with Walter Noble Burns. Junius B. Wood represented the *Chicago Daily News;* Frank Elser and L. A. Speers, the *New York Times;* William A. Willis, the *New York Herald;* Byron Utecht, the *New York World;* Clare Kenamore, the *St. Louis Post-Dispatch;* and Mrs. Henrietta Eleanor Goodnough Kinley, writing under the name of Peggy Hull, the Newspaper Enterprise Association.

The only foreign newsman present, so far as is known, during this second period of U.S.–Mexican involvement, was Hamilton Fyfe of the London *Daily Mail.* He had reported the first phase of the European war in Belgium and France and later returned there. In the United States on a British government mission in 1916, he took time to visit the Mexican border briefly, perhaps to assess the quality of the U.S. Army in the field.

As the troops were withdrawn from the border in February 1917, those correspondents remaining also were redeployed. Just as some who had been at Vera Cruz in 1914 had gone to Europe to report the war there, some of those at the Texas border did the same in 1917 and 1918. Among them were Gibbons, Miller, O'Flaherty, Wood, Turner, Kenamore, Walker, and Peggy Hull.

The difficulties in Mexico were not at an end in February 1917 when most of the troops left the border, nor were the border incidents. Coverage of Mexican affairs reverted to those correspondents working in Mexico City, while the attention of the press and people of the United States turned primarily to events relating to the war in Europe.

Confrontation: The Great War, 1914–18

11

On Sunday, June 28, 1914, the Archduke Francis (Franz) Ferdinand, heir to the Austrian-Hungarian throne, made a ceremonial visit to Sarajevo, capital and administrative center of the provinces of Bosnia and Herzegovina, annexed by Austria in 1908. He was accompanied by his wife, the former Countess Sophie Chotek.

Bosnia and Herzegovina were Slav states. So was adjacent Serbia. The successes of Serbia in the recent Balkan wars, reversed by Austrian intervention, had revived Pan-Slav enthusiasm in those areas. The archduke, nephew of the aging Hapsburg Emperor Francis Joseph I, symbolized the anti-Slav policy of the Vienna government, and was viewed with little affection in Serbia.

In these circumstances, members of a patriotic society and students in Sarajevo, aware of the archduke's visit, made plans to assassinate him. The first attempt failed. One of the conspirators tossed a bomb into the open automobile in which the archduke and his wife were riding, but he himself tossed it out before it exploded. An hour later, after a ceremony at the City Hall, another of the conspirators, Gavrilo Princip, fired three revolver shots at the royal pair in the automobile as it stopped nearby. The archduke was killed; his wife was wounded and died soon after.

The assassination received full attention in the world press, although political assassinations were not uncommon. King George I of Greece had been killed in March of the previous year, and President Madero of Mexico in February. After the first shock, Europe relapsed into what seemed a normal summer calm, and the rest of the world gave the matter little further thought.

Vienna did not forget, however. Although the assassination of the heir to the throne had occurred in the capital of Bosnia and was accomplished by Bosnian conspirators; they were racially Serbian Slavs, and had obtained their weapons in Serbia. Austria held Serbia responsible for inciting and supporting the act. Urged further by Germany, Austria-Hungary delivered an altimatum to Serbia on July 23 demanding the right to determine Serbian government policy on some matters. A reply was called for within twenty-four hours.

Serbia appealed for support to Russia, also a Slav state sympathetic to Slavic interests. Russia, however, advised Serbia to agree to the demands, and it did so, almost entirely. Because it did not agree completely, Austria broke off diplomatic relations with the Belgrade government. Then on July 28, one month after the Sarajevo shooting, Austria declared war on Serbia. The next day, Austrian-Hungarian forces shelled Belgrade, just across the frontier. Thus began the Great War of 1914–18—now commonly referred to as World War I.

Russia ordered mobilization of its forces on July 29. Coincidental Russian and British proposals to the European powers for a discussion of the situation, looking to its peaceful solution, were rejected by Austria, and also by Germany, which supported the Austrian action. At the same time, Germany demanded that Russia demobilize at once. It further demanded a statement from France as to whether it would or would not remain neutral in the event of war. Great Britain, for its part, asked both Germany and France to assure respect for the neutrality of Belgium if war should occur. France replied that it would do so. Germany made no reply.

The wires hummed from July 29 through July 31 with these demands and counter-demands, and diplomatic representatives in all capitals were busy moving to and from the various foreign ministries on their assigned errands.

When Germany failed to receive assurances within the specified twelve hours that Russia would reverse its mobilization orders, it declared war on Russia on August 1.

France, in an agreement with Russia in 1893 and 1894, reenforced in 1912, had established an assurance of mutual military support in any controversy by which either was attacked by Germany or Austria or, indeed, Italy. This accounted for Germany's demand upon France July 29 for a statement of its neutrality. With no such assurance received within the specified eighteen hours, Germany moved troops into Luxembourg on August 2, and declared war on France on August 3. Great Britain had assured France on August 2 that if the German fleet attacked the French coast along the English Channel, the British fleet would aid France.

Germany not only ignored a British ultimatum that it respect Belgium's neutrality, but declared war on Belgium August 4, and sent troops into that country. Britain declared war on Germany that same day, and so aligned itself with France, Belgium, Luxembourg, and Russia, not to mention Serbia. The countries of the British Empire also promptly extended their support to the mother country.

The dominoes continued to fall. Austria-Hungary on August 6 declared war on Russia, aligning itself with Germany. Both France and Great Britain responded by declaring war on Austria-Hungary on August 12, in support of Russia. Serbia meanwhile was resisting Austrian aggression as best it could. Montenegro joined with Serbia on August 5, and both also declared war on Germany. Japan, which had formed a mutual defense alliance with Great Britain in 1902, with treaties also in 1910 with both Great Britain and Russia, declared war on Germany August 23, and on Austria two days later.

Germany had signed a treaty of alliance with Turkey on August 2, and Turkey joined in a naval attack on Russia on October 29. Between November 2 and 5, Russia, Serbia, Great Britain, and France declared war on Turkey. Britain also proclaimed the annexation of the island of Cyprus in November, and in December proclaimed a protectorate over Egypt for its defense against Turkey, and for the defense of the Suez Canal, long since viewed as "the lifeline to India." Turkey, with Germany's encouragement, declared a Jihad, or holy war, on November 14. Australian and New Zealand (Anzac) troops arrived in Egypt to support the Allied position in the Mediterranean area.

Italy, although joined with Austria and Germany in a Triple Alliance since 1882, with the last of several renewals in 1912, nevertheless proclaimed its neutrality on August 3, taking the position that it was not obligated by the terms of that alliance to join in any "aggressive war." In May 1915, however, Italy deserted the Triple Alliance entirely by declaring war on Austria, thus joining with France, Great Britain, and Russia. On August 21, 1915, Italy also declared war on Turkey.

If Italy's move had come as something of a surprise in a switch of loyalties, another came in October 1915 when Bulgaria, previously at odds with Turkey, joined with that country, as with Austria and Germany, and declared war on Serbia, with which it had been both allied and then in conflict during the Balkan wars. Within the week, Montenegro, Britain, France, Russia and Italy all declared war on Bulgaria, in support of Serbia.

A further complication of belligerencies occurred in 1916. In March, Germany and Austria both declared war on Portugal, which had been allied by treaty with Great Britain. In August, Rumania gave support to Russia by declaring war on Austria. Germany, Bulgaria, and Turkey responded promptly by declaring war on Rumania. In the same period, Italy, already at war with Austria and Turkey, added its declaration of war on Germany.

The years 1917 and 1918 brought a further involvement of nations. The United States, departing from its earlier neutrality, broke diplomatic relations February 3 and declared war on Germany on April 6, 1917, and on Austria December 7. Greece, on June 27, 1917, declared war on Austria-Hungary, and also on Bulgaria and Turkey. Turkey had severed diplomatic relations with the United States in April. Between April 1917 and July 1918, declarations of war against Germany came from Panama, Cuba, Siam, Liberia, China, Brazil, Guatemala, Nicaragua, Costa Rica, Haiti, and Honduras. Of these, Siam, China, Panama, Cuba, and Nicaragua also declared war on Austria. Short of war, Bolivia, Peru, Uruguay, and Ecuador all severed diplomatic relations with Germany. Of all these latter countries, Brazil was alone in sending forces to the battle zone in Europe.

With nations of all continents so involved, what began as a European war became a world war, in the literal sense. One of the most significant events of the war years, an event transcending almost anything else in its lasting influence, was the revolution that began in Russia in March 1917, with the abdication of Czar Nicholas II. This was a prelude to a second or Bolshevik revolution in October. With German complicity, this had the effect of removing Russia from the war as one of the Allied powers. The official withdrawal came in December, followed by the establishment of a new Communist government in Moscow in March 1918.

The Russian desertion from the alliance released German and Austrian forces previously engaged on the eastern front for service on the western front, with the prospect of breaking the long stalemate there and bringing victory for the Central Powers. That this did not occur was because British and French forces were able to check a strong March 1918 offensive directed by Germany's General Ludendorff, and because U.S. forces by then present in sufficient numbers were prepared to join effectively in the campaign by June. A turning point came in July in an Allied counter-offensive, and an end of the war was in sight by August, with the balance then on the side of the Allied and Associated powers.

Allied advances in the south of Europe and in the Middle East, proceeding from June 1918, brought the surrender of Bulgaria in September and both Turkey and Austria-Hungary in October.

In that month, Germany also appealed to President Wilson for an armistice. Heavy fighting proceeded, nevertheless, in France. Ludendorff resigned his command, the Germans retreated in France and in Belgium, German naval forces mutinied at Kiel and then in other ports, and a revolution broke out in Munich. Prince Max of Baden, chancellor and foreign minister since October, advised Kaiser Wilhelm II to abdicate. The abdication was announced November 9, and Philipp Scheidemann, Social Democratic party leader, proclaimed a new German republic. Advised by Field Marshal von Hindenburg that the loyalty of the army was uncertain, Wilhelm II took refuge on November 10 in neutral Holland. A German armistice commission, headed by Mathias Erzberger, leader of the Center party, already had been received on November 8 by France's General Ferdinand Foch, since April the commander-in-chief of the Allied armies in France. Erzberger had no option except to sign the terms of an armistice designed to make renewal of hostilities impossible. It called for the cessation of fighting at 11 A.M. on November 11, 1918, and brought an end to the war. The last German troops left France November 18 and Belgium November 26. At the same time, French, British, and U.S. troops began an occupation of Western Germany between November 25 and December 1. A Peace Conference followed in Paris in 1919, with the last treaties signed in 1920.

Governmental changes of a relatively routine sort occurred in the belligerent countries during the war years, although some were important and significant, involving elections and appointments. But unpredictable changes also occurred, notably the abdication of Czar Nicholas in March 1917, and the second Russian revolution of October, with the withdrawal of that country from the war, and the establishment of a Communist government. Lord Kitchener, British minister of war, also had been lost at sea while on a journey to Russia in May 1916. Austria's Emperor Francis Joseph died in November of that year, aged eighty-six, and because the heir-apparent, the Archduke Francis Ferdinand, had been assassinated at Sarajevo in 1914, his grandnephew succeeded as Charles I.

In Greece, King Constantine, on the throne since 1913, abdicated in June 1917 in favor of his second son, who became King Alexander. In Turkey, the Sultan Abd ul-Hamid II had been dethroned in 1909, following a military revolt, after thirty-three years of despotic rule. His brother took his place as Mohammed V. In July 1918 he died, succeeded in turn by his brother as Mohammed VI. King Ferdinand of Bulgaria abdicated in October 1918, with his son becoming Boris III. Kaiser

Wilhelm II in November became the fourth ruler to abdicate during the war years, and Charles I of Austria-Hungary also abdicated on November 12, after two years on the throne, and found refuge in neutral Switzerland.

The new German republic, as formally proclaimed on November 9, 1918, was directed provisionally by Philipp Scheidemann and Frederick Ebert, also a Social Democratic party leader. In Austria, the abdication of Charles I was followed the next day by the proclamation of an Austrian republic. An independent Hungarian government under Count Michael Károlyi had been announced in Budapest on November 1, but proclamation of a Hungarian republic on November 12 left him without authority.

Austria's attack on Serbia in July 1914 had triggered World War I. King Peter I of that country, seventy years of age and unwell, had yielded power the previous month to his son, Crown Prince Alexander. On November 24, 1918, three weeks after the Austrian surrender, a United Kingdom of Serbs, Croats, and Slovenes was proclaimed, with Belgrade as its capital. On December 1, a Yugoslav National Council recognized Crown Prince Alexander as head of the new kingdom, virtually a realization of the Pan-Slav concept of earlier times. King Nicholas I of Montenegro was deposed so that country might become part of the united kingdom. In 1921 both the retired King Nicholas I and King Peter I died at the ages of eighty and seventy-seven, respectively. Alexander, the prince-regent, became Alexander I. The kingdom included Serbia, Montenegro, Bosnia, Herzegovina, Croatia, Slovenia, and Macedonia. In 1929 it was renamed Yugoslavia, meaning "south Slav."

The more than four years of war that ended in November 1918 had mobilized more than 65 million persons for military service. Casualties exceeded thirty-seven million, including more than ten million deaths, not counting certainly another million civilians killed, wounded, or dead of hardships. In addition there were more than 400,000 also victims of a 1918 influenza epidemic in the United States alone, far from the scene of the fighting. More were made homeless and even stateless. The monetary cost of the war, greatly exceeding any previous conflict, was estimated at more than $1,500 billion, much still remaining as part of the tax burden borne by a second and third generation.

The Peace Conference, bringing an official end to the war, assembled in Paris on January 18, 1919, and continued until August 10, 1920. The Treaty of Versailles was signed between the Allies and Germany on

June 28, 1919. That with Austria, the Treaty of St. Germain, was signed September 10. The Treaty of Neuilly with Bulgaria was dated November 27. Hungary signed a separate document, the Treaty of the Trianon, on June 4, 1920. The last was the Treaty of Sèvres with Turkey on August 20, 1920, but it was replaced by the Treaty of Lausanne on July 24, 1923.

The Covenant of the League of Nations was included as a part of each of the treaties. Intended to prevent future wars, the League was established in 1920, with its headquarters at Geneva.

New frontiers were set and new nations created in the peace settlements. Austria and Hungary were made separate republics. Yugoslavia and Czechoslovakia became new nations, including areas formerly Austrian, Hungarian, and Bulgarian. Out of territory formerly Russian, German, and Austrian there came Poland, Finland, the three Baltic republics of Latvia, Lithuania, and Estonia, and the port of Danzig, made a free city under the League's administration. Rumania gained territory. The independence and identity of Albania was confirmed.

In the Middle East, out of what had been Turkish territory, there came Syria, Lebanon, Palestine, the Transjordan, Iraq, and part of Saudi Arabia. Mandates were established under the League whereby Syria and Lebanon were administered by France; Palestine, the Transjordan and Iraq by Great Britain. Areas once German in Africa, Asia, and the Pacific, were mandated to Great Britain, France, the Union of South Africa, Belgium, Australia, New Zealand, Japan, and the United States.

Germany was placed under restraints and obligations set by the terms of the Treaty of Versailles. Occupation of the Rhineland by Allied troops under the Armistice terms continued, pending satisfaction of certain of the Treaty provisions. Germany was not to rearm. A monarchy was not to be restored. The provinces of Alsace and Lorraine, lost by France in the Franco-Prussian War, were returned. Germany also was required to make reparations for war damages both by payments in kind and by cash payments over a period of years. This called for the surrender of a great portion of her shipping, submarine cables, certain industrial holdings, and the delivery of tangible goods. The cash payments were to be made in an amount later set at the equivalent of about $25 billion. These provisions, particularly as calling for what soon proved unrealistic payments and deliveries, held within themselves seeds from which new difficulties were to grow.

The war, when it began in 1914, came as a surprise to most persons. Since the Franco-Prussian War of 1870–71, more than a generation had lived in peace in western Europe. Such wars as had occurred had been far from the more populous centers of the world; had been conducted, for the most part, by relatively few fighting men, usually volunteer professional soldiers and sailors; had tended to be short, with limited casualties, and at costs placing no great burden upon the national economies of the countries. There also was a disposition to believe that civilization had attained a point at which major wars were unthinkable.

In retrospect, it is clear that some rulers and some professional military men did not share this latter view, notably in Germany. Among others to whom the war came as less of a surprise were a number of experienced news correspondents. But even they could not grasp what was in store for the world. Henry Wickham Steed, who became foreign editor of the *Times* in 1913 after seventeen years as a correspondent in Rome and Vienna, was not surprised by the war's outbreak, but still did not at first sense the determination of Austria, backed by Germany, to press its campaign on Serbia; nor did he envision the manner in which the war would escalate. Salvatore Cortesi, representing the Associated Press in Rome, recognized the hazard existing from the time of the shooting at Sarajevo. Ellis Ashmead-Bartlett of the *Daily Telegraph,* also saw the danger. James D. Bourchier of the *Times,* long based in Sofia, was professionally prepared as the fighting began, but he was both astonished and dismayed when Bulgaria, which he thought he knew so well, chose to align itself with Austria-Hungary and Germany in 1915.

The immediate preliminaries of the war and its beginnings were reported by correspondents in each of the capitals directly concerned. The speed and scope of the events, however, were beyond the experience of a generation raised in a world where the impact of war and crisis had touched very few. Except for neutral correspondents, those representing the press of the Allied countries had to leave the capitals of the Central Powers countries, and vice versa. Generally, they were evacuated along with diplomatic representatives similarly affected, and with such private citizens as were able to leave, travelers among them.

Even correspondents who had been in the field during the Balkan wars in 1912 and 1913 had no way of knowing how different the coverage of the Great War was to be; they could only assume that the procedures would be much as they had been since 1900. In England, Bennet Burleigh, Frederic Villiers, and Henry W. Nevinson, experienced as they were, began to prepare themselves for new assignments by riding in London's Hyde Park, supposing that they would again need to move about on horses. They began to gather field kits. Some other correspondents imagined themselves consorting with kings and generals, and duplicating or exceeding the feats, by then legendary, of William Howard Russell, Archibald Forbes, and other earlier war correspondents.

Ashmead-Bartlett of the *Daily Telegraph* was summoned from the English countryside on Sunday, July 26, to meet with John Merry LeSage, editor of that newspaper and also once a war correspondent, to be sent off for Vienna to cover what then seemed no more than a possible Austro-Serbian conflict. He took two trunks and five bags of clothing and equipment for all occasions. A fortnight later, with Great Britain itself by then engaged in a suddenly far-spreading war, Ashmead-Bartlett managed to return to London, minus all baggage, having passed through eleven countries, traveled on twenty-nine trains and three ships, expended about £500 (about $2,000), and yet having written no single dispatch.

None of the assumptions of publishers, editors, correspondents, or others, as entertained in July and early August of 1914, in whatever country, survived for long. World War I took on a form unlike any before it. Much of the fighting was to be in some of the most highly populated areas of the world. Rather than a war of movement fought with small arms and cavalry action, the war in France, particularly, became a long stalemate after the first few weeks, with well-entrenched troops in relatively fixed positions. There were new great long-range guns, high explosives, barbed-wire entanglements, machine guns, tanks, U-boats, airplanes, zeppelins, and poison gas. Men were living and dying like rats in fields and farmlands transformed into mudholes, soaked with rain, blood, and snow. Homes, farms, and forests were destroyed; villages and towns reduced to rubble; civilians killed or forced to flee with such small possessions as they could save. Ships at sea were sunk by torpedoes, with hundreds drowned.

Great capitals did not escape. Paris was shelled by long-range guns. London and other British cities were bombed from zeppelins. Propaganda became a far more organized weapon of war. At sea, too, great naval powers were engaged, and convoys moved men and supplies. Ships, both great and small, were sunk; and submarines even threatened coastal areas with gunfire. Manpower and wealth were conscripted.

Numberless families were visited by tragedy. Much of an entire generation was lost, and financial burdens were placed upon millions yet unborn. The brunt of the war was felt in France, but the impact bore heavily upon Great Britain and Russia, the Balkans and Italy, Turkey and the Middle East, Germany and Austria-Hungary, and on other parts of the world where no shots were fired, including British Empire countries and the United States.

It was Sir Edward Grey (later Viscount Grey of Falloden), then British foreign secretary, who sensed the horror ahead. His prophetic remark of August 3, as he looked out the window of his room in the Foreign Office as dusk came over St. James's Park, was to be remembered. "The lamps are going out all over Europe," he said. "We shall not see them lit again in our lifetime." Symbolically, they were to go out over more of the world even than Europe. While they were, in fact, to be relighted long before his own death in 1933, Grey was still correct, in essence, because they never were to burn quite as before, and they lighted a different world.

The people of Europe, however, could not see into the future. Many of them went to war in that beautiful August of 1914 with a song and a cheer, moved by patriotism and the excitement of what seemed a great adventure. Besides, it would not last long, they assured themselves. Two weeks, some said; a month, or six months at most.

If the peoples of Europe were not able to see into the future, or to understand the issues at stake, it is not surprising that peoples in other parts of the world failed to do so. The assassination at Sarajevo in June had seemed to many of those who took note of it at all as "just another fuss in the Balkans."

In the United States, Melville E. Stone, general manager of the Associated Press, discounted warnings from Cortesi that there was serious trouble ahead. When Austria-Hungary presented its July 23 ultimatum to Serbia, Karl H. Von Wiegand, United Press correspondent in Berlin, cabled 138 words on the subject to New York. He was promptly reprimanded for his extravagance in sending a message costing as much as $13.80, at ten cents a word, on such a matter. William Philip Simms, United Press correspondent in Paris, was ordered at the same time, in cablese terminology, to "downhold warscare."

There was more interest in the United States at that time in the events that had been proceeding in Mexico since April, with U.S. forces occupying Vera Cruz. People also were talking about a new motion picture called "The Birth of a Nation," and the Panama Canal was to open in August. There never had been a more exciting baseball season, with the Boston Braves making a sensational late-summer advance to win the National League pennant. They then met the Philadelphia Athletics of the American League, winners of the last four World Series, and defeated them in four straight games out of seven, the first time such a thing had ever happened.

By contrast, the war in Europe seemed secondary at that point. Henry Wood, assisting Simms in the United Press Paris bureau, had received a message from New York: "War interest diminishing. Hold down. World Series begins Monday."

Such reactions did not survive for long, as the importance of the war was recognized. For the first time in history, many persons attending newly popular motion picture performances not only became familiar with Beverly Bane and Francis X. Bushman and followed "The Perils of Pauline," but they also saw Hearst-Selig newsreels and other films of war, increasingly grim in their portrayal of events and of battlefields.

For the press in the United States, some scholars have credited the *Portland Oregonian* with having been the first newspaper to give its readers an intelligent understanding of the storm in Europe.

The *New York Times,* however, was prepared to report the war, and prompt to do so in several ways. It increased its staff in Europe. It used its Sunday rotogravure section to present photos of the war. It established a new *Mid-Week Pictorial* magazine, also in rotogravure, to provide wider distribution of a weekly illustrated report of the war. It established a monthly *Current History* magazine to present supplemental information, including a virtual day-by-day record of events, special articles by qualified writers, and texts of important documents and addresses. It also established a cumulative quarterly index of the entire news content of the daily editions of the paper.

Among newsmen in the United States better prepared than most to understand the issues and events of the war was Frank H. Simonds, then editor of the *New York Evening Sun* and foreign editor of the New York monthly *Review of Reviews.* Following his graduation from Harvard in 1900, after earlier military service during the Spanish-American War, he had worked for the *New York Tribune* and the *New York Evening Post.* With a special interest in history, and particularly of European wars, he had used vacation periods through ten years or more to walk and cycle over old battlefields, many of which were about to become new battlefields.

As he wrote of the war in the *Evening Sun,* Simonds's articles attracted attention. He returned to the *New York Tribune* early in 1915 as a special analyst of war reports, with his articles syndicated for use by newspapers throughout the United States and in other countries. It may be said that he became the first special columnist in the United States to write of international affairs. He later was presented with honorary degrees, received decorations from France, Belgium, and other countries, and continued after the war as editor of the *Review of Reviews* and was the author of books on the war and the postwar world.

Because of the personal interest Victor F. Lawson had conceived some fifteen years earlier in the provision of an international news service for his paper, the *Chicago Daily News* was ready to meet the new challenge. Edward Price Bell in London, Paul Scott Mowrer in Paris, Albert C. Wilkie in Berlin, and John Foster Bass in St. Petersburg were key figures in the European representation.

Mowrer, in the field during the First Balkan War, was concerned with war coverage in France. He also observed the change in the attitude of U.S. editors and readers toward world affairs. When Mowrer accepted the appointment to Paris in 1910, it was contrary to the advice of fellow newsmen in Chicago. Neither they nor readers of the *Daily News* paid much attention to foreign news at that time, and Lawson's concern for such coverage was regarded in the office as an expensive personal eccentricity. Even the managing editor, Charles H. Dennis, supervising foreign coverage, instructed Mowrer not to occupy himself "too much with European politics." What the readers wanted, he said, were "feature stories, quaint episodes illustrative of French life, human-interest stories, stories of Americans abroad." The *Daily News* Paris office, prominently marked, was at the corner of the Rue de la Paix and the Avenue de l'Opera, where American visitors passed, and the paper regularly reminded Chicagoans going to Paris that they might use the office as a kind of headquarters and a place to have mail delivered.

When Italy declared war on Turkey in September 1911, Mowrer and Bell were informed that cabled comment was not desired; the AP reports would be more than sufficient. Mail copy might be acceptable, within limits. And Mowrer was instructed to select the best jokes each week from Paris publications and forward them to Chicago.

In fairness, it must be said that other newspapers, whether in the United States or in Great Britain, gave little space to the news of the Italo-Turkish War. But this very fact began to bother Mowrer. Men were dying in the Libyan desert. Informed persons in Paris were concerned lest the Italian moves should lead to an outbreak in the Balkans, and even a German invasion of France. In his book, *The House of Europe* (1945), Mowrer recalled:

For the first time, I began to discern in the rivalries of nations, a kind of plot or sequence. Things didn't just happen. One led to another. . . . In a dispatch to the *Daily News,* I tried, without editorializing, to indicate the gravity of events; but my dispatch was relegated to the editorial page, as if it were only a bit of philosophy.

When the First Balkan War began in 1912, Mowrer suggested to Bell in London, director of the paper's European coverage, that the situation in that part of Europe might be no less important than that which had resulted in the *Daily News* sending four men to report the Russo-Japanese War eight years earlier. Bell agreed, cabled Chicago, and Mowrer himself went to Serbia, and later to Macedonia and Albania. In addition to dispatches, he took photographs. Both were well displayed in Chicago and in other newspapers receiving the *Daily News* service by syndication, with Mowrer's by-line frequently used.

"Yet it was remarkable," he wrote later, "how soon the public's interest died away." He was not sent to report the Second Balkan War in 1913. During the first war, moreover, Mowrer became a target for a kind of organized pressure, with propaganda purposes, which was to become more common in later years. The *Daily News* received letters signed by persons of Greek origin living in the Chicago area. They protested, for example, because of a reference in one of Mowrer's dispatches suggesting that Albania was Albanian, with the writers contending that it was Greek territory. This disturbed Mowrer when he learned of it, since it seemed to bring his integrity into question, as well as his accuracy. He received reassurance, however, from his more experienced Paris colleague, Elmer Roberts, of the Associated Press. Roberts suggested, probably quite correctly, that the letters to the paper may have been inspired by the Greek consul in Chicago, acting under instruction from Athens, that those who signed them actually knew nothing of the facts and wrote because they had been persuaded to do so, perhaps also under pressure in a diplomatic ploy to shape the news.

When the Great War began in 1914, Mowrer was immediately involved in reporting from Paris, and was presently in the field, but he recalled that quite soon

> The same American public that had been indifferent to the signs and portents were fascinated now by the cyclonic fury of this war in which they had not believed. The papers told of little else. A few editors, resenting the impertinent usurpation of the front page by the foreign interloper, still lay in wait for opportunities to play up again the local fires, accidents, murders and scandals to which they were accustomed.[1]

---

1   Paul Scott Mowrer, *The House of Europe* (Boston, 1945), p. 245.

As Mowrer observed, it was not long before the news of the war was receiving major attention in the newspapers and many periodicals in the United States and in other countries. Understandably, the war received great attention in the newspapers of the nations directly involved. Reports from those countries were at times quoted in the wider, world service, but were received with some skepticism because it was recognized that censorships and self-interests existed.

As the nations declared war between July 28 and August 6 of 1914, the first casualty was an interruption in what had been a well organized flow of information and general communication. There was an immediate halt of telegraphic, cable, and telephone transmissions across frontiers of the countries at war; commercial wireless service was stopped by the Allied governments; postal deliveries were blocked between nations, as well as normal rail, road, and ship movements. There was an end to the news exchange between the Reuter and Havas agencies, on the one side, and the Wolff and Austrian Korrbüro and its Hungarian subsidiary, on the other. The Wolff service to the Russian agency, Westnik, ceased, and Havas provided that world service to Russia through Stockholm.

All German cables in the Atlantic were cut by the British Navy within a few hours after the British declaration of war on August 4, and German cables in Asian and Pacific waters were seized by Japan after its declaration of war on August 23. The use of the Great Northern Telegraph Company line across Russia and Siberia, between Copenhagen and Shanghai, was immediately denied German use because it crossed Russian territory.

The severed end of one of the German Atlantic cables was towed to a French port and assigned to France for use in communication with the United States. Another was used by the British government, with one end towed to make a Canadian landing, and the other end, in the Azores, spliced to a cable from the English shore. The one German South Atlantic cable, from Liberia to Brazil and Argentina, also was reconnected for British use. Those in the Pacific were used by Japan. After the U.S. entrance to the war in 1917, the German submarine U-151 cut two cables off the New York harbor entrance, but they were soon repaired.[2]

---

2 None of the German cables ever was returned to Germany. After the war, the Versailles Treaty provisions for German reparations assigned them to five of the Allied and Associated powers, and particularly to Great Britain, France, and Japan. This was formalized late in 1920 at an International Conference on Communications in Washington.

Despite Germany's loss of its cables, wireless transmission was sufficiently developed by 1914 to provide a certain alternative. Its use across the North Atlantic between England and Newfoundland was ended for Anglo-American press and commercial purposes, although it continued in government wartime use. The relatively new and powerful German transmitter at Nauen was used, however, and was available to U.S. correspondents remaining in that country as neutrals until 1917 as a means of sending their reports to New York. It also was used by the German government-sponsored Syndikat Deutscher Uberseedienst, or Transozean Nachrichten, as it became in 1915, to disseminate a service of news and propaganda by wireless for use without cost wherever received. A second German propaganda agency, Europa Presse, was formed in 1916. News and other messages also moved in and out of Germany during the war by telegraph through adjacent neutral countries—Switzerland, Holland, Denmark and Sweden—and also to and from Austria-Hungary, Turkey, and the Balkan countries.

Correspondents for the press of the United States were more numerous in Europe in 1914 than for any other nation's press, except that of Great Britain. They formed a group of fifty to seventy-five staff and stringer representatives. The number increased as the war continued. As neutrals, they were able to cover all capitals, including Berlin and Vienna, until the United States entered the war in 1917.

In 1914, there were almost no German or Austrian correspondents in the United States, and those in London and Paris left, as did those in Rome in 1915. The total Berlin foreign press group, about thirty in 1914, had declined to about twelve in 1916, with the British, French, Russian, and Italian correspondents gone. It naturally dropped further in 1917 with the departure of the U.S. group. A few Swiss, Swedish, and Dutch correspondents remained. The same erosion occurred in Vienna and Constantinople.

Each capital and country had its own media engaged in reporting the war, and each capital and a few other major cities had active foreign press correspondents and stringers. This obviously was true of London, already the greatest single world news center, and of Paris, the capital nearest the main fighting front and later the center for the peace negotiations. New York and Washington attained new importance, especially in the last two years of the war. Berlin, Vienna, Rome, Petrograd (as St. Petersburg was renamed as the war began), and Warsaw were regularly in the news, especially until 1917. Constantinople, Belgrade, Bucharest, and Athens were among other news centers, and scores of place names became familiar, figuring in the reports of war action.

The media were obliged to extend their efforts to meet the demand for information. The costs were high. Indicative was the expense of the foreign report alone reaching the New York headquarters of the Associated Press. This increased from $225,543 in prewar 1913 to $801,157 in wartime 1918. The total AP expenditure for war coverage from 1914 through 1918 has been estimated at $2,685,125. Costs for other agencies and newspapers rose in proportion. Although annual expenditures by agencies and newspapers were to become greater in later years, the wartime figures represented an enormous outlay, especially considering the purchasing power of the dollar, or other units of currency, at that time. Special assessments upon the press were essential to assure coverage.

The actions of the war receiving the greatest press attention were those on the western front in Belgium and France. Coverage was less intensive on the eastern front, where Russian forces contested with those of Germany, Austria-Hungary, and Turkey.

There never was any direct press coverage of naval action, except around the Dardanelles in 1915, during the Gallipoli campaign, with two or three newsmen then aboard ships involved in the action. It was a campaign authorized by the British War Council, conducted as a joint British-French operation to divert Turkish forces, then exerting pressure on Russia, by sending ships and men into the Straits of the Dardanelles to "take the Gallipoli peninsula, with Constantinople as its objective."

The campaign began with a naval bombardment of the straits in February 1915 and an attempted entrance on March 18. This first effort failed. In April a landing was made on the Gallipoli Peninsula, with a second landing in August, with British, Australian, and New Zealand (Anzacs), and French forces involved. The entire campaign was marked by delays, errors, and failures. Ships were sunk. Allied troops, once landed, were unable to advance against greater Turkish forces, and were driven to entrench themselves. They lacked ammunition and supplies, were plagued by autumn rains, and suffered inevitable casualties. By October 1915, it was generally agreed by members of the War Council that the campaign should be abandoned. But the evacuation was delayed until the nights of December 18–19 and January 8–9, 1916. Miraculously, it was a bloodless evacuation.

Rumania, which had entered the war in support of Russia in August 1916, was crushed four months later by Austro-German forces under

Germany's General Erich von Falkenhayn. A new Russian offensive in the south in 1917 also failed. The revolution, combined with Austrian and German attacks, led to Russia's withdrawal from the war, to all intents in December 1917, and fully on March 3, 1918, when Bolshevik representatives signed the Treaty of Brest-Litovsk.

Meanwhile, Italy also had entered the war in 1915 in association with the Allies, but was stalemated and severely hurt in contests with Austrian and German forces until 1918. Under Allied pressure, and with troop support, Greece entered the war on the Allied side in June 1917. Press coverage in those areas of southern Europe did not extend into the field, with some exceptions, until 1918. Military action against Turkish forces in the Middle East was better reported from October 1917, but such action as occurred in Africa and the Pacific received virtually no direct coverage.

The manner in which the war was to be reported, and the relationship between press correspondents and the military, was a subject of importance from the moment the first shots were fired in 1914. The need for some policy governing that relationship had arisen originally at the time of the Napoleonic wars, and various methods had been followed by governments and military leaders since then. Press representatives had, in fact, provided coverage in almost all war situations, and with growing effectiveness.

Even as late as 1914, however, some military leaders felt that newsmen tended to get in the way. Some feared they might reveal vital information, however inadvertently, and so threaten the security or the success of planned maneuvers. There was concern over the availability and use of communications facilities. Assuming that the correspondents could care for themselves in matters of housing, food, and transportation, if they were in personal danger they still might also become an additional burden on the military.

It was recognized, however, that the press was the only medium through which the public could be informed about a war they were expected to support. The press therefore could not be ignored and its representatives needed to have access to information and opportunity to observe. It was a problem that assumed new proportions in a war to be conducted, as no other before it, in the populous areas of Europe, on an unprecedented scale, and with newsmen of neutral as well as belligerent countries involved. Each government found its own way to meet this problem.

In Great Britain, the press was as highly developed and free as any in the world, and it was greatly experienced in the reporting of wars. The government and the military establishment nevertheless considered restrictions and controls essential, rather than leaving news reporters and correspondents largely to their own devices, as on earlier occasions.

As the war began, Parliament rushed through a Defense of the Realm Act (DORA). It gave new teeth to censorship regulations prepared in 1913 by a committee representing the War Office, the Admiralty, and members of the press, and designed to be put into effect in the event of war. With war a fact, those regulations were immediately applicable. They specified that war reports were to be submitted to an official Press Bureau for approval before publication.

Such a Press Bureau was set up in London, originally under the direction of Frederick Edward Smith (later Lord Birkenhead), a member of Parliament, and his was the final authority in the approval of reports. The Press Bureau also was to issue official war communiqués and to provide information and answers to the press about the war. Through the Press Bureau, further, the government or its military command might issue so-called "D notices" to the press requesting that certain specified items of information be withheld from publication "in the national interest."

These regulations were strengthened by an amendment to the Defense of the Realm Act in 1915. From the outset, also, an Official Secrets Act of 1911 was relevant to press coverage. It made it illegal for any person in government service, at any level, to give information to an unauthorized person, or for a person receiving such information to pass it on to others.

The War Office and the Admiralty were logical sources of information about British war action on land and at sea. The War Office also controlled the accreditation of correspondents who might provide direct coverage of such action on land. Lord Kitchener, greatly honored as a field marshal and statesman in a long military and administrative career and recently granted an earldom, became secretary of state for war as hostilities began. This meant that he headed the War Office. Winston Churchill was the first lord of the admiralty.

Contrary to the views of most others, Kitchener made no secret of his belief that the war would continue for four years, as in fact it did. He performed great feats of recruitment and organization. A dislike for war correspondents was conceived during his service in the Sudan in the

1890s. By his orders, no credentials were granted to newsmen applying to the War Office to accompany the British Expeditionary Forces, whose first members arrived in France on August 9. Further, Kitchener and the War Office ruled that any British correspondents reporting the war in Belgium and France were to be regarded as "outlaws," subject to arrest and prosecution.

So that the press might receive information not only through the Press Bureau but through the War Office, the latter office appointed Colonel Sir Ernest Swinton of the Royal Engineers and author of two books to prepare daily reports on what the military leadership wanted to make known, or have believed, about the progress of the war. These were distributed to the press, bearing the line, "By Eyewitness."

Information did reach the British press from other sources, however. Neutral correspondents and British correspondents already in Paris wrote from there, and some hastened to Belgium or reported from the field in France. Others defied the War Office ruling and went from England to the continent.

It soon became clear to editors in Great Britain that the War Office "Eyewitness" reports conveyed no sense of the reality of the war. This, and objection to the "outlaw" ban on correspondents in France, brought an appeal by editors to Churchill for support in modifying the War Office ruling. Although having gained his own first reputation and political advancement through his correspondence for the *Morning Post* during the South African War, Churchill now shared Kitchener's view. He obstructed any accreditation of correspondents to observe naval action, and recommended London as the place to write about the war. The result was that the denial of accreditation for British correspondents by the War Office continued through the first ten months of the war, until May 1915. They were tightly controlled even after that.

British outlaw correspondents nevertheless were numerous during those ten months, and their reports were published. Despite the War Office ruling, they had the support of their principals in London. This was especially true of Lord Northcliffe, publisher of the *Daily Mail* and of the *Times*. Hubert Walter, of the founding family of the *Times*, with John Walter V still sharing in the ownership of that paper, personally directed its outlaw coverage in the field. Sir Max Aitken, publisher of the *Daily Express* and a native of Canada, went personally to France with Canadian troops and wrote his own eyewitness reports.

Even though the Press Bureau, exercising censorship authority, might have been expected to support the War Office ban on outlaw correspondents, it did not halt publication of their reports. Smith, its director, even supported the use of accounts almost certainly stronger than the War Office wanted to see in print.

The outlaw correspondents faced problems in getting their reports to London, however. Quite apart from the disorganized situation in Belgium in the first weeks of the war, normal communications channels were subject to French and British governmental controls. Some correspondents were able to use the telephone. For a time, a special courier system was maintained, but the War Office halted its operation. Occasionally, with no alternative, and an important story to tell, an outlaw would return personally to London with his report. Philip Gibbs, then representing the *Graphic,* so returning in 1915, was arrested on Kitchener's orders, but was held only briefly.

British outlaw correspondents in Belgium and France, in addition to Gibbs and Walter, included George Jeffreys Adams and Arthur Moore of the *Times.* A considerable group represented the *Daily Mail.* Northcliffe, owning both papers, made personal visits to Belgium and France. The *Daily Mail* group included Joseph M. N. Jeffries, G. Ward Price, William Beach Thomas, George Curnock, Hamilton Fyfe, Ferdinand Tuohy, F. W. Wilson, photographer James Grant Marshall, and playwright Frynwyd Tennyson Jesse, one of the few women correspondents.

Other outlaws included Ellis Ashmead-Bartlett of the *Daily Telegraph,* Percy J. Philip and H. M. Tomlinson of the *Daily News,* Gordon Gordon-Smith of the *Daily Herald,* a Mr. Milligan of the *Morning Post,* and W. T. Massey of the *Daily Telegraph.*

Had it not been for these correspondents, some assigned to Paris before the war began, the British press and public would have been deprived of much information during the first months of the war. More information reached the country and the world through correspondents for the press of the United States also in Belgium and France, and bearing no outlaw designation.

In passing through the official Press Bureau for censorship, reports rarely were cut or changed, but neither the Press Bureau nor the DORA regulations assured accuracy, much less the full truth. Rumors sometimes gained currency as fact. Also, whether because of the loyalty and caution of editors or of correspondents themselves, or because the correspondents were unable to comprehend or verify the full horror of the war, readers were spared the worst of the news and, to that extent, were denied information. When the time came to explain this flaw in reporting it was ascribed to a need to maintain public morale and a willingness to bear the sacrifices of the war.[3]

In the spring of 1915 the war was going very badly for the Allies. Losses of men in France were astronomic. The Gallipoli campaign undertaken in the Mediterranean in February turned into a disaster, resulting among other things in Churchill's replacement as first lord of the admiralty by Arthur Balfour. German submarines were working havoc on ships at sea, greatly dramatized by the sinking on May 7 of the 32,000-ton Cunard liner *Lusitania* off the Irish coast, eastbound from New York, with 1,198 persons lost. One of the victims was Herbert Stone, son of Melville E. Stone, general manager of the AP; another was Patrick L. Jones, en route to join the INS staff in London.

Northcliffe had never ceased to insist upon the right of the British people to know the truth about the war. He denied the official view that they could not stand up to bad news. The loss of the *Lusitania* was one matter, at least, that could not be hidden. But Northcliffe knew from Arthur Moore, *Times* correspondent in France, and from Tuohy of the *Daily Mail,* and others familiar with the Gallipoli failure, that the British had been unable to conduct effective warfare in either place for lack of sufficient ammunition. He held Kitchener especially responsible for a blunder that had cost thousands of lives, and also blamed Churchill, chief advocate of the Gallipoli campaign.

Although a shortage of shells in France as well had first been reported by Colonel Charles à Court Repington, military correspondent for the *Times,* it was verified by others. Northcliffe, at some personal risk, made it a subject of vigorous attack in the *Daily Mail.* This was effective in bringing a change of government, with the Asquith cabinet reorganized as a coalition in May 1915, and a new Ministry of Munitions set up in July.

The Northcliffe campaign also resulted in a reluctant agreement in May by Kitchener by which the War Office authorized the accreditation of correspondents to the British Expeditionary Force headquarters in France, then located at St. Omer. There were conditions attached, however, and the agreement was intended, originally, to be temporary, a mere concession to press demands. In fact, it became permanent, and some of its first limitations also were eased.

This change, spurred by Northcliffe, had the support of the potent London Newspaper Proprietors' Association. Contributing further was

---

3 This is well explained in Philip Knightley, *The First Casualty* (New York, 1975), chapters 5–7.

the fact that F. E. Smith, as chief censor in the Press Bureau, had passed some of the most revealing reports for press use without change, and occasionally even added details. Some members of the cabinet, beyond that, had been persuaded that the British position in world opinion was being harmed by the denial of full press coverage of the war. Foreign comment had supported this view. Former President Theodore Roosevelt, for one, had made his feelings known to Sir Edward Grey, foreign secretary.

Correspondents at last accredited to the British Expeditionary Force headquarters, under the arrangement demanded by the War Office, were classified in three separate groups, British, French, and neutral, each limited in numbers. The correspondents were to wear uniforms and identifying armbands, were to move into the field only with conducting officers, and were to submit their reports to censorship. In turn, they would be housed and fed, provided with transportation and communications facilities.

It was agreed that other British correspondents might be accredited to the French, Russian, Serbian, and Italian forces, since Italy also joined the Allies at this period in May 1915. All of this had the effect of ending the outlaw classification of British correspondents.

Correspondents were not assigned to ships at sea, however. This meant that the naval aspects of the war were reported primarily on the basis of official reports from the Admiralty. One of the notable accounts, unique in its way, was of the Battle of Jutland, fought in May 1916, and the greatest wartime encounter between British and German ships. It was an account written and signed by Rudyard Kipling. Although not a correspondent, in the usual sense, he became a reporter, and received his information from British naval personnel who had participated in the action and were authorized to assist him. The long account was published in four parts in the *Daily Telegraph* of October 19, 23, 26, and 31 of 1916, and reprinted or quoted from that source throughout the world. Despite its official sponsorship, it was regarded as a major story of the war.

The British correspondents accredited to BEF headquarters in France in May 1915 were received there with skepticism and even hostility by British army personnel assigned to assist them. As with those pioneer war correspondents undertaking to report the Crimean War seventy-five years before, they were regarded as a nuisance and possibly a threat to security in the conduct of the war. It was not long, however, before that attitude changed completely, with correspondents welcomed, trusted, and accepted as friends. Henry Lytton was the chief censor of copy.

Near the war's end he was succeeded by Charles Edward Montague, formerly of the *Manchester Guardian,* but then a British officer. These and others who examined the copy usually were men of judgment and wisdom, and correspondents rarely encountered difficulties arising from their treatment of stories. This, it must be said, was also because the correspondents themselves exercised that restraint already noted as having obscured some of the harsh realities of the war.

The British press was permitted only five correspondents at BEF headquarters. One was for Reuters, with his reports going to the entire British press, distributed in the provinces through the Press Association, Ltd., and also going to the Ring Combination agencies in other countries able to receive it. Beyond that, only eight British newspapers were directly represented, but in four pairs, with each of the other four correspondents serving two newspapers. The individual correspondents might change.

The first representative for Reuters was Douglas Williams, son of the former chief editor for the agency, George Douglas Williams. He soon joined the British army, however, and was succeeded by Herbert Russell, who remained throughout the rest of the war.

For the *Times* and the *Daily News,* under the pairing arrangement, John Buchan was the first. He produced a notable report on the Battle of Loos in September 1915. Shortly after that he returned to London, succeeded by M. H. H. Macartney, briefly, and then by Harry Perry Robinson, who remained until the end of the war, except for a brief period when he was relieved by Gerald Fitzgerald Campbell.

For the *Daily Telegraph* and *Daily Chronicle,* Philip Gibbs, most recently returned to the staff of the latter paper, was at BEF headquarters throughout the war, except for a brief period of recuperation in July-August of 1918, when Henry W. Nevinson substituted for him. With the consent of the War Office and of the Newspaper Proprietors' Association, Gibbs's dispatches were syndicated for use in British provincial papers and in some other countries, including the United States. There the *New York Times* published them and also distributed them to subscribing newspapers in the United States and Canada. Gibbs thus became the most widely known British war correspondent, establishing a basis for postwar popularity as a lecturer and a novelist.

For the *Daily Mail* and the *Standard,* Valentine Williams was the first representative at BEF headquarters. A brother of Douglas Williams of Reuters, and a former *Daily Mail* correspondent in Paris and Berlin, he had organized that paper's war coverage in London before moving to France. Like his brother, he also joined the British army in December 1915. He was succeeded at headquarters by William Maxwell of the *Standard,* who had been a war correspondent in the Sudan in the 1890s. His term at headquarters was relatively short, and he was followed by William Beach Thomas, who remained until the end.

For the *Daily Express* and the *Morning Post,* Percival Phillips of the former paper, matched Gibbs in remaining at BEF headquarters throughout the war. U.S.-born, he had reported wars since 1897, and had been with the *Daily Express* since 1901, had covered the Russo-Japanese War, both from Tokyo and later with Russian forces in Manchuria, had written from Japan and China, Jamaica, Spain, and Portugal, had been with President Roosevelt on his European tour in 1910, and with George V on his India visit in 1911, and had covered the Balkan wars.

Russell, Robinson, Gibbs, Thomas, and Phillips, serving at BEF headquarters through some of the most critical periods, all were awarded knighthoods after the war by King George V.

The long tradition of anonymity attaching to the work of British correspondents, only occasionally breached, was almost completely abandoned during the war. Even the *Times,* ultra-conservative on that point, and to become so again after the war, made frequent use of by-lines. This change was almost essential because correspondents, working as they did, were unable to avoid the introduction of a considerable amount of subjective material in describing what they observed. From this, it was both easy and logical to use by-lines on objective reports as well. One result was that some correspondents, and not Gibbs alone, became widely known by name, not only to readers in the United Kingdom, but in British Empire countries and others where their reports were used.

One advantage of the control exercised over correspondents at BEF headquarters in France was that they suffered no casualties. They had a full share of hardship and risk on expeditions in the field, but were compensated by comforts and conveniences at headquarters. There was less opportunity than in some other wars for individual initiative, enterprise, or derring-do. But they could elect to go to certain parts of the line, were provided with transportation and assisted by conducting officers, would hear from responsible officers a review of the situation, and possibly produce exclusive eye-witness accounts. Some brilliant writing emerged, and dispatches were promptly transmitted through army communications facilities. As the tide of the war changed, the headquarters were moved so that the distance from the lines remained much the same. With the Germans in retreat in the last months of 1918, the correspondents, who had been at Rollancourt for some time, moved to the Château of Vauchelles, near Abbeville, until the end of the war.

Henry W. Nevinson, who relieved Gibbs as a correspondent during July-August 1918 at the turning point of the war, presented a picture of the manner in which those at the headquarters worked at that period, when the system was well established. With experience in other wars and on other fronts also giving him a basis for comparison, he wrote:

> In the old days half one's time, or more than half, was spent in finding food and shelter for one's horses, men and self. Now I was welcomed into the stately Château of Rollancourt, near Hesdin—stately in front, but having little more inside than a knifeblade. Copious food was provided three times a day, not to speak of afternoon tea! I had a real bedroom to myself, and servants to make the bed, wash up and cook.
>
> Every evening I need only tell my officer where I wanted to go next day, and at dawn a motor would be snorting at the gate, ready for both of us. When I had driven out, and seen or heard what I could in the time, I returned to the château at about 1:30, and met with the other correspondents (there were only five or six of us). Each told where he had been and what he had seen or heard. Knowledge was equally pooled. There was no rivalry, no 'scooping'.
>
> After lunch all retired to write composite dispatches, the only chance of personal distinction being the 'style,' that is, the way of looking at things, and the proportion kept. By 3:30 our own Press Officers, acting as censors, and living in the château, had read and approved or disapproved. They handed the messages to the despatch-rider, waiting at the door with his motor-cycle, and the thing was done. All had been organized and paid for by the Newspaper Proprietors' Association, and the strain of the war correspondent's life was relaxed until it almost ceased.[4]

The correspondents accommodated in this fashion were not limited to the British press representatives. There also were the French and neutral correspondents at BEF headquarters. For the French there were five also. One served the Agence Havas, and Henri Ruffin filled that assignment throughout the 1915–18 period. The four others, operating on a somewhat less precise pairing system, represented Paris dailies, with their dispatches going also to provincial dailies. Those accredited changed from time to time, but the basic group included Philippe Millet for *Le Temps*, Henri Bidou for the *Journal des Débats*, André Tudesq for *Le Journal*, Raymond de Maratray for *Le Petit Journal*, Serge

---

4 Henry W. Nevinson, *Fire of Life* (London, 1935), pp. 348–49.

Basset and Jean Nignaud for *Le Petit Parisien,* and Jules Hedeman at times for *Le Matin.*

The neutral unit was slightly larger, but was limited to only one representative each for the press of the United States, Norway, Sweden, Denmark, Holland, Switzerland, Spain, and Italy. With Italy entering the war almost immediately after the press accreditation began to the BEF, its status was modified to give it slightly more representation.

The first correspondent for the press of the United States at BEF headquarters was Frederick Palmer, experienced in war coverage since 1897, and in Europe since 1914 for the United Press. He was succeeded in 1916 by Robert T. Small of the Associated Press, formerly in Washington and in Mexico for that agency. He remained until the United States entered the war in 1917. As a belligerent, its press then gained a new status, with a special section at the BEF headquarters. DeWitt Mackenzie, in the AP bureau in London since 1916, moved to the BEF post at that time and remained until the end of the war.

All correspondents with the BEF operated in the same fashion as the British correspondents. There was a change of directions and policy at the headquarters in 1916, however. Lord Kitchener was lost at sea in June while on a journey to Russia, and was replaced as head of the War Office by David Lloyd George. Events themselves brought an increase in the number of representatives accredited. Photographic and cinematographic sections were added and writers for magazines and special services were received. Publishers and other visitors from Allied and neutral nations were given brief tours of the war area in France. Provision also was made through the War Office for the accreditation of press representatives and others to British forces engaged in the Middle East and Italy.

In London, the Press Bureau became a Department of Information in 1917 and then a Ministry of Information early in 1918, performing a wide variety of functions. There also were changes reflecting greater recognition of the importance of information in support of the British and Allied position at home and abroad. The ministry itself, when formed, was headed by Lord Beaverbrook, formerly Sir Max Aitken, who was raised to the peerage in January 1917, and was publisher of the *Daily Express.* Lord Northcliffe was made director of propaganda in enemy lands. John Buchan became director of intelligence.

The urgency of events that brought the Department of Information into being in 1917, and then the cabinet-level ministry in 1918, included an acceptance of propaganda as a weapon of war. It was spurred not only by the hard facts of the war itself, but by the new threats posed by a diversion in Ireland, beginning with a so-called Easter rebellion in Dublin in 1916, and by the Russian Revolution bringing the abdication of Czar Nicholas in March 1917. Other results included the end of the Asquith ministry in December 1916, with Lloyd George becoming prime minister in a new government, and Churchill recalled in 1917 to succeed him as war and air minister.

The issues relating to correspondents representing the British press during the war years applied also to correspondents of other countries, or to correspondents serving in those countries.

In France, the military command at the outset was scarcely more cordial to correspondents seeking to report the war than the British War Office had been. French military commanders were directed to arrest correspondents in their areas, regardless of nationality. This placed British outlaw correspondents in double jeopardy. The French military concept was that the press of France itself, and of other countries as well, should take reports of the war from the Agence Havas, semi-official in its relationship to the government, and that Havas would be given only such information as the military deemed proper. Also, the press was to indulge in no critical comment about the conduct of the war and, in any case, should be subject to censorship.

This concept was not accepted even by the Agence Havas, much less by the French press in general. Georges Clemenceau, recently premier of France (1906–09) and to become so again from 1917–20, but also a journalist, helped to block the designs to control the press. His own political daily of 1914, *l'Homme Libre* (The Free Man), was suspended by government action in September because of Clemenceau's outspoken views. He promptly started another, *l'Homme Enchainé* (The Man in Chains), and continued to make himself heard. He was not alone, and the French government and military modified their original positions.

Credentials were granted to French and other correspondents. In practice, the French press demonstrated only limited initiative in direct coverage of the war. It had correspondents at the BEF headquarters, beginning in 1915, but it was generally willing to accept and use information on the war as provided by the French government, distributed through Havas, even though that information frequently proved wrong or misleading.

Like the War Office in London, the French military command, beginning early in 1915, also made concessions. As the Grand Quartier Général (GQG), it formed its own Information Section to produce and distribute reports of action as "News from the Front" or "Letters from the Front." These, like the British "Eyewitness" reports, were unsatisfactory to the press and did not continue. The Ministry of Foreign Affairs created a Maison de la Presse to provide information, although more political than military. At length, a French press headquarters, comparable to the BEF headquarters, was established at Chantilly, near Paris, also the site of French G.H.Q. during 1914–16, under General Joseph Joffre. The ancient Condé family chateau there had accommodations for French, British, Italian, and neutral correspondents. In theory, Russian correspondents would have been received at either headquarters, but no such correspondents appeared. The chateau, attractively furnished, in beautiful grounds, and with excellent meals, became much favored by correspondents.

Freedom of the press in France vanished during the war, however. The military was able to maintain a strict censorship throughout the period. Centering originally at the Hotel Continental in Paris, it was referred to colloquially, and often bitterly, as "Anastasia." The name derived from Sainte-Anastasia, allegedly the patron saint of censors, and personified in cartoon form as a sour-visaged lady of some age wielding a pair of oversized scissors. Some papers manifested their disapproval of her attention by permitting white spaces to appear in their columns where words or sentences had been excised in the original copy, but this did not continue. The censorship later was moved to the government's Bureau de la Poste, Télégraphe et Téléphone, in the Place de la Bourse.

If the British and French military commands were unwilling as the war began to have press correspondents reporting action in the field, the third major Allied government of the time was even less willing. The Russian government policy had been traditionally hostile to the press, whether foreign or domestic, in peace or war. Despite a certain easing in that respect just before and during the first period of the Russo-Japanese War, the policy existed in 1914.

Foreign correspondents in Petrograd, as St. Petersburg had been renamed to rid it of the German connotation, had limited sources of information and their outgoing reports were subject to censorship. The Russian press was subject to control and received nearly all of its reports through the official Petrograd Telegraph Agency (PTA or Westnik), including a selection from the Havas service, received by way of Stockholm, as a substitute for the German Wolff agency service previously received.

At least one opportunity to observe troop action was granted to foreign reporters early in the war when they were taken in two railway cars to the Galicia battle zone. The effort backfired because of Russian losses on that occasion, and it was not repeated. Correspondents seeking to report the war on the eastern front made Warsaw an advanced base, but rarely went into the field and had to withdraw entirely in August 1915 when German troops took that city. Russian correspondents were rarely permitted to observe battle action and the newspapers were under such close censorship that they were of little informative value.

Germany and Austria, by contrast to the Allied governments, were more lenient and cooperative in their relations with foreign press representatives as the war began. Their own media were under restraint. The German General Staff accredited correspondents from neutral countries, however. They were permitted to go into combat areas under the supervision of conducting officers, and were provided with transportation and communications facilities.

The Wolff-CNB agency, and the Austrian and Hungarian news agencies were under official control, as were the newspapers, but they had their own correspondents covering the war. Special battle reports were provided by a group of correspondents serving also as members of the German armed forces. With the possible exception of some Japanese correspondents during the Russo-Japanese War, they were the first combat correspondents to serve in any war, and ultimately were several hundred in number.

Austria also had a special army section to provide war coverage, and relations with the correspondent group were easier in that country than in any other during the early period of the war. A Presse Quartier in Vienna provided assistance to accredited correspondents. An advanced press headquarters was set up at a village in Hungary, from which correspondents were conducted to battle areas on the eastern front. News was not forthcoming in great volume, but the conditions of life for correspondents were beyond compare. Attractive accommodations, motor transport, servants, good food, wines, and tobacco were provided without cost. Communications facilities were at hand. Horses and even firearms were available for use. The newsmen could relax, enjoy simple recreations, and even go to Budapest or Vienna if they wished.

Sampling these advantages during the first year of the war were more than one hundred correspondents representing the press of Austria and Germany, the United States, Sweden, Denmark, and other neutral countries. Present at various times were Dr. Paul Goldmann, widely known as a writer for the *Neue Freie Presse* of Vienna; a Mr. Siosteen of the *Göteborg Tidning* of Sweden; Robert Atter, Vienna correspondent for the Associated Press; F. C. Bryk, Vienna correspondent for the United Press, and William G. Shepherd, also of the UP; Arthur Ruhl, of *Collier's Weekly;* Constantine Brown, an American and therefore a neutral, but writing for the London *Times;* and Ferenc Molnar, noted playwright and novelist, writing articles for the press of his native Hungary.

News from Austria normally moved through Berlin and, like Berlin news itself, reached other parts of the world by wireless or by telegraph to and through such neutral capitals as Berne, Stockholm, Copenhagen, or Amsterdam and The Hague. Reports from Constantinople likewise moved by way of Vienna and Berlin. War news and general news also moved in a reverse flow through the neutral countries to Germany, Austria-Hungary, and Turkey.

The easier policy in the accreditation of newsmen in the first period of the war in Germany and Austria was moderately advantageous to those governments because it meant a more complete and perhaps earlier and more colorful treatment of the issues and actions of the conflict from their point of view than from countries where the correspondents were obliged to operate under greater restraint. Sources of information were reasonably open, and neutral correspondents were given opportunities to visit both fronts, where the forces of both countries then were advancing successfully.

Whereas the British and French government press policies were eased in 1915, the reverse became true in Germany and Austria toward the end of that year. The first expectation in Berlin for a quick victory had ended in the stalemate on the western front. There followed an establishment of a War Press Office (Kriegspressamt), controlled by the General Staff, to manage all domestic press activities. A comparable office soon was set up within the Ministry of Foreign Affairs, its objective being to shape what neutral correspondents wrote of the war.

Correspondents in Berlin were asked to sign statements promising to remain in Germany throughout the war, and promising that their agencies or publications would use only such dispatches as had been approved by the German censorship. The inference was that only those correspondents giving such assurances would continue to receive information from official sources, be permitted to visit the fronts, or enjoy such other advantages as might exist to the benefit of their personal as well as professional lives.

Correspondents could not properly give any such assurances, of course. They had no authority to do so, nor would any reputable agency or publication approve such commitments. Even though such assurances therefore were not forthcoming, news continued to be made available, and visits to the front were not halted. The censorship became tighter, however, and a major problem was obtaining information about the war at sea, including submarine warfare. A serious issue, particularly after the torpedoing of the *Lusitania* in May 1915, such news was cleared through the German Admiralty and was far more closely controlled than the news of land action.

The war brought a great change in news coverage and news exchange affecting all countries of the world, belligerent or neutral. The exchange through the Ring Combination was nothing like what it had been before the war. The entrance of the United States to the war in 1917 meant the withdrawal of the largest group of neutral correspondents in the countries of the Central Powers. The only correspondents remaining as neutrals were representatives of the press in Sweden, Denmark, Norway, Holland, Switzerland, and Spain. This meant that newspapers of such countries were read with unusual interest in the warring nations. It meant that the capitals of some of those countries became listening posts to which correspondents of the warring countries were assigned to read the newspapers more promptly and to talk with persons leaving or entering the countries at war.

The chief listening posts were Berne and Basel in Switzerland, Amsterdam and The Hague in Holland, Copenhagen, and Stockholm in Scandanavia. Correspondents for the press in the Allied and Central Powers countries were equally involved. This created some curious situations, with correspondents for enemy countries rubbing elbows at the bar or dining at adjoining tables in such places, for example, as the Grand Hotel in Stockholm.

Among correspondents for the Allied countries so assigned, William J. Maloney of Reuters and Thomas Stockwell of the Associated Press were in Amsterdam; Robert E. Berry of the AP and Enid Wilkie of the *New York Times* were in The Hague. The *Daily Mail* and other British newspapers also maintained coverage in Holland. Ludovic Péricard of the Agence Havas was in Basel. Ulrich Salchow of the AP, Carl Sandburg of the NEA, Cyril Brown of the *New York Times,* and Oswald Schuette of the *Chicago Daily News* were in Stockholm, with Brown and Schuette also in Copenhagen at times.

As the German invasion of Belgium began, correspondents for the Anglo-American press, and some for the French press, mobilized there. They moved also to France and, in a more limited degree, to Russia.

The peoples of British Empire countries, with their own men soon on the fighting fronts, were deeply concerned, and newspapers of Australia, New Zealand, Canada, India, and South Africa also were represented. Keith Murdoch, director and editor of the United Cable Service of Australasia, became particularly involved at the scene of the Gallipoli campaign in 1915, and later was in London and in France. Reports for the empire press cleared through London, for the most part, and included accounts by the British correspondents at BEF headquarters in France.

The assignment of correspondents and general media performance during the war years may best be described as relating to the chronology of events in the chapters immediately following.

A Change at Reuter

It is not a digression to examine the special position of the Reuter agency in 1914 and 1915, with wartime influences and an internal crisis bringing an important change in its position.

War coverage sent costs skyrocketing. The news exchange between the Wolff agency of Germany and Reuter as well as Havas, was immediately blocked. The German invasion of Belgium ended the news position long shared by Reuter and Havas in that country.

Other financial problems arose. The British wartime Defense of the Realm Acts of 1914–15 prohibited the use of codes in private telegraphic and cable communication. This brought an end to the profitable Telegraph Remittance system operated by Reuter since 1891 between London, India, and Australia. More serious, the Reuter Bank, or British Commercial Bank, only just formed early in 1914 as a subsidiary, with shares sold to the public, was promptly in difficulties. All foreign investments were frozen, share values declined and no dividends could be paid. The manager of the bank, of Hungarian nationality, happened to be in Austria as the war began and he was conscripted into the Austrian-Hungarian army. German and Austrian staff members of the bank in London were interned. The bank had to be closed for a time, and it became a burden to the agency.

Coincidentally, another sort of problem arose. The war had hardly begun when it was revealed that Otto Hammann, for many years chief of the press department in the German Foreign Ministry, anticipating the war situation, had been organizing a program to use the Wolff-Havas-Reuter news exchange and the Ring Combination to inject propaganda useful to German designs into the world service of news. The intent was to use the Wolff agency, already standing in a semi-official relationship to the German government, as a channel for such reports as suited the policy and purposes of the government. Secret funds also had been used to support the formation of the new German agency, or service, the Syndikat Deutscher Uberseedienst, to broadcast news by wireless by means of the transmitting station at Nauen, near Berlin, with the reports available for use without cost to newspapers or agencies throughout the world. This service, with its propaganda objective, was retitled in 1915, becoming the Transozean Nachrichten. It was further arranged that in neutral countries German industrialists would advertise their products or services only in such newspapers as used dispatches provided through that service.

Just after the war began, also, information was circulated in neutral countries by design or indirection that the Agence Havas had agreed to distribute news prepared in Germany, channeled through Wolff, as in the Hammann program, and disseminated by wireless. Reuter also was said to have been approached with a view to a similar arrangement. Both Havas and Reuter denied any part in such negotiations, which would have made them propaganda agents of the German government. The matter was viewed seriously enough by the British government for it to publish a White Paper in September 1914 with a rebuttal of the charges.

Through the Wolff agency, the Agence Havas apparently had in fact been approached with some such proposal before the war began, although Reuter had not. There is no reason to doubt that the Havas management rejected the proposal. Unauthenticated indications suggested, however, that Léon L. Pognon, with the agency since 1876, and a top administrator in Paris, had held discussions with Wolff that touched upon the possibility of ceding controlling shares in Havas to the German agency. Again incredible, suspicion that there may have been some truth to the matter was not reduced at the time when Pognon committed suicide, and some suspicion fell, however wrongly, on the Reuter agency as well.

The fact that Havas and Reuter, even more particularly, were under constant attack in the German press throughout the war years became the best answer to what ultimately was judged to have been a German government and propaganda effort to discredit and embarrass those agencies as a calculated wartime measure. If so, it was an effort that failed because Reuter reports were given special credence as the war proceeded, not only in Allied and neutral countries, but even by those few persons in Germany and Austria who were in a position to see them in the neutral press or otherwise.

As if these problems were not enough, the Reuter agency was faced with the necessity of a considerable reorganization in the midst of some of the most critical months of the war. The need arose when Herbert de Reuter, sixty-three years old and director of the agency since 1878, inconsolable over the death of his wife three days before, shot and killed himself on April 18, 1915.

The only member of the Reuter family surviving as a possible successor was Reuter's son, Hubert de Reuter, then thirty-nine. He had worked for the agency in Constantinople, schooled by Werndel, an able correspondent, and then in Australia and London. As the war began he went as a correspondent to Belgium and France. His personal interests were in scholarship, rather than in news work, and he had been a schoolmaster. His father had been equally disinterested in news work as a youth, with a preference for music and mathematics. He had yielded to his own father's wish that he assume direction of the agency, where he served with distinction. It is possible that Hubert de Reuter might have done the same. As it happened, however, he had entered the British army early in 1915, was in France at the time of his father's death, and was himself killed in the Battle of the Somme in 1916 while attempting to rescue a wounded companion under heavy machine-gun fire. So ended any prospect of a family member continuing with Reuter in any capacity.

Following the death of Herbert de Reuter in April 1915, and with Hubert in military service, W. F. Bradshaw, with the agency since the 1870s or earlier and secretary of the company for many years, became acting manager. He served until September, at which time the board of directors named Roderick Jones as manager. Bradshaw retired, and was replaced as secretary by S. Carey Clements.

With Hubert de Reuter's death on the battlefield in 1916, a reorganization of the agency was essential and was accomplished in November of that year. The Reuter's Telegram Company, Ltd., so titled since 1865, became more simply Reuters, Ltd. Roderick Jones was confirmed in his position as managing director, a position he was to occupy until his retirement in 1941, during most of which time he also was chief proprietor, with a substantial share interest in the company.

Jones, although born in England in 1878, had been in South Africa almost exclusively from the time of his youth until 1915. Before he was eighteen he had worked for the *Pretoria Press* and the *Pretoria News* in the South African Republic (or Transvaal) and had become an assistant to William Hay Mackay, correspondent in Pretoria for Reuter. He served as a correspondent for the agency throughout the South African War, transferring in that period to the Reuter bureau in Capetown, where he also worked for the *Cape Times*.

With the war at an end in 1902, a new South African Department was established in the Reuter headquarters office in London. Jones, by then twenty-four, was brought to London to head that department. He remained until 1905, when he was named general manager for the agency in South Africa, returning there in charge of news coverage and administration for the following ten years. In that time he played a major role in the formation and direction of the Reuter South African Press Association (RSAPA).

In July 1915, three months after Herbert de Reuter's death, Jones returned to London "to advance his claims for succession" in direction of the agency, as put by Graham Storey in his official centennial history of *Reuters: The Story of a Century of News-Gathering* (1951). What those "claims" may have been, other than his twenty years with the agency and his position as general manager for South Africa, is not specified. He arrived in London, however, bearing a recommendation from Viscount Gladstone,[5] the first governor-general of the Union of South Africa, directed to Mark F. Napier, a member of the Reuter board of directors for more than twenty-six years and its chairman.

Napier believed that Reuter needed a young man to direct its fortunes. Jones, possessing long and solid experience with the agency, and yet only thirty-seven years old, met Napier's specifications. The two agreed that the Reuter news service needed improvement if the agency was to survive, and needed to be made staunchly British. They agreed that with the war in progress a proper course needed to be charted in support of the British government and the Allied cause while avoiding government restraints compromising the agency's reporting of the war. The financial problems that had arisen so suddenly, bearing upon general costs and also upon the critical position of the Reuter-sponsored

---

5   Viscount Gladstone was Herbert John Gladstone, son of William Ewart Gladstone, British prime minister in 1868–74, 1880–85, 1886, and 1892–94.

British Commercial Bank, seemed to call for a full reorganization of the agency's corporate structure. Yet, to do that, capital had to be found to buy outstanding shares in the Reuter's Telegram Company, Ltd., preliminary to the creation of any new company.

With Napier's support, Jones had been named by the board of directors in September 1915 as manager for Reuter. The death of Hubert de Reuter in France in the summer of 1916 made the prompt reorganization of the agency doubly essential. Late in that year financial arrangements were made, with bank loans of £550,000 (almost $2.7 million) approved. This made it possible to purchase 50,000 outstanding stock shares from 1,200 holders. The new private company, Reuters, Ltd., was thereupon formed. Jones was confirmed in the managerial position. A separate sale of the British Commercial Bank was negotiated for £500,000, the total bank loans were reduced accordingly to £50,000 by 1917, and this remaining indebtedness was removed after the war.

Apart from Jones, as its new director, the staff of Reuters, Ltd., remained as it had been previously, including Dickinson as chief editor, Clements as secretary, and Napier as chairman of the board. The board itself was somewhat changed, however. One of its new members was John Buchan, who had already served as a war correspondent in France for the *Times,* and returned to London when the Reuter crisis arose. He continued on the board until 1935, when he became governor-general of Canada, known by then also as a novelist and bearing the title of Lord Tweedsmuir.

The British wartime Department of Information became a full Ministry of Information early in 1918, headed by Lord Beaverbrook, with Lord Northcliffe and John Buchan also holding positions in the ministry.

Jones was knighted early in 1918, becoming Sir Roderick Jones. He was asked to join the ministry to supervise cable and wireless services, and did so for several months in 1918, while also continuing to exercise his full responsibility with Reuters. This particular combination drew criticism, however, viewed by some as making Reuters appear to be an arm of the government, and bringing the independence of its news reports into question. Accordingly, Sir Roderick withdrew from his post in the ministry in September.

Reuter had been reluctant in 1914 to respond to a government suggestion that it include in its service special matter reflecting subjects of wartime concern to the government. Ultimately, however, it did distribute within its world territories reports supportive of the Allied cause. Sincerely concerned with preserving its independent position, it made a distinction by omitting the usual "Reuter" logotype on such reports. Instead, it substituted an "Agence Reuter" logotype. With this small difference, almost certainly overlooked by most receivers or readers, or with its significance obscure, Reuter distributed Allied war communiqués and official news releases to British Empire points, Allied troops, and Ring Combination agencies in Allied and neutral countries.

The agency occupied a favored position in its access to government information. For its special service under the "Agence" logotype it received a government payment of about £120,000 (approximately $600,000), marked to cover communications costs. The agency also received a fee from the United States government after 1917, through the U.S. wartime Committee on Public Information, to distribute a special service of reports bearing upon the role of the United States in the war from that time.

The criticisms directed at Reuters for such minor departures from complete independence of government were naturally echoed, if not originated, in German wartime propaganda. They were sufficiently noted so that beliefs lingered in some minds long after the war, and assertions sometimes were made, that Reuters was at least a semi-official arm of the British government, and receiving subsidies. This charge was vigorously denied by Reuters.

Mark Napier, Reuters board chairman, died in 1919. Under the terms attaching to the formation of Reuters, Ltd., in 1916, Sir Roderick Jones became the principal proprietor. It was an agreement intended to safeguard the agency against stock control passing into the hands of persons who might not adhere to the principles of objective news treatment, and who might not even be British citizens. It gave Jones sixty per cent of the shares in his own name, and control of the remaining forty per cent under a trusteeship. Thus Reuters, Ltd., proceeded as a private company and a commercial enterprise, as contrasted, for example, to the cooperative ownership by member newspapers of the Associated Press in the United States, or some other agencies partly or wholly owned by governments, and therefore semi-official or official in character.

Coverage of a World at War, 1914–17

12

The great gray tide of the German army began to move into Belgium on August 4, 1914. Although the first shots had been fired on Belgrade July 29, the Belgian invasion marked the onset of full war in Europe and the world.

Well prepared for the war, the German military command moved in general accordance with a plan of attack directed primarily against France. It had been devised, originally, in the early 1890s by Count Alfred von Schlieffen (1833–1913), son of a Prussian army officer, and in military service himself throughout his adult years. Chief of the German general staff from 1891 to 1906, he played an important part in creating a powerful modern army.

Schlieffen viewed Germany as surrounded by enemies, Russia, Austria-Hungary and France, posing a great potential danger. His plan called for a strategy combining defensive positions with an an aggressive attack designed utterly to destroy the forces of that country regarded as most dangerous, and then turn to any other. In 1905 he saw France as that most dangerous enemy, adjusted his plan accordingly, and put it in written form in 1907, the year following his retirement from active service. It became a major document within the military establishment, outlining in detail the procedures to be taken against France when, but not necessarily if, the appropriate time came for its use.

The plan called for German forces to strike at France by way of the relatively level terrain of Belgium, and swing to the left, with Metz as a pivot, driving toward Paris and Verdun. This was intended to force the French to do battle from what for them would be a reverse position and a disadvantage, as contrasted to meeting a frontal attack, more difficult for the Germans, by way of the Vosges Mountains between Belgium and Luxembourg on the north and Switzerland on the south.

(Basil Henry) Liddell Hart, a British historian of the war,[1] with later access to the Schlieffen document, noted that its author "considered that the military advantages of the plan outweighed the moral stigma of violating Belgian neutrality, and also the practical dangers of British hostility."[2] Both issues, of course, arose as the German army entered Belgium. Schlieffen himself did not live to see that occur, having died in 1913. Also, changes had been made in the plan between 1907 and 1914, and it was not carried out as Schlieffen had proposed. Perhaps for that reason, what he had projected as a German victory over France in less than six weeks was turned to a stalemate and an eventual defeat.[3]

German press correspondents and army combat correspondents were with that country's forces in Belgium in 1914. The Belgian press itself was unable to function after the first few days. Those few staff and stringer correspondents in Belgium for the foreign press were equally handicapped. They did what they could to report events, however, and were joined by French, British, and U.S. correspondents, some moving in from Paris and London.

All except the German correspondents were operating at great risk, in a chaotic situation. Attired as civilians, and mingling with a civilian population often in panic and flight, some were mistaken for spies, as was George Curnock of the *Times,* who was seized and narrowly escaped being shot. In a war of swift movement, they lacked financial means and had problems of transport, food, lodging, and communication. They were in danger of capture. This was the fate of Harry A. Hansen of the *Chicago Daily News,* along with two French correspondents, Maurice Gerbault and Jacques Obels, even though they tried to remain inconspicuous as the Germans moved into Brussels. The French correspondents were placed in a prison camp, but Hansen, a neutral, was released. Percy J. Philip, a British outlaw correspondent in Belgium for the *Daily News,* was nearly captured, but escaped to Holland aboard a barge.

The sources of information in Belgium were completely disorganized. Such information as correspondents were able to obtain even through

---

1   Also a British army officer throughout the war, twice wounded, and later military correspondent for the *Daily Telegraph.*

2   Liddell Hart, *The War in Outline, 1914–1918* (New York, 1936), p. 23.

3   A version of the Schlieffen plan was applied with greater success by German forces on the Russian front in 1914, first at Tannenberg in August and then at Lodz in November, both important German victories attained in a few days. The Schlieffen plan was revived by the German army in 1940, with the Wehrmacht invading Belgium on May 10 and France signing an armistice on June 22, less than six weeks later.

public officials or military personnel often was mere rumor and beyond verification. There were times when they were able to observe certain actions, and therefore to report with accuracy. But errors and distortions were inevitable. Reports appeared of things that never happened. Even what may have been carefully specified as "unverified" sometimes was accepted by readers as fact and repeated as such. Out of such circumstances there came stories of atrocities attributed to both sides. Such reports also became the subject-matter of propaganda, widely disseminated, whether by the Allied or Central Powers, with the deliberate intent to arouse or maintain the fighting spirit and to win sympathy and support in neutral countries. There were some stories horrendous enough, and quite true, but it was to be years before the false were to be distinguished from the true.

Correspondents regularly assigned to Brussels were the first to report the entrance of German military forces to the country. They included representatives of Reuter and Havas, so long as they could remain. Ed Traus and Thomas T. Topping reported for the Associated Press. Dutch-born Hendrik Willem van Loon, also of the AP, was with German troops entering Belgium. So was Herbert Bayard Swope for the *New York World*.

One of the first new correspondents to report from Belgium was Granville Fortescue, a U.S. Army reserve officer, vacationing with his family at Knocke on the North Sea coast when the invasion began. During the Russo-Japanese War, on active duty as a military observer, Fortescue had formed a friendship with Ellis Ashmead-Bartlett, representing the *Daily Telegraph*. Later, after serving as military aide at the White House both to Presidents Roosevelt and Taft, Fortescue had been in Morocco at the time of the Agadir crisis of 1911. Through Ashmead-Bartlett, again present at that time for the *Daily Telegraph,* Fortescue arranged to act as a correspondent for the London *Standard*. In Belgium in 1914, he himself became a correspondent for the *Daily Telegraph,* and produced striking eye-witness accounts of early action, and also became a correspondent for the *New York Tribune*.

In addition to George Curnock, Percy J. Philip, and Fortescue, all writing for the London press, Philip Gibbs moved into Belgium for the *Graphic* and then for his old paper, the *Daily Chronicle*. Percival Phillips of the *Daily Express* was with the Belgian army, and Edward Cleary also wrote for that paper from Antwerp until the port was captured by the Germans in October. The *Daily Mail* had a number of representatives in Belgium, among them William Beach Thomas, Hamilton Fyfe, G. Ward Price, William M. McAlpin, and Ferdinand

Tuohy, son of James M. Tuohy, London bureau chief for the *New York World* since 1899.

As a neutral, Fortescue was not subject to the War Office ban as an outlaw. Other U.S. correspondents were engaged by British newspapers because of that advantage, and some also received favored treatment in London. Gerald Morgan of the *New York Tribune* joined Fortescue in reporting for the *Daily Telegraph*. He had represented both papers during the Russo-Japanese War. Will Irwin of the *New York Sun*, who had hastened to Belgium for that paper and for *Collier's Weekly*, became closely identified with the *Daily Mail* for the remainder of the war. Richard Harding Davis, moved directly to Belgium after reporting the U.S. military action at Vera Cruz to cover his sixth war. He wrote both for the Wheeler Newspaper Syndicate of New York and the London *Daily Chronicle*.

Other U.S. correspondents, apart from those mentioned, were prompt to arrive in Belgium. They included three for the *Chicago Tribune:* Joseph Medill Patterson, recently become the paper's copublisher; John T. McCutcheon, on a fourth war assignment as an artist-correspondent; and James O'Donnell Bennett, who had been on a special assignment in England. Patterson and McCutcheon had been among those at Vera Cruz.

Irvin S. Cobb, formerly of the *New York Sun* and the *New York Evening World*, but writing since 1911 chiefly for the *Saturday Evening Post*, gained accreditation for that magazine and again for the *New York World*. Lincoln Eyre, Arno Dosch, and Henry Noble Hall also represented the *World*, while Wythe Williams switched from the *World* staff in London to represent the *New York Times*. Arthur Ruhl of the *New York Tribune* was accredited to *Collier's Weekly* for coverage in Belgium.

Added AP coverage in Belgium was provided by Robert E. Berry and Scottish-born Roger Lewis. Mary Boyle O'Reilly, writing for the Newspaper Enterprise Association (NEA), became one of two women correspondents in Belgium, the other was Frynwyd Tennyson Jesse of the *Daily Mail*. William G. Shepherd of the United Press, and James H. Hare, British-born photographer, both among the Vera Cruz contingent, were in Belgium, with Hare serving *Leslie's Weekly* of New York, rather than *Collier's Weekly,* as he had in three previous war situations. Donald C. Thompson was another photographer, then representing the Hearst newspapers.

Remarkable as perhaps the last example of a kind of free enterprise, individualistic approach to war reporting was a joint experience in

Belgium shared by Bennett and McCutcheon, both of the *Chicago Tribune,* along with Cobb of the *Saturday Evening Post* and the *New York World,* then known primarily as a writer of fiction and humorous articles.

These three crossed the Channel from England together and attached themselves to the Belgian army. In Brussels on August 20, when German forces entered that capital, they were cut off, and left without accreditation. As neutrals, however, they presented themselves to the German command and were permitted to remain. Further, they managed to get a message to Kaiser Wilhelm, personally. The result was their accreditation to German headquarters, with the right and opportunity to travel freely behind the German lines with an automobile and driver provided for their use. They also were flown in a military plane. Under such favored conditions, they were able to observe the German advance through Belgium and into France before the end of August. Their highly readable reports, along with photos and McCutcheon sketches, appeared in the *Chicago Tribune* and the *New York World,* and in the *Saturday Evening Post.* They portrayed the war as a kind of personal adventure, in a style that might once have been acceptable, but ceased to be so after that time as inappropriate to the reality of battle.[4]

The grim aspects of the war in Belgium and northern France through August 1914 were reported by the British outlaw correspondents, by the neutral U.S. group, and a few others. Richard Harding Davis gained special recognition because of a memorable account of the massive German army march into Brussels on August 21. Davis described it as "not men marching, but a force of nature like a tidal wave, an avalanche or a river flooding its banks." He also reported the German army occupation of Louvain, a week later, with the burning of the city and of its famed fifteenth century university and library. Mary Boyle O'Reilly of NEA was present on both of those occasions and produced her own moving reports.

---

4   One somewhat comparable adventurous approach to war reporting was undertaken by Geoffrey Pyke, Reuter correspondent in Copenhagen when the war began. Joining the *Daily Chronicle* at that time, and obtaining a false U.S. passport so that he might seem to be a neutral, he entered Germany, posing as a salesman for printing equipment. Fluent in German, and proceeding to Berlin, he mixed with the people in cafés and other public places, presumably to learn how the Germans were reacting to the war. After six days, he was arrested, threatened with death as a spy, jailed for six months, and transferred to an internment camp at Ruhleben. He escaped and walked to Holland and freedom. The story of his adventures appeared in the *Daily Chronicle* of July 26, 1915, and was told at greater length in a book, *To Ruhleben and Back* (London, 1915), a wartime best-seller. See also Philip Knightley, *The First Casualty* (1975).

Will Irwin and Arno Dosch were with Belgian forces as they were driven back. Despite reports inevitably tragic for Belgium, both were able to return to Brussels as neutrals without objection from the occupying Germans. Hansen of the *Chicago Daily News,* and Lewis of the AP, also went north as far as the German frontier and on into Holland, proceeding then to London. Richard Harding Davis and Arno Dosch did the same, arriving together at Buxtel in Holland.[5]

In the first weeks of the war, attitudes and policies were in flux. Apart from the expectation that the conflict could not continue for long, there was nevertheless a disposition in the major capitals to seek a favorable opinion in the United States as a large neutral country and a potential source of support. This was evidenced by the German concessions to U.S. correspondents in Belgium. Such concessions also were made in London.

William G. Shepherd of the United Press, for example, arriving in London from his Mexican assignment, but before proceeding to Belgium, had a remarkable interview with Winston Churchill, then first lord of the Admiralty. Technically bound by the principle of "Cabinet responsibility," meaning that any statement by a member of the cabinet was to be regarded as an expression of government policy binding upon all other members of the government, Churchill nevertheless spoke with the utmost frankness. Not only did he grant an interview, in the first place, but he went beyond responding to Shepherd's questions by adding further information obtained from Prime Minister Asquith and possibly from King George. When Shepherd, in the interest of accuracy, showed him a draft of the interview prior to its transmission, Churchill called the chief censor in the Admiralty, directing him to pass the story and, in turn, instruct the cable censors to do the same. Released to the British press as well, it was used with credit to the United Press.

Irvin Cobb had a less happy experience. After his return from Belgium and Germany, he was granted an interview with Lord Kitchener at the War Office. This was a concession in itself, and he was quite willing to submit his questions in advance, as requested. How the interview itself proceeded is not clear. Perhaps Kitchener merely

---

5   Davis, then fifty, gave Dosch, hardly half his age, a capsule lesson in how to succeed in journalism. Strolling in the town while waiting for luncheon to be prepared, as Dosch recalls (p. 32) in his book, *Through War to Revolution* (1920), and "walking past a stagnant canal, I commented idly that the Dutch seemed to be forever washing everything with dirty water." He quotes Davis as then counseling him, "Don't look at the dirt. Admire the picturesque. That is what I do, and that is why I am getting a thousand dollars a week and you are getting—whatever it is that you are getting."

dictated answers to some questions. Surprisingly, even so, he never was shown a draft of the final story. Curiously, also, Cobb seems not to have been aware that Kitchener did not wish to be quoted directly. When the interview appeared in the *Saturday Evening Post,* already a weekly of two million circulation reaching a world audience, quotes were used throughout the text. Kitchener promptly denied that he ever had been interviewed.

As the war moved from Belgium into France in the last days of August 1914, most of those correspondents who had been in Belgium followed along. They were joined by others already in France or arriving there. The British correspondents were still outlaws, so far as the War Office was concerned—and would be until May 1915. The French military command was almost equally hostile to field correspondents of any nationality until early 1915.

George Jeffreys Adams, recently transferred from Reuters service in Paris to the *Times,* arranged for a group of representatives of that paper to move behind the French lines on bicycles, or by any other means they could find. These were Harry Perry Robinson, M. H. H. Macartney, and Gerald Fitzgerald Campbell, all later at BEF headquarters, and Arthur Moore, Charles Dawburn, and Christopher Dittmar Rawson Lumby.

Campbell and French-born F. Lamur worked together to report German military action in France between August and October of 1914, and also did a series of reports on French army maneuvers in 1914–15. So long as they kept clear of British sectors they were safe from arrest as outlaws. With French officers then also instructed to arrest correspondents, however, they had to be constantly on guard.

As it was, Curnock, also of the *Times,* was nearly shot as a spy. William Beach Thomas of the *Daily Mail* was one of several arrested in France by the British. Six correspondents were arrested by the French near Rheims in May 1915 and jailed briefly in Paris. These were Ashmead-Bartlett and Granville Fortescue, both of the *Daily Telegraph,* Luigi Barzini of the Milan *Corriere della Séra,* Richard Harding Davis and Gerald Morgan, of the *Telegraph* and the *New York Tribune,* and Wythe Williams of the *New York Times.* After that time, however, correspondents bearing proper accreditation were able to move freely in France.

Place-names, centers of wartime action, had appeared in reports from Belgium—Liége, Brussels, Louvain, Tirlement, Namur, Charleroi, where the French first met the Germans on August 21, and Mons, where the British Expeditionary Force met them two days later.

In France, too, place-names began to appear—Longwy, Montmédy, Soissons, Laon, Rheims, Maubeuge, and the Marne River. The German forces advanced with such speed and power toward Paris that the French government moved to Bordeaux, far to the southwest, on September 3, and many civilians also retreated from the capital, at least temporarily.

The Battle of the Marne, fought within ten miles of Paris, thirty miles from its center, continued from September 5 to 12, with French and British troops at last forcing a German withdrawal. It was an historic engagement remembered, among other reasons, because nearly all of the taxicabs of Paris were used to transport about 11,000 French infantrymen to the front.

Although the capital was damaged then and later by shellfire and aerial bombing, it never was entered or captured, and the fighting in France and on the western front moved farther eastward from that time. British forces in the north of France and the northwest of Belgium, and French forces in the central part of the country southward to the Swiss border were able to hold the German armies in a relatively fixed position for the next three years, with a line of entrenchments extending from the Belgian North Sea coast to Switzerland. Both sides tried repeatedly to break that line. Many thousands of men died on both sides in single operations.

A variety of other places, early and late in the war, became tragically familiar in this time—datelines on news stories, with some of them fought over in repeated campaigns. In no particular order, there were the Aisne, Picardy, Artois, Verdun, St. Mihiel, the Meuse, Yser, Ypres, Dixmude, Noyon, Montdidier, Peronne, Bapaume, Arras, Armentières, Passchendaele, the Somme, Vimy Ridge, Flanders, and more.

In the same period to 1917, the names of generals commanding on the western front became familiar in the news, among them were von Moltke, von Kluck, von Bülow, von Falkenhausen, Ludendorff, and von Hindenburg for the Germans; Joffre, Foch, Gallieni, Pétain, and Nivelle for the French; and Sir John French and Sir Douglas Haig for the British.

William Philip Simms, manager of the United Press bureau in Paris as the war began, observed the first bombing of that city from the air, the first such attack on any western capital. He was the first U.S. correspondent accredited to the French forces and the first to visit the front. He also was to go to Russia briefly in 1915, and to visit that eastern front.

Paul Scott Mowrer, heading the *Chicago Daily News* office in Paris, was early in the field with French troops, later at frequent intervals, and sometimes for extended periods throughout the war. A youthful-appearing twenty-seven when the war began, he grew an impressive titian beard to gain a greater air of maturity designed to command respect from military and government personnel. It was an adornment he was to wear until the mid-1920s.

The *Chicago Daily News* coverage in France in the first weeks and months was augmented by Harry A. Hansen, following his experience in Belgium. Percy J. Philip of the London *Daily News,* another who had been in Belgium, also wrote for the Chicago paper and its service, as did both E. Percy Noël, H. M. Tomlinson, A. R. Decker, a young American engineer, and Paul Rockwell, both newly employed, and René Arcos and Charles de la Garde, French correspondents—the latter twice wounded. Edgar Ansel Mowrer, younger brother of Paul Scott Mowrer, studying at the Sorbonne as the war began, became an assistant in the bureau. When Italy entered the war in 1915, the younger Mowrer, Rockwell, and Decker transferred to Rome. Decker, at one point, went aboard an Italian submarine seeking Austrian naval craft in the Adriatic. Louis Edward Browne was in the Balkans for the paper, and with Serbian forces in Albania.

Frederic Villiers, representing the *Illustrated London News,* and the most senior of all British correspondents in terms of service, was with the French forces from 1914 until his retirement in 1916. For that London illustrated paper, Seppings Wright also was in the field as an artist-correspondent. As for others, Gilbert Holiday was with the French for the *Graphic.* The *Sphere* was represented by Philip Dadd, who died at the front, the first casualty among correspondents. Henry Beech Needham, formerly in Washington for the *New York Evening Post* but in France for *Collier's Weekly,* was killed in an airplane accident near Paris in 1915, possibly the first correspondent to lose his life in such a manner in the history of news reporting.

For the Central News of London, Alfred Rorke, still classified as an outlaw correspondent, wrote the first story of British troops in action at Mons in August 1914. Oliver Madox Hueffer of that agency, in returning from coverage at Vera Cruz in 1914, became active in France, as did B. J. Hodson and Edward Lyell Fox. The British Exchange Telegraph Company (Extel) had French-born André Glarner in Paris.

Arno Dosch, after covering action in Belgium for the *New York World,* returned to France to report the German drive toward Paris and the Battle of the Marne in early September 1914. He was with the French army. Although a native of Oregon, his mother was French-born. The Teutonic flavor of his surname induced him, as a matter of prudence, to add his mother's maiden name to his own, so that he became Arno Dosch-Fleurot. Under that hypenated name, he reported the war from France, later from Russia, and continued as a correspondent in Europe for many years.

Harrison Sprague Reeves, in Paris for the *World* from 1910 to 1914, was joined and followed by Henry Wales, formerly of the Paris edition of the *New York Herald,* but who soon moved to the International News Service. Lincoln Eyre, who had been in Belgium, succeeded Wales, with British-born William Cook as second man in the bureau.

The *Daily Mail* coverage in France was substantial, with Joseph M. N. Jeffries as Paris bureau chief. Others serving there and in the field, some following experience in Belgium, included Ferdinand Tuohy, Thomas, Fyfe, Price, McAlpin, Jesse, and James Grant Marshall, a photographer. Its manpower was augmented through the staff of the *Continental Daily Mail* of Paris, edited during the war years by Sisley Huddleton and its staff, including: W. L. Warden, later editor of the *Daily Mail* in London, Harry J. Greenwall, Arthur Glynn, W. J. Deeth, Roland Atkinson, and Peter Goudie. Fyfe and Price reported the war from other fronts in later years, and Jeffries set a record in that respect by covering the fighting in no less than seventeen countries before 1918, including Egypt, Albania, Greece, Italy, and Austria, as well as Belgium and France.

A chance meeting in London between Will Irwin and George Moore, Irish novelist and a friend of Sir John French, first commander of the British Expeditionary Forces (later viscount and then Earl of Ypres), enabled Irwin to play a part in revealing the shortage of munitions that was placing British forces in France at a serious disadvantage. This became the subject of a campaign directed by Lord Northcliffe through the columns of the *Daily Mail.* It also resulted in Irwin, a correspondent for *Collier's Weekly,* being engaged personally by Northcliffe to write also for the *Daily Mail.*

As a neutral, Irwin covered the first Battle of Ypres, during October-November 1914, in one of the classic reports of the war. He also covered the second Battle of Ypres in April 1915 and was credited as the first correspondent to report the use by the Germans of poison gas as a weapon of war. The same "first" was attributed to William G. Shepherd, however, who reported the action for the United Press. Shepherd was credited also with the first report of Zeppelin raids on London in September of that year.

The entrance of Italy into the war in May 1915 introduced a new element, as did the entrance of Bulgaria in October and the earlier and unsuccessful Allied campaign at Gallipoli in the Dardanelles, which had extended the fighting to the Middle East. Although the western front in France continued to receive major attention, the range of activity by correspondents took some to other fronts, and London, Berlin, Vienna, and Petrograd all drew correspondents in greater numbers.

The importance of the western front gave special significance to Paris as a center for coverage. For the French Agence Havas, directed by Charles Lafitte, the general news service was in charge of Henri Houssaye until his retirement in 1915, and then supervised by his nephew, Charles Houssaye. Others prominent in the administration during the war years included Elié Mercadier, a veteran in the service, André Meynot, Ernest Barbier, Léon Rénier, and Léon Rollin. Herbert Jacques and Jean de Pierrefeu were with French troops.

The French newspaper press tripled and quadrupled its staff coverage in the war years. Apart from those mentioned as active at BEF, others writing as correspondents for Paris papers included Pierre Millet and Serge Basset for *Le Temps,* Henri Barby for *Le Journal,* André Géraud and Marcel Hutin for *l'Echo de Paris,* Stéphane Lauzanne and M. Caro for *Le Matin,* M. Bonnefon for *Le Figaro,* and others for *Le Petit Parisien* and *Le Journal des Débats.*

In Paris, Reuters, the Associated Press, and the United Press were well represented. For Reuters, Lester Lawrence, with the Allied forces during the Dardanelles-Gallipoli campaign in 1915, was later with the French army. E. Lacon Watson was in Italy. Fergus Ferguson and W. H. G. Werndel were in the Middle East and Mediterranean areas. Werndel also reported on the activities of Serbian forces, covered the Allied offensive from Salonika, and produced the first report of Bulgaria's surrender in September 1918. Ferguson was in Egypt, later accompanied General Allenby and British forces from Jerusalem to Damascus, and reported the Turkish surrender in October 1918.

Keith Murdoch and Charles Bean, representing the Australian press, covered the 1915–16 disasters at Gallipoli, where Australian and New Zealand troops shared with British forces in the setback. Murdoch, who was obstructed and arrested and also torpedoed, made common cause with Ashmead-Bartlett of the *Daily Telegraph,* whose accreditation was cancelled for revealing the failures of the campaign. This interference with the reporting of unwelcome events was to become an element in Northcliffe's attack of 1915 on the conduct of the war.[6]

---

6   For further details, see Knightley, *The First Casualty,* pp. 100–03.

For the Associated Press, Charles Thaddeus Thompson, heading the Paris bureau from 1902 to 1911, moved between Paris and Rome during the war, with Elmer E. Roberts, formerly in Berlin, as bureau chief in Paris since 1911. Salvatore Cortesi, bureau chief in Rome, was assisted by Thomas B. Morgan; Patrick Hibben was in Athens; and Robert M. Collins was bureau chief in London. Thomas T. Topping, formerly in Brussels, joined the Paris staff. Ulrich Salchow was in Stockholm and Thomas Stockwell in Amsterdam.

In London, Collins had the assistance of Ben S. Allen, Frank America, Frank B. Elser, who came from the Vera Cruz assignment, Robert T. Small, formerly in Latin America and Washington, Charles Stephenson Smith, formerly in Washington, and DeWitt Mackenzie, who arrived in 1916 from the AP bureau in Cleveland. Others came and went between London and the continent.

Allen went to Ireland to give special coverage to the arrival at Queenstown of survivors of the sinking of the *Lusitania* in May 1915. A native Californian and a Stanford University graduate, like Herbert Hoover, Allen also reported upon Hoover's activities in London in the organization of the Belgian Relief Commission of that period, and was associated with Hoover in postwar undertakings. Mackenzie, almost immediately after his arrival in London in 1916, proceeded to Dublin to report upon the Easter Rebellion there in which the Sinn Fein began its harassment of the British government in the cause of Irish independence, which continued through the war years. Mackenzie later went to Egypt and to France, where he succeeded Small at BEF in 1917 until the end of the war.

For the United Press, Simms in Paris worked with Edward L. Keen, London bureau chief. Wilbur Forrest, in the Washington bureau since 1912, moved to London in 1915 as assistant general European manager. He was the first U.S. correspondent to reach Queenstown in May to interview survivors of the *Lusitania* sinking. He also reported the Sinn Fein rebellion in Dublin in April 1916, and was in France in July and August of that year to report the critical Battle of the Somme, in which the British introduced the use of tanks.

Roy Howard, director of the UP, was in London in 1916 and obtained a widely quoted interview with David Lloyd George, recently become secretary of state for war, following Kitchener's loss. Henry Wood, a member of the Paris bureau, had gone to Rome in 1916 to direct the UP bureau headed since 1914 by Alice Rohe, a sister of Mrs. Roy Howard. Wood later covered aspects of the war in Italy, and held a roving commission that took him to Serbia, to Turkey during the Gallipoli campaign, and also into Armenia. A new member of the war staff was Demaree Bess, with General Allenby and British forces in the Middle East, and beginning a long career as a correspondent.

The International News Service, the youngest and smallest of the U.S. news agencies, claimed 400 newspaper clients in the country in 1914, as compared to 500 for the UP and 894 for the older AP. William Randolph Hearst, founder of the agency in 1909, owned nine daily newspapers in 1914. Although the INS was to become an important world news agency in later years, its own news coverage beyond the boundaries of the United States did not become effective until after 1916.

As the war began in 1914, INS had British-born W. Orton Tewson, a former London stringer for the *New York Times,* as its London representative. It had George Allison, also British, and formerly a member of the *New York Herald* bureau in London, writing from the European continent, chiefly from Paris. William Bayard Hale, Paris correspondent for the *New York Times* from 1907 to 1909, was in Berlin for INS. Donald C. Thompson, a news photographer, represented the Hearst newspapers and therefore INS in Belgium and Germany until he joined the *Chicago Tribune* staff in Berlin in 1915.

Aside from these few representatives, the INS was not prepared to cover the war when it began. The editorial position taken by the Hearst papers on the conflict was considered so sympathetic to Germany as to be offensive to the Allied countries. The British government, early in the war, protested dispatches sent by Hale from Berlin as being "distorted" and "pro-German."[7] In 1915, the INS and the Hearst newspapers were accused of faking reports from the countries at war by using accounts bearing what were held to be fictitious by-lines of nonexistent correspondents. Cited were "Herbert Temple, London and European manager of INS"; "Frederick Werner, Berlin staff correspondent of INS"; "Brixton D. Allaire, Rome"; "Franklin P. Merrick, Paris"; "John C. Foster, London"; and "Lawrence Elston, London."

These charges were carried further in 1916–17, when the INS was accused by the Associated Press of pirating AP war dispatches as received by Hearst newspapers holding AP membership, rewriting some to give them a slightly different character, and distributing them under the INS logotype. Although this was neither the first nor the last time

---

7   Hale indeed was paid by the German government to try to keep the United States from entering the war. With this revealed, he ceased to write for the INS, and made his home in Germany where he died in Munich in 1924, at fifty-five.

that news piracy was charged, it was the first occasion on which the matter was taken to court, and it became a classic case in press law bearing upon property rights in the news. The Associated Press carried the case to the United States Supreme Court on appeal. The decision returned in 1918 was essentially in support of the AP, turning on the issue of unfair competition. For a time a question also existed as to whether the Hearst newspapers might be expelled from membership in the AP. They never were, and by 1918 the INS had become a more mature and responsible agency.

In October 1916, the British government had denied INS the use of the mails and cables for transmission of news dispatches from that country. The French government took similar action, followed by Portugal and Japan. In addition to some protests against the Hearst newspapers in the United States, they were barred from distribution in Canada.

Hearst responded in several ways to these events. He countered the British and French ban on communication for the INS by engaging leading British, French, and Italian writers and political figures to contribute special articles, at generous fees, for use in his papers and for distribution by his service. Among them were Rudyard Kipling, George Bernard Shaw, René Viviani, a former French premier, Edmond Rostand, Gabrielle d'Annunzio, and Guglielmo Ferrero. Hale left the staff of INS, but new members were recruited. One of the first was Henry Wales, who moved from the *New York World* staff, but remained in Paris. Another was William Welton Harris, formerly of the *New York Herald* and the *New York Sun,* who briefly joined the London staff. Earl Reeves was sent to London in 1916 to replace Tewson as bureau chief. Patrick L. Jones, dispatched from New York to the London bureau in 1915, had sailed in the *Lusitania* and was one of those lost when that ship was torpedoed. With these and other changes, the INS had a small but solid staff by 1917. When the United States entered the war in April, INS freedom to operate was restored in Great Britain and elsewhere. For war news, however, even the Hearst newspapers still depended chiefly upon the AP and the UP.

Among newspapers reporting from France, Italy, the Balkans, and the Middle East, beyond what already has been described, Gerald Fitzgerald Campbell and F. Lamur, working together for the *Times,* remained with French forces until 1917. Campbell so established himself in the confidence of the French military that there was reluctance at command levels to permit him to transfer at that time to the Italian front, even though Lamur remained. Campbell did return later to France, but for assignment to the BEF headquarters.

The *Times* staff, although mobile, remained generally unchanged throughout the war. One exception was the retirement of William Francis Hubbard, Rome correspondent, who was replaced by William K. McClure, second man in the bureau. Another exception was the departure of James David Bourchier from his post in Sofia, occupied since 1892, when Bulgaria chose in October 1915 to ally itself with the Central Powers. It was an action he had not expected, despite his experience and his sources of information in the area. His reports never had suggested such a decision, and the *Times* almost dispensed with his services, despite his long association with the paper and the high regard in which he had been held.

Moving to Bucharest, in neighboring Rumania, Bourchier remained until the spring of 1917. Rumania meanwhile joined the Allies in August 1916, but was overrun, looted, and occupied early in 1917 by the forces of Bulgaria, Austria-Hungary, and Germany. In a second move, Bourchier went to Odessa, in the south of Russia, on the Black Sea coast. Russia was then entering upon the first phase of its revolutionary period. The czar abdicated and a provisional government struggled to continue the war against Germany and Austria-Hungary. The effort failed in the October revolution, when the Bolsheviks took power under Lenin. An armistice ended Russia's participation in the war in December 1917, although the Treaty of Brest-Litovsk was not signed until March 1918.

Bourchier moved a third time in November 1917 from Odessa to Petrograd. There he observed the results of the October revolution, had rare interviews with Lenin and Trotzky, the new leaders of government, and then moved to Sweden and Norway. There, in Christiania (now Oslo), he wrote reports based upon his Petrograd observations and interviews. These were his last dispatches to appear in the *Times*.[8]

For the *Daily Telegraph,* Ashmead-Bartlett, Fortescue, and Morgan, Lawrence Gerrold, and W. T. Massey were in France. Fortescue and

---

8   Bourchier returned to England, but did little for the paper. With the war ended in 1918, and with fond associations in Bulgaria, he became a self-appointed, unofficial spokesman for that country and other Balkan states at the Paris Peace Conference in 1919, and at subsequent and related conferences. His concern for Bulgaria and Macedonia resulted in his being asked in 1920 to become Bulgaria's Consul-General in London. Before taking up the post, however, he returned to Bulgaria for a visit, and died there December 20, 1920. He was paid high honors by the people and government of that country.

Morgan also were writing for the *New York Tribune.* Ashmead-Bartlett had been at Gallipoli, and Fortescue was in Russia early in the war. G. T. Stevens was in the Balkan area for the paper, and Massey went to the Middle East.

The London *Daily News* had Percy J. Philip in Paris, writing also for the *Chicago Daily News.* H. T. Cozens-Hardy was also in Paris for the paper, and Hugh Martin was in Egypt.

The *Daily Chronicle* had Martin Donohoe in Paris, and also Philip Gibbs and, later, Henry W. Nevinson. Alan Botts served the paper in France early in the war, but joined the British army and was captured later by the Turks in Palestine. Percival Gibbon, an experienced man, was in France and later with British troops in Italy. George Herbert Perris, George Renwick, and Charles Sarolea also wrote for the *Chronicle* from the war fronts.

The *Standard* had William Maxwell in the field in France before he went to BEF headquarters. The *Manchester Guardian* was represented in Paris by John G. Hamilton, who was succeeded by Robert Dell, and the paper had Nevinson in France, at Gallipoli, and in Egypt before he switched to the *Chronicle.* The *Daily Express* was represented in Paris by Harry J. Greenwall, who switched from the *Continental Daily Mail.*

Among newspapers of the United States, the *New York Times,* under Van Anda's news direction in New York, authorized correspondents to send war dispatches at double-urgent rates when events warranted. Its cable charges rose to about $780,000 a year. If reports required extra space, the paper sometimes omitted as much as sixty to seventy columns of advertising in a day, at great sacrifice in revenue. It received, used, and distributed the reports of the London *Daily Chronicle,* including dispatches from Philip Gibbs at BEF headquarters. Its general news coverage and its concern for recording the events of the war, including publication of full texts of documents and addresses, gained for the *New York Times* the top award in the Pulitzer Prizes of 1918 for the "most disinterested and meritorious public service" by a newspaper during the preceding year.[9]

---

9   The year 1918 was the first for Pulitzer Prize awards, recognizing accomplishments in 1917. The prizes were provided from an endowment set up under the will of Joseph Pulitzer, publisher of the *New York World* and *St. Louis Post Dispatch,* as he also provided an endowment for the establishment of a Graduate School of Journalism at Columbia University in New York, opened in 1912, a year after his death. The Pulitzer Prizes gave recognition not only to "meritorious public service," but to reporting, editorial writing, and books of history, biography or autobiography, fiction, and drama. Other

Wythe Williams, who became Paris correspondent for the *New York Times* in 1914, directed the paper's coverage from France in the first years of the war. He was assisted by British-born Walter Duranty. George LeHir, a French journalist, also joined the bureau in 1915. He and Williams produced a notable account of the Battle of Verdun in 1916. Ernest Marshall headed the London bureau, as he had since 1908.

The *New York Herald,* long a leader in news-gathering enterprise at home and abroad, continued actively, but was matched or overmatched in the war years by other U.S. papers. James Gordon Bennett, Jr., its publisher, with his home in Paris since 1877, died there in May 1918, four days after his seventy-seventh birthday, and six months before the end of the war.

The Paris edition of the *New York Herald,* dating from 1887, played a part in the coverage of French news for the parent paper. When the war began, its long-time editor, G. H. (Gaston Hanet) Archambault, a native of France, entered military service. As the German army approached Paris in September most members of the staff left the city, along with the government itself. A few managed to keep the paper going, however, and Bennett himself, then seventy-three, was out reporting the news. With the immediate danger to the city soon ended, the staff was restored and enlarged. British-born Eric Hawkins, already a staff member and a resident of Paris since his youth, who had been a stringer or correspondent there since 1906 for the *Standard* and other London papers, became managing editor. He remained in charge of the Paris *Herald*'s news function until his retirement thirty-six years later.

Staff members with the Paris edition during the war years included John Burke, former *Herald* city editor in New York; Henry Wales, until he joined the *New York World* staff; George Seldes, until he joined the Edward Marshall Syndicate in London; Hugh Muir, Burr Price, Julian LaRosa Harris, Don Martin, and two British journalists, John Jeffrey and Lewis Glynn, who moved from the *Continental Daily Mail,* and both remained with the paper for many years. The *New York Herald* also had Harry S. Brown in London.

---

categories were added in later years, including Washington or foreign correspondence, international reporting, national reporting as distinct from local reporting, cartoon, news photography, poetry, non-fiction, music, and a special citation. The prizes are awarded by the trustees of Columbia University on the basis of recommendations by an Advisory Board on Pulitzer Prizes. Awards may be omitted. A gold medal is awarded for "meritorious service." The prize in the other categories, originally $500, is now $1,000.

The *New York Tribune* had Charles Inman Barnard in Paris when the war began, and he remained there. Gerald Morgan, who had served the paper during the Russo-Japanese War, wrote from Belgium and then from France. He also served the London *Daily Telegraph* until 1917. Gordon Gordon-Smith wrote from France and also went to the Balkans. Fred B. Pitney and C. L. Garvan moved about Europe. Philip Patchin was in London, but Arthur Draper, Sunday editor in New York, was assigned there in 1915 and remained until 1925 as the paper's European manager, not only organizing war coverage but bringing distinction to the foreign service. The *Tribune* was among U.S. newspapers receiving reports from the Wheeler Newspaper Syndicate from the time of its organization in 1913. It also published and distributed the special columns of war analysis by Frank H. Simonds, who became associate editor of the paper in New York in 1915.

The *New York Sun* and *Evening Sun* had provided a service of foreign reports also reaching other papers through its subsidiary Laffan News Bureau since 1897. As the war began, *Sun* coverage from Paris was provided by Frank B. Grundy. He was transferred there from the London bureau in 1912, at which time Judson C. Welliver, former Washington correspondent for the *Des Moines Leader,* became London bureau chief. Both men remained at those posts throughout the war. Hal O'Flaherty, who had reported the Mexican border incident for the United Press early in 1916, then went to London for that agency, but soon switched to the *New York Sun* bureau. He left in 1917 to join the U.S. Army Air Force, but returned after the war. In 1916, the *Sun* papers were bought by Frank A. Munsey, who merged the morning *Press,* owned since 1912, into the morning *Sun,* and suspended the Laffan News Bureau. The *Evening Sun* also continued.

The *New York World,* in addition to Eyre, Dosch-Fleurot, and others mentioned as active in Belgium and France, had British-born James M. Tuohy as chief of the London bureau directing the paper's wartime staff in Europe. Joseph Grigg was second man in the bureau as the war began. Karl H. von Weigand, in Berlin for the United Press, returned briefly to New York in 1916 to work for the *World,* then for the INS, and was back in Berlin in 1917 for the *New York Sun.*

For the *Chicago Tribune,* Henry Norman and Arthur L. Clarke were in London when the war commenced, and James O'Donnell Bennett was on special assignment there. Joseph Medill Patterson, who had just become copublisher of the paper, and John T. McCutcheon, artist-correspondent, both arrived directly from coverage of U.S. military action in Vera Cruz and hastened to Belgium along with Bennett.

Patterson remained briefly, but McCutcheon and Bennett, and Irvin S. Cobb of the *Saturday Evening Post* and the *New York World,* proceeded as previously described. McCutcheon returned to Europe in 1915 to write and produce sketches from France and the Balkans.

Robert R. McCormick, cousin of Patterson and copublisher of the *Tribune* since 1914, visited Europe in 1915. Where Patterson's interest had been in the news itself, McCormick was more concerned with issues and policies, and he met with leaders of government in England, France, Russia, and Germany, including Prime Minister Asquith and Czar Nicholas. His one departure from such high-level associations was to have a motion picture cameraman accompany him on expeditions in Germany to make newsreels of the war to be shown in the United States.

Wartime coverage for the *Chicago Tribune* in western Europe was provided by T. P. O'Connor, an experienced London journalist, Carolyn Wilson in Paris and later in Rome, Inez Milholland Boissevain also in Rome, Henry J. Reilly, a former U.S. Army officer writing from the Balkans, and Robert J. Thompson, former U.S. consul in Aix-la-Chapelle writing from The Hague. The *Tribune* also used reports written for the *Daily Mail* by Will Irwin, Frederic William Wile, and others.

The *New York Evening Post* received reports from Paris from Robert Dunn, who had arrived in 1914 directly from Vera Cruz, and from Stoddard Dewey, in Paris since the 1870s. Dewey was dean of the foreign press corps there, in point of service, and a stringer for various newspapers.

Most of the agencies and newspapers mentioned here as having coverage in the years between 1914 and 1917 in Belgium, France, Italy, the Balkans, and the Middle East, also were represented in Germany, Austria-Hungary, and Russia. The major difference was, of course, that there could be no British or French or Italian correspondents in the Central Powers countries. For example, Frederick A. Mackenzie, in Berlin for the *Times* since 1899, was forced to leave when war was declared in 1914. Wile, Berlin correspondent for the *Daily Mail* since 1906, also was forced to leave, even though he was a neutral citizen of the United States, and a correspondent for the *New York Times.* In London, and at times in The Hague, Wile was chiefly engaged throughout the war in preparing a regular column of news on German affairs used in the *Daily Mail* under the title "Germany Day by Day," based largely upon information obtained through sources in Holland.

Mackenzie did a comparable column for the *Times* titled "Through German Eyes," analyzing current conditions in Germany.

So long as the United States remained neutral, correspondents for its press were active in Central Powers countries. For the Associated Press, Seymour Beach Conger was Berlin bureau chief, Robert Atter was Vienna bureau chief, and Theron J. Damon was in Constantinople. George Abel Schreiner, already experienced in Europe for the agency and returned from the Vera Cruz assignment, assisted Conger and Atter. He and Atter were together in reporting the Gallipoli-Dardanelles campaign from the Turkish side in 1915, along with Damon. Hendrik Willem Van Loon returned to AP service after a decade, and moved with German troops into Belgium. S. Miles Bouton and Guido Enderis were in the Berlin bureau. Bouton and Atter went to the front on occasion. Enderis, although reared in the United States, held Swiss citizenship, and chose to remain in Berlin after the United States entered the war. There he acted as custodian of AP property until the bureau was reopened after the war.

The United Press had Karl H. von Wiegand in Berlin when the war began. He went both to the eastern front and to the western front, where he had an exclusive interview with the German Crown Prince Wilhelm. When he returned to the United States in 1915, he was replaced in Berlin by Carl W. Ackerman. Walter Niebuhr, also in the bureau, accompanied the German army in its drive against Warsaw in 1915. F. C. Bryk was Vienna correspondent until 1917. William G. Shepherd moved both with the German and Austrian armies.

With the forced departure of Wile from Berlin in 1914, the *New York Times,* in extending its European coverage, named Cyril Brown to replace him. He went to every German battlefront between 1914 and 1917, and was in Stockholm and Copenhagen throughout the rest of the war. He was assisted in the Berlin bureau by Garet Garrett from 1915, by Oscar King Davis from 1916, and by Joseph Herrings. Enid Wilke was in The Hague throughout the war.

The *New York World* was represented in Berlin when the war began by D. Thomas Curtin, who also wrote for the *Daily Mail* during 1914–15, following Wile's departure, with his dispatches reaching London by way of New York. E. Alexander Powell, another U.S. neutral and a correspondent for the *World* during the Balkan wars of 1912–13, and also previously in North Africa and Latin America for the paper, became another staff writer in Germany, and his reports also went to the *Daily Mail.*

Herbert Bayard Swope, already known as an able reporter on the *World* staff in New York, became a notably effective member of the Berlin bureau from 1914 to 1917. He was with the German armies moving into Belgium, and later was on the eastern front as well. A series of articles, the fruit of his experience, appeared in the *World* in 1917, after the United States entered the war. They were republished the same year as a book, *Inside the German Empire in the Third Year of the War.* These articles won for Swope the first Pulitzer Prize for "a distinguished example of a reporter's work," awarded in 1918.[10]

For the *Chicago Daily News,* Raymond E. Swing (later known as Raymond Gram Swing), on his first foreign assignment, was in Berlin from 1914 to 1917. Oswald Schuette was second man in the bureau. Swing was able to visit the German fronts and in 1915 he also went to Constantinople to report the Dardanelles-Gallipoli campaign. Reporting from the Turkish side, he was aboard a transport torpedoed by a British submarine in the Sea of Marmara. Schuette was the last U.S. correspondent to leave Berlin in 1917. He went to Copenhagen and later to Stockholm, listening posts, for the rest of the war.

For the *New York Sun,* Dr. Stanley Shaw was in Berlin until 1917. He was joined by von Wiegand, formerly there for the UP and returning after two years in New York, but was soon forced to leave when the U.S. declared war on Germany.[11] The *New York Herald* had Sidney Whitman in Berlin through 1917. Aubrey Stanhope, with a roving commission for the *Herald* for some years before the war, also was in Berlin in 1917, although Irish-born and of British nationality. He chose to remain there through 1918 in charge of an English-language propaganda weekly, the *Continental News,* sponsored by the German Ministry of Foreign Affairs.

When James O'Donnell Bennett of the *Chicago Tribune* entered Germany with McCutcheon and Cobb after their experience in Belgium in 1914, he remained until 1917, representing the paper as its first Berlin correspondent. Joining him were two photographers, Donald C. Thompson, formerly in Belgium and Germany for the Hearst newspapers, and Edwin F. Weigle. Both men moved widely on assignments. Also joining Bennett in the new bureau was Sigrid Schultz,

---

10   Swope saw the war from both France and Russia in 1918, one of the few correspondents to observe actual fighting from both sides. He served as executive editor of the *World* from 1920–29.

11   Back in Berlin in 1919, von Wiegand represented the Hearst newspapers from that time, and the INS as well, with Berlin as his base of operations for almost twenty years.

a young woman of U.S. citizenship in Germany with her father when the war began, and unable to leave at the time. Although both were forced to depart in 1917, Miss Schultz returned after the war and was ultimately to head the *Tribune* bureau in Berlin.

More will be said presently of coverage of the Russian front, but correspondents based in Petrograd or visiting the eastern front during 1914–17 included Guy Beringer for Reuters, Horace Trouvé for the Agence Havas, Roger Lewis, Walter C. Whiffen, D. B. McGowan, and Charles Stephenson Smith all for the AP at various times, and William Philip Simms for the UP. For newspapers, Robert Wilton and then George Dobson wrote for the *Times*, L. B. Golden for the *Daily Mail*, Dr. Emile Joseph Dillon for the *Daily Telegraph*, joined by Edwin H. Wilcox, who was forced out of his post for the paper in Berlin. Arthur Ransome represented the *Daily News*, and Alan Ostler the *Daily Express* until he left to join the British army, when he was succeeded by Herbert Bailey. The *Manchester Guardian* had three representatives, M. Phillips Price, Michael Farbman, and Francis McCullagh, who also wrote for the *New York Herald*.

The *Chicago Daily News* had John Foster Bass in Petrograd. Wounded on a visit to the front in 1916, he was succeeded by Isaac Don Levine and Basset Digby.

Three British newspapers formed news exchange arrangements with New York dailies for mutual advantage, including the provision to the London dailies of reports by neutral U.S. correspondents in the Central Powers countries. Thus, the London *Daily News* resumed a relationship it had had with the *New York Tribune* at the time of the Franco-Prussian War. The *Daily Chronicle* had an arrangement with the *New York Times*, and the *Daily Mail* with the *New York World*.

Both before and after Italy entered the war in May 1915, *Il Corriere della Séra* of Milan led in news and editorial substance in that country and had Luigi Barzini and Guglielmo Emanuel producing reports from the fighting fronts. *La Stampa* of Turin and *Il Messaggero* were almost equally enterprising. Benito Mussolini, editor since 1912 of *Avanti*, official Socialist party paper, and of a review, *Utopia*, which he established in 1913, exercised considerable influence upon opinion in Italy. His support of the Allies, once the war began, forced him to leave the Socialist party and the editorship of *Avanti*, but in November 1914 he established his own paper at Milan, *Il Popolo d'Italia*, in which he advocated Italy's entrance into the war against Austria and Germany. With some who followed his leadership, there was formed an organization, the Fasci d'Azione Rivoluzionaria, engaging in propaganda in support of his views. When Italy actually entered the war in May 1915, Mussolini became a private in the Bersaglieri, or light infantry, in which he had served as a youth. Wounded by a grenade explosion during training exercises, he was hospitalized for months, but returned to the editorship of his paper late in 1917.

Among newspapers in neutral countries of Europe, some were important throughout the war. Notable in the group were *De Telegraaf* of Amsterdam, presenting reports from a Mr. Simons in Germany as well as widely reprinted political cartoons by Louis Raemakers; the *Nieuw Rotterdamsche Courant* of Rotterdam; the *Neue Zürcher Zeitung* of Zurich; *Der Bund* of Berne; the *Journal de Genève* of Geneva, with editorial comment by William Martin; the *Berlingske Tidende* of Copenhagen; the *Morgenbladet* of Christiania; the *Dagens Nyheter* of Stockholm; and the *Gotëborgs Tidning* of Gothenburg.[12]

Beyond the coverage of the war by news agencies and individual newspapers, several syndicate services, particularly in the United States, had representatives and correspondents actively engaged. Some magazines, again chiefly in the United States, became involved. Not only were photographers more numerous than ever before on any war front, but motion picture photography and newsreels became fully established in the area of public information.

The McClure Newspaper Syndicate, one of the first, formed by Samuel S. McClure in New York in 1884, presented some accounts of the war for distribution to subscribers. John L. Balderston was its wartime representative in London.

The Curtis Brown News Bureau, organized in 1900, with offices in New York and London, had Irish-born John S. Steele as its London manager during the war years. He was assisted for a time by George Seldes, formerly of the Paris edition of the *New York Herald*. Curtis Brown News reports went by mail to the *New York Press*, the *Chicago Tribune*, the *Philadelphia Press*, the *Boston Post*, the *Detroit Free Press*, the *St. Louis Globe-Democrat*, the *Atlanta Constitution*, and others, and also to some British newspapers.

In 1916, the Curtis Brown bureau was purchased by Edward Marshall,[13] former *New York Journal* correspondent during the

---

12 Sven Anders Hedin, a Swedish explorer of some fame, with cordial relations with German leaders, wrote from Berlin for the Swedish press. A book derived from his early dispatches, *With the German Armies in the West* (1915), was so full of praise for Germany as to draw criticism even from his own countrymen.

13 Not to be confused with Ernest Marshall, then chief of the *New York Times* bureau in London.

Spanish-American War. He had experience since 1885, both in the United States and Europe, and also with the *New York American, New York Herald, New York Press,* and with the McClure Newspaper syndicate. Under his direction, the bureau became the Edward Marshall Newspaper Syndicate, Inc. Steele remained in charge in London with Seldes, and the service went to approximately the same list of newspapers, except for the *New York Press,* which was merged in 1916 by Munsey with the morning *Sun.*

The Scripps-owned Newspaper Enterprise Association (NEA), formed in Cleveland in 1902 and directed from there by Robert Paine, also was actively represented in Europe during the war years. Harold E. Bechtol was in London as European manager. Mary Boyle O'Reilly produced major reports from Belgium in 1914, and Carl Sandburg, already known as a poet and editor in Chicago, was in Stockholm for the NEA. Charles Edward Russell and George Randolph Chester, both known authors, wrote from Europe early in the war. W. H. Durborough, a news photographer, was with the German armies on the eastern front for a time. Others representing NEA arrived after the U.S. entrance to the war.

A group of U.S. newspapers had joined in 1911 to form the Associated Newspapers. They included the *New York Globe,* the sponsor, the *Boston Globe,* the *Philadelphia Evening Bulletin,* the *Chicago Daily News,* the *Kansas City Star,* and others totalling twenty-eight from coast to coast. This service was headed in London by Herbert Corey.

The Wheeler Newspaper Syndicate was established in New York, also in 1911, by John N. Wheeler, formerly of the *New York Herald.* The key newspaper in the group, however, was the *New York Tribune.* Its editor and manager in London was Guy T. Viskniskki. The particular star of the syndicate was Richard Harding Davis, known for his colorful writing since the 1890s, including coverage of wars since 1897. Having been reporting in the Vera Cruz area as war clouds appeared in Europe in July, he had hastened to New York in time to sail aboard the *Lusitania* on August 4, 1914, to report the German invasion of Belgium, and to write from France and Greece through 1915. Back in the United States in 1916, but about to return to Europe, Davis died suddenly of a heart attack on April 11, a week before his fifty-second birthday.[14] With

---

14 The seizure came as he was speaking on the telephone with Martin Egan, former AP correspondent in Tokyo from 1901 to 1907. Editor of the *Manila Times* from 1907 to 1914, Egan then had returned to the United States to become public relations adviser to J. P. Morgan & Co. in New York, until his death in 1938.

Davis's death, the Wheeler syndicate was merged later in 1916 with the Bell Newspaper Syndicate, Inc., also a Wheeler enterprise. Wheeler himself joined the U.S. Army in 1917 as an artillery officer, serving with the AEF in France until 1919.

Among U.S. periodicals, *Collier's Weekly* had taken a lead in presenting articles with a strong news emphasis, beginning at the time of the Spanish-American War. James H. Hare, British-born photographer, had served it since then. In Vera Cruz in 1914, he had been one of those moving promptly to Europe. In this case, he made photos, not for *Collier's* but for *Leslie's Weekly,* also of New York. First in Belgium and then France, he went to Greece and Serbia in 1915. Returning to the United States, he was again in France late in 1916 and in Italy in 1917.

Photos were subject to censorship, and so was the work of artists. The latter were present in considerable numbers throughout the war, despite the new emphasis on photos and motion pictures, and more than ninety were estimated to be in the field during the last year of the war.

For *Collier's,* Webb Waldron became European editor. Arthur Ruhl was the most active correspondent. Formerly a music critic of the *New York Tribune,* he gained high respect for the quality of his writing from Belgium and France in 1914, Germany and Austria in 1915, and Russia in 1916 and 1917, thus covering the war from both sides. He was in France again in 1918, and in the Baltic States in 1919. Will Irwin wrote for *Collier's* as the war began, but became more particularly identified with the London *Daily Mail.* He also did some writing for the *New York Tribune* and for the *Saturday Evening Post.* Henry Beech Needham, representing *Collier's,* was killed in an airplane accident near Paris in 1915. Stanley Washburn, with experience for the *Chicago Daily News* in the Russo-Japanese War and for that paper and the London *Times* in Russia in 1905, went to Europe for *Collier's* in 1914, but soon became a neutral correspondent serving the *Times* again. Wythe Williams left the *New York Times* service in France in 1917 to write for *Collier's,* and James Hopper also served the magazine in France in the latter part of the war.

The *Saturday Evening Post* of Philadelphia, also a weekly and owned by Cyrus H. K. Curtis, began during the war to give more attention to world affairs than previously. Irvin S. Cobb, already established as a writer of fiction and humor for the magazine, wrote from London and from Belgium in the first weeks, but did not remain in Europe. Will Irwin sometimes wrote for the *Post.* The entrance of the United States into the war spurred the *Saturday Evening Post* to new efforts, with writers sent to France. Among them were George Pattulo and Mary Roberts Rinehart, previously known for fiction alone, and Isaac F. (Ike) Marcosson, a staff member, interviewing leaders of government in various countries.

The *New York Times* had sponsored the formation of the *Mid-Week Pictorial* and the monthly *Current History* immediately after the war began in 1914. Neither had any direct representation in Europe, but the London bureau of the newspaper channeled photos and textual material to New York for their use.

A beginning had been made shortly before the war in the preparation and distribution of newsreels to be shown at motion picture theaters, then growing in numbers, supplementary to the entertainment features shown. In France, Charles Pathé and Léon Franconi had been producing such *actualités* since 1909. In the United States, the Edison Company had sponsored news films since 1896. Parallel advances had occurred in Great Britain, Germany, and elsewhere.

In December 1913, William Randolph Hearst formed a Hearst-Selig Company in Chicago to produce and distribute a weekly newsreel as the first such fully organized venture in the United States. Film clips were brought together in Chicago as promptly as possible from any and every part of the nation and the world to be processed and distributed to theaters throughout the country. Clips of U.S. military action in Mexico in 1914 gained attention for the Hearst-Selig Newsreel, and views of the war in Europe soon were added. Other newsreels were standard fare in motion picture theaters of the world from about 1915 until about 1950, after which time the delivery of television news in homes made them seem redundant. All gained voice and sound after about 1928.

Media Changes and
U.S. Agency Extensions

13

By necessity or otherwise, media changes occurred during the war years. Some newspapers within the zones of combat were forced to suspend or take new forms. News exchange between some countries was interrupted. Censorship had its influence. Deliveries of newsprint were affected in certain areas. The costs of news coverage rose.

The death of Herbert de Reuter in 1915 brought the reorganization of the agency bearing his name, as described. Within the Agence Havas, Charles Houssaye succeeded his uncle, Henri Houssaye, in 1915 as news director. That same year, the London *Sunday Times* was purchased by William E. Berry, and put on its way to importance and prosperity as a quality paper.

The death of Lord Burnham in 1916 meant that the full direction of the *Daily Telegraph* passed to his son, the Honorable Harry Lawson, already its director. He became the second Lord Burnham. Sir Max Aitken assumed full direction of the *Daily Express,* and in 1917 became Lord Beaverbrook. William Waldorf Astor, born in the United States, but a British subject since 1899, and owner of the London Sunday *Observer* since 1911, was made a peer; he became Baron Astor of Hever Castle and in 1917 a viscount. George Allardice Riddell, proprietor of the Sunday *News of the World,* became vice-president of the Newspaper Proprietors' Association, and was knighted in 1918, as was Roderick Jones of Reuters. In the United States, the morning and evening *New York Sun* papers were purchased in 1916 by Frank A. Munsey, resulting in the suspension of the *New York Press* and the *Sun*-related Laffan News Bureau.

The *Daily Chronicle* of London in 1918 came under the control of David Lloyd George, then prime minister. In that year, James Gordon Bennett, Jr., proprietor of the *New York Herald,* its Paris edition, and of the afternoon *New York Telegram,* died in Paris. The *New York Evening Post,* owned since 1900 by Oswald Garrison Villard, was purchased by a group headed by Thomas Lamont, a member of the J. P. Morgan & Company banking firm. In the sale, Villard retained and continued as editor of the *Nation,* a weekly magazine long published under the wing of the newspaper.

U.S. Agency Service in South America

The media change during the war years that was to have the most far-reaching significance was the entrance of the United Press and the Associated Press of the United States into the service of the press in South America. Not only did this give new directions to the transmission of world news, but it opened the way toward improvement of news reporting by the introduction of backgrounding and factual interpretation, led to an extension of news services in other countries, and contributed to the eventual end of the regional limitations on news exchange long maintained within the Ring Combination.

When the war began in 1914, both the Agence Havas and Reuters refused to distribute German and Central Powers war communiqués as part of their services. Although those communiqués were available by wireless from Germany itself, this omission in the Havas service was objectionable to *La Nación* and *La Prensa* of Buenos Aires, which were among the quality papers of the world. They took special pride in their complete foreign reports, largely obtained through the French agency service, and they served as models for many other dailies in Latin America.

Argentina, Brazil, and all other countries of South America were neutrals. But many of their peoples had close personal, cultural, and commercial ties with Europe, and the papers wanted to provide them with full accounts of the war. If the communiqués from the German and Austrian commands were omitted from the Havas report, perhaps other things also were being omitted, or given a special slant.

The United States then also was neutral. The Associated Press was one of the oldest news agencies in the world. It was well represented in Europe by 1914, and the organization even then was being augmented to report the war. In September 1914, Jorge A. Mitre, proprietor of *La Nación,* invited the AP to provide his newspaper with a supplementary, disinterested news report covering the war and including the communiqués of all belligerents.

The Associated Press was disposed to respond favorably to this overture. But because of contractual arrangements within the Ring Combination, of which it was a member, South America was recognized as an exclusive territory wherein the Agence Havas alone might distribute a world news service. For this reason, the AP was obliged to reply regretfully that it could not serve the Buenos Aires newspaper.

Doubtless having been aware of the Ring Combination restriction, Mitre made a similar request to the United Press. Formed in 1907, and only starting to develop its own foreign service in 1910, the UP representation abroad was still small. It was an aggressive and enterprising service, wholly independent of the Ring Combination, and was able for that reason to consider Mitre's request. Roy W. Howard, the UP general manager, was hesitant about limiting the service to war news alone. Since *La Nación* was able and willing to meet the costs for what would be a special, tailor-made service, it was finally agreed, however, that the United Press would undertake to provide such a report.

Up to that time there had been virtually no direct relations between the press organizations of North and South America. Howard sent Charles P. Stewart to Buenos Aires to determine what would be required and to make arrangements for provision of the reports. By 1915 the UP service was moving to Buenos Aires for use by *La Nación*. Stewart remained to supervise operations.

The results were sufficiently favorable to induce Howard to go to Buenos Aires himself in the summer of 1916. There he signed a ten-year contract with *La Nación* for continuation of the service. The contract also provided that reports from *La Nación*'s own correspondents in Argentina, and from others writing as stringers in South America and Europe, might be combined to enrich the full United Press service. That total report was made available to other newspapers in Latin America, and to some extent in the United States.

The door thus was open for use of UP service beyond the boundaries of the United States. Also in 1916, the UP formed an exchange arrangement with the Nippon Dempo Tsushin-sha (Dentsu) agency of Japan, with the small but independent Agence Télégraphique Radio (Agence Radio) of Paris, with the Exchange Telegraph Company (Extel) of London, and with the Australian Press Association (APA). Meanwhile, the United Press coverage itself was extended in Europe and beyond, as well as at home, including a far more intensive coverage of the war as the United States became a belligerent. By then, also, the UP service was being used widely in Latin America.

Stewart left Buenos Aires in 1918 and was replaced by James Irvin Miller, an engineer rather than a newsman, who supervised the agency service there. Howard also returned to South America soon after Miller took charge. The war in Europe was at its gravest point, with the United States fully involved. But there were several reasons for Howard's attention to Latin America at that time.

Most serious were rumors, soon substantiated, that Mitre of *La Nación* was planning to establish a news agency of his own, take over the United Press clients, and squeeze that agency out of Latin America, despite the ten-year contract of 1916. Second, Mitre had visited New York a few weeks earlier to discuss personally with the Associated Press once again the provision of service to *La Nación,* with the proposal then to cancel the UP service. Third, there was reason to believe that conversations were taking place between the AP and Havas with a view to its agreement to the AP entrance into the Latin American field. Fourth, some newspapers in South America that had been receiving the UP service were indeed switching to a new service already being offered through *La Nación.* Howard was concerned lest the United Press might indeed be forced to retire entirely from South America. Its position there had become important, as a matter both of prestige and profit, and he went south to explore means by which that possibility of its forced withdrawal might be reversed.

In July, Kent Cooper, traffic manager of the Associated Press, also arrived in Buenos Aires, and the issue was joined. Although the AP was not a commercial agency but a nonprofit cooperative, the necessity of rejecting Mitre's original request for service had continued to bother Melville E. Stone, AP general manager, as it also bothered Cooper and members of the AP board of directors. The alternative entrance of the UP into the South American field was doubly disturbing. Conversations looking toward a possible compromise agreement with the Agence Havas had indeed been opened between Stone and Henri Houssaye of that agency, and continued with his nephew, Charles Houssaye, as he succeeded to the post of news director in 1915.

An element entering into the matter also arose from personal conversations between Howard for the UP and Cooper for the AP. Both had worked for newspapers in Indianapolis at the same period in the early years of the century, as well as for the Scripps-McRae Press Association, and long had been friends. When Howard visited South America in 1916, he had studied the Havas reports being distributed for use throughout that continent and considered them so slanted as to distort the facts on subjects of importance, and specifically to create misunderstanding and even ill-will toward the United States. Returning to New York, he discussed this matter with Cooper and suggested that the AP as well as the UP should in fact enter South America with services to correct the Havas influence. Cooper agreed that this was desirable, and renewed his own efforts to find a means by which the AP might reach an agreement with Havas to share the South American field, as it had shared the Central American field along with Reuters since 1893.

Another element bearing upon such a change related to the communication rate for the delivery of a world news report to South America. Cooper explains in his book, *Barriers Down* (1942), that it was costing Havas twenty-five cents a word to cable news from Paris to Buenos Aires during the war period. By then the New York–Buenos Aires rate, using U.S.-owned cables, was sixteen cents a word. With the UP service moving at that rate, it could provide reports to South American newspapers at a cost considerably below what Havas needed to charge simply to meet expenses. This became a point in the discussions between Stone and Cooper for the AP and Charles Houssaye for Havas.

The AP suggested to Havas that it might be forced out of the South American field by the UP because of this cost differential, but if the AP were permitted to enter the field, while paying Havas for the right to use its full world report, it would be to the advantage of both agencies. Havas continued to insist, however, upon its exclusive rights, and Houssaye explained that the French government itself would make up any difference in costs, and would even go so far as to pay the entire communications costs if necessary to maintain the position of the French news agency in South America.

Negotiations between the Associated Press and the Agence Havas lagged, but were not discontinued. The entrance of the United States into the war gave the AP a new position of strength. Mitre's second approach to the AP early in 1918, his intent to suspend UP service as an element in the establishment of his own agency in South America, and the influence he exerted in matters of press and communication in Argentina and, potentially, throughout the continent all added further to the AP position. Houssaye and the Agence Havas were obliged to reconsider that agency's opposition to the entrance of the Associated Press to South America.

An agreement was sufficiently near in July 1918 for Cooper to go to South America for the AP, and was indeed reached at that time. The Associated Press was permitted to provide a world news report to *La*

Nación and other newspapers prepared to receive it on that continent, with the understanding that the AP would compensate Havas for any loss of income caused by a switch of subscribers from Havas to the AP, but that Havas also could incorporate AP reports into its own service.

Howard, of the UP, was still in Buenos Aires when Cooper arrived. Both remained in South America until October, and traveled together much of the time, although they were in competition. Mitre's intent to establish a news service of his own never came to fruition. But the AP service not only replaced that of the UP in *La Nación;* Cooper also completed arrangements by which twenty-five other newspapers, large and small, in Argentina, Brazil, Chile, Peru, and elsewhere, were to become AP clients, some lost by the UP. To put a capstone on his success, he won *La Prensa* of Buenos Aires, the most prestigious daily, as a client. Thus the AP established a solid position in South America.

Meanwhile, Howard and Miller gained as clients *O País* and *O Imparcial* for the United Press, the two most important and highly-competitive dailies of Rio de Janeiro, Brazil. These contracts were signed despite an effort by Mitre to sabotage the arrangement in the interest of his own syndicate project, still in prospect. Miller also brought three small Buenos Aires papers into the UP service.

These five newspapers were not sufficient, however, to compensate the UP for the loss of *La Nación* and other clients. Efforts to persuade *La Prensa* to subscribe to the UP service were defeated when that paper elected to receive the AP service. The outlook for the UP was dark when Howard left Buenos Aires in October, taking passage in a ship bound for Spain because he could not find a sailing at that time to New York.

Prior to his own departure from South America somewhat earlier, Cooper had a confrontation with a representative of a small agency recently formed in Buenos Aires under the name of La Prensa Asociada, a Spanish version of "The Associated Press." It was, in fact, a propaganda service supported by the German government. Its representative sought to bargain with Cooper for the right to distribute the AP service under the Prensa Asociada name. Cooper naturally refused, but was concerned both by the fact that Havas had not exposed the nature of the agency, and that some newspapers and readers of South America, confused by the similarity in name, were being misled by its slanted news.[1]

---

1   An Associated Press subsidiary of that same name was established in Buenos Aires in 1939.

Miller, remaining in Buenos Aires for the United Press after Howard left, continued the effort to restore the agency's position. Lawrence S. Haas was an assistant, and Harry Robertson was placed in charge of the service in Rio de Janeiro. Some additional small dailies were gained as clients. Miller concentrated his efforts, however, on trying to win *La Prensa* as a client, even though it had so recently chosen to receive the AP service.

Don Ezequiel Paz, publisher of *La Prensa,* was not favorably impressed by the news agencies of the United States. He was especially disdainful of "feature stories, quaint episodes . . . and human interest stories" such as then formed a part of the total UP report. This was a competitive advantage in the United States, where the AP report, by Stone's insistence, was so conservative in content and style as to make dull reading for many, however informative and accurate. The livelier UP style appealed to many editors in the U.S. and, as they believed, to readers.

Aware as he was of Don Ezequiel's views, Miller called regularly at the *La Prensa* office and met with the publisher at times, as well as with editors and staff members. He studied the paper, learned more of its news needs, tastes, and policies, and indicated ways in which the UP service might be useful, or made useful with certain changes. He also pointed out regularly that, since both *La Nación* and *La Prensa* were using the same Associated Press reports, *La Prensa* lacked a service that would be distinctive and exclusive. This was a weighty argument.

Ultimately, Don Ezequiel yielded to Miller's persuasions and agreed to subscribe to the United Press service on a one-year trial basis, beginning June 1, 1919. The AP service was to continue, and it was understood that the UP service would involve special coverage and would be more substantive and interpretative than its service going to newspapers in the United States. Winning *La Prensa*'s acceptance was important enough to the UP in itself as a matter of prestige, not to mention the financial payment, to warrant both special effort and expense to prepare what was a virtually a custom-made report for the paper.

The war in Europe was near seven months ended when the UP service to *La Prensa* began, and the Paris Peace Conference was in session. The service was less than a month in operation when the Versailles Treaty was signed. A lengthy report on this event was sent from Paris to *La Prensa* at the urgent rate, delivered in advance of any other service, and so giving the paper first publication of the news. The full text of the treaty also was cabled on June 9 at substantial cost, and *La Prensa* became the only newspaper in the world, except for the *New York Times,* to present the full document. This was a good beginning for the UP in its relationship with *La Prensa.*

Meanwhile, Miller's special understanding of *La Prensa* and a desire to assure the paper's satisfaction with the service led him to give personal attention to the prompt translation into Spanish of all arriving dispatches and their immediate delivery. He also worked with Furay, UP foreign editor in New York, and with Keen, director of the European service in London, to provide reports on news situations wherever they might arise that might be of special interest to *La Prensa,* and which were written in a manner to meet its standards and requirements.

The trial period for which *La Prensa* was to receive the UP service became a permanent association. When the Associated Press contract with the paper expired in 1920, it was not renewed because the AP refused to grant an exclusive service in Buenos Aires. The UP did grant such an exclusive service to *La Prensa,* delivering at least 5,000 words of cable news a day. In return, it also gained the right to incorporate within its service *La Prensa*'s own reports, obtained through staff and stringer correspondents throughout Argentina, elsewhere in Latin America, and some in Europe.

As a prosperous newspaper, *La Prensa* was able to pay for reports from the United Press beyond the basic service. To meet the requirements of *La Prensa* alone, the UP had to increase its staff and stringer representation, but the payments received over a period of time met the costs. They rose to as much as $550,000 a year. As Joe Alex Morris surmises in *Deadline Every Minute: The Story of the United Press* (1957), this was "probably the largest sum that any newspaper in the world paid to any news-gathering organization" for service.

The prestige that accrued to the United Press because of its selection by *La Prensa* enabled the agency to gain other newspaper clients throughout South and Central America. This more than restored the position it had occupied there from 1916–18, prior to the termination of its relations with *La Nación.* To meet the requirements for gathering as well as distributing the news, the UP established bureaus with staff or stringer correspondents in a number of Latin American capitals.

The Buenos Aires bureau, which processed the agency's flow of news to and from as well as within South America, was expanded under Miller's direction. As UP manager there from 1920, he also became a vice-president of the agency in 1923, and director of the entire Latin

American service in 1927. Others serving there in the early years included A. L. Bradford and Miles W. Vaughn, both of whom held important posts with the UP in the next decade, and Joshua Powers, subsequently to become an advertising representative in New York for a large group of Latin American newspapers.

The Associated Press, although losing *La Prensa* as a client, continued its association with *La Nación* and a group of leading Latin American newspapers. Some of the more prosperous papers arranged to receive both the AP and UP services, even as in the United States. The Havas service also continued to be widely used.

The third U.S. news agency, the International News Service, strengthened and extended in the last year of the war and the decade following, also entered the Latin American field. Both the UP and the INS likewise entered upon news coverage and distribution in parts of Asia, Europe, and elsewhere. The Associated Press became free to do the same after 1934, when the Ring Combination ceased to exist, with an end to exclusive territories for member agencies.

The United Press, having played so important a part in breaking the barriers on international news distribution through the extension of its service in South America, had also provided reports at that time to two of the larger Paris dailies, *Le Matin* and *Le Journal*. It had formed an exchange arrangement in 1916 with the Dentsu agency of Japan, and later with the Extel agency of Great Britain, the APA of Australia, and the Agence Télégraphique Radio of France. The latter agency was formed in Paris in 1918 and reorganized in 1919 by Henri Turot, with the support of Aristide Briand, a former journalist as well as a political leader, but lost its associations with the UP in 1929 when it came under the control of the Havas agency.

_____

Factual Interpretation in the News

The war-born entrance of the three U.S. news agencies into the provision of current information to the press and peoples of other countries was beneficial. It advanced the volume and quality of that information and corrected some earlier elements of distortion. In addition, however, a second significant improvement in the information process emerged, resulting largely from the efforts of the United Press to provide reports to meet the wishes of Ezequiel Paz of *La Prensa*. This was the appearance of "factual interpretation" or "background" added to the raw facts of a day's event or happening, thus giving meaning to the bare bones of the news.

As a concept, this was not wholly without precedent and already favored by *La Prensa* itself, by the *Times* in reports by its own special correspondents, and by some other newspapers. It was not acceptable for news agencies, however, because their services went to a variety of newspapers with a variety of viewpoints.

Historically, when the press was young and newspapers were small, with little staff help and limited financial resources, such "news" as they published was casually obtained locally and, for the rest, usually was reprinted or rewritten from other news sheets arriving late from other cities or other countries. The availability of telegraphic reports brought a new era. By that time, in the mid-nineteenth century, there existed a certain number of prosperous dailies with enough staff members to obtain news more systematically and of greater scope. The writing of that news still tended to be subjective, nevertheless, and sometimes partisan.

To obtain nonlocal news by telegraph was expensive. Most cities then had several daily newspapers, and competition required that any newspaper must use the telegraph if it were to survive in such a competitive situation. The solution was for newspapers to share the costs of telegraphic service bringing the nonlocal reports by joining in the formation of a news agency, or obtaining the service of such an agency. News agencies therefore developed as a means of providing telegraphic news reports with greater economy.

It soon became clear, however, that subjective writing of news was unacceptable in reports prepared for distribution by a news agency. The same reports went to a considerable number of newspapers. If a report was written in a subjective style, it might be acceptable to some editors, but not to others. To avoid protests from editors who might view a subjective news report as partisan, not to say inaccurate, the news agency discovered that its only recourse was to report the facts alone, with a concern for demonstrable accuracy. This meant reporting the who-what-when-where-why-&-how of a day's occurrences, minus adjectives, personalities, and opinion, and extending to the most careful choice of words. This manner of reporting and writing became known as an "objective" style, as distinct from the "subjective." If that was to be the style of telegraphic reports provided by the news agency, it became desirable, as a matter of consistency, that the newspaper's own reporters, writing of local matters, use the same style.

As the objective style thus evolved, it became the practice to write a news story by beginning with the most striking element in the event or situation reported. This might be the most interesting or the most important element, the factor most likely to capture the attention of the prospective reader at once and induce him to read the entire story, whether three paragraphs or a column or more. Known as the "lead" (or "lede"), it might be one sentence, or two or three, but hardly more, and in preferably short sentences. Considering interest or importance or both, it would provide an immediate answer to the who-what-when-where-why-how of the event, with an opening emphasis on whichever of those questions most particularly required an answer. As the story passed beyond the "lead" and got into the "body" of the story, the full account would be presented to the length required to cover all relevant points, with those points recounted in order of diminishing importance.

From about 1860 this form of objective news writing was fully accepted by newspapers and news agencies in the United States. It met the favor of readers, who found its directness and brevity satisfying. From about 1870, the same could be said for the people and press of Europe, introduced to the style at the time of the Franco-Prussian War largely through the association of the *New York Tribune* with the London *Daily News* in the coverage of that war.

Long before World War I, the objective style of writing was accepted in the most advanced countries, used by the best papers and by news agencies. An outright political paper might disregard objectivity altogether. Any well-made general newspaper, however, maintained a strict separation between news and opinion, political or otherwise. Any expression of opinion, any subjective articles, or special signed columns went on its editorial page, where readers were expected to understand the difference between the facts of the news columns and the point of view of the editorial page columns.

For all the value that objectivity brought to the presentation of the news, in this fashion, and the general dedication to that concept of reporting, there was a recognition by a growing number of editors and reporters in the mid-1920s that facts alone were not always enough to make complex subjects clear to all readers of the news columns. Some further explanation might be required to put those facts in perspective. Given the facts as to what happened today or yesterday, a reader might have forgotten, or never have known, what had happened on an earlier day or month or year. He needed to be reminded or told, if he was to understand the latest report or be led to read it at all. He might need to know more of the "why" or "how" of the event, to clarify its meaning, while the writer still avoided injecting elements of personal opinion.

The recapitulation of such relevent facts, briefly told, constituted background, *factual* background. Was such a form of writing possible? Editors and writers faced that question in a world of growing complexities. There were other questions. Was a reporter or correspondent, following a subject in the news from day to day, to repeat that background each day? Was all of this to be telegraphed or cabled, repeatedly, at great cost, or might it be prepared or inserted legitimately by an editor processing the report in a news agency or a newspaper office? Would the addition of such background make the original story too long and therefore one to be cut by an editor or, if used, ignored by a reader? Should the background be provided in a so-called "sidebar," a separate account to be used adjacent to the new report? Even so, would the reader take time to look at it? If not, might the space be used more profitably in other ways? Should it be left to a magazine to provide such background? If so, how many newspaper readers would see that magazine?

Such questions were of sincere concern to conscientious and responsible news personnel. Most editors were agreed that news agency reports must be objective, in the strictest sense of the word. Some, however, were prepared to permit staff reporters or correspondents in whom they had full confidence, on the basis of demonstrated professional competence, to place more stress in their writing on the "why" and "how" of a story, or to go into causes and meanings of events, as well as presenting factual background. Properly done, this could put an event in a "frame of reference," to make the report more informative, more understandable, more useful, even more interesting, and no less accurate, while neither subjective nor partisan. This might be called "interpretation" by some, but it was to be *factual* interpretation as distinct from an *editorial* interpretation, such as might include personal opinion or advocacy.

It was and is a test of the highest professionalism in journalism for a writer thus to produce a clear and well-informed report on a difficult, complex, and possibly controversial subject while retaining balance and writing impersonally. Fortunately, many reporters and correspondents are able, and have been able to meet the test.

The London *Times* was one newspaper that gained much of its prestige by developing a staff of writers at home and abroad able to meet the standards of factual interpretation. In Buenos Aires, *La Prensa* was made very much in the image of the *Times*. A great difference was that

La Prensa did not yet have its "own correspondents" permanently at major capitals of the world in 1920, although it would have some later. It already had a somewhat comparable service from representatives in cities of Argentina, however. To supplement that service, it was "factual interpretation" from the world capitals that Don Ezequiel wanted from the United Press at that time.

Few newspapers in 1920 were prepared to attempt any sort of interpretation of the news beyond some outright editorial comment or the publication of special signed articles. If they published interpretative reports from their own staffers, it almost certainly would be with the writer's name attached, with his effort used as a special column, and probably placed on the editorial page or in a Sunday section. It was considered inappropriate then for a news agency to attempt any such reporting whatever.

The United Press nevertheless responded to *La Prensa*'s desire for a special service. Not only was *La Prensa* satisfied with the service, but it was an element in the extension of UP service to other newspapers in Latin America. Although designed for that part of the world, it was a development of which editors in the United States soon became aware. Some recognized the value of adding factual background to the raw news of the day, particularly at a time when a new depth of reporting of public affairs in a postwar world was gaining recognition. Some of those editors therefore requested the UP to provide such a service to their own papers, again supplementary to the regular report, and the UP proceeded to do so.

By then, the Associated Press had been asked to provide a comparable supplementary service of factual interpretation of the news for *La Nación* and other newspapers in South America, and to some member newspapers in the United States. Nor was that treatment of events to be ignored by the International News Service. Some U.S. editors also asked for an application of factual interpretation to the news out of Washington by their own correspondents there, as well as through the news agencies. Some experimented in the introduction of background reporting bearing upon affairs in their own communities. Those newspapers with foreign correspondents were prepared to receive more "interpretative" reports from them.

There were many editors in the United States who remained wholly dedicated to the concept of objectivity, unable or unprepared to accept the possibility that there could be such a thing as factual interpretation, while still retaining objectivity. To them, interpretation meant editorializing, with the uncertainties of personal opinion. For almost another decade there was a sharp division between U.S. editors, in particular, on this point. But the concept of factual interpretation gained ground, with special adaptation to the growing foreign and Washington services of individual newspapers. Complex problems arising at home and abroad in the late 1920s and 1930s tilted the balance toward general acceptance and application of factual interpretation, the backgrounding of the news, and "depth reporting" locally, nationally, and internationally.

Objectivity remained basic, and still does, but the events of the national economic depression in the United States after 1930, and a growing world crisis, changed matters. A public acceptance of news magazines with their emphasis on background, and notable attention to radio news reporting, commentaries, and analysis combined to spur newspapers, news agencies, and syndicates to present far more background and factual interpretation in a variety of ways. The net result was an opportunity for the people of the United States and of many other countries to gain an improved understanding of every sort of event and situation, wherever it might arise.

Russia, the Eastern Front and Revolution, 1914–18 14

Russia, holding itself as a protector of the Slavic peoples, supported Serbia in the face of Austria's ultimatum of July 23, 1914, correct in its belief that Austria intended to partition that country. With Austria's July 29 attack on Belgrade, Russia mobilized its forces. Germany, supporting Austria, demanded Russia's immediate demobilization. Receiving no assurance of such action, Germany declared war on Russia on August 1, and Austria followed on August 6. With Germany also at war by August 4 with Belgium, France, and Great Britain, the conflict was joined on two fronts, east and west, and in the south in Serbia, and soon in Turkey and the Middle East, and then in all of the Balkan area.

On the eastern front, Russian armies, with a two-to-one superiority in manpower, under the command of Grand Duke Nicholas, an uncle of the czar, entered East Prussia on August 17 and were on the frontier of Austria's northeastern province of Galicia. German and Austrian troops suffered reverses in both areas, but only briefly. Generals Ludendorff and Hindenburg were sent from the western front, and German troops under General August von Mackensen were moved in October to bolster those of Austria in Galicia. Ludendorff and Hindenburg had great successes in late August and September in the battles of Tannenberg and the Masurian Lakes, in the north.

To relieve the Austrian position in the south, a joint German-Austrian attack from Galicia into the south of Poland was undertaken on October 4. This was so effective that forces under Mackensen even reached Warsaw on October 12. Pressure on the Austrians in the south, however, forced the Germans to leave Warsaw and to combat heavy Russian reinforcements through November. With new divisions of their own, the Germans captured Lodz, near Warsaw, in December 1914.

A second offensive in both the north and south resumed in the spring of 1915. The Germans again took Warsaw in August and held it. By September the Russians had lost all of Poland and Lithuania, had suffered about a million casualties, and the Grand Duke Nicholas had been replaced as supreme commander by Czar Nicholas II himself.

In the south of Poland, meanwhile, Russian forces had taken Lemberg on September 3, 1914, and within another week the Austrians had been forced to abandon eastern Galicia. The Russians took Czernowitz and Jeroslav and threatened the fortress of Przemysl and the Carpathian mountain passes into Hungary. Farther south, Serbian forces were able to drive out Austrian troops, following the July shelling of Belgrade and a tentative invasion, and Serb troops even moved into Austrian territory.

Just as a German-Austrian campaign was undertaken successfully in October to protect Galicia, so Austrian forces in December contested the Russians threatening Cracow, and also struck back at the Serbs, entering Belgrade on December 2. This was a brief success, however. In a December 3–6 battle, the Austrians were forced to retreat. They lost Belgrade again on December 15, and were engaged in a winter campaign with heavy casualties on both sides.

The Russians had some successes in the winter and spring of 1915, including the capture of Przemysl, at last, in March. But the Russian position was compromised by a lack of guns, ammunition, and transport. A new Austrian offensive, beginning in July, along with the German-dominated drive in Poland, cost the Russians dearly by the end of 1915.

Austrian forces, strengthened by new German divisions under Mackensen also directed a new attack on Serbia in October 1915, with Belgrade again changing hands. Bulgaria, not forgetting its territorial losses in the Second Balkan War of 1913, had joined with the Central Powers in September 1915, and its forces also crossed into Serbia in October. Under attack by the forces of three countries, the Serbian army was driven out of its own land by the end of 1915. It was pursued into Montenegro, whose King Nicholas surrendered and took personal refuge in Italy, which had joined the Allies in 1915, and into Albania, whose government likewise took refuge in Italy in February 1916, based in Naples. Others of the fleeing Serb forces in 1915 moved to the island of Corfu, off the Albanian coast, and to the Aegean port of Salonika. Both of these were in Greek territory, and Greece, then a neutral in the war, protested.

The French and British, with naval forces in the Mediterranean, had brought pressure on Greece to enter the war in support of the Allies, but King Constantine refused. With the private consent of the king, however, British and French divisions were landed at Salonika in October 1915. Despite Greek opposition, the French also occupied Corfu in January 1916. Serb forces in both places were reorganized and returned to action at Salonika in July 1916, and in November a Greek provisional government organized in Crete under Eleutherios Venizelos, former premier, declared Greece at war with Germany and Bulgaria. The British recognized that government in December. King Constantine abdicated in June 1917, with his second son becoming Alexander I, with Venizelos as premier, and with Greece actively engaged with the Allies.

Not only had the Allies brought Italy and Greece into the war as Associated powers, but Rumania also had cast its lot with the Allies in August 1916, declaring war on Austria-Hungary. Germany, Turkey, and Bulgaria almost immediately declared war on Rumania. The Rumanians had scarcely begun an invasion of the Transylvanian province in Hungary when they faced a counter-attack by Austro-German forces. Bucharest, the capital, was captured in December, and the country was forced to sign a treaty of peace in May 1917. By its terms, the Dobrudja area, on the Black Sea coast, lost to Bulgaria in the Second Balkan War, was returned, and concessions were made to Austria-Hungary and to Germany, which obtained a ninety-year lease on the Rumanian oil wells near Ploesti.

Even as the 1916 actions were proceeding in the Balkans, but before Rumania's entrance into the war in August, a new Russian offensive was directed at Austrian forces. Under General Alexei A. Brusilov, it began June 4, coordinated with an Allied offensive in France and also intended to relieve some of the pressure then being exerted by Austria upon Italian forces in the Trentino. Between June and September there were some Russian advances, but they were later reversed, partly because of transport problems, but also because fifteen German divisions were moved in from the western front to assist the Austrians. Again, Russian casualties totalled about a million, and both army and civilian morale was seriously affected.

The Empress Alexandra, exercising power in Petrograd in the absence of the czar, was hostile to the Duma as an arm of government representative of the people. She also was under the influence of Gregory Rasputin, a monk, and a religious fanatic of low moral standards. To remove that threat and obstacle to the conduct of the war, he was assassinated in December 1916 by a group of aristocrats headed by Prince Felix Yussupov.

The war had not gone well for Russia. Its first gains of 1915 had been reversed, and by the end of that year it had lost all territory previously controlled in Poland and the Baltic area. Two attempted offensives failed in 1916. Rumania, as an ally, was crushed within six months after entering the war in that year. Millions of men had been lost. The armies were ill-equipped, and there were rumors of corruption. These circumstances combined to bring Russia to a crisis point as 1917 began.

Strikes and riots in the cities, and a mutiny of troops occurred early in March. The Duma, disobeying an imperial order to dissolve, instead gave its support to the formation of a new provisional government on March 12. Three days later, Czar Nicholas abdicated. He and members of the royal family were placed under arrest. They were to be held at three locations, the last at Ekaterinburg (now Sverdlovsk), 1,100 miles east of Petrograd in the Ural Mountains, and near the Trans-Siberian Railway line. There they were executed July 8, 1918.

The provisional government was headed by Prince George Lvov. It supported a continuation of the war, and a new offensive was undertaken in June 1917 against the Austrians in Galicia, and in September against the Germans in the north. Alexander Kerensky, the only Socialist member of the government, was minister of justice, but in May became minister of war.

Although a revolutionary sentiment within Russia against the czarist government was nothing new, the actual March revolution, along with Czar Nicholas's prompt abdication, was a surprise to the revolutionary group, as it was to the entire world.

An element in the German wartime propaganda program, as directed by Mathais Erzberger, leader of the Center party, had been to persuade the revolutionary group in Russia to work for a separate peace. This failed in that the group forming the provisional government acted without reference to any German influence and, moreover, favored continuation in the war.

As the provisional government was formed in March, an independent Petrograd Soviet, a Council of Workers' and Soldiers' Deputies, also was organized by the more extreme (Bolshevik) wing of the Socialist party. As contrasted to the more moderate (Menshevik) wing, its members favored ending the war, without any concern for annexations or indemnities. This brought the Petrograd Soviet immediately into conflict with the provisional government.

Germany, observing the course of events in Russia, and aware of the readiness of the Bolshevik group to make an independent peace, entered upon a program designed to advance the power of that group. Certain of the most dedicated and experienced revolutionists among the Bolsheviks were living outside Russia, seeking safety and opportunity to make their own propaganda through a voluntary exile.

Documents captured or discovered in the years after the war, and even after World War II, reveal that at least as early as March of 1915 Russian Social Democrats (Bolsheviks) were in contact with German government and military leaders to the level of Kaiser Wilhelm himself, and were provided with passports and generous financial allowances. Moving not only in Berlin, and in Russia itself, but in Constantinople, Bucharest, Copenhagen, Stockholm, and in Switzerland and elsewhere, they were responsible for acts of sabotage, sponsored pro-German newspapers, spread defeatist and separatist propaganda, conducted secret trade operations and currency transfers, and even sought to subvert Russian prisoners of war, held by the Germans and Austrians.

Most important, in the final analysis, however, were the arrangements made in March 1917 by which Nikolai Lenin, the recognized leader of the Bolsheviks, was moved from his place of exile in Zurich, Switzerland, and across Germany to Sweden, and so to Petrograd. With him went Gregory Zinoviev, Karl Radek, Anatole Lunacharski, and others forming a party of thirty-two. It was a passage in a special "sealed" railway carriage, from April 9 to April 16, and a passage in which Kaiser Wilhelm and General Ludendorff took a personal interest. Lenin was received with great enthusiasm by the Petrograd Soviet.[1] As history records, he was to take the leadership in what became the second, or Bolshevik revolution of October.

In May, Leon Trotsky, another Socialist leader less extreme in his views than the others, although a Bolshevik, arrived in Petrograd from New York. He had collaborated with Lenin in the publication of *Iskra* (The Spark). Joseph Stalin, then thirty-three in 1912, became editor of another revolutionary paper, *Pravda* (Truth), produced within Russia

---

1 See Edmond Taylor, *The Fall of the Dynasties; The Collapse of the Old Order, 1905–1922* (Garden City, N.Y., 1963), pp. 282–88; George F. Kennan, *Russia Leaves the War* (Princeton, 1956); and Alexander Kerensky, *Russia and History's Turning Point* (New York, 1965), pp. 258–67, 295–300, and chapter 18.

itself. Trotsky, of the same age, had been in New York in 1916 editing the revolutionary *Novy Mir* (New World). When the provisional government was formed in March 1917, friends collected funds to send him back to Russia. En route, he was arrested and interned at Halifax when his ship put in there, but was released at the request of the provisional government in an appeal to London, and so reached Petrograd by way of England.

Meanwhile, between March and July of 1917, sharp differences had arisen within the provisional government over proposed reform measures and over war policy. The campaign in Galicia failed in mid-July, and the Petrograd Soviet, by then dominated by Lenin and the Bolshevik group, attempted to seize power, with intent to end the war. The attempt failed, and Lenin took refuge in Finland, but Trotsky and others were arrested. At the same time, Prince Lvov resigned as head of the provisional government and was succeeded by Kerensky.

With the Kerensky, or Menshevik, wing of the Socialist party directing the provisional government, and a strong war position still supported, General Lavr Kornilov was appointed as commander-in-chief of the armed forces. In September an effort was made to drive the Germans out of Latvia, but the first result was the loss of Riga. Kerensky immediately dismissed Kornilov from his command. A week later, Kornilov turned against him and led a military attack on Petrograd in an effort to oust the government. That failed when Kerensky was joined by Trotsky, freed from prison. Speaking on behalf of the Bolsheviks, he made a direct appeal to the troops. This halted Kornilov, and it gave the Bolshevik group influence in the government.

The following month of October 1917 brought the provisional government to a new crisis and to an end. The Petrograd Soviet, following the Bolshevik extremist Socialist policy, had gained added support among factory workers and among soldiers in the Petrograd garrison. Confidence in the provisional government was indeed undermined, as the Germans had foreseen, and its status was not improved by the military reversals in Galicia and Latvia. Many also had been led to believe that, given an opportunity, it would reverse the revolutionary moves that had brought an end to the czarist rule and might restore that monarchy.

So it was that on October 24–25 (or November 6–7 by the Gregorian calendar, which only superceded the Julian calendar in Russia after the Soviet government became established), there occurred in Petrograd the second revolution of that year, the "Bolshevik revolution" or what since has been referred to as the Russian Revolution.

On those days soldiers, sailors, and the workers' Red Guards, acting under Bolshevik leaders, including Lenin, returned from Finland, captured most of the provisional government offices, located in the czar's former Winter Palace. Members of the government were arrested, but Kerensky escaped and, for a time, was with armed forces trying to retake Petrograd. When this failed, he reached London, Paris, and later the United States, where he remained.

In Petrograd on October 25 (November 7), there was organized a Council of People's Commissars, a new government, headed by Lenin. Among its members, Trotsky was commissar for foreign affairs and Stalin was commissar for national minorities. In December the Council formed an Extraordinary Commission to Combat Counter-Revolution, known briefly as the Cheka, later as the G.P.U., and by other names, but functioning as a secret police concerned with the security of the government.

Trotsky, as foreign commissar, proposed to the Allied Powers that an armistice be concluded with the Central Powers. The Germans were prepared to negotiate, but the western Allies were unwilling to approve an armistice under conditions then favorable to Germany. The Russian Council therefore acted independently and an armistice with Germany was concluded at Brest-Litovsk on December 5, 1917. It soon broke down, however, when the Russians learned that Germany would demand the surrender of Poland and other territorial concessions.

On February 9, 1918, the Germans negotiated a separate peace with the Ukraine, the large province dominating central European Russia. In Petrograd the Bolsheviks protested this, but nonetheless they then announced the end of the war by proclamation. This unilateral action did not satisfy the Germans, who resumed the war on February 18, and began a march on Petrograd. Since the Bolsheviks were unprepared to resist such a move, they were forced to sign a harsh treaty, again at Brest-Litovsk, on March 3, 1918. Under its terms they lost Poland, the Ukraine, Finland, Latvia, Lithuania, and Estonia, all formerly parts of czarist Russia.

To avoid further possible disaster, the Bolsheviks promptly moved the capital from Petrograd, on the Gulf of Finland, 400 miles inland and southeastward to Moscow (Moskva), which had been the administrative center and capital of Russia from the fourteenth century or earlier until the government was moved to St. Petersburg in 1712. There they felt less exposed to German designs, and better able also to resist possible counter-revolutionary moves by members of the old privileged, propertied, and politically moderate elements in Petrograd, as well as by those living in areas lost in the peace settlement. In Moscow the Bolshevik party became the Communist party, officially, in March 1918. The Council of People's Commissars formed the Soviet government of the Union of Socialist Soviet Republics (USSR).

So long as the war continued elsewhere in Europe until November 1918, the new Soviet government continued to have trouble. German forces moved into the Ukraine seeking food, supplies, and munitions. They might conceivably have gone elsewhere, and might have recruited labor or even military manpower. Aware of the potential, the Allied governments sent troops into Russia from the north, south, and east. This led the Communist government to declare war upon Russia's former allies on July 29, 1918. Meanwhile, anti-Bolshevik elements within Russia ("Whites") contested with the Communists ("Reds") for a restoration of an alternative regime. They sometimes made common cause with the Allied forces in the country.

From the time of the second Brest-Litovsk Treaty of March 3, 1918, and indeed from the time of the first treaty of December 5, 1917, Russia no longer was involved in the European war. Its withdrawal released German, Austrian, Turkish, and Bulgarian forces for action on other fronts. These forces presented a special threat on the western front in France and to Italy in its contest with Austria, and could tilt the balance of victory.

As on the western front, so on the eastern front from 1914 to 1917, the names of places and personalities figured in the news. Among them were the areas of East Prussia, Poland, and Galicia, the Vistula River, and such places as Lemberg, Przemysl, and Warsaw. But there also were Lublin and Cholm, Kovno and Grodno, Gumbinnen and Ivangorod, Cracow and Lodz, Lowicz and Limanova. Some of these places were in those sections where the important battles of Tannenberg and the Masurian Lakes were fought in 1914. Some figured in later action, but other place-names also appeared. There were Riga and Vilna, Tarnopol and Dvinsk, the areas of Bukovina and Courland, the Dunajec River, Memel and Jaroslav, Minsk and, of course, Brest-Litovsk. Among military figures there were the Grand Duke Nicholas, the czar, Rennenkampf, Samsonov, Alexeiev, and Brusilov on the Russian side; Ludendorff and Hindenburg, Prittwitz, Hoffmann, Falkenhayn, Moltke, Mackensen, and Below, for the Germans; Conrad and others for Austria; and still others for Bulgaria and Turkey.

With the declaration of war between Russia and the Central Powers, at least four Russian correspondents were obliged to leave Berlin, and German correspondents left St. Petersburg, including a representative of the Wolff news agency. Wolff ceased to provide service to the official Sankt-Petersburgskoye Telegraphnoye Agenstvo (Westnik), with the Agence Havas replacing it in the provision of that world service routed through Stockholm.

St. Petersburg itself was promptly renamed Petrograd to rid it of the Germanic version of the saint's name, and the Westnik agency name also was modified, becoming the Petrogradskoye Telegraphnoyve Agenstvo. Of about fifty dailies published in Russia, a dozen appeared at Petrograd, with *Novoye Vremya* and *Ryech* regarded as the most important. Two others of some standing were the *Russkoye Slovo* of Moscow and *Kievskaya Muysel* of Kiev. The importance of any Russian paper was only relative, however, since none was greatly enterprising, depending chiefly upon government releases of information and upon the official news agency for its reports. They lacked that freedom to comment enjoyed by most newspapers in western Europe.

Allied and neutral correspondents in Petrograd, as the war began, included Guy Beringer of Reuters; Alexandre Gorline, present for Havas since 1907; Roger Lewis, Associated Press; Dr. Emile Joseph Dillon, the *Daily Telegraph;* Robert Wilton and George Dobson, the *Times;* L. B. Golden, the *Daily Mail;* Arthur Ransome, the London *Daily News;* Francis McCullagh, the *Manchester Guardian* and the *New York Herald;* John Foster Bass, the *Chicago Daily News;* Alan Ostler, the *Daily Express;* and Ludovic Naudeau of *Le Journal,* Paris.

Other correspondents hastened to Russia, and still more were there for certain periods as the war continued. Early arrivals included Walter C. Whiffen of the AP, coming from Vera Cruz and replacing Lewis, who went to Belgium and northern France; Horace Trouvé, who replaced Gorline for Havas; F. H. Wilcox of the *Daily Telegraph,* forced to leave his former post in Berlin and joining Dillon for that paper; and Herbert Bailey, joining Ostler for the *Daily Express,* who departed in 1915 to join the British army and was killed in service in 1918. Bailey, later writing also for the *New York Times,* remained in Petrograd until early 1917, and later represented the *Daily Mail* in France in 1918.

Neither the Russian government nor the military leadership was notably cooperative with the press, domestic or foreign. Early in the war, however, the high command did give some foreign reporters a quick tour behind the lines, but they were permitted to see very little. The critical August Battle of Tannenburg received no direct press attention at all from the Russian side, but it was reported from the German side. By December 1914, correspondents attempting to report Russian action on the eastern front made Warsaw the center of their efforts, with the Hotel Bristol as a place of residence and work. They remained there until the city was taken by the German army in October 1915.

During those months, some correspondents had opportunity to go into the field. One was William Philip Simms, chief of the UP bureau in Paris, who was in Russia briefly. Granville Fortescue, an American representing the *Daily Telegraph,* visited the Russian front after earlier coverage in Belgium and France. Stanley Washburn, also an American correspondent, who represented the *Chicago Daily News* during the Russo-Japanese War, and who wrote from Russia for the *Times* in 1905, again served that paper. He complained that never had he known "any place where more false reports and misinformation circulated at par than here in Warsaw."[2] Gregory Mason, writing for the *Outlook Magazine* of New York, and formerly reporting from Vera Cruz, was in Russia in 1915 and returned in 1917. McCullagh of the *Manchester Guardian* and the *New York Herald,* along with Basset Digby, who had arrived to assist Bass for the *Chicago Daily News,* produced notable reports of the German capture of Warsaw. Robert Liddell of the *Sphere,* a London illustrated weekly, was perhaps longest in Warsaw and saw most but wrote relatively little.

Petrograd, which remained the only base for correspondents after the capture of Warsaw, was little better as a center for reporting. News never had been a commodity easy to obtain in Russia, and the critical developments there since 1905 had made it no easier. Reliable information on the war was difficult to obtain. There was small opportunity to verify reports and a strict censorship was in effect. Occasional opportunities to visit the front were not always happy in their results. Bass of the *Chicago Daily News* was wounded in 1916, and Isaac Don Levine took his place as bureau chief for the paper in Petrograd. Whiffen of the AP, accompanied by D. B. McGowan, also was wounded and replaced as bureau chief by Charles Stephenson Smith, formerly of the AP staff in Washington, who had hastened to London when the war began. He had been in Belgium and then on an assignment in Peking

---

2 Son of Minnesota Senator William Drew Washburn (1831–1912), Washburn's correspondence and notes were presented to the Library of Congress in 1955 by his widow.

prior to moving to Petrograd. H. L. Rennick was another AP correspondent assigned to Petrograd.

Arthur Ruhl of *Collier's Weekly,* in moving widely over the war areas, included Russia in his travels in 1916 and again in 1917. Hamilton Fyfe and Joseph M. N. Jeffries, equally mobile as correspondents for the *Daily Mail,* also were in Russia. John Reed, who had reported events in Mexico for the *El Paso Herald* and as a stringer both for the UP and the *New York Times,* was in Russia from 1914 writing for the *Metropolitan Magazine,* then for the *Masses,* New York Socialist magazine, and for the *New York Evening Call,* Socialist party daily dating from 1908. He was sometimes with Russian forces, accompanied by Boardman Robinson, an artist. Herbert Bayard Swope of the *New York World,* who had been on the Russian front with German troops as Berlin correspondent for that paper, moved to Petrograd early in 1917 and spent some time with Russian forces. David Fraser, in China for the *Times,* visited Vladivostok to report aspects of the war in Asiatic Russia.

News of military action on the eastern front was overshadowed progressively during 1916–18 by news of political action and revolution. Information on the position of Rasputin in the court as it leaked out, and his assassination in December 1916, was the subject of many stories. The strikes, riots, and military defections in early 1917 made for news that reached the world despite the censorship. The formation of a new provisional government immediately following, and the abdication of Czar Nicholas was, of course, a major event.

The sequence of events through the next year was complex and often confusing. The first revolutionary period from March to October 1917, with the provisional government attempting to maintain Russia's role in the war, and with Kerensky as its prime minister from July, produced many news reports. Not only were there continuing failures in battle, but more significant in retrospect was the opposition to the new government aggressively advanced by the Petrograd Soviet, also formed in March 1917, and soon directed by Lenin, Trotsky, and other Bolshevik Socialists who returned to Russia from foreign exile. Their ultimate success came in October in the second revolution that ended the provisional government, put the Bolshevik element in complete power, and led to the treaties of Brest-Litovsk that took Russia out of the war and established a new Soviet (Communist) government in Moscow in March 1918.

These months gave correspondents in Petrograd a great deal to do, with fact to be sifted from rumor, with a variety of political and social viewpoints to be identified and analyzed, with sources of information to be found to cast light on the interplay of forces within the country, and always without forgetting that military action was still in progress. Further, the problems continued after Brest-Litovsk, somewhat changed, but equally confusing.

The complex and sometimes violent events in Russia from March 1917 affected the domestic press organization and affected the position of foreign reporters in the country. Existing newspapers ceased to appear, brought under restraint as Bolshevik rule was extended. Their publishing plants were nationalized and converted to the production of approved papers in Petrograd, which were later moved to Moscow. The first, made the official paper, was *Pravda* (Truth), which dated from 1912 as an underground revolutionary paper, usually forced to operate clandestinely because it was repeatedly suppressed when it attempted normal publication. The second was *Izvestia* (News), started in March 1917 as the provisional government began, and almost equally official.

With the October revolution, the Petrogradskoye Telegraphnoye Agenstvo (Westnik) agency was seized and retitled, as one of its parts had been before the 1904 merger, to become the Rossiyskoye Telegraphnoye Agenstvo (Russian Telegraph Agency), or Rosta. It was an official agency, without ties to Havas or any other agency, and merely used to distribute official reports and information.[3]

Arno Dosch-Fleurot of the *New York World,* arriving in Petrograd from France early in 1917, spoke with Ludovic Naudeau, long in Russia for *Le Journal* of Paris. Dosch-Fleurot expressed amazement over certain of his first impressions. In his book, *Through War to Revolution* (1920), he cites Naudeau's reply, which he credits as helping prepare him for much that he was to observe in months to follow. Naudau remarked:

> You will not know enough about Russia to explain it until you have been here so long you are half-Russian yourself, and then you won't be able to tell anybody else anything about it at all. You won't want to, ...
> Think of Russia as a country where nobody ever grows up, where no man ever reaches twenty though he lives to be a hundred. . . . You will be tempted to compare Russia with other countries. Don't. Keep only in mind that it is very young, with the headlong aspirations and the blind follies of youth. [Pp. 103–04]

---

3 In 1925 Rosta was reorganized under the Soviet government as the Telegrafnoie Agenstvo Sovietskavo Soyuza (Telegraph Agency of the Soviet Union), but known almost exclusively as TASS.

Herbert Bailey, in Petrograd since 1915 for the *Daily Express* and also writing for the *New York Times,* forecast the ultimate Bolshevik revolution after Kerensky had become head of the provisional government in July 1917. The *Daily Express* editors in London, disbelieving his forecast, refused to use his story. Bailey thereupon resigned, left Petrograd, and represented the *Daily Mail* in France in 1918.

Russian-born Herman Bernstein, formerly on the staff of the *New York Times* and in St. Petersburg for the paper at intervals from 1908–12, then founder and editor of the *New York Day,* a Jewish daily, during 1914–16, arrived in Petrograd early in 1917 as a representative of the *New York Herald.* He uncovered the so-called "Willy-Nicky" letters, prewar correspondence between Germany's Kaiser Wilhelm II and Czar Nicholas II, which became a chapter in the retrospective history of Europe.[4] They were edited and published by Isaac Don Levine in 1920, then a correspondent for the *Chicago Daily News.*

James D. Bourchier of the *Times* arrived in Petrograd in November 1917, following the October revolution. He came from Sofia by way of Bucharest and Odessa, and gained rare interviews with Lenin and Trotsky, which he forwarded to London from Christiania as his last dispatches in the newspaper he had served since 1892.

Gregory Mason of *Outlook Magazine,* having been in Russia in 1915, returned briefly in 1917. One of his fellow passengers aboard ship eastbound from Halifax and onward from London was Leon Trotsky, traveling under circumstances already described, but his identity and status went unrecognized on that voyage. Other correspondents arriving in Petrograd in 1917 prior to October included Swope of the *New York World,* M. (Morgan) Phillips Price, one of the best-informed and most effective, and David Soskice, a later arrival, both for the *Manchester Guardian.* Soskice almost immediately became Kerensky's secretary. Michael Farbman, also for the *Guardian,* but writing for the *Chicago Daily News* as well, was another arrival. Rita Childe Dorr came as a representative of the *New York Evening Mail,* a paper dating from 1867, but purchased secretly by German agents shortly before the entrance of the United States into the war. Bessie Beatty, accredited to the *San Francisco Chronicle,* also arrived in Petrograd.[5]

---

4 Bernstein served as U.S. minister to Albania from 1930–33.

5 In Russia at the time of the revolution, representing a London business firm in Petrograd, was Negley Farson, an American then without news experience, but to become a post-war correspondent for the *Chicago Daily News.*

Robert Wilton, Petrograd correspondent for the *Times,* returned to London shortly before the October 1917 revolution because he found the censorship too limiting, and his paper traditionally had resisted submission to censorship. Although Bourchier passed through Petrograd in November, the paper had no representative in Russia from 1917 until 1940, and even then for less than a year when censorship again brought a withdrawal.

Correspondents in Petrograd for the Allied press or any other were in an increasingly uncomfortable position after the October revolution, and were unable to produce much news of substance because of lack of sources and censorship. In the circumstances, most left the country. Among them, Guy Beringer of Reuters made what was deemed an escape from Petrograd with his wife after the revolution, reaching Finland and London. He returned alone to Russia, but was arrested and imprisoned for six months. This was a new hazard for correspondents.

George Dobson, a member of a British family long resident in Russia, and representing the *Daily Mail* at this period, also was seized by the Bolsheviks after the signature of the Brest-Litovsk Treaty in March 1918. He was held with members of the British consular staff, and imprisoned for five weeks in Moscow, where the new Bolshevik government moved on March 9, six days after the treaty signature. Meanwhile, Maxim Litvinov, representing the Bolshevik government in London since the October revolution, along with Georghy Chicherin, were arrested there and held as hostages for British persons detained in Russia. Both men, later to become foreign commissars in the Soviet government, were exchanged for Dobson, Robert Bruce Lockhart, British consul-general, and other British subjects in Russia.

Those very few correspondents who did remain in Russia after March 1918, moving to Moscow with the new government, were in an almost intolerable situation. They could not function as reporters and some were to see the inside of jails, McCullagh among them, as well as Beringer and Dobson. At least one German correspondent ventured to visit Moscow, Alfons Pacquet of the *Frankfurter Zeitung,* but he remained only briefly. Among others, the last correspondents to leave Russia at this period appear to have been Soskice, Ruhl, and Ransome.

The one correspondent remaining, and favored by the new regime, was John Reed, writing for the Socialist *New York Evening Call.* He lived in Moscow with his wife, the former Louise Bryant. Both had come from well-to-do families in Portland, Oregon. Graduated from Harvard in 1909 and entering journalism, Reed had become a Socialist. Among the correspondents in Petrograd in 1917, he and Ransome of the London *Daily News,* Levine of the *Chicago Daily News,* and Price of the *Manchester Guardian* have been credited with producing the most authoritative information and demonstrating a greater understanding of the course of events under the Bolsheviks. Reed had become an outright partisan and was given special opportunities to obtain information from headquarters. Out of the country for a time late in 1918, he returned and worked in a newly formed Soviet propaganda bureau in Moscow. There he died of typhus in 1920 at thirty-three, and was given an honored burial and a commemorative plaque on the Kremlin wall.

News Reporting in Post-Revolutionary Russia

In Moscow, the new Soviet government established its headquarters in March 1918 at the Kremlin, walled and protected as a citadel within the city, its original twelfth century center, and one resisting destruction even by the army of Napoleon in 1812. It was regarded as a haven against possible new German aggression or dissidents within Russia. As a further safeguard against any attempt to restore the monarchy, the czar and members of the royal family, held captive since the March 1917 abdication, were moved to a more remote and secure place of detention at Ekaterinburg.

Communist concern about internal opposition was warranted. An attempt to assassinate Lenin on August 30, 1918, brought a reign of terror in which great numbers of intellectuals and members of the middle class were killed. It spurred the formation of the secret police as a powerful arm of government. Opponents of the Bolshevik regime, of whom there were many, sought to defend their property, possessions, and privileges. These so-called "Whites" organized against the Communist "Reds," so far as they were able, with military forces led by General Anton Deniken, who had been the czar's chief of staff, General Anton Ivanovich, General Lavr Georgivich Kornilov, Admiral Aleksandr V. Kolchak, and others.

For the Communists, Trotsky became commissar for war as 1918 began, and he developed a small volunteer force into a disciplined conscript Red Army, including some 40,000 former czarist officers, growing in strength through the two years of civil war that followed. Campaigns in that war of 1918–20 proceeded in the Ukraine, in the

Caucasus, in southern Russia, in the Baltic area and Poland, in Siberia, and in eastern Russia. There were both victories and defeats for the Red Army. Early aid from Germany was offset by an Allied blockade and by Allied forces that gave some support to the "Whites."

Meanwhile, it was impossible for the new Soviet regime to organize the economy. This led to widespread famine, with peasant uprisings and rioting among city workers that kept the country in turmoil until 1923.

Two factors added to the problems of the as-yet uncertain Communist regime. Czech soldiers, unwilling conscripts in the Austrian army, had been taken as prisoners by the Russians on the East Galician front in 1917 in the first campaign undertaken by the provisional government. Under Kerensky, it was agreed that they should be granted their freedom to fight with the Russian provisional forces as a Czech Legion. After the October revolution, however, and the first Brest-Litovsk Treaty by which Russia withdrew from the war, it was agreed that the Czechs should be permitted to move eastward by the Trans-Siberian Railway to Vladivostok and return to Europe by ship to join the Allies in the war still proceeding against Germany and Austria.

The first group of about 100,000 Czechs proceeded according to this plan, and were indeed to fight in France. Elements starting later, however, met interference from the Bolsheviks, and fighting ensued. The Czechs gained control of a section of the rail line eastward to Irkutsk in Siberia, and of a wide area in the foothills of the Ural Mountains. They also formed an alliance with anti-Bolshevik White forces and posed a threat to Ekaterinburg, where the czar was being held. It was this situation, and the possibility that he might be freed, that brought Bolshevik orders to execute all members of the royal family, as was done on July 16, 1918. Admiral Kolchak, leading the combined White Russian and Czech forces, continued in an advance in eastern Russia until December, but was overcome by the Bolsheviks in 1919. Kolchak was captured and executed, and the Czechs, never properly accounted for, are believed also to have died.

The second factor arose because Russia's full and official withdrawal from the war at the time of the signature of the second Brest-Litovsk Treaty in March 1918 caused the Allies concern lest the Germans gain foodstuffs, general supplies, munitions, and even labor in Russia. This the Germans had immediately undertaken to do in the Ukraine following the separate peace there in February. Since the Allies were still at war with Germany, French, British, Japanese, and U.S. military elements moved into Russia from ports in the north, south, and east.

They could and sometimes did join forces with the White Russian groups. This led the Communist government in Moscow to declare war on the Allies on July 29, 1918. There were to be some clashes in the months following between Allied forces and elements of the growing Red Army.

The Allied expeditions into Russia were reported by some of the correspondents previously in Petrograd, but they were joined by others. Between June and August 1918, British, French, and U.S. forces landed at Murmansk and Archangel, in the north of Russia. With this group were Roger Lewis and H. L. Rennick, of the AP; Douglas Williams of Reuters, recovering from wounds received while in British army service; Carl W. Ackerman, formerly in Germany and Russia for the UP, but now representing the *New York Times;* and Frazier ("Spike") Hunt of the *Chicago Tribune.* Ackerman managed to move into Russia as far as Ekaterinburg, joined the Czech Legion there, and also verified the execution of the czar and the royal family.

At the same time, French and British forces landed in the Black Sea area in the south and occupied Odessa. These landings were reported by Joseph M. N. Jeffries of the *Daily Mail,* Walter S. Hiatt of the AP, and Paul Williams of the *Chicago Tribune.*

In the east, Japanese, U.S., and British troops landed at Vladivostok and moved into Siberia. This action was reported by David Fraser, Peking correspondent for the *Times.* He was soon relieved by Robert Wilton, formerly in Petrograd for the paper, and who arrived by way of the United States and the Pacific, joining on the last leg of the journey with U.S. troops assigned from the Philippines, Wilton, in turn, was replaced for the *Times* by Andrew Soutar, formerly in British military service, and on his first news assignment. John Sherwood-Kelly, another veteran of British military service, and much decorated for valor, represented the *Daily Express* in Siberia while also commanding troops.

Walter C. Whiffen of the AP, who had been in Petrograd, and who recovered from wounds received on that front, reported the U.S. landing at Vladivostok and proceeded into Siberia with Frank King of the AP Tokyo bureau. Joseph E. Sharkey, wartime chief of that bureau, joined in the Siberian move and also made a difficult and hazardous journey westward to Omsk to report an attempt there to form an autonomous Siberian government under Admiral Kolchak. When this failed, with Kolchak's execution by the Communists, Sharkey made the equally difficult return eastward to complete a 2,800-mile expedition.

Herman Bernstein, also formerly in Petrograd for the *New York Herald,* joined the Siberian press group. Others present were Wilfrid Fleisher of the *Japan Advertiser* in Tokyo, and also then writing for the *New York World;* John D. Ryan for the *Chicago Tribune;* Peggy Hull (Mrs. Henrietta Kinley) for NEA, with earlier experience in France; and Junius B. Wood of the *Chicago Daily News,* who was formerly accredited to the AEF in France.

White Russian and Polish forces, with some aid from the French, were aligned against Red Army units in the Ukraine and Poland during 1918–21. Hiatt, of the AP, and Williams, of the *Chicago Tribune,* who had been in the south of Russia, witnessed some of this action. Others present in Poland in 1919 included Vernon Bartlett, recently engaged by the *Times,* and Hal O'Flaherty of the *Chicago Daily News,* formerly on the Mexican-Texas border for the UP, in London for the UP and the *New York Sun,* and now returned to news work after service in the U.S. Army Air Force.

With the German armistice and the formal end of the war in Europe in November 1918, the Allied need for troops in Russia lost its point, and they were eventually withdrawn. French troops were only driven out of Odessa by Red Army forces in April 1919, and some still remained in Poland. Japanese forces remained in Vladivostok and the east until October 1922, seeking to establish a position in that area adjacent to Korea and Japan itself. The involvement of some Allied units with White Russian forces, along with uncertainties as to the course to be taken, led to confusion and delays that resulted in some troop mutinies. The formation by the Communist government in March 1919 of the Third International, with the announced purpose of propagating the Communist doctrine in other countries, created an atmosphere of hostility that induced the Allies to maintain a blockade of Russia until January 1920.

The Germans, in the Ukraine from February 1918, lost their position there with the Armistice in November. White Army units were active in that central area, however, until December 1919, and Polish forces until 1920. Only then did the Ukraine become a republic within the USSR. It was only then, also, that the Red Army gained control in the Caucasus.

Russia, by the terms of the final Treaty of Brest-Litovsk, had been forced to yield control of Poland, Finland, Latvia, Lithuania, and Estonia to Germany. Under the terms of the 1918 armistice, Germany in turn was obliged to yield those areas to the Allies, with a final determination of their sovereignty to be made in the Treaty of Versailles in 1919. By those terms, independent republics resulted in all five areas. French forces remained in Poland and the Baltic areas to assist in preserving their independence in the face of Red Army attacks during 1918–20.

Meanwhile, with the Armistice of 1918, two representatives of the *Chicago Tribune,* Floyd Gibbons and Richard Henry Little, made their way from France across Germany to Poland and beyond. They were followed on this journey by a woman correspondent, Marguerite Harrison, with credentials from the *Baltimore Sun,* for which she had worked, but also from the Associated Press and the *New York Evening Post.* Little, seeking to observe battle action, was wounded near Petrograd. Gibbons and Harrison risked a crossing of the battle lines to reach Moscow.

The Communist government declaration of war against the Allies in July 1918, although not formally renounced until 1921, ceased to stand as a technical ban on the presence in Russia after November 1918 of correspondents representing the press of the Allied countries. They were not welcomed, however, nor were those who appeared formally admitted or accredited, and some were arrested. A number spent some time in Moscow, nevertheless, in 1919 and 1920.

McCullagh, of the *Manchester Guardian* and *New York Herald,* had managed to remain, although unable to work as a journalist, and in prison much of the time. John Reed was there from 1918 until his death in 1920, but in the Communist service. Gibbons and Mrs. Harrison were the first to enter. Gibbons left after a short time. When it became known that Mrs. Harrison was not quite a *bona fide* correspondent, and was making reports to the U.S. Army military intelligence branch concerning her observations in Germany, Poland, and Russia, she was arrested and spent many months in a Moscow prison.

Others arriving included Michael Farbman of the *Manchester Guardian* and *Chicago Daily News,* who had been in Petrograd earlier, Edwin Ware Hullinger also of the *Chicago Daily News,* Frank J. Taylor of the United Press, Samuel Spewack of the *New York World,* and John Clayton of the *Chicago Tribune.* They were in an extremely uneasy position. Clayton was expelled, and by 1920 all foreign reporters had departed. Not until November 1921 were others admitted formally.

The Last Year of the War, 1917–18

As the war began in Europe in August 1914, Woodrow Wilson was in the second year of his first term as president of the United States. His administration had recently entered a period of critical relations with Mexico, with U.S. military forces in Vera Cruz from April to November.

The United States announced its neutrality, and Wilson used his office to seek a settlement of the differences between the nations at war. Through 1915 and 1916 he acted personally to try to establish a basis for restoration of the peace. Edward M. House, a wealthy Texan and an honorary colonel in the militia of that state, went repeatedly to Europe as the president's friend and representative in that cause. Meanwhile, the United States became an arena in which sympathies and loyalties to the European belligerents were tested and contested; an arena in which propaganda efforts and persuasions of both sides received expression.

There was no denying that Austria-Hungary and Germany had been the aggressors in the war and that Germany, in particular, had been following a "militaristic" policy for at least a decade, with a view to extending its power. This circumstance tended to create a sympathy for the victims of that aggression, beginning with Serbia and "little Belgium," and for the Allied nations under attack. The strong British heritage, so much a part of the social and political structure of the United States, and an attachment to France deriving from that nation's assistance in the attainment of independence in the eighteenth century, combined to create a sentiment favorable to those countries under attack. This support was particularly strong in the Atlantic coastal states, nearest to the scene of the war and with the closest ties to Great Britain and France.

While the war seemed far away and without clear significance to most persons in the United States, the great flood of immigration since about

1870 had brought more than twenty-five million persons into the United States from Europe and other parts of the world. Among them were more than three million from Germany and others from Austria. Adding second-generation persons of that origin, the total was perhaps five or six million, with great concentrations in such cities and surrounding areas as New York, Baltimore, Cincinnati, St. Louis, Chicago, and Milwaukee. With cultural and family attachments to the fatherland, their sympathies not unnaturally were involved.

Yet other first and second-generation groups also were present with ties to other countries. Immigrants in the 1870–1910 period from Russia, Poland, and the Baltic states exceeded two and a half million, more than three million from Italy, perhaps two and a half million from Great Britain, close to a million from Canada and Australia, and others from France, Belgium, Turkey, Greece, and the Balkan states.

Tensions soon were felt in the United States, and were expressed and sometimes acted upon by the diverse groups of national origins or background. There were well publicized reports of "atrocities" committed by the German forces in Belgium, and later in France. Arising in part because of the chaotic conditions of war, and the difficulty of checking rumor against fact, these stories were presented circumstantially through the British and French press and information services as a means both to spur the war effort at home and to win support and sympathy from neutral peoples and governments, not least in the United States. The Germans at the same time put out stories of their own, using their sympathizers and agents and diplomatic representatives in neutral countries. False or exaggerated as some of these stories were, there was virtually no way to verify or disprove or correct them until after the war.

Tensions also arose because of the German use of submarine warfare. As the war began, merchant ships and passenger ships of the belligerents sought shelter in their home ports or neutral ports, including New York harbor. The United States, as a neutral nation, held to the view that its own ships had the right to move without interference, and they continued to do so, even though some were challenged by the British, and some later were sunk by German submarine action.

The British, out of necessity, but with a strong navy to provide defense and convoy protection, continued to send ships to sea. Some were lost, and the sinking of the great Cunard liner, *Lusitania* (31,938 tons), off Ireland in May 1915, became a turning point in the war. Bound from New York to Liverpool, the ship had sailed despite a notice published in New York newspapers by the German Embassy in Washington informing travelers that "vessels flying the flag of Great Britain, or any of her allies, are liable to destruction" in the "waters adjacent to the British Isles." Among 1,198 drowned in the sinking were 114 U.S. citizens.

There was indignation in the United States following the torpedoing of the *Lusitania,* and a possibility of U.S. entrance into the war. A series of notes was exchanged, with the Germans insisting that the ship carried munitions and was armed, but the British denied the latter. President Wilson's protest to Germany was so strong that even his own Secretary of State William Jennings Bryan resigned, fearing U.S. involvement in the war. He was succeeded by Robert J. Lansing.

The U.S. protest over the *Lusitania* sinking brought some restraint in the German submarine warfare, but it was not halted, and was later resumed full scale. Meanwhile, in July 1915, New York financier J. Pierpont Morgan, who had organized loans to support the Allied war effort, was shot and wounded by a German sympathizer, who was identified as also having placed a bomb the day before that destroyed the Senate reception room in the Capitol Building in Washington.

In the same month, the U.S. Secret Service found evidence of an extensive German propaganda and espionage group in the United States involving members of the German Embassy staff in Washington, German consuls, officials of the Hamburg-America Steamship Line in New York, and a number of Americans of German descent, including George Sylvester Viereck, editor of a periodical, *The Fatherland,* in New York[1] The group had plans to gain control of companies and supplies relating to the war potential of the Allies. One result was the departure from Washington of two German Embassy military attachés, Captain Franz von Papen and Captain Carl von Boy-ed, and also the Austrian-Hungarian ambassador, Dr. Constantine Dumba.

Other evidences of German action touching the United States in 1916 included the arrival of the German submarine *Deutschland* at Baltimore on July 9 and again at New London, Connecticut, on November 1, bringing goods for trade. The armed submarine U–53 also put in at Newport on October 7 for three hours; six ships were sunk the next day off nearby Nantucket Island. Further, on July 30, 1916, an explosion destroyed munitions destined for the Allies at Black Tom Island in New Jersey, and another occurred at the Canadian Car and Foundry Plant at Kingsland, N.J., on January 11, 1917. Both were traced to German sabotage, with damages estimated at $55 million.

The growing crisis arising both from the war in Europe and the

---

1   Vierick later described his effort in *Spreading Germs of Hate* (New York, 1930), with a foreword by E. M. House.

involvement of the United States since March 1916 on the Texas-Mexican border had recommended a policy of military preparedness, even though no responsible person or group wished to see the country at war. A National Defense Act was passed by Congress in June to increase the army and the National Guard. In a parade giving support to the preparedness theme in San Francisco on July 22, a bomb was thrown that killed ten persons and wounded forty.

Through the years from 1914 to 1916 the press of the United States presented the news of the war and of the developments at home. Editorially, none favored direct U.S. participation in the war, but their views and policies varied, nonetheless, so that some seemed to favor the Allies, while others were regarded as pro-German. The *Literary Digest,* in the autumn of 1914, with the war three months old, undertook a survey that seemed to show 105 pro-Ally newspapers in the United States, 20 pro-German, and 230 neutral out of a total of 2,457 dailies. If the 2,105 unclassified newspapers were not also neutral, the *Literary Digest* did not make clear what else they might be.

Support for the Allied cause was reflected in newspapers as the war proceeded, particularly in the eastern cities. The *New York Times* led in reporting, not only through its own pages but through its sponsorship of the *Mid-Week Pictorial* and *Current History* magazines, both stressing war material. The first Pulitzer Prizes were awarded in 1918. The top-category prize for "the most disinterested and meritorious service" by a newspaper went to the *New York Times* for its reporting of the war from 1914 through 1917. The second such award, in 1919, went to the *Milwaukee Journal* in recognition of its editorial campaign from 1914 through 1918 against anti-Americanism and German propaganda in Wisconsin. This was cited as a courageous action in an area where the German element was large and influential.

As the war began, William Randolph Hearst directed his nine newspapers, with a tenth added in 1917, and his International News Service into what was widely regarded as a pro-German position. It was actually more than that because he held anti-British sentiments. Until the United States became involved in the war, the policy of his newspapers was viewed by many as inimical to the Allied cause, and the INS was denied facilities for normal operation in Great Britain, France, Portugal, and Japan, and his papers were barred from Canada.

Other U.S. papers regarded as pro-German prior to the U.S. entrance into the war in 1917, and certainly prior to the sinking of the *Lusitania* in May 1915, are noted by Frank L. Mott as having included the *Chicago Tribune,* the *Cincinnati Enquirer,* the *Cleveland Plain Dealer,* the *Washington Post,* the *San Francisco Chronicle,* the *New York*

Evening Mail, which had in fact been secretly purchased by German agents, and most of the German-language newspapers, then fifty-five in number.

President Wilson had continued efforts through 1916 to bring a restoration of peace in Europe, with Germany seeming not totally unresponsive, but proposing terms that Wilson found unacceptable. On February 1, 1917, Germany announced the resumption of unrestricted submarine warfare against neutral as well as belligerent shipping. The President had had reason to protest since 1914 to Great Britain, as well as to Germany, against what he viewed as unwarranted interference with U.S. shipping, but British submarine activity was never an issue. The new Berlin threat was another matter, and on February 3 the United States severed diplomatic relations with Germany.

Matters moved rapidly from that time. The arming of U.S. merchant ships was approved. General John J. Pershing, commanding 150,000 men on the Texas-Mexican border, had been ordered to Washington on January 28, 1917, and most of the troops were withdrawn early in February to form the nucleus of what would become an American Expeditionary Force in France, if war were declared.

Late in February, the British Secret Service intercepted and decoded a message from the German Foreign Office to the German ambassador in Mexico instructing him to offer an alliance between Germany and Mexico, if the United States entered the war, with support assured to Mexico in the recovery of territory in Texas, New Mexico, and Arizona lost in the U.S.–Mexican War of 1846–1848. It also was proposed that Mexico seek to persuade Japan to leave the Allies and give its support to the Central Powers.

Meanwhile, since February 1, Germany had proceeded with its unrestricted submarine warfare. U.S. ships were among others sunk in February and March. By that time, with Wilson inaugurated for his second term, it was believed in Washington that U.S. participation in the war was the only recourse. A new government also had just been formed in Great Britain, with David Lloyd George succeeding Herbert Asquith as prime minister. Czar Nicholas had just abdicated the Russian throne. There was some feeling that U.S. entrance into the war would give strength to the provisional government of Russia in its announced intent to continue the war against Germany, and that it might also create a sentiment in Germany for a peaceful settlement.

In a message to Congress on April 2, President Wilson called for a declaration of war on Germany, which was declared on April 6, and on Austria-Hungary on December 7. A Selective Service Act was approved by Congress on May 18, providing for the conscription of men for military service. General Pershing arrived in France on June 13 and the first troops arrived June 26. Admiral William F. Sims was placed in command of U.S. naval forces. A unit of U.S. infantry participated in action in France on November 3, and the 42nd (Rainbow) Division arrived at the end of that month, with men from every state of the Union. It was several months, however, before the U.S. forces in France were large enough, or sufficiently prepared to enter the lines.

With a total strength of about 200,000 when war was declared, the U.S. Army training program was activated in 1917, an aviation program was added, and a navy training program. By the end of the war in November 1918, the personnel in the U.S. Army, Navy and Marine Corps totalled 4,791,000, with more than two million transported to France. A Liberty Loan Act, approved by Congress in April 1917, helped provide for the financing of the war, including loans to the Allies. Five series of Liberty Bonds were sold between May 1917 and April 1919, with twenty-five million purchasers, producing more than $21 billion in revenue.

In January 1918, President Wilson presented to Congress a statement on "War Aims and Peace Terms" in which he outlined fourteen points he regarded as necessary for a proper peace. These were to become important in later negotiations, particularly with Germany. The last of them, calling for the "formation of a general association of nations," became the basis for the League of Nations, made a reality in 1920.

Washington as a Wartime News Center

The development of Washington as a major news center has been described. By March 4, 1913, when President Wilson was inaugurated, the Press Gallery of the Congress of the United States included more than 200 members. Hardly more than twenty-five were full-time resident staff correspondents representing the U.S. news agencies, New York and Chicago newspapers, and the foreign press. Others were attached to the Washington papers. Many were stringers, and a few were foreign correspondents based in New York and visiting the capital only occasionally.

Unlike major capitals in Europe, Washington was a relatively small city of perhaps 300,000, still with a relaxed southern air, often uncomfortably hot and humid in summer, cold and sometimes snow-bound in winter. It was a city almost exclusively concerned with government and politics. It possessed limited cultural and intellectual resources, and a social life revolving largely around the diplomatic corps. For members of the press, a National Press Club of Washington, organized in 1908, was a center.

Woodrow Wilson opened a new era in White House relations with the press. A great advance in that respect had taken place during the administration of Theodore Roosevelt, and those relations continued favorably, although less actively, under President Taft. Wilson, however, introduced the .first formal and regular White House press conferences. Correspondents were received in his office twice each week at scheduled times, with no favorites among them. Foreign correspondents were welcome and had opportunities to ask questions.

Although working space had been set aside earlier in the White House for the use of correspondents by then regularly assigned there by agencies and newspapers, a White House Correspondents Association was formed in 1914, partly to regularize arrangements having to do with the new press conferences, including special accreditation for those attending. This in turn was to bring the formation of comparable associations for correspondents covering the Department of State and other government agencies.

As governor of New Jersey from 1911–13, Wilson had enjoyed a generally cordial relationship with the press. An educator from 1885 to 1910, he taught history, political economy, and jurisprudence at Bryn Mawr, Wesleyan, and Princeton. He was president of Princeton from 1902 to 1910. He recognized the importance of the press as an aid to keeping the people informed and in making the democratic process more effective. It was this concept that underlay his proposal for White House press conferences. His secretary during his term as governor, Joseph P. Tumulty, a lawyer by profession, continued with him at the White House, and also was available to reporters to answer questions and make information available.

The first of Wilson's press conferences met at the White House on March 15, 1913, only eleven days after his inaugural. Those reporters responding to his invitation were told something of his philosophy and hopes. He indicated that through such conferences he wished to take the people of the country into his confidence, to inform them on current matters requiring government attention, and to share his thinking on the policies followed in dealing with those matters.

He expressed the hope that reporters and correspondents would ask questions consistent with that objective, which he regarded as part of a responsibility to advance public understanding of current issues and problems. The president added his hope that the newsmen would use the allotted time to ask questions bearing upon matters of substance and importance, avoiding trivialities, that they would not dwell on the inevitable skirmishes forming part of political life, and particularly would avoid publicizing the activities of members of his family.

The results were not all that Wilson had hoped. The reasons were several. Most correspondents accepted the news conferences in the spirit the president intended, and some useful reporting resulted. This was still a time in the practice of journalism in the United States, however, when experience covering police headquarters was commonly regarded as providing the best and most realistic training in preparation for any sort of reporting. A "police reporter" was expected to be quick and aggressive, to ask sharp no-nonsense questions most likely to produce the facts, whatever they might be, even though the reporter possibly had no basic knowledge of the subject. With that approach, the accepted belief was that the reporter could go anywhere, cover any sort of story, and get the news.

There were well-informed, tactful, and sensitive reporters in Washington, of course. Some possessed qualities represented later by so-called "diplomatic correspondents," competent in handling international news with understanding. But there also were reporters, young and old, who affected the police reporter manner, with primary concern for a sharp lead or a human interest angle.

Whether the police reporter approach by some was responsible it is difficult to say, but President Wilson was irritated when reporters persisted in dwelling upon what he regarded as trivialities, or on subjects he was not ready to discuss. This, in turn, irritated some reporters, who felt the news was being suppressed or issues avoided. The president also objected to questions he viewed as too personal, and of no concern to the public. Some had to do with his three daughters, all then in their twenties. In August 1914, his wife, Ellen Louise Axson Wilson, died quite suddenly, at fifty-four. Unpleasant stories and rumors were circulated that hurt him further, beyond the hurt of his personal loss. This also was at a time when the war in Europe was just beginning, demanding the president's careful attention, and when U.S. forces were in Vera Cruz.

The president was not wholly blameless for the failure of the press conferences to meet his expectations. He did not fully understand the press and its operation. He did not grasp the concept of objectivity. When reporters inquired further about statements made, whether during a press conference or from sources outside the White House, or when they reported contrary viewpoints, or questioned him on such differing views, the president was unable to accept the matter with good grace. He persuaded himself that the press was "inventing" facts, was "lying," or was "untrustworthy." He did not like to see stories involving speculation on statements made at press conferences. If politically partisan reports appeared these annoyed him further, perhaps sometimes with reason, but he still held himself ill-treated.

All of this, of course, was part of an adversary relationship between public officials and the press that neither began nor ended with Wilson, and a relationship inevitable in a country possessing a free press. It may even be regarded as an element of press responsibility, with reporters acting as representatives of the people in the performance of a "watchdog" function, observing the activities of officials conducting the business of government at any level.

President Wilson, in any case, after six months, had come to regard his press conferences as a "waste of time." He felt they were not accomplishing the purpose he had hoped they might in advancing public understanding of government procedures. He also learned that some attending the conferences had gone directly to the telephone to convey information to persons in New York to be used in speculating in the stock and produce markets before that same information became public knowledge, and that some foreign newsmen also had given immediate reports to the embassies or legations of their countries, with the reporting of news a secondary consideration.

In these circumstances, the president's conferences became less frequent. With the crisis brought by the sinking of the *Lusitania* in May 1915, and the war situation impinging increasingly upon the United States, they were abandoned entirely after two years and two months. The president again was to feel the sort of personal attention he so disliked when he remarried in December 1915 with Edith Bolling Galt of Washington as the new bride. Further, he was subjected to personal and political abuse during his campaign for re-election in 1916.

Ray Stannard Baker, a highly competent investigative reporter, and later one of Wilson's advisers at the time of the Paris Peace Conference in 1919, has said that the president never was greatly respected by newsmen, nor did he respect many of them. Wilson did, however, have confidence in Frank I. Cobb, editor of the *New York World,* and sometimes sought his advice. He submitted to a major interview with Samuel G. Blythe of the *Saturday Evening Post.* He was on good terms with David Lawrence, then twenty-five, whom he had known as a student at Princeton and who covered the White House for the Associated Press and then, from 1916 to 1919, for the *New York Evening Post*. He carried on a correspondence with John St. Loe Strachey, editor of the weekly *Spectator* in London, who also had maintained regular correspondence with President Roosevelt and had been his guest at the White House. He became a reader of the *Manchester Guardian* and of the *Times,* and in 1918 gave an exclusive interview to Arthur Willert, correspondent for the *Times* in Washington.

For the domestic press, the Associated Press bureau became the largest and busiest in the capital. Edwin Milton Hood, its chief and one of its senior members, continued to work cooperatively with S. Levy Lawson, New York representative of the Reuters agency, to provide reports for that service. Bureau members included Robert T. Small, Charles Stephenson Smith, Stephen T. Early, and David Lawrence, until he joined the *New York Evening Post* bureau. Others were Kirke Simpson, Byron Price, Jackson S. Elliott, and Lionel C. Probert, all destined for major assignments with the AP.

Coverage for the United Press in Washington was provided, among others, by Carl D. Groat, Robert J. Bender, formerly of the *Springfield Evening News* in Illinois, a family-owned newspaper, Charles McCann, Wilbur Forrest, until he moved to the London bureau in 1915, and Webb Miller, following his coverage on the Mexican border.

Correspondents writing from the capital for individual newspapers included Richard V. Oulahan for the *New York Times,* Clinton Gilbert and later Carter Field for the *New York Tribune,* Louis Seibold for the *New York World,* Laurence Hills for the *New York Sun,* Oswald Garrison Villard, as well as Lawrence, for the *New York Evening Post,* Raymond Carroll for the *Philadelphia Public Ledger,* Charles D. Warner for the *Christian Science Monitor,* J. Fred Essary for the *Baltimore Sun,* and Arthur Sears Henning for the *Chicago Tribune.*

The involvement of the United States with Mexico from April 1914, and the beginning of the war in Europe in August, had immediate echoes in Washington. These became louder as the war continued, accentuated in 1915 by the *Lusitania* crisis and, in 1916–17, by the second Mexican involvement along the Texas border and southward.

William Jennings Bryan, secretary of state, revived the Hay-Root practice of the Roosevelt administration and improved upon it by receiving correspondents almost daily, including foreign correspondents, more of whom were appearing in Washington. Robert Lansing, succeeding Bryan in 1915, continued that practice, with individual meetings becoming more useful conferences. Some other government officials also began to conduct press conferences more or less regularly, including Newton D. Baker, secretary of war from 1916, and Josephus Daniels, publisher of the North Carolina *Raleigh News and Observer* and secretary of the navy, with Franklin Delano Roosevelt as assistant secretary. News sources thus were improved, with practices established that were to become permanent and at that time unmatched in any other world capital.

When the United States broke diplomatic relations with Germany in February 1917, and especially after the declaration of war in April, Washington became a news center of the highest importance, and has remained so. The very few German correspondents in the United States left when war was declared, along with Count Johann Heinrich von Bernstorff, German ambassador, and other diplomatic representatives. Still others, representing the Allied countries arrived, however, and more foreign newsmen soon were in New York and Washington than ever before.

On April 14, 1917, shortly after the declaration of war, the president by proclamation created a government Committee on Public Information (CPI), with George Creel, an experienced newsman most recently with the *Rocky Mountain News* of Denver, as its chairman. Its function was to shape public opinion in support of the war, a propaganda purpose, and it also assisted in the drafting of a code of wartime censorship, developed with the voluntary cooperation of the press. Assistants and specialists in the CPI included Edgar Sisson, editor of *Cosmopolitan* magazine, and Carl Byoir and Edward L. Bernays, both later widely known for their work in what became known as "public relations." A flood of information was produced by a well-staffed news division, distributed in an "Official Bulletin," while an advertising division arranged for the production and placement of advertising in support of Liberty Bond sales and other war needs. Lowell Thomas, then twenty-five, with experience as a reporter in Colorado and on the *Chicago Journal* and as a lecturer and an instructor in English at Princeton from 1914–16, became a staff reporter and writer for the CPI in the News Division. Later he was dispatched to Europe and the Middle East on special informational missions.

Wilson also issued a proclamation in April 1917 underlining the obligation of publishers and others to avoid "giving aid or comfort to the enemy," within the meaning of treason as specified in Article III, Section 3, of the Constitution. An Espionage Act passed by Congress in June, a Trading-with-the-Enemy Act in October, and a Sedition Act in May 1918 all gave the government power to exercise control over the press and publications. The Code of Censorship, formed with the collaboration of press representatives, along with a censorship of mails and cables, established guidelines for correspondents and publications.

The Hearst newspapers, although modifying their earlier news and editorial content considered pro-German by some, still were sometimes at odds with the CPI and military authorities. So was the *Washington Post,* then owned by John R. McLean, wealthy Cincinnati and Washington publisher, banker, and utility operator. Foreign-language papers proceeded on their good behavior, but three editors of the *Philadelphia Tageblatt* went to prison, and more than half of the fifty-five German-language dailies of 1916 ceased to appear. More than seventy-five newspapers and periodicals were threatened by the Post Office Department with denial of mailing privileges, under the provisions of the Espionage Act. About fifty of them were Socialist publications, and some, in fact, did lose their mailing privilege, including the *New York Evening Call,* the *Milwaukee Leader,* owned by Victor L. Berger, a member of Congress from 1911–13 and again after the war, and the magazine, *The Masses.*

Creel, as chairman of the CPI, encouraged foreign correspondents in New York and Washington to form an association comparable to those already existing in such capitals as London, Paris, and Berlin. Thus there was organized in New York in 1917 an Association of Foreign Press Correspondents in the United States (AFPC). It became a permanent association, although reorganized in 1941, and its name simplified to the Foreign Press Association (FPA).

The original membership of the AFPC in 1917 included a dozen or more correspondents, virtually the entire staff and stringer foreign press representation in the United States at that time. They included nine correspondents for the British press and six others. These were A. Maurice Low of the *Morning Post,* senior in service, Percy S. Bullen and Sydney J. Clarke of the *Daily Telegraph,* S. Levy Lawson of Reuters, Arthur Willert of the *Times,* Walter Fred Bullock of the *Daily Mail,* P. Whitwell Wilson of the *Daily News,* Frank Dilnot of the *Daily Chronicle,* who presided at the first meeting of the association, and Warren Mason of the *Daily Express,* who drafted the rules for the organization. Others were William M. Davies, representing the Australian press, Leonce Levy of *Le Matin,* Paris, Romeo Roncini of *La Prensa,* Buenos Aires, A. Arib-Costa of *La Tribuna,* Rome, Severo

Salcedo of *La Union,* Valparaiso and Santiago, Chile, and R. de Llanto of *Excelsior,* Mexico City.

Most of these correspondents were based in New York, which explains why the association established its headquarters there. Low and Willert were permanently in Washington, however. Creel took some of the correspondents to meet with President Wilson at the White House on April 5, 1918. It was the first occasion of the sort in Washington, although the president had met some of the men individually. On this occasion, he explained aspects of the government's foreign policy, and expressed his personal views with considerable frankness.

Creel suggested that the president see other groups of correspondents, and he did receive a visiting party of Italian journalists later in April. He was reluctant to make a practice of doing so, despite the increased world interest in the United States, because he was not even meeting with U.S. reporters at that period. Also, he did not wish to be put in a position where he was almost certain to be asked about pending matters involving wartime security and seem over-reticent if he failed to respond.

When the Armistice was signed in November 1918, Wilson soon sailed for Europe, the first president to leave the country during his term of office. His announced intention was to help make the peace, with "open covenants, openly arrived at." Another expression of the same idealism with which he had undertaken news conferences in 1913, this too was to become a disappointment to him, as to others, with the Paris Peace Conference of 1919 becoming anything but open in its conduct.

Decision on the Western Front

Manpower and shipping losses since 1914, along with economic pressures, had brought the Allies close to the breaking point in 1917. The Central Powers, however, were equally exhausted.

The first revolution in Russia in March 1917 was followed by an effort of the provisional government to combat Germany and Austria-Hungary in new campaigns. These failed, and the second or Bolshevik revolution of October took Russia out of the war in December, and officially so in March 1918. The prospect of a shift of those forces of the Central Powers previously engaged on the eastern front to France, with the possibility that their added weight might end the long stalemate there and overwhelm the French and British, was a current threat to the Allies and a spur to the morale of the Central Powers.

The entrance of the United States to the war in April 1917 provided the Allies with new hope. The British treasury was so drained that London did not wait so much as a half-hour after the formal declaration of war by the United States to appeal by cable to Washington for loans or credits essential to support its continuing effort. The question also existed even in December 1917, as the Russians withdrew from the war, as to whether U.S. manpower and armor could be organized and made available in France in time to counterbalance the anticipated increase in German strength on the western front.

Major General John J. Pershing, commander of the American Expeditionary Force (AEF) in France, had arrived there in June 1917, two months after the U.S. declaration of war. The general and a small staff of officers had sailed from New York on May 28, 1917, in the Cunard liner *Baltic*. They arrived in Liverpool on June 9, and reached Paris four days later. The first U.S. troops, part of the First Division and a Marine regiment, arrived at the French port of St. Nazaire on June 26 and went into training at Gondrecourt and La Valdahon, near Besançon, in east-central France, not far from the Swiss border. In October, Pershing was made a full general, and on November 3 a U.S. infantry contingent participated with the French in a first engagement—the only such participation until March 1918.

Months were required to organize, train, and equip the necessary forces for the AEF, and to move them to France. By the spring of 1918, however, a half million U.S. troops were in position and entered combat. Others followed in a flood, with more than two million in France by the end of the war, plus four million tons of supplies and equipment, all moved across the Atlantic by a navy of 500,000 men and a merchant fleet under constant threat of German submarine attack.

All of this came none too soon. David Lloyd George had been British prime minister since December 1916 in a coalition government. In November 1917 Georges Clemenceau became French premier. The war was going badly for the Allies then and grew worse in the first months of 1918. The German army, at last reinforced by troops released from the eastern front following the Russian signature of the Treaty of Brest-Litovsk, opened a new offensive in France, as had been anticipated. A heavy attack at St. Quentin advanced forty miles through the British lines before being checked with the help of French reserves.

With British, French, Belgian, and U.S. forces in France, and some Brazilian flyers, it had been proposed that a unified military command be established to coordinate the Allied efforts. With the new German offensive under way, General Sir Douglas Haig, commander-in-chief of the British forces, urged that such action be taken. A conference on March 26 approved France's General Ferdinand Foch, a member of the Supreme War Council, to become commander-in-chief of all the Allied forces. That appointment was confirmed April 14, although leaving substantial authority to Haig, for the British, King Albert, for the Belgians, and General Pershing, for the United States.

By the time Foch assumed the supreme command, the German forces, directed by General Ludendorff, had advanced to Armentières, after breaking through British and French lines near Ypres. In May the French were driven back thirteen miles in one day on a line between Soissons and Rheims. German forces pushed on by May 30 to the Marne River, only thirty-seven miles from Paris, where they had been turned back in September of 1914.

Marshal Foch, already faced with a real danger in March, had wanted at that time to use fresh U.S. troops as reserve reinforcements wherever and whenever he felt they could be helpful. General Pershing contested this plan. He wished to see the U.S. divisions operating as an independent force to provide clear evidence to the Germans that the United States was in the war, and so to shake their confidence. Also, he wished to maintain the full morale of the U.S. troops themselves, retaining their own identity, and fighting with a spirit then lacking among the war-weary men on both sides of the lines.

Recognizing the desperate need, however, Pershing permitted some of the U.S. troops to be used as Foch wished. Even so, the AEF had its own successes. The 26th (Yankee) Division was the first in the line on April 20–21, near the village of Seicheprey, in the French army area in northeastern France. It was bloodied but did well. A victory was attained by the First Division at Cantigny, also in the French army area, with the town taken on May 28 and held against a counter-attack the next day.

The third involvement was that of the Second Division's Marine Brigade, which scored a solid triumph over the Germans at Chateau-Thierry and nearby Belleau Wood between June 1 and June 4. When it was again contested, Belleau Wood was recaptured June 25, with support by elements of the Third Division.

As the critical Battle of the Marne proceeded after May 30, Pershing also committed nine U.S. divisions, about 85,000 men, to assist in the vital contest to save Paris and reverse the German drive. Between July 15 and August 7 they played a major part in forcing the Germans back, with the French also retaking Soissons on August 7. By then Pershing had committed 270,000 U.S. troops to action within the Aisne-Marne area, and 54,000 on the Somme. The results upset Ludendorff's original plan to drive into Flanders with the Channel coast as an objective. It also enabled the Allies to gain the initiative.

The results of the AEF participation in the war were so obvious by July that General Pershing was able to proceed with his preferred battle plan from that time, with U.S. divisions fighting independently of the French or British. They advanced on the St. Mihiel salient in September and through the Meuse-Argonne in the weeks from late September to early November, and U.S. troops reached Sedan on the Franco-Belgian frontier on November 10. British troops farther north broke through the Hindenburg line, reached the Channel, and moved into Belgium. The French also regained great areas of their country.

As German troops retreated along the western front from August 1918, the resistance of the Central Powers also gave way elsewhere. A steady British drive and advance in Palestine and other parts of the Middle East from October 1917 brought Turkey's surrender in October 1918. In the Balkans, British, French, Italian, Serbian, and Greek forces in September 1918 joined in a concerted action eastward from Albania to Salonika. Troops of Austria, Germany and Bulgaria retreated, and Bulgaria surrendered on September 30. An Italian campaign against Austrian positions in October brought an armistice with Austria-Hungary on November 3. Meanwhile, Rumania, one of the Allies in 1916–18, which was forced to surrender on May 7, 1918, re-entered the war on November 10, again on the Allied side.

The German military position in France had so far deteriorated by the end of September 1918 that General Ludendorff urged Berlin to seek an armistice while it still might be able to negotiate on favorable terms. On October 4 Prince Max of Baden, only just named chancellor of the German government, and a cousin of Kaiser Wilhelm, made an appeal to President Wilson through the Swiss government. On behalf of the German and Austrian governments, he sought an armistice looking toward a peace based upon the "14 points" Wilson had presented to the U.S. Congress the previous January as a basis for such a settlement. Wilson, in his reply on October 14, noted that the fourteen points called for an end of such arbitrary rule as represented by the monarchies of both countries, and also that only an outright surrender could be acceptable to the United States.

On October 16, Austria's Emperor Charles, who had succeeded to the throne of the Dual Monarchy in 1916 upon the death of Francis-Joseph, proclaimed a reorganization of the empire, with separate self-government for Austria and Hungary, and self-government for the subject nationalities. What followed was that the Czechoslovaks within the empire declared their independence on October 21, and a republic was proclaimed October 30; a Yugoslav National Council at Zagreb proclaimed the independence of the Serbs, Croats, and Slovenes, also on October 21, and a kingdom was proclaimed November 24. An armistice was concluded between Austria-Hungary and the Allied powers on November 3. The Emperor Charles did not abdicate, but on November 12 he renounced all authority and retired to Switzerland. An independent Hungarian government, under Count Michael Karolyi was announced November 1, but this became a Hungarian Republic on November 16.

Germany meanwhile had yielded on October 20 to a U.S. demand that it recall its submarines. Turkey, on October 14, had appealed to President Wilson to arrange an armistice. Receiving no reply, it nevertheless signed armistice terms with the British on October 30. The Bulgarian armistice, on September 30, had been followed by the abdication of Tsar Ferdinand, who was succeeded by his son Boris III.

When Austria accepted an armistice with all of the Allied Powers on November 3, Germany remained as the only surviving belligerent among the Central Powers. German troops were retreating in France and on that same day a mutiny occurred among members of the German fleet at Kiel, with crews refusing to put to sea. The mutiny spread to the ports of Hamburg, Bremen, and Lübeck, with related disorders in much of northwestern Germany. A revolution occurred in Munich on November 7, with Bavaria proclaimed a separate republic.

The pressure in Berlin rose to such a pitch that the German government, with Prince Max of Baden as chancellor, advised Kaiser Wilhelm that his abdication was necessary if there was to be any hope of saving the monarchy. The kaiser resisted, but his abdication was announced on November 9 and a German republic proclaimed. Further advised by Field Marshal von Hindenburg and General Wilhelm von Gröner of the high command that they could no longer guarantee the loyalty of the army, the kaiser fled Germany on November 10, taking refuge in Holland. There he was to live at Doorn until his death in 1941.

A false report of an armistice with Germany caused premature celebrations in the Allied countries on November 7. The Armistice actually was signed at 5 A.M. on November 11, with German emissaries meeting Marshal Foch in his railway car in the Compiègne Forest, fifty miles northeast of Paris. A cease fire, sounded all along the western front at 11 A.M. of that day, ended the war. The Armistice had the effect also of abrogating the March 1918 Russian-German Treaty of Brest-Litovsk, with Germany yielding to the Allies territories gained through that treaty. These included Poland, the Baltic States, and Finland.

All German troops were out of France by November 18 and out of Belgium by November 26. French, British, and U.S. troops began an occupation of the German Rhineland areas on December 1, and German military forces were disbanded. The German fleet was surrendered to the British under the terms of the prospective treaty, but the major vessels were scuttled by crew members at Scapa Flow on June 21, 1919, before the treaty was signed.

Emperor Charles of Austria-Hungary in October 1921 made an attempt to regain the throne in Hungary. This failed and he was exiled by the Allies to Madeira, where he died on that Portuguese island in 1922 at thirty-four, survived by the former Empress Zita and several children. The eldest, Otto, was claimant to the Hapsburg thrones in later years.

Press Coverage in the Final Year

The sequence of events through 1917–18 was, of course, reported at every step by the press. With the United States becoming a belligerent in April 1917, U.S. correspondents, no longer neutral, left Berlin, Vienna, Constantinople, and other Central Powers areas, as those very few Central Powers news representatives in the United States also either left or ceased to report as stringers.

The U.S. correspondents already reporting from the Allied countries, then still including Russia, remained. Transfers soon occurred, however. Allied correspondents in Russia at the time of the October revolution departed. Europe received a great new influx of correspondents from the United States, arriving chiefly in France, but also in Great Britain and Italy. Some British, French, and Italian correspondents were reassigned to report the activities of U.S. forces in France.

Headquarters for the American Expeditionary Force and General Pershing's base was established at Chaumont in July 1917. AEF press headquarters was established about thirty miles away at Neufchâteau, attached to the Army Intelligence section, G-2, with living quarters at the Hôtel de la Providence. An AEF press headquarters also was

established in Paris, first at Castellane House, 31 rue de Constantine, off
the Quai d'Orsay and adjacent to the French Ministry of Foreign
Affairs, across the Seine from the Place de la Concorde. Soon, however,
it was moved to 10 rue Sainte Anne, just off the Avenue de l'Opera, a
short distance above the Place du Théâtre Française.

The administration of press matters, within the chain of command
under Pershing, rested with Colonel W. C. Sweeney of the General
Staff, who directed the Censorship and Press Division of the AEF.
Under him were Colonel Dennis E. Nolan, chief of G-2-D, Major E. R.
W. McCabe, and Lieutenant Joseph C. Green, both of the regular army
and G-2-D.

The AEF press headquarters at Neufchâteau was placed in charge of
Frederick Palmer, who had long experience as a correspondent, and who
was in Europe for the United Press since leaving his Vera Cruz
assignment in 1914. He had moved with the German and Austrian
armies, and then had become the first U.S. neutral observer at British
Expeditionary Force headquarters, serving from May 1915 until
yielding to Robert T. Small of the AP in 1916. Temporarily in
Washington when the U.S. declared war in April 1917, Palmer received
an offer from James Gordon Bennett, Jr., to become chief correspondent
in Europe for the *New York Herald* at an unprecedented salary of
$40,000 a year. But at the War Department he also came upon Pershing,
whom he had known since they both were in the Philippines in 1899.
Palmer, then twenty-six, was writing for the *New York World* and
Collier's Weekly, and Pershing, then thirty-nine, held rank as a captain.
They renewed their friendship, and Palmer was able to give Pershing an
informed report on the war situation in France.

When Pershing sailed in the *Baltic* on May 28, Palmer was with him
and joined in discussions with staff officers aboard. Pershing urged that
he accept a commission and take charge of the Press Section of G-2,
under Colonel Nolan. As a patriotic duty, he felt obliged to accept and
was commissioned a major at a fraction of the salary he would have
received from the *New York Herald,* knowing also that he would have
the responsibility of directing a censorship, as well as supervising the
accreditation of correspondents for coverage of the AEF.

Palmer's first assistant at Neufchâteau was Gerald Morgan, also an
experienced correspondent, who had been in Japan at the time of the
Russo-Japanese War. He represented the *New York Tribune* and the
London *Daily Telegraph* in Belgium and France from 1914 until 1917.
Morgan returned to the United States to enter officers' training camp,
and held a commission as a first lieutenant assigned to G-2. From

December 1917, Palmer became increasingly concerned with assignments for General Pershing, and Morgan, advanced to the rank of captain, assumed his role at Neufchâteau.

Other newsmen in uniform later attached to AEF headquarters to handle censorship, act as conducting officers, and generally to assist, included Lieutenant Arthur E. Hartzell, formerly of the *New York Sun,* Lieutenant Mark S. Watson, formerly of the *Chicago Tribune,* and Major Bozeman Bulger, formerly of the *New York Evening World.*

A daily AEF communiqué began to appear on May 15, 1918, and a special army news roundup was made available to correspondents regularly after mid-September. Both reflected the extension of U.S. troop participation in war action.

The press headquarters at Neufchâteau, at some distance from Chaumont, and even farther from the areas where the first U.S. troops were in training, required that correspondents spend considerable time being transported in motor cars from their base, which bothered some. While certain amenities were not lacking at the Hôtel de la Providence, some formally accredited there often preferred to work from Paris, to move about independently when they could, or alternatively to seek accommodation in the more lush French press headquarters at Chantilly, pending the time U.S. troop activity began to produce more solid subject-matter for the news.

One of the first correspondents accredited to the AEF was Robert T. Small of the Associated Press, who had succeeded Palmer at BEF headquarters, and was succeeded there in turn by DeWitt Mackenzie, also for the AP. The total number of correspondents accredited to the AEF at any one time was held to about fifty, approximately as at BEF headquarters. One major difference was that, whereas only five writing correspondents for the British press itself were accredited at BEF, twenty-one of those accredited to the AEF were writing representatives. This was the result of a compromise demanded through Washington whereby each of the three U.S. news agencies was granted its own correspondent, as were certain of the larger dailies (with no pairing arrangements), a number of periodicals, and ultimately even some smaller dailies and special services. The remaining accreditations went to photographers and artists, and to correspondents for the press of Allied countries. As at British headquarters, special accreditation also was granted for limited periods to prominent visitors.

Well before the arrival in France of the great mass of military personnel, the army established a daily newspaper in Paris for distribution to the American forces. It was to provide information from home, along with general news and war reports, and to give special emphasis to the role of the United States in the war. This was the *Stars and Stripes,* the official paper of the AEF. It appeared daily in eight pages, produced from the presses of the *Continental Daily Mail.*

It's staff was organized from among members of the army possessed of prior news experience. The first editor was Major Guy T. Viskniskki, former editor and manager of the Wheeler Newspaper Syndicate bureau in London. Later editors were Harold Ross, with prior news experience in Salt Lake City, New Orleans, and San Francisco, and later to become the founding editor of the *New Yorker* magazine in 1925, and Lieutenant Mark S. Watson, formerly of the *Chicago Tribune,* reassigned from AEF headquarters. Watson remained active in journalism in later years, gaining a Pulitzer Prize for international correspondence in 1945 as a World War II correspondent for the *Baltimore Sun.*

The *Stars and Stripes* staff included enlisted men already established in journalism, some to become widely known after the war. Among them were Hudson (Boz) Hawley, former editor of the *Yale Record* and later of the *New York Sun,* who was one of the first on the new army paper; Albian A. Wallgren of the marines, a cartoonist; John T. Winterich, formerly of the *Springfield Republican,* and later historian of the *Stars and Stripes;* Alexander Woollcott, drama critic for the *New York Times* and later also a radio personality; Franklin P. Adams, known later as a columnist ("F.P.A.") for the *New York Tribune* and also a radio personality; Grantland Rice, also of the *New York Tribune,* known as a sports writer; C. Leroy Baldridge, an artist, known for his later work; Stephen T. Early, formerly of the AP Washington bureau, who became assistant editor of the paper and later was press secretary for President Franklin D. Roosevelt; and Hilmar R. Baukhage, later to have a career as a radio newsman.

Other publications for the military were introduced. The *Baltimore Sun* produced a special weekly overseas edition in tabloid size mailed to Maryland men in the AEF to keep them informed of home events. The most ambitious privately sponsored effort of that sort, and one that survived the war until 1934, was a so-called Army Edition of the *Chicago Tribune,* which began publication in Paris on July 4, 1917, and was produced from the presses of *Le Petit Journal.* The *Chicago Tribune* had been only moderately active in original foreign news reporting before the war, although it used the service of the London *Times.* Its enterprise increased in that respect from 1914, however, with coverage of the U.S. involvements in Mexico, and then with the war in

Europe. The introduction of the Army Edition in Paris in 1917 was accompanied by an extension of direct coverage and the formation of what became a permanent and active foreign service.

Controlling ownership of the *Chicago Tribune* in the summer of 1914 had come into the hands of Robert Rutherford McCormick and Joseph Medill Patterson, then thirty-five and thirty-four years old, respectively. They were cousins and also grandsons of Joseph Medill, editor and publisher of the *Tribune* for many years prior to his death in 1899. Patterson's father, Robert W. Patterson, son-in-law of Medill, had succeeded him as publisher from 1899 until his own death in 1910.

McCormick's father, Robert Sanderson McCormick, also Medill's son-in-law, and heir to the McCormick Harvesting Machine Company and the International Harvester Company fortune, served in U.S. diplomatic assignments in London from 1889 to 1893, and as U.S. ambassador to Austria, Russia, and France from 1901 to 1907. Robert Rutherford McCormick and his elder brother (Joseph) Medill McCormick, spent some years with their parents in England, and attended school there prior to going on to Yale. Medill McCormick, graduated in 1900, joined the *Tribune* as a reporter, and succeeded Patterson as publisher upon his death in 1910. Married in 1903 to Ruth Hanna, daughter of Senator Mark A. Hanna of Ohio, a potent figure in the Republican party, Medill McCormick also became active politically in 1912. He served two terms in the Illinois State Assembly, was a member of Congress (1917–19) and a member of the U.S. Senate from 1919 to his death in 1925.

Robert McCormick, three years younger than his brother, had returned from England to enter Groton and also proceed to Yale. His cousin, Joseph Medill Patterson, a year younger, was with him at both institutions. Their family and personal experiences made them quite different, however, in general outlook and life styles. McCormick prepared himself for a career in law, was admitted to the bar in Illinois in 1907, and became active in civic affairs. Patterson showed more interest in journalism. In the summer of 1900, while still at Yale, he went to China for the *Tribune* to report the Boxer relief expedition. He joined the staff of the paper following his graduation in 1901. His service was interrupted in 1903–04, when he was a member of the Illinois state legislature, and through 1905–06, when he was commissioner of public works in Chicago. Unlike McCormick, who was utterly conservative and business-minded, Patterson had liberal political leanings and left the *Tribune* in 1908 to write a novel and coauthor a play, both reflecting Socialist views.

With the death of Patterson's father in 1910, Joseph Medill Patterson and Robert R. McCormick became coeditors of the *Tribune*. Medill McCormick was publisher until 1914, when he chose to retire from any active role with the paper to concentrate on his career in politics. With his withdrawal, the two editors also became joint-publishers of the paper. At the same time, an increased stock interest went to Patterson's sister, Eleanor Medill Patterson.[2]

Patterson and McCormick differed in appearance as well as in personality. McCormick was six foot four, slim, reserved but assertive, and aristocratic in manner. Patterson, although nearly as tall, was more squarely built, and far more casual, unceremonious, and approachable. He was possessed of his own eccentricities, one of which was a style of dress at times highly informal. McCormick, although married, left no children. Patterson's daughter, Alicia (Mrs. Harry F. Guggenheim) established *Newsday* in 1940, which became a successful newspaper based in Garden City, New York.

Patterson had gone to report the U.S. troop activity at Vera Cruz in 1914, and went directly from there to Belgium in the first weeks of the war in Europe. It was at that time that he and McCormick became copublishers of the *Tribune*. It was then, also, that James Keeley, able managing editor and general manager since 1898, left the *Tribune* to direct the *Chicago Herald,* a reorganization of the *Record-Herald,* which was sold to Hearst in 1918 and merged with his morning *Examiner.* Keeley then moved to the Pullman Company to direct public relations. In 1915 McCormick also went to Europe, but his interest was in the leaders of governments more than in the events on the fighting fronts.

When the United States became engaged in the Mexican punitive

2   Then thirty, Eleanor (Cissy) Patterson took no active part in the *Tribune*. In her youth, visiting in Vienna, where her uncle, Robert S. McCormick was ambassador (1901–02), she met a Polish nobleman, Count Josef Gizycki, at the Austro-Hungarian court, and they were married. Their later divorce, with diplomatic negotiations to win her custody of their daughter, Felicia, became a subject of international news. The Countess Gizycki, later remarried, but taking the name Mrs. Eleanor Patterson in 1930, entered then into newspaper publishing in Washington, D.C. She first leased the morning *Washington Herald* from William R. Hearst and conducted it as editor and publisher. In 1937, when she was fifty-three, she leased both the *Herald* and the afternoon *Washington Times* from Hearst, with an option to buy. She bought both in 1939 and combined them as an all-day paper, the *Washington Times-Herald,* which she directed to the time of her death in 1948. In those years, also, Felicia Gizycki, was married in 1925 to Drew Pearson, at that time moving about the world as a writer for syndication, but who joined the staff of the *United States Daily* in 1926. They had one child, Ellen, but were divorced in 1928. See Ralph E. Martin, *Cissy: The Extraordinary Life of Eleanor Medill Patterson* (New York, 1979).

expedition of 1916, Patterson rejected the offer of a commission in the Illinois National Guard. McCormick, however, accepted such a commission, became a major in the cavalry and joined Pershing's staff. After the United States entered the European war in 1917, Patterson enlisted as a private in the artillery and worked up through the ranks to become a second lieutenant, going to France in that grade in 1918. He served through five engagements, was gassed and wounded and advanced to the rank of captain. Meanwhile, McCormick went to France as a colonel in the 61st Field Artillery of the 1st Division, remaining until July 1918. He then returned to the United States to serve through the rest of the war as Commandant at Fort Sheridan, just north of Chicago.

Shortly before McCormick left France, he and Patterson met near Mareuil-en-Dôle to discuss their newspaper interests. Patterson had recently met in London with Lord Northcliffe, whose *Daily Mirror,* a tabloid-size morning daily, at the time had a circulation of 800,000 and was growing. Northcliffe suggested that such a newspaper, stressing illustrations and photos, would do well in New York.[3] Patterson agreed, and he proposed to McCormick that they join in the establishment of such a paper after the war. Their first issue of the *Illustrated Daily News* appeared there June 26, 1919, and was soon known more simply as the *New York Daily News.*

By 1924, the *New York Daily News* had attained circulation leadership in New York and in the United States, a position it still holds. Its success also brought the tabloid newspaper into fashion throughout the United States and elsewhere. From the time of the establishment of the *Daily News,* Patterson made his home in New York, concerned primarily with the newspaper there, while McCormick remained in Chicago as director of the *Tribune.* The two papers shared news reports provided through the *Tribune* service, and special features developed by both papers. They made both news and features available through a Chicago Tribune–New York Daily News Syndicate, Inc.

---

3   Northcliffe, arriving in New York in December 1900 when he was still Alfred Harmsworth, but highly successful as publisher of the London *Daily Mail* and other publications, was invited by Joseph Pulitzer, publisher of the *New York World,* to take full charge of that newspaper for one day and make it what he believed a newspaper should be in the new century about to begin. Harmsworth did so, and produced the *New York World* of January 1, 1901 as a tabloid newspaper. A novelty at the time, it created lively interest, nationally. It was in 1903 that he started the *Mirror* as his own London tabloid. For details and an illustration see Reginald Pound and Geoffrey Harmsworth, *Northcliffe* (London, 1959), pp. 266–68. See also W. A. Swanberg, *Pulitzer* (New York, 1967), p. 276–77.

The *Chicago Tribune* had shown news enterprise since the time of the Civil War, but its major activity in foreign news reporting began in 1914. Medill McCormick, Patterson, John T. McCutcheon, and Floyd Gibbons all represented the paper in Mexico at the time of the Vera Cruz occupation. Gibbons was again in Mexico in 1916–17 at the time of the punitive expedition, along with Walter Noble Burns. As the European war began in August 1914, Patterson, McCutcheon, and James O'Donnell Bennett were in Belgium. McCutcheon was again in Europe in 1915 and 1918, while Bennett remained in Berlin for the paper from 1914 to 1917, joined there by Donald C. Thompson, a photographer, and Sigrid Schultz, who was beginning a long career with the paper. McCormick visited England, France, Russia, and Germany in 1915.

If the *Chicago Tribune* had been regarded by some as pro-German during 1914–17, it may have been because of an anti-British sentiment on McCormick's part, stemming from unpleasant experiences as a schoolboy in England. With the entrance of the United States to the war, however, it became staunchly pro-Allied.

When diplomatic relations were broken with Germany on February 3, 1917, Floyd Gibbons was recalled from the Mexican border to be reassigned to London in a first move to augment the war staff, and perhaps to head the London office. A reporter on the *Tribune* staff since 1912, Gibbons, born in Washington, D.C., in 1887, had attended Georgetown University and subsequently worked for the *Milwaukee Free Press* and the *Minneapolis Tribune*. At thirty, he was experienced, aggressive, and adventurous. This he had demonstrated on his Mexican assignment. Now posted to London, Gibbons saw the possibility of a story of German submarine action even as he crossed the Atlantic. Quite deliberately, he chose to sail from New York in the 18,000-ton Cunard liner *Laconia,* which was carrying munitions. The ship was torpedoed and sunk 200 miles off the Irish coast on the night of February 25, with two U.S. citizens among those lost. After six night hours in an open lifeboat on the wintry seas, Gibbons reached the Irish coast and filed a 4,000-word story from Queenstown. It was a vivid personal account and established his reputation as a daring and enterprising reporter.

Based in London, Gibbons was among those in Liverpool to meet General Pershing on his arrival in June. He followed Pershing to Paris, where he remained from that time. He helped to establish the Army Edition of the *Tribune* there in July. That paper was organized and edited, however, for the first several months by Joseph Pierson, assistant city editor of the *Tribune* in Chicago. When he returned to Chicago to become cable editor of the paper to handle the greater flow of war reports, Spearman Lewis became editor of the Army Edition in Paris through 1919. The paper received its own news reports by cable from the United States, and also published the war reports by the *Tribune*'s own correspondents.

Gibbons became the chief war correspondent for the paper, one of the first accredited to the AEF, on October 9. He carried on somewhat in the tradition of Richard Harding Davis, who had died in 1916 in New York. Constantly active, he was in the field with the U.S. 2nd Division at Château-Thierry in June 1918. There he was shot in the arm by German machine-gun fire and lost the sight of his left eye. He was back in action within a month, but ever after wore a black eye-patch. Gibbons remained in Paris as director of the *Tribune* foreign service until 1927. He then became one of the early personalities in radio until his death in 1939.

Other *Tribune* correspondents in France in 1918 included Richard Henry Little, who had covered the Russo-Japanese War, Parke Brown, Frederick A. Smith, M. Farmer Murphy, Paul Williams, Frazier ("Spike") Hunt, John Clayton, John D. Ryan, transferring from the NEA service, Ring Lardner, primarily a sports writer for the Chicago paper, and McCutcheon, making a third return to the war. Williams reported the Allied Black Sea landing in the south of Russia in 1918. Ryan was in the landing in Siberia, and Hunt at Archangel. Gibbons and Little crossed Germany to Poland and Russia early in 1919. That same year, Henry (Hank) Wales, formerly with INS, moved to the *Tribune* staff in Paris, where he succeeded Gibbons as director of the European service in 1927.

In May 1918, the Army Edition of the *Tribune* had as staff members in London George Seldes, Howard Kahn, Lloyd Ross Blinn, Gerald (Jed) Kiley, Howard Williams, Victor Frank, and Ruth Hale (Mrs. Heywood Broun), whose husband was in France for a time as a correspondent for the *New York Tribune*. Seldes was accredited later to the Marshall Syndicate but returned to the *Tribune* parent paper after the Armistice. Peggy Hull (Mrs. Henrietta Kinley), formerly writing for NEA from the Texas-Mexican border, and on terms of friendship both with General Pershing and Colonel McCormick, wrote at times for the Army Edition, although without full accreditation. Later she was with U.S. troops in Siberia, writing there for the NEA.

The *New York Times* had maintained a small group of correspondents in Europe since 1908. Ernest Marshall headed the London bureau, assisted by W. Orton Tewson until he joined the INS. Frederic William

Wile was in Berlin, where he had also represented the *Daily Mail.* Because of that connection, he was forced to leave when the war began, even though a U.S. citizen. He was replaced there for the *New York Times* by Cyril Brown, assisted first by Garet Garrett, until he returned to the United States in 1916 to join the *New York Tribune* staff, and then by Oscar King Davis, who went to the paper's Washington bureau after all U.S. correspondents were forced out of Berlin in 1917. Brown at that time joined the *New York World* bureau in Paris.

Wythe Williams, in the *New York Times* London bureau when the war began, moved to Paris, where he was assisted by British-born Walter Duranty. As the war proceeded, he was able to provide the *Times* with some exclusive reports through an ingenious series of innocent-seeming cables to Van Anda in New York. He was among the first correspondents accredited to the AEF headquarters in July 1917. Duranty followed French army action. Charles A. Selden, also in the Paris bureau, wrote of French political matters.

Williams, also writing for *Collier's Weekly,* ran afoul of AEF censorship regulations because of an article for that periodical not submitted for advance inspection. Since it was concerned with French military and political subjects, unrelated to the AEF, and had been based upon information provided by Premier Clemenceau himself, Williams contended that it did not require AEF censorship, and he was supported in this position by Clemenceau. Williams's AEF accreditation nevertheless was suspended in February 1918, the third correspondent so disciplined. Thus barred from the field, he remained in Paris for the paper.

Succeeding Williams as *Times* correspondent accredited to the AEF, beginning in March, was Edwin L. (Jimmy) James, then twenty-eight, and selected by Van Anda for assignment to France on the basis of his work as a reporter on the staff in New York and in covering the news at Albany, the state capital. James began what was to be a long period of service for the paper in Europe, and later was managing editor in New York.

Another member of the Paris bureau in 1917–18 was Charles H. Grasty. Then fifty-four, he had more than thirty years of news experience, including more than twenty years as the vigorous owner and editor, successively, of the *Baltimore Evening News,* the *St. Paul Dispatch* and *Pioneer Press,* and the *Baltimore Evening Sun.* For ten of those years he was a member of the Associated Press board of directors, and he long had been a personal friend of Adolph S. Ochs, publisher of the *Times.* In 1914, Grasty chose to dispose of his Baltimore newspaper, and in 1915 he went to Europe to write special articles on the war for the *Times,* the AP, and the *Kansas City Star.* He then became treasurer of the *New York Times* from 1916–20. In 1917 he returned to Europe, sailing with General Pershing and staff officers, along with Frederick Palmer, and remained there in the *Times* Paris bureau until after the Peace Conference in 1919.

Carl W. Ackerman, who had been in Berlin for the United Press until 1917, then joined the *New York Times.* He was with the Allied expedition landing at Archangel in 1918, and became the first to verify the execution of the czar and his family at Ekaterinburg in July.

The *Chicago Daily News* had a solid news service through the years of the war, with Edward Price Bell in London, Paul Scott Mowrer in Paris, John Foster Bass in Petrograd, and Raymond E. Swing in Berlin. The Paris staff was augmented by Mowrer's younger brother, Edgar Ansel Mowrer, A. R. Decker, and Paul Rockwell. All three later were reassigned to report the war in Italy and the Balkans. Other staffers included Louis Edgar Browne, Percy E. Noël, and Junius B. Wood. Noël had gone to France in 1914 as a member of a British Red Cross unit for service at the front, had been wounded, was invalided out, and began to write for the *Daily News* in 1915 in France and Italy. Wood, with experience on the Mexican-Texas border, joined the Paris staff, was accredited to the AEF in July 1917, but was with the Allies in Siberia in 1918.

Bass, wounded on the Russian front, was succeeded in Petrograd by Isaac Don Levine, who later yielded to Michael Farbman, writing also for the *Manchester Guardian.* When Bass recovered from his wounds, he represented the *Daily News* in France, Italy, and the Balkans, served on a government mission to the Italian front in 1918, covered the Peace Conference, and represented the U.S. press in Poland in 1919. Swing, leaving Berlin in 1917, moved through Switzerland and Paris to Washington. There he went on leave from the paper, returning to France on a confidential mission for Colonel Edward M. House, special adviser to President Wilson. Swing was chiefly occupied with government assignments in Washington throughout the rest of the war.

The *New York World* was represented in London by James M. Touhy, with Joseph Grigg as an assistant. It had received reports from Belgium in the first weeks of the war from Lincoln Eyre and Arno Dosch (later Arno Dosch-Fleurot), both of whom then were to write from France, and Dosch-Fleurot also from Egypt and Russia. Herbert Bayard Swope and E. Alexander Powell were in Berlin until 1917. Henry (Hank) Wales, formerly of the Paris edition of the *New York Herald,* became Paris correspondent for the *World* during 1914–16, but then switched to the INS. He was succeeded in Paris by Eyre, with William Cook, a British newsman, as an assistant. Eyre was accredited to the AEF in October 1917. Grigg was transferred from London to the Paris bureau, also augmented by Cyril Brown, formerly in Berlin for the *New York Times,* by J. Carlisle MacDonald, formerly in New York, and by Martin Green, Edwin Emerson, Jr., and Samuel Spewack. Brown, accredited to the AEF in December 1918, after the Armistice, followed U.S. forces into Germany, and Spewack reached Moscow for the paper in 1919, where he remained briefly.

The *New York Tribune* had Charles Inman Barnard in Paris as the war began. He was then sixty-four and dean of the correspondent group, president of the Anglo-American Press Association, and preparing to retire. Fred Pitney was in London, and Gerald Morgan reported from Belgium. The *Tribune* also received reports by Richard Harding Davis through the Wheeler Newspaper Syndicate. George W. Smalley, Boston-born, but London correspondent for the paper for nearly thirty years before switching to the London *Times* service in the United States in 1895, and retired from that position since 1906, returned to live in London and write again from there for the *Tribune* until his death in 1916. In New York, Frank L. Simonds, editor of the *Evening Sun,* rejoined the *Tribune* as associate editor, and wrote a daily analysis of war reports.

As the war proceeded, the *Tribune* sent Philip H. Patchin and C. L. Garvan to London, followed in 1915 by Arthur Draper, who had been Sunday editor in New York. He later became London bureau chief. Gordon Gordon-Smith was sent to the Balkans. Following the U.S. entrance to the war Morgan left the paper to join the army, was commissioned and assigned to the Press Section of G-2 at AEF headquarters. He served with Frederick Palmer. Two members of the *Tribune* staff who were in the army, Grantland Rice and Franklin P. Adams, became identified with the *Stars and Stripes.*

Heywood Broun, a *Tribune* sports writer, was accredited to the AEF in July 1917. He was not happy in the assignment, ignored the censorship, and his accreditation was suspended in February 1918, whereupon he returned to New York. His wife, an early feminist who insisted upon using her maiden name, Ruth Hale, managed to get to France, and was associated with the Army Edition of the *Chicago Tribune.* With Broun's departure, the *New York Tribune* engaged Wilbur Forrest, who had been in London with the United Press. He was to report on the AEF throughout the remaining period of the war, and continued with the paper for many years, chiefly in Paris and New York. Deems Taylor, assistant editor of the paper's Sunday magazine, also went to France as a correspondent in 1918. Casper Whitney was in Paris through 1918, producing substantial background articles. Isaac Don Levine, who had been in Petrograd for the *Chicago Daily News,* became foreign editor for the *Tribune* in New York in 1917.

The *New York Herald* took its general direction from its publisher, James Gordon Bennett, Jr., who lived in Paris until his death there on May 14, 1918, at seventy-seven. The *Herald* was not the enterprising newspaper it had been in previous years, and was largely dependent upon the Associated Press for its war reports and general news. Harry S. Brown was London correspondent for the *Herald,* and Sidney Whitman was in Berlin until 1917. Francis McCullagh wrote from Petrograd, also serving the *Manchester Guardian,* and was one of the few correspondents to remain after the revolution, although he had no means of getting reports out of the country at that time. Herman Bernstein also wrote for the *Herald* from Petrograd prior to and during the revolution, and he went into Siberia for the paper in 1918 with the U.S. forces.

The staff of the Paris edition provided coverage for the paper from that capital. With the U.S. entrance into the war, Donald Martin, a former political reporter for the *Herald* in Albany and Washington, also was accredited as its correspondent with the AEF in May 1918. He was soon active in covering U.S. troop action, including that at Château-Thierry in June, a difficult and hazardous involvement, along with Gibbons of the *Chicago Tribune* and James of the *New York Times.* Martin, past his youth, contracted pneumonia as a result and died. He was replaced as AEF correspondent by Burr Price, who had arrived recently from the New York staff to become editor of the Paris edition of the *Herald,* but was accredited to the AEF in October. May Birkhead, a member of the Paris edition staff since 1912, following her part in reporting the loss of the *Titanic,* became acquainted with General Pershing and, through that social relationship and other established sources, was able to write some exclusive reports, even though she never was an accredited correspondent.

The *New York Sun* had Judson C. Welliver in London as the war began. Hal O'Flaherty joined the bureau in 1916, transferring from the United Press, but left in 1917 to serve in the U.S. Army Air Force. He returned to the *Sun* bureau in London in 1919, but switched almost immediately to the service of the *Chicago Daily News,* with which he remained for many years. Dr. Stanley Shaw was in Berlin for the *Sun* until 1917. British-born Frank B. Grundy was in Paris, and Thomas M. Johnson arrived there and was accredited to the AEF in October 1917.

The *Philadelphia Public Ledger* and the weekly *Saturday Evening Post,* both under the proprietorship of Cyrus H. K. Curtis, had introduced their own direct foreign coverage as the war began, and it became active during 1917–18. Henri Bazin was an early writer from France for the *Ledger,* and reference has been made to articles for the *Saturday Evening Post* by Irvin S. Cobb and Will Irwin. Raymond G. Carroll, formerly in Washington for the *Ledger,* and representing that paper in France after the U.S. entrance to the war, became one of the first correspondents accredited to the AEF in July 1917. Harold Learoyd also was in France for the paper. Irwin, writing earlier for *Collier's Weekly,* and extensively for the *Daily Mail,* also wrote regularly for the *Saturday Evening Post* in 1917–18. Isaac F. Marcosson, a member of the magazine staff since 1907 and known for his interviews with public figures, conducted in-depth interviews with political and military leaders in several countries. George Pattullo, also a staff writer for the *Post* since 1908, was in France in 1917–18 and wrote of the AEF and the war in general. Mary Roberts Rinehart, known primarily for her fiction in the *Post,* and Elizabeth Frazier both wrote descriptive articles from France.

The *New York Evening Post* was represented in Paris early in the war by Robert Dunn, already an experienced war correspondent, and Stoddard Dewey; both continued beyond the 1917–18 period. Other correspondents for magazines and syndicates included four for *Collier's Weekly:* Irwin, until he switched to the *Saturday Evening Post,* the very active Arthur Ruhl, William Slavens McNutt, and James Hopper, accredited to the AEF. Webb Waldron became European manager for *Collier's.* Frazier Hunt arrived in France for the *Red Cross Magazine,* but switched to the *Chicago Tribune.* Herbert Corey, in Europe since 1914 for the Associated Newspapers, was accredited to the AEF for that group, among the first, in July 1917. George Seldes was accredited in May 1918 for the Marshall Syndicate. C. C. Lyon was accredited for the NEA in October 1917, with E. D. Thierry and John D. Ryan also writing for that syndicate, although Ryan switched to the *Chicago Tribune* late in the war and reported the Allied move into Siberia.

Many U.S. newspapers never before active in foreign reporting, such as the *Philadelphia Public Ledger,* gained accreditation for war correspondents in 1917–18. The *Ledger*'s morning competitor, the *Philadelphia North American,* for one, received accreditation in

September 1917 for Reginald Wright Kauffman. That accreditation was suspended in April 1918 because of a controversy over censorship policies, but Kauffman continued to write from France.

For the *Brooklyn Eagle,* Swedish-born Naboth Hedin was accredited to the AEF in March 1918, but was replaced in September by Guy C. Hickok. The paper also was represented at The Hague in that period by Henry Suydam. For the *Cincinnati Enquirer,* Bernard J. O'Donnell was accredited in August 1918. George S. Applegarth was accredited for the *Pittsburgh Post,* and Charles J. Doyle for the *Pittsburgh Gazette-Times,* both in October, and Edwin A. Roberts for the *Cleveland Plain Dealer* in November. Ward Greene of the *Atlanta Journal* and Clare Kenamore of the *St. Louis Post-Dispatch* were accredited in December after the Armistice.

Other correspondents in France for U.S. newspapers in 1918, but not accredited to the AEF, included Burris Jenkins and Otto Higgins for the *Kansas City Star;* Frank P. Sibley, *Boston Globe;* Walter S. Ball, *Providence Journal;* Raymond S. Tompkins, *Baltimore Sun;* Adam Breede, *Hastings Daily Journal* (Nebraska); Cecile Dorian, *Newark Evening News;* Harry A. Williams, *Los Angeles Times;* Joseph Timmons, *Los Angeles Examiner;* and David W. Hazen, *Portland Oregonian.*[4]

The three U.S. news agencies were well represented and actively competitive in Europe during 1917–18. The AP and UP were providing reports to the press in South America, as well as in the United States, under circumstances described earlier.

For the Associated Press, Robert T. Small became the first correspondent for that agency accredited to the AEF. Previously with the British forces at BEF, Small nearly lost his life in an action shortly before transfer to the AEF, and was exhausted. To give him relief, he was succeeded at AEF in October 1917 by Norman Draper. Crozier, in his book, *American Reporters on the Western Front,* reports Draper as arguing that he should have special access to information and priority in transmission of his reports because, as he contended, the AP service reached more readers than all others combined. He set the figure at ninety million, and so earned the nickname of "Ninety Million Draper." His attitude induced some other correspondents to form a coalition to beat him on volume, quality, and speed of reporting, and also to counter what some believed to be his inducements to French telegraph operators

---

4 A listing of correspondents, accredited and otherwise, appears in Emmet Crozier, *American Reporters on the Western Front, 1914–1918* (New York, 1959), pp. 279–81.

at AEF headquarters to let him see stories filed by others and, as they also believed, to lift some items for his own use. Draper, in any case, was succeeded at AEF in March 1918 by John T. Parkerson. In July, Parkerson was in turn replaced by James P. Howe, then by Burge McFall and, at the end of that month, by Charles E. Kloeber, formerly chief of the news desk in New York.

The Paris bureau itself, headed by Elmer Roberts, was well-manned in 1918, not only by Small, Draper, Parkerson, Howe, and McFall after their separations from the AEF, but by Philip M. Powers, Samuel Wader, Stanley W. Prenosil, formerly in Boston, Robert Berry, formerly in Petrograd but then reporting on the French army, and Martin Egan, former AP bureau chief in Tokyo from 1902 to 1907 and on leave from the J. P. Morgan Company, in New York.

For the AP, Walter C. Hiatt followed the Italian-Austrian battle in the last period of the war. S. Miles Bouton, formerly in Berlin, was in Stockholm. Charles T. Thompson, AP correspondent in Paris since 1902 and until 1911, was in Rome with Salvatore Cortesi supervising coverage of the Italian war action. Robert M. Collins, London bureau chief, had assistance there in handling a heavy volume of news from Ben S. Allen, Frank B. Elser, and Frank America.

The International News Service, its cable rights restored in 1917, had Earl Reeves directing its London bureau, assisted by George Allison. Charles F. Bartelli, formerly of the *New York Times* bureau, and Henry Wales, formerly of the Paris edition of the *New York Herald,* were in Paris. Dennis B. Ford was accredited to the AEF for INS in March 1918, but was succeeded in that position in April by Newton C. ("Archie") Parke. Daniel Dillon joined the Paris bureau in June 1918, one of several correspondents crossing the Atlantic with a large contingent of AEF troops.

From 1910 to 1917 the INS served both morning and afternoon papers in the United States. This was modified in 1918 when a Universal Service was formed by the Hearst organization to serve the morning papers. H. H. Stansbury was named as director and Plautus I. Lipsey, Jr., became foreign editor. Damon Runyon, who had been on the Texas-Mexican border for the Hearst press, was in Paris in July 1918, representing Universal Service. The INS service then went to afternoon newspapers.

The United Press coverage grew substantially during 1917–18, with dramatic successes and one dramatic error. Keen in London and Simms in Paris continued in their executive positions. Shepherd, active as a correspondent on the war fronts in 1914–16, had joined Pershing's staff in 1917, and Forrest, who had been in the London bureau, joined the *New York Tribune* in Paris in February 1918. The London staff had been augmented in 1917 by five men coming from the United States. These were Arthur Mann, Lowell Mellett, Robert Getty, Westbrook Pegler, coming from Chicago, and Webb Miller, moving from his assignment on the Texas-Mexican border by way of the Washington bureau.

In the summer of 1917 Pegler and Mellett were sent to the Paris bureau. There Henry Wood had been representing the UP at the French press headquarters at Chantilly, while Frank J. Taylor had been reporting early AEF developments. Pegler was with the first correspondents at Neufchâteau, accredited to the AEF in July 1917. Youngest of the correspondents at twenty-two, his experience was comparable to that of Heywood Broun of the *New York Tribune*. He also became involved in a controversey over censorship regulations and by early 1918 was in such disfavor with Pershing himself, and others at AEF headquarters, that his accreditation was withdrawn. Pegler returned to London and left the UP to join the U.S. Navy. He rejoined the agency after the war.

To provide more experienced men in France, Fred S. Ferguson, manager of the UP news desk in New York, along with Webb Miller in London, arrived in Paris early in 1918. Henry Wood was reassigned to report the war in Italy, with Mellett replacing him at Chantilly. Ferguson, accredited to the AEF in April, and Taylor in May, both moved into battle areas. Ferguson, with U.S. forces at St. Mihiel in September, scored a major news beat for the UP by his early report of the success there that marked one of the turning points of the war. Miller, active in the Paris bureau, was accredited to the AEF on November 19 after the Armistice.

The success of the United Press in 1918 was attributable to advance planning for the transmission of reports, to the transmission of some at the urgent rate, and to the discovery of a means to transmit reports in advance of others. Serving its client newspapers in South America, some UP dispatches were routed directly to Buenos Aires, and relayed from there to New York. The cost was higher, but South Atlantic cables were less heavily used, and delays were reduced to a minimum. One further result was that some UP reports were cabled back to London and Paris by way of New York before that same news had appeared in those cities. This became a great trial to the Associated Press, which suffered competitively, with its own member papers in the United States using

UP reports by preference, or subscribing to the UP service if they were not already receiving it.

The key to this success rested in the agency's good fortune in gaining the right to use what Webb Miller later described as "the only private leased wire between Paris and Brest, the cable head."[5] It was an exclusive right, and kept as a precious secret. The wire was controlled by Louis Condurier, publisher of *Le Dépêche de Brest,* which had become a UP client newspaper. It was a wire in operation only four or five hours a day, but those hours, by chance, coincided with a number of important wartime news developments. Its use on such occasions permitted messages to move from Paris to Brest, and thence to New York or Buenos Aires, without delays attendant upon dispatches passed through the censorship in the normal way at the French government Bureau de la Poste, Télégraph et Téléphone, in the Place de la Bourse.

Allowing time for that government censorship, and taking account of the mass of dispatches to be handled, as much as an hour's delay was usual for news moving from Paris to New York through the Place de la Bourse. Arrangements with the French government's chief of censorship, however, permitted the elimination of that step for dispatches originating in the U.S. sector at the front and already passed by U.S. military censors, for dispatches based on matter that had appeared in Paris newspapers, and for official communiqués. It was only necessary, in such cases, to send copies of the dispatches, later, to the French censorship as a matter of record.

Under this arrangement, United Press dispatches meeting the qualifications specified, never went directly to the Bureau de la Poste. They were simply "taken across the street" to the telegraph office handling matter for the private wire, went forward to Brest without delay, were recognized there as having proper clearance for further transmission, and so could be forwarded immediately to New York or Buenos Aires from the Brest cable-end.

The use of this leased wire system, successful as it was on other occasions, also involved the UP in an error that became classic in the history of journalism, if nothing more. It was an error, also, that involved no less a personage than Roy W. Howard, president and director of the United Press.

Howard had been in South America for several months in 1918 to oversee and protect the position established there by the UP. Unable to

---

5   See Webb Miller, *I Found No Peace: The Journal of a Foreign Correspondent* (New York, 1936), chapter 5.

arrange a sailing direct to New York when he was ready to leave Buenos Aires in October 1918, Howard took a ship to Spain and proceeded to Paris. Intending to sail for New York, he was in Brest on the morning of November 7.

Secret negotiations looking toward an armistice had been initiated by Germany and Austria early in October. By November 3 all Central Powers nations had concluded armistices and were out of the war, except for Germany, and mutiny and riot proceeded there. On the morning of November 7, German Field Marshal von Hindenburg sent a message to Marshal Foch, commander of all Allied forces, requesting a meeting to discuss an armistice. German emissaries were to arrive at Foch's field headquarters in the Compiègne forest on the morning of November 8.

In some manner never wholly clarified, the German request on the morning of November 7 for a meeting to discuss an armistice was distorted in its secondary repetition in Paris and beyond. With what he believed to be reliable information from the U.S. Embassy in Paris, U.S. Admiral Henry B. Wilson, commanding U.S. Naval forces in France and based at the port of Brest, informed Howard that an armistice actually had been signed that morning between Germany and the Allied Powers, and that fighting would end at 2 P.M. that day. Wilson also caused an announcement of the Armistice to be made to the citizens of Brest, with a public celebration immediately ensuing.

Howard assumed that a report of the Armistice would have been transmitted by the UP from Paris, but he asked Admiral Wilson's permission to send a backup cable from Brest. Wilson regarded the announcement of the Armistice as official, and told Howard to proceed, detailing a French-speaking officer to accompany him to the cable office to assist in clearing the message through the censorship.

At the office of *Le Dépêche de Brest,* Howard prepared a brief dispatch on a regular cable blank, signed with his name and the name and press card number of Simms, the Paris bureau manager. At the cable office, the censor himself was out celebrating the Armistice. An operator, acquainted with the Navy officer who delivered the message and satisfied with the *bona fides* attached, transmitted it, with a Paris dateline. It arrived at the UP office in New York at 11:20 A.M., on November 7. Immediately placed on the network wires, the news touched off a celebration of the war's end all across the United States, in Canada, then in South America, and also in London and Paris, as the report was cabled eastward again from New York.

In Brest, meanwhile, Howard had gone to dinner, when an orderly arrived from Admiral Wilson's office with a message from the admiral informing him that a second report from the Paris embassy said that the original account of the Armistice was "unconfirmable." Howard filed another cable to New York, two hours after the first, with that report. But it did not reach the UP office until almost noon of November 8, a day late.

The Associated Press had been under pressure by member papers in the United States from noon of November 7 to provide its own report of the Armistice, but could only say that the news of such an event could not be confirmed. Those AP papers with confidence in the agency accordingly refrained from publishing reports of the war's end. In the emotional reaction of the moment, some such newspapers became targets of public displeasure. The INS was in the same position as the AP. In Washington, the Department of State announced officially that no Armistice terms had been signed.

With no confirmation from Paris or elsewhere, the UP office in New York became increasingly tense. The desire was to believe in the accuracy of Howard's reports. But that straw of hope vanished when his second cable at last arrived on November 8. It was small comfort to be able to publish a statement from Admiral Wilson accepting responsibility for the premature report and absolving both Howard and the UP from error.[6] When the real Armistice came four days later, signed early on November 11, and effective at 11 A.M., Paris time, on that date, the news was joyfully received, but came as something of an anticlimax.

Apart from correspondents for the U.S. press, the news of the last year of the war naturally continued to be reported by agency and press representatives of other Allied countries, of the Central Powers, and of some neutral countries.

Among correspondents for the British press accredited to the AEF in France were Cameron Mackenzie of the *Daily Telegraph,* Herbert Bailey of the *Daily Mail,* H. Noble Hall, formerly writing for the *New York World* but in this period for the *Times,* H. Warner Allen of the *Morning Post,* and H. Provost Battersby of Reuters until he was gassed and invalided home.

Others based in Paris and added to the corps already there were George Renwick and Percival Gibbon for the *Daily Chronicle;* Ellis

---

6   The story of the "false armistice" was told later by Howard in a special chapter appearing as a supplement to Webb Miller's *I Found No Peace.* References also appear in Joe Alex Morris, *Deadline Every Minute: The Story of the United Press* (Garden City, 1957). Oliver Gramling, *AP: The Story of News* (New York, 1940), and in Emmet Crozier, *American Reporters on the Western Front* (New York, 1959).

Ashmead-Bartlett of the *Daily Telegraph,* and Robert Dell of the *Manchester Guardian.* Those attached to French and Italian forces were on the move as battle lines changed, and BEF headquarters itself was moved, and so was AEF press headquarters. Still centered at Neufchâteau, and with a branch in Paris, temporary bases were established at Chepoix in Picardy, at Beauvais, at Meaux near Paris, at Nancy in September 1918, and finally at Bar-le-Duc.

With the Armistice effective on November 11, an advance AEF press headquarters was moved to Verdun on November 16, to Luxembourg on November 21, and on December 8 to the German Rhine city of Coblenz, which became the headquarters for the American Army of Occupation. At approximately the same time, Cologne was made the headquarters for the British Army of Occupation, and Frankfurt-am-Main for the French army, with press representatives following.

A few adventurous and courageous correspondents preceded the troops into Germany, and also went beyond the zones of occupation, fanning out through Germany, into Austria, and as far east as Poland and Russia. Some neutral correspondents had remained in Berlin and Vienna, but there was no assurance as to how the people might relate to Allied correspondents, arriving independently and actually contrary to the terms of their accreditation, but none was molested or harmed.

The first U.S. correspondents to enter Germany drove across the German border from Luxembourg on November 21, using army cars and drivers assigned to them as a perquisite of their accreditation to the AEF. They were Lincoln Eyre of the *New York World,* Herbert Corey, Associated Newspapers, C. C. (Cal) Lyon, NEA, George Seldes, Marshall Newspaper Syndicate, and Frederick A. Smith, *Chicago Tribune.*

After an early involvement with a column of retreating German army troops, they professed to be on a mission to examine the food needs in Germany, which were urgent. They were well enough received at Trier to risk returning their army cars and drivers to Luxembourg with a note explaining their absence from the AEF base. They went on to Frankfurt and Kassel. There they found Field Marshal von Hindenburg and induced him to grant an interview, brief and monosyllabic, but newsworthy. Eyre, a former Berlin correspondent, acted as interpreter. From Kassel, Seldes returned to Luxembourg, but the other four went on to Berlin. They were soon returned from there, perforce, by agreement with the German military under the terms of the Armistice agreement.

The AEF headquarters was both alarmed and outraged by the unauthorized move of the "runaway five" correspondents into Germany.

They were subject to formal interrogation, and might have been imprisoned for six months. A letter in their support from Colonel Edward M. House, then in Paris as an adviser to President Wilson, saved them from any such fate, and their accreditations were restored. It was late December, however, before they were permitted to send the stories they had obtained in Germany in November, with the "news value" much reduced.

A comparable venture into Germany, but with different results, involved Lowell Thomas and Webb Waldron, a novelist and at the time European editor for *Collier's Weekly*. Thomas had returned to Paris in November 1918, after a long assignment during 1917–18 to Creel's U.S. government Committee on Public Information. With Harry Chase, a motion picture cameraman, he had made films and prepared material for talks in support of the war effort, first on the Italian front and then in Egypt and the Middle East, where they had joined with General Sir Edmund H. H. Allenby and British forces in the advance on Jerusalem and its surrender without violence. There also Thomas had become acquainted with Thomas Edward Lawrence, Oxford-educated archeologist who had become a leader of an Arab Bedouin revolt against the Turks—a great aid to Allenby in the Palestine campaign. Virtually ignored by correspondents, Lawrence became Thomas's friend, with Lawrence's exploits made known later, largely through Thomas's book, *With Lawrence In Arabia* (1924), and also through films and lectures presented by Thomas in London and around the world.

In Paris shortly after the Armistice, Thomas and Waldron conceived the idea of moving into Germany, aware that Foch wanted no reports from there that might arouse possible sympathy for the defeated enemy, and aware of the disfavor visited upon the "runaway five." The two nevertheless went by rail to Strasbourg. The frontier was closed, but they found an American-born ambulance driver with a French infantry unit then assigned to drive along the frontier to pick up Allied soldiers released from German prison camps. He was persuaded to drive them to the Swiss border, where they managed to get through the barbed wire on a moonless night and reach Basel. There they were arrested, but gained the support of a U.S. consular officer, who agreed that it would be useful for them to enter Germany and let the American public know of conditions there. In uniform, they went by train to Freiburg in early December, were well received, and reached Prince Max, the last German imperial chancellor, on his Baden estate, where they heard his story.

They went on to Stuttgart, Munich, and Oberammergau for Christmas Eve, and soon to Berlin, where they remained about a month. As Thomas recalls in his book, *Good Evening Everybody* (1976), the capital was in the midst of revolution, strikes, and violence. The two were under fire at times. They observed much, however, and talked with many persons, including a journalist who had worked for the AP and may have been Enderis, who had remained in Berlin. In any event, by way of Copenhagen, stories went out of the visit of what were described as the first returning U.S. correspondents. One such report published in the United States gave the erroneous impression that Thomas had been shot. In Berlin, Thomas and Waldron talked with Karl Liebknecht and Rosa Luxemburg, Spartacist leaders advocating a Communist government in Germany, with Friedrich Ebert, prospective president of the new Weimar Republic, and with Count Johann Heinrich von Bernstorff, former German ambassdor to the United States, whom they found at the Adlon Hotel.

From Berlin, Thomas and Waldron went on to Hamburg in January, and were able to get transportation to LeHavre aboard a French cruiser. Since they had been in Germany without authorization, and had no proper papers, the cruiser put them off at night in a longboat to be landed in France some miles from the port. When they reached Paris they still had to gain some form of accreditation if they were to be able to report what they had seen and heard. Again, this was accomplished through Colonel House, who also had them tell their stories to Herbert Hoover and to General Tasker H. Bliss, chief of staff. Their interviews with Prince Max, Ebert, and others were of such substance that they were given full clearance. Waldron also wrote of their experiences and observations. Thomas, who had been able to buy four reels of motion picture showing street battles in Berlin, disposed of them to Pathé News as exclusive and still newsworthy.

By that time, the AEF headquarters had been moved to Coblenz, and General Pershing conducted a conference there for correspondents. The need for censorship was ended, and other correspondents by then not only had traveled in Germany, but some were returning to Central European posts in what was to become a resumption of regular coverage, with the focus of interest upon matters other than military.

Apart from Smith of the *Chicago Tribune,* a "runaway" correspondent, and the Thomas-Waldron visit, S. Miles Bouton of the Associated Press was perhaps the first *bona fide* correspondent to reach Berlin. He approached from Stockholm and was unrestricted by AEF accreditation

requirements. Arno Dosch-Fleurot of the *New York World,* Henry
Wood of the United Press, and Wythe Williams, then representing the
Daily Mail, were other early arrivals. Williams may have been the first
writing for the British press.

Floyd Gibbons and Richard Henry Little, both of the *Chicago
Tribune,* followed by Marguerite Harrison, with accreditation to the
Baltimore Sun, the AP, and the *New York Evening Post,* made their
way across Germany, ending in Poland and Russia. Little was wounded
near Petrograd and Harrison jailed in Moscow. Gibbons returned from
Moscow to Paris. There he succeeded Spearman Lewis for a time as
director of the Army Edition of the *Chicago Tribune.* Little, following
recovery from his wounds, became the first postwar resident correspondent in Berlin for the *Tribune,* but returned to Chicago in 1920.

Other correspondents moving into the areas of the Central Powers,
beyond the Allied-occupied zones along the Rhine River, included Cyril
Brown of the *New York Times,* Junius B. Wood, *Chicago Daily News,*
and Ben Hecht, newly arrived in Europe, also for the *Daily News.* Hecht
remained as Berlin correspondent for the paper for several months.
Harry J. Greenwall of the *Daily Express* was in Germany for five
months, where he witnessed the Spartacist demonstrations of January
1919 in support of a German Soviet Republic, and which were put down
with violence. He was in Weimar in February to report the assembly
drafting the constitution for the Weimar Republic. Vernon Bartlett of
the *Times* was another who saw Spartacist violence. He moved on to
Austria and Hungary.

Robert Atter of the AP was the first Allied correspondent to return to
Vienna, where he resumed his prewar post. Walter G. Hiatt, also of the
AP, and Joseph M. N. Jeffries of the *Daily Mail,* were not far behind.
G. Ward Price of the *Daily Mail* may have been the first into Bulgaria.
He and W. H. G. Werndel of Reuters were early arrivals in Turkey.

As the occupation forces themselves took their positions in Germany
in December 1918, they were accompanied by correspondents. Those
with the British forces included Philip Gibbs of the *Daily Chronicle* and
Percival Phillips of the *Daily Express.* Those with U.S. forces included
James P. Howe of the AP, Webb Miller, UP, Wilbur Forrest, *New York
Tribune,* and Edwin L. James, *New York Times.* Three experienced
Havas men, Ludovic Péricard, Horace Trouvé, and M. Cartier, were
with the French forces.

Among other correspondents reporting the uneasy period in Germany
and the former Austro-Hungarian area immediately after the Armistice
were Frank J. Taylor, followed by Carl D. Groat, both for the United

Press, Guido Enderis, resuming representation for the Associated Press in Berlin, Gibbs of the *Daily Chronicle* moving out from Cologne, and Gregory Mason for *Outlook* magazine.

The events transpiring in Central Europe during 1918–19, like those in Russia in the same period, were reported so far as the chaotic conditions of the time permitted. Those conditions left much to be desired in the quality of coverage. Meanwhile, the news spotlight was focused sharply upon the Peace Conference in Paris.

The Peace Conference, 1919–20 16

The tragedy of the Great War was fully recognized long before the shooting stopped on November 11, 1918. More than four years of horror had largely decimated a generation and left a trail of destruction and a heritage of debt. Those surviving the war were weary and disillusioned, regardless of nationality. It soon became a question as to whether there were any real victors. Not surprisingly, the phrase characterizing the conflict as "the war to end war" gained hopeful acceptance. The concept of a League of Nations, intended to assure future world peace, gained wide favor.

President Wilson was the exponent of the League of Nations. It was proposed as one of the "14 points" enunciated in January 1918 as the basis for a peace settlement. The president himself arrived in France on December 13, crossing the Atlantic in the liner *George Washington,* accompanied by Mrs. Wilson. He represented a nation whose troops had tilted the balance and brought victory to the Allies, even as Germany's Field Marshal von Hindenburg had told Lincoln Eyre of the *New York Times* in the interview at Kassel with the five "runaway" AEF correspondents in November 1919. In coming to participate in the conference to make peace, Wilson was received in European countries almost as a new Messiah. He and Mrs. Wilson made what became a triumphal tour, acclaimed by crowds as he visited Paris, London, Manchester, Rome, Milan, and Brussels.

The Peace Conference was formally opened in Paris on January 18, 1919, with seventy delegates representing the victorious Allied and Associated Powers. Their task was to draft the terms of treaties to be submitted separately to representatives of each of the five defeated Central Powers.

President Wilson soon discovered that his "14 points" were not taken with a view to their literal application by France's Premier Clemenceau or Great Britain's Prime Minister Lloyd George, nor was the concept for a League of Nations fully accepted. He learned of secret treaties and agreements made before the United States entered the war to win the support of Italy, Rumania, and other governments, and which complicated settlements. He became aware of nationalistic sentiments so strong as to bring a temporary departure from the conference, for example, of Italy's Premier Vittorio Orlando when certain of his claims were resisted. He discovered that France was to demand conditions and reparations threatening a secure peace. He recognized that his hopes for "open covenants openly arrived at" were in vain. He was forced to compromise on a final treaty with Germany written in such terms that, while accepted perforce by a defeated nation and approved by other Allied powers, it was never ratified by the United States Senate.

Wilson persuaded the Allied leaders, who formed a Council of Ten, to give unanimous adoption to a resolution supporting creation of a League of Nations, but the details remained to be negotiated. Two weeks later in mid-February 1919, Wilson returned to the United States to attend to domestic business, and Lloyd George returned to London. Both were back in Paris before the end of March, and the Council of Ten thereafter became a Council of Four, the so-called "Big Four," with Wilson, Clemenceau, Lloyd George, and Orlando working privately and intensively on the terms of the treaties.

A Covenant of the League of Nations, drafted by a Covenant Committee headed by Wilson, and specifying its objectives, organization, and administrative details, was approved by a full session of the Council of Ten on April 28, 1919. The Covenant was incorporated as forming the first twenty-six articles in each of the five peace treaties to be concluded with Germany, Austria, Bulgaria, Hungary, and Turkey. When the Treaty of Versailles with Germany, the first to be signed, became effective on January 10, 1920, the League of Nations also came into formal existence, with its headquarters at Geneva, Switzerland. Since the United States Senate declined to ratify that treaty, however, or any of the others, the United States never became a member of the League.

Even before the Peace Conference began its sessions in Paris in January 1919, a new German republic had been proclaimed in Berlin by Philipp Scheidemann, Socialist leader, on November 9, 1918, the day following the abdication of Wilhelm II and two days before the Armistice. A National Assembly, elected in January, met at Weimar in February 1919 and elected Friedrich Ebert as president. A constitution was adopted there in July. These actions occurred amid internal disorder in Germany as differing elements advanced their own views. In addition to the Communist-directed Spartacist revolt in January 1919, the Kapp Putsch by monarchists erupted in March 1920.

Before the Weimar Constitution was adopted in July 1919, the German delegation selected to sign the peace treaty was summoned and arrived at Versailles on April 29. The document was presented on May 7. After a study of its terms, the German delegation protested that they did not reflect Wilson's "14 points," and that certain of the provisions were unrealistic and could not be fulfilled, including the reparations demands. Some slight modifications were made on the basis of these protests. The terms were still regarded by the Germans as harsh and unrealistic, yet they had no alternative but to sign. The formal ceremony was held in the Hall of Mirrors at the Palace of Versailles on June 28. This was the fifth anniversary, as it happened, of the assassination at Sarajevo that had provided the spark to touch off the war.

Although the peace treaty was opposed in Germany, the National Assembly at Weimar voted its reluctant ratification on July 7. It acted under the pressure of an Allied blockade causing hunger and hardship among the people, with a military occupation along the Rhine, and with an Allied invasion as the alternative. The same treaty then also was ratified for the Allies in October by France, Great Britain, Italy, and Japan, but not by the United States. Instead, Congress at last adopted a resolution on July 2, 1921, declaring peace with the Central Powers, and without membership in the League of Nations.

The other four treaties were completed and signed by representatives of Austria in September 1919, Bulgaria in November, Hungary in June 1920, and Turkey in August. The first three of these also were duly ratified, except by the United States. The treaty with Turkey was not ratified and was renegotiated at Lausanne in July 1923.

The conference which had begun in Paris on January 18, 1919, thus continued through August 10, 1920. These nineteen months of hard work were marked by frustration, controversy, disillusionment, and considerable bitterness between individuals and governments. There was no general satisfaction with the treaties. It was enormously satisfying, however, that the war had ended, and President Wilson, for one, saw the establishment of the League of Nations as one solid accomplishment holding prospects for good. The defeat of his hope for U.S. participation was the tragedy of his life, and may have been fatal to the peace itself.

Returning from Paris and presenting the Treaty of Versailles to the U.S. Senate in July 1920 following the German ratification, Wilson encountered opposition based in part on partisan politics, on isolationist sentiments, and on objections to some treaty provisions. There also was Wilson's own unwillingness to accept certain proposed amendments. Instead, he set out on a speaking tour of the United States to rally public support for the treaty and particularly to explain the potential value of the League. Between September 3 and September 25 he made seventeen speeches in twenty-nine cities of the Middle West and Far West. At Pueblo, Colorado, on September 25 he suffered an apoplectic stroke and was returned to Washington. In the more than six months between that time in 1920 and the end of his term in March 1921 Wilson was unable to function effectively, although a fiction was maintained that he could perform the essential duties of his office. He died in 1924, aged sixty-seven, a bitter and broken man.

Even before Wilson died, difficulties had become apparent in the world, related largely to the harsh provisions in the Versailles Treaty. The decade following brought a sequence of events, escalating into what became World War II. In 1919, any such thing would have been beyond belief.

The Conference and Public Information

The Paris Peace Conference of 1919–20 was the first international gathering to receive massive press attention and something approaching world coverage. The nearest previous parallel may have been the Berlin Conference of 1878, following the Russo-Turkish War, but the press representation there was relatively small, and the relationship between those representatives and the governments was quite different.

As the Paris Conference began, the French government made a center available where all correspondents might meet socially, exchange information if they wished, and occasionally receive information on a semi-official or official basis. The center was at the Hôtel Dufayel, 80 Avenue des Champs-Élysées, the private residence of a wealthy French manufacturer, recently deceased. Formally designated as the Cercle Française de Presse Étranger, it was a kind of press club. Although literally translated as a French Club for the foreign press, it was not for foreign journalists only, of whom there were more than 500 in Paris at the time, but included French journalists also. It had a membership list of about 2,200 before the conference ended in 1920. News photographers and motion picture photographers were among them. The total fluctuated during the nineteen months, beginning with a substantial number, dwindling as negotiations continued without producing any significant news, rising again when the Treaty of Versailles was about to be signed, and then declining sharply.

The British press, at its high point, was represented by about 100 correspondents. For the U.S., at least 250 correspondents, coming and going, requested recognition at one time or another. A large number understandably represented the French press, while those for Italy, Japan, and other Allied and neutral countries were present in smaller numbers.

Press representatives of the Central Powers were not permitted to appear until the treaties had been prepared. Then, in April 1919, the German plenipotentiaries arriving in Versailles were accompanied by fifteen correspondents. Others came with the Austrian, Bulgarian, Hungarian, and Turkish delegations.

The Paris Conference provided a forum and testing ground for a world press that had attained new stature during the years since 1914, and was on the brink of further advances. Before the war, press coverage had been demonstrating a growing concern for a wide variety of substantive matters—political, administrative, economic, diplomatic, social and cultural. Government officials unaccustomed to such searching inquiries as were being made, and sometimes fearful or even resentful, often tried to keep reporters at arm's length.

The press in Great Britain and the United States, where it was strongest, showed the greatest enterprise and independence, and was most effective in countering efforts to curb its inquiries. Reporters and correspondents representing the media of both countries were aggressive and successful in the pursuit of news at home and abroad. British and U.S. newspapers therefore became the models upon which many others patterned themselves, both in physical appearance and, where possible, in general practice and content. The French press, and certain Paris dailies in particular, also served as models in countries sharing French heritage and interests, some as information papers and others as political papers in the sense previously described.

There were defensible reasons for officials to limit their direct relations with reporters or correspondents even for the most reputable papers. One was the increase in the number of correspondents in some capitals, bringing such demands upon the time of officials as to require protective measures. Another was the rise of the popular press with such stress on human interest and personalities, even in the reporting of serious subjects, as to cause some officials to avoid their representatives, whose efforts they saw as contributing to the publication of trivia, and to sensational or irresponsible accounts.

This still did not mean that an official might refuse to see any correspondent ever, or perhaps meet with a group of correspondents. Many officials at last were aware that a public right to and need for information meant that correspondents required a regular available source in any one of the departments of government. Awareness of the need did not arise in every capital at the same time, and not much was done about it in more than a few.

Considering the historical precedence of London as a world news center, it is understandable that William E. Gladstone, British prime minister on several occasions between 1868 and 1894, would seem to have been the first major official of a national government to name an assistant specifically to undertake the duties of what would later become known as a "public information officer" (PIO) or "public relations officer" (PRO) dealing with press inquiries. Algernon Turner, occupant of that position at 10 Downing Street, was rather uncharitably referred to at the time as a "deputy mop-squeezer" for the prime minister. After 1920, however, a public information office and staff existed there, at the British Foreign Office, and later in other departments of the government, with press officers appointed to meet with reporters.

Count Otto von Bismarck had been notorious for his manipulation of the press in Germany in the late nineteenth century, acting as his own press officer while serving as chancellor. By 1910, a press bureau was established in the Ministry of Foreign Affairs in the Wilhelmstrasse, ostensibly to assist or inform foreign correspondents. Its value was slight, if one may judge by the recollection of Raymond Swing, Berlin correspondent shortly thereafter for the *Chicago Daily News*. Swing recalled that if he sought news at the ministry "a man with a long beard, standing at a desk, received me and invariably told me there was no news. If I asked a question he invariably was unable to answer it. If I took him a report that I wanted verified, he invariably said that the report was not true."

As a capital, Washington was relatively less important as a source of news prior to the war, and the number of correspondents present there for the foreign press posed no problem. The number of domestic reporters had increased, however, and President Theodore Roosevelt had introduced informal press conferences at the White House as early as 1901. John Hay had done so at the Department of State even earlier, and Woodrow Wilson had undertaken regularly scheduled conferences in 1913. Reporters and correspondents in Washington were able by then, to obtain information with general ease and freedom through conferences with officials in many departments of the government or from staff secretaries.

When the European war began in 1914, the relations between governments and the press in capitals other than Washington remained casual and ill-defined. Personal relationships between officials and selected reporters and correspondents still determined very largely the style, quality, and tone of existing news reports on public affairs. What became immediately important was the war itself, and how it was to be reported. Military leaders were concerned lest a conflict conducted so close to the major capitals and in populous areas would introduce unprecedented problems relating to information, which in fact it sometimes did. Some such problems, especially in the face of unceasing demands for the accreditation of more correspondents, led to the establishment of firmer rules and regulations than had ever before been needed, even in a war situation. The correspondents and their principals were obliged to accept certain restraints and regulations, with none of the evasions that had occurred in other wars.

As already explained with reference to BEF headquarters, the correspondents were obliged to wear uniforms and identifying armbands or symbols and be unarmed. Even with accreditation, they could go only where they were permitted to go, and then only in the company of officers assigned to guide them, and they had to submit what they wrote for censorship. In turn, they were provided with food, shelter, transportation, and communication facilities. The same general procedures were introduced at AEF press headquarters, and applied also within the Central Powers.

There was a certain logic to this departure from the older practices, and it carried advantages and benefits not offered in earlier wars, notably in providing greater safety for correspondents. It also was argued that it did not deprive the public of any essential information. As to this, contrary views later were expressed.

Whether it would have made a difference or not, possibly shortening the war, is difficult to say, but the errors of military and civilian leadership and the catastrophic manpower losses were so obscured by censorship and by considerations of morale that the full truth rarely was communicated to the people in any one of the warring nations. This was well-summarized a half-century later, not only with reference to the war of 1914–18, but to all wars, by Philip Knightley of the London *Sunday Times* in his book *The First Casualty* (1975). His thesis was that truth is the first victim of wars and war-reporting.

It did not require more than a half-century, however, to have this unhappy fact made clear with reference to World War I. A. J. Cummings, distinguished British journalist, identified with the London

News-Chronicle, and a veteran of army service in France, referred to the matter in *The Press and a Changing Civilization* (1936). Even as the war proceeded, he said, those men engaged in the fighting, and knowing what it meant, were at times "nauseated to read, day after day, the lying official communiqués in the press," and "to read the solemn but silly editorial comments based upon those official lies." It was, he wrote, "more nauseating still to read the endless drivel despatched by G.H.Q., whose business it was, by striking a loud and continuous note of light-hearted optimism, to cheer the spirits of the troops at the front and to stimulate the morale of the civilians at home."

Cummings did not point the finger at any individual correspondent, for the movements of the correspondents usually were controlled, as the price of their accreditation. What they were able to report also was determined by the censorship under which they operated, and to which their agencies or newspapers were subject. With no reflection upon their own competence or honesty, important elements might be omitted from dispatches, or removed by the censorship.

This also was indicated by the very titles of books written by some correspondents after the war, perhaps in part to ease their own consciences. Examples are: Philip Gibbs, *Realities of War* (1920), published in the United States as *Now It Can Be Told,* and *More That Must Be Told* (1921); Thomas M. Johnson, *Without Censor* (1928); Charles Edward Montague, *Disenchantment* (1928); and Webb Miller, *I Found No Peace* (1936). Much was written after the war about the operation of censorship and the impact of propaganda, including Harold D. Lasswell's *Propaganda Technique in the World War* (1927), Arthur Ponsonby's *Falsehood in War-Time* (1928), and James Morgan Read's *Atrocity Propaganda, 1914–1919* (1941).

Correspondents and reporters for much of the European press, who were reared in a tradition respectful of official authority, tended to accept with little question the rules and regulations imposed upon them. Those associated with the British press were more independent-minded; their spirited resistance to War Office edicts during the first year of the war, and the independent revelations of munitions shortages stand as evidence. French journalists also showed independence, Clemenceau himself among them. Even so, the rules were generally respected.

In the United States, another tradition existed among journalists. Authority received its due, but there was less hesitation about questioning rules and regulations, if there seemed reason to do so. Wartime censorship regulations were observed, but it was a voluntary censorship, with the press having a voice in setting the rules. Any pretension to superior wisdom on the part of an official was certain to be challenged, and military personnel were not exempt from critical appraisal. A newsman of experience held himself as equal to anybody else, and better than most. He deemed such self-confidence, even arrogance, an essential of his craft. Some viewed themselves as serving a high purpose as representatives of the people, acting on their behalf in obtaining and publishing information to which the public had a transcendant right. The "watchdog" function of the press was regarded as a part of its responsibility to its readers, and elected or appointed officials were viewed as public servants.

With this attitude widely shared and rarely abused, and also generally accepted by officials themselves in the U.S. government, those U.S. news executives and correspondents in Europe in 1914–17, proceeding in that spirit, had battered down some doors and produced news reports of substance. In fairness, it must be said that both the Allied and Central Powers were contesting in that period for the support of the United States. Allowances therefore were made for attitudes and actions that might otherwise have been self-defeating on the part of some brash or naive correspondents, little acquainted with protocol and the history and background of the European countries, or with their languages and way of life.

When the United States entered the war in 1917, the more experienced U.S. correspondents, some present long before 1914, had adjusted to European ways. But they were outnumbered during 1917–18 by a wave of new arrivals who had to learn their own lessons. Some used the police reporter approach, assuming that they could obtain information in the same direct fashion as in cities of the United States. Few understood military procedures, and some assigned to the AEF were not disposed to accept its rules and regulations. A number were disciplined and deprived of accreditation, something almost unimaginable at BEF or other headquarters.

Not to overstress this element, however, some of the older and wiser British and American correspondents were troubled and even shocked by attitudes occasionally encountered among officials and press representatives in European centers, and by practices of some segments of the European press. It cannot be said that either party survived the impact of this collision without some change, slow though it was in coming. There was compromise and accommodation on both sides, possibly with mutual benefits.

Illustrative of the beginning of that change was an incident in Paris early in 1918 at a time when the reinforced German army attack on the western front was causing alarm in France. Franklin D. Roosevelt, U.S. assistant secretary of the navy, was on an official visit in Paris. He let it be known that he would be pleased to make himself available for a conference with French newsmen, and others. This he might have done in Washington at that period, under what had become normal procedure there. In Paris, however, it was unusual. Individual members of the French cabinet sometimes met with a small and carefully selected group of Paris newsmen with whom they could speak in confidence, establishing certain points the government wanted to have presented to the public, but without specific attribution to source.

The Roosevelt conference, by contrast, was open to any who might wish to attend, with no restriction on attribution. A considerable group of French and Italian newsmen arrived. They came expecting no more than a formal statement, which would have been the procedure had a French official of equal stature received any such general press group. Instead, however, Roosevelt spoke informally, sometimes in French, and invited questions, which he answered informally, with no ban on the publication of his remarks. He also explained that President Wilson had conducted open press conferences in Washington, and that the secretary of state and some other U.S. cabinet members did the same. The newsmen left the meeting pleased and impressed, and with material for stories that appeared in their newspapers.

A near crisis followed. France's Premier Clemenceau, though a journalist himself, protested personally to Roosevelt that the style of his conference, with its informality, ready response to random questions, and remarks about the manner of such conferences in Washington, was inexpedient. French journalists, he complained, might now be encouraged to demand similar opportunities to meet with members of the French government and question them.

The Roosevelt conference in Paris had been conducted not only in the pattern of Washington conferences by then common, but in the spirit suggested in the first of President Wilson's "14 points" looking toward a peace settlement and calling for "open covenants openly arrived at." This was not acceptable to Clemenceau, Lloyd George, or some others. But it appealed to the public as a concept, and it was already accepted by British and U.S. correspondents. With the return of peace and wartime censorship no longer existing, they joined in a rather concerted demand that they be given improved access to information. French, Italian, and other correspondents followed that lead, as Clemenceau had feared, with impressive changes to come.

George Slocombe, Paris Peace Conference correspondent for the London *Daily Herald,* a British Labour party paper established in 1912 and entering a period of importance and strength in 1919, was one of several observers taking note of the new insistence by correspondents upon answers to their questions. In his book, *The Tumult and the Shouting* (1936), he wrote that correspondents at the conference had "a hand in the reporting of history, and sometimes in making it."

First, with reference to British correspondents, he said:

> As a body they were loyal, intelligent, conscientious, hard-working and patriotic. On the whole, they were as familiar with the questions at issue as the British ministers who crossed the Channel to represent Great Britain at the Peace Conference and at the many subsequent meetings with Allied statesmen. On the whole they reported the proceedings of those conferences fairly and intelligently, doing justice to the rival claims of contestants, and treating information imparted in confidence with the discretion imposed by the unwritten law of the Press. . . .

Slocombe then went on to refer to the U.S. correspondents:

> Able and enterprising, experienced and much-travelled as these British journalists in Paris and other capitals were, they were, however, out-numbered, out-paced, out-dared and out-travelled by their American colleagues.
>
> The war, in a great degree, discovered Europe to American newspapers as a field for news. It was a rich and exciting discovery, even if the field was to some extent closed by Allied censorships, and the difficulty of communications. The Armistice changed all that. Every boat from America brought fresh recruits to an army of correspondents.
>
> The American newspaper men swarmed all over the still-ravaged territories of the European belligerents. They came hungry for adventure, for news, for experience, for sensation, for novelty, for sex. They came with their bright and cynical eyes, their calm, unworried faces; their tireless industry, their cool courage; their infinite capacity for drinks, jesting, poker, and work; their insatiable curiosity, their generosity to a comrade, American or European; their professional pride, their calm assumption of equality with any king, president, statesman or newspaper reporter under the sun. . . .
>
> Their work was taken with the same zest that they showed in their pleasures. It was performed with intelligence, conscientiousness and honesty. . . . [Pp. 65–67]

As Slocombe indicated, both British and U.S. correspondents turned in 1919 from war correspondence, with its stress upon happenings, to the reporting of the highly complex political, economic and social problems of the peace-making and of a new world order. It was a concern not entirely new, but one that was to mark the next decade in the reporting of national and international subjects. It brought greater depth and substance to journalism than ever before, with more information and background on a host of subjects made available to the peoples of many lands. The degree to which those peoples actually paid attention to the riches offered them is another matter; some did, but many did not. Differences continued to exist between newspapers and in the relations between the press and governments. But the general quality of the press advanced from that time in countries where it was free to do so, where enough literate readers existed and enough who appreciated its contributions to knowledge.

From that period, the demands of the press for information, and its enterprise in seeking information, brought a new relationship between government officials and representatives of the press. The changes came in France, as elsewhere, and there was no general return to the older, more secretive relationship, except as all freedoms were compromised in some countries. Even there, for better or for worse, governments were obliged to pay new heed to public opinion, with some undertaking to manipulate it, rather than ignore it.

As 1920 dawned, only two countries in the world maintained a censorship—the new Soviet Union and Venezuela. The League of Nations, coming into existence then, also introduced a cordial working relationship with the press, and soon set an example for the peoples and governments of all nations as to what such a relationship might be, and might accomplish for the benefit of all mankind.

Patterned somewhat after practices already existing in Washington, an Information Section within the permanent Secretariat of the League was directed by Pierre Comert of France, and then by Arthur Sweetser, a citizen of the United States, even though the United States was never a member of the League. Comert had been Berlin correspondent for *Le Temps* of Paris. Sweetser had been assistant director of a Press Department attached to the United States Commission at the Paris Peace Conference, and he was familiar with the Washington press situation.

The League Information Section was well staffed and well conducted. Once organized, it went beyond anything known even in Washington to assist correspondents to report League activities in Geneva or elsewhere. It provided working space and the best in communication facilities, documents, and prompt summaries relating to all sessions of the League Assembly, Council, auxiliary committees, and special conferences. The League itself sponsored meetings concerned specifically with topics looking toward improved international news reporting.

Officials of most governments of the world, appearing repeatedly in Geneva, and correspondents also present for news agencies, newspapers, syndicates, and periodicals became personally acquainted. They dined together, drank together, and formed friendships. Old barriers thus vanished. The quality of information improved within the many areas of public affairs occupying the attention of the League and touching upon the human condition world-wide.

It was inevitable that observance of these benefits should encourage an adaptation of the League Information Section methods within the governments of many countries. Press bureaus or offices appeared in various capitals, staffed to provide information to the domestic press and to foreign correspondents, and with press conferences scheduled by officials or by their spokesmen as public information officers. Documents and texts of addresses were made available in advance, and communications facilities improved.

Such advances were by no means universal. Neither did they always exist or survive in a form dedicated to the provision of objective information and honest public guidance. Some information offices were turned to propaganda purposes, or the system was otherwise abused or misused. Yet the existence of an Information Section in the League Secretariat, along with the enterprise and determination of individual reporters and correspondents, brought a recognition by most governments of a need to improve communication with their own peoples, and those of the rest of the world. Given a proper freedom, along with a professionalism on the part of the press, the advantages of these changes outweighed their misuse by some governments.

Conference
Press Coverage

The war was not the only newsworthy event in the years between 1914 and 1918, but it did occupy the center of the stage, as did the Peace Conference in 1919. Once the Armistice had been signed, correspondents in Paris resumed civilian attire. Many turned to reporting the peace negotiations, and they were joined by specialists on international affairs coming from London, Rome, Washington, and elsewhere in the Allied and neutral world, but not at first from Berlin or other places in the Central Powers countries.

It is the newsman's task, at any time, to discover and isolate the essential facts. Notable skill was required to do that in the months of the

Peace Conference. The issues often were abstruse, frequently rooted in a long history, and possibly dull. The problem was made no easier by elements of controversy, nationalism, and secrecy in the negotiations. There was the added difficulty of making the subject matter of the reports clear to the reading public, and of adding meaning and interest. This needed to be done with sufficient brevity to assure use of a report competing for space with other news, and without doing violence to accuracy and perspective within a very limited period of time.

The correspondent's task was to obtain the facts each day about the progress of the peacemaking. He might look to the Cercle Française de Presse Étranger as one center of information. The French Bureau de la Presse, in the Quai d'Orsay, near the French Foreign Ministry, also continued during the conference as an information center. More important, however, each national press group had its own particular center or source attached to its official delegation to the conference.

The French press contacts remained largely indirect, in keeping with past practice. Premier Clemenceau and other government officials provided information as it suited their purpose to do so, but only to selected French journalists. There was an understanding that some of that information would be passed along, orally, to journalists of other countries. Under this system, information from the French delegation was channeled, among others, through André Tardieu, then foreign editor of *Le Temps,* and André Géraud, writing as "Pertinax" for *l'Echo de Paris,* and through the Agence Havas.

The official British delegation at the conference established itself in the Majestic and Astoria hotels. A press center there was headed by Sir George Riddell, publisher of the *News of the World* and also vice-president of the Newspaper Proprietors' Association. Riddell, closely associated with Prime Minister Lloyd George, was in effect his liaison man with the press. George Herbert Mair, formerly of the *Manchester Guardian,* was assistant to Riddell, and commonly met with correspondents to inform them of developments. Philip Kerr (later Lord Lothian), a secretary and adviser to the prime minister, was at times helpful to individual correspondents, within the discretionary limits of his position. Ralph Norman Angell (later Sir Norman Angell), first editor of the *Continental Daily Mail,* was a member of the British delegation and also helpful to correspondents. Contrary to the generally closed situation surrounding the French delegation, the British delegation's press center was open for guidance and information not only to British correspondents but to others as well. The same was true within the U.S. delegation and press center.

The United States delegation had its headquarters at the Crillon Hotel on the Place de la Concorde. President Wilson was in residence at the Villa Murat, several miles away, near the Porte de St. Cloud, but Robert Lansing, secretary of state, heading the official delegation, was at the Crillon. A Press Department was established adjacent to the Crillon at 4 Place de la Concorde, with a work room for correspondents included. The department was headed by Ray Stannard Baker, an experienced magazine writer and editor, who also had been a special commissioner in Europe for the Department of State in 1918. Arthur Sweetser, his chief assistant prior to the League's establishment, met regularly with correspondents.

The U.S. Press Department staff included Stephen Bonsal, correspondent for the *New York Herald* from 1885 to 1893, when he entered diplomatic service. Bonsal had been attached to Pershing's headquarters in 1918, with rank as a major and lieutenant-colonel, and then became confidential interpreter for President Wilson and for Colonel Edward M. House, aide and adviser to the president.[1] The staff also included Walter Lippmann, on leave from the *New Republic* and holding rank as a captain in the U.S. Army; Frank I. Cobb, chief of the editorial page of the *New York World,* a post to which Lippmann succeeded in 1929; and Charles Merz, also on leave from the *New Republic* and later editor of the *New York Times* in 1938.

Colonel House, Henry White experienced in the U.S. diplomatic service since 1883, and General Tasker H. Bliss, U.S. chief of staff, were members of the U.S. delegation and helpful in the provision of information to correspondents.

The Italian delegation conducted its press relations in somewhat the same indirect fashion as that used by the French. Under this arrangement, Luigi Barzini and Guglielmo Emanuel, correspondents for the *Corriere della Séra* of Milan, were prominent among Italian journalists meeting with Premier Orlando, while also transmitting certain information to journalists of other countries. The Italian situation differed from that of the French in one respect, for Salvatore Cortesi, representing the Associated Press in Rome, also had his own special relations with members of the delegation.

As the Peace Conference began, the French government made a suitable room available at the Ministry of Foreign Affairs on the Quai d'Orsay. There Clemenceau, Lloyd George, Wilson, and Orlando, the "Big Four," conducted their private conversations. Full publicity was

---

1   Bonsal's book, *Unfinished Business, Paris-Versailles, 1919,* telling the story of the conference, but only published in 1944, was awarded the Pultizer Prize in 1945 for letters, as the most distinguished book of the year relating to the history of the United States.

not to the taste of any of them. In the circumstances, it was doubly necessary for correspondents to find such indirect sources of information as they could. These usually were members of their own national delegations. Sometimes information was obtained from members of the other six delegations. Some such members might speak or reveal matters out of dissatisfaction or disillusionment with the course of negotiations. Journalists of the various nationalities, with their own sources, also exchanged information to their mutual advantage. With many news leaks, there was no shortage of subject matter for the press.

This means of reporting an international conference was not wholly satisfactory, nor did it assure accuracy. It was realistic, however, and was matched at later conferences and on other occasions where newsmen of various countries were concerned with bringing out facts for the information of the public, rather than lending themselves to a game of international politics and secret diplomacy.

With the Paris conference still limited to negotiations between the Allied and Associated Powers, but with differences obviously existing on certain points, the British and U.S. press departments—more open than the French or Italian—turned to holding some joint sessions to explain, so far as possible, the results of a day's discussions between the Big Four. Such Anglo-American sessions were not widely attended, however, because correspondents by then had become increasingly knowledgeable and many had developed their own sources of information.

Some British journalists had background and personal associations enabling them to write extremely well-informed reports without reference to what might be said by press officers of any government or delegation. This was notably so for Henry Wickham Steed, foreign editor of the *Times*. He was in Paris from January to April of 1919, when he returned to London to become editor of the paper. During his months in Paris, he was able to reach certain informed conclusions and turn to such sources as enabled him to write with unusual authority.

The Reuters agency was in a favored position. Not only was it represented by experienced correspondents, but the British government, having disbanded its wartime Ministry of Information immediately after the Armistice, requested Reuters to assume the special task of preparing official reports on the Paris negotiations for distribution to all British officials at home and abroad, as well as to the British press. The Press Association, working with Reuters and representing both the British provincial press and the Newspaper Proprietors' Association, joined in this arrangement.

Reuters had a considerable staff at the conference directed by William Turner, formerly in South Africa for the agency. As his chief assistants, he had Douglas Williams and Lester Lawrence, seasoned

European correspondents, and A. Kerr Bruce, Paris bureau chief. Sir George Riddell, head of the British delegation's press office, worked closely with these representatives. He provided information at all times, arranging, among other things, to relay to Reuters a verbatim report on the climactic ceremony during which the Treaty of Versailles was presented to the German plenipotentiaries in the Hall of Mirrors on June 28, 1919.

For the British newspapers, the *Times* representation in Paris was directed by George Jeffreys Adams, who also had directed the war staff in France. In addition to Steed, there was Arthur Willert. As Washington correspondent, he had been among those sailing with President Wilson in December 1918. He remained in Paris until the Versailles Treaty was signed in June 1919, and then returned with the president to Washington. Wythe Williams, wartime correspondent for the *New York Times*, was transferred after the Armistice to the service of the *Times* and the *Daily Mail*, both Northcliffe papers, and continued through the period of the conference.

Coverage for the *Daily Mail* was briefly in charge of George Curnock, and then of Valentine Williams after February. The staff included G. Ward Price, Douglas Crawford, Roland Atkinson, then editor of the *Continental Daily Mail,* and W. L. Warden, its assistant editor. Frederic William Wile, who had been in the London office of the *Daily Mail* through the war, after previous service as Berlin correspondent since 1906, had covered President Wilson's arrival in France in December 1918, his tour of European cities, and the early aspects of the Peace Conference. He returned to London in February 1919 and resigned from the *Daily Mail* in June to return to the United States as chief of the Washington bureau of the *Philadelphia Public Ledger.*

Sisley Huddleston, who had been wartime editor of the *Continental Daily Mail,* was another who left the Northcliffe organization after the Armistice. Depending largely upon his own sources, like Steed, he wrote of the Peace Conference for the Sunday *Observer,* the *Graphic,* and the *Westminster Gazette,* all of London, and also for the *Christian Science Monitor* of Boston. He later represented the *Monitor* in Paris after the peace settlement.

Other British correspondents reporting the conference included the veteran Dr. Emile Joseph Dillon, on virtually his last assignment for the *Daily Telegraph,* and W. A. Campbell, also for that paper. Philip Gibbs, Martin Donohue, John Hamilton, and G. H. Oerris, all wrote for the *Daily Chronicle;* Harry J. Greenwall, Hugh L. Mair, and Sidney Dark for the *Daily Express;* John Bell, H. Wilson Harris, General Sir

Frederick Maurice, A. F. Whyte (later Sir Frederick Whyte), and Norman Venner for the *Daily News;* Gordon D. Knox for the *Morning Post;* and George Slocombe for the *Daily Herald.* The *Manchester Guardian* was represented by J. L. Hammond, C. M. Lloyd, Rosalind Toynbee—one of the few women correspondents—and William Bolitho Ryall, a South African wounded during the war and entering upon a relatively brief but distinguished period as a writer and international news reporter under the foreshortened name of William Bolitho.

U.S. correspondents in Paris were joined at the time of the conference by a number of others arriving from London, New York, and Washington. They had the advantage of material especially prepared by the U.S. delegation press office to clarify subjects under discussion as the negotiations proceeded.

Whereas Clemenceau, Lloyd George, and Orlando met rather often with selected correspondents representing the press of their countries, Wilson did so only once, in February. On that occasion, he felt that one correspondent then had betrayed his confidence and, perhaps for that reason, held no other meetings, individually or collectively.

Baker, who saw the president each evening to go over the day's developments, was helpful to correspondents, and so was Sweetser. But they were not always fully informed, or at liberty to speak with complete freedom. U.S. correspondents, more than others, therefore had to try to develop such sources of information as they could, whether in or out of their own delegation.

News reporting was complicated for all because the issues were complex and because there was not always agreement even among members of the same delegation, or among press representatives of the various countries, as to what was happening at a given time, why it was happening, or whether members of the delegations were pursuing the "right" policy. Conflicts also arose between some delegations and newspapers of their own countries.

In England, for example, Lord Northcliffe and his newspapers, the *Times* and the *Daily Mail,* stood at odds on some points with Prime Minister Lloyd George. At the same time, Lloyd George had gained control of the *Daily Chronicle* in 1918, and was using its columns to support his purposes. President Wilson had encountered opposition to his views both from Lloyd George and Clemenceau. His differences with Clemenceau doubtless contributed to attacks upon him in some Paris newspapers, to criticism of the behavior of U.S. troops remaining in France, and even to interference with the dispatch of some news reports from Paris to the United States. Wilson also was under fire at home through the columns of the Hearst newspapers and some others.

Charles T. Thompson, Associated Press correspondent in France since 1902, saw Colonel House each day and received news matter and background information. But this ended in August 1919 when House had differences with President Wilson and left Paris. Secretary Lansing was helpful to correspondents, but on a selective basis, and with a certain stiffness, perhaps reflecting the stiffness in relations between Wilson and other members of the Big Four. This was not eased by an occasion when Clemenceau brought to Wilson a news report by a U.S. correspondent to which he found objection. It developed that the report had never been sent, in fact, but had been held up by a French censorship that supposedly had ended with the Armistice.

When the Treaty of Versailles was completed, whether in summary or in full text, it seemed to correspondents and many others to include some dubious provisions. This brought questions addressed to members of delegations that were not happily received in the closing period of the conference.

Among the estimated 600 correspondents in Paris for the world press during the height of the conference period, about 200 represented the U.S. agencies, newspapers, and services.

The Associated Press staff was headed by Elmer E. Roberts. Charles T. Thompson, his predecessor, actually in Italy during much of the war and wounded there, returned to Paris to direct conference coverage, following which he became head of the AP foreign service in New York. Salvatore Cortesi, chief of the AP Rome bureau, was in Paris for the conference, giving close coverage to the Italian delegation. Seymour Beach Conger, chief of the AP bureau in Berlin from 1911 to 1917, and then an adviser to the War Trade Board in Washington, returned to Europe as a member of the AP conference staff. Edwin Milton Hood, long chief of the Washington bureau, and Lionel Probert, also of that bureau, traveled to Paris with President Wilson. Melville E. Stone, general manager of the AP, arrived from New York. Seven AP correspondents who had covered aspects of the war also were members of the Paris staff: DeWitt Mackenzie, Charles Stephenson Smith, Norman Draper, Thomas P. Topping, Griffin Henry, Frank B. Grundy, formerly of the *New York Sun,* and L. F. Curtis.

The United Press conference staff was headed by Edward L. Keen, London bureau chief since 1911, with William Philip Simms, wartime Paris bureau chief, as his chief assistant. James H. Furay, foreign editor in New York, arrived in Paris, along with Carl D. Groat and Robert J. Bender of the Washington bureau, and Clarence Axman. Correspondents who had reported the war and continued in Paris included Fred S. Ferguson, Lowell Mellett, Henry Wood, and Webb Miller.

The International News Service coverage, bolstered in 1918–19, was directed by Fred J. Wilson, who was assisted by Henry Wales until he joined the *Chicago Tribune* staff in 1919, and by Newton C. Parke, Robert J. Prew, and John E. Nevin. For the Hearst Universal Service, established in 1918 to serve morning papers, Jay Jerome Williams, formerly of the INS Washington staff, was in Paris during the conference, along with Naboth Hedin, who had been accredited to the AEF during the war for the *Brooklyn Eagle.*

For the *New York Times,* conference coverage was directed by Richard V. Oulahan, normally chief of the paper's Washington bureau, along with Edwin L. James, Paris bureau chief. Others assisting were Walter Duranty and Charles A. Selden, both in Paris through the war years, Ernest Marshall, chief of the London bureau, and Gertrude Atherton, a novelist engaged to write special articles.

The *New York Tribune* reports of the conference were provided by Arthur S. Draper, London bureau chief, and Wilbur Forrest, Paris bureau chief. Frank H. Simonds, coming from the New York office, produced accounts going not only to the *Tribune* but to about 100 other newspapers through the McClure Newspaper Syndicate. Clinton Gilbert of the paper's Washington bureau had arrived with President Wilson. *Tribune* writers in Paris also included Willmott H. Lewis, Frederick Moore, Samuel Crowther, Ralph Courtney, Arthur M. Brece, and Bampton Hunt. The paper further used special articles by André Cheradame, a French writer, and George W. Wickersham, U.S. attorney general during the Taft administration and a member of the U.S. conference delegation.

The *New York World* coverage was directed by James M. Tuohy, chief of the London bureau, along with Lincoln Eyre, formerly of the *New York Times,* but then Paris correspondent for the *World.* Present also were Herbert Bayard Swope, formerly in Germany and Russia and Pulitzer Prize winner in 1917, who became editor of the morning *World* in 1920, Joseph Grigg and William Cook, correspondents during the war, and Louis Seibold and Charles M. Lincoln, both of whom arrived from New York.

The *Chicago Daily News* was served during the conference by Paul Scott Mowrer, Paris bureau chief, assisted by John Foster Bass, Louis Edgar Browne, E. Percy Noël and Harry Hansen, all of whom had reported aspects of the war. Charles H. Dennis, managing editor of the paper in Chicago, was present until the Treaty of Versailles was signed. Henry Justin Smith, news editor, followed Dennis and remained about six months, for Mowrer had a long overdue home leave.

The *Chicago Tribune* conference coverage was in charge of Floyd Gibbons at the outset, and then of Spearman Lewis, editor of the Army Edition of the *Tribune,* when Gibbons also took a home leave. Gibbons engaged Henry Wales, formerly of the INS, to help cover the conference. Others who assisted were Frederick A. Smith, Farmer Murphy, Parke Brown, T. S. Ryan of the Army Edition, John T. McCutcheon, again in Europe, and three others from the Chicago staff, Arthur M. Evans, Tiffany Blake, and Percy Hammond.

For the *New York Herald,* conference coverage was provided by J. Carlisle Macdonald, formerly of the *New York World,* Cameron Mackenzie, Herman Bernstein, formerly in Russia, Burr Price, Truman Talley, Paul Tyher, and May Birkhead of the Paris Edition of the *Herald.* The paper was operating at this time under a trusteeship following the death in May 1918 of James Gordon Bennett, Jr., its publisher. Under some financial stress, its future was uncertain and it was purchased in 1920 by Frank A. Munsey, along with the Paris Edition and Bennett's *New York Evening Telegram.*

The morning and evening *New York Sun,* already owned by Munsey since 1916, was represented at the conference by Thomas M. Johnson, who had been accredited to the AEF in 1917–18, and by Laurence Hills, who came from the Washington bureau as one of the group of correspondents accompanying President Wilson, and one of those accompanying him on his preconference tour of European cities. Hills became editor and general manager of the Paris Edition of the *New York Herald* when that paper became a Munsey property in 1920. A third member of the *Sun* conference staff was Burnet Hershey, formerly accredited to the AEF for the *New York Times.*

The *New York Evening Post* coverage of the conference was dircted by William G. Shepherd, who switched from the United Press, and was aided by Stoddard Dewey, long in Paris. David Lawrence, also for the *Post,* was another Washington correspondent arriving with the president. Harold P. Stokes and Simeon Strunsky came from the New York office. Oswald Garrison Villard, owner of the paper from 1900 until its 1918 sale, arrived to write for the weekly magazine, the *Nation,* long published under the wing of the newspaper and retained when the sale was made.

Other U.S. correspondents included some who had reported the war and some who came to cover the conference. Among them was Arthur B. Krock, editor of the afternoon *Louisville Times,* who wrote for that paper and for the companion morning *Louisville Courier-Journal.* Raymond S. Tompkins, with the AEF for the *Baltimore Sun,* was joined by J. Fred Essary, Washington correspondent for the paper. For the *Brooklyn Eagle,* in the same fashion, Guy C. Hickok was joined by C. C. Brainerd. Herbert Corey continued as a representative of the Associated Newspapers, and E. M. Thierry and Harold Edwin Bechtol for the NEA. Will Irwin was present for the *Saturday Evening Post,* and H. R. Baukhage for the Army newspaper, the *Stars and Stripes.* New arrivals also included James Montague, *New York American,* Jay G. Hayden, *Detroit News,* William Allen White for the Wheeler Newspaper Syndicate, Mark Sullivan and Berton Braley for *Collier's Weekly,* and Lewis Gannett for *Survey* magazine.

The French press naturally was fully represented at the conference, although primarily through the Agence Havas and the major Paris information papers. The agency was under the direction of the elderly Charles Lafitte. Charles Houssaye, as news manager, exercised broad control over conference coverage. Executives André Meynot and Ernest Barbier worked closely with the French government and its delegation and controlled staff assignments. For the Paris newspapers, André Tardieu of *Le Temps* and André Géraud of *l'Echo de Paris* have been mentioned, but reporters and editorial commentators were active for such other dailies as *Le Matin, Le Journal, Le Petit Parisien,* and *Le Figaro.*

Among about forty-five correspondents for the Italian press, there were Barzini of *Il Corriere della Sèra;* Virginio Gayda for *Il Messaggero* of Rome, Emmanuele Ceria, long-time Paris correspondent for *Il Stampa* of Turin and other newspapers, and representatives of the Agenzia Stefani.

There were about twenty correspondents each for the Belgian, Greek, and Spanish presses, although some were stringers. There were approximately a dozen each from Switzerland and Portugal, and about a dozen from Norway, Sweden, and Denmark combined. There were almost as many for the press of Holland, and a few from Finland and from the Baltic areas of Latvia, Lithuania, and Estonia, soon to become independent republics. About thirty-five came from what also would soon be the Polish republic, about twenty-five from what would become Czechoslovakia, and several from Serbia and the area that would become Yugoslavia. The press of Rumania was represented by about twenty-five correspondents, and there even were representatives of the new Soviet Russia press.

From Japan, Seziko Uyeda, chief editor of the Nippon Dempo Tsushin-sha (Dentsu) agency was in Paris. So was J. Russell Kennedy, director of the Kokusai agency. There were correspondents for the leading Japanese dailies, *Asahi, Mainichi,* and *Yomiuri.* Several correspondents represented the press of China. About twenty-five were in Paris for the Brazil press, fourteen were writing for *La Prensa, La Nación,* and other papers in Argentina, and still another twenty-five for newspapers of other countries in South America and Central America.

When the German delegation arrived in Versailles in May, it was accompanied by fifteen correspondents, including Dr. Heinrich Mantler, director of the Wolff-Continental agency, and also including Theodor Wolff, distinguished editor of the *Berliner Tageblatt* and formerly its Paris correspondent. The Austrian delegation, arriving in September, also brought its own press group, including Dr. Joseph Karl Wirth, director of the Korrburo agency of that country.

The Treaty of Versailles, completed late in April 1919, and presented to the German plenipotentiaries at Versailles on May 7, remained a confidential document in its full text until early June. It might have remained so at least until signed at Versailles on June 28, had it not been for the press.

The first hint of the treaty's terms came in a report in the *New York Sun* of May 8 by its correspondent Burnet Hershey, and regarded by Knightley as "one of the few scoops of the whole peace conference." Hershey tells of it in his own book, *How I Got That Story* (1967). It arose from a desire to know how the German plenipotentiaries might react to the provisions of the treaty once they received it.

The German delegation, under Count Ulrich von Brockdorff-Rantzau, was housed at the Hôtel des Réservoirs. The German press correspondents were at the adjacent Hôtel Vatel. Both were surrounded by tight security. Each morning, the correspondents moved in a group from the Vatel to the Hôtel des Réservoirs for a briefing by some member of the delegation.

Hershey became familiar with this pattern of procedure. In a manner reminiscent of earlier exploits of Dillon, *Daily Telegraph* correspondent in Russia and a master of disguise when it proved useful in obtaining information, Hershey dressed in a pair of striped trousers, a frock coat, Tyrolean hat, wore heavy spectacles and carried a well-worn briefcase. So attired, he used his own press pass to enter the Hôtel Vatel. There he waited for the German correspondents to assemble and joined them as they set off for the other Versailles hotel.

Speaking in German, he introduced himself to the nearest in the group, a correspondent for the *Berliner Tageblatt,* possibly Wolff, who apparently admired Hershey's enterprise and helped him gain entrance to the press room at the Hôtel des Réservoirs. There he talked with other correspondents, agreed to do some shopping for them in Paris, and joined them again in the same fashion a few days later.

What Hershey wanted was an interview with Count von Brockdorff-Rantzau. This he never gained. On May 7, however, he was among the Allied and German correspondents present at Versailles when Clemenceau presided at the ceremony during which the treaty was given to the German delegation. In his disguise, Hershey returned to the Hôtel des Réservoirs with the German correspondents. Quite without intending it, he found himself seated next to Brockdorff-Rantzau as he spoke to the correspondents. The count expressed his resentment of the treaty terms and "insults" by Clemenceau. This was not an interview, but it was an exclusive account of the first official German response to the general terms of the treaty, and Hershey hastened to the U.S. press room near the Hotel Crillon to write his story.

Paul Scott Mowrer, of the *Chicago Daily News,* through the cautious interposition of Colonel House, was permitted to see a copy of the full treaty a few days later in May, and he cabled essential parts of it for publication in the *Daily News.* This provided more information than had so far been available about some terms of the treaty. But it still was not the whole document awaited by many.

An official summary was released in Paris later in the month, which received wide publication. Running to 16,000 words, it was cabled to New York, the longest single press message so transmitted up to that time. But it was still only a summary. The German delegation had received the full text on May 7 and the United States Senate, for one, thought it had a right to see that same text. Pending its actual signature by the Germans, however, President Wilson chose to withhold it in accordance with a decision by the Big Four.

The delegations of the ten Allied and Associated Powers represented in Paris all had received full-text copies of the treaty. It seemed possible that at least one delegation or one official might not approve withholding that treaty from the public until the time of its signature. Late in May, Spearman Lewis of the *Chicago Tribune* found that one, a member of the Chinese delegation. Rather duplicating the feat of Henri de Blowitz, who had obtained an advance copy of the full treaty concluded at the Congress of Berlin in 1878 following the Russo-Turkish War, with its first publication in the *Times,* Lewis obtained a full copy of the Treaty of Versailles.

At that juncture, Frazier Hunt, who had been in the Archangel area of Russia as a *Tribune* correspondent with U.S. forces there, returned to Paris. As Donald Mackenzie Wallace had carried that Treaty of Berlin in great secrecy from Berlin to London, so Hunt acted as a courier in 1919 and carried the Treaty of Versailles from Paris to Chicago as promptly as ship and rail allowed. The *Tribune* did not use the treaty, but Colonel McCormick directed Hunt to proceed to Washington and give the text personally to Senator William E. Borah of Idaho, chairman of the Senate Foreign Relations Committee.

Borah, a Republican party member, who was a leader in later Senate action to deny ratification of the treaty by the United States and thus foreclose its membership in the League of Nations, acted immediately to have the full text of the treaty published in the *Congressional Record* of June 9.

The Washington bureau of the *New York Times,* learning of the prospective publication and working from wet proofs of the *Congressional Record* pages, opened twenty-four telephone and telegraph lines to New York to transmit the complete text to the paper. Even as that transmission was proceeding, Edwin L. James who was visiting Germany, cabled New York that he probably could get a copy of the treaty from sources there if the paper wished. Van Anda was able to reply that the paper already had the treaty. It was published in the *Times* of June 10, occupying nearly eight solid pages of type in a forty-eight page edition. Only one other newspaper in the world published the full text. *La Prensa* of Buenos Aires received the text from New York through the United Press and published it also on June 10.

The publication of the full text of the treaty in the *Congressional Record* of June 9 and in the two newspapers made possible extensive and accurate reports on its terms throughout the world.

Despite German opposition to parts of the treaty, its representatives signed the document with minor changes in the Hall of Mirrors ceremony on June 28, with the world press represented. It was ratified at Weimar on July 7 and in the Allied countries, except for the United States, in October. By that time, a treaty with Austria had been signed, and those with Bulgaria, Hungary, and Turkey were in prospect.

By October 1919 it became possible to consider restoring a normal international exchange of news. Before the end of the year new contracts were signed between Ring Combination agencies in the countries formerly at war. Again, they recognized various exclusive and shared territories for the distribution of service and were to be effective for ten years.

The contracts differed in some respects from those of 1914, however.

The Associated Press by 1919 occupied an unquestioned position of equality with Reuters and Havas as a world agency. The Wolff agency lost some of its former exclusive territory, which was now shared by Reuters and Havas. There also were changes in some associated agencies within the Ring Combination. Soviet Russia was uninvolved for the time being. The Norsk Telegrambyrå of Norway, formerly a Wolff subsidiary, in 1918 had become a cooperative agency owned by Norwegian member papers. Other changes came in 1920. The Svenska Telegrambyrå of Sweden, also formerly of Wolff subsidiary, became a new independent agency in 1921, Tidiñiñgarñas Telegrambyrå (TT). New agencies were established in Austria and Hungary to replace the Korrburo and the UTB, and also in Belgium, Poland, the three new Baltic republics, in newly formed Czechoslovakia, and in what was to become Yugoslavia.

The four years of war, followed by a year and a half of peace negotiations, created a vigorous and continuing appetite for information among a very substantial segment of the world's people. It had stimulated and required a greater effort by the press on an unprecedented scale, almost regardless of expense.

The Paris conference had demanded an examination of political, economic, social, and ethnic topics, with an extension of public awareness and thought. There was to be no retreat to a world of simpler times or lesser issues—rather the contrary. A greater attention went also to scientific matters and cultural interests. The press and public had no choice other than to move with events. A new generation had received a painful induction into a new period of history, but entered it with a greater maturity. There was reason to believe that the peoples of the world would be better informed and therefore prepared to conduct their affairs more wisely. Problems existed, and others were to be expected, but if human intelligence had validity, and surely it did, there was hope for a brighter era.

Part III
New Dimensions in Information

As the year 1920 dawned, a fresh page was spread upon which to begin a new chapter in history. The Great War was at an end. It left reasonable persons persuaded that modern weaponry had made war too high a price to pay for whatever conceivable gain it might bring even to the victors. The war had made it apparent that no people, wherever they might dwell, were unaffected by events in other parts of the globe. Such events did not need to reach the point of war to shape the relationships between peoples of a world that had become suddenly close-knit and complex—almost frighteningly so.

The end of the war did not heal its scars or restore the economies of nations. Unemployment, hunger, misery, and fear were the lot of millions. Even those most hopeful of solutions for the world's ills could not fail to be aware of the fallibility of the human species, and of the alternate gains and reverses recorded in the sweep of history. In 1920, if there were to be gains, many saw these as attached to a greater availability of formal educational opportunities, along with a greater service of public information and understanding provided by a free and responsible press. Thus people might be prepared to cope with events, be prepared to view them in an informed perspective, and to respond with wisdom.

Advances were made in fact in both respects, beginning in the 1920s. Schools, colleges, and universities in many countries opened their doors, raised the level of literacy, and provided a larger and better prepared audience for the media of information. At the same time, there was a wider and more sympathetic recognition in the 1920s than ever before of the role the press might play in establishing a general understanding beneficial to peoples everywhere. Further, the press and companion media growing in professional competence and prosperity provided an improved report.

Highly significant, in that respect, were new dimensions brought to the information process in the decade or two following the war. These included great improvements in communications: the introduction of radio broadcasting, notable advances in photography, photo-engraving, motion pictures, and in recording, changes in periodicals by which greater attention was given to public affairs, and new ways of focusing attention on such affairs.

Radio-telegraphy, Beam Wireless, and the RCA

With the Armistice of November 1918, the wartime restriction placed upon the commercial use of wireless by the Allies came to an end. Its wartime use by governments and military elements had brought technical advances, and its development proceeded rapidly in a variety of applications. News transmission and radio broadcasting were among them.

The coverage of news has point only as current information reaches the public with the least possible delay. The science and technology of communication seemed to have attained something close to perfection by 1920. One wonder had followed another since about 1840, with the telegraph, the submarine cable, the telephone, wireless telegraphy, and the teleprinter all in the service of the press and the people. But there was more to come.

The first use of wireless in 1898, as given practical application by Guglielmo Marconi, had suffered because the spark-and-arc method of transmitting code signals was noisy and difficult to control. The signals spread in concentric circles from the point of transmission, or "radiated"—from which the term "radio" was to derive. The signals faded over distances, and were lost. If two or more transmitters were operating at the same time, there was interference, with no signal readable and lost in the scramble of noise.

Experiments had proceeded through the years, conducted by pioneers of wireless communication. These included Marconi himself, R. A. Fessenden, Edwin H. Armstrong, Thomas A. Edison, Lee DeForest, Sir John Ambrose Fleming, C. S. Franklin, and Michael Pupin.

Important contributions also were made by John J. McCarty, engineer for the American Telephone & Telegraph Company (AT&T); by Swedish-born Ernst F. W. Alexanderson and by Irving Langmuir, both with the General Electric Company (GE) in Schnectady, N.Y.; by Frank Conrad of the Westinghouse Electric and Manufacturing Company (Westinghouse) in Pittsburgh; and Alexander Meissner of the German Telefunken Company.

Experimentation and invention by 1920 had solved most of the problems mentioned. It had been recognized from the outset that electrical energy emitted in wireless transmission moved in the form of waves. Experimentation revealed that the waves varied in length and in breadth and were subject to atmospheric influences, but could be controlled. The control was made possible through the use of a high-frequency generator devised by Fessenden, a vacuum audion amplifer tube invented by DeForest, with refinements added by Armstrong, and an alternator device developed by Alexanderson.

These particular inventions had been produced and patented in the United States between 1906 and 1915. With the control of signals that they made possible, the International Telegraphic Union (ITU) in Berne, exercising a regulatory authority over electrical communications, also could assign various wavelengths upon which individual transmitters might operate worldwide without signals overlapping, thus avoiding interference and chaos in transmission.

The electromagnetic waves generated for the transmission of wireless signals are classified as to frequency within the total spectrum as "low," "medium," and "high," and indeed as "very high," "ultra high," and beyond. The length of the waves, from crest to crest, varies in the same respective order, from "long" to "medium" to "short."

In the assignment of frequencies, under the authority of the ITU, amateurs, or "ham" operators, had been given the right to transmit within the short wave "band" of high frequency, rather than in the more commonly used medium wave band, or the long-wave band of low frequency. Each of those bands was subject to divisions by which transmitting stations even within the band might each broadcast signals on its own assigned frequency. This meant that signals were carried on waves of a particular length, measured in meters, with a frequency range measured in kilocycles or megacycles.

In England, Marconi and Franklin of the British Marconi Wireless Telegraph Company undertook experiments in 1916 involving the use of the short waves. They learned that such signals were better received over long distances than those transmitted within the long-wave band, then in general use. They learned also that by placing what amounted to a reflector behind a transmitter the shortwave signal could be focused or "beamed" in a particular direction, rather than being diffused in all directions like ripples on a pond. Given a focused projection in a desired direction, the signal thus concentrated gained strength, traveled farther, and was received with greater clarity, while actually using less power.

Contributing greatly to the effectiveness of beamed transmission was Fessenden's high frequency generator utilizing a continuous wave principle, Alexanderson's alternator, and of course the DeForest and Armstrong audion amplifier tube. The great potentialities of these devices in world wireless developments was obvious to specialists in the field, and not least to Marconi. In 1917 and 1918, therefore, the British Marconi Company in concert with other British interests long prominent in communications sought to buy control of the patents to those inventions.

Whether they would have been sold is a matter of conjecture. In any case, alert individuals in the United States brought the issues involved to the attention of President Wilson and others. It was pointed out that such a sale would give British interests, already dominant in world cable communications, a disproportionate control of wireless and other means of communication then recognized as in prospect—radiotelegraphy, radiotelephony, and voice radio.

Because the United States government then held extraordinary wartime controls over communications and finance alike, action was taken to block any sale of the patents. Official pressure was brought on the American Telephone & Telegraph Company, which controlled the DeForest patents involved, and on the General Electric Company, controller of the Alexanderson patents, to prevent their transfer to any interests outside the United States.

With the direct encouragement of the government, a Radio Corporation of America (RCA) was organized in 1919 as an independent business venture to hold and develop the DeForest and Alexanderson patents, and others in the communications and electronics field. Associated in the formation and control of the new RCA were the AT&T, the General Electric Company, and the General Fruit Company of Boston. The latter company operated a limited wireless service under the name of the Tropical Radio Telegraph Company, with circuits between its Boston headquarters and Miami, New Orleans, and ports in the Caribbean. It was one of four small U.S. companies operating wireless services in the interests of private corporations, handling some commercial messages, but never any press business.[1]

The RCA opened a wireless service in March 1920 on a New York–London circuit, with Paris, Berlin, and Rome included in 1921. The 1920–22 period was enormously active for the new corporation,

---

1   The other three were: Globe Wireless, Ltd., for the Robert Dollar Steamship Company, operating chiefly in the Pacific and Caribbean; the United States–Liberia Radio Corporation, for the Firestone Tire and Rubber Company; and the South Porto Rico Sugar Company, with an otherwise untitled circuit between Puerto Rico and points in the West Indies and to Venezuela.

even though it was faced with great complexities. These had begun with the Marconi company's attempt to gain control of U.S.-registered patents, but relations with the Marconi enterprises continued.

The original Marconi Wireless Telegraph and Signal Company, formed in England in 1897, had been reorganized in 1900 as the Marconi Wireless Telegraph Company, with a separate Marconi International Marine Communication Company concerned with ship-to-shore and ocean wireless communication. A Marconi Wireless Telegraph Company of America was formed in 1901, and a Marconi Company of Canada. In 1906 a subsidiary of the British Marconi Company was formed in Argentina and later undertook to erect a transmitter near Buenos Aires, but its completion was interrupted by the war. The British company also had entered into a contract with the young Chinese Republic early in 1914 to erect and equip wireless stations in China, but this project also was interrupted by the war.

Meanwhile, the German Telefunken system had organized a government-controlled Gesellschaft für Drahtlose Telegrafie. This company had a part in the establishment of a German-owned wireless station in Argentina during the war. Early in 1917, it also contracted with the Chinese government to erect stations in that country, thus moving into areas in Argentina and China that the Marconi Company had felt temporarily unable to develop. In China, however, the German company was no more successful and, in the end, wholly unsuccessful in both countries.

In August 1917, China declared war on Germany and Austria-Hungary. Germany's surrender in 1918, and the terms of the Versailles Treaty resulted in the German company's contract with the Chinese government being taken over by Mitsui Bussan Kaisha, Ltd., of Japan. At the same time the Marconi Company renewed its 1914 contracts and, in association with the Peking government, formed a Chinese National Wireless Telegraph Company in 1919, with a twenty-year contract to manufacture equipment as required. The German company's interest in the Argentine station also was brought into question under the provisions of the Versailles Treaty.

All of these circumstances bore upon the development of the Radio Corporation of America in its own establishment of international wireless circuits. First, the British Marconi Company, in part because of its failure to obtain the DeForest and Alexanderson patents, was prepared to sell its own interest in the Marconi Wireless Telegraph Company of America, founded in 1901, and that company accordingly was taken over as a part of the RCA. The RCA joined with the British

Marconi Company, the French Compagnie Générale Télégraphie sans Fil, and the German Gesellschaft für Drahtlose Telegrafie in a consortium whereby, rather than erecting separate transmitters in South America, they joined in sharing the facilities of the German-owned station near Buenos Aires. This station was enlarged to handle the traffic of the four companies.

A third and more complex element arose in China, reflecting the politics of international communications. There in January 1921 the Chinese government concluded an agreement with the Federal Telegraph Company, a California enterprise, by which that company was to erect and operate wireless stations in Shanghai, Peking, Canton, Hankow, and Harbin for communication within China, in the Pacific area, and beyond.

This brought immediate protests from the British, Japanese, and Danish governments. They held it in violation of contractual rights granted to the British Marconi Company in 1914 and reaffirmed in 1918–19, of rights granted to the Japanese Mitsui Company in 1919, and of rights granted in 1896 by the former Chinese imperial government to the Danish Great Northern Telegraph Company, as well as to the British Eastern Extension, Australasian and China Telegraph Company, Ltd., and due to continue until 1930.

The United States government, responding to these protests on behalf of the Federal Telegraph Company, denied the validity of any exclusive foreign rights to engage in the communications business in China. The matter was argued at the Washington Naval Conference of 1921–22. Contrary to the wishes of the United States, but as an element in the political pressures involved, British support was given to Japan's bid for control under a League of Nations mandate over the former German-held island of Yap, a Pacific cable point in the Caroline Islands group. By agreement in 1922, the mandate did go to Japan, but the United States gained compensating cable and radiotelegraphic rights. The RCA also took over the Federal Telegraph Company contracts in China in 1922. It did not receive the right to operate there, however; until 1927, and only then by reason of new agreements at an International Radiotelegraphic Conference in Washington in that year. Even with that, because the British and Danish contracts of 1896 with the former Chinese imperial government did not expire until December 31, 1930, the RCA did not begin to construct wireless stations in China until 1931.

When the RCA was formed in 1919, the Westinghouse Electric and Manufacturing Company of Pittsburgh, chief competitor of General

Electric, was omitted from the group and undertook in 1920 to build a communications empire of its own. It had use of patents held by Frank Conrad, Westinghouse engineer, and also gained the right to use certain Armstrong and Pupin patents. It also made an arrangement with the International Radio and Telegraph Company (IRTC), which was inactive but controlled important Fessenden patents. It soon became evident, however, that the Westinghouse-IRTC combination was not going to be able to gain foreign agreements that would be needed to assure a satisfactory world radiotelegraphic service. The result was that Westinghouse-IRTC joined the RCA group of companies in July 1921, with the patents it held also made available to the RCA.

With the Westinghouse addition, and the Federal Telegraph Company contracts in China, plus the consortium in South America, the basic RCA structure was established by 1922. It possessed rights to more than 2,000 patents in the wireless and radio communications field, and that number was doubled by 1930. To handle its international wireless and radiotelegraphic business, a subsidiary was formed— R.C.A. Communications, Inc. (RCAC). A second subsidiary was formed to handle ship-to-shore communications, the Radio Marine Corporation of America (RMCA). Supplementing its wireless service between New York and European capitals, as opened in 1920–21, RCA developed service in 1922 between San Francisco, Honolulu, and Tokyo and, by 1927, Manila and Hong Kong were included. The service was further extended to Latin American points in 1930, to China in 1931, and by 1939 RCAC had fifty-two international circuits in operation, with that number to continue to rise.

The only major competition for RCA from any U.S.-owned enterprises in international wireless communication came after 1927 from the International Telephone and Telegraph Company (IT&T), formed in 1921, and two of its subsidiaries, All-America Cables and Radio, Inc., and the Mackay Radio and Telegraph Company, in ship-to-shore communications. The IT&T, a highly successful enterprise, might have acquired ownership of the RCA in 1930 had it not been for congressional intervention, mindful of the reasons for the organization of the RCA in 1919. Although not precisely competitive, the United States Navy wireless stations, by special congressional authorization, carried some non-governmental traffic, including press dispatches, between Peking, Manila, Guam, Honolulu, and San Francisco, both eastward and westward, in the years between 1921 and 1930.

Meanwhile, the British Marconi Company, even though having failed to gain control of the DeForest and Alexanderson patents, was enabled to use those patents under license and to continue in the development of the beam system of point-to-point transmission. That system had so demonstrated its superiority by 1924 that the British government approved the construction of a chain of shortwave transmitters throughout the empire, or the British Commonwealth of Nations, as it became in 1926. Keyed from a station built by the British Marconi Company at Hillmorton, near Rugby, and under the ownership of the British General Post Office, the system went into operation in 1926. The Rugby station then was the most powerful in the world, superceding both the U.S. Navy transmitter constructed at New Brunswick, New Jersey, in 1917, and a Dutch government transmitter completed soon after the war near The Hague, to link Holland with its colonial possessions in the East and West Indies.

The beam system of transmission, developing rapidly, was used not only in the British service, but by the RCA and others. This manner of transmission of code signals by wireless became known after 1926 as "radiotelegraphy," by way of distinguishing it from the earlier method under which signals, carried by long waves, spread in concentric circles from the point of transmission, even though on assigned wavelengths. The term distinguished such transmission from the conventional landline telegraphy, from voice radio, then growing in importance throughout the world, and from radiotelephony, also beginning to appear as an alternative to the transmission of telephone messages by wire or cable.

The League of Nations had established its own communications facilities at Geneva. Correspondents might use shortwave wireless to transmit their reports to any part of the world. Shortwave voice broadcasts could be made by 1932, and radiotelephone service became available. At the same time, the Swiss Helvetian wireless was open for use by the Swiss national news agency, ATS, to disseminate reports to the press within the country itself.

Multiple-
Address
Transmission   A system of news transmission had its origin in 1931 that combined the advances of beamed radiotelegraphy with parallel advances in the automatic teleprinter by which it might become a "radioprinter,"

activated by wireless or radio signals, rather than by impulses moving by wire or cable. It was referred to variously as "multiple address," "multiple-direction transmission," "multiple-directional broadcasting," "multiple destination transmission," and as "Scheduled Transmission Service" or STS.

The system made it possible for a news agency to broadcast from a central transmitter, or to beam the service to a particular segment of the globe, for direct reception by newspapers or other agencies in their own offices on radioprinters equipped to receive the radiotelegraphic signals and convert them into typewritten copy for immediate editing and use. It was a system that eliminated intermediate point-to-point circuits for the relay of dispatches, as well as any concern for cables and telegraph lines. It therefore had the effect of reducing transmission costs and avoided isolated delays. The teleprinter replaced by the radioprinter, permitted the delivery of news reports even in places where no telegraph service was available, made the reports available to any number of papers simultaneously, and greatly sped the process.

The technical development of the principles of the multiple address system occurred earlier, but the Agence Havas was the first to put it to practical use in 1931. It then introduced a "Havasian service" broadcast to South America, and to North America and Asia. The service was improved and extended in 1933 following the completion of a new and powerful shortwave transmitter operating twenty-one hours a day at Pontoise, near Paris.

Léon Rollin, inspector general for the agency, later said that "Havas was the first great news agency that thought radio transmission could be useful and helpful to press associations." The Havas agency, he said, had experimented for several years and had concluded that by its use the agency could sell its service at a lower price. "South America is covered with one transmission from Paris," he said. "There is no cable cost. All cities of the continent are covered simultaneously."

The low rates that the Agence Havas was able to set for its service to South American dailies in 1931 dismayed the three U.S. agencies by then also active there, the UP, AP, and INS. They suspected that Havas was receiving an added subsidy from the French government with a view to supporting France's position in a world of growing crisis. That subsidy was in fact increased, but it was the technology of the system that made the low-cost service possible, as it soon did also for other agencies.

In Great Britain, the Reuters agency established a "Reuterian toll service" beginning in November 1932 that made effective use of the multiple address system. From transmitters at Rugby and Leafield, its news reports and its service of commercial information and stock and commodity prices were beamed to newspapers and other subscribers throughout the world on a twenty-four-hour schedule. Starting modestly, it was in full operation by 1939.

With news agency services being broadcast by the multiple address system, there was nothing to prevent almost any newspaper in the world, given possession of a radioprinter, from pirating dispatches without payment. There is no evidence that this occurred, but it was a possibility. Also, the system tended to threaten the sanctity of the exclusive territories for the distribution of news by the big three agencies, as maintained since 1870 within the Ring Combination association of national and world news agencies. Yet two of those world agencies, Havas and Reuters, were using multiple transmission by 1932.

The Deutsches Nachrichten Büro (DNB), which replaced the Wolff agency, the third of the big three, following the National Socialist assumption of government control in Germany in 1933, also then entered into multiple transmission to South America, Asia, and other parts of the world. In this it was joined by the Transozean service. As official Nazi government enterprises, both departed from Ring Combination standards and injected propaganda into their services. This combination of circumstances contributed to the suspension of the Ring Combination in 1934.

Something rather comparable to a multiple-address system had been used in the Soviet Union as early as 1925 to enable the official TASS agency, formed in that year, to distribute its reports to publications appearing in areas of the U.S.S.R. not then served by telegraph or telephone. The TASS reports were read over the radio at dictation speed at certain times of the day, with notes made by staff members of newspapers and transcribed for publication. It was a radio version of the "pony service" provided in telephone hookup by the AP and UP in parts of the United States prior to the war.

In Italy, a first use of shortwave voice radio was made in 1930 by the Agenzia Stampa, a small agency unrelated to the official Agenzia Stefani, but equally controlled by the Fascist government of the country at that time. Its reports were directed to South America, had a distinct propaganda content, and marked the beginning of an air-borne propaganda war due to increase in scope, tempo, and virulence.

The landline telegraph and telephone systems after 1920 were even more important than they had been before as elements in the world communication network. The development of radiotelegraphy and radiotelephony became greatly competitive, however.

Press dispatches long had formed a large part of the volume of telegraphic and cable traffic. The diversion of a considerable part of that transmission to wireless or radiotelegraphic circuits after the war was a matter of concern to cable communication companies. British cable companies, controlling more than half of the world's undersea lines, were losing an important revenue return to the radiotelegraphic services, and radiotelephony soon threatened also to compete seriously with telephone cables. There was some glum speculation that cables might become obsolete as a means of moving information. Ocean cables were expensive to lay and maintain; wireless stations were less costly, and one station also could handle traffic to and from many places. This permitted lower rates for transmission, and invited even greater patronage.

The high per-word rates set for the transmission of messages in the nineteenth century had been greatly reduced by 1920, and special press rates were even lower. Through the use of leased wires and teleprinters, news agencies were able to deliver a full news report to any one newspaper within a country at a reasonable cost. In Europe, where the telegraph lines were government-owned and where news agencies might also receive government subsidies, the cost was particularly low. This, however, did not necessarily save costs for an individual newspaper maintaining a service of its own, to supplement the news agency service, or receiving other services by telegraph.

The cost for dispatches received from points requiring cable transmission across the Atlantic or Pacific or by way of the Arabian Sea and the Mediterranean was another matter. There were no cable lease arrangements to be made, even by a news agency. The regular rates and the press rates had been reduced for cable transmission, as for telegraphic transmission, but those rates were not necessarily low, and the volume of news transmitted also had increased greatly, with expenses in proportion.

In North Atlantic cable transmission it sometimes was possible for a news agency to arrange for segments of time for cable use. The only real economy for cable use, however, beyond that provided by the press rate, was to prepare dispatches in that abbreviated form of writing known as "cablese." It was necessary, also, for correspondents to cope with delays. In the 1920s, a U.S. correspondent in Paris, for example, was obliged to prepare and file copy with an allowance of five hours for delivery in New York. The same applied to news copy moving eastward from New York or Washington to London or Paris. Delays even greater applied to Pacific traffic, with costs also higher.

The cables in operation world-wide in 1920 totalled approximately 320,000 nautical miles. Of these, about 242,000 miles were controlled by private companies and the rest by governments. Of about twenty-seven companies, ten in four countries controlled close to 208,000 nautical miles, or 68 percent of the total. Testimony before the U.S. Senate Naval Affairs Committee in 1919 ascribed 51 percent of all cables to British interests, both private and governmental, 26½ percent to private companies in the United States, 9 percent to France, 7½ percent to Germany, presumably on the basis of prewar figures, and 1 percent each to Italy, Spain, and Japan.

Later estimates varied. German cable holdings were reduced, under the terms of the Versailles Treaty, from 23,000 nautical miles to about 2,400 miles. The largest individual holding in 1923 was by the British Eastern Telegraph Company, with 153 cables totalling 52,000 nautical miles and operated by three inter-related Eastern companies. The Western Union Telegraph Company of the United States was second, operating 21,000 nautical miles of cable. French interests then held 18,000 nautical miles, of which 14,000 miles were government-owned.

Most cables were short, linking coastal points and islands. Of the longer cables, those spanning the North Atlantic numbered twenty-one by 1929, of which sixteen were U.S.-owned or operated under lease from British owners, notably by Western Union. Two were British-owned and operated, and three were French. The South Atlantic then was spanned by four cables, three British and one Italian. But four other British cables from England to the West Indies also had connections with Latin American points, and another extended northward to the Bahamas, Bermuda, and Halifax. North America also was linked to the West Indies and Central and South America by ten U.S.-owned cables, of which the first to provide direct communication with the east coast of South America went into operation in July 1925.

Apart from the long 1865 Indo-European overland telegraph line and the 1868 Great Northern Telegraph Company line across Siberia, other Asian points, Australia and New Zealand, and points in Africa as well, were brought into cable connection with Europe and with the rest of the world between 1869 and 1874. The first long cables across the Pacific between North America and Asian points became operative between 1902 and 1905.

As 1920 began, cables had been in operation in parts of the world since 1851, greatly extended since the 1870s, and replaced where necessary with improved construction and armoring for durability and efficiency. Cables laid before 1902 could carry messages at the rate of only about twenty-five words a minute. Duplex, quadraplex, and multiplex systems, permitted two, four, and more messages to move simultaneously and in either direction over the same cable. The traffic was doubled on further improved cables after 1903, and more than doubled when they were laid in pairs, as became the practice on the busier routings to provide reassurance against stoppages. In 1923, the Commercial Cable Company put down a North Atlantic cable with a copper core, producing a great advance in potential traffic volume, and three Western Union permalloy cables laid in 1924 and 1925 were judged able to handle as much traffic as the other eighteen North Atlantic cables combined.

The costs for messages passing between points in Asia and points in Europe or North America were far higher, even at press rates, than on the more heavily used North Atlantic circuits. The Pacific cables were technically inferior in the 1920s to those newer cables in the North Atlantic. They operated at only about 100 *letters* a minute, whereas the best of the Atlantic cables were carrying up to 2,500 *words* a minute. To lay such an improved cable across the Pacific, however, would cost from $10 to $16 million, and the advances already in view for radiotelegraphic communication made such an expenditure questionable when there seemed a possibility that wireless transmission might make all cables obsolete.

At the same time, the need for effective Pacific communication was obvious. Neither the United States government, the U.S. press, or commercial interests wished to be handicapped by slow or inefficient transmission of messages, or to accept the prospect of a permanent dependence, or even supplementary dependence, on the use of British and Danish communications facilities. The conflict in 1921 over the introduction of a Pacific wireless service by the RCA gave added point to this issue, with still more importance arising from a desire and a need for prompt reports on new situations taking shape in China, Japan, and India.

Admiral W. H. G. Bullard, director of the United States Naval Communications Board, was one of those particularly aware of this need. He had represented the government in the negotiations that led to the formation of the RCA. Another who saw the need, and representing the press, was Valentine Stuart McClatchy, then publisher of the *Sacramento Bee* in California, and a member of the Associated Press board of directors.

Together, they enlisted the support of members of Congress in a proposal that existing U.S. Navy wireless stations in Asia and the Pacific be made available, at least temporarily, for use in the transmission of press dispatches to and from the United States at greater speed and at far lower cost than then was possible by cable, and at a time when no commercial wireless service was yet available in the area. It was anticipated that Navy stations could provide service in Peking, Cavite (near Manila), Guam, Honolulu, and Alaska, where a U.S. Army cable also might be available for use to Seattle. Cables and telegraph lines could also be used between Tokyo, Shanghai, and Hong Kong to handle reports to or from Peking or Manila, to be handled further by navy stations in San Francisco or San Diego.

Congress voted in 1920 to authorize the use of navy wireless transmitters in this fashion to move press dispatches from 1921 to 1923, "under the theory that daily exchanges of news reports was necessary for the promotion of understanding between the United States and its insular interests, and because private agencies seemed unprepared to furnish full service." It was specified that the arrangement would end "whenever privately owned and operated stations are capable of meeting the normal communications requirements." Such stations in 1923 were still unprepared to meet those requirements, and the right of the press to use the navy transmitters was therefore extended and re-extended until 1930.

Westbound transmission of news by U.S. Navy radio stations began in January 1921, and eastbound traffic from Asian and Pacific points to the United States began about three months later. It was not as fast a service as some had wished or expected, but it was faster than by cable, and considerably less costly. The navy radio press rate between Manila and San Francisco, for example, was set at 6 cents a word as against 33 cents by cable, at 3 cents a word to or from Honolulu as against 16 cents by cable.

Press messages moved between Peking and Manila, and then to the United States at an equally reasonable rate until January 1, 1924. Use of the Peking transmitter for press traffic had to be halted at that time, however, because of U.S. government agreements, or concessions, at the Washington Naval Conference of 1921–22. With the use of the commercial cable facilities between Shanghai, Hong Kong or Tokyo and Manila, however, and the navy wireless at Cavite, near Manila, the press rate for that distance still was 24 to 27 cents a word, as contrasted to 32 cents by cable. This was further trimmed to 22 cents in 1925, and to 18 cents in 1927. Commercial wireless service also was available eastbound to Manila through Marconi and through a French government station established in Shanghai's International Settlement in June 1921.

RCA Communications, Inc., although barred from operating in the Chinese Republic until 1930, did institute a San Francisco–Tokyo circuit in 1922, and a San Francisco–Manila–Hong Kong circuit in 1927. Use of the wireless circuits to and from Manila also allowed for a rate lower than by cable and assured a saving in time. The RCAC circuit between Tokyo and San Francisco was used from its establishment in 1922, since the U.S. Navy had no wireless facilities in Japan, and again at a rate lower than the cable.

The navy wireless, in addition to bringing press reports eastward into San Francisco, carried an average of about 3,000 words a day in a reverse flow to Honolulu, and about 2,500 words beyond that to Guam and Manila. The Associated Press was sending about 1,000 words a day, in cablese, to Honolulu in 1922, and about 800 words to Manila. In 1923 the AP was sending about 5,000 words a month to Japan by way of the navy transmitter in Guam and commercial cable relay to Tokyo for use by the Kokusai agency and, after its reorganization in 1925, the Rengo agency. The United Press was sending a brief general report by the same routing for use by the Dentsu agency and by two newspapers, the *Nichi Nichi* of Tokyo and the *Mainichi* of Osaka. In 1927 the navy wireless was carrying both AP and UP reports from San Francisco to Manila, with a drop-off at Honolulu, at a cost of $96 a day for 1,600 words at each reception point.

RCAC also carried some AP and UP dispatches to Japan after 1922. There B. W. Fleisher, publisher of the *Japan Advertiser,* a Tokyo daily, established a Trans-Pacific News Service to receive a daily report of 250 to 400 words, either by way of RCAC or navy wireless via Guam. This matter was used in the *Advertiser,* distributed to some other foreign language and vernacular papers in Japan, and forwarded to still others in China.

News executives in the United States, McClatchy among them, in 1920 had advocated a transpacific cable press rate of 9 cents a word, as contrasted to the existing rate of approximately four times that figure. Japanese correspondents reporting the Washington Naval Conference in 1921 complained that they sometimes were obliged to pay an urgent rate of $3.24 per word, and even then a dispatch might not reach Tokyo short of 100 hours.

By 1925 the RCAC was prepared to set a San Francisco–Tokyo press rate of 10 cents a word. The Japanese press would have welcomed it, but the Tokyo government would not agree, believing it would result in so sharp an increase in the volume of communications as to overburden existing facilities. The RCAC also was prepared in 1927 to handle San Francisco–Manila press traffic at 8 cents a word, San Francisco–Honolulu traffic at 3 cents, or the same message to both places at 9 cents. Manila publishers, then receiving reports by navy wireless at 6 cents a word, contended that even an 8 cent rate might make enough difference to force suspension of some papers, or at least curtail the news service received from the United States. The San Francisco–Honolulu rate of 3 cents was made effective. Under U.S. government pressure, the RCAC agreed to set a 6 cent rate on Manila traffic, matching the navy rate, so that either service might be used there.

By 1929 the Japanese government-owned Pacific cable spur from Guam to Yokohama, originally made operative in 1905, had been modernized to handle an increased volume of traffic. The concern felt by the Tokyo government in 1925 about reduced press rates was removed, whether with reference to cable or wireless. The Commercial Pacific Cable Company, with which the Guam-Yokohama line was joined, therefore announced a new San Francisco–Tokyo press rate in 1929 of 12 cents a word, with a 9 cent deferred rate. The regular commercial rate remained at 72 cents a word, however, and the urgent rate at $2.16.

The Canada-to-Australia Pacific cable of 1902 was so routed that it did not carry a volume of news traffic to compare with the Commercial Pacific Cable Company line. Both the Canadian and Australian governments provided some financial support, in part to underwrite an empire news exchange. Running from Bamfield, near Vancouver, to Sydney, a 6 cent press rate applied in 1927, with a 5 cent night deferred press rate introduced in 1929.

By then the Marconi Company also beamed press messages over a Canadian–Australian radiotelegraphic circuit at a 7 cent press rate, or 4½ cents at night. The entire Commonwealth press benefitted when an all-British beamed radiotelegraphic service become operative after 1929. For example, the London–Melbourne cable press rate had already come down in 1922 to 15 cents a word (7½d), but by 1930 it was about half that by radiotelegraph, and the Shanghai–London rate was reduced from 25 cents to 16⅔ cents.

Competition and prospective competition had the same general result even where considerations of Commonwealth unity were not involved. In 1929, for example, the German government-subsidized the Transozean service, not at that time supporting a propaganda line, as it had from 1913 to 1918. It began to transmit a wireless news report available for use at the equivalent of only $35 a month, and rather widely used at that rate by the Asian press.

Radiotelegraphic transmission was bringing reduced rates on circuits throughout the world, as evidenced on the Vancouver–Sydney, Melbourne–London, and London–Shanghai exchanges mentioned, and the rates as trimmed by RCAC in areas of the Pacific where it was able to operate. The London–New York commercial radiotelegraphic press rate in 1927 was 5 cents a word. Press dispatches could be moved from Tokyo to New York for 21 cents, and from Shanghai for 31 cents. It was recognized after the expiration on December 31, 1930, of the British and Danish contracts with the Chinese government that there no longer would be any barrier to the establishment of wireless communications facilities in China by RCAC or other interests.

Congress was prepared to believe by 1930 that the RCAC and the Commercial Pacific Cable Company were able to offer effective Asian service at reasonable rates and therefore to meet "normal communications requirements" so that the navy radio service to the U.S. press might be halted, as it then was. Since RCAC and Commercial were private business enterprises, rather than tax-supported, it was accepted that their rates would be higher than those set by the navy radio.

A third Pacific service was begun in April 1934 by Globe Wireless, Ltd. Formed originally as the Dollaradio Communications System by proprietors of the Dollar Line of the United States for use in the conduct of that company's world trade and shipping business, it extended its operations to handle some commercial wireless traffic, but virtually no press matter. By contract with the new Nationalist government of China, a New York–San Francisco–Honolulu–Shanghai circuit also was opened in 1930 with Marine Station XSG in Shanghai, providing a twenty-four-hour commercial service, but again with no press traffic.

So long as rates remained high and, lacking events of such drama or importance as to warrant unusual expenditures, the news of Asia and Latin America as reported in the United States and Europe remained limited in volume. The reverse was equally true. So little was transmitted, apart from reports of critical, sensational, or bizarre events, that readers in either part of the world had only slight awareness of the peoples and problems in the other. The resulting lack of understanding and interest meant, further, that a proportion of the news transmitted was not used, or was used so inconspicuously as to escape general notice.

Transmission rates, however important as a budgetary matter, have no essential relation to the importance of the subject-matter of the news. High rates nevertheless stand as an invitation to public misunderstanding in that they tend to discourage full reporting. Recognition of that fact had induced the Congress to approve the use of U.S. Navy facilities from 1921 to 1930 to move news between Asia and the United States at a lower rate.

To illustrate how rate variations may operate as an "invitation to misunderstanding," a New York daily in 1920 could receive a 300 word cablese news report from London at 7 cents a word, or $21. But a 300 word report from Tokyo at the cable press rate of 39 cents a word to San Francisco then cost $117, to which telegraph tolls to New York would add another $15. A New York editor with a budget to consider would tend to be six times as cautious about ordering a report from Tokyo, and a correspondent there would hesitate to report more than the barest of facts.

By 1927 the rates had come down so that a press dispatch could be moved from Tokyo to New York for 21 cents a word, or from Shanghai for 31 cents. But the London–New York rate also had dropped to 5 cents a word. Even so dedicated a newspaper as the *New York Times* observed at that time that its news from London cost about $50 a column, whereas that from Tokyo still cost about $200 a column, and that from Shanghai cost from $300 to $350 a column.

Despite these variations, the greater importance attaching to the news of the Far East in the decade of the 1920s, and the availability of better and somewhat less costly Pacific communications, brought a sharp increase in the volume of news entering the United States from that part of the world. The volume rose from 301,000 words in 1920 to 726,000 words in 1929. In the same period, news reports leaving the United States by way of the Pacific rose even more, from 481,000 words to 1,229,000 words. Those figures rose further after 1930, as full radiotelegraphic service became operative and as cable rates were trimmed.

By comparison, however, the North Atlantic traffic continued at a far greater volume. News entering the United States from Europe between 1920 and 1929 increased from 10,405,000 words to 20,731,000 words.

This included not only news of Europe itself and Great Britain, but news relayed by way of Europe from Africa, the Middle East, even from the Far East, notably India, and most of the news from South America then moving on a triangular course. The outgoing news to Europe, chiefly news of the United States and Canada, but also some from Mexico and Central America and the Pacific, increased in the same period from 3,690,000 words to 9,781,000 words. Another significant figure indicates that the volume of news matter entering the United States from all points between 1916 and 1929 increased by 250 percent, while outgoing traffic increased by 400 percent. The volume of news traffic on most routings continued to rise after 1930, and although rates were reduced, the total costs increased because of the volume.

Record figures on single dispatches had been set from time to time and continued to be set, or particular events taxed the available communications facilities. A new record for a single dispatch was set, for example, when the full text of the Treaty of Versailles, exceeding 50,000 words, was cabled from New York to Buenos Aires in 1919 by the United Press for publication in *La Prensa*. Other long dispatches in the 1920s and early 1930s included the text of the Dawes Reparations Committee report, again nearly 50,000 words, cabled from London to New York in April 1924 at a cost of $5,000 shared by the AP and UP, and relayed from New York to Buenos Aires. Ten men were kept busy for sixteen hours preparing the report for transmission from London. Other long reports included a 10,000-word encyclical by Pope Pius XI in 1931, and also the League of Nations report by the commission headed by Lord Lytton on the Japanese invasion of Manchuria. It was 15,000 words in length, broadcast by the League's own transmitter in Geneva in February 1933, and published by the *New York Times,* the only newspaper to use it in full.

By 1929, apart from cables, there were about seven million miles of telegraph line and nearly sixteen million miles of telephone line operating throughout the world. From 40 to 60 percent of these lines were in the United States and Canada, under private ownership and direction. It was estimated in 1934 that there were 32,445,855 telephones in the world, 60 percent controlled by private companies, and 50 percent of them in the United States, even though its population was only about 6 percent of the world total. These figures were to grow larger, of course, in later years.

Both the technical possibilities and clarity of telephone communication advanced dramatically after 1920. The American Telephone &

Telegraph Company, the British General Post Office, and the post and telegraph ministries of most other countries were active in extending and improving telephone facilities.

By the 1920s it was common practice for newspapers reporters in the United States to use the telephone to gather information, calling offices and individuals to do so. This practice was rarely used in Great Britain or elsewhere, in part because there was little disposition on the part of persons in those other countries to respond to questions put to them by telephone. Reporters in the United States, particularly for afternoon papers, also telephoned their offices from their various points of assignment, in the late morning and early afternoon, to provide verbal reports of news. The details were noted by "rewrite men," or sometimes women, who then prepared the stories. This permitted the reporter to remain at the source of the news, rather than coming into the office. British newspaper reporters did the same, on occasion, with the difference that their verbal reports were usually recorded in shorthand, rarely used in newspaper offices in the United States.

As the telephone system became more highly developed in the United States, with long-distance circuits offering greater clarity and flexibility, correspondents in Washington or other cities sometimes telephoned their home offices. Also, it was not uncommon for a reporter or a rewrite man to telephone great distances in seeking additional information.

These practices, with some modifications, also were used in Europe. As telephone connections were made between European capitals, they were used on occasion by correspondents. Until about the mid-1920s the technical problems caused difficulties, with quick connections and clarity of tone wanting. By about 1926, however, British, French, German, and Italian correspondents in the various capitals telephoned their home offices regularly in the evenings to convey or dictate their reports, but still with some difficulties. By the early 1930s, however, the clarity of the connections was near perfection.

Technicians throughout the world had been busy extending the distances over which telephone conversations might be conducted. The technology of wireless and radio communication, as advanced during and immediately after the war and adapted to telephony, resulted in the first two-way transatlantic telephone conversations on January 14, 1923. These were between telephone officials in New York and London. With the AT&T, RCA, and the British GPO collaborating, conversations took place between press representatives in London and New York on March 7, 1926. A commercial radiotelephone circuit between those cities went into operation on January 7, 1927, and later in the year was extended to Paris. The United States was also in radiotelephone communication with Canada, Cuba, and Mexico. By July 1928 commercial circuits existed between the United States, Great Britain, France, Switzerland, and other European countries. New York and Buenos Aires were linked in 1930, New York and Tokyo in 1931, and New York and Shanghai in 1934. By 1936 there were twenty-seven direct international radiotelephone circuits out of New York. London provided switchboards through which most countries of the world could be reached. The same was true in Geneva, where the League of Nations maintained an international switchboard.

As with other communications advances, the press was quick to use the radiotelephone, at first as a novelty but soon as a conventional aid to news reporting. The New York–London rate in 1927 was $75 for three minutes, but this figure was progressively reduced in later years, as had been true for the telepgraph and cable, but never with any special press rate for the telephone, for which the three-minute unit of time remained the basis for charges.

As a novelty, the *Chicago Journal* established radiotelephone contact with the London *Daily Mail* in February 1927. Soon after, the *New York Evening Post* telephoned *Le Quotidien* in Paris. In March the *New York Herald Tribune* telephoned its Paris edition, the *New York Herald*. These transatlantic conversations were reported as matters of interest, even though lacking in substance. With the new and powerful Rugby station handling radiotelephonic as well as radiotelegraphic transmissions, both Reuters and newspapers in Great Britain after 1927 telephoned points in the United States and other parts of the world to verify or supplement news reports.

The establishment of radiotelephone communications between the United States and Argentina in September 1930 was marked by a journalistic coup when the *New York Times* used it to obtain information on the seizure of the Argentine presidency, despite a censorship on outgoing cable reports.

The *New York Herald Tribune* may have been the first to use the radiotelephone on a contract basis to receive international reports regularly over major distances. In January 1927 a regular service began between its New York office and its London bureau, and in July between New York and the Paris bureau. Connections were made at a fixed time each day—6 P.M. in New York (11 P.M. in London), and 7:30 P.M. in New York (12:30 midnight in Paris). With radiotelephone service established in 1931 between New York and Tokyo, and in 1934 between New York and Shanghai, comparable scheduled calls were set up with the paper's correspondents in those cities.

The radiotelephone was a flexible instrument, as the *Herald Tribune* demonstrated somewhat later, when telephone technology had made further advances. When Amelia Earhart was attempting to set a new record for flight around the world in 1937, on what proved to be her last air exploit, the paper reached her from its New York office by telephone at Batavia, in the Dutch East Indies, within five minutes of her landing there, and obtained her personal comment on that leg of the flight. Also, when Leland Stowe, of the paper's own staff, landed at Lisbon June 19, 1939, on the first Pan American Clipper flight from New York to Europe, he was dictating a story to New York within fifteen minutes of arrival, and his story was relayed back to Paris for use in the *New York Herald* edition there.

A telephone contract service was used after 1930, both on the landline long-distance circuits and on the radiotelephone circuits. The calls were scheduled for particular times from the home office to a bureau, or sometimes the other way around. Correspondents for London papers in New York or Washington, for example, called their offices at perhaps 2 P.M. (7 P.M. in London), time enough to prepare reports for morning papers there.

By the mid-1930s, with Europe in a period of crisis, U.S. correspondents there found the use of the telephone to be a way of speeding the news, and an assurance that it would reach its destination promptly. It was especially effective as used in such disturbed capitals as Rome and Berlin, but also in Vienna and Geneva, although not yet in Moscow or in Spain. The practice was made more effective because of the almost coincidental appearance of systems for recording telephoned reports on a disk or on a wire-recorder, a first step toward the introduction of tape-recording.

It became the practice for a U.S. correspondent in Berlin or Geneva to prepare his dispatch and read it over the telephone to his paper's bureau in Paris. There it would be recorded, then transcribed, and relayed by radiotelegraph or cable to New York. The system worked well, and was adopted by British correspondents and others. It was a method also adopted for use on radiotelephone circuits.

The advantages of this system were several. For the correspondent, the time of the contract call became a deadline when his copy must be ready. Completion of the call gave assurance both to the correspondent and to his office that the dispatch would be available when required, with no possibility of transmission or censorship delays, and with no errors or omissions attributable to either. The contract arrangement tended to eliminate a possible delay or denial of a noncontract call, whether placed to the correspondent or by the correspondent.

If a censorship was formally established and acknowledged, a government would require that the correspondent's copy be censored in advance, regardless of how it was to be sent. If to be telephoned, that censorship would need to be completed in advance of the call. The correspondent in preparing his copy would need to allow for the censorship process. Once that was completed, he would know that what he had written, or what had survived the censorship, would go through, so long as he did not depart from the approved text. He would have to assume that a government censor, holding a duplicate copy, would be monitoring his call and would break the connection in such an event.

Another advantage of telephone transmission of copy, with the use of the recording at the receiving end, was an actual saving of cost. If a telephone transmission was recorded by a shorthand reporter it would require speaking at a moderate dictation speed. As recorded on disk or wire or tape, however, the experience of the *New York Herald Tribune* demonstrated that a correspondent could speak clearly and distinctly at 200 words a minute, or more. In its own international use of the system, the recording room in New York was taking 10,000 to 25,000 words daily on six machines. The original copy, written in cablese, became far more in actual text when the cablese was put into full English. The recording could be played back at dictation speed for transcription, and repeated if necessary to clarify a word or phrase. Even with relatively high telephone charges, the *Herald Tribune* calculated the savings over telegraphic or cable transmission of the same volume of material at about $2,000 a month. By March 1940 the paper estimated it was receiving as much as 90 percent of all reports from its own correspondents outside the United States by radiotelephone in this fashion.

The *New York Times,* with an equally sophisticated system of communications, supervised and directed by Fred E. Meinholtz, used a variant of the telephone method of news transmission early in 1940. Cyrus L. Sulzberger, then in Turkey as a correspondent, arranged for fifteen minutes of time each afternoon for several successive days on a shortwave radio station in Istanbul. He broadcast his dispatch for the day. The broadcasts were monitored and recorded in the *Times* building in New York for use in the paper. Even though sent in the clear, they never were pirated for other use, and the saving in time and money for the paper was considerable.

An important new private company entered the field after 1921 to advance telephone communications in several countries, and telegraph and cable communications as well. This was the International Telephone and Telegraph Corporation (IT&T), organized in New York at that time by the brothers Sosthenes and Hernand Behn, both originally of the Virgin Islands when they were Danish territory and before their purchase by the United States in 1917.

Educated in Europe, and linguistically gifted, the Behn brothers were in business together from 1906 in Cuba and in Puerto Rico. There they became bankers and owners of a small telephone company in 1914. In 1920 they joined with the AT&T in extending a telephone cable between the United States and Cuba. In forming the IT&T the year after, they proceeded to extend their communications interests.

The first major IT&T venture came in 1924 when a contract was signed with Spain to replace that country's government-owned telephone system with a modern system to be constructed and owned by IT&T. With financing handled by J. P. Morgan & Company in New York, the IT&T paid $30 million for the AT&T European manufacturing subsidiary, the International Western Electric Company, with a right also to use AT&T patents in the production of equipment in Spain.

Three years later in 1927 the IT&T also bought a two-thirds interest in All-America Cables, linking North and South America. This enterprise, developed by James Alexander Scrymser, a native of New York, a veteran of the Civil War, and a pioneer in telegraph and cable development between 1865 and his death in 1918, was renamed All-America Cables and Radio, Inc. It included five cables between the United States, Mexico, Central America, Cuba, and other islands of the Caribbean, and both the east and west coasts of South America. It also brought application of the new radio and radiotelegraphic techniques to the original Behn brothers operation of what became the Radio Corporation of Puerto Rico. A radiotelephone circuit was added between islands of the West Indies, with a tie to the AT&T lines in the United States.

The All-America Cables had formed a working arrangement in 1922, before its purchase by the Behn brothers, with the Postal Telegraph Company and its allied Commercial Cable Company of the United States, directed by Clarence H. Mackay. In 1926 All-America Cables had sold a 60 percent interest in part of its network, the Mexican Telegraph Company, to Western Union. This gave Western Union a one-third interest in the reorganized All-America Cables and Radio, Inc., in 1927, with IT&T holding the other two-thirds.

The Postal Telegraph Company, in existence since 1884, and possessing a network of wires in the United States, was nevertheless handling less than 20 percent of the telegraph business of the country in 1928. In that year, Mackay sold the company to IT&T. With it went Postal Telegraph contracts with the Canadian Telegraph Company, the Mackay Radio and Telegraph Company, in ship-to-shore service, and the Commercial Cable Company, controlling North Atlantic cables, and holding a quarter-interest in the Commercial Pacific Cable Company. The latter company, formed in 1902–03 by Postal Telegraph-Commercial Cable, operated the only Pacific cable from U.S. shores to Manila, with its link to Tokyo, and connections by British cables to Shanghai and Hong Kong. By 1928, however, half the stock in the company already was controlled by the British Eastern Company, and the remaining quarter was held by the Great Northern Telegraph Company, primarily Danish-owned, along with British interests.

The IT&T had become a great holding company by 1929, and negotiations were proceeding looking toward its acquisition of the radiotelegraphic facilities of the Radio Corporation of America. But the Congress of the United States, in recalling the reasons for the formation of the RCA in 1919, intervened in 1930 to halt any such sale.

At about the same time, the IT&T suffered temporary reverses arising from the general national and world economic dislocations of that period. Later, it was forced to divest itself of its holdings in Spain, and holdings it had gained in Rumania and Italy and in Argentina, all because of political changes in those countries. In 1943, it sold the Postal Telegraph Company to Western Union, with its suspension following, leaving Western Union with a telegraph monopoly in the United States.

On balance, however, the IT&T gained in strength and size. Its control of All-America Cables and Radio, Inc., continued. It retained its quarter interest in the Commercial Pacific Cable Company. The Mackay Radio and Telegraph Company service was augmented with forty-two circuits to many parts of the world. The Radio Corporation of Puerto Rico continued to operate an IT&T controlled telephone system there. The corporation also had interests in Cuba, and some South American cities and regional areas, as well as in Great Britain, France, Belgium, Norway, China, and Japan. It retained and extended its manufacturing interests in the electronics field, and its stock was widely held by citizens of many countries.

The American Telephone & Telegraph Company also prospered. Its primary concern was with telephone communication, nationally and then internationally. At the same time in 1930, it became involved in the nation-wide operation of teleprinter circuits, connected by telephone wires, rather than telegraph. In this, it converted the former Morkrum-Kleinschmidt Company into the Teletype Corporation as a subsidiary, transmitting messages not only for the press, but for business and government. It gained an early and active role in voice radio broadcasting, with WEAF as its station in New York. This it sold to RCA in 1925, however, as it had sold its interest in RCA itself in 1923. From 1926, however, AT&T was to provide the long lines for network radio broadcasting in the United States. It also entered into the transmission of photographs by wire, and into facsimile reproduction by wire.

Despite the great use of radiotelegraphy, and the development of radiotelephony from the mid-1920s, the concern felt by cable companies lest their services become redundant proved unjustified. The cables were unaffected by atmospheric conditions that sometimes interfered with clear transmission by wireless. Technical advances assured good cable service in terms of speed and quality of transmission. International telephony by cable matched radiotelephony in quality and assured greater confidentiality. The growing volume of world communications and new needs, as for photo transmission and voice radio transmission across the seas, worked in their favor. The rates also became comparable.

Even so, it cannot be said that the cables survived without change, technologically and otherwise. Since many of the British cables had been laid originally with the direct encouragement of the government, the cable companies of that country, seeking to protect their investments, urged upon the government a plan to place all British communications, whether government-owned or privately owned, under a unified direction. The domestic telegraph lines had been government-owned since 1872, and some cables also were government-owned. By making privately owned cable and wireless companies equally a part of one organization, it was argued, any adverse competition would be eliminated between the government-owned services and the privately owned services.

The British government actually had favored some such move to bring the cable lines under the same GPO direction as the telegraph lines. Since 1910 a half dozen official studies had been made, with recommendations in the matter. Responding to the new interest manifested by the privately owned companies themselves, an Imperial Wireless and Cable Conference met in London in 1927–28. The result was the organization of two so-called "chosen instruments," that is, two companies, one to own and the other to operate all British communications. The first was Cable & Wireless, Ltd., a holding company. The other was Imperial and International Communications, Ltd., as the operating company. They were known jointly as Cable & Wireless, Ltd. (C&W).

Cable & Wireless took control in 1929 of three privately owned and related cable companies. Known as the Electra House Group, since that was the London headquarters location, they included the Eastern Telegraph Company, dating from 1872, the Eastern Extension, Australasia and China Telegraph Company, Ltd., the largest single unit in the world's cable network, with 50,000 nautical miles of line linking Europe with Asian and Pacific points, and the Western Telegraph Company, Ltd., with lines linking the United Kingdom with African and Latin American points.

The C&W organization also included the British Marconi Wireless Telegraph Company, with its stations and circuits, and its manufacturing interests. The domestic telegraph lines, already under GPO control, were omitted from the combination, however, and so was the GPO wireless station at Rugby, soon to become an important center for the multiple-address transmission of news, for radiotelephony, and for other communications purposes.

This giant C&W combination included 165,000 nautical miles of cable formerly under private direction, plus 25,000 nautical miles of British government-owned cable, and it included all British wireless stations and circuits except the Rugby transmitter. It was a grouping estimated to have a value of $875 million, although capitalized at only $250 million. The British private cable companies held a 44 percent interest in C&W, and the radiotelegraph organizations also held 44 percent at the outset. Shares in the remaining 12 percent were offered for sale to the public, with an indication that purchasers might expect a 6 percent return on their investments.

To conduct the actual operation of the cables and the wireless circuits, the staff personnel of the various companies continued as before, but under the umbrella of the new subsidiary, Imperial & International Communications. This, like C&W itself, was regarded as a kind of public utility. Messages that formerly would have been carried by the various independent companies continued to be designated for transmission as they would have been previously, based in part upon destination, and therefore on forms marked for "Imperial," "Eastern," "Western," "Marconi," or "Empiradio."

The combination of cables and point-to-point or beamed wireless (radiotelegraphic) circuits linked all parts of the British Empire or Commonwealth in what was variously called the "All-British Network" or the "All-Red System." It was possible for messages to go around the world, and to many parts of the world, without passing through or requiring relay in any non-British territory. This was regarded as possessing political value, contributing to empire or commonwealth unity and assuring security of message-transmission, while also providing a counter to the new strength of the United States in international communication.

The economic turn in world affairs in the early 1930s affected C&W adversely. Public investors in the company stock failed to receive the 6 percent return they had been led to expect. The British government also found it expedient in 1936 to cancel rental charges for use of government-owned communications facilities in the amount of £250,000 ($1,215,000) annually to ease the financial pressure on C&W. Further benefits were granted. In return, however, the government accepted 9 percent of C&W shares, and the communication services continued effectively.

The Evolution of Press Wireless, Inc.

During the last year of the war, the United States government had erected a wireless transmitting station for official use near Bordeaux, France. Known as the Lafayette station, it shared a position with the U.S. Navy station at New Brunswick, New Jersey, as the most powerful at that time. In the chronology of postwar press communication, some of the first news reports were sent by U.S. correspondents in France by special arrangement from that Bordeaux station. They were received not at the New Brunswick station but at another U.S. Navy station at Bar Harbor, Maine.

There were delays, however, in the handling of these messages, some of the first of which were directed to the *New York Times*. Carr Van Anda, managing editor, arranged to have a wireless receiving station installed in the *Times* building in 1919 to permit direct reception, without going through Bar Harbor. As the Peace Conference proceeded in Paris, dispatches from the paper's correspondents there were routed through Bordeaux and also through a station in Lyons and received regularly in the *Times* building.

Soon, the *New York Times* correspondents in Germany were sending their reports directly to New York by way of transmitting stations at Nauen and Eilvese. From the paper's London bureau, news reports also were moved through stations at Leafield, England, and Carnarvon, Wales. All of these messages received in the *Times* building were recorded on dictaphones at more than 100 coded words a minute for later transcription. A receiver also was installed to receive messages from ships at sea. The system enabled the *New York Times* to receive reports from its own correspondents both promptly and inexpensively.

This undertaking by the *Times* was of interest to other newspapers in the United States. In Chicago, Joseph Pierson, cable or foreign editor of the *Chicago Tribune,* who had established the Army Edition of the *Tribune* in Paris in 1917 and edited it for a time, gained approval for a plan whereby dispatches from *Tribune* correspondents in Europe might be routed through Paris for transmission from Bordeaux directly to Chicago. The *Tribune* arranged for its own receiving station, designated as 9ZN, and received the first dispatch on October 14, 1920.

For about three months, weather conditions permitting, the *Tribune* received all of its dispatches from continental Europe in this fashion, totalling about 3,000 words a day. This saved three to six hours in delivery time over the alternative use of the cable to New York and the telegraph to Chicago, and it meant a saving of about 30 percent in cost. If atmospheric disturbances obscured portions of a dispatch, the operator of 9ZN would telephone Great Lakes Naval Training Station, a few miles north of Chicago, and its powerful naval transmitter would "break" Bordeaux and have the doubtful portion repeated. The *Tribune* also arranged to receive other dispatches through the Lyons station and through the German Nauen station.

Early in 1921 the French government took control of the Lafayette station at Bordeaux. Arrangements followed between the French government-controlled Compagnie Général Télégraphique sans Fil and RCA Communications (RCAC), just formed in the United States, whereby dispatches between France and North America would have to go either by cable or be handled by RCAC. In either case, west-bound messages reaching North America would then need to be forwarded to inland destinations by telegraph.

For the *Tribune,* this would be more costly, and would provide no assurance of prompt handling or delivery. That had been made evident by an informal test of the alternative routing. For a time, the Bordeaux station continued to act unofficially in sending *Tribune* dispatches. They were monitored in Chicago, although the paper's 9ZN station no longer had official sanction. As a matter of form, paid duplicate dispatches were sent by the commercial routing, but often arrived hours after the *Tribune* had appeared with the same reports as received directly from Bordeaux.

The three U.S. news agencies and U.S. newspapers with their own correspondents in Europe were plagued during 1919–21 by delays of from twelve to thirty hours in the delivery of cable dispatches. Complaints on this matter and other inequities led the Department of State to sponsor a meeting of news executives and publishers in Washington in 1922 to explore the situation. The outcome was the formation of an American Publishers' Committee on Cable and Radio Communication based in New York, with Pierson of the *Tribune* as chairman.

Pierson had talked previously, late in 1921, with news personnel and with communications company officials in the United States and Europe about the possible establishment of special radio circuits for the exclusive handling of news. In December the *Tribune,* the *New York Times,* and the *Philadelphia Public Ledger,* all of which had been experimenting in the wireless transmission of news, joined to finance the establishment of their own cooperative wireless receiving station at Halifax, Nova Scotia. That station became operative on February 22, 1922.

For a period of six to nine hours daily, the Halifax station received press messages only, sent by the British General Post Office transmitter at Leafield, near Oxford. Circuits presently were added between Halifax and both Paris and Rome. The speed was twice that of cable transmission, even allowing for some atmospheric problems and use of the telegraph between Halifax and the newspaper offices in Chicago, New York, and Philadelphia.

The effectiveness of the Halifax station naturally interested the members of the American Publishers' Committee when it was formed later in 1922. Some joined in the undertaking, assuming a share of the cost. These were the United Press, International News Service, Universal Service, the *New York World,* and the *Christian Science Monitor.* The *New York Herald Tribune,* formed in a merger of those two newspapers in 1924, then also became a member.

The participants in the Halifax venture formalized their association in 1924, establishing a Canadian corporation, the News Traffic Board, Ltd., with Pierson continuing as director. By 1926 the station was handling about 20,000 words of press matter daily. The speed and reliability of the service was greatly advanced through an automatic relay system, which moved the message directly from the wireless receiver to the telegraph lines. Since the wireless facility was controlled by the press itself, the cost for transatlantic transmission was lower than by the privately owned commercial cables, RCAC, or other wireless services.

The diversion of so substantial a volume of press traffic to the press-sponsored service introduced related problems. Western Union handled most of the telegraphic business from Halifax to cities in the United States. In also operating North Atlantic cables, however, Western Union was not interested in aiding an enterprise it had to regard as competitive on the transatlantic circuit. Telegraphic transmission delays on the delivery of incoming dispatches over its wires between Halifax and cities in the United States became common, and other complications arose.

Some press messages from Rome, for example, were received at Halifax in Italian. In 1926 Western Union ruled that such messages, if they were to be forwarded by telegraph in Italian could only be handled at triple the usual rate. The contention was that matter in any foreign language was not entitled to move at the domestic press rate in an English-speaking area. Although Italian was a "recognized" language within the regulations of the International Telegraphic Union, the United States government was not a signator of the pertinent ITU convention. On that technicality, the Western Union ruling had to be accepted, and Italian-language messages no longer were directed through Halifax.

What might have become more serious, Western Union announced in 1927 that Halifax was not a gateway for U.S. communications, and the U.S. domestic press rate therefore could not apply to press messages moving from there by telegraph and would be tripled. The Halifax reception center promptly rerouted all press traffic to points in the United States over the lines of the competitive Canadian Pacific Telegraph Company and the associated Postal Telegraph Company of the United States. After three nights of this, Western Union reconsidered and ruled that the press rate would apply as before.

High frequency or shortwave wireless transmission had proved itself more satisfactory over long distances by 1927 than the longwave transmission previously used. That same year, applications were made to the newly established U.S. Federal Radio Commission (FRC) for the use of shortwave bands to carry press traffic exclusively. In 1928 the

FRC announced that it was prepared to assign such bands for use by the press, both domestically and internationally, but with the proviso that any agency or newspaper using an assigned waveband be a "public service corporation," prepared to carry any press message offered.

By that time in 1928 the membership of the Canadian-based News Traffic Board had increased to include the *Los Angeles Times,* the *San Francisco Chronicle,* and the Scripps-Howard Newspapers, then about fourteen in number, from coast to coast. Of the dozen members of the Board, all except two had correspondents outside the United States, and all were interested in rapid international press communication. This seemed to them to require a fully operative wireless system, independent of landline telegraph. They saw this as possible through the use of a shortwave band such as might be assigned by the FRC. The Board members therefore agreed to form a new public service corporation as specified to replace the News Traffic Board, and with a U.S. base rather than a Canadian one. This was the American News Traffic Corporation, Ltd., for which Pierson presented a request to the FRC for shortwave frequencies.

As this request was pending, a second public service corporation, backed by five of the News Traffic Board members, also was formed under Delaware law. Known as Press Wireless, Inc., with Pierson as its president, it was superimposed upon the American News Traffic Corporation, Ltd., which thereupon vanished from the scene, having served its brief purpose as a transitional organization.

On December 29, 1929, the FRC granted twenty clear channels in the shortwave spectrum for intercontinental press dispatches and service messages, and it also granted twenty additional channels for intracontinental, or domestic transmission. Each of the forty wavelengths was to be split into two twelve-hour night and day services. Existing transmitting and receiving stations were to be used, including such stations as already belonged to newspapers or news agencies in the United States. But all were to be open for the unrestricted use of any other newspaper, agency, or press service.

The twenty intercontinental shortwave bands were assigned by the FRC to Press Wireless, pursuant to the earlier application by the American News Traffic Corporation. It was specified that the organization would act as trustee of the assigned channels so long as it operated them in a manner acceptable to the FRC—or the FCC (Federal Communications Commission) as it was to become in 1934.

Some protests were made to this plan. Existing commercial communications companies in the United States objected that the assignment of shortwave channels to the press would interfere with a "truly national system of domestic communication." The Hearst organization also found some objections, even though the INS and the Hearst-owned Universal Service were members of the corporation. Six months of legal controversy followed and it was two years before a general agreement was reached. It the end, the allocation of the twenty intracontinental press channels was cancelled. But Universal Service had been granted its own wave band in December 1929, and in 1931 the Hearst Newspapers received permits and licenses from the FRC to organize an independent domestic American Radio News Corporation.

Press Wireless, as formed earlier in 1929, began to operate on September 15 of that year, even before the FRC assignment of intercontinental channels. It used the existing transmitters of its five charter members. These were the *Chicago Tribune,* the *Christian Science Monitor,* the *Los Angeles Times,* and the *San Francisco Chronicle,* all of which had been members of the Traffic News Board in 1928, and the *Chicago Daily News,* which had not. It was a million-dollar corporation from the outset, although only $116,000 was actually paid in to provide operating capital.

Other earlier members, the *New York Times,* the *New York Herald Tribune,* the UP, and the INS soon rejoined. New members added were the Associated Press, the Hearst-owned King Features Syndicate (KFS), and the North American Newspaper Alliance (NANA), a special service formed in 1922. These additions brought about $400,000 further capital into the operating budget within a few months. Stock in the organization could be purchased by U.S. newspapers, news agencies, or other news organizations in amounts from a minimum of $1,000 to a maximum of $25,000, but no one group was permitted to own in excess of 20 percent of the stock.

Construction of five wireless stations to handle Press Wireless business began in 1929, and were in operation by April 1930, with about 15,000 words handled daily. They were near New York, Boston, Chicago, Los Angeles, and San Francisco. Litigation instituted by RCAC and Mackay Radio curtailed operations, however, until January 1931. At that time it became possible for the FRC to grant Press Wireless permission to erect nineteen shortwave transmitters to be used both for national and international business. Still other delays attaching to the FRC channel assignments in 1929 persisted until September 1931, when Press Wireless (P.W. or Prewi) was at last able to operate with full freedom.

Direct service between stations in Europe and the Press Wireless stations in the United States was begun. Powerful transmitters were made available for use near Paris, London, and Berlin, and also near Havana, Mexico City, and Honolulu. Contracts were made later with stations near Rome, Amsterdam, Capetown, Buenos Aires, Manila, Tokyo, and Shanghai. Incoming messages from these various points were received at the Press Wireless stations at Needham, Mass., near Boston; at Little Neck, L.I., or Baldwin, L.I., near New York, and at stations near Chicago, Los Angeles, and San Francisco.

Canadian newspapers were able to use Press Wireless facilities, as were European newspapers and agencies reporting from the United States. About three million words moved to Europe through Prewi in 1932. The incoming volume was far greater, however, with fifteen million words of press matter moved into the United States in that year. By 1935 about twenty-five million words were received, of which 65 percent was for the seven members. Prewi had become a common carrier for the U.S. press and began to show a profit in 1934. By the late 1930s, it was handling traffic between the United States and points in Asia and Latin America, as well as in Europe.

Owned and operated by the press itself, and serving the press exclusively, Press Wireless provided convenience and speed. Able to ignore the per-word charge maintained by commercial companies and governments operating cable and radiotelegraphic services, the cost was lower, estimated at about three cents a word on the transatlantic service, and hardly higher elsewhere.

Press Wireless was not a news-gathering organization, and it was not a news agency. Its function was to transmit the news as a "public service corporation," as specified by the FRC/FCC. It was a communications cooperative owned and operated by the press. Under Pierson's direction, it proved flexible enough to adapt its operations to advances in press requirements and in media development and technology. Its facilities were used not only for the transmission of textual matter, but for the international transmission of photographs and voice radio transmission, beginning in the very early 1930s. In short, it became a key in the advancement of international news coverage for the press and radio of the United States and other countries.

Press Wireless matched the Agence Havas in the early use of the multiple address system in 1931, beaming U.S. news agency reports from its own transmitter at Hicksville, L.I., to newspapers in Canada, Europe, and South America. Later, it was to do the same for newspapers in Asia and the Pacific through its stations in Los Angeles, San Francisco, and Manila. Press Wireless was to attain major importance during World War II.

Electronic Journalism:
News on the Air 18

Those early experiments in the broadcasting of voice and music mentioned as having taken place between 1906 and 1916 did not go unnoticed by scientists, engineers, and amateur wireless enthusiasts. Experimentation continued and the end of the war brought a burst of activity. Those interested and with sufficient understanding put together equipment for sending and receiving simple broadcasts. They used phonograph records to broadcast music, as Fessenden, DeForest, and Herrold had done. They called upon friends to play the piano, sing, or speak. They took microphones into places where choral or musical groups were performing.

Others on the receiving end invited their friends and families to listen. The receiving sets were battery-powered and used a quartz crystal oscillator, with headphones for listening. The range and frequency of broadcasts was limited and the quality mixed, but the novelty of hearing music and speech come "out of the air" captured popular interest as early as 1919, and also made it a subject of news interest. Some who could do so constructed their own receiving sets, but it soon became possible to purchase them.

Newspapers began to publish program logs to inform readers of stations on the air, their wavelengths, the times of broadcast, and perhaps the subject of scheduled broadcasts. Some newspapers in the United States began to present broadcasts from their own buildings, usually including live music and brief news reports. For listeners, it became a kind of game and a topic of conversation to tune in stations, especially at night when transmission was clearer. The more distant the station, the greater the wonderment. This form of broadcasting, known as "radio" in the United States, and equally of interest in other countries, was referred to as "wireless" in Great Britain, and in France as "TSF" or *télégraphie sans fil* (telegraphy without wire).

In 1915 David Sarnoff, then assistant traffic manager of the Marconi Wireless Telegraph Company of America in New York, had been one of those experimenting personally in radio. He proposed officially to the Marconi Company that it manufacture a "Radio Music Box" to operate on several wavelengths to bring news, entertainment, and perhaps advertising into homes. With the war then in progress and wireless use under restrictions, nothing was done. In 1920, however, Sarnoff had become commercial manager of the new Radio Corporation of America. He repeated his suggestion at that time, and results soon were to follow, with RCA becoming among the first to manufacture radio receiving sets for sale to the public.

The development of radio broadcasting seems to have been most rapid in the United States. The very size of the country meant that the number of stations broadcasting grew. All were privately sponsored by individuals, universities, newspapers, and manufacturing, or retail companies. To assure order on the air, wavelengths were assigned and stations licensed after 1919 by a newly formed Federal Radio Commission (FRC) and the Department of Commerce. Station interference was a problem, nevertheless, as the number multiplied. Although largely solved by 1927, full control and clarity came only after the FRC was replaced by the Federal Communications Commission (FCC) in 1934.

The first permanent radio station in the United States probably was that conducted by Herrold at San Jose from 1909, and licensed by the FRC in 1919 under the call letters SJN. That same year the University of Wisconsin at Madison opened a transmitter broadcasting weather reports and farm market quotations, with musical programs and talks added. It was licensed as station WHA.

The DeForest organization set up an experimental station, 8MK, in Detroit, financed by the *Detroit News* and located in its building. Broadcasts began on a limited daily schedule on August 20, 1920, and included news reports, music, and talks. This later became station WWJ. It provided the first regular broadcasts of news reports, and also marked the beginning of newspaper ownership of radio stations. Other daily newspapers in the United States established stations within a few months, beginning in 1921, with the *Kansas City Star*, the *Chicago Tribune*, the *Chicago Daily News*, the *Milwaukee Journal*, the *Atlanta Journal*, the *Louisville Courier–Journal*, the *Los Angeles Times*, and others. Some large department stores also sponsored stations, among them Bamberger's of Newark, N.J., with a station in New York known as WOR. The American Telephone & Telegraph Company established station WEAF in New York in 1922.

Meanwhile in Pittsburgh, Dr. Frank Conrad, assistant chief engineer with the Westinghouse Electric and Manufacturing Company, had been experimenting on radio development since 1916, and the company had made radio equipment for use by the United States government and others during the war years. In 1919 Conrad set up his own experimental station in the garage attached to his home. Designated as 8XK, it broadcast both phonograph music and voice, and was heard by "ham" operators. Licensed for regular public broadcasting in November 1920, and designated as KDKA, Pittsburgh, a Westinghouse station, it began by broadcasting the November 2 presidential election returns. KDKA has frequently been referred to as the first radio station in the United States, and the first to broadcast news. It may have been the first to maintain a regular air schedule, but in the other respects it was in fact preceded by the stations cited at San Jose, Madison, and Detroit. The Westinghouse Company soon established another station, WJZ in New York. This was taken over in 1923 by the General Electric Company, which already had station WGY in Schenectady, where its main plant was located. General Electric also established both WRC in Washington, D.C., and KOA in Denver.

In 1923 the AT&T, an original part of the Radio Corporation of America when it was formed in 1919, sold its stock interest to the RCA and in 1925 also sold WEAF, its New York station, to RCA. It disposed, likewise, of forty other stations that had been licensed to it throughout the country in 1922. In this, the AT&T withdrew from direct participation in broadcasting. It retained a vital part in radio, however, because its wires were used to carry what became network broadcasts, in a close contractual alliance with RCA, beginning in 1926.

Radio had made vast advances. The DeForest audion tube brought clarity of reception, reception over greater distances, greater selectivity, and more stations to be tuned in by turning the dials on improved radio sets. The quartz sets were outmoded, with tubes replacing crystals. "Loudspeakers," and then built-in speakers, replaced earphone headsets and permitted all persons in a room to hear a broadcast. Power came from electric outlets, rather than from batteries. By 1925 there were 530 licensed stations in the United States, and 2,500,000 radio receiving sets already were owned; this was to become 51 million by 1940, including small portable sets and sets installed in motor cars and boats.

The quality and variety of programs on the air also advanced. Musical programs were standard radio fare from the outset, but became more elaborate. Drama and comedy, serials, and "live" events followed. News reports and sports broadcasts were among regular offerings. The *Detroit News* and the seven other newspaper-owned stations of 1921 presented brief bulletins adapted from their own columns and read at intervals by announcers. Newspaper-owned stations had become forty-eight in number by 1927, ninety by 1930, and nearly 250 by 1940, out of a total of 814 in the United States at that time. One of the early sports events to be reported as it was in progress was the Dempsey-Carpentier heavyweight championship fight of July 2, 1921, at Newark, N.J., with a telephone-line hookup between enough stations to reach an estimated 300,000 listeners. Baseball and World Series coverage followed, and football, with a coast-to-coast network broadcast of the Rose Bowl game at Pasadena, California, on January 1, 1927.

On some occasions, newspapers assigned staff members to listen to events broadcast live from other cities and to take notes, with a view to presenting some reports even before being received through regular news agency service. This was done by the *Milwaukee Journal,* for example, when the Republican National Convention was in session at Cleveland in June 1924, with broadcasts through a station in that city. Shortly after, as the Democratic National Convention met in New York, broadcasts through WEAF were widely heard through one of the early station hookups.

Such live and special events broadcasts became standard after 1921. Warren G. Harding in 1923 was the first president whose voice was heard on radio. An address by President Coolidge in February 1927 was heard nationwide over forty-two stations. The first coast-to-coast broadcast of an opera, *Faust,* which originated in the Chicago Civic Auditorium, had occurred in January. Live sports coverage brought two of the first widely recognized names and familiar voices to radio as broadcasters, Graham MacNamee and Milton Cross, both with station WEAF in New York. Special events reporting was given new impetus in 1927 when Charles A. Lindbergh arrived in New York aboard the U.S. Navy cruiser *Memphis,* on his return from France after his solo flight across the Atlantic. He was acclaimed in one of the first ticker-tape parades up Broadway from the Battery, and MacNamee, with an open microphone, provided a running account of the day's events. Lindbergh's later reception in Washington by President Coolidge also was fully reported by radio.

Other early names in the treatment of news on the U.S. radio stations were those of four correspondents, Frederic William Wile, William Hard, David Lawrence, and H. R. (Hilmar Robert) Baukhage. Wile, a correspondent in Europe for 20 years for the *Chicago Record* and *Chicago Daily News,* and for the London *Daily Mail* and the *New York Times,* had returned to the United States in 1920 to head the

Washington bureau of the *Philadelphia Public Ledger,* but had switched in 1922 to the staff of the *Washington Star.* He was invited in the fall of 1923 to broadcast the news of the capital once a week, originally without pay, over the newly established station WRC in Washington. His voice soon was carried also over station WJZ in New York. Both stations then were owned by the General Electric Company and became part of the National Broadcasting Company (NBC) network of stations as formed in 1926. Wile, by then paid for his broadcasting, continued with WRC and the NBC until 1928, when he switched to the Columbia Broadcasting System (CBS), formed in 1927 as a second network. He broadcast from that network's Washington station until 1938.

William Hard, in the capital since 1906, chiefly for *Collier's Weekly,* replaced Wile for WRC and the NBC network in 1928. Lawrence and Baukhage, both experienced in Washington, became contemporaries of Wile in broadcasting from the capital. Lawrence, already active for the Associated Press and then for the Consolidated Press in producing a syndicated service, turned to newspaper publishing in 1929 as director of a newly established *United States Daily* in Washington. Baukhage continued in radio and had a long career in news broadcasting for NBC.

A departure in the style of radio news reporting was introduced in 1924 in a promotional venture by *Time,* then in its first year as a weekly news magazine. A program bearing the strange title of "Pop Question," was prepared and voiced by Briton Hadden, the magazine's cofounder and copublisher along with Henry R. Luce, but it did not continue for long. In 1928 *Time* tried another approach by providing a daily ten-minute script for broadcast consisting of items culled from newspapers, processed for voice broadcast, and distributed by wire to forty radio stations. To describe this service, *Time* coined and copyrighted the term "Newscasting." In 1929 a modified treatment was provided and described as "Newsacting," with current news events re-enacted in dramatic form. Further modified in 1930, this became "The March of Time,"[1] with Ted Husing and Harry Von Zell, by then both familiar radio names and voices, as announcer-narrators. It was continued until 1931, but then voiced by (Cornelius) Westbrook Van

---

1 In 1935 "The March of Time" became exclusively a monthly motion picture documentary film examining one newsworthy subject for twenty minutes, and given general theater screening as a "short subject" preceding the feature film. Like the radio program, it was narrated by Van Voorhis in a distinctive "voice of doom," produced by Louis de Rochemont, and continued through World War II.

Voorhis. In 1932 this program, formerly a promotion for *Time* magazine, was jointly sponsored by *Time* and CBS and carried over that network.

The FRC regulations for the licensing of radio stations in the United States required that each station announce its identity, with call letters and location, every fifteen minutes. It was made permissible, during such so-called station breaks, to use a limited time to introduce spot announcements to advertise products or services, with payment to be made to the radio station for the time on the air. The first such broadcast was made over WEAF, New York, then owned by the AT&T, on August 28, 1922, on behalf of a Long Island real estate firm. Other stations introduced the practice, and the radio "commercial" was born.

The first wire hookup between radio stations came in October 1923, linking WEAF, New York, and WJAR in Providence, and then WEAF and WRC in Washington. With the number of stations increased, this kind of "chain broadcasting" proceeded in 1924 and 1925, and was soon to become "network" broadcasting, with regional and nationwide connections. It became useful to companies manufacturing products used nationally to broadcast spot announcements or advertising messages regionally or nationally and then to "sponsor" programs. The public response was rewarding and so was the financial return to radio stations for the sale of time. It became clear that the more appealing the program, the greater the listening audience, and the greater the audience the greater the response to the advertising messages and the greater the return to the stations for the sale of air time. It was therefore in the interest of the stations to present programs of entertainment and news that would be well received by the public. Advertising agencies, previously concerned with newspapers and magazines, soon reorganized their operations to give major attention also to radio advertising, not only in its writing and placement, but in the actual sponsorship and origination of programs. Thus radio ceased to be a novelty and became highly commercial.

It was obvious by 1925 that stations joined to broadcast the same program and reaching a very large audience could set a higher rate for the air time used for the commercial announcements or, indeed, for the sponsorship of the program, and especially for broadcasts at those evening or Sunday afternoon hours when more persons found it convenient to listen. To provide such audiences, RCA bought station WEAF in New York from the AT&T in September 1926, and made it the key station in a network of twenty-four stations in twenty-one cities between New York and Kansas City. This was the National Broadcasting Company (NBC), with its first network broadcast on November 15, 1926. The AT&T provided the long lines to carry the programs, in some cases supplemented in the early period by the wires of the Western Union and the Postal Telegraph companies, previously used for more limited regional station connections.

The NBC was so successful, both technically and in the revenue it brought both to advertisers and to stations, that other radio stations beyond the original twenty-four sought membership. A second NBC network was established January 1, 1927, based on WJZ in New York, originally a Westinghouse station, and including KDKA, Pittsburgh, also a Westinghouse station, and others, to provide another NBC network of forty-two stations from coast to coast. The first grouping, based on WEAF, was designated as the "Red" network, the other based on WJZ was the "Blue" network.

With more than 600 radio stations in the United States in 1927, some competing for listeners and advertising in the same cities, it was impractical for all to join the NBC, or for all to broadcast the same program at the same time. A second national network therefore was formed in 1928 by William S. Paley, then twenty-seven, and associated with the Congress Cigar Company of Philadelphia, a family business. This second national network was the Columbia Broadcasting System (CBS), evolving from an unsuccessful United Independent Broadcasters (UIB) of New York, originating in 1927 with some financial support from the established Columbia Phonograph Company. That company retained an interest in the CBS, which became active under Paley's direction on January 8, 1929. With WABC, New York, as the key station, it began with 49 affiliated stations in 41 cities from coast to coast, linked by the wires of the AT&T. In 1929, also, the Paramount-Publix Corporation, film producers and theater operators, became associated with CBS, with a 49 percent stock interest.

A third national network was started in 1934, the Mutual Broadcasting System (MBS). The key station was WOR, New York, owned by the Bamberger department store of Newark, but with its main radio studio in Manhattan. Equally important, however, was station WGN, Chicago, owned by the *Chicago Tribune,* with its call letters derived from that paper's slogan, the "World's Greatest Newspaper." Within a year, the MBS had nineteen affiliated stations, increased to thirty-eight by 1938. Eventually it became the largest network. Many of its affiliates were small stations in small cities, and the operation was less tightly knit in the national broadcast of programs. This permitted a more flexible schedule and a more modest rate structure.

Meanwhile, the RCA had extended its interests to the motion picture field in 1928, joining in ownership of the Radio-Keith-Orpheum group of theaters and the formation of RKO film studios. It was involved in the introduction of sound-on-film through application of certain of its patents, with "talking" motion pictures then beginning to appear. Again, as with CBS, the RCA gained an interest in the phonograph and recording field in 1929, when it assumed control of the prestigious Victor Talking Machine Company. As another subsidiary, it became known as RCA-Victor, producing RCA radio receiving sets, combination phonograph and radio consoles, and recordings.

In addition to NBC, CBS, and MBS, regional radio networks developed in the United States. In New England, a group of radio stations joined in a Yankee Network, operated by the Shepherd Broadcasting Company, with KNAC, Boston, as its key station. A Don Lee Network was formed in California, and smaller networks in Texas and Michigan. They brought national as well as local advertising to the support of the programs and stations.

The return from the sale of advertising time on the air, increasing in volume and effectiveness, provided full support for the stations and networks. It made possible the presentation of programs in great variety and many of high quality.

By 1930 the RCA itself had become so large, with its various interests and subsidiaries, including the NBC, that even though it had been formed a decade earlier with direct government support, the government now brought an anti-trust suit against it. The result was that in 1932 both the General Electric and Westinghouse companies disposed of their stock interests in RCA, as the AT&T had done in 1923. Both continued to manufacture broadcasting equipment, however, and receiving sets and tubes. This put them in direct competition with RCA-Victor, also manufacturing such equipment.

RCA retained its control of RCAC and RMCA in the communications field. The government had intervened in 1930 to halt the possible purchase of RCA by the IT&T. The Federal Communications Commission ruled that competition between U.S.-owned communications companies in foreign countries was contrary to the public interest. For example, it refused to permit the Mackay Radio and Telegraph Company, a subsidiary of IT&T, to establish a direct circuit to Oslo, which had been served by RCAC since 1921.[2]

---

2   Much later, in 1943, the FCC forced the RCA to dispose of the NBC "Blue" network, which became the independent American Broadcasting Company (ABC) in 1945, under the direction of Edward J. Noble. The "Red" network remained as the one and only NBC.

Radio broadcasting developed in other countries as it did in the United States from 1919 to 1930. In some respects, France actually pioneered in the field. DeForest had broadcast a program from the Eiffel Tower in Paris in 1908. A Societé Française Radio-Electrique had been formed there in 1916, and was absorbed in 1918 by a new Compagnie Générale de Télégraphie sans Fil that constructed stations for radiotelegraphic and radiotelephonic communication, and then for voice radio, with a powerful transmitter on the Eiffel Tower after 1922. In March 1924 a Radio-Paris station was established, with a transmitter in the Port-de-Clichy area of the city, and stations presently were established at Toulouse, Lyons, and elsewhere in France.

In Great Britain, it was natural that Guglielmo Marconi, in making his home there, should have played a role in the development of voice radio. In cooperation with the *Daily Mail,* he arranged a special broadcast in London on June 15, 1920, and his voice was heard as far away as Persia. The first station in the United Kingdom was sponsored by a private group, the Radio Society of Great Britain. Known as 2MT Writtle, it was on the air from London for a half hour each week, beginning early in 1922. It was joined in August 1922 by another experimental station, 2LO, London.

Largely through the initiative of Canadian-born William Stephenson (later Sir William Stephenson), who had already provided impetus for the formation of a Canadian Broadcasting Corporation (CBC), a British Broadcasting Company, Ltd., was formed to begin operations in November 1922.[3] He was joined in the effort by Lord Beaverbrook, a fellow Canadian and publisher of the *Daily Express,* by Gladstone Murray, a member of that paper's staff, with the further support of Lord Northcliffe and Charles P. Steinmetz, German-born scientist. He also arranged for the manufacture and sale of radio receiving sets to the British public.

The new British Broadcasting Company absorbed station 2LO in London, and established stations at Manchester (2ZY), Birmingham (5IT), and later at Daventry (5XX). Regular broadcasts, beginning in November 1922, included music, talks, and news. The public responded, with nearly 36,000 receiving sets owned in the country by the end of that

---

In 1949, the NBC had 170 affiliated stations, ABC had 272, CBS had 179, and MBS had 519. The total number of standard radio broadcasting stations in the United States at that time was 1,867, with 80 million radio sets in use in 94 percent of all U.S. homes, plus some 12 million automobiles.

3   Stephenson later played a key role in secret diplomacy during World War II. See William Stevenson, *A Man Called Intrepid* (New York, 1976), pp. 14–17.

year. In 1927 the company was reorganized as the British Broadcasting Corporation (BBC), with a royal charter, as a government-controlled undertaking. John Charles Walsham Reith, who had been general manager and managing director since 1922 (later Lord Reith of Stonehaven) was director-general until 1938. The BBC became one of the most effective of the world's radio organizations.

Other strong radio stations were established in cities of Europe by the Reichs-Rundfunkgesellschaft (RRG) in Germany, and the Radio Audizioni Italia (RAI) in Italy. They existed in Austria, Switzerland, Holland, and every other European country, including Soviet Russia, where Radio Moscow was broadcasting by 1925.

In Japan the first broadcasts were made March 22, 1925, over station JOAK, Tokyo, and other stations were established in Osaka and Nagoya, with the three merged before the end of the year into the Nippon Hoso Kyokai (NHK) (Broadcasting Corporation of Japan). Stations appeared at the same period throughout much of Latin America. Some in Brazil were owned by newspapers, as in the United States, with the Chateaubriand group, the Diarios Asociados, becoming especially active in that respect as the years passed.

The number of stations and the number of receiving sets multiplied in all countries of the world. In some, the stations and networks were privately owned, but in many they were controlled, if not owned, by the governments. Where the government owned or controlled the medium, it might also provide financial support, but did not necessarily do so.

Radio broadcasting generally was financed in one of two ways. One was by the sale of time on the air for advertising, such as began in the United States in 1922. The second system evolved in Great Britain. There commercial sponsorship of programs, or any advertising on the air was barred. Instead, to provide operating funds, an annual license fee was assessed against each radio receiving set. Originally, this was ten shillings (about $2.50), with the amount raised later. The public was led to believe that unlicensed radio sets could be detected by a system of triangulation, and generally the fee was paid faithfully in the same manner as annual automobile license fees were paid. In some countries, both methods were used in some combination. In Holland, churches and institutions gave financial support to the system with their own stations. In countries where radio sets were not sufficiently numerous to meet revenue requirements, even under the license system, partial support or full support came out of the national budget, but with radio then usually operating only for a limited time each day and serving special government interests. A Vatican Radio was supported entirely from Vatican sources.[4]

The press had given news attention to radio as a novelty in the first years, and some newspapers in the United States were among the first station owners. Soon, however, concern arose lest radio become a direct competitor both as a news medium and, in the United States, as a competitor for the advertising dollar. Those papers publishing program logs began to wonder if they were turning readers to this new competition to their own disadvantage. Newspapers presenting news reports by radio over their own stations and taking those reports from their own columns or from the agency reports also wondered about the wisdom, propriety, and even the legal right to do so. News agencies themselves, so long associated with the daily newspapers, were forced to consider whether their reports should go out on the air, whether as used by a newspaper-owned station or as provided directly to a radio station as a client of the service. Considering the cost of obtaining, distributing, and publishing the news, what was the legal position of a newspaper-owned station broadcasting those reports without payment, and what was the position of a radio station obtaining and using such reports for the price of a copy of the newspaper?

It became clear, in the earliest days of radio, that listeners enjoyed getting early news reports by radio, often before the newspapers reached them. For newspaper-owned stations it was simple for an announcer about to go on the air to turn to the news agency teleprinter and take off some copy to use, to "rip and read," as the the phrase was used, or for so-called "news readers" in London to do the same. It also was clear that a radio station with a news agency teleprinter available could report an occurrence before a newspaper could put that same information into type, prepare the pages and the press, and distribute printed copies. Long before that process was completed, the radio had reported the essentials of the event and of others over a vast radius. The newspaper practice of publishing "extras" as a way of reporting occasional events of special interest occurring after normal publication hours became quite pointless in the new radio age, and that practice ended almost at once. Radio news reporting became increasingly competitive with

---

4   Some "pirate" radios operated from ships in the North Sea and the English Channel, broadcasting advertising messages as a part of their programs. The Luxembourg radio, accepting advertising, included such messages directed to listeners in adjacent countries and in Great Britain.

newspaper reporting, even within normal hours, and newspapers were forced to re-examine their positions.

When advertising spot announcements and sponsorship of programs began the publishers of newspapers felt a further alarm, whether they also owned radio stations or not. Radio advertising promptly demonstrated its effectiveness in stimulating the sale of goods and services. There was a rush by business organizations to make the most of what appeared to be a great new opportunity for profit. Publishers saw readers turning to radio at no cost, with a possible circulation loss also forcing a reduction in advertising rates. Further, they saw advertisers turning to radio, with a possible loss in advertising revenue threatening the very survival of the newspaper. This was a threat to magazines as well.

These worst fears were not realized, but the number of daily papers did decline from 2,042 in 1920 to 1,878 in 1940, even though census figures showed a population growth in the same period from 105,710,620 to 131,669,275. But the loss of papers was at least as much a result of the national economic depression of 1929–38 as of radio competition. The readership of newspapers actually grew, with total combined circulations rising from 27.8 million daily in 1920 to 41.1 million in 1940. Radio advertising, starting from zero in 1920 represented 10.5 percent of the total national advertising expenditure by 1940, but newspapers still led widely in the latter year, both in percentage and in dollar volume of advertising. This was partly because added funds were budgeted to advertising by the business and industrial community, with all media benefitting. Further, almost 250 radio stations in the United States in 1940 were owned by or affiliated with newspapers, about one-third of all stations, with the papers also receiving revenue from that source.

The fact remained that the 60,000 radio receiving sets in the United States in 1920 had become 40 million by 1940; the 30 broadcasting stations had become 700. Radio stations and networks had profited enormously from the sale of advertising time, and also had become progressively more active in the broadcasting of news. Further, they were active in the direct coverage of news at its source, both at home and abroad. Experienced newsmen were recruited to assist as reporters, as writers processing the news, and as actual broadcasters. The names and voices of many became familiar to listeners, and some attained fame comparable to stars of the theater and the motion picture screen.

Popular and useful as radio became, newspapers retained certain advantages. The scheduled radio news broadcasts, originally limited to five minutes, could not offer more than a few items of information in so brief a time, hardly more than the lead paragraphs of the most important and interesting stories of the hour. This was changed only in degree when news broadcasts became more frequent and changed to a fifteen-minute format, allowing thirteen minutes apart from the advertising or commercial messages. It still remained necessary for any person more than casually interested in the news to turn to the newspaper. Only there did he find the full account, the far greater variety of news, supplementary photos, diagrams, charts, and statistical tables, and full texts of important addresses or documents, editorials, and special articles. Even in advertising, radio could not match the appeal of published display advertising, much less the service of classified advertising. Also, the radio listener had to have his set tuned in at the right moment, to pay strict attention, and to be undisturbed by extraneous sounds and voices. By contrast, the newspaper reader could choose his own time, suit his own convenience, and reread an item if necessary for full understanding. Thus each medium had its values.

Radio stations, in the early years, were not staffed to obtain news for broadcast except through the newspapers themselves, or through the news agencies. In the United States, the United Press and the International News Service, parts of the corporate structures of the Scripps and Hearst newspaper organizations, respectively, found no objection to the sale of their news services for use by radio stations, and the United Press was particularly active in doing so. The Associated Press, however, as a nonprofit, cooperative agency owned by its member papers, was reluctant to provide such service, although many of its members also owned radio stations. In 1922 the AP specifically warned its member papers against broadcasting news appearing in their columns, or permitting others to do so.

Even though the British radio was not dependent for support upon revenue derived from the broadcast of advertising messages, as in the United States, the potential rivalry of radio as a news medium was recognized by the press. Lord Riddell of the *News of the World,* speaking for the Newspaper Proprietors' Association as late as 1928, cautioned against publication of the daily program logs as an encouragement to readers to turn to the other medium. He noted that the BBC was paying Reuters only £8,000 a year for the use of news reports costing that agency and the newspapers £5 million to obtain, yet with news broadcasts threatening the newspapers with circulation losses. Reuters continued to provide service to BBC, however, nor were limitations placed upon the use of news agency services by radio in other countries.

As radio stations in the United States began to sell spot announcements on the air after 1922, and then to find sponsors for
programs, a possibility arose that a special news service or agency might
be formed by or for the new medium. To forestall any such thing,
competitive as it might become, and recognizing that the UP and INS
were providing reports for radio use, the Associated Press modified its
ban on radio in 1925 to permit a conditional use of important bulletins,
and in 1928 to approve the preparation of two special daily broadcasts
through the period of that year's presidential campaign. In 1929 the AP
policy was further eased when it agreed to join with the UP and INS in
the formation of a National Radio Press Association, with Herbert
Bayard Swope, former executive editor of the *New York World,* as
director. The concept was that the association would have its own
correspondents reporting important events and that these accounts,
along with a general report based upon dispatches by the three agencies,
would be processed for radio, that is written for oral delivery and
listening rather than in conventional newspaper style, and distributed to
radio stations for a suitable fee.

The National Radio Press Association existed from 1929 to 1934, but
without much success. It failed to satisfy the radio stations or to meet the
public interest. Radio by then had attained a strong position, with NBC
and CBS both well established as networks, and with ninety newspapers
operating their own stations in 1930. Some of the earlier alarms felt by
the press about radio competition had abated. A study by the American
Newspaper Publishers Association (ANPA) had concluded that radio
news broadcasts actually were stimulating public interest in newspaper
reading. Circulations were indeed rising. Radio was attracting a
growing volume of advertising, but new money had placed the
newspapers' advertising dollar volume at a record level in 1929 of $80
million. This exceeded radio twice over, and also exceeded every other
medium—magazine, outdoor, and direct mail advertising.

The depression years that followed in 1930–38 were less favorable,
relatively, with newspapers and magazines losing advertising, while
radio gained. The number of newspapers declined, but the survivors
gained in circulation and maintained a strong advertising position.
Newspapers in other countries suffered during the same years, not
because of a shift of advertising to radio, since radio advertising did not
exist in most, but rather because of the general economic decline.

Meanwhile, events themselves were stimulating public interest in
radio news. Radio stations and networks in the United States undertook
to supplement the reports of the National Radio Press Association

through efforts of their own. In 1930, KMPC of Beverly Hills, California, a station then owned by the MacMillan Petroleum Corporation, offered three daily broadcasts of local news gathered through its own subsidiary organization, the Radio News Service of America, with ten persons covering the news of the Los Angeles area, plus some coverage elsewhere. In New England, the Yankee Network of Boston formed a regional news-gathering service directed by Richard D. Grant, formerly of the *Boston Transcript*. Such efforts did not continue for long, however. They were soon made unnecessary by later developments in news agency services and network-related activities.

William Hard for NBC and Frederic William Wile for CBS even then were broadcasting from Washington.[5] Both networks undertook to develop added coverage of their own in 1933. Early in the year, NBC engaged Jack Levy, a former reporter for the *United States Daily,* which was published in Washington from 1926 to 1933 by David Lawrence. Levy was to report the news of Congress for the network. He was denied entrance to the press galleries, however, since a radio reporter was not recognized by the Press Galleries of the Congress of the United States. The rules specified that admission to the galleries should be limited to "bona fide correspondents . . . who represent daily newspapers or news associations requiring telegraphic service." The Standing Committee governing admission took the position that since radio obviously was not a "newspaper" and that "telegraphic service" was not an element in radio coverage, Levy's application should be denied.

Listening to debates from the visitors' galleries of the House and Senate, Levy nevertheless became the first radio correspondent at the Capitol itself. He was able to follow the business of Congress further by direct approach to senators and representatives and their staff assistants. He telephoned information to WRC, the NBC station in Washington, where it was processed for use.

In the autumn of 1933, CBS announced the formation of a subsidiary, the Columbia News Service, Inc., which was intended to provide independent coverage of the news. Based in New York, the corporation was to be headed by William S. Paley, president of CBS, with Edward Klauber, former city editor of the *New York Times,* as first vice-president. Paul White, publicity director for CBS, a former member of the United Press staff in New York and a columnist for that

---

5 One of the members of the NBC board of directors then was Edward W. Harden, formerly of the *Chicago Tribune,* who had reported the Battle of Manila Bay for that paper and for the *New York World* in 1898, a major action of the Spanish-American War. See Desmond, *The Information Process,* pp. 396ff.

agency, was to be general manager. L. L. Trumbull, a former Chicago newsman, was to be in charge of New York City coverage, assisted by Edward G. Angly, formerly of the AP staff in Paris, and Herbert S. Moore, formerly in the UP London bureau. Wells Church, in Washington, was to be assisted there by Cecil Owen and Frank Connor, Jr. Actually, the Columbia News Service never became operative. An application for accreditation of a correspondent to the Press Galleries of the Congress was rejected, as it had been for Levy. That action, along with other delays and developments, resulted in the suspension of plans for the service.

The American Newspaper Publishers Association, late in 1932, had recommended that news agencies at least withhold their reports, or the use of their reports, from radio stations or networks until after those news reports had appeared in the newspapers, and that even then the news should be presented by radio only in bulletin form. In 1933 the ANPA, along with the Associated Press, went further and proposed the denial of agency reports to radio altogether, except for occasional urgent bulletins. This would have been a return to the AP's policy of 1925–28, but now the UP and INS joined in accepting the proposal.

The prospect threatened radio stations and networks with a crisis in the matter of news broadcasts. It spurred the NBC effort in Washington as a beginning of independent action, and it spurred CBS in the organization of the Columbia News Service. It also placed the existing National Radio Press Association in an anomalous position, even beyond the fact that its service was not satisfactory to stations or networks at the time.

Nothing actually was done to resolve this uncertain situation until 1934. Radio, however, had reached such a position of strength and public acceptance that it was unrealistic to suppose so vital a medium could be denied the opportunity to include news broadcasts as a part of its programming. They had become enormously important. Some were sponsored by advertisers. If some elements might seek to block that service, other elements, including about 100 newspapers by then operating their own radio stations, took an opposite position. Some stations were undertaking their own local or regional news coverage, and NBC and CBS were moving in that direction. The Mutual Broadcasting System (MBS) began operations in 1934, and other independent news services designed especially for radio were in prospect. Five appeared in 1934 and 1935. A compromise therefore was to be expected to assure the provision of radio news reports.

Through an agreement between the American Newspaper Publishers Association and the American Society of Newspaper Editors, a Press

Radio Bureau was organized. The full title was the Press-Radio Bureau of the Publishers' National Radio Commission. The service operated out of New York, beginning in March 1934, and was directed by James W. Barrett, former city editor of the *New York World,* which suspended in 1931. When it began, the former National Radio Press Association was suspended, and the projected CBS Columbia News Service also died before it began to operate.

The function of the Press Radio Bureau was to prepare scripts for two five-minute news broadcasts each day, based upon material drawn from the full reports of the AP, UP, and INS. Those broadcasts were to be made, however, only after the newspapers had appeared, morning or afternoon. They also were to be used without advertising sponsorship. In the event of extraordinary occurrences, it was understood that special bulletins would be released for radio use.

This service never was fully effective. Two five-minute news broadcasts each day meant a retreat by radio stations from practices already well established. They looked elsewhere for news, and no more than 245 radio stations, less than half of those then in operation, ever used the Press Radio Bureau service. The Yankee network in its territory, and other stations, were obtaining news through their own enterprise. The NBC and CBS networks were naming staff and stringer correspondents throughout the country, and even in Europe, and broadcasting their reports. The MBS soon followed suit. Independent services also appeared, the most important of which was the Transradio Press Service (TP), established in New York in 1934, even as the Press-Radio Bureau also was formed. Transradio Press was organized and directed by Herbert S. Moore. He had been associated with the short-lived Columbia News Service and, prior to that, the UP London bureau. Moore found financial backing and engaged correspondents in New York, Washington, London, and elsewhere. The Ring Combination of news agencies came to an official end on March 31, 1934, after sixty-four years of existence. With the provision for "exclusive territories" for news distribution thus abolished, Moore also was able to receive a world news report for Transradio Press from the French Agence Havas. A year later, a similar relationship was established with the Reuters agency.

By 1935 the Transradio Press was providing service to 160 U.S. radio stations, then also free to present the news with commercial sponsorship. By 1938 it was going to 288 stations and forty-six newspapers as well, not only in the United States but to the *Daily Telegraph* in London and the *Daily Express* in Johannesburg. It had a staff of forty in New York and thirty-four bureaus in the United States and abroad, manned by 132 writers and editors, plus stringers.

The three established U.S. news agencies locked into the Press Radio Bureau arrangement were feeling substantial competition from Transradio Press. Moore became a controversial figure under attack along with the TP itself from the ANPA and other sources. The competition of the TP was such that by May 1935, hardly a year after it began operations, the UP and INS asked and received permission to be released from the Press Radio Bureau arrangement so that they might return to the sale of full news reports directly to radio stations and to the networks. The UP re-entered the field with vigor, establishing a special wire to carry reports to radio stations and was fully prepared to meet the needs of broadcasting. The INS followed suit.

The desertion of UP and INS naturally reduced the effectiveness of the Press Radio Bureau. It still had available the excellent AP service as a basis for preparing its two daily five-minute broadcast scripts. But radio stations and networks understandably preferred to receive services they could use as they wished, with no limitations on the time, length or frequency of broadcasts, and with no restriction on sponsorship or the use of spot commercials.

By the summer of 1935, the Pacific Coast bureau of the Press Radio Bureau was closed, and most of the sixty-five radio stations that had been receiving reports from that source in the western area turned directly to the UP and INS services. According to one estimate, by 1936 500 stations out of 635 then operating in the United States were broadcasting news programs based upon reports from UP and INS.

The Associated Press, so long insistent upon restricting use of its service by radio, at last felt compelled by May 1939 to make its reports generally available for broadcast, with or without sponsorship, and without time limitations. A cooperative news agency, with strict membership restrictions for newspapers, it entered into full competition with UP and INS in the sale of news for radio use. Radio stations, unlike newspapers, were not "members" of the AP, but received its service on a commercial basis. Further, in January 1941, the AP formed a subsidiary, Press Association, Inc., to maintain a twenty-four hour national teleprinter circuit to distribute a special news report processed for radio.

The radio networks and major stations commonly received news reports on teleprinter circuits from two or more agencies. The Press Radio Bureau, operating on a limited basis after 1935, was suspended in 1940. Transradio Press also suffered a loss of patronage after 1935, but continued a service for press and radio clients alike until December 1951.

News programs, as broadcast originally, were read in the United States by anonymous announcers, and by news readers in Great Britain. The voices of many announcers became familiar to listeners and their names soon began to be used. Certain of the news programs also were identified with sponsors, networks, and sometimes with individual stations, newspapers, or magazines.

One of the first familiar names was that of Frederic William Wile, who began broadcasting from WRC in Washington in 1923, and then from WJZ, New York, as well, for the NBC network of stations from the time of its formation in 1926 until 1928, when he switched to the CBS network until 1938. Having started without pay in 1923, he joined CBS in 1928 at a salary of $10,000 annually. This was indicative of the growth that had come to radio in five years, and of what the use of spot announcements and commercial sponsorship was bringing financially to stations, networks, and those persons appearing on the air.

In addition to Wile, and William Hard, who replaced him in Washington for NBC in 1928, another newsman of experience entering early into broadcasting in the United States was Hans von Kaltenborn, a member of the *Brooklyn Eagle* staff since 1910, and associate editor in 1922. In that year, simplifying his name to H. V. Kaltenborn, he became the first news commentator for station WJZ in New York, and a news analyst and commentator for the NBC network from 1926 through 1929. He was then with the CBS network from 1929 to 1940, and returned to NBC in 1940 until almost the time of his death in 1965. The radio news analyst or commentator was a phenomenon of the 1930s.

Floyd Gibbons, with a decade of experience as a reporter and correspondent for the *Chicago Tribune,* primarily in Paris, made his first appearance on radio on Christmas night of 1925 in Chicago, when he broadcast over WGN, the *Tribune* station, recounting some of his personal adventures in the news field. In the spring of 1929, he left the *Tribune* to begin an association with NBC. His broadcasts were related to the news only on certain occasions, but they were informational. He was primarily a spokesman for corporate sponsors, the General Electric Company, the *Literary Digest,* the Libbey-Owens-Ford Glass Company, the Johns-Manville Company, the Standard Oil Company, Nash Motors, and RCA. Larry Rue, also formerly of the *Tribune* staff in Europe, worked with him on the preparation of his earlier broadcasts.

Gibbons's rapid-fire, informal style of delivery became familiar to radio listeners throughout the United States and Canada. His contract with NBC permitted him to cover any event he wished. Under this provision, he reported the arrival of the Graf Zeppelin at Lakehurst, New Jersey, in 1929 after its eastward flight around the world from Friedrichshafen, Germany, by way of Russia, Japan, and the Pacific, and across the United States. He reported an army pageant in Washington in 1932, the Republican and Democratic national conventions of that year, made the first broadcast from a moving train, described the inauguration of Franklin D. Roosevelt as president in 1933, and made a series of broadcasts on the Chicago "Century of Progress" World's Fair of that year.

Lowell Thomas was another radio news broadcaster and commentator to enter the field, originally in 1930, following Gibbons at that time as spokesman for the *Literary Digest*. He continued as a news broadcaster until his retirement in 1976. During many of those years, he also narrated the Fox Movietone newsreel, was a key figure in the establishment of Cinerama, and active in television.

Another broadcaster familiar to network listeners in the United States in the early 1930s was Boake Carter. Born in Baku, in southern Russia, and son of a British consular officer, he had been a staff member of the London *Daily Mail,* and then a Philadelphia newsman. It was there he entered broadcasting. Heard over the CBS network, he became widely known in 1932 for his direct reporting on the continuing and deeply moving story of the kidnapping of the first child of Charles A. Lindbergh and Anne Morrow Lindbergh from their home near Hopewell, N.J. Going beyond the news itself to add subjective interpretation of the event, Carter became one of the first radio commentators.

Among other early news broadcasters and commentators heard on the networks were Edwin C. Hill, previously on the staff of the *New York Sun,* Gabriel Heatter, formerly of the *New York American* and *Brooklyn Eagle,* and John B. Kennedy, identified with *Collier's Weekly*.

The *Christian Science Monitor* in 1930 began the preparation and distribution of a somewhat interpretative news script each day, useful and informative for broadcast any time within several days of its preparation. Based largely upon reports from the *Monitor*'s own correspondents in the United States and overseas, it was prepared under the direction of Volney D. Hurd, then the paper's radio editor—a new position on some papers. It went to as many as 400 radio stations in the

United States for a number of years, available for use without cost.

By the early 1930s the radio medium and the print medium, taken together, were providing a better report on the news than the public ever before had available, not only in the United States, Canada, and Great Britain, but in many other countries.

Technological advances involving a recording or taping process permitted the broadcast and rebroadcast of radio programs at periods convenient for listeners in various time zones. This produced audiences of millions for some programs. Radio, in this fashion, introduced a very literal form of mass communication. This term, of course, meant that the program was reaching a vast number of persons, not that the audience represented the masses in a pejorative sense, as some persons mistakenly assumed even after the terms mass media and mass communications were in general use.

Sarnoff's magical "music box" opened new vistas for much of the world's population, including the illiterate, the blind, the elderly, the lonely, and persons living in remote places. It also opened previously unimagined commercial opportunities.

Illustrative of these circumstances was a sequence of events originating in Canada. There radio news broadcasting had developed after 1920 much as in the United States. The Canadian Broadcasting Company (CBC) represented a network of stations, privately owned but licensed and able to accept advertising announcements and sponsorship of programs. The Canadian Press (CP) and BUP services were available to the stations as a basis for the preparation of news broadcasts.

Working in Ottawa, Toronto-born Roy Herbert Thomson had been active in the sale of radio receiving sets there and in areas surrounding. So that purchasers of such sets in the smaller towns might be assured of programs, he also had established radio station CFCH at North Bay in 1931, another at Timmins, a gold field town in northern Ontario in 1932, and then CJKL at Kirkland Lake. Further, to provide an added means to advertise his radio sets and to provide program listings for purchasers, he bought a weekly paper, the *Press,* at Timmins in 1934. Then forty years old, Thomson was successful in these efforts. The radio stations brought him a financial return from the advertising time sold on the air. His weekly paper also prospered so that it soon was appearing twice a week, and became a daily in 1936. He acquired a fourth radio station, CJCS at Stratford, Ontario, and formed the Northern Broadcasting and

Publishing Company, with an office in Toronto. He added other papers as well, and three more radio stations in 1940.[6]

By the late 1930s, radio held every prospect of advancing public understanding at a new pace. To some, the oral presentation of news and information seemed preferable to print and sufficient to satisfy their interests. It was quick, convenient, and without cost. For all, there was an undeniable appeal in being able to listen to some events as they occurred, to hear the actual voices of those previously known only by name or seen in photographs. By listening attentively, many may have become more aware of events than ever before.

In the United States, the voices of Presidents Harding, Coolidge, and Hoover had been heard by millions. President Roosevelt became known to virtually all. The same familiarity with the voices of leading personalities applied in other countries, and the growth of international broadcasting made many known to listeners throughout the world.

Radio correspondents increased in number in Washington after 1933, and a Radio Correspondents' Association was formed. Its president in 1938 was Fulton Lewis, Jr., formerly a member of the INS bureau in the capital, who switched in 1937 to the Mutual Broadcasting System as a news commentator. Lewis, in December 1938, revived the matter of admitting radio correspondents to the Press Galleries of the Congress. Although Levy had made such a request in 1933, Lewis was able to cite two precedents in 1938. The International Association of Journalists Accredited to the League of Nations in Geneva had given full recognition to radio correspondents. In London, the BBC had been granted a seat for its correspondent in the parliamentary press gallery of the House of Commons in 1936.

---

6   Thomson was on his way to a fabulous media empire. He became a member of the board of directors of the Canadian Press, and later its president, and president of the Canadian Daily Newspaper Publishers Association in 1950. By 1953 he not only owned radio and television stations in Canada, but controlled 19 newspapers there, and several in the United States. In 1954 he extended his interests to the United Kingdom, purchasing the *Scotsman* of Edinburgh, and entered also into television at a time when the BBC position was modified to permit a second Independent Television (ITV) network, able also to broadcast commercial advertising messages. Thomson became a British citizen in 1963, by which time he also owned the London *Sunday Times* and the many other newspapers and magazines previously conducted by Lord Kemsley (formerly Sir James Gomer Berry). In 1964 he was created a baron, and took the title of Lord Thomson of Fleet. In 1966 he was able to purchase the *Times*. He continued to develop his holdings and when he died in 1976, at eighty-two, he owned 148 newspapers and 138 magazines in seventeen countries of all five continents, as well as radio and television stations and other enterprises. No other media holdings by any one man or company ever had been so large. His son, Kenneth Thomson, carried the business forward, with further additions. See Russell Braddon, *Roy Thomson of Fleet Street* (New York, 1966).

The Standing Committee of the Press Galleries again rejected the application for accreditation of radio correspondents, however, and also rejected a proposal that a separate Radio Correspondents Gallery be established. In this instance, however, Lewis persisted in his appeal on behalf of the Radio Correspondents' Association. He had the matter referred to the Rules Committee in the House of Representatives, and also gained the support of Neville Miller, president of the National Association of Broadcasters, an organization formed in 1923. Further, he made direct appeals to individual members of the House and Senate.

The House Rules Committee in reviewing the issue agreed that radio, by then well established in its news function and well represented in the capital, should have equal facilities for covering both houses of Congress and other Washington sources, including the White House. The proposal for a separate Radio Correspondents Gallery, originally presented in 1933, was revived and approved by congressional action in April 1939, with twenty-six radio correspondents promptly accredited.[7]

Radio broadcasts moved over the standard AM medium wave frequency bands within the various countries. The radius within which programs could be heard was limited, with transmitters holding to their assigned frequencies, which was essential to prevent signal interference. In Europe, where distances were not great between countries, radio programs inevitably crossed many frontiers, but audiences tended to be self-selective because of language differences.

Experimentation proceeded. The benefits deriving from the use of higher frequencies, or short waves, had been demonstrated in application to beamed radiotelegraphic transmission. This led to speculation as to whether comparable benefits might be realized in voice-radio transmission by the use of short waves.

In 1927 the BBC began to beam such programs experimentally from London to listeners anywhere in the British Commonwealth. This, if it could be accomplished, was expected to advance the sense of Commonwealth unity. But it also would open the frontiers of the world so that millions of persons might hear news, music, commentaries, cultural programs, and live events, directly or by delayed broadcast,

---

7 This now operates as a Radio-TV Correspondents Gallery. As originally established, it became a precedent for the addition of a Press Photographers Gallery and a Magazine Correspondents Gallery. Members are listed in the *Congressional Directory*.

from any part of the earth. There was no reason why shortwave frequencies might not be assigned, as with medium wave frequencies, to make that possible while avoiding signal interference.

The BBC experiments proved that all this was feasible. Similar experiments followed in other countries and by 1930 direct international transmissions over the greatest distances became standard radio fare. The programs might be heard directly by those with suitable receiving sets, but also could be recorded for rebroadcast on the standard medium wave bands at hours convenient for general listening audiences in any given time zone of the world.

The London Naval Conference opening in the British House of Lords on January 21, 1930, became an historic occasion in shortwave radio broadcasting of the news. Although there had been three earlier voice transmissions across the Atlantic between 1924 and 1929, this marked the first live news event to be reported, and the first heard so broadly, with the BBC providing the facilities. It began with an address of welcome by King George V, whose voice was heard internationally.

The groundwork for the conference had been laid in Washington in 1929 at a meeting between President Hoover and British Prime Minister J. Ramsay MacDonald. Frederic William Wile, who had reported that meeting for CBS, proposed to William S. Paley, president of the network, that he go to London to report the conference itself, and Paley agreed. William Hard, then representing the NBC in Washington, also was assigned to the story for that network. The two men accompanied the U.S. delegation to London. Through arrangements with Reith at the BBC, they broadcast from separate studios, with their comments rebroadcast from New York over the networks. They began with eye-witness accounts of the opening day ceremonies, along with explanations of the purpose of the conference.

The Naval Conference continued from January to April, meeting after that first day in St. James's Palace. During those weeks, Wile and Hard broadcast frequent reports. They also brought to the microphone members of the U.S. delegation and such prominent British personalities as Prime Minister MacDonald, Philip Snowden, chancellor of the exchequer, Viscount Cecil of Chelwood, president of the League of Nations Union, and Henry Wickham Steed, former editor of the *Times*.

Direct coverage of news and special events by shortwave continued from that time. Ceremonies in Paris on Bastille Day, July 14, 1930, were broadcast internationally. A sharp earthquake the following week in the Melfi region of southern Italy, with a thousand deaths and injuries and damage, was reported in broadcasts by Philip Lemont of Universal Service, and Frederick L. Abbott, manager of the INS Paris bureau, who happened to be in Italy at the time. Prince Pignatelli, Rome correspondent for Universal Service, also spoke of the event from aboard the yacht of Guglielmo Marconi, standing off the coast.

This particular coverage was provided through a new Hearst Radio Service, directed by Emile J. Gough, former managing editor of the *San Francisco Call,* and George C. Williams, former managing editor of the *Albany Times-Union,* both Hearst papers. The broadcasts from Italy were picked up by a General Electric shortwave station, W2XAF, Schenectady, N.Y., and rebroadcast over WGY, Schenectady, a General Electric AM station within the NBC network, and carried nationally by that network. The Hearst Radio Service did not continue for long, but the enterprise it displayed in reporting the Italian earthquake was typical of shortwave radio news service in the years to follow.

When Wile left London in April 1930, after coverage of the Naval Conference, a permanent CBS representative remained. César Saerchinger, a former Berlin and London correspondent for the combined *Philadelphia Public Ledger–New York Evening Post* news service and a music authority, was named director for the network in London and Europe, a position he was to occupy until 1937. Hard's departure from London was followed by a similar appointment for NBC, with Fred Bate, an artist and cosmopolite, as its representative. Their assignments were to arrange shortwave broadcasts of special events, musical performances, and addresses by prominent individuals.

Through the facilities of the BBC and the British General Post Office, and occasionally through the League of Nations transmitter or others on the European continent, the CBS and NBC networks in the United States, along with the CBC network in Canada, carried talks by personalities and leaders. Among them were the Prince of Wales, Viscount Grey of Falloden (formerly Sir Edward Grey), Rudyard Kipling, Bernard Shaw, H. G. Wells, Gilbert K. Chesterton, Stanley Baldwin, Eamon De Valera, and Thomas Masaryk.

The BBC and shortwave stations in France, Germany, Italy, and Holland both originated and received broadcasts, with an international exchange growing through the years. From London, for example, George V introduced the practice of making Christmas broadcasts in 1932, extending greetings and good will to the peoples of the British Commonwealth and all nations through 1935, a few weeks before his death.

On January 1, 1931, Benito Mussolini in Rome broadcast a special address in English. The following month, Pope Pius XI, speaking in Latin, broadcast world-wide from a new Vatican shortwave station. Later in the year, at the time of the Indian Round Table Conference in London, Mahatma Gandhi was heard in an address. The results of the British general election in October were reported by shortwave radio. Queen Wilhelmina of the Netherlands, addressed the people of that country and of the Dutch East Indies and Dutch West Indies from The Hague. Late in the year, the Reichs-Rundfunkgesellschaft (RRG) (German Broadcasting Company), completed a study preparatory to initiating a weekly broadcast from the United States. Before the plan became effective, however, the German government had changed and the idea was abandoned.

A major news event of 1932 was a World Disarmament Conference meeting at Geneva in February under League of Nations auspices and adjourning in July. Wile of CBS and Hard of NBC returned to Europe to provide coverage, and were joined by radio correspondents of other countries. Their broadcasts were transmitted by the League's own powerful radio installation, Radio Nations, built at a cost of 4.2 million Swiss francs (about $1 million) and only just put into operation, with its transmitter at Prangins, on Lake Geneva's shore.[8]

The year 1932 also brought shortwave broadcasts including an address in Copenhagen by Leon Trotsky, who had been exiled from the Soviet Union in 1929. Broadcasts by Floyd Gibbons for the NBC were made from Manchuria and from Shanghai. Amelia Earhart was interviewed on the air immediately after her arrival in Ireland on a solo flight from Newfoundland in May, the first ocean flight by a woman. The 1932 presidential campaign in the United States included shortwave coverage from the time of the two national conventions through the November election and Franklin D. Roosevelt's victory over Herbert Hoover.

The 1932–34 period was transitional in world affairs and in measures taken to report them by radio, both medium wave and short wave. Technical advances permitted an improved reporting of the unfolding events. Radio reporters, able to move about with open microphones, gave listeners a sense of being present themselves at the scene.

Systems of disk, wire and tape recording were introduced to capture the story and the sound of events for later broadcast and rebroadcast.

---

8   When the League of Nations became a casualty of World War II, this transmitter was sold to the Swiss government in 1942 for less than 300,000 Swiss francs (about $75,000) and became Radio Suisse, a semi-official government station.

Cue channels could be set up on separate wavelengths to permit discussion of arrangements and details of broadcasts, even across oceans. Press Wireless became able to handle voice transmission, as well as text messages in code. It also became common to supplement the broadcast of news by offering a news analysis or commentary by a radio reporter or correspondent possessed of the requisite background and experience.

The voices of leading personalities in the drama of those years became familiar to listeners throughout the world, Roosevelt and Hitler among them. The broadcast of Britain's Edward VIII on December 10, 1936, announcing his abdication, made history. So did the broadcast of ceremonies at Westminster Abbey in May 1937 when George VI and his queen were crowned. In the same year, there was a ninety-second eye-witness broadcast by George Hicks of NBC from the Canton Islands describing a total eclipse of the sun, the only one anticipated by astronomers for some 1,200 years. There also was an account of the wedding of King Farouk in Egypt, and a broadcast from the pyramids, both by an NBC unit.

The economic and political crises occupying the 1930s, including events of war in China, Ethiopia, and Spain, and not least the Munich conference of 1938, were reported both by radio correspondents and by those of the press. Many of the radio correspondents were recruited from among those very press representatives. The volume and costs of radio coverage rose in proportion to the growing activity in electronic journalism.

For the BBC, Vernon Bartlett became a regular broadcaster from Geneva from 1927 to 1933, and was heard in the United States after that. Percy J. Philip, also British, and in Paris for the *New York Times,* broadcast from there for BBC listeners. Arthur Ernest Baker, formerly of the *Times,* became overseas news editor for the BBC in 1938. Sir Frederick Whyte, S. K. Ratcliffe, Gerald Barry, and Stephen King-Hall, broadcasting for the BBC, were heard in the United States and Canada. Richard Dimbleby moved abroad on BBC assignments from early 1939. Pierre de Lanux was heard from Paris. In the same period, Raymond Gram Swing in New York broadcast an "American Commentary" for rebroadcast by the BBC in the United Kingdom. Pierre Bédard, Percy H. Winner, and John B. Whitton, of Princeton University, broadcast to France.

All three U.S. networks advanced their service of broadcasts, particularly from Europe, in the 1930s. The NBC, with A. A. Schechter in New York as director of news and special events, named George

Holmes, formerly of INS, to succeed Hard in Washington in 1933, with
Levy added to the staff. Dr. Max Jordan, of U.S. nationality, but
Italian-born and German-educated, a former New York correspondent
for the *Berliner Tageblatt* and then an INS staffer in Central Europe,
became NBC correspondent in that area after helping report the Geneva
Conference in 1932, but established in a permanent bureau at Basle, as
Bate was in London. Frank E. Mason, former general manager in
Europe for INS in 1928–31, became vice-president for NBC. Paul
Archinard became correspondent in Paris. Alex Dreier, formerly of the
AP, Warren Irvin, and Paul Fischer broadcast from Berlin, Charles
Lanius, Reynolds Packard, and Philip McKenzie from Rome, and G. E.
R. Gedye of the *New York Times* from Prague.

For CBS, Paul W. White was in New York as director of news
coverage from 1934 to 1939. Saerchinger, in London since 1930,
resigned in 1937, and was succeeded by Edward R. (Roscoe) Murrow,
who had been in New York as "director of talks" for the network since
1935. E. Percy Noël, manager in Paris since 1932, was succeeded there
by Thomas B. Grandin, formerly of INS. H. V. Kaltenborn, usually in
New York, had made special broadcasts from Spain. Murrow, taking
charge in London, promptly engaged William L. Shirer, in Europe and
India since 1925 for the *Chicago Tribune* and Universal Service, first to
broadcast from Vienna and then from Berlin. He picked Eric Sevareid,
in Paris for the UP, to succeed Grandin there. Others added to the CBS
staff in Europe in the next three or four years included Kenneth T.
Downs and Cecil Brown, both formerly of INS, Howard K. Smith,
Harry Flannery, Larry LeSueur, Richard G. Hottelet, Charles L.
Collingwood, and Walter Cronkite, all formerly on European
assignments for the UP. Elmer Davis, formerly of the *New York Times*,
became a broadcaster in New York.

For MBS, David Driscoll became director of news and special events
in the New York headquarters in the late 1930s. John Steele, London
correspondent for the *Chicago Tribune*, became European representative in 1935, although not a broadcaster, and Sigrid Schultz, *Tribune*
Berlin correspondent, was Central European representative. Raymond
Gram Swing became commentator for the network in New York. Others
called upon to broadcast from Europe for MBS included William
Hillman, formerly of INS and *Collier's*, Edmond Taylor, formerly of
the *Chicago Tribune*, Waverly Root, formerly of the Paris edition of the
Tribune, Patrick Maitland of the *Times*, Maurice Hindus, and John
Paul Dickson.

These were among the correspondents heard in international
broadcasts in the late 1930s. There were others, including some on other

continents, and more would be drawn into broadcasting as events proceeded, some temporarily but many permanently. Most were recruited, as nearly all of those mentioned, from previous positions with news agencies, newspapers, and magazines.

Communications Regulation

The great and varied use of wireless communication after World War I demanded international regulation, if confusion on the air was to be avoided. This had been obvious since the earliest wireless signals began to be transmitted shortly before 1900. The two conferences in Berlin in 1903 and 1906, approached the problem, and more was accomplished at an International Telegraphic Union conference in Lisbon in 1908. The ITU had been meeting at five-year intervals, but the events of World War I delayed the next meeting until 1925 in Paris. A related International Radiotelegraphic Union (IRU) meeting had occurred in London in 1912, but the war delayed the next until 1927 in Washington.

The ITU conference of 1925 recommended that the ITU and the IRU conventions for the regulation of communications be combined, and this proposal was approved by the IRU at a 1927 meeting. The control of wavelength assignments improved notably from that time, and improved further after 1934.

A wide awareness had emerged from the war of a need for inexpensive as well as technically effective world communications, and for a means to obtain and disseminate news of current affairs without censorship interference or propaganda distortion. An unprecedented number of meetings between 1920 and 1940 brought together specialists in communications technology and specialists in news. Some of these meetings were sponsored by the League of Nations, but they included those of the ITU and the IRU.

Meetings in Madrid in 1932 of the ITU and the IRU were notably important. It was the thirteenth ITU conference, and the first "diplomatic" conference since the St. Petersburg meeting of 1875, with delegates authorized to sign a treaty binding upon their governments. Some eighty countries were represented, plus sixty-two private companies and various international organizations. The IRU conference was its fourth, also diplomatic in character, and brought together representatives of sixty-five countries and sixty-four private companies and organizations. The conferences were separate, but liaison was maintained. Ten joint plenary sessions were held, and a joint convention followed, establishing regulations to govern what then became officially known as "telecommunications," embracing all forms of electrical communication. The treaty included a fourth revision of the basic St. Petersburg agreement of 1875 bearing upon rates, conditions, and priorities of service.

The Madrid meeting gave formal approval to the merger of the ITU and the IRU, with a new title as the International Telecommunications Union, still the "ITU," which became effective January 1, 1934. The Berne administrative ITU bureau was correspondingly retitled. Continuing as the center for the regulation of international communications, the bureau held responsibility for the assignment of radio frequencies, as well as for transmission rates and other matters necessary and helpful in maintaining orderly communications. Henri Etienne, head of the ITU bureau, was succeeded in 1934 by Dr. Franz von Ernst, who served as secretary general until his retirement in 1950.

At the suggestion of the United States, it was agreed at Madrid that privately owned communications companies in future might participate actively in ITU discussions, rather than be represented merely as observers as before. The United States and Canada had been unable, previously, to vote or even to accept all regulations governing telegraph, cable, and telephone communications because the facilities were not government-owned in those countries. The convention at Madrid, however, was drafted in terms sufficiently general so that both countries were able to sign. For radio communication neither country was hindered in its IRU participation because those governments did in fact exercise control over the transmitting stations through regulations and the system of licenses required for the control of wavelength assignments. This government control meant that radio news broadcasting was not free in the same legal or constitutional sense as news published in the press, even in the United States.

An important accomplishment of the Madrid meetings was to review and establish new assignments of shortwave frequencies throughout the world. These related not only to point-to-point radiotelegraphic transmissions and to voice broadcasts, but to distress signals on land and sea, police radio, amateur broadcasting, and other electronic emissions. The ITU bureau at Berne subsequently published these assignments, as well as itemizing all telegraph, cable, and telephone lines, and it maintained a current listing of all circuits and changes.

A second important specification approved at Madrid was that in the event of any message being delayed in transmission, for whatever reason, notice of that delay was to be given promptly to the sender. In practice, this was to have special importance in application to press dispatches delayed by censors. It was a regulation generally observed, but not always with prompt notification.

Discussions at Madrid had ventured into matters bearing both upon censorship and propaganda, and upon the control a government might exercise over messages moving within its jurisdiction. Proposals by some governments would have increased such control over the content and handling of messages. These proposals were blocked, however, largely through the insistence of the U.S. delegation, headed by Robert T. Pell, then press attaché in the U.S. Embassy in Paris.

The IRU meeting in Washington in 1927, aware of experiments then in progress relating to shortwave voice broadcasts, adopted resolutions recommending that precautions be taken to avoid the international transmission of material likely to injure good relations between peoples and governments. The League of Nations, at the request of the IRU, had brought this recommendation to the attention of its member governments, then including all major countries except the United States and the Soviet Union. The League suggested that governments enact national regulations to prevent the broadcast of political, economic, religious, cultural, or other references that might cause ill feelings between nations. These particular efforts and recommendations had small effect. The only specific response was a 1931 German-Polish agreement intended to prevent broadcasts of such prejudicial or tendentious nature, but even that agreement was ignored, particularly after 1933.

The need for regulation of radio communication, regionally as well as internationally, had brought the formation of an Inter-American Union of Electrical Communications at Mexico City in 1924. In 1933 an IRU-ITU Technical Committee met at Brussels. A European Broadcasting Conference met at Lucerne, also in 1933, and other regional meetings occurred at Lisbon in 1934, Bucharest in 1937, and Montreux in 1939. An Inter-American Radio Conference met at Havana in 1937, and a second at Santiago in Chile in 1940. Special meetings relating to telephone, cable, and telephone usage met at Prague and Budapest in 1934, and at Warsaw and Copenhagen in 1936.

A full-dress fourteenth ITU conference met at Cairo in the spring of 1938, with separate sessions to consider telegraph-cable-telephone matters and radio matters. Both sessions were concerned with rates, but the radio session gave major attention to a further reallocation of frequencies to meet increased needs in communications, medical, and other fields.

Censorship and shortwave radio propaganda had by then become even more serious problems than at the time of the 1932 conference at Madrid. The subjects were discussed again, but with no effective result. The matter also had been introduced at the League of Nations Disarmament Conference in Geneva in 1932–33, and was referred to that conference's Moral Disarmament and Political Commission, where it languished. A League-sponsored International Institute of International Cooperation in Paris took an interest in the subject and in 1933 initiated action that led to a special League conference in 1936 at which representatives of twenty-eight nations signed a draft convention, positive and constructive in its measures, and relative to the use of broadcasting as an instrument of peace. Comparable action was taken at an Inter-American Conference for the Maintenance of Peace meeting at Buenos Aires also in 1936. These efforts came too late, however, to reverse a negative trend. The countries guilty of the misuse of radio as a propaganda weapon, notably Fascist Italy and Nazi Germany, were unprepared to join in any commitment to refrain from such action.

The Pact of Paris, popularly known as the Kellogg-Briand Pact, signed by almost all nations in 1928, which renounced war as an instrument of national policy, was virtually forgotten by 1933. Japan that year announced its withdrawal from the League of Nations, after League condemnation of its 1931 invasion of Manchuria. Germany was admitted to the League in 1926, but under a National Socialist government in 1933 immediately announced its withdrawal. Italy, the first to use shortwave radio in international propaganda broadcasts, announced its withdrawal in 1937, after League condemnation of its 1935–36 invasion of Ethiopia. Soviet Russia, admitted to the League in 1934, despite its uses of censorship and propaganda since 1917, was expelled from the League in 1939 because of its invasion of the Baltic states and Finland in the shadow of Germany's invasion of Poland in that year. Other countries also withdrew from the League and it faded and vanished by 1940 as a viable organization.

An ITU conference scheduled to meet in Rome in 1940 was cancelled because of the war then dividing Europe, and the ITU did not meet again until 1947 in Atlantic City.

In its concern with communications rates, including special press rates, the ITU had served since the St. Petersburg Conference in establishing certain basic procedures. That 1875 conference had approved a special press rate at half the regular telegraph and cable rates, and an even lower deferred press rate for transmissions during the hours of the night from 6 P.M. to 6 A.M. Later ITU conferences modified the rates. The deferred rate was made applicable in the daylight hours as well. An urgent rate for the press, with equal priority, was set at half the regular urgent rate by action at the Lisbon meeting in 1908. Although no special press rate ever has been established for telephone use, the general rate for three-minute units on long lines was progressively reduced.

The use of leased wires, teleprinters, and radioprinters had the effect of reducing the average per-word cost of transmission on domestic circuits, while also speeding delivery. The press rate on the heavily used North Atlantic cable, already reduced to ten cents a word in 1886, was seven cents by 1926, with a five-cent deferred rate. The San Francisco–Tokyo Pacific cable press rate dropped from thirty-nine cents in 1921 to nine cents in 1929.

With shortwave radio transmission by radiotelegraphy and multiple transmission, and the even lower net rate set by Press Wireless, the cost of transmission on some circuits was averaging one-and-a-half to two cents a word by 1932. This was exceptional, however, with rates remaining relatively high on other circuits, and a greater volume of copy transmitted raised costs, in any case. By 1932, nevertheless, the per-word cost of international news transmission had reached the lowest point in the history of electrical communication.

There then came a certain reversal. The Madrid ITU and IRU conferences of 1932 reaffirmed the special press rates existing. But qualifications were introduced. Press messages filed at press rates were no longer to have equal priority with messages filed at regular rates. The use of cablese on press messages filed for radiotelegraphic transmission was ruled out, as it had already been ruled out for use on the Western Union North Atlantic cables in 1926. It also was ruled at Madrid that, whereas ten letters transmitted had been counted as one word, five letters now would be counted as a word. Further, payment for messages was based upon the French gold franc, as had been specified in 1875, then equal to about twenty cents in U.S. currency.

All of these rulings meant higher press transmission costs. The change in priority meant that the press might need to use the full urgent rate to assure prompt handling of messages, and sometimes the higher double urgent rate. Cablese never had been used in domestic telegraph transmissions on teleprinter transmission. But if cablese contractions continued to be used on the cables, it was to be understood after 1932 that they would be charged for on a per-word basis equal to the true meaning of the contraction. That might still permit an economy in the use of letters, but the five-letter count rather than the ten-letter count in computing the per-word charge obviously had the effect of doubling the cost for whatever was sent, except where Press Wireless circuits were available. The specified use of the French gold franc as a basis for charges was only confusing because no such currency unit had existed in France since 1919, and several countries also were off the gold standard by 1932, and more would be by January 1, 1934, when the Madrid regulations were to go into effect.

Advocacy of those changes in the Madrid discussions had come chiefly from smaller countries, especially in Europe. The United States representatives had opposed them, but the United States was not then a voting member of the ITU. The increased costs resulting had their greatest impact upon the media in the United States. By at least one estimate, those media then were bearing 80 percent of the charges for world news transmission.

Even with these increases, the press was able to trim its communications costs. This it did through the use not only of leased wires, through cables leased for certain time periods, through the use of the telephone and radiotelephone in combination with recording disks, wire, or tape, through economies introduced by Press Wireless operating with full effectiveness after 1931 on a non-profit basis, and after 1934 through the use of multiple-address systems by news agencies to move dispatches to overseas clients.

Even denied cablese, savings still could be made through brevity of writing and the omission of articles, conjunctions, some prepositions, of full names and titles or identifications of persons and officials commonly in the news, of locations of familiar places, and of other elements easily inserted by an editor at the receiving end in a news agency headquarters or on a newspaper foreign desk. The development of commercial airmail service, including ocean flights in the 1930s, also made it possible to forward topical reports and advance copy, as well as photos, by airmail.

When the 1938 Cairo conference met, another possible reversal was forestalled. A proposal was introduced that would have authorized the assessment of point-to-point word rates at each separate receiving point for matter actually moved in one multiple-address transmission. This would have meant a charge of as much as $1 a word for some dispatches, and could have halted transmission to some places.

Actually, the Cairo conference approved one constructive measure by recognizing the growth of radio as an important new medium of information, greatly advanced in its international application since the Madrid conference of 1932. Accordingly, it authorized the extension of press rates to messages moving within the radio broadcasting organizations by radiotelegraphy or by cable, whether as service messages or as news reports to be voiced at the receiving end.

Since the beginning of electrical communication in the 1840s, the media had been engaged in an unceasing effort to keep communications costs within reason and this effort was to continue.

Quite apart from the newspaper press, literally thousands of periodicals were appearing throughout the world in 1920. They were concerned with every sort of subject and made to meet every sort of reader-interest. Most were small and of limited circulation, serving a special purpose and designed for a special audience. A great many, however, were made for a general reading audience, usually published weekly or monthly, with a few quarterly publications.

In the United States, some had been active since about 1900, or had become active in the provision of current information, supplementing the newspaper press. Of that variety, reference has been made to *Collier's Weekly*, the *Saturday Evening Post, Outlook, World's Work*, the *Review of Reviews*, the *Literary Digest*, the *Pathfinder, Current History*, the *Nation*, the *New Republic, Asia*, and the *National Geographic*. Others dealing significantly with public affairs included at least three quarterlies: *Foreign Affairs*, published by the Council on Foreign Relations of New York, the *Annals* of the American Society of Political and Social Science, Philadelphia, and the *Yale Review* of New Haven. Magazines of quality appearing monthly also included the *Atlantic, Harper's, Century, Scribner's*, and *North American Review*, among others.

The interests of the business community, served since early times by news-letters and newspapers, were reflected in a variety of periodicals and special reports. In the United States, the McGraw-Hill Publishing Company of New York produced periodicals concerned with engineering and technical subjects, and was served by stringers and staff writers in various parts of the world. It also published a *Magazine of Business*. The Fairchild Publications, also of New York, which specialized in news of the garment trade and of retailing, had Ivor B. Boggis in London and Bertram J. Perkins in Paris in the 1930s. The monthly magazine *Vogue*, published by Condé Nast in Greenwich, Connecticut, and *Harper's Bazar,* a Hearst publication produced in New York, both were concerned with high style in women's attire, and had representatives in London and Paris.

The periodical as a form of journalism had its beginning in the seventeenth century, particularly in Paris, London, and Rome, but it existed in many other countries by the eighteenth century, including the United States. They were literary, philosophical, and critical in their content. The nineteenth century brought a far greater variety, some popular in appeal, and some featuring illustrations and caricatures, and bearing upon current events. Poetry and fiction were common fare in many, even from the eighteenth century.

From the time of Joseph Addison and Richard Steele, writers and publishers of the *Tatler* and the *Spectator* in eighteenth century London, whose style was widely imitated, British periodicals became numerous. Charles Philipon, with his daily *Le Charivari* and other periodicals featuring caricatures and the satire of Honoré Daumier and others in 19th century Paris, spurred the use of art work relating to current events in the periodical and newspaper press as a form of social commentary in many countries. Periodicals in great variety were appearing throughout the world by the twentieth century, with the United States rivaling Great Britain in that respect by the 1920s.

British periodicals of general readership at that time, old and new, into the 1930s, included *Blackwood's, Punch,* a satirical weekly, *Cornhill,* which had introduced serial fiction, the *Illustrated London News,* the *Sphere, Queen,* the *Strand Magazine,* with articles and fiction, a new version of the *Tatler,* the weekly *Economist,* dealing effectively with commerce and finance, the *New Statesman and Nation,* one of a number of politically oriented weeklies, and many more.

France had its well-established reviews: the *Mercure de France, Revue des Deux Mondes,* and *l'Europe Nouvelle* among them, the distinguished monthly, *l'Illustration,* the popular *Gringoire* and *Candide,* the impudent *La Vie Parisienne,* its own high style publications, and scores of others.

Germany had the well-printed and colorful *Illustrirte Zeitung,* such serious publications as *Die Literatur,* the *Deutsche Vierteljahrschrift,* and *Die Neue Rundschau,* until suppressed by the Nazi government in 1933, and others. Italy had *La Critica,* established in 1903 by Benedetto Croce as a very personal journal, *La Rassegna Italiana,* and others. Indeed, there were magazines of both serious and popular interest in virtually every major country.

The history of newspaper and magazine publishing is replete with stories of short-lived ventures, of changes of ownership and policy, of mergers and combinations. For every solid success there have been scores of failures. The 1920s and 1930s, however, produced a number of new magazines in the United States that gained special importance, including some as media of information, supplementing others already existing, but blazing new trails.

Among these new publications, eight in particular must be mentioned, *Time, Newsweek,* and the *United States News,* generally referred to as news-magazines, *Life* and *Look,* both picture magazines also rich in text matter, *Reader's Digest,* both a digest and a pocket magazine, the *New Yorker,* and *Fortune.* Three others might be added, *Liberty, Business Week,* and *Esquire.* Of these eleven, three appeared monthly, one semimonthly, and the others were weeklies. Two were sponsored by newspaper publishers. Three of them, *Time, Fortune,* and *Life,* were produced by the same publisher. Of the eleven, eight continue to be published.

The first of these magazines to appear was the *Reader's Digest,* started in 1922 by DeWitt Wallace, with the active assistance of his wife, Lila Acheson Wallace. Wallace, then twenty-three, had prior experience with the Webb Publishing Company of St. Paul, his native city, in producing farm magazines and textbooks. After wartime service with the army in France, during which he was wounded, he was in the publicity department of the Westinghouse Electric Company in Pittsburgh. There, and later in New York, he and his wife planned and worked and finally produced the *Reader's Digest.* Its announced purpose was to reprint by permission condensed versions of articles they deemed of "lasting interest," which had been originally published in a variety of magazines. They were articles "constructive" in subject matter and edited for easy reading. The *Reader's Digest* was pocket-size in format and included no advertising. It was dependent for revenue entirely upon sales at twenty-five cents a copy, or by subscription. This was a new concept for a magazine.[1]

---

1   E. W. Scripps had attempted to publish two small daily newspapers without advertising, the Chicago *Day Book,* started as a tabloid in 1911, with Negley D. Cochrane as publisher and Carl Sandburg as chief reporter, and the Philadelphia *News-Post,* started in 1912. The rising cost of newsprint at the time of World War I forced both to suspend.

Among magazines, the existing *Literary Digest* had reprinted excerpts from magazines and newspapers as fillers in the back pages, but the *Reader's Digest* was the first to make such reprints and excerpts the main content. Generous payments were made for the right to do so. Later, books were condensed.

Wallace was not alone in recognizing the prospective appeal of a magazine containing selected reprints, but he was the first to act effectively. The early years were difficult. By 1930, however, the *Reader's Digest* was well-established, with a large circulation, including foreign sales, and was published in Pleasantville, New York. A British edition was added, and then other editions in a variety of languages. It named foreign representatives and also appointed staff writers to produce original articles. Among them were newsmen and foreign correspondents of experience and reputation, some holding status as roving editors. By 1940 *Reader's Digest* had a circulation of nearly three and a half million in the United States and Canada, a figure that was to rise. With its foreign editions, it attained the largest total circulation of any publication in the world, approaching eighteen million in 1955. The success of *Reader's Digest* brought the appearance of other pocket and digest magazines, usually in special-interest subject fields.

Liberty was the third of the new magazines. Introduced in 1924 as a venture backed by Colonel Robert R. McCormick and his cousin, Captain Joseph Medill Patterson of the *Chicago Tribune* and the thriving *New York Daily News,* it was conducted as a weekly presenting articles and fiction in a pattern somewhat comparable to *Collier's* and the *Saturday Evening Post,* although matching neither in quality. It attained a circulation exceeding a million, but is estimated to have lost about $12 million in the years from 1924 to 1931, when McCormick and Patterson sold it. *Liberty* continued under several other owners until 1951, when it suspended.

The *New Yorker* was the fourth of the magazines to appear. Established in 1925, it was a weekly intended originally for readers in the New York metropolitan area, sophisticated in style and content and assertedly not made for "the old lady in Dubuque." It was edited during its first twenty-six years by Harold Ross. A native of Colorado, he had worked on newspapers in several western cities prior to World War I, had become editor of the army newspaper *Stars and Stripes* in Paris during the war, and afterward was an editor of *Judge,* a New York satirical weekly.

With financial backing from Raoul Fleischmann, wealthy New York baker and yeast manufacturer, and after a difficult introductory period, Ross made the *New Yorker* a magazine of rare quality, gathering about him writers of talent, and artists who produced socially trenchant and amusing cartoon panels. The magazine had its own distinctive character, but was roughly comparable, in some respects, to the successful London weekly magazine *Punch.* Although primarily concerned with the New York scene, and profiting as an advertising medium reaching a selected consumer group, the *New Yorker* produced national and international articles and personality sketches. They included letters from "our far-flung correspondents," who might or might not be staff members, writing from almost any part of the world. Included were regular letters from Washington by Richard Rovere, from Paris by Janet Flanner writing under the name of "Gènet," from Mollie Panter-Downes in London, and sometimes from A. J. Liebling, who wrote about the vagaries of the New York press in a column, "The Wayward Press." In time, the *New Yorker* gained a substantial national readership, became highly profitable, and had its own imitators, not only in New York, but in other cities.

The News Magazine

The second of the magazines established, and the most significant in terms of public information as well as the most successful, was *Time*. Appearing in March 1923, it was subtitled "The Weekly News-Magazine." The climate of the period itself, and the flow of news was such that newsmen, talking among themselves, speculated on the need and prospects for a publication such as *Time* became, providing the kind of background and perspective then gaining recognition as essential, but still generally denied readers of newspapers in the United States because of a strict adherence to objectivity.[2] It remained, however, for Henry Robinson Luce and Briton Hadden, then both twenty-four, to bring the concept to reality.[3]

Luce had been born April 3, 1898, near Penglai, China, in Shantung province, where his parents were missionaries and educators at Tengchow College. They were forced to flee at the time of the Boxer uprising in 1900, but returned to Tengchow after the rebellion was ended. In 1904 they moved to Weihsien College, still in Shantung

2   This writer recalls consideration of the need for a magazine such as the *Reader's Digest* shortly before its actual appearance, and observed some actual experimentation independent of Wallace's effort. He recalls discussion among members of the staff of the *Milwaukee Journal* concerning the need and prospects for a magazine such as *Time*, even as its first issue was nearing publication in New York, and further conversations, two years later, following its establishment, with expressions of envy for its free style of writing and approach to the news, and a wish that both might be applied locally. Similar wishes were expressed by newsmen in other cities, including New York itself.

3   W. A. Swanberg, *Luce and His Empire* (New York, 1972); John Kobler, *Luce, His Time, Life and Fortune* (New York, 1968).

province. There the boy lived until he went to a British boarding school at Cheefoo for his primary education.

The Luce family spent 1906–07 in Chicago, which was Henry Luce's first view of the United States. He did not return again until 1913. Then, after a year at St. Albans School near London, he entered Hotchkiss preparatory school at Lakeville, Connecticut, where he was graduated in 1916. There he formed a friendship with Hadden, a fellow student, and they both entered Yale that September. Hadden, a native of Brooklyn and a young man determined to make journalism his career, turned Luce's interest in that direction. They both worked for the *Yale Daily News*, with Hadden becoming chairman and Luce managing editor. Both were tapped for Skull and Bones, and Luce made Phi Beta Kappa.

With the entrance of the United States into World War I in 1917, their Yale experience was interrupted. They went to officers' training camp together at Camp Jackson, near Columbia, South Carolina, and with their commissions as second lieutenants were assigned to Camp Zachary Taylor, near Louisville, Kentucky. While they were there, the war ended.

In the time at Camp Jackson, Luce and Hadden conceived the idea for a magazine such as *Time* was to become. Returning first to Yale, however, in January 1919, they were graduated in 1920. Hadden then persuaded Herbert Bayard Swope to give him a job as a reporter on the *New York World*. Luce went to England for a year of study at Oxford and to travel in Europe. Returning to the United States in 1921, he got a job on the *Chicago Daily News* as assistant to Ben Hecht, recently returned from a postwar year as Berlin correspondent for that paper, and conducting a daily column about Chicago and its people.[4]

Luce and Hadden had not forgotten their plan for a weekly magazine, and they soon contrived to work together on the staff of the *Baltimore News*, a Munsey-owned afternoon paper. They were able to experiment in the writing and design of their proposed venture, and to seek financial support. Their intent was to summarize each week's news, adding background material not present in newspaper stories, and to inject perspective on the personalities figuring in the news—all to advance a reader's understanding of events. They hoped also to report on subjects little touched upon in the average daily newspaper or general magazine, and to present all material in a fashion that would add interest to the content and gain a reader response.

---

4   Some of the columns were republished in Hecht's book, *1001 Afternoons in Chicago* (Chicago, 1922).

No publication then existed to do quite what the magazine they envisioned would attempt or in the manner they had conceived. Several were on the fringe, however, all in the United States.

In a prospectus issued in 1922, Luce and Hadden solicited charter subscriptions and financial support. The idea was to meet what was described as a need by busy people to be kept informed on subjects growing in variety and complexity. All news of importance and interest would be presented in a logical departmental arrangement, it was said, including topics otherwise largely ignored. The emphasis would be on brevity, facts, balance, and meaning, and without editorial comment. It was estimated that $100,000 would be required to establish and maintain the magazine until it could become self-supporting from circulation and advertising revenue. Actually, only $86,000 was raised from friends and acquaintances, and only 9,000 charter subscribers were obtained, but the first issue of *Time* nevertheless was published in New York on March 2, 1923.

Economy was essential as the magazine proceeded in its first years. Hadden and Luce did most of the work, and alternated in handling the editorial and business functions. They traded upon their youth, personal charm, Hotchkiss-Yale background, and friendships to gain advice and guidance, as well as support from persons of position, experience, and financial means. The staff was small, mostly young men three or four years out of college, working with enthusiasm but for small salaries. Manfred Gottfried, fresh out of Yale, became national affairs editor. Thomas J. C. (John Cardell) Martyn, of British nationality, was brought to New York as foreign editor, at a somewhat higher salary, in the belief that he was an experienced correspondent.[5] Roy Larsen, a year out of Harvard, became circulation manager, and persuaded several debutantes to help, at little or no cost.

The magazine was printed as inexpensively as possible, with few illustrations and no color for some time. The offices were moved from New York to Cleveland in 1925, where costs were lower, and remained there until 1927. The news itself was rewritten from newspapers, and especially from the *New York Times,* at no expense beyond the purchase of the copies used. This was supplemented by matter obtained from reference books and libraries. Within the first two years, however, *Time* also became a subscriber to the Associated Press service. Regional

5 Luce is believed to have confused him with C. J. Martin, Paris correspondent for the *Daily Telegraph* and later for the *Daily Mail.* Martyn left *Time* in 1927 to go to the staff of the *New York Times* and in 1933 established *News-Week* (later *Newsweek*) as a competitor with *Time.*

offices were established in several other cities, with staff or stringer correspondents.[6] It was not until about 1940 that *Time* added correspondents outside the United States.

By 1927, the major hurdles had been cleared. The circulation of *Time* had risen to 136,000 weekly, and advertising revenue returned $501,000 in that year. It had grown in number of pages, had improved its appearance as well as its content, included more illustrations, and made generous use of color. It was available throughout the country on newsstands in small towns and villages as well as in the cities at 15 cents a copy, and it had a large mail subscription list. From 1928 its success was never in doubt and those who had invested in the experimental publication of 1923 were richly rewarded as Time, Inc., developed through the years both as a magazine and as a publishing company.

Theodore Peterson in his study of *Magazines in the Twentieth Century* (1956) credits Hadden and Luce with recognizing that there existed a market for such a magazine as they established. Factors included the emergence of a new generation of readers from the colleges and universities after World War I, a tempo of life faster and tighter-knit, with a better-informed national audience wanting more information and more understanding about a changing nation and world, but wanting it in a hurry.

Time seemed to meet that need, with its departmentalized and brief news reports. Promptly delivered and in step with events, its treatment of those events was fresh, interesting, and entertaining. This was in part because of a writing style devised by Hadden, "brash and irreverent," as Peterson describes it, with non-objective adjectives, coined words, "hyperactive verbs," sentences sometimes running backward, terms and phrases repeatedly introduced but still meaningful, and amusing footnotes never before used in magazines. The style was lively enough in itself and sufficiently original to cause comment, even to raise objections, but also served to advertise the magazine. A flood of letters from readers poured in, some from persons of note and those figuring in the news, protesting, applauding, commenting, and supplementing the content. These were used in great numbers, protests included, in a manner unlike other publications, and added interest as well as confidence in the magazine.

---

6 Experienced Washington correspondents, offered what then was a good salary to represent *Time* in the capital, hesitated for several years to become identified with a publication that sometimes referred to members of the government in a style deemed over-personal and offensive by some.

Radio was developing as a news medium at the same period, and
Time, in its venturesome way, started its own radio programs in 1924
and 1928. Newspapers were less concerned competitively about *Time* as
a news-magazine than about radio news programs. It was recognized
that individuals wanted their news each day, while it was still news,
rather than days later in a weekly magazine. It was believed that such
a magazine might even stimulate interest in reading the news each day,
so it was not to be feared. Since *Time,* in the very nature of things, could
not present local news in any degree, there was nowhere else for the
resident of a particular community to turn for such news except to the
local paper.

The news magazine, nevertheless, had a great impact upon the daily
newspaper press. Its style of writing, irreverent though it seemed at
times, its sometimes non-objective treatment of public affairs, its stress
on personalities, its use of background material, and its departmentalization of news were well received by the public and forced the
newspaper press to review its established and rather formalized content.
Radio was exercising a somewhat comparable influence upon the press,
especially when news analysis and commentary became a part of its
offering after 1930.

The attention given by *Time* to background material on national and
international news developments was welcomed by readers, and revealed
an unsuspected appetite for such additional information as contributing
to an understanding of current news events. The solid value of this form
of factual interpretation as a departure from the strict objectivity of
news agency and newspaper treatment of the news was at last
demonstrated beyond question. The reception of radio news commentaries provided further evidence that such background matter need not
necessarily be editorial in character.

A few newspaper editors had seen the possibilities of such news
treatment at least as early as 1919, when the United Press was
persuaded to provide its interpretative service for *La Prensa* in Buenos
Aires. Now a new generation of editors in the United States recognized
that objectivity need not be lost by the introduction of background
material.

In its departmentalization of the news, *Time* magazine also gave
attention increasingly to some subjects that had been little noted by the
daily press. This induced newspaper editors to look again at their local
coverage and at what was being provided by news agencies. What
resulted was, for example, a better balance in the treatment of
labor-management relations, more attention to science, arts and

education, law, business and finance, and even to the press and radio. It brought more investigative reporting in depth on urban and social problems in home communities, more detailed attention to grass root standards of living and administration. The very irreverence of *Time* in treating of public affairs led the media, in general, to deal both objectively and subjectively with current topics in a manner sometimes in questionable taste, but more often useful in casting light upon the conduct of government at every level, and upon international relations.

The manner in which *Time* was made, and its departmentalization of the news, led some to believe that local and regional magazines following the same pattern might be effective and popular. Some such attempts were made, as they also were made to produce local versions of the *New Yorker*. They did not survive, but local adaptations of the news summary were undertaken. A weekly review was made a feature in the *Pittsburgh Bulletin-Index,* a newspaper published from 1933 to 1949. A number of other newspapers added a weekly summary of news, departmentalized and backgrounded and including close attention to local affairs. One of the first to do so was the *New York Times,* where Lester Markel, Sunday editor, introduced a "News of the Week in Review" section to the Sunday Editorial Section. Actually proposed in the late 1920s, it was started in January 1935 and was notably well received. Newspapers from Boston to San Francisco followed this lead, and news agencies also began to distribute weekend news reviews for use by the press, with each paper free to add its own local review. Such local summaries were largely ended, beginning in the 1940s, as local television news programs began to provide some such daily coverage.

It was a great loss to *Time* when Briton Hadden became ill and died in February 1929 at thirty-one, and the magazine was deprived of his skill as a writer and editor and of his imaginative contributions. From that time, Luce was the effective proprietor, but the securely established magazine included many other bright minds among its staff members. Time, Inc., grossed more than $3 million in advertising revenue in 1930, paid its first dividend to stockholders, and went on to greater profits despite a general decline in the national economy during the depression years,

Even as the depression began, Time, Inc., produced the first issue of a second magazine in February 1930. Titled *Fortune,* and a monthly, it had been in the planning stage since 1928. The new magazine was devoted to aspects of industry, business, and commerce as "the greatest single common denominator among the active leading citizens of the

United States." Large in format, beautifully printed in full color on the highest quality paper and bound with a square back a half inch thick and using the finest illustrations magnificently reproduced, its subscription rate was an unheard of $10 a year, or $1 a copy. It began, nevertheless, with 30,000 charter subscribers and a substantial advertising volume. Despite the depression, and despite the shattered image of business and industry, it went on successfully. By 1941 it had a circulation of 162,000, more than $2 million in advertising revenue, and proceeded to even more impressive figures.

Time, Inc., in 1927, had established an advertising trade publication, *Tide,* a weekly resembling *Time* in general format. It also had a financial interest in the weekly *Saturday Review of Literature,* established in 1924, which was a spinoff of a *New York Evening Post* literary supplement and an interest of Henry Seidel Canby, Yale professor of literature, author, and supporter of the Luce-Hadden establishment of *Time* magazine. The Time, Inc., relationship to these publications was brief, however. *Tide* was sold in 1930 to Raymond Rubicam, New York advertising agency executive, and the *Saturday Review* went its independent way after 1932.

Meanwhile, Time, Inc., purchased an established industry magazine in 1932, the monthly *Architectural Forum,* and in 1936 it established *Life* as a weekly photo magazine, which was to have the same kind of runaway success as *Time* magazine.

The three Luce-owned publications, *Time, Fortune,* and *Life,* separately and in combination, contributed notably to the prose and pictorial treatment of news and public affairs, nationally and internationally. The bureaus established by Time, Inc., in regionally located cities of the United States were used to serve the three publications. The news matter intended for *Time,* as written by its growing number of staff and stringer correspondents, was prepared in the New York office, delivered there over a teleprinter service. Editors in New York used all the matter received to write the final accounts as they appeared each week. In this they were assisted by "researchers," a new specialization in journalism, most of them young women graduated from eastern colleges and universities. They sought out background information requested by the editor-writers, and they checked and double-checked all the written material for factual accuracy.

This was a new system devised by *Time,* referred to as "group journalism." It was not necessarily satisfying to the ego of correspondents, whose original prose underwent great change in the final writing, if used at all, and whose names only appeared in small print on the masthead of the magazine but rarely elsewhere. The same degree of anonymity attached to the editors and writers. The system resulted in a magazine possessed of a consistency of style. This in fact had become known as "Timestyle" during Hadden's regime and invited parody. Later modified, it still had its own character. The final product had its critics, and occasionally with reason, since the selection and treatment of subject matter at times could be regarded as reflecting an editorial bias. But it usually provided a fair, brief, and useful total report, informative and interesting to readers as evidenced by the steady rise in circulation.

Although directed and written in New York, *Time* was printed in Chicago in mid-week from the R. R. Donnelly Press, a vast commercial enterprise. *Life* also was produced there, and the Time, Inc., circulation department was based in Chicago as a central point of direction and distribution. The publishing schedule of *Time* and *Life* magazines required a tightly-organized work week, including a busy weekend, and a system of deadlines and leased wire teleprinter circuits, but it was successful. Colorful covers, usually featuring a photo or art rendering of an individual prominent in the news, were distinctive on the newsstands.

Photographers were providing coverage for the Luce publications, not only domestically but also from abroad, in some degree from about 1928. *Time,* as a news magazine, depended chiefly upon the AP and UP for international reports until after the outbreak of the war in Europe in 1939. But those reports were supplemented by background material prepared in New York. From 1940, *Time* developed its own staff coverage of the world, eventually to match that of the most active daily newspapers.

The success of *Time* as a news magazine and of *Life* as a picture magazine brought adaptations in the content and style of newspapers and of other magazines, and inspired imitations in more than one country. Successfully competitive with those several other magazines in the United States touching the field of current news, it also had a certain impact.

The monthly *Review of Reviews,* edited from 1914 to 1933 by Frank H. Simonds, absorbed the monthly *World's Work* in 1932. The weekly *Literary Digest* had absorbed the weekly *Current Opinion* in 1925. The monthly *Forum* absorbed the monthly *Century* in 1930. The monthly *Current History* was sold by the New York Times Company in 1936 to M. E. Tracy, formerly of the Scripps-Howard Newspapers, and in 1940 it absorbed the monthly *Forum*.

The *Literary Digest*, perhaps the strongest publication dealing with current affairs, with gross revenues exceeding $12.7 million in 1920, had been losing ground since that time. The depression accelerated that decline, and there can be little doubt that the livelier appeal of *Time* contributed further. William Seaver Wood, editor since 1905, resigned in 1933, and was replaced by Arthur Draper, formerly of the *New York Herald Tribune*. Changes in design, typography, and content intended to brighten the magazine did not halt its decline, and Draper resigned in 1935. He was replaced by Morton Sevell and then by Wilfred Funk, of the Funk and Wagnalls publishing family, owners of the magazine. In 1937 the *Literary Digest* was purchased by Albert Shaw, Jr., of the *Review of Reviews,* which was itself then merged with the *Literary Digest,* and published under the simpler name of the *Digest*. But the decline in its fortunes continued.

The *Literary Digest* from 1920 had conducted a so-called "straw vote" preceding national presidential elections, a kind of forerunner of what became public opinion polls. The results, based upon the return of millions of postcards sent to names of persons in the telephone directories, had been accurate until 1936. In that year, however, the returns showed that Alfred Landon would defeat President Roosevelt, then running for re-election. The result, of course, was quite the opposite, with a landslide victory for Roosevelt. Some asserted that this error brought the *Digest* to an end. Peterson, in his history of magazines, differs, contending that "the poll was but the blow that finished an already tottering publication." Its last issue appeared in February 1938, and in May *Time* bought its title and subscription list, then about 250,000, and added the *Literary Digest* name inconspicuously to its own masthead.

The *Pathfinder* of Washington, D.C., another of the news-oriented magazines described earlier was of such character as to be noncompetitive with *Time*. Dating from 1894, it continued until the 1950s. Among weeklies attempted in imitation of *Time,* one was *Events,* started in 1937 by Spencer Brodney, who had edited *Current Opinion* until its purchase by the *Literary Digest* in 1925. He was then with *Current History* until its purchase by Tracy in 1936. *Events* survived only four years. It was purchased and merged with *Current History* in 1941.

The first successful weekly made in the image of *Time* appeared in 1929. The *Magazine of Business* was published by the McGraw-Hill Company of New York and then converted into *Business Week*. It was restyled to resemble *Time* in format, departmentalization, brevity, informality of writing style, and the introduction of background material. The magazine was announced as "preeminently the businessman's journal of business news, vital and vivacious, informative and dynamic" and "keyed to the new tempo of business." That tempo was sadly reduced by the end of the year as the depression began, but *Business Week* survived and became a highly successful news-magazine within its own framework. That framework was indeed the business world. For that reason, it was not precisely competitive with *Time,* offering a specialized content, and with its circulation deliberately restricted, so far as possible, to business executives likely to be personally responsive to its advertising messages.

The success of *Time* was noted abroad, and two imitations appeared in 1933. In Shanghai, Joseph Coughlin, a former California newsman, established *East, Newsweekly of the Orient.* In London, Francis Yeats-Brown established *Everyman, World News Weekly.* Both were short-lived. Two other frank imitations appeared in London in 1936, the *News-Review* and *Cavalcade.* As the European war began in 1939, both were forced to suspend because of a shortage of paper, all of which was imported and had to be rationed.

In the United States, two news weeklies began in 1933, competitive with *Time.* The first of these, *News-Week,* appeared in New York in February, and was directed by Thomas J. C. Martyn, already noted as one of the early *Time* staff members. With the *New York Times* since 1927, he formed an association with Samuel Thurston Williamson, formerly of that paper's Washington bureau. They obtained substantial financial backing, reportedly $2.25 million, and undertook to produce a weekly digest of the news differing somewhat from the *Time* treatment. By 1937 their magazine had a circulation of 250,000, about one-third that of *Time,* and their original capital was reduced almost to zero.

Meanwhile, another weekly had been started in November 1933 to publicize the Roosevelt administration's "New Deal" program. Titled *Today,* it was edited by Raymond Moley, a Columbia University professor who had been an assistant secretary of state and a member of the so-called "brain trust" in the first months of the administration. It was financed by Vincent Astor and W. Averell Harriman, both of great personal wealth. Although a publication of some substance, and by its very nature giving attention to aspects of the news, it was not actually a news-magazine. It failed to capture a reader following, never exceeding 75,000 in circulation. Late in 1937, *Today* was merged with *News-Week* under an arrangement by which the latter publication was reorganized in a new company with Astor as its president, and Malcolm Muir, former president of the McGraw-Hill Publishing Company, as publisher. Martyn left the magazine. Williamson remained as executive editor. Moley remained as editor, and Edward W. Barrett, formerly of the *Birmingham News* and of the Columbia Broadcasting System publicity department but with *News-Week* since its establishment, was named as associate editor.

Under this new regime, *News-Week* was retitled as *Newsweek,* with a subline describing it as "The Magazine of News Significance." It became more like *Time* in that it presented the news along with background and with a departmentalization covering much the same range of subject-matter. It received a full service from the United Press, had staff and stringer correspondents at regional bureaus, and used the group journalism method of producing the stories as they were to appear, with researchers to assist the writers in the main office in New York. Although appearing in the same size and format as *Time,* each magazine had its own distinctive cover style. Unlike *Time, Newsweek* used the names of some writers, not over news reports but over certain columns or pages. Moley wrote in that fashion as editor, and Ernest K. Lindley, formerly of the *New York Herald Tribune* bureau in Washington, who became *Newsweek* representative there, wrote a signed article occupying a page each week.

Newsweek preceded *Time* in providing some original coverage of foreign news. In 1937 Joseph B. Phillips was brought from the Moscow bureau of the *New York Herald Tribune* to become foreign editor in New York. Bradish B. G. Johnson, Jr., went to cover the Spanish Civil War and was killed there in January 1938. Mark J. Gayn, China-born of Canadian parentage, but educated chiefly in the United States, had worked for the *China Weekly Review* in Shanghai and served briefly as a *Newsweek* correspondent. Harold Isaacs also wrote from Chungking, the new Nationalist government capital, in 1939. These assignments were exceptional, however, since *Newsweek* waited to develop extensive foreign coverage of its own, as *Time* did, until after direct U.S. participation in World War II began at the end of 1941.

The second news weekly to be established in 1933 was the *United States News* of Washington, D.C. Always distinctive from *Time* and *Newsweek* in its treatment of current affairs, it was the product of a sequence of events that began in May 1917 when David Lawrence, a correspondent in the capital since 1910 and then writing for the Associated Press, was appointed a member of the wartime U.S. Committee on Public Information, directed by George Creel. Lawrence produced an Official Bulletin for the News Division of the CPI. This was continued after the war, but privately published by Roger W. Babson, an economist, under the name of the *United States Bulletin.* Its purpose was to disseminate information about the business of the United States government, and it continued until 1921.

Meanwhile, Lawrence became proprietor of a syndicate, the Consolidated Press Association, based in Washington and operating from 1919 to 1933. Although the *United States Bulletin* had suspended in 1921, the concept of reporting comprehensively upon the conduct of government affairs was revived on a more ambitious scale in 1926 with the establishment in Washington of the *United States Daily,* also under Lawrence's direction. Supported by private contributions and subscriptions, it went to government departments and officials, business and corporation executives, organizations with offices in the capital, newspapers, news agencies and their correspondents, public libraries, universities and faculty members, and students and individuals with special interests relating to government.

Recognized as a useful publication, the *United States Daily* was costly to produce. Its subscription rate was high; its circulation limited, and its advertising volume as well. Understandably, it became a casualty of the economic depression and was suspended in 1933. Its function in reporting systematically and seriously on government matters, however, was carried forward in later years by such separate and independently produced publications as the *Federal Register* and the *Congressional Quarterly.* For a more general audience, however, Lawrence in 1933 salvaged something of the *United States Daily* by introducing what he called the *United States News,* a weekly magazine of the same general format as *Time,* but differing in other respects. He disposed of the Consolidated Press Association, which was absorbed by the North American Newspaper Alliance (NANA), created in 1922 by the *New York Times* in association with a group of other large dailies as a cooperative organization to handle the distribution of articles and series of articles of special substance. From that time, Lawrence gave his full attention to the magazine.

Another magazine established in the United States in October 1933 reflected *Fortune* in some degree, as well as the *New Yorker. Esquire* was an outgrowth of *Apparel Arts,* an elaborately printed Chicago quarterly designed for the men's clothing trade. *Esquire* began as a quarterly but soon became a monthly. Published by David Smart and edited by Arnold Gingrich, it was large both in size and number of pages, heavy with advertising, rich in color, and well illustrated. It was in no sense a news publication, but did publish substantial articles and fiction by leading writers and authors. It also was known for colorful drawings of curvaceous girls, the so-called Petty and Vargas girls, named for their artists. Despite the depression, and what then was a high price of fifty cents a copy, its circulation rose to 184,000 a month in its first year.

The company added a monthly pocket magazine in 1936, *Coronet,* and in 1938 attempted a somewhat sensational news-oriented monthly, *Ken,* soon made a bimonthly and then a weekly. Its first editor was Jay Cooke Allen, who had been a correspondent in Europe for the *Chicago Tribune.* George Seldes, also formerly of the *Tribune,* was a contributing editor. Both soon left the staff, however, displeased with the policy outlined by the company, and *Ken* was suspended in August 1939, even though its circulation was reasonably good.

Among other established magazines previously mentioned as dealing with public affairs and appearing in these years were *World's Work,* suspended in 1932, the *Review of Reviews,* suspended in 1937, and the *Forum,* suspended in 1940. Continuing also were the *New Republic* and the *Nation.* Oswald Garrison Villard, editor and publisher of the latter weekly, wrote informed and sometimes controversial articles from Washington and abroad. Louis Fischer and Maurice Hindus wrote from the Soviet Union, and Fischer also wrote of the Spanish Civil War.

The Hearst-owned *Cosmopolitan* and *Hearst's International* magazines, both monthlies with considerable fiction content, also published some articles on world subjects. The *International* in 1925 was merged with *Cosmopolitan,* which published editions both in New York and London. Frazier Hunt, previously abroad for the *Chicago Tribune* and INS, represented the magazine in London for five years, during which time he also moved about Europe and journeyed to the Far East.

Collier's Weekly, one of the first magazines to attempt coverage of current news developments from the time of the Spanish-American War, and the *Saturday Evening Post,* which had undertaken to do the same from the beginning of World War I, continued actively to provide topical coverage. As inexpensive weeklies of large general circulation, both presented fiction of quality but also included substantial articles, chiefly by staff writers.

For *Collier's,* Charles Merz, formerly of the *New Republic,* ranged much of the world as a correspondent during 1920–24, at which time he also wrote for the *New York World,* later joining its editorial page staff. Thomas R. Ybarra, formerly of the *New York Times,* wrote for *Collier's* from Europe and the Middle East in 1927–28. He served as European editor from 1931 to 1937, except for a period in 1933–34 when he was in South America, familiar to him from his youth. Martha Gellhorn, who had free-lanced in Mexico and Europe for several years, and had been with *Vogue* and the United Press in Paris, wrote for *Collier's* from Spain during the civil war, and later from Czechoslovakia, France, Finland and the Far East, all between 1937 and 1941.[7] British-born but reared in the U.S., James D. (Jim) Marshall[8] was a roving correspondent for *Collier's* in the Far East during the 1930s. In 1938 and 1939 *Collier's* added to its European staff William Hillman and Frank Gervasi, both formerly members of the INS staff in London.

For the *Saturday Evening Post,* Isaac F. (Ike) Marcosson, a staff member since 1907, continued at home and abroad to produce articles and interviews of significance. Will Irwin, formerly of the *New York Sun,* continued as a regular contributor from overseas, as he had done since 1914. Sam Blythe (Samuel George Blythe), writing from Washington for the *New York World* since 1900 and also for the *Saturday Evening Post* since 1903, wrote exclusively for the *Post* from 1907 to 1938. Garet Garrett, formerly of the *New York Tribune,* wrote political and economic articles in the U.S. and abroad. William Allen White, editor of the *Emporia Gazette* in Kansas, was a frequent contributor, chiefly of political articles. Kenneth Roberts, formerly of the *Boston Post,* was a staff correspondent moving about the world in the 1920s, after which time he devoted himself to the writing of historical novels.

Cyrus H. K. Curtis, publisher of the *Saturday Evening Post* since 1897, died in 1933. George Horace Lorimer, editor of the *Post* since 1899, retired in 1936 and died in 1937. He was succeeded by Wesley W. Stout. After 1934 the magazine had Edgar P. Snow as a special correspondent writing from China and Russia. In 1938 Demaree Bess, then Moscow correspondent for the *Christian Science Monitor,* became European correspondent for the magazine, and subsequently associate editor with headquarters in Paris. The *Post* also published articles during the 1930s by such experienced correspondents as Hallett E. Abend, in China for the *New York Times,* and by Frederic William

---

7 In 1940, Miss Gellhorn became the third wife of Ernest Hemingway, whom she had met when both were covering the war in Spain. Divorced about five years later, in 1953 she became the second wife of Thomas S. Matthews, a member of the *Time* staff since 1929, and its editor in 1949–53. They also were divorced. She continued as a respected correspondent, later for the *Guardian* of London, through the 1960s, and as the author of several books based on her coverage of wars and public affairs.

8 Not to be confused with Raymond Gifford (Ray) Marshall of the United Press, also active in China and Japan in the 1930s.

Wile, Raymond G. Carroll, Wythe Williams, and Dorothy Thompson.

Correspondents for newspapers and news agencies had contributed articles to general and specialized magazines through many decades, and had written books bearing upon their experiences and special areas of knowledge. This they continued to do. As indicated in the foregoing, developments within the periodical press and developments in radio news broadcasting as well took many experienced correspondents into both of those media fields in the period of the 1930s and beyond.

Photo-Journalism:
A New Era 20

Illustrations made from wood engravings had received public attention in Asia and Europe long before the development of printing from movable type. The caricaturist and sketch artist were contributing to printed publications before photography existed.

Photography became a practical art after 1840 and by 1900 was greatly perfected, with motion picture photography also possible. The reproduction of photos in printed form began in the 1870s, but it was near 1900 before they could be reproduced in newspapers, using relatively coarse paper and printed on fast-moving rotary presses. Cameras, lenses, and photographic and photo-engraving processes improved steadily, so that by 1920 the general information process was about to be enriched in ways that brought into existence what became known as photo-journalism.

The sketch artist and the photographer already had contributed to the success of such magazine-type publications as the *Illustrated London News* and the *Graphic* in London, *l'Illustration* in Paris, *Illustrirte Zeitung* in Berlin, and *Frank Leslie's Illustrated Newspaper* in New York. The new era was perhaps foreshadowed by the establishment in London in 1903 of the *Daily Mirror*. It was introduced by Alfred Harmsworth (later Lord Northcliffe), already successful with his *Daily Mail* and other publications.

The *Daily Mirror* was a tabloid newspaper, that is, roughly half the page size of the standard-size newspaper or broadsheet. It was not the first tabloid-size paper, nor was it an immediate success. But it was perhaps the first daily to feature illustrations, both sketches and photographs, presented in generous space. It did set a new pattern, and it did gain readers. By the period of World War I it could be counted a success, the prototype for the illustrated tabloid newspaper widely introduced throughout the world after 1920.

Shortly before World War I, a second major advance occurred in pictorial journalism. The process of rotogravure reproduction of photographs was demonstrated in Germany. It was not a high-speed process, but it produced beautiful results in detailed illustrations and was promptly adapted elsewhere. In the United States, the *New York Times* added a special rotogravure section to its Sunday editions, and dailies elsewhere in the country did the same, as well as papers in Argentina and other countries. When World War I began, the *New York Times* also produced a weekly rotogravure magazine, the *Mid-Week Pictorial,* primarily but not exclusively to present photographs relating to the war. The gravure process was also adopted by other magazines.

Captain Joseph Medill Patterson and his cousin, Colonel Robert R. McCormick, copublishers of the *Chicago Tribune,* had agreed in 1918 that they would establish a tabloid newspaper in New York after the war. Accordingly, the first edition of the *Illustrated Daily News* appeared on June 26, 1919, but the name was soon changed to the *New York Daily News.* Like the *Daily Mirror* in London, the New York tabloid made a feature of illustrations and photographs. As with the *Mirror* in 1903, the success of the *Daily News* was not immediate in 1919. It was in competition with the *Times,* the *Herald,* the *Tribune,* the *World,* and the *American,* all long established in the morning field, not to mention the business papers the *Wall Street Journal* and the *Journal of Commerce.* Numerous magazines existed, bright with pictures, and the *Times*'s Sunday rotogravure section could scarcely be improved upon for photographic reproduction of news-related photographs.

Unlike any other daily newspaper, the *Daily News* commonly used its entire front page to display one striking photo along with a bold banner line, both inviting street sales among New Yorkers bound for their morning activities. The inside pages supplemented the page-one display and were packed with other photos, news, and features not to be found in other New York papers. The selection and use of photos, many by the paper's own growing staff of photographers, was marked by dramatic effect. News subjects and news stories also were selected, written, and displayed for their emotional impact, sometimes meriting the use of the word sensational. A staff of high professional competence, enterprising, and aggressive was backed by strong financial resources and produced a paper that soon gained a substantial circulation, which in turn produced a heavy volume of advertising. By 1924, the *Daily News* had become the newspaper of largest circulation in the United States. By 1930 the figure was 1,300,000 daily and rose above the 2,000,000 mark.

Other newspapers, ascribing the success and prosperity of the *Daily News* largely to its use of photographs, increased their own use of such art. Throughout the United States standard-sized papers advertised a daily page of pictures. Most dailies had photographers as staff members or available on call, but many began to develop photographic staffs and to install elaborate photo laboratories and better photoengraving equipment. Syndicate services and news agencies extended their efforts to obtain and distribute pictures, and to do so more and more promptly.

As had happened in London when the *Daily Mirror* circulation began to rise, competing tabloids appeared in New York, in other cities of the United States, and in other countries. In New York, William Randolph Hearst established the *New York Daily Mirror* as a morning tabloid in 1924. It also became successful. In 1937 he halted publication of the morning *American* and the name was merged with his afternoon paper as the *New York Journal-American.* Later in 1924, Bernarr Macfadden, publisher of *Physical Culture, True Story,* and other magazines, established a tabloid *New York Evening Graphic.* It was more sensational than either of the others, but less successful, and was suspended in 1932.

Not all tabloid-size newspapers were sensational in their treatment or display of the news. The *Chicago Times* (1929) was conservative, for one, and the *Daily News* itself became relatively sober after 1930, as the economic depression began in the United States. Patterson commented that the people's major interest had turned to "how they're going to eat" and directed his staff that "from this time forward, we'll pay attention to the struggle for existence that's just beginning." Photos, nevertheless, remained a prominent feature of most tabloid papers, and were important to all newspapers.

Out of the great emphasis on photographs came a desire to have news photos appear as promptly as the news itself. This was no problem with local pictures. Photos of events occurring elsewhere were moved as rapidly as possible by airmail and by the fastest ships between continents. Commercial air service over great distances and across the seas began about 1930 and helped to speed photos. Even so moved, such photos could only appear a day after an event, and often as much as a week or more after. The answer to this problem became part of the story of the electronic age, leading to the transmission of photographs by wire and by radio.

As with the other means of electrical communication, that relating to photo transmission emerged from experimentation dating back many years. At least as early as 1849, Alexander Bain, Scottish inventor, had demonstrated a method of transmitting a facsimile of handwriting by telegraphic impulses, and a somewhat similar device appeared in London in 1851. The Abbé Jean Caselli, an Italian-born priest living in France, received financial support from Emperor Napoleon III in evolving a process about 1865 whereby elaborate hand-drawn portraits or other illustrations could be sent by wire. In the United States, illustrations were sent experimentally in 1891 through a method originated by N. S. Armstutz of Valparaiso, Indiana. Elisha Gray, one of the earlier contributors to the development of the telegraph, produced a "teleautograph machine" in 1893, making it possible to reproduce pencil messages or illustrations. It was used to transmit line drawings to the *Chicago Times-Herald* on June 21, 1895. Edouard Belin of France demonstrated a machine known as the Telesterograph in the United States in 1920.

The key to successful transmission of actual photographs, illustrations, and printed or written matter proved to be the "photoelectric eye," utilizing radioelectronic principles. A picture attached to a revolving cylinder was scanned by the photoelectric eye, a sharply defined beam of light, as the cylinder turned. The dark and light areas of the photo set up varying impulses transmitted by wire. At the receiving end a matching pinpoint of light was focused on a photographic film wrapped about the same size cylinder as the original picture and revolving at the same speed; the intensity of the light varied with the changing impulses transmitted. When the film was developed and a print made, a reproduction of the original photo resulted. From this a halftone could be made in the usual fashion, suitable for reproduction in print. A drawing, chart, or any black and white illustration could be transmitted in the same manner.

Perhaps the first photo transmission for press use was to the London *Daily Mail* in 1922. In the United States, experiments being conducted by the American Telephone & Telegraph Company, among others, centered in Cleveland. A photo was transmitted from there to New York on May 19, 1924, using the telephone line. The Republican National Convention met in Cleveland soon after. A photo of that gathering was transmitted to the *New York Times* for use on June 9. Picture transmission by wireless was accomplished experimentally in 1925. The cost of transmission was high, the quality of the picture received, whether by wire or wireless, was not good, and facilities were not generally available. For those reasons the press did not make further immediate use of the method.

The AT&T experimentation continued, however, with a New York–Chicago–San Francisco wire moving pictures in 1926. Five other cities were added by 1933. By that time the quality and speed of picture transmission was much improved. Efforts to interest a number of photo syndicates in using the advanced system, however, were not immediately successful. These included an A.P. Picture Service organized by the Associated Press in 1928, a Wide World Photos syndicate formed by the *New York Times* in 1919, International News Photos, a Hearst enterprise, and Acme Newsphotos, owned by the Scripps organization.

The Associated Press and the A.P. Picture Service found that about thirty-five member papers were then prepared to enter into an agreement for the transmission of photos, using the improved AT&T telephoto system. Because of prospective costs, most AP member papers were not yet prepared to join in the venture. For that reason, a separate subsidiary organization was formed, the AP Wirephoto Service, effective January 1, 1935. Using the AT&T system, and with a 10,000-mile leased wire network, photos were made available in a national exchange between dailies in thirty-nine cities. Editors were able to talk on a supplementary national intercom network to report pictures available and pictures desired, with delivery following within minutes. Most pictures were transmitted in an 8×10 inch size, but could be as large as 11×17 inches. The quality improved, and the photo received was soon almost indistinguishable from the original. This encouraged more papers to subscribe to the service, rather than wait for prints to arrive by mail. Transmission could be made by telegraph wires, as well as by telephone wires, and also by cable and radiotelegraphy. Color photography also had developed by the mid-1930s, and a color photograph was transmitted from London to New York in May 1937 depicting the coronation ceremony of King George VI. Moved nationally by AP Wirephoto, it was reproduced in color by a few newspapers.

The AT&T and the Associated Press were not alone in working on photo transmission. For the Hearst organization, Walter Howey, who had edited the *Chicago Herald Examiner* and the *New York Mirror,* developed a Soundfoto system in December 1935, working with International News Photos, Inc., and had twenty papers receiving spot news pictures by the end of 1936.

The *New York Times* worked with Austin G. Cooley of the Massachusetts Institute of Technology in Cambridge to develop an experimental system for photo transmission between 1934 and 1936. In the latter year this system was put to use by Wide World Photos, a *Times* subsidiary, retitled Wide World Wired Photos. Newspapers in six cities were served originally, and twenty before 1941. At that time, the service was sold to the Associated Press and made part of the AP Wirephoto network.

For the Scripps organization, a United Feature Syndicate was formed in 1919 as a subsidiary of the United Press. In 1930 it absorbed the Metropolitan Newspaper Service, then eleven years old, and in 1931 it acquired the World Feature Service when the *New York World* newspapers were sold to Scripps-Howard and suspended.

A United News Pictures syndicate was established in 1928, also a Scripps enterprise, directed by Monte Bourjaily. The Newspaper Enterprise Association (NEA), conducted since 1902, distributed news photos as part of its service. In March 1936, it absorbed the Scripps Acme Newsphotos to become NEA-Acme, Inc., with an Acme Telephoto service also operating in conjunction with United News Pictures.

Systems for picture transmission by wire were introduced in Great Britain and some parts of the European continent during the 1930s. All systems permitted the use of portable equipment carried in suitcases, large at first, but later of smaller size. The equipment could be hooked to any telephone and, after a line connection had been made, a photo could be transmitted to a newspaper or news agency bureau. It became possible to transmit pictures also by radiotelegraphy from airplanes in flight, ships at sea, moving trains, and automobiles.

Photo transmission was of concern because of the new emphasis on pictures used to accompany current reports of events at home and abroad. Public interest in photographs so presented was stimulated both by the immediacy with which they appeared and by the quality of the pictures themselves. Excellent photographs had been available for a decade or more, but the 1920s and 1930s brought such further technical advances as to produce pictures far more effective and holding new elements of interest.

Cameras, lenses, and films were improved, adding speed and definition so that photographs could be made under almost any circumstance. Aerial photography produced striking views. Wide-angle and telephoto lenses opened new vistas. Every sort of sports event could be captured in detail, showing close-up action. The awkward and sometimes hazardous use of flash powder was ended with the introduction of flash bulbs. Photography in full and accurate color became as convenient as black-and-white photography, and under the same conditions of light and weather.

Perhaps most important in advancing the art of photography and creating photo-journalism was the invention of the compact, hand-held camera loaded with 35-millimeter film and with an f.3.5 and then an f.2 lens permitting most photographs to be made under available or adverse light conditions, whether in black and white or in color. First produced in Germany, the camera was easy to carry, quick and inconspicuous to use. For news purposes, it produced views of prominent persons, unposed and unaware of the camera, and at various distances. Yet it was equally effective in making pictures of the highest artistic quality or of any sort of event, and of capturing the most rapid motion. It did not replace other cameras, but it supplemented them and was put to great use.

Early notice of the 35-millimeter camera arose from its use in Germany by Dr. Erich Solomon making photos of private individuals and public officials in the most natural and informal of circumstances. Solomon became known for his "candid camera" photographs, beginning in 1928. The camera was used in London, with photographs of the royal family made even in the available light as they watched a theatrical performance. Thomas McEvoy, a photographer for *Time* magazine, made a series of candid photographs of President Roosevelt in his office at the White House as he examined letters awaiting signature on his desk. The President was not wholly pleased when the pictures were published showing him grimacing over his task.

The 35-millimeter camera was established as an alternative tool of the trade, and was adopted by news photographers throughout the world. Solomon himself produced notable candid views of Hitler, Mussolini, Chamberlain, Daladier, and others at the Munich Conference in 1938, and these were given prominent display in many countries.

McEvoy's use of the 35-millimeter camera in 1928 was just one example of the prompt interest of *Time* magazine in taking advantage of the advances being made in photography. When Time, Inc., started *Fortune* in 1930, one of its features was a generous use of photographs, many in full color, large in size, and as perfectly reproduced as the art of printing permitted. The first issue included a series of dramatic photos made by Margaret Bourke-White, U.S. photographer already known for her accomplishments, portraying aspects of the Soviet Union's first Five Year Plan.

Aware of the growing importance of the photographic medium, and with *Time* and *Fortune* successfully established, Luce began planning in 1933 for a new and elaborate illustrated magazine to make full use of what he saw as an original approach to the communication of information. In considering a title for the magazine, he favored "Life" as appropriate, but that was the name of a satirical weekly already in existence in New York since 1883. It had been in financial difficulties since 1930, however, and Luce was able to buy the magazine and its title from Clair Maxwell for $92,000.

As a Time, Inc., venture, *Life* appeared in a new format as a picture magazine on November 23, 1936, a weekly selling for ten cents. Large in size, on fine paper, its circulation passed the million mark within a few weeks, twice what had been anticipated. The advertising rate, set in expectation of the lesser circulation, did not bring in revenue sufficient to meet the costs of publication until contracts could be renegotiated later at a more realistic figure. As the years passed the circulation ultimately reached seven million.

Even though there had been illustrated publications for many years, and photos were being used increasingly, the success of *Life* is generally credited with having introduced photo-journalism in the modern sense, both for magazines and newpapers. Using every means to speed the receipt and publication of photographs, its editors learned how to give them full value in illustrating current news subjects, and to use them in series to tell "picture stories." In addition, *Life* provided substantial articles under the bylines of known writers and specialists, using maps, charts, diagrams, and tables, where appropriate, as well as photos in black and white and in color. They provided background on current news subjects, on subjects not previously explored, on persons of interest, on science, art, places, religion, archeology, and numerous other topics, all presented in a manner earning respect from specialists, while holding the interest of the general readership. Some of the photos and art reproductions were of such quality as to be circulated for school and museum displays, and preserved for reference. Old photos recovered and displayed proved as interesting and informative as current pictures.

Even as radio was giving personal reputations to individual broadcasters, so staff photographers and contributing photographers for *Life* became widely known. Some also were represented in the pages of *Time* and *Fortune,* McEvoy and Bourke-White among them. Dr. Solomon covered assignments for the magazines both in Europe and in the United States. Among others who became known were German-born Alfred Eisenstaedt, Carl Mydans, and James Abbe, a reporter and broadcaster as well as a photographer. Abbe was the first foreigner to make photos of Joseph Stalin, and one of the first to interview and photograph Adolf Hitler after he became chancellor of Germany.

Another was Hungarian-born André Friedmann. Taking the name of Robert Capa, he gained first fame through photo coverage of the Spanish Civil War, where his wife was killed while assisting him. Levon West, respected as an engraver, also became a specialist in photography under the name of Ivan Dmitri. His work appeared not only in *Life,* but later even more particularly in the *Saturday Evening Post.*

The work of great photographers, some of earlier times, and of various countries, was given public exposure through *Life, Fortune,* and other magazines. These included Edward Steichen, Peter Stackpole, Ansel Adams, Therese Bonney, Henri Cartier-Bresson, Alfred Steiglitz, Edward Wesson, Yousuf Karsh, and others. Photos made during the U.S.–Mexican War of 1846–48, the Crimean War of 1854–56, and the American Civil War of 1861–65, but never seen at those times because a photo-engraving process did not exist, were given publication in *Life,* along with many other early photos.

The prompt public acceptance of *Life* in 1936 had even more immediate results than the success of *Time,* the first Luce publication, in inspiring imitators, not only in the United States but in other countries as well.

One that might have been competitive already existed, the *Mid-Week Pictorial,* a weekly rotogravure magazine established in 1914 by the New York Times Company. Early in 1936 it had been sold to Monte Bourjaily, formerly of the United News Picture Syndicate. Responding to the same interest in photographs that was moving Henry R. Luce, he planned a larger magazine in a more attractive format. The first issue appeared in October 1936 and was well received, the circulation jumping from 30,000 for the old weekly to 117,000 for the new. In November, however, the first issue of *Life* appeared, and soon had a million circulation. Bourjaily suspended the *Mid-Week Pictorial* in February 1937 "to restyle it," but it never was resumed.

One of the many daily newspapers in the United States publishing a Sunday rotogravure supplement presenting photographs and advertisements in high-quality reproduction since 1920 was the *Des Moines Register* in Iowa, a morning paper. With the *Des Moines Tribune* in the afternoon, it was published by Gardner Cowles, assisted by his sons, John Cowles and Gardner Cowles, Jr., both graduated from Harvard in the early 1920s.

George H. Gallup, a native of the state, graduated in journalism from the State University of Iowa at Iowa City in 1923. He also completed work for an M.A. there in 1925. As a part of his graduate work, he pioneered in a study of readership of newspapers to learn the manner in which readers responded to news stories, illustrations, advertisements, and to their placement on pages throughout an edition. Using the Des Moines papers, morning and evening, as the basis for his investigations, he was encouraged and assisted by Cowles and his sons.[1]

In Des Moines, Gallup had learned, among other things, that readers responded particularly to photographs. This led Gardner (Mike) Cowles, Jr., to assign a staff group of the *Des Moines Register,* under Vernon Pope, to begin experimenting with pictures, first to produce them in a series to tell a story. This was successful enough for the paper to begin to syndicate such picture-stories in 1933. It also used its own Sunday rotogravure section to test ideas looking toward the production of a separate picture magazine.

It was at this same period that Luce was making plans for what would become *Life.* He was seeking ideas on every hand. This led to extended meetings with Mike Cowles. Luce also met with editors of the magazine *Vanity Fair,* a monthly established in 1892, but published since 1913 by Condé Nast, former advertising manager for *Collier's Weekly,* owner since 1907 of the Home Pattern Company, and publisher since 1909 of *Vogue* and *House and Garden* magazines.

Vanity Fair, as edited by Frank Crowninshield in the 1930s and published at Greenwich, Connecticut, had become an elegantly printed and illustrated publication presenting articles on a variety of subjects, including national and world issues by the ablest of writers. Nast himself suffered serious losses in the stock market crash of 1929, but was saved professionally in 1933 when Sir James Gomer Berry (later Lord Kemsley), proprietor of the *Sunday Times* and other British periodicals, invested in Condé Nast Publications, Inc., which included a British edition of *Vogue.*

In his investigation of the manner in which *Vanity Fair* handled illustrations, Henry Luce in 1933 became acquainted with its managing editor, Clare Boothe, who had been divorced since 1929 from George Brokaw of a profitable New York clothing manufacturing firm. Luce also had recently been divorced from the former Lila Ross Hotz of

---

1   Gallup received a Ph.D. at Iowa in 1928. He headed the Department of Journalism at Drake University, Des Moines, from 1929–31, and was a professor at the Medill School of Journalism, Northwestern University, in Evanston, Illinois, in 1931–32. It was as an outgrowth of the studies, also, that Dr. Gallup went on to direct market research for the Young & Rubicam advertising agency, in New York, from 1932–47, to other assignments in teaching and research, to the origination of public opinion polling techniques, to the establishment of the American Institute of Public Opinion in 1935, and to the syndication of public opinion poll results on innumerable subjects. A British Institute of Public Opinion was established under his direction in 1936.

Chicago, whom he had met in England and married in 1923. He and Clare Boothe Brokaw, both with children by their first marriages, were themselves married in November 1935. In addition to writing three successful plays between 1937 and 1940, Clare Boothe Luce also wrote for *Life*.

In his discussions with Mike Cowles, Luce discovered that while both were planning picture magazines their concepts differed. Since the two did not regard their prospective publications as likely to become directly competitive, they exchanged ideas freely. Peterson, in his history of magazines, dismisses a story sometimes circulated that Luce held a financial interest in the Cowles's picture magazine, *Look,* later established. He explains, rather, that "Luce favored pictures that transmitted news or information; . . . Cowles thought that good pictures were inherently interesting. . . . Their different concepts resulted in magazines of different characters . . . ."

Life appeared first in November 1936 as a weekly. Cowles produced his picture magazine *Look* as a monthly, beginning in January 1937. *Life* was in letter press, *Look* in gravure, with Vernon Pope as its editor. Made cautious by *Life*'s experience in setting too low an advance advertising rate, *Look* accepted no advertising at all for the first ten months, pending the time when it became possible to estimate the circulation and set the rate accordingly. Beginning with 705,000 circulation, it reached 2 million before the end of its first year. It also soon changed from monthly to biweekly publication. In 1940 Pope was replaced as editor by Harlan Logan, previously editor of *Scribner's,* a former Rhodes scholar, and New York University faculty member. Pope became editor of *Pageant,* a pocket monthly. Outgrowing the space available for its publication in Des Moines, most of *Look*'s operations were moved to New York in 1941, where it proceeded as another of the largest U.S. magazines in circulation.

Observing the success of *Life* and *Look,* other picture magazines appeared in the United States, most of them in 1937, bearing names such as *Focus, Photo History, Now and Then, Foto, Picture, Click,* and *Pic.* Varying in emphasis, size, and quality, some attained substantial circulations but none survived beyond 1948.

In other countries also, new picture magazines appeared after 1936, most of them made in the general style of *Life* but some produced in gravure. In London, the established Edward Hulton Press produced *Picture Post,* edited by Tom Hopkinson and published from 1938 until 1957. In France, Jean Prouvost, publisher of *Paris Soir,* established *Match,* which suffered interruption during World War II, but resumed publication in 1945. The war obstructed some such publishing ventures throughout Europe, in part because paper supplies were limited. But picture magazines resumed in strength after the war in many countries. Some also appeared or continued to stress photography as an art, such as *U.S. Camera,* rather than photography as a news or informational service.

The Public Affairs Column

A phenomenon of the 1930s, was the appearance in most daily newspapers of the United States of the "public affairs" column, usually syndicated and usually written from Washington by an experienced capital correspondent for a newspaper or news agency.

There had been special columns of great variety supplementing the general news content of newspapers in the United States and other countries, both signed and unsigned, for almost as long as newspapers had existed.[1] But the public affairs column had characteristics of its own. It emerged from a need of the times, and represented one of the new dimensions of journalism.

Some London newspapers had political gossip columnists prior to 1930, but the term was misleading because their contributions tended to be informed, serious, and responsible. Political writers in certain Paris information papers were read attentively, as well as some in the political press itself, and the same was true in certain other countries. But they tended to be polemicists, sometimes writing with great style, but still

---

1 Pamphleteers and editorial writers were columnists of a sort, and did concern themselves with public affairs. From the time of Addison and Steele, in London in the early eighteenth century, from John Wight's "Mornings at Bow Street" columns in the London *Morning Herald* in 1823, and from Solon Robinson's "Hot Corn" columns in the *New York Tribune* of 1853, readers were attracted and held to newspapers by features other than the news reports alone. There were sober financial columns, columns of political commentary, society, literary, and humor columns, some using contributions from readers. Sports columns, often written with great freedom of expression, more informal than anything else in the paper, long have been popular with readers. Columns of "advice to the lovelorn," and others on health, fashions, cooking, theatrical and motion picture news and "gossip," the glamor and color of cities, and virtually every other subject of human interest have been, and continue to be presented.

In the United States alone, the writers or columnists have gained their own fame. They have included Eugene Field, Finley Peter Dunne, Kin Hubbard, Don Marquis, O. O. McIntyre, Bert Leston Taylor (BLT), Franklin P. Adams (FPA), Christopher Morley, George Ade, Ring Lardner, Grantland Rice, Ben Hecht, Beatrice Fairfax, Dorothy Dix (Elizabeth N. Gilmer), and many more prior to 1940 and later.

with a partisanship quite different in purpose from the U.S. public affairs columnists of the 1930s.

Among those writing for the London press in that period were Vladimir Poliakoff (Augur), variously contributing to the *Times,* the *Daily Telegraph,* and the *Evening Standard,* and Robert H. Bruce Lockhart, writing anonymously in the *Evening Standard*'s leader page "Londoner's Diary." In Paris, they were somewhat matched by André Géraud (Pertinax), identified with *l'Echo de Paris,* and Geneviève Tabouis (Cassandra), of *l'Oeuvre* in the late 1930s.

Any correspondent writing from a capital was almost certainly writing largely of public affairs. For U.S. correspondents, the accepted concern for objectivity set a line rarely overstepped. Even the new allowance given a special newspaper correspondent by the 1930s for the introduction of background and factual interpretation did not reduce his objectivity.

If there were exceptions among U.S. writers, they were to be found chiefly in writers for magazines, such as Mark Sullivan of *Collier's Weekly,* Sam Blythe of the *Saturday Evening Post,* Frank Simonds of the *Review of Reviews,* and later such writers as Janet Flanner (Genêt) in Paris, Mollie Panter-Downes in London, or A. J. Liebling in New York or sometimes abroad, all three for the *New Yorker.* For the newspaper press, an added freedom of reporting was injected by David Lawrence in a syndicated Washington column in 1916, later distributed more widely through his Consolidated Press Association. Frank Kent of the *Baltimore Sun* also took some liberties in another syndicated column beginning in 1923. Meanwhile, Arthur Brisbane of the Hearst newspaper group in 1917 introduced a column titled "Today," which appeared in the first column of page one of the Hearst newspapers seven days a week and was syndicated to many others, some outside the United States. The column was highly subjective in style, consisting of a series of news-related items, some touching upon what could properly be called public affairs. It continued until his death in 1936.

Willis J. Abbot, editor of the *Christian Science Monitor,* wrote a public affairs column, "Watching the World Go By," wide-ranging in its subject matter and appearing on the editorial page of that newspaper in the 1920s and until his death in 1934. A Sunday column was produced by Cyril Arthur Player for the *Detroit News.* Another was introduced by Clinton Gilbert, in Washington for the *Philadelphia Public Ledger.* Constantine Brown, an experienced European correspondent, did the same for the *Washington Star.* Arthur Krock, in Washington for the *New York Times,* began an editorial page column, "In the Nation." By the time the Brown and Krock columns began to appear in the early 1930s, the public affairs column as a syndicated feature was accepted by newspapers throughout the United States responsive to circumstances of the time.

First, the United States was deep in an economic depression by 1931, with the lives of millions of persons disrupted. Publishers, editors, and correspondents, no less than others, felt a desperate need to know and understand what was happening to their lives and beliefs, and what was being done, or could be done, to control or repair the uncertainty and even the misery and hunger that had so suddenly overtaken many members of a generation of confused men, women, and children. The Hoover administration was replaced by the Roosevelt administration in 1933, and a "New Deal" program was undertaken. This in itself was so far-reaching and complex as to defy understanding. There could only be a hope and an almost religious faith that by some magic the problems might be resolved, that somewhere a wisdom existed to restore the nation to economic and social stability. The people turned to the press and to the radio for answers. There was a feeling that things might be happening behind the scenes that they should know about. It appeared that any solution must come through actions that could only be taken by the national government to meet a national problem, or perhaps even an international problem.

Second, by 1931 the radio had become an enormously important medium in the United States, a source of news as well as of entertainment, and a potent force in advertising. Also *Time* magazine had become a widely read and quoted medium of information, and *News-Week,* as it then was titled, would become a second weekly news magazine. These two publications presented much the same news as appeared in the daily press, but in a different focus and sometimes a useful perspective. They added background and interpretation, departing from the strict objectivity of the news agency and newspaper treatments of the same subjects. The public found this helpful in advancing understanding, and many newspaper writers and editors wistfully regretted that they remained bound by the rules of objectivity.

Further, radio was offering the public a form of news analysis or interpretation supplemental to the basic news broadcasts in the commentaries of competent observers such as Raymond Swing, Edward R. Murrow, H. V. Kaltenborn, Lowell Thomas, William L. Shirer, Eric Sevareid, Elmer Davis, and others. Here, again, the newspaper and news agency writers were by the demands of objectivity held within bounds.

Third, in 1931 the book *Washington Merry-Go-Round* was published that did "go behind the scenes" in an irreverent but informative way to cast new light on personalities in the capital and on the administration of government. Somewhat gossipy and superficial, it demonstrated that neither press nor radio was presenting some aspects of procedures in the capital. This was not because of any deliberate or sinister suppression or censorship, but once again because of the limitations of objectivity. The book became a best-seller, widely discussed and influential.

Although published anonymously, it was soon known that the book's authors were Drew Pearson, then of the Washington staff of the *Baltimore Sun,* and Robert S. Allen, then Washington bureau chief for the *Christian Science Monitor.* Once revealed, Allen was dismissed by the *Monitor,* partly because what he had written in the book bore slight resemblance to what he had written for the paper, again bound by the rules of objectivity. Pearson's position with the *Baltimore Sun* became no less questionable. For the two writers, however, the result was an invitation to write a syndicated column from Washington in somewhat the same spirit as the book, with "personal" and "exclusive" revelations bearing upon events in the capital. Also titled "Washington Merry-Go-Round," and with the impetus provided by the popularity of the book, the column beginning in 1932 was an immediate success, and was used by many newspapers.

This broke the log jam that had previously obstructed the news agencies and newspaper press alike in going beyond the facts alone, however accurately reported, to look more deeply into national affairs in the capital and elsewhere. It was not that they departed from the accepted objectivity in their basic reporting; that remained unchanged, and properly so. But they did feel able to support the publication of a new-style supplementary "public affairs column" doing what they had previously felt they could not do themselves. Some experienced Washington correspondents, above all others, followed Pearson and Allen in producing columns for distribution by the agencies or by syndicates. Thus they also matched in some degree what was being done by the radio commentators and by the news magazines. The public was given a further source of information, much of it useful.

When the *New York World* newspapers were sold in 1931, Walter Lippmann, who had been editor of the morning *World,* turned to writing a public affairs column for the *New York Herald Tribune.* Titled "Today and Tomorrow," sober and well-informed and appearing three days a week, it also became widely syndicated. Lippmann's column continued for some thirty years until his retirement. It was written from Washington through most of that time.

In between the Pearson-Allen column, offering several items somewhat gossipy in style, and the Lippmann column, dealing seriously with a single topic, scores of columns appeared after 1931 dealing with public affairs, national and international. There were columnists to suit every taste, most of them writing conscientiously.

One of the first in the new group was Paul Mallon of the United Press staff in Washington, who wrote effectively in a column titled "News Behind the News." A second was Raymond Clapper, also of the United Press, and formerly of the *Washington Post,* with his column titled more simply, "In Washington," which he continued until his death in 1944.

Other public affairs columnists entering the field in the 1930s included Marquis Childs, in Washington for the *St. Louis Post–Dispatch;* Ludwell Denny of the Scripps Howard Newspapers; Samuel Grafton, Doris Fleeson, and Thomas L. Stokes, all experienced in Washington; Robert Kintner and Joseph Alsop writing for the *New York Herald Tribune* and its syndicate, joined by Stewart Alsop later; Ernest K. Lindley, formerly of the *New York World* and the *New York Herald Tribune,* a Rhodes scholar, later writing exclusively for *Newsweek* magazine; Jay Franklin (John Franklin Carter, Jr.), formerly in the Department of State and with diplomatic assignments in Europe, writing for the *New York Times, Vanity Fair,* and other publications, including the London *Daily Chronicle;* and George E. Sokolsky, formerly in China for various newspapers, and writing largely on international affairs.

Anne O'Hare McCormick, experienced as a correspondent in Europe, became a columnist for the *New York Times,* writing of international subjects in a column titled "Abroad" and alternating on the editorial page with Krock's "In the Nation." Dorothy Thompson, also experienced as a correspondent in Europe, became a columnist for the *New York Herald Tribune,* with her "On the Record" syndicated. Eleanor Roosevelt herself wrote a more personalized column, "My Day," with wide syndication, during her years in the White House.

Other columns on a personal level, marginally concerned with public affairs, included those by Heywood Broun, formerly of the *New York World,* and Westbrook Pegler, formerly of the United Press, both former sports writers; Walter Winchell, primarily a Broadway gossip columnist for the *New York Mirror;* Will Rogers, basically an entertainer but bringing a note of humor to current affairs; and Ernest T. (Ernie) Pyle, formerly of the *Washington News,* writing columns chiefly of human interest while moving about the country.

What Pearson and Allen had done in writing of Washington in 1931 was done on a broader canvas, also anonymously, by John Gunther, then of the *Chicago Daily News*. His book, *Not to Be Repeated; Merry-Go-Round of Europe* (1932), was followed in much the same style by his highly successful *Inside Europe* (1936), and other "inside" books dealing with Asia, Latin America, the United States, Africa, Russia, and South America.[2]

In practice, the public affairs column bearing the name or names of the writers and written daily or weekly, but usually three times a week, was distributed by telegraph, supplementary to a news agency service or by a syndicate as an independent commercial enterprise or as a newspaper subsidiary. The column was, in fact, about a column in length, roughly 800 to 1,000 words. It presented a series of items or, more commonly, dealt with a single subject. As the receiving newspaper elected, it might be published as a straight column or spread over parts of two or three columns. It appeared usually under a set title, rather than a special headline reflecting its subject matter, as in a news story. It also appeared in a fixed position in the paper, usually on the editorial page or on the facing or opposite ("op ed") page.

The reason the public affairs column represented a new dimension in journalism at the period of its introduction in the 1930s, and why it brought something new and useful to the public understanding of events, was well summarized by Raymond Clapper:

> The writer of the column can move into his piece naturally, shading the emphasis, keeping the elements of the piece in perspective, interjecting qualifying statements, looking behind the scenes to show the reader what is really there.
>
> The columnist having a fixed position in the paper is relieved of the pressure to strain his copy to make page one. He doesn't have to write for headlines. He doesn't have to treat the pompous utterances of a tin-horn politician with the solemn gullibility that the news tradition seems to demand. The columnist can take that for what it is worth and then go on and tell where the body is. ... This kind of realistic reporting by the columnists is driving the politicians crazy. ...
>
> Newspapers need both reporters and columnists. ... The ... news columns are so stereotyped in the news reporting formula that the regular reporter cannot tell his story in the paper as he tells it to his colleagues in the press room. The columnist, unchained by the news writing formula, is free to write the rest of the story that the regular reporter has to leave out.[3]

---

2   For their work as public affairs columnists, Pulitzer Prizes were to be awarded to Krock (1935, 1938), McCormick (1937), Stokes (1939), Pegler (1941), and Lippmann (1962).

3   Raymond Clapper, "Hysterical Headlines!" *Quill* (September, 1939), 3–4.

What began in this fashion in the 1930s became a permanent feature of the daily newspaper press in the United States, contributing to an understanding of events growing more complex through the years.

The public affairs column was useful and probably necessary to that understanding in places where it was available in 1930, and later, because the world atmosphere was changed, and unfortunately not for the better.

Except in the Soviet Union, the prospect for public understanding through the press was better almost anywhere in the world in 1920 than it ever had been before. Temporarily, at least, there existed a greater freedom to seek and publish information. News sources were more open than ever before. Correspondents were able to move at a faster pace, by motor cars and airplane, as well as by ship and rail. Some traveled so constantly that the "roving" correspondent and the "swing man" became known internationally. Moved like pawns in a chess game, they met and met again for conferences, not only in Geneva and in the capital cities, but in such places as Lausanne or Rappalo, Cannes or Genoa. Their arrival at places where trouble had occurred, or was brewing, made them seem like birds of ill omen, but they gathered equally on occasions that held promise for good. They wrote of happenings and they wrote of situations, sometimes the hard facts of the day, and again a so-called "thumb-sucking piece" in which the correspondent speculated upon or interpreted the meaning of an event or circumstance.

All things considered, it is possible that the reporting of world affairs, in point of relationships between representatives of the media and their sources of information—particularly at the level of national governments—may have reached the highest effectiveness of all time in the four-year period from about 1925 to 1929. Marcel W. Fodor, in Vienna and elsewhere for the *Manchester Guardian* and the *Chicago Daily News* for three decades following World War I, and who was greatly respected by all who knew him, observed that those four years were the only ones in his experience when a correspondent could "live and work like a gentleman." For some, that happy circumstance extended to about 1932.

Until that time, a correspondent was able to work in or visit most countries and obtain information in what might be called a normal fashion. He could sample various points of view, live and move without personal hazard or calculated inconvenience, and write without concern for censorship or serious delays in transmission of his reports. Exceptions were, again, the Soviet Union and, by then, Fascist Italy, Spain, and parts of China. After 1932, however, the correspondent's problems increased throughout much of the world. Problems also increased for the press, the media generally, and the peoples of many lands. These matters will be explored in the next volume of this study of the information process.

Bibliography

Abbe, James. *Around the World in Eleven Years.* New York, 1936.

_____ . *I Photograph Russia.* New York, 1934.

Abend, Hallett. *My Life in China, 1926–1941.* New York, 1943.

Abbot, Willis J. *Watching the World Go By.* Boston, 1934.

Adam, Gerald. *Behind the Scenes at the Front.* London, 1915.

Allen, Frederick Lewis. *Only Yesterday: An Informal History of the Twenties.* New York, 1931. New ed. 1957.

_____ . *Since Yesterday.* New York, 1940.

[Allen, Robert S. and Pearson, Drew.] *Washington Merry-Go-Round.* New York, 1931.

Archer, Gleason L. *Big Business and Radio.* New York, 1939.

_____ . *History of Radio to 1926.* New York, 1938.

_____ . *Defense of Freedom.* New York. 1952.

Ashmead-Bartlett, Ellis. *Some of My Experiences in the Great War.* London, 1918.

_____ . *With the Turks in Thrace.* New York, 1913.

Baehr, Harry W., Jr. *The New York Tribune Since the Civil War.* New York, 1936.

Bainbridge, John. *Little Wonder, or The Reader's Digest and How It Grew.* New York, 1946.

Baker, Ray Stannard. *American Chronicle: The Autobiography of Ray Stannard Baker (David Grayson).* New York, 1945.

_____ . *Woodrow Wilson and World Settlement.* 3 vols. Garden City, N.Y., 1922.

Barnouw, Erik. *A History of Broadcasting in the United States.* 3 vols. New York, 1966–70.

Barns, Margarita. *The Indian Press.* London, 1940.

Barrett, James W. *The World, the Flesh, and the Mssrs. Pulitzer.* New York, 1931.

Barry, David S. *Forty Years in Washington.* Boston, 1924.

Bartlett, Vernon. *This Is My Life.* London, 1937. Published in U.S. as *Intermission in Europe: The Life of a Journalist and Broadcaster.* New York, 1938.

Bass, John Foster and Moulton, Harold Glenn. *America and the Balance Sheet of Europe.* New York, 1921.

Bass, John Foster. *The Peace Tangle.* New York, 1920.

Baxter, A. Beverly. *Strange Street.* London, 1936. (The London press.)

Beals, Carleton. *The Crime of Cuba.* Philadelphia, 1933.

Bechhofer, C. E. *In Denikin's Russia.* London, 1921.

Bell, Edward Price. *World Chancelleries.* Chicago, 1926.

Bell, E. H. C. Moberly. *The Life and Letters of C. F. Moberly Bell.* London, 1927.

Bell, Enid. *Flora Shaw.* London, 1947.

Bellanger, Claude, Godechot, Jacques, Guiral, Pierre, and Terrou, Fernand. *Histoire Général de La Presse Française.* 5 vols. Paris, 1969–76.

Bent, Silas. *Ballyhoo, The Voice of the Press.* New York, 1927.

———. *Strange Bedfellows.* New York, 1928.

Berger, Meyer. *The Story of The New York Times, 1851–1951.* New York, 1951.

Bernays, Robert. *"Special Correspondent."* London, 1934.

Bickel, Karl A. *New Empires: The Newspaper and the Radio.* Philadelphia, 1930.

Bickford, Leland. *News While It Is News: The Real Story of the Radio News.* Boston, 1935.

Blumenfeld, Ralph D. *R.D.B.'s Dairy.* London, 1930. Published in U.S. as *In the Days of Bicycles and Bustles.* New York, 1930.

_____ . *The Press in My Time.* London, 1933.

Blythe, Samuel G. *The Making of a Newspaperman.* Philadelphia, 1912.

Bok, Edward W. *The Americanization of Edward Bok.* New York, 1921.

_____ . *A Man from Maine.* New York, 1923. (Biography of Cyrus H. K. Curtis.)

Bolitho, William. *Camera Obscura.* Preface by Noel Coward. New York, 1930.

_____ . *Italy Under Mussolini.* New York, 1926.

Bömer, Karl. *Das Internationale Zeitungswesen.* Leipzig, 1934.

Bonsal, Stephen. *Unfinished Business, Paris-Versailles 1919.* Garden City, N.Y., 1944.

Boorstein, Daniel J. *The Americans: The Democratic Experience.* New York, 1973.

Bourke-White, Margaret. *Portrait of Myself.* New York, 1963.

Briggs, Asa. *History of Broadcasting in the United Kingdom.* 2 vols. Oxford, 1961, 1965.

Britt, George. *Forty Years—Forty Millions: The Career of Frank A. Munsey.* New York, 1935.

Brown, Frank James. *The Cable and Wireless Communications of the World; A survey of present day means of international communications by cable and wireless.* London, 1927.

Brucker, Herbert. *Freedom of Information.* New York, 1949.

Bruntz, George C. *Allied Propaganda and the Collapse of the German Empire in 1918.* Hoover War Library Publication No. 13. Stanford, Calif., 1938.

Buck, Sir Edward. *Simla, Past and Present.* Calcutta, 1904.

Buell, Raymond L. *Europe: A History of Ten Years.* New York, 1928.

_____ . *International Relations.* Rev. ed. New York, 1929.

Bullard, F. Lauristan. *Famous War Correspondents.* Boston and London, 1913.

Burleigh, Bennet. *Empire of the East; or Japan and Russia at War, 1904–1905*. London, 1905.

———. *The Natal Campaign*. London, 1900.

Burnham, Lord [Edward Frederick Lawson]. *Peterborough Court: The Story of the Daily Telegraph*. London, 1955.

Busch, Moritz. *Bismarck: Some Secret Pages of His History*. 3 vols. London, 1898.

Busch, Noel F. *Briton Hadden: A Biography of the Co-Founder of Time*. New York, 1949.

Campbell, Gerald. *Verdun to the Vosges*. London, 1916.

Canham, Erwin D. *Commitment to Freedom: The Story of the Christian Science Monitor*. Boston, 1958.

Carnes, Cecil. *Jimmy Hare, News Photographer: Half a Century With a Camera*. New York, 1940.

Carter, Boake. *This Is Life*. New York, 1937.

Carter, Thomas Francis. *The Invention of Printing in China and Its Spread Westward*. 2d ed. Rev. by L. Carrington Goodrich. New York, 1955.

Casey, Robert J. *Baghdad and Points East*. New York, 1928.

———. *Cambodian Quest*. New York, 1931.

———. *Easter Island*. New York, 1931.

Chamberlin, William Henry. *Confessions of an Individualist*. New York, 1940.

———. *The Russian Revolution, 1917–1921*. 2 vols. New York, 1935.

———. *Russia's Iron Age*. Boston, 1934.

———. *Soviet Russia*. Rev. ed. New York, 1931.

Chambers, Julius. *News Hunting on Three Continents*. New York, 1921.

Chao, Thomas Ming-Heng. *The Foreign Press in China*. Shanghai, 1931.

———. *My Fifteen Years as a Reporter*. London, 1944.

Charnley, Mitchell V. *News by Radio*. New York, 1948.

Chase, Francis, Jr. *Sound and Fury: An Informal History of Broadcasting*. New York and London, 1942.

Chester, Edmund A. *A Sergeant Named Batista.* New York, 1954.

Childs, Harwood L. *Public Opinion: Nature, formation, role.* Princeton, 1965.

Childs, Marquis. *I Write from Washington.* New York, 1942.

———. *Sweden, The Middle Way.* New York, 1948.

———. *Washington Calling.* New York, 1937.

———, and Reston James B., eds. *Walter Lippmann and His Times.* New York, 1959.

Chirol, Sir Valentine. *Fifty Years in a Changing World.* London and New York, 1928.

Clapper, Raymond. *Watching the World, 1934–1944.* Ed. by Mrs. Raymond Clapper. Introd. by Ernie Pyle. New York, 1944.

Clark, Delbert. *Washington Dateline.* New York, 1941.

Clark, Keith. *International Communications: The American Attitude.* New York, 1931.

Clark, Ronald W. *Edison: The Man Who Made the Future.* New York, 1978.

Clarke, Joseph I. C. *My Life and Memories.* New York, 1925.

Close, Upton [Josef Washington Hall]. *Behind the Face of Japan.* New York, 1942.

Cobb, Irvin S. *Paths of Glory.* New York, 1915. Published in London as *The Red Glutton.*

———. *Speaking of Prussians.* New York, 1917.

Cochrane, Negley D. *E. W. Scripps.* New York, 1933.

Codding, George Arthur, Jr. *The International Telecommunications Union: An Experiment in International Cooperation.* Leiden, 1952.

Codel, Martin, ed. *Radio and Its Future.* New York, 1930.

Collins, Henry M. *From Pigeon Post to Wireless.* London, 1925. (Reuter agency growth.)

Colquhoun, A. H. U. *Press, Politics and People: The Life and Letters of Sir John Willison, Journalist and Correspondent of The Times.* Toronto, 1935.

Colquhoun, Archibald Ross. *China in Transformation.* Rev. ed. London and New York, 1912.

Conference on the Press. Princeton University, April 23–25, 1931. Washington, D.C., 1931.

Cook, Sir Edward. *Delane of The Times.* London and New York, 1916.

———. *The Press in War-Time, with Some Account of the Official Press Bureau.* London, 1920.

———, Willert, Sir Arthur, Long, B. K., and Hobson, H. V. *The Empire in the World.* London and New York, 1937.

Cooper, Kent. *Barriers Down, The Story of the News Agency Epoch.* New York, 1942.

———. *Kent Cooper and The Associated Press; An Autobiography.* New York, 1959.

Cortesi, Salvatore, *My Thirty Years of Friendships.* New York and London, 1927.

Cowles, Virginia. *The Astors.* New York, 1980.

Creel, George. *How We Advertised America: The First Telling of the Amazing Story of the Committee on Public Information That Carried the Gospel of Americanism to Every Corner of the Globe.* New York, 1920.

———. *Rebel at Large: Recollections of Fifty Crowded Years.* New York, 1947.

Creelman, James. *On the Great Highway: The Wanderings and Adventures of a Special Correspondent.* Boston, 1901.

Crozier, Emmet. *American Reporters on the Western Front, 1914–1918.* New York, 1959.

Cruttwell, Charles R. M. F. *History of the Great War, 1914–1918.* Oxford, 1936.

Cummings, A. J. *The Press and a Changing Civilization.* London, 1936.

Current, Richard N. *The Typewriter and the Men Who Made It.* New York, 1954.

Curtin D. Thomas. *The Land of Deepening Shadow.* New York, 1917.

Dafoe, John W. *Clifford Sifton in Relation to His Times.* Toronto, 1931.

Dale, Edgar and Vernon, Norma. *Propaganda Analysis: An Annotated Bibliography*. Columbus, Ohio, 1940.

Davis, Charles Belmont, ed. *Adventures and Letters of Richard Harding Davis*. New York, 1918.

Davis, Elmer. *History of The New York Times, 1851–1921*. New York, 1921.

Davis, Oscar King. *Released for Publication: Some Inside Political History of Theodore Roosevelt and His Times, 1898–1918*. Boston and New York, 1925.

Davis, Richard Harding. *The Cuban-Porto Rican Campaign*. London, 1899.

———. *The Notes of a War Correspondent*. New York, 1910.

———. *With the Allies*. New York, 1915.

———. *With the French in France and Salonika*. New York, 1916.

———. *A Year from a Correspondent's Note-Book*. New York and London, 1898.

DeBeaufort, J. M. *Behind the German Veil; A record of a journalistic war pilgrimage*. London, 1917.

DeForest, Lee. *Father of Radio: The Autobiography of Lee DeForest*. Chicago, 1950.

Demartial, Georges. *La Guerre de 1914: Comment on Mobilisa les Consciences*. Paris, 1922.

Dennis, Charles H. *Victor Lawson, His Time and His Work*. Chicago, 1935.

Desmond, Robert W. *The Information Process: World News Reporting to the Twentieth Century*. Iowa City, 1978.

———. *The Press and World Affairs*. New York and London, 1937. Reprinted, New York, 1972.

Dickens, Charles. *American Notes*. New York, 1842.

Diehl, Charles Sanford. *The Staff Correspondent: How the News of the World is Collected and Dispatched by a Body of Trained News Writers*. San Antonio, 1931.

Dillon, Emile Joseph. *The Inside Story of the Peace Conference*. London and New York, 1920.

Donald, Robert, ed. *The Imperial Press Conference in Canada, 1920.* London, 1921.

Dosch-Fleurot, Arno. *Through War to Revolution, Being the experiences of a newspaper correspondent in war and revolution, 1914–1920.* London, 1920.

Dovifat, Dr. Emil, ed. *Handbuch der Deutschen Tagespresse.* Leipzig and Frankfurt-am-Main, 1937.

Downey, Fairfax. *Richard Harding Davis: His Day.* New York and London, 1933.

Dresler, Adolph. *Geschichte der Italienischen Presse.* 2 vols. Munich and Berlin, 1933 and 1934.

Driberg, Tom. *Beaverbrook: A Study in Power and Frustration.* London, 1956.

Dunlap, Orrin. *The Story of Radio.* New York, 1935.

Dunn, Robert. *Five Fronts: On the Firing-Lines With English, French, Austrian, German and Russian Troops.* New York, 1915.

Eder, Joseph Maria. *History of Photography.* Translated from German by Edward Epstean. New York, 1945.

Eliassen, Peter. *Ritzaus Bureau, 1866–1916.* Copenhagen, 1916.

Elson, Robert T. *Time, Inc.: The Intimate History of a Publishing Enterprise, 1923–1941.* New York, 1968.

Emery, Edwin. *History of the American Newspaper Publishers Association.* Minneapolis, 1950.

Emery, Edwin and Emery, Michael C. *The Press and America; An Interpretative History of the Mass Media.* 4th ed. Englewood Cliffs, N.J., 1978.

Escott, T. H. S. *Masters of English Journalism: A Study of Personal Forces.* London, 1911.

Essary, J. Fred. *Covering Washington; Government reflected to the public in the press, 1922–1926.* Boston, 1927.

Faber, John. *Great Moments in News Photography.* New York, 1960.

Ferguson, George V. *John W. Dafoe.* Toronto, 1948.

Fessenden, H. M. *Fessenden—Builder of Tomorrow.* New York, 1940.

Fielding, Raymond. *The March of Time, 1935–1951.* New York, 1978.

———. *The Newsreel.* New York, 1972.

Fine, Barnett. *A Giant of the Press.* New York, 1933. Reprinted with epilogue by Robert W. Desmond. Oakland, Calif. 1968. (Short biography of Carr Van Anda.)

Fischer, Heinz-Dietrich and Merrill, John C., eds. *International and Intercultural Communication.* Rev. ed. New York, 1976.

Fischer, Louis. *Men and Politics: An Autobiography.* New York, 1946.

Fisher, Charles. *The Columnists.* New York, 1944.

Forrest, Wilbur F. *Behind the Front Page.* New York, 1934.

Fortescue, Granville. *At the Front With Three Armies.* London and New York, 1914.

———. *Front Line and Deadline; The experiences of a war correspondent.* New York, 1937.

Fox, Edward Lyell. *Behind the Scenes in Warring Germany.* New York, 1915.

Frédérix, Pierre. *Un Siecle de Chasse aux Nouvelles; De l'Agence d'Information Havas à l'Agence France-Presse, 1835–1957.* Paris, 1959.

Freidel, Frank. *The Splendid Little War.* Boston, 1958. (Spanish-American War.)

Fyfe, Hamilton. *My Seven Selves.* London, 1935.

———. *Northcliffe: An Intimate Biography.* London and New York, 1930.

———. *Sixty Years of Fleet Street.* London, 1949.

Gardner, Gilson. *Lusty Scripps: The Life of E. W. Scripps, 1854–1926.* New York, 1932.

Garvin, Katherine. *J. L. Garvin, a Memoir.* London, 1948.

Gelatt, Roland D. *The Fabulous Phonograph.* 2d ed. New York, 1965.

Gelb, Barbara. *So Short a Time: A Biography of John Reed and Louise Bryant.* New York, 1973.

Gerard, James W. *My Four Years in Germany*. New York, 1917.

Gibbons, Edward. *Floyd Gibbons, Your Headline Hunter*. New York, 1953.

Gibbons, Floyd. *And They Thought We Wouldn't Fight*. New York, 1918.

Gibbs, Philip. *Adventures in Journalism*. New York, 1923.

———. *More That Must be Told*. New York, 1921.

———. *Now It Can Be Told*. New York, 1920. Published in London as *Realities of War*.

———. *The Pageant of Years*. London, 1946.

Gies, Joseph. *The Colonel of Chicago*. New York, 1979. (R. R. McCormick.)

Gilbert, Douglas. *Floyd Gibbons: Knight of the Air*. New York, 1930.

Gollin, A. M. *The Observer and J. L. Garvin, 1908–1948*. Oxford, 1960.

Gossin, Albert. *La Presse Suisse*. Neuchatel, 1936.

Gorham, Maurice. *Broadcasting and Television Since 1900*. London, 1952.

Gould, Lewis L. and Greeve, Richard. *Photojournalist: The Career of Jimmy Hare*. Austin, Texas, 1977.

Gramling, Oliver. *AP: The Story of News*. New York and Toronto, 1940.

Grandin, Thomas. *The Political Use of Radio*. Geneva, 1939.

Greenwall, Harry J. *Scoops; Being Leaves from the Diary of a Special Correspondent*. London and New York, 1923.

———. *Round the World for News*. London, 1936.

Grogan, Lady Ellinore. *The Life of J. D. Bourchier*. London, 1926.

Groth, Otto. *Die Zeitung, ein System der Zeitungskunde*. 3 vols. Mannheim, Berlin, and Leipzig, 1928.

Haley, Sir William et al. *C. P. Scott, 1846–1932; The Making of The "Manchester Guardian."* London, 1947.

Hanazano, Kanesada. *The Development of Japanese Journalism*. Osaka, 1924.

Hapgood, Norman. *The Changing Years: Reminiscences of Norman Hapgood.* New York, 1930.

Hardman, Thomas H., comp. *The First Imperial Press Conference: A Parliament of the Press, 1909.* London, 1909.

Harlow, Alvin E. *Old Wires and New Waves: The History of the Telegraph, Telephone and Wireless.* New York, 1936.

Harrison, Marguerite. *There's Always Tomorrow: The Story of a Checkered Life.* New York, 1935.

———. *Marooned in Moscow.* New York, 1921.

Hart, Liddell. *The War in Outline, 1914–1918.* New York, 1936.

Haslett, A. W. *Radio 'Round the World.* New York, 1934.

Hawkins, Eric and Sturdevant, Robert N. *Hawkins of the Paris Herald.* New York, 1963.

Hedin, Sven Anders. *With the German Armies in the West.* Trans. from Swedish by H. G. de Walerstroff. London and New York, 1915.

Herd, Harold. *The March of Journalism; The Story of the British Press from 1622 to the Present Day.* London, 1952.

Hershey, Burnett. *How I Got That Story.* New York, 1967. (Relating to Paris Peace Conference.)

Hettinger, Herman S., ed. *Radio: The Fifth Estate.* Annals of American Academy of Political and Social Science. Philadelphia, 1935.

Hicks, Granville. *John Reed, the Making of a Revolutionary.* New York, 1936.

Hicks, Wilson. *Words and Pictures, An Introduction to Photojournalism.* New York, 1952.

Hindle, Wilfrid. *The Morning Post.* London, 1937.

History of the London Times, 1785–1948, The. 5 vols. London and New York, 1935–48.

Hodges, Charles. *The Background of International Relations.* New York, 1931.

Hodgetts, E. A. B. *Moss from a Rolling Stone.* New York, 1924.

Hoge, Alice A. *Cissy Patterson.* New York, 1966.

Hohenberg, John. *Foreign Correspondence: The Great Reporters and Their Times.* New York, 1964.

———, ed. *The Pulitzer Prize Story.* New York, 1959. (With commentaries.)

House, Edward M. *The Intimate Papers of Colonel House.* Boston, 1930.

Howe, Quincy. *The News and How to Understand It.* New York, 1940.

Huddleston, Sisley. *In My Time, An observer's record of war and peace.* New York, 1938.

———. *Peace-Making at Paris.* London, 1919.

Hunt, Frazier. *One American and His Attempt at Education.* New York, 1938.

Huntford, Roland. *Scott and Amundsen.* New York, 1980.

———. *This Bewildering World, and Its Search for a New Rhythm.* New York, 1936.

Ireland, Gordon. *Boundaries, Possessions and Conflicts in South America.* Cambridge, Mass., 1938.

Irwin, Will. *The City That Was: A Requiem of Old San Francisco.* New York, 1906.

———. *The Making of a Reporter.* New York, 1942.

———. *A Reporter at Armageddon: Letters from the Front and Behind the Lines of the Great War.* London and New York, 1918.

Ito, Masanori. *The Japanese Press—Past and Present.* Tokyo, 1949.

"Iwanaga Kun." Tokyo, 1941.

James, Lionel. *High Pressure.* London, 1929.

———. *Times of Stress.* London, 1929.

———. *With the Conquered Turk.* London, 1913.

Jeffries, J. M. N. *Front Everywhere.* London, 1935.

Jeffrey, William H. *Mitre and Argentina.* New York, 1952.

Johnson, Gerald W. *An Honorable Titan, a Biographical Study of Adolph S. Ochs.* New York, 1946.

Johnson, Thomas M. *Without Censor, A New Light on Our Greatest World War Battles.* Indianapolis, 1928.

Jones, Kennedy. *Fleet Street and Downing Street.* London, 1920.

Jones, Sir Roderick. *A Life in Reuters.* London, 1951.

———. *A Note on Reuters; International Conferences on the Press.* London, 1932.

Josephy, Alvin M., Jr., ed., et al. *The American Heritage History of World War I.* New York, 1964.

Journalism; By Some Masters of the Craft. London, 1932.

Jouvenal, Henri de, Martin, Kingsley, Mowrer, Paul Scott, Cano, Sanin, and Sieburg, Friedrich. *The Educational Role of the Press.* Paris, 1934.

Juergens, George. *Joseph Pulitzer and the New York World.* New York, 1966.

Kaplan, Justin. *Lincoln Steffens, a Biography.* New York, 1974.

Kawabe, Kisaburo. *The Press and Politics in Japan: A Study of the Relation Between the Newspaper and the Political Development of Modern Japan.* Chicago, 1921.

Kendrick, Alexander. *Prime Time: The Life of Edward R. Murrow.* Boston, 1969.

Kennan, George. *The Tragedy of Pelée.* New York, 1902.

Kennan, George F. *The Decision to Intervene.* Princeton, 1958.

———. *Russia Leaves the War.* Princeton, 1956.

Kennedy, Malcolm Duncan. *The Changing Fabric of Japan.* London, 1930.

Kirk, Betty. *Covering the Mexican Front: The Battle of Europe Versus America.* Norman, Okla., 1942.

Kirkland, Wallace. *Recollections of a Life Photographer.* Boston, 1954.

Kitchin, Frederick Harcourt. *Moberly Bell and His Times; The London 'Times' Under the Management of Moberly Bell. An Official Narrative,* London and New York, 1925.

Knight, Oliver. *I Protest; Selected Disquisitions of E. W. Scripps.* Madison, Milwaukee, and London, 1966.

Knightley, Philip. *The First Casualty: From the Crimea to Vietnam: The War Correspondent as Hero, Propagandist, and Myth Maker.* New York and London, 1975.

Kobler, John. *Luce, His Time, Life, and Fortune.* New York, 1968.

Koenigsberg, Moses. *King News: An Autobiography.* New York, 1941.

Kohler, Wolfram. *Der Chef-Redakteur: Theodor Wolff.* Dusseldorf, 1978.

Kramer, Dale. *Ross and the New Yorker.* Garden City, N.Y., 1931.

Krieghbaum, Hillier. *Facts in Perspective.* New York, 1955.

Krock, Arthur. *Memoirs: Sixty Years on the Firing Line.* New York, 1968.

Landry, Robert. *This Fascinating Radio Business.* New York, 1946.

Lane, Margaret. *Edgar Wallace: The Biography of a Phenomenon.* New York, 1939.

Laney, Al. *Paris Herald: The Incredible Newspaper.* New York, 1947.

Langford, Gerald. *The Richard Harding Davis Years.* New York, 1961.

Laski, Harold J. *The American Presidency.* New York, 1940.

Lasswell, Harold D. *Propaganda Technique in the World War.* New York, 1927.

——, with Casey, Ralph D., and Smith, Bruce Lannes. *Propaganda and Promotional Activities; An Annotated Bibliography.* Minneapolis, 1935.

Laufer, Berthold. *Paper and Printing in Ancient China.* Chicago, 1931.

Lawrence, David. *Diary of a Washington Correspondent.* New York, 1942.

——. *The True Story of Woodrow Wilson.* New York, 1924.

Lazarsfeld, Paul F. *Radio and the Printed Page: An Introduction to the Study of Radio and Its Role in the Communication of Ideas.* New York, 1940.

The League of Nations: Ten Years of World Co-operation. Geneva, 1930.

Lee, Alfred McClung. *The Daily Newspaper in America: The Evolution of a Social Instrument.* New York, 1937.

Leiter, Friedrich. *Die Zeitung im Kriege und nach dem Kriege.* Vienna, 1915.

Levine, Isaac Don. *Eyewitness to History.* New York, 1973.

———. *Red Smoke.* New York, 1932.

Lewis, Alfred Allen. *Man of the World, Herbert Bayard Swope: A Charmed Life of Pulitzer Prizes, Poker and Politics.* New York, 1978.

Liang, Hubert S. *Development of the Modern Chinese Press.* Nanking, 1937.

Lin Yu'tang. *History of the Press and Public Opinion in China.* Chicago, 1936.

London, Joan. *Jack London and His Times, An Unconventional Biography.* New York, 1939.

Lord, Walter. *The Good Years; From 1900 to the First World War.* New York, 1960.

Lovett, Pat. *Journalism In India.* Calcutta, 1927.

Lowe, Charles. *The Tale of a "Times" Correspondent.* London, 1927.

Lucas, Reginald. *Lord Glenesk and the Morning Post.* London, 1910.

Lundberg, Ferdinand. *Imperial Hearst, A Social Biography.* New York, 1936.

Lytton, Neville. *The Press and the General Staff.* London, 1921.

Macartney, M. H. H. and Cremona, Paul. *Italy's Foreign and Colonial Policy, 1914–1937.* London and New York, 1938.

Mackenzie, F. A. *Beaverbrook: An Authentic Biography.* London, 1931.

———. *The Mystery of the Daily Mail, 1896–1921.* London, 1921.

Maclaurin, W. Rupert. *Invention and Innovation in the Radio Industry.* New York, 1949.

Magnus, Philip. *Kitchener: Portrait of an Imperialist.* New York, 1959.

Mance, Brig. Gen. Sir Osborne and Wheeler, J. E. *International Telecommunications.* London and New York, 1944.

Manevy, Raymond. *Histoire de la Presse, 1914 à 1939.* Paris, 1945.

Marcosson, Isaac F. *Adventures in Interviewing.* New York and London, 1923.

_____ . *Before I Forget, a Pilgrimage to the Past.* New York, 1959.

_____ . *Turbulent Years.* New York, 1938.

Markham, James W. *Voices of the Red Giants: Communications in Russia and China.* Ames, Iowa, 1967.

Marshall, Walter P. "Printing Telegraphy, Stock Tickers." In *Encyclopedia Americana.* Vol. 26. New York, 1959.

_____ . "Teleprinters." In *Encyclopaedia Britannica.* Vol. 21. Chicago, 1959.

Martin, Frank L., ed. *The Press Congress of the World: Regional Meeting in Mexico City. 1931.* Columbia, Mo., 1934.

Martin, Ralph C. *The Extraordinary Life of Eleanor Medill Patterson.* New York, 1979.

Mathews, Joseph J. *George W. Smalley, Forty Years a Foreign Correspondent.* Chapel Hill, N.C., 1973.

_____ . *Reporting the Wars.* Minneapolis, 1957.

McCabe, Charles R., ed. *Damned Old Crank, A Self-Portrait of E. W. Scripps.* New York, 1951.

McClure, Samuel S. *My Autobiography.* New York, 1914.

McCormick, Anne O'Hare. *The World at Home: Selections from the Writings of Anne O'Hare McCormick.* Edited by Marion Turner Sheean. Introd. by James B. Reston. New York, 1956.

McCutcheon, John T. *Drawn From Memory.* Indianapolis, 1950.

McKenzie, Vernon, ed. *Behind the Headlines; Journalistic Adventures of Today.* New York, 1931.

_____ . *Through Turbulent Years.* New York, 1938.

McMurtrie, Douglas C. *Printing History, Typography and Techniques of Printing: A List of Books and Pamphlets.* Chicago, 1935.

McNaught, Carlton. *Canada Gets the News.* Toronto, 1940.

McRae, Milton A. *Forty Years of Newspaperdom: The Autobiography of a Newspaperman.* Preface by Arthur H. Vandenberg. New York, 1924.

Meister, Alois. *Die Deutsche Presse im Krieg und Später.* Münster, 1916.

Merrill, John C. *The Elite Press: Great Newspapers of the World.* New York, Toronto, and London, 1968.

———. *"M.E.S." His Book.* New York, 1918. (Melville E. Stone's first 25 years with the Associated Press.)

Miller, Webb. *I Found No Peace: The Journal of a Foreign Correspondent.* New York, 1936.

Millis, Walter. *The Martial Spirit.* Boston and London, 1931.

———. *The Road to War.* Boston, 1935.

Mills, J. Saxon. *The Press and Communications of Empire.* New York, 1924.

Mills, William Haslam. *The Manchester Guardian: A Century of History.* Preface by C. P. Scott. London, 1921; New York, 1922.

Mitarai, Tatsuo. *Shimbun Taiheiki.* Tokyo, 1950. (History of the press in Japan.)

Mock, James R. *Censorship 1917.* Princeton and London, 1941.

———, with Larson, Cedric. *Words That Won the War; The Story of the Committee on Public Information, 1917–1919.* Princeton, 1939.

Montague, Charles Edward. *Disenchantment.* London, 1928.

Moorhead, Alan. *Gallipoli.* London, 1956.

———. *The Russian Revolution.* New York, 1958.

Moran, James. *Printing Presses. History and Development from the Fifteenth Century to Modern Times.* Berkeley, Calif., 1973.

Morison, Samuel Eliot. *The Oxford History of the American People.* New York, 1965.

Morris, Joe Alex. *Deadline Every Minute, The Story of the United Press.* Garden City, N.Y., 1957.

Mott, Frank Luther. *American Journalism: A History of Newspapers in the United States.* 3d ed. New York, 1962.

———, with Casey, Ralph D., eds. *Interpretations of Journalism; A Book of Readings.* New York, 1937.

Mowrer, Edgar Ansel. *Triumph and Turmoil: A Personal History of Our Times.* New York, 1968.

Mowrer, Paul Scott. *Balkanized Europe—A Study in Political Analysis and Reconstruction.* New York, 1921.

———. *Our Foreign Affairs—A Study in National Interest and the New Diplomacy.* New York, 1924.

———. *The House of Europe.* Boston, 1945.

Murthy, Nadig Krishna. *Indian Journalism.* Mysore, 1966.

Myers, Dennis P., ed. *Handbook of the League of Nations.* Boston, 1935.

Nafziger, Ralph O. *Foreign News Sources and the Foreign Press: A Bibliography.* Minneapolis, 1937.

———. *International News and the Press: Communications, Organization of News Gathering, International Affairs and the Foreign Press—an Annotated Bibliography.* New York, 1940.

Nevinson, Henry W. *Changes and Chances.* London, 1923.

———. *Fire of Life.* London, 1935.

———. *Last Changes, Last Chances.* London and New York, 1929.

———. *More Changes, More Chances.* London and New York, 1925.

Newhall, Beaumont. *Photography, 1839–1937.* New York, 1937.

Nicolai, Walter. *Nachrichtendienst, Presse und Volksstimmung im Weltkriege.* Berlin, 1920.

Nichols, M. E. *(CP) The Story of The Canadian Press.* Toronto, 1948.

Nicholson, Harold. *Peacemaking 1919, Being Reminiscences of the Paris Peace Conference.* London and New York, 1933.

Noble, George B. *Policies and Opinions at Paris, 1919.* New York, 1935.

Northcliffe, Lord. *At the War.* New York, 1916.

———. *Lord Northcliffe's War Book.* New York, 1917.

O'Brien, Frank M. *The Story of the Sun, 1833–1928.* Rev. ed. New York, 1928.

O'Connor, Richard. *The Scandalous Mr. Bennett.* Garden City, N.Y., 1962.

Older, Mrs. Fremont. *William Randolph Hearst, American.* New York, 1936.

Olson, Kenneth E. *The History Makers; The Press of Europe From Its Beginnings Through 1965.* Baton Rouge, La., 1966.

Orchard, J. E. *Japan's Economic Position.* New York, 1930.

Owen, Russell. *The Antarctic Ocean.* New York, 1941.

———. *South of the Sun.* Foreword by Roy Chapman Andrews. New York, 1934.

Paine, Ralph D. *Roads of Adventure.* Boston, 1922.

Paley, William S. *As It Happened: A Memoir.* Garden City, N.Y., 1979. (Development of the Columbia Broadcasting System.)

Palmer, Frederick. *America in France: The Story of the Making of an Army.* London, 1917.

———. *My Year of the Great War.* New York, 1915.

———. *Our Greatest Battle; The Meuse-Argonne.* New York, 1919.

———. *With Kuroki in Manchuria.* New York, 1904.

———. *With the New Army on the Somme: My Second Year of the War.* London and New York, 1917.

———. *With My Own Eyes, A Personal Story of Battle Years.* Indianapolis, 1932.

Patmore, Derek. *Balkan Correspondent.* New York, 1941.

Patterson, Don D. *The Journalism of China.* University of Missouri Journalism Series, No. 26. Columbia, Mo., 1922.

Pemberton, Max. *Lord Northcliffe: A Memoir.* London, 1922.

Peterson, H. C. *Propaganda for War: The Campaign Against American Neutrality, 1914–1917.* Norman, Okla., 1939.

Peterson, Theodore. *Magazines in the Twentieth Century.* Urbana, Ill., 1956.

Pethybridge R., ed. *Witness to the Russian Revolution.* London, 1964.

Pictured Encyclopedia of the World's Greatest Newspaper. Chicago, 1928. *(Chicago Tribune.)*

Pierrefeu, Jean de. *French Headquarters, 1915–1918.* Translated from French by Major C. J. C. Street. London, 1924.

Pollard, James E. *The Presidents and the Press.* New York, 1947.

Ponsonby, Arthur. *Falsehood in War-Time.* New York, 1928.

Poore, Benjamin Perley. *Reminiscences of Sixty Years in the National Metropolis.* 2 vols. Philadelphia, 1886. (Washington news reporting.)

Potter, Pittman B. *This World of Nations.* New York, 1929.

Pound, Reginald and Harmsworth, Geoffrey. *Northcliffe.* London and New York, 1959.

Powell, E. Alexander. *Adventure Road.* Garden City, N.Y. 1954.

——. *Fighting in Flanders.* New York, 1914.

——. *Slanting Lines of Steel.* New York, 1933.

——. *Twenty Years of Travel and Adventure.* New York, 1937.

Powell, John B. *My Twenty-Five Years in China.* New York, 1945.

Prando, Alberto. *A Century and a Half of Journalism in Argentina.* Austin, Texas, 1961.

Price, G. Ward. *Extra-Special Correspondent.* London, 1957.

Price, Morgan Phillips. *My Three Revolutions.* London, 1969.

Price, Warren C., comp. *The Literature of Journalism; An Annotated Bibliography.* Minneapolis, 1959. Rev. ed. 1977.

Pupin, Michael I. *From Immigrant to Inventor.* New York, 1923.

Ralph, Julian. *The Making of a Journalist.* New York, 1903.

——. *War's Brighter Side: The Story of the Friend Newspaper Edited by Correspondents with Lord Roberts's Forces.* London and New York, 1901.

Ransome, Arthur. *The Crisis in Russia.* New York, 1921.

Rathert, Helmut. *Die deutsche Kriegsberichtstattung und Presse als Kampfmittel im Weltkreig.* Berlin, 1934.

Read, James Morgan. *Atrocity Propaganda, 1914–1919.* New Haven, 1941.

Reed, John. *Ten Days That Shook the World.* New York, 1919.

——. *The War in Eastern Europe.* Illustrations by Boardman Robinson. New York, 1917.

Regier, C. C. *The Era of the Muckrakers.* Chapel Hill, N.C., 1932.

Reith, Lord. *Into the Wind: His Autobiography.* London, 1947. (Relating to the British Broadcasting Corporation.)

Remak, Joachim. *"Sarajevo."* New York, 1959.

Repington, Colonel C. C. *The First World War, 1914–1918.* 2 vols. London, 1920.

Report on the British Press. London, 1938. (Political and economic planning.)

Richardson, J. Hall. *From the City to Fleet Street.* London, 1927.

Riddell, Lord. *Lord Riddell's Intimate Diary of the Peace Conference and After, 1918–1923.* New York, 1934. Published in London as *Lord Riddell's War Diary.*

Robinson, H. Perry. *The Turning Point.* London, 1917.

Rosenstone, Robert A. *Romantic Revolutionary.* New York, 1975. (Relates to John Reed.)

Rosewater, Victor. *History of Co-operative News-Gathering in the United States.* New York and London, 1930.

Ruhl, Arthur. *Antwerp to Gallipoli, A Year of War on Many Fronts—and Behind Them.* New York and London, 1916.

———. *White Nights and Other Russian Impressions.* New York, 1917.

Saerchinger, Cesar. *Hello America! Radio Adventures in Europe.* Boston, 1938.

Salisbury, Harrison E. *Black Night, White Snow: Russia's Revolutions, 1905–1917.* Garden City, N.Y., 1977.

Salmon, L. M. *The Newspaper and Authority.* New York, 1922.

———. *The Newspaper and the Historian.* New York, 1922.

Schanz, Dr. Joachim. *Die Entstehung Eines Deutschen Presse-Gross Verlages.* Berlin, 1933.

Schechter, Abel A. and Anthony, Edward. *I Live on Air.* New York, 1941.

Schreiner, George Abel. *Cables and Wireless, and their role in the foreign relations of the United States.* Boston, 1924.

———. *The Craft Sinister.* New York, 1920.

Schuster, M. Lincoln. *Eyes on the World: A Photographic Record of History-in-the-Making.* New York, 1935.

Schwarte, Max, ed. *Presse; Der Weltkreig im seiner Einwirkung auf das Deutsche Volk.* Leipzig, 1918.

Scott-James, R. A. *The Influence of the Press.* London, 1926.

Seldes, George. *You Can't Print That! The Truth Behind the News, 1918–1928.* New York, 1929.

———. *World Panorama, 1918–1933.* Boston, 1933.

Seldes, Gilbert. *The Seven Lively Arts.* New York, 1924.

Seton-Watson, R. W. *The South Slav Question and the Hapsburg Monarchy.* London, 1911.

Sharp, Eugene W. *International News Communications: The submarine cable and wireless as news carriers.* University of Missouri Bulletin. Columbia, Mo., 1927.

Shepherd, William G. *Confessions of a War Correspondent.* New York, 1917.

Slocombe, George. *The Tumult and the Shouting.* New York, 1936.

Smith, Bruce Lannes, with Lasswell, Harold D., and Casey, Ralph D., eds. *Propaganda, Communication and Public Opinion: A Comprehensive Reference Guide.* Princeton, N.Y., 1946.

Smith, Gene. *When the Cheering Stopped; The last years of Woodrow Wilson.* Introduction by Allen Nevins. New York, 1964.

Snyder, Louis L. and Morris, Richard B., eds. *A Treasury of Great Reporting: "Literature Under Pressure" from the Sixteenth Century to Our Own Times.* Preface by Herbert Bayard Swope. New York, 1949.

Squires, James Duane. *British Propaganda at Home and in the United States from 1914 to 1917.* Cambridge, Mass., 1935.

Strachey, John St. Loe. *The Adventure of Living.* London, 1922.

Steed, Henry Wickham. *Through Thirty Years, 1892–1922, A Personal Narrative.* 2 vols. London, 1924.

Steevens, George Warrington. *Things Seen: Impressions of Men, Cities and Books.* Selected and edited by G. S. Street, with a Memoir by W. E. Henley. Indianapolis, 1900.

Steffens, Lincoln. *The Autobiography of Lincoln Steffens.* 2 vols. New York, 1931.

———. *The Letters of Lincoln Steffens.* Edited by Ella Winter Steffens and Granville Hicks. 2 vols. New York, 1938.

———. *Lincoln Steffens Speaking.* New York, 1936.

Stewart, Irwin, ed. *Radio.* Supplement to Annals of American Academy of Political and Social Science. Philadelphia, 1939.

Stewart, Kenneth and Tebbel, John. *Makers of Modern Journalism.* New York, 1952.

Stillman, William J. *The Autobiography of a Journalist.* 2 vols. New York and London, 1901.

Stone, Melville E. *Fifty Years a Journalist.* New York and Toronto, 1921.

Storey, Graham. *Reuters, The Story of a Century of News-Gathering.* New York, 1951. Published in London as *Reuters' Century, 1851–1951.*

Stuart, Sir Campbell. *Secrets of Crewe House.* London, 1920.

Sullivan, Mark. *Education of an American.* New York, 1938.

———. *Our Times: The United States.* 7 vols. New York, 1926–1932.

Sukhanov, N. N. *The Russian Revolution, 1917.* New York, 1955.

Sutton, F. A. *One-Arm Sutton.* London, 1933.

Swanberg, W. A. *Citizen Hearst; A Biography of William Randolph Hearst.* New York, 1961.

———. *Luce and His Empire.* New York, 1972.

———. *Pulitzer.* New York, 1967.

Swanson, Walter S. J. *The Thin Gold Watch; A Personal History of the Newspaper Copleys.* New York and Toronto, 1964.

Swettenham, John A. *Allied Intervention in Russia.* London, 1967.

Swope, Herbert Bayard. *Inside the German Empire in the Third Year of the War.* New York, 1917.

Sydney Morning Herald. *A Century of Journalism: The Sydney Morning Herald and Its Record of Australian Life, 1831–1931.* Sydney and London, 1931.

Tarbell, Ida M. *All in the Day's Work.* New York, 1939.

Taylor, A. J. P. *Beaverbrook.* London, 1972.

Taylor, Edmond. *The Fall of the Dynasties: The Collapse of the Old Order, 1905–1922.* Garden City, N.Y., 1963.

Tebbel, John. *An American Dynasty, the Story of the McCormicks, Medills and Pattersons.* Garden City, N.Y., 1947.

———. *George Horace Lorimer and the Saturday Evening Post.* Garden City, N.Y., 1948.

_____. *The Life and Good Times of William Randolph Hearst.* New York, 1952.

Thayer, William Roscoe. *The Life and Letters of John Hay.* 2 vols. Boston, 1908.

Thomas, Lowell. *Good Evening Everybody; From Cripple Creek to Samarkand. An Autobiography.* New York, 1976.

_____. *Magic Dials.* New York, 1939.

_____. *So Long Until Tomorrow: From Quaker Hill to Kathmandu.* New York, 1977.

Thompson, Charles T. *The Peace Conference Day by Day: A presidential pilgrimage leading to the discovery of Europe.* Introduction by Colonel E. M. House. New York, 1920.

Thompson, Charles Willis. *Presidents I've Known.* Indianapolis, 1929.

Thurber, James. *The Years With Ross.* Boston, 1957.

Tomlinson, John D. *The International Control of Radio-Communications.* Ann Arbor, Mich., 1945.

Tong, Hollington K. *Dateline: China; The Beginning of China's Press Relations with the World.* New York, 1950. Published in Taiwan as *China and the World Press.*

Torres, Teodoro. *Periodismo.* Mexico City, 1934.

Townsend, George Alfred. *Washington Outside and Inside.* Hartford, Conn., and Chicago, 1873.

Tribolet, Leslie Bennett. *The International Aspects of Electrical Communications in the Pacific Area.* Baltimore, 1929.

Tuchman, Barbara. *The Guns of August.* New York, 1962.

Turner, H. E., ed. *The Fifth Imperial Press Conference (South Africa), 1935.* Foreword by T. W. Mackenzie. London, 1935.

_____. *The Fourth Imperial Press Conference (Britain), 1930.* London, 1930.

_____. *The Imperial Press Conference in Australia, 1925.* London, 1927.

Valdés, Miguel Valasco. *Historia del Periodismo Mexicano.* Mexico City, 1955.

Valenzuela, Jesus Z. *History of Journalism in the Philippine Islands.* Introduction by Willard G. Bleyer. Manila, 1933.

Viereck, George Sylvester. *Spreading Germs of Hate.* New York, 1930.

Villard, Oswald Garrison. *Fighting Years: Memoirs of a Liberal Editor.* New York, 1939.

Villiers, Frederic. *Villiers; His Five Decades of Adventure.* 2 vols. London and New York, 1920.

Wagner, H. *With the Victorious Bulgarians.* Translated from German. London, 1913.

Waldrop, Frank C. *McCormick of Chicago.* New York, 1966.

Washburn, Stanley. *The Cable Game; The Adventures of an American Press-Boat in Turkish Waters during the Russian Revolution.* Boston, 1912.

———. *Field Notes from the Russian Front.* London, 1915.

———. *The Russian Campaign, April to August, 1915.* London and New York, 1915.

———. *The Russian Offensive.* New York, 1917.

———. *Victory in Defeat, The Agony of Warsaw and the Russian Retreat.* New York, 1916.

Watson, Elmo Scott. *A History of Newspaper Syndicates in the United States—1865–1935.* Chicago, 1936.

Wendt, Lloyd. *Chicago Tribune: The Rise of a Great American Newspaper.* New York, 1979.

WGN, The. Chicago, 1922. (Relates to the *Chicago Tribune.)*

White, Llewellyn. *The American Radio.* Chicago, 1947.

White, Paul. *News on the Air.* New York, 1947.

White, Theodore H. *In Search of History: A Personal Adventure.* New York, 1978.

———. *The View from the Fortieth Floor.* New York, 1960.

White, William Allen. *The Autobiography of William Allen White.* New York, 1946.

———. *Woodrow Wilson; The Man, His Times and His Task.* Boston, 1924.

Whitman, Sidney. *Things I Remember.* New York and London, 1916.

Whyte, Frederic. *The Life of W. T. Stead.* 2 vols. London and Boston, 1925.

Wildes, Harry Emerson. *Social Currents in Japan, With Special Reference to the Press.* Chicago, 1927.

Wile, Frederick William. *Emile Berliner, Maker of the Microphone.* New York, 1926.

_____ . *News Is Where You Find It; Forty Years' Reporting at Home and Abroad.* Indianapolis, 1939.

Wilkerson, Marcus M. *Public Opinion and the Spanish-American War: A Study in War Propaganda.* Baton Rouge, La., 1932.

Willey, M. M. and Rice, S. A., *Communications Agencies and Social Life.* New York and London, 1933.

Williams, Francis. *Transmitting World News.* Paris, 1953. (UNESCO publication.)

Williams, Walter, ed. *A New Journalism in the Far East.* University of Missouri Bulletin, Journalism Series No. 52. Columbia, Mo., 1928.

_____ . *Press Congress of the World.* 3 vols. Columbia, Mo., 1922, 1928, 1934.

Williams, Wythe. *Dusk of Empire; The Decline of Europe and the Rise of the United States, as observed by a foreign correspondent in a quarter-century of service.* New York, 1937.

_____ . *Passed by the Censor; Experiences of an American Newspaperman in France.* Introduction by Myron T. Herrick. New York, 1916.

_____ with Van Narvig, William. *Secret Sources: The story behind some famous scoops.* Chicago and New York, 1943.

Winterich, John T., ed. *Squads Write! A selection of the best things in prose, verse and cartoon from The Stars and Stripes.* New York and London, 1931.

Wisan, Joseph E. *The Cuban Crisis as Reflected in the New York Press (1895–1898).* New York, 1934.

Wolff, Theodor. *Through Two Decades.* Translated from German by E. W. Dickes. London, 1936. (Editor of *Berliner Tageblatt,* 1906–33.)

Wood, Alan. *The True Story of Lord Beaverbrook.* London, 1965.

Wood, James Playsted. *Magazines in the United States.* 2d ed. New York, 1956.

Woodhead, Henry George W. *Adventures in Far Eastern Journalism: A Record of Thirty-Three Years' Experience.* New York, 1935. Published in London as *A Journalist in China.*

Woodward, J. L. *Foreign News in American Morning Newspapers.* New York, 1930.

Wrench, John Evelyn. *Geoffrey Dawson and Our Times.* London, 1955.

Ybarra, Thomas R. *Young Man of Caracas.* New York, 1931.

——. *Young Man of the World.* New York, 1942.

Young, James R. *Behind the Rising Sun.* New York, 1941.

Young, Kenneth, ed. *The Diaries of Sir Robert Bruce Lockhart.* Vol. 1, 1915–38. London and New York, 1973.

Young, Kimball and Lawrence, Raymond D. *Bibliography on Censorship and Propaganda.* University of Oregon Publication, Journalism Series. Eugene, Ore., 1928.

Zobrist, Benedict Karl. *Edward Price Bell and the Development of the Foreign Service of the Chicago Daily News.* Master's thesis, Northwestern University, 1953.

Index